risk management & insurance

mcgraw-hill insurance series

C. ARTHUR WILLIAMS, JR., CONSULTING EDITOR

FACTORY MUTUAL SYSTEM · Handbook of Industrial Loss
  Prevention
FAULKNER · Health Insurance
HOWARD · Cases on Risk Management
MACLEAN · Life Insurance
MICHELBACHER and ROOS · Multiple-line Insurers:
  Their Nature and Operation
MOWBRAY, BLANCHARD, and WILLIAMS · Insurance
PATTERSON · Essentials of Insurance Law
WILLIAMS and HEINS · Risk Management and Insurance
WINTER · Marine Insurance

Ralph H. Blanchard was editor of the series from its inception
until his retirement in 1958. Since this time he has maintained
editorial responsibility for Mowbray, Blanchard, and Williams's
Insurance and Maclean's *Life Insurance.*

risk management & insurance

second edition

c. arthur williams, jr.
University of Minnesota

richard m. heins
University of Wisconsin

McGraw-Hill Book Company

New York   St. Louis   San Francisco   Düsseldorf   Johannesburg   Kuala Lumpur   London
Mexico   Montreal   New Delhi   Panama   Rio de Janeiro   Singapore   Sydney   Toronto

This book was set in News Gothic by Kingsport Press, Inc.
and printed and bound by Kingsport Press, Inc.
The designer was J. E. O'Connor;
the drawings were done by John Cordes, J. & R. Technical Services, Inc.
The editors were R. Bruce Kezer, Jack R. Crutchfield, and Sonia Sheldon.
Annette Wentz supervised production.

risk management & insurance

Library of Congress Catalog Card Number 79-146478

07-070556-9

567890KPKP79876543

contents

preface

Like the first edition of *Risk Management and Insurance,* this second edition is designed primarily for introductory one-semester or one-quarter courses in risk management and insurance. Its contents and its structure are based on the twin beliefs (1) that the study of insurance, a major tool of risk management, should be preceded by an understanding of the procedures and concepts of risk management itself, and (2) that most of the students in these introductory courses will take only one course in this area, which should cover both risk management and insurance. For students interested in risk management or insurance as a career, this balanced treatment of both subjects also provides a comprehensive introduction to the field, which can be followed by more intensive studies of particular parts and case courses.

The text is divided into four parts. Part 1 acquaints the student with risk—its nature and its effects—and discusses the purposes and scope of risk management. Part 2, which deals with business risk management, describes the risk management function in business, how a business can identify and measure its potential losses, the types of potential losses faced by a typical firm, the five major tools of risk management, how to select among these tools, how to analyze insurance contracts, some leading policies, and insurers and their operations. Part 3 covers the unique aspects of family risk management. Part 4 deals with government regulation of insurers, social insurance, poverty, automobile compensation, and other public policy issues of importance to all citizens.

Significant changes from the first edition include the following:

1. The text is shorter. The number of chapters has been reduced from thirty-seven to thirty-three.
2. The treatment of property and liability insurance contracts has been shortened and restructured. The first edition contained nine chapters in the business risk management part covering six types of property insurance and three types of liability insurance. This edition contains two chapters describing how to analyze insurance contracts, one on package property and liability insurance contracts and one on other types of property and liability insurance contracts. In the family risk management part, one chapter on property and liability insurance contracts has replaced the former two-chapter discussion.
3. More space is devoted to quantitative approaches to risk measurement and selecting the proper tools of risk management. This expansion both clarifies and simplifies the discussion in the first edition, and it introduces new material. Furthermore, in both cases the quantitative discussion is preceded by a nonquantitative analysis. Those teachers and students who prefer can skip Chapters 5 and 13 on quantitative approaches without affecting the rest of the text.
4. Part 4 has been expanded from a single chapter on government regulation of insurance to four chapters.

Although Professor Heins' contributions to the revision have been substantial, the major portion of the text reflects Professor Williams' views and work, as was true for the first edition.

The authors are indebted to many persons who have contributed directly or indirectly to the completion of the first edition and this revision. We again express our appreciation to the persons named in the preface for the first edition. For this revision, specific mention should be made of the contributions of Prof. Donald L. Strand of Illinois Wesleyan University, who sent us his well-marked copy of the first edition with suggestions for changes; Prof. John Neter of the University of Minnesota, who co-authored an article on which Chapter 13 is based; and Prof. Andrew F. Whitman of the University of Minnesota, who shares with one of the authors the pleasant task of teaching an introductory course in which this text is used. Most of the manuscript was typed by Miss Jane Borosewicz and Miss Diane Helleland, who must now be the most accomplished handwriting interpreters in the nation. Our wives have contributed in numerous ways, and our dedication reflects our continuing thanks for their support. Any errors, of course, are the responsibility of the authors.

Revising this text has been a more demanding task than we expected, but we appreciate the opportunity to publish what we consider an improved product. We hope that teachers and students agree.

C. Arthur Williams, Jr.
Richard M. Heins

part 1
introduction to
risk management

Risk exists whenever the future is unknown. Because the adverse effects of risk have plagued mankind since the beginning of time, individuals, groups, and societies have developed various methods for managing risk. Since no one knows the future exactly, everyone is a risk manager not by choice, but by sheer necessity.

The purpose of this text is to examine carefully one important class of risks. Restricting the detailed analysis to a limited class of risks permits the discussion to focus sharply on certain concepts, many of which will also be applicable to other types of risks. Once certain fundamental ideas have been presented, the text will explain in some detail the need for, and the application of, various tools of risk management, first by a business firm and second by a family.

Part 1 of the text introduces the reader to the general subject of risk and risk management. After defining risk and analyzing its adverse effects, the scope and nature of the risk management function are examined.

1
risk: its nature and its effects

The quest for security is the eternal concern of man. The history of civilization reveals how individuals, groups, and even nations have expended their resources and energies toward this quest. History also discloses how time after time such plans temporarily succeeded but eventually went awry.

This book proposes to examine carefully a major class of risks confronting business firms and families as they function in a free-enterprise economic system. Such a system grants more freedom in decision making than other societies, but it also imposes upon its citizens greater responsibility for dealing with risk.

This introductory chapter defines and analyzes the concepts of risk, uncertainty, and reaction to risk, discusses various classifications of risk, and describes the economic costs of risk that risk managers attempt to curtail.

Risk Defined

Textbook writers and other authors have defined "risk" in various ways.[1] There is no "correct" definition. In order to emphasize the major objective

[1] For example, risk has been defined as (1) the subject of insurance, whether a person or a thing, (2) chance of loss, or (3) uncertainty concerning the outcome. For a more complete discussion see p. 4 of the first edition of this text and Part I, "The Meaning and Measurement of Risk," in J. D. Hammond (ed.), *Essays in the Theory of Risk and Insurance* (Glenview, Ill.: Scott, Foresman and Company, 1968).

Although the authors of this text continue to distinguish among chance of loss, risk, and uncertainty, they have altered their definitions slightly from the first edition.

of risk management, the authors have chosen to define risk as *the variation in the possible outcomes that exists in nature in a given situation.* When the risk is small, one's ability to predict the future is high; when the risk is great, one's ability to predict the future is low. This definition has some support in the literature of insurance and economic theory.

Illustration   To illustrate the concept, consider the two probability distributions shown in Figure 1.1. A probability distribution shows for each possible outcome its probability of occurrence. The probability associated with a certain outcome is the relative likelihood that that outcome will occur. If the probability is zero, that outcome will not occur. If the probability is 1, that outcome will occur. The closer the probability is to 1, the more likely it will occur. Because one and only one of the outcomes included in a probability distribution will occur in a given time period, the sum of the probabilities must equal 1.

One of the two distributions in Figure 1.1 is characterized by a concen-

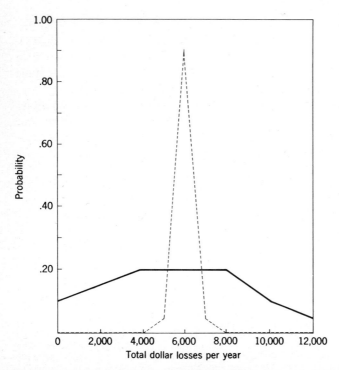

Figure 1.1   Hypothetical probability distribution of total dollar losses per year.

tration of possible outcomes; in the second distribution the outcomes can vary widely. In a situation characterized by the peaked curve one can predict with some confidence a narrow range within which the outcome will fall. In the other instance it is difficult to predict the outcome. Consequently the risk in the first situation is small and in the second situation large.

A formula for measuring risk is presented in Chapter 5. For the moment it is sufficient to understand the intuitive concept.

RELATIONSHIP TO PROBABILITY

Another way to clarify this definition of risk is to distinguish between risk and probability. Risk is a property of the entire probability distribution, whereas there is a separate probability for each outcome. In a two-outcome situation for which the probability of one outcome is 1 and the probability of the second outcome is zero, the risk is zero because the outcome is known. Clearly, therefore, the two concepts, as defined in this text, are not the same.

OBJECTIVE AND SUBJECTIVE ASPECTS

Both risk and probability have their objective and subjective interpretations. The true state of the world often differs from a person's assessment of that state. Because a person acts on the basis of what he believes to be true, it is important to recognize this distinction. To the extent that a person's estimates are incorrect, he bases his decisions on false premises. Consequently risk managers must constantly strive to improve their estimates. Even with perfect estimates, decision making under risk is a difficult task.

Probability   Objective probability is the proportion of total ventures that would result in a particular outcome in the long run under a constant cause system. Objective probability is the same for all persons in a given situation. Under certain special circumstances this probability can be determined by a priori reasoning. There must be a number of equally likely outcomes, some of which represent the particular outcome whose probability is being determined. For example, the probability of obtaining a head when a "fair" coin is tossed is $\frac{1}{2}$ because (1) there are two equally likely outcomes—a head and a tail[2]—and (2) one of these outcomes is a head. The probability of drawing a king from a deck of cards is $\frac{1}{13}$ because (1) there are 52 equally likely outcomes and (2) four of these outcomes are kings. The probability of drawing a king of hearts is $\frac{1}{52}$, a king of hearts or a king of spades $\frac{1}{26}$, and any card in the suit of hearts $\frac{1}{4}$. The probability of obtaining an ace when a die is thrown is $\frac{1}{6}$.

[2] It is assumed that the coin will not remain standing on its edge.

Many persons, however, do not know how to calculate these probabilities in all of the situations where a priori reasoning is possible. Instead they *estimate* these objective probabilities in some other way. Estimates of objective probabilities are called "subjective" probabilities because they may differ among persons facing the same objective probabilities. In situations where a priori reasoning is not possible, actions must be based on estimates of the underlying probability, these estimates being based upon statistical evidence or judgment. These estimates may vary widely among persons, depending upon the information they have, their ability to analyze this information, their biases, and so on. For example, the objective probability that a certain loss will occur may be $\frac{1}{50}$, but one person may estimate this probability to be $\frac{1}{100}$ while another estimates it to be $\frac{1}{20}$.

Various studies suggest that even when they are told the objective probability, subjects may use a different subjective probability in their decision making. One study revealed that when the objective probability was below about .20, the subjects tended to use a higher subjective probability. When the objective probability was above .20, the subjects tended to use a lower subjective probability.[3] Ward Edwards, who has conducted many experiments in this field, has observed that when a person assigns subjective probabilities to all of the possible outcomes, the sum of these probabilities often exceeds 1, an impossibility with objective probabilities.[4] In an experiment with school children Cohen and Hansel discovered "an inability to regard an independent event as separate and detached from a series of similar events in which it occurs."[5] If each of ten tosses of a coin have resulted in a head, the probability is still $\frac{1}{2}$ that the next toss will produce a head, assuming a fair coin. Nevertheless most persons prefer a subjective probability lower than $\frac{1}{2}$, apparently because they believe it is time for a tail to appear. This group often mistakenly cites the law of large numbers or law of averages, which is described in the next paragraph. Others prefer a probability higher than $\frac{1}{2}$ because they believe the tosser is lucky or skillful.

In many situations where a priori reasoning is not possible, statistical evidence may be available, at least to some persons, that will shed some light on the objective probabilities. For example, one cannot determine a priori the probability that a light bulb coming off a production line will be defective, that the number of phone calls a day through a specified exchange will exceed 100, or that a person, aged 35, will die in the coming

[3] M. G. Preston and P. Barrata, "An Experimental Study of the Auction Value of an Uncertain Income," *American Journal of Psychology*, LXI, No. 2 (April, 1948), 183–193.
[4] See, for example, Ward Edwards, "Subjective Probabilities Inferred from Decisions," *Psychology Review*, LXIX, No. 2 (March, 1962), 109–135.
[5] J. Cohen and M. Hansel, *Risk and Gambling* (New York: Philosophical Library, Inc., 1956).

year. In cases such as these, if it is assumed that there is no change in the underlying conditions, the probability can be estimated by computing the proportion of times the outcome in question occurs in a long series of repeated observations. For example, the statistician can compute the proportion of defective light bulbs among a large number of tested bulbs, the proportion of days over a long period of time in which the number of phone calls at the exchange exceeded 100, and the proportion of deaths in a large group of men, all of whom were aged 35 at the beginning of the year. Probability can be measured in this way because, according to the law of large numbers, which may be proved mathematically or demonstrated empirically, as the number of observations increases, the proportion of times a certain outcome occurs tends to approach the underlying probability. If the underlying conditions are changing, statistical evidence is sometimes available that would indicate the trends, cycles, or seasonal fluctuations that should be taken into account. However, not everyone has the same amount or kind of information available, and those who have the same information may not interpret it in the same way. For example, if the probability of a certain loss has increased steadily during the past five years, will the probability next year reflect a continuance or a correction of this trend?

Up to this point attention has been limited to situations in which the event is repeatable. Otherwise one cannot speak about the proportion of outcomes in the long run. Probability, however, can also be interpreted as a degree of belief. Under this interpretation, it is reasonable to apply the concept to unique events. For example, one can talk about the probability that a certain candidate will be elected president, that a specific product will be a success, or that a particular person will die. In these cases objective probabilities do not exist, but it may still be useful to make decisions as if they did. Some statisticians believe that this concept of subjective probability has little value and may, in fact, be misleading.

In summary, objective probability is the proportion of times a particular outcome would occur in the long run assuming that underlying conditions remain unchanged. In some special circumstances this probability can be calculated exactly through a priori reasoning. In all other instances, subjective probability estimates must be used. One way to estimate the underlying objective probability is to observe the proportion of times that a particular outcome has occurred in the past under basically the same conditions. The closer the experience approximates a long-run situation, the more reliance one can place in this indicated probability. If experience of this sort is not available or is unreliable, probability estimates must be based on other factors, some of which are extremely subjective. In events that are not repeatable, it may be useful to state subjective probabilities as degrees of belief, but there is no underlying objective probability.

Risk This has been defined as the variation in the possible outcomes that exists in nature in a given situation. In order to measure this variation one would have to know the underlying probability distribution and how to assess the variation inherent in that distribution. For example, a mathematical statistician-gambler may be able to calculate precisely the probability of each hand that he might be dealt in a game of cards. Nevertheless, he still does not know what cards he will receive; there are many possible outcomes. He can measure the variation in the results using one or more commonly accepted yardsticks, to be described in Chapter 5, which will enable him to compare the risk in one situation with the risk in another. Because these measurements are not subject to variations among persons, they represent a state of the world. Thus risk is an objective concept.

In most situations, however, one does not know the risk inherent in the situation. Instead he must estimate this risk. For example, if one must rely upon subjective probability distributions instead of objective probability distributions, he must clearly rely upon subjective estimates of risk. The variation in the estimated probability distribution might be calculated in the same manner as the risk in an objective probability distribution. Even if he knows the underlying probability distribution, he may not know how to calculate the variation in the potential outcomes, and thus he forms a subjective estimate of the risk.

Uncertainty Defined

Uncertainty is the doubt a person has concerning his ability to predict which of the many possible outcomes will occur. Uncertainty is a person's conscious awareness of the risk in a given situation. It depends upon his estimated risk—what he believes to be the state of the world—and the confidence he has in his belief. A person may be extremely uncertain about the future in a situation where in reality the risk is small; on the other hand, he may have great confidence in his ability to predict the future when in fact the future is highly uncertain.

Reaction to Risk Defined

A person's reaction to risk is the way in which he behaves or responds in an uncertain situation. One factor affecting this reaction is the person's uncertainty. Other things being equal, one would expect the person to react more strongly, either positively or negatively, the greater his uncertainty. Other factors that may be of equal or greater importance are the potential gains or losses involved and the effect of these gains or losses upon the person's economic status. For example, one may react more strongly to a situation where the uncertainty is the same but the potential gains and losses are $\pm\$1,000$ instead of $\pm\$10$. He may also react differently if he is a wealthy man instead of a poor man. A wealthy man may be more uncertain than a poor man about the future but he may fear the future less because of his greater ability to withstand adversity.

Even if all these conditions (uncertainty, potential gains and losses, and economic status) are the same, however, people may react differently because their personalities, as determined by their heredity and their environment, vary. Indeed, the same person may have a different affinity for or aversion to risk at different ages and in different situations.

Individuals making decisions under risk should be aware of the effect of their own risk attitudes upon their decision. Upon closer inspection they may decide to alter these attitudes. Persons delegating these decisions to someone else should know that person's attitudes toward risk and whether he makes decisions in accordance with his own attitudes toward risk or with his estimate of his principal's attitudes.

FACTORS AFFECTING RISK ATTITUDES[6]

Many experimenters have focused their attention upon the factors that cause persons to make different decisions under uncertainty. What personality traits or environmental conditions are likely to be associated with a willingness to assume risk? Some of the more interesting results are summarized below:

1. Wallach and Kogan constructed a "deterrence of failure" index for subjects who varied by age and sex.[7] The index was determined by asking each subject what minimum probability of success he would require ($\frac{1}{10}$, $\frac{3}{5}$, $\frac{5}{10}$, $\frac{7}{10}$, $\frac{9}{10}$, or $\frac{10}{10}$) in each of 12 life situations before he would accept the more risky of two alternatives. The higher the sum of the required probabilities, the higher the index. The findings indicated that the disutility of failure increases with age for both sexes, but that, whereas this increase may occur gradually for women, it tends to happen abruptly to men. Wallach and Kogan speculate that this difference between the sexes may be associated with the greater impact of retirement upon men. The scores for younger men were almost the same as for the younger women. Older men also scored about the same as older women.

2. The effect of education and intelligence upon risk taking is not clear One experiment showed an inverse relationship between intelligence and

[6] For a collection of articles on risk-taking behavior, some of which are specifically cited below, see Part II in J. D. Hammond, *op. cit.*
[7] M. A. Wallach and N. Kogan, "Aspects of Judgment and Decision Making: Interrelationships and Changes with Age," *Behavioral Science,* VI, No. 1 (January, 1961), 23–26.

the risk a person is willing to accept;[8] another indicated a positive relationship between good grades and risk taking.[9] Preston and Barrata found that mathematicians, statisticians, and psychologists who were well acquainted with probability overestimated and underestimated objective probabilities to the same degree as their other subjects.[10]

3. Torrance and Ziller found a close relationship between certain personality traits as measured by a biographical inventory and the willingness to select the more risky alternative in a military situation.[11] In general, risk takers learned skills such as dancing and driving a car early, were born in small towns or on farms, were more independent, enjoyed and were good at physical activity, were socially aggressive, enjoyed competition and bets, gave free expression to their sexual drives, and were divorced and remarried.

4. Many psychologists have argued that man does not necessarily strive to achieve the optimum result. The immediate objective may be a "satisfactory" outcome. If this outcome is achieved, the next goal may be a more satisfactory outcome.[12] Consequently they argue that in experiments it is not always reasonable to assume optimum behavior with respect to risk taking.

People also differ in their level of aspiration, which may affect the amount of effort they will put forth in making a decision and their willingness to take risk. Some people set levels just a little above their probable level of performance. Others set goals that it is impossible for them to attain because they seek approval for the goals themselves. Still others set goals below their abilities because they fear failure.[13]

5. In a book-length treatment of "Risk Taking,"[14] Kogan and Wallach emphasize the complexity of the decision-making process, but they believe that a person's willingness to assume risk and his consistency in this behavior are influenced greatly by (1) his "test anxiety," or his desire to avoid failure, and (2) his "defensiveness," or the degree of his concern with maintaining his image.

6. Wallach, Kogan, and Bem conducted a study in which they determined "deterrence of failure" indexes for individual subjects and for groups

[8] A. Schodel, P. Ratoosh, and J. Mines, "Some Personality Correlates of Decision Making under Conditions of Risk," *Behavioral Science,* IV (1959), 11–18.
[9] D. Kipnis and A. S. Glickman, "The Development of a Non-cognitude Battery: Prediction of Radiomen's Performance," *Bureau of Naval Personnel Technical Bulletin,* United States Navy, June, 1959.
[10] Preston and Barrata, *op. cit.,* p. 193.
[11] E. P. Torrance and R. C. Ziller, "Risk and Life Experience: Development of a Scale for Measuring Risk-taking Tendencies," *Research Report AFPTRC-TN-57-23, ASTIA Document No. 098926,* Air Force Personnel and Training Research Center, Lackland Air Force Base, Texas, February, 1957.
[12] H. A. Simon, "Theories of Decision-Making in Economics," *American Economic Review,* XLIX, No. 3 (June, 1959), 253–283.
[13] C. T. Morgan and R. A. King, *Introduction to Psychology* (3d ed., New York: McGraw-Hill Book Company, 1966), p. 234.
[14] N. Kogan and M. A. Wallach, *Risk Taking* (New York: Holt, Rinehart and Winston, Inc., 1964).

composed of these individual subjects. The indexes for the groups were significantly lower than the average individual index for the subjects in the group. Perhaps the individuals with lower indexes are the more persuasive members of the group or perhaps people are more willing to take chances when their individual responsibility appears less.[15]

7. Hermann and Stewart discovered that their subjects underwent a definite change in their willingness to gamble as they participated in a game involving wagers. The subjects became increasingly conservative when they were winning. They took greater chances when they were losing.[16]

Pervasiveness of Risk

Most human activities involve some risk and uncertainty. This pervasiveness of risk can be illustrated by the following examples, which could be multiplied almost without limit. Placing a new product on the market or purchasing a new plant may prove to have been an unwise business decision; a gambler may lose on a particular bet; increasing use of technology may affect the social structure of our population in some unpredictable and unfortunate ways; because of a new statute or court decision, certain persons may unexpectedly become guilty of violating the law; a hopeful suitor may receive a negative response to a proposal; certain forms of exercise may damage a middle-aged heart; and the actions of one nation may cause another to respond with overwhelming force.

The potential losses in a situation involving risk can be classified according to whether their effects are economic, social, political, psychological, physical, or legal. Of course the same loss could be economic and social or involve some other combination of types. Since it is impossible to handle all these aspects of risk in this book, the text deals primarily with the economic aspects. On the other hand, most of the general discussion on the principles and tools of risk management will also be of value in handling the other aspects of risk. Furthermore, the economic effects of risk can seldom be completely isolated, and in discussing the handling of economic risks, it is necessary to pay some attention to the associated noneconomic effects and costs.

Classes of Economic Risks

Economic risks and uncertainties can be classified in several ways—according to their cause, their economic effect, or some other dimension. Five

[15] M. A. Wallach, N. Kogan, and D. J. Bem, "Diffusion of Responsibility and Level of Risk Taking in Groups," *Journal of Abnormal and Social Psychology*, 68, No. 3 (March, 1964), 263–274.
[16] C. C. Hermann and J. B. Stewart, "The Experimental Game," *The Journal of Marketing*, XXII (July, 1957), 12–20.

important methods classify risks according to whether they are (1) property, liability, or personnel risks; (2) physical, social, or market risks; (3) pure or speculative risks; (4) static or dynamic risks; and (5) fundamental or particular risks.

PROPERTY, LIABILITY, AND PERSONNEL RISKS

The first method classifies risks according to the type of potential losses. *Property* risks exist when property in which the firm or family has a financial interest, other than a liability interest, may be damaged, destroyed, reduced in value, or lost. For example, a property risk exists when a building may be destroyed by fire or when the value of a business may be reduced by a change in government purchases of its products. *Liability* risks exist when the firm or family may be held legally responsible for property or personnel losses suffered by others. For example, the owner of an automobile may be held responsible for injuries suffered by a pedestrian, or a business may have to pay the medical expenses of an injured workman. *Personnel* risks exist when the firm or family may suffer a loss to their persons. For example, the family may fear the possible unemployment of the bread-winner, or a firm may fear the death of a key engineer or salesman. Because this classification provides a simple, logical way of looking at the potential losses facing a firm or family, it will be developed in more detail later and used extensively in this text.

PHYSICAL, SOCIAL, AND ECONOMIC RISKS

The second method classifies risks according to the cause or origin of the loss. In his classic book on all forms of risk and risk bearing, C. O. Hardy has described five types of risks classified according to their origin.

1. Risks of destruction of property through the physical hazards of nature, such as a storm, a flood, or a fire
2. Uncertainties in the production process, such as variations in the strength of materials or the effectiveness of labor
3. Social risks caused by deviations of individual conduct from what is expected, such as theft, or negligence, and by the impossibility of predicting the behavior of social groups, such as strikes, riots, wars, and tax reforms
4. Risks caused by the failure or inability of individuals to use knowledge which is accessible to them or their competitors, such as failure to use market research information
5. Market risks, such as price reductions between the dates of purchase and sale of commodities[17]

[17] Charles O. Hardy, *Risk and Riskbearing* (Chicago: The University of Chicago Press, 1923), pp. 2–3.

These five classes are not mutually exclusive. An employee's negligence may lead to a fire; faulty planning by an individual may intensify the results of a business depression; or a strike may result in an explosion. The classification does, however, illustrate the widespread sources of risk. If the second and fourth classes are combined with the fifth class on the ground these three classes are concerned with economic risks, risk can be classified as (1) physical, (2) social, or (3) economic.

PURE AND SPECULATIVE RISKS

A. H. Mowbray is responsible for the classification of risks as pure or speculative.[18] A *pure* risk exists when there is a chance of loss but no chance of gain. For example, the owner of an automobile faces the risk of a collision loss. If a collision occurs, he will suffer a financial loss. If there is no collision, the owner does not gain. His position remains unchanged. A *speculative* risk exists when there is a chance of gain as well as a chance of loss. For instance, expansion of an existing plant involves a chance of loss and a chance of gain. Pure risks are always distasteful, but speculative risks possess some attractive features.

Pure risks also differ from speculative risks in that they are more amenable to the law of large numbers, already described in the section "Probability" under "Risk Defined." This means that one can more successfully predict the proportion of units that will be lost if they are exposed to a pure risk than if they are subject to a speculative risk. One notable exception to this statement is the speculative risks associated with games of chance, which are highly amenable to this law.

Finally, in a situation involving a speculative risk, society may benefit even though the individual is hurt. For example, the introduction of a socially beneficial product may cause a firm manufacturing the product it replaces to go bankrupt.[19] In a pure-risk situation society suffers if any individual experiences a loss.

As explained in Chapter 2, risk management is concerned primarily with pure risks. Consequently this text will concentrate on the nature and treatment of these risks. Much of what is said, however, can also be applied to speculative risks.

There is some evidence that people may react differently in pure-risk and speculative-risk situations. Professor Mark Greene has reported an experiment in which he measured attitudes toward risk by a "deterrence of failure" test similar to that of Kogan and Wallach and by the Torrance-Ziller

---

[18] A. H. Mowbray, R. H. Blanchard, and C. A. Williams, Jr., *Insurance* (6th ed., New York: McGraw-Hill Book Company, 1969), pp. 6–8.
[19] Wagers always result in some winners and some losers. Other speculative-risk situations may result in all winners or all losers.

biographical inventory test.[20] Scores of these tests were correlated with one another and with the scores on an insurance-mindedness test which was designed to measure probable insurance-buying behavior. Because the insurance risks included in the test were pure risks, the score on the insurance-mindedness test depends upon the person's attitude toward pure risk. Although Greene warned that his conclusions were tentative, he found no significant relationship between the two sets of risk-attitude scores or between each set of risk-attitude scores and insurance-mindedness.

A more recent experiment also suggests that attitudes toward speculative risks may not be a satisfactory indicator of pure-risk attitudes.[21] For example, one group of graduate students in business administration was unwilling to participate in a venture that presented a possible gain of $100 and a possible loss of $4,900 unless the probability of winning was at least .99; i.e., the probability of losing was .01 or less. On the other hand, they were unwilling to pay a fee of $100 to avoid a loss of $5,000 unless the probability of loss was .10 or more. For lower probabilities of loss they preferred to retain the risk of a possible gain of $100 (the premium saving) or a net loss of $4,900 (the $5,000 loss less the premium saving). In the first instance the subjects were "buying" a gamble; in the second they were "selling" a gamble. The importance of this distinction has been noted elsewhere in the literature on risk attitudes,[22] but this may not be the only explanation for the difference. Additional experiments in which the subjects are required to make decisions involving pure risks are needed to shed more light on the relationship between pure-risk attitudes and attitudes toward speculative risks.

STATIC AND DYNAMIC RISKS

A. H. Willett, in another classic treatise, divided risks into static risks and dynamic risks.[23] *Static* risks are "connected with losses caused by the irregular action of the forces of nature or the mistakes and misdeeds of human beings."[24] They would be present in an unchanging economy. *Dynamic* risks are associated with changes, especially changes in human wants and improvements in machinery and organization. Static losses usually result

[20] Mark R. Greene, "Attitudes toward Risk and a Theory of Insurance Consumption," *The Journal of Insurance*, XXX, No. 2 (June, 1963), 165–182.
[21] C. A. Williams, Jr., "Attitudes toward Speculative Risks as an Indicator of Attitudes toward Pure Risks," *The Journal of Risk and Insurance*, XXXIII, No. 4 (December, 1966), 577–586.
[22] G. M. Becker and C. G. McClintock, "Value: Behavioral Decision Theory," *Annual Review of Psychology*, XVIII (1967), 239–286. Howard Raiffa, *Decision Analysis* (Reading, Mass.: Addison-Wesley, 1968), pp. 89–91.
[23] Allan H. Willett, *The Economic Theory of Risk and Insurance* (New York: Columbia University Press, 1901; and Homewood, Ill.: Richard D. Irwin, Inc., 1951), pp. 14–23.
[24] *Ibid.*, p. 14.

in a loss to society; dynamic losses generally do not. A static loss usually affects directly a few individuals at most, while dynamic losses have more widespread effects. Finally, static losses exhibit more regularity over a specified period of time. They are always pure risks, whereas dynamic risks include pure and speculative risks.

FUNDAMENTAL AND PARTICULAR RISKS

Dean C. A. Kulp has distinguished between fundamental risks and particular risks.[25] Although the dividing line between the two groups is not always clear, the basic idea is that *fundamental* risks are group risks, impersonal in origin and effect, and, at least for the individual, unpreventable, whereas *particular* risks are personal in origin and effect and are more readily controlled. Examples of fundamental risks are those associated with uncertainties, inaccuracies, and disharmonies in the economic system, risks associated with major social and political changes, and risks associated with extraordinary natural disturbances such as droughts and tornadoes. Examples of particular risks are the risk of death or disability from nonoccupational causes, the risk of property losses by such perils as fire, explosion, theft, and vandalism, and the risk of legal liability for personal injury or property damage to others. Particular risks are always pure risks, whereas fundamental risks include pure and speculative risks.

Economic Costs of Risk

Life without any risk or uncertainty would be difficult and not entirely pleasant to think about. We take pleasure in anticipating gains that may never be realized and even more pleasure in realizing unexpected gains. Life is more interesting, and the human race more alert and imaginative, because of risk and uncertainty. As Friedrich Nietzsche has said, "A heart full of courage and cheerfulness needs a little danger from time to time or the world gets unbearable."[26]

Still, we do not enjoy being concerned about losses even if they never occur, and to suffer unexpected losses is clearly painful. Life is insecure, and the human race is more frustrated, worried, and afraid because of this insecurity. The problems of human existence thus require the balancing of a little danger to avoid boredom against assuming a great danger that may threaten even physical or mental security.

The economic costs of uncertainty have been discussed by many writers

[25] C. A. Kulp and J. W. Hall, *Casualty Insurance* (4th ed., New York: The Ronald Press Company, 1968), pp. 3–7.
[26] R. Flesch, *The Book of Unusual Quotations* (New York: Harper & Row, Publishers, Incorporated, 1957), p. 55.

in this field. A. H. Willett, in his discussion of the economics of insurance, refers to the costs of uncertainty arising out of (1) the unexpected losses that do occur and (2) the uncertainty itself even if there are no losses.[27]

COSTS OF UNEXPECTED LOSSES

All business managers, from the small, one-man single proprietorship to the large corporate giants, recognize the serious consequences that may result from an unexpected loss. Newspapers often carry stories of small business firms that are forced to close their doors as a result of uninsured or inadequately insured fire or automobile liability losses. The disastrous effects of earthquakes, floods, and serious business depressions upon firms and families alike are well known. Finally, almost everyone knows at least one family that has suffered an important financial reverse because of the death, disability, or unemployment of the breadwinner.

The costs of these unexpected losses to the individual economic unit, the firm or family, and in many instances to society (e.g., through decreased taxes and increased welfare payments), are clear to most people, but the more important costs associated with uncertainty itself are less often appreciated.

COSTS OF UNCERTAINTY ITSELF

The first cost of uncertainty itself is a tendency to reduce the total satisfaction associated with a given economic status. This reduction may result from (1) "diminishing marginal utility," (2) overestimating the chance of loss, or (3) fear and worry.

Economists have introduced into their literature the highly useful concept of utility.[28] The *utility* associated with a given economic status is the total satisfaction a person obtains from that status. The reason the concept is so useful is that it consolidates the effects of all the factors which determine the satisfaction associated with a given economic status. Economists have also noted that for most persons utility or satisfaction does not increase proportionately with increases in economic status. For example, if a person's wealth were to double from $5,000 to $10,000,

---

[27] Willett, *op. cit.*, pp. 24–31.

[28] For a more comprehensive but elementary discussion of this concept by an economist, see Paul A. Samuelson, *Economics* (6th ed., New York: McGraw-Hill Book Company, 1964), pp. 427–429. The utility concept introduced in Chap. 13, "Selecting the Proper Tools," differs from the one described here in that, in addition to indicating the relative satisfaction derived from different certain wealth positions, the utility function reflects the person's attitude toward risk. In other words, the person's attitude toward risk affects the shape of his utility curve. The concept employed above, which is the older concept of utility, is useful because it permits a distincton between the effects of relative satisfaction with various outcomes and attitudes toward risk.

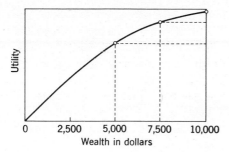

Figure   1.2   A   hypothetical   utility function.

his satisfaction level would probably less than double. Figure 1.2 presents a typical utility curve of this type. The curve is said to be characterized by diminishing marginal utility because as the wealth increases, the increase in utility associated with each dollar increase in wealth gets smaller and smaller.[29]

In order to apply this concept to the problem at hand, assume that a person commands a wealth of $7,500 with no uncertainty involved. Now introduce uncertainty about the amount of wealth he will possess in the next minute and assume that there are two equally likely outcomes, $5,000 and $10,000. This sounds like a fair exchange, since the average of the two dollar amounts is the same as his present position; however, because of diminishing marginal utility, the gain in satisfaction associated with the increase to $10,000 is less than the loss in satisfaction associated with the drop to $5,000. The person, therefore, has reason to prefer the certain $7,500 position or even a reduced certain position.

For some persons, a dollar gained is more important than a dollar lost, and for these people the same reasoning leads to the opposite result.

The certain position may also be less desirable if it is assumed that the person is overoptimistic and overestimates by a considerable degree his chance of improving his economic position.[30] Overpessimistic estimates, on the other hand, reinforce the effect of diminishing marginal utility.

The third reason why uncertainty reduces the total satisfaction associated with a given economic status may be the most important. The concern

[29] Professors Friedman and Savage have argued that for many people, as their wealth increases, the marginal utility first diminishes, then increases, and finally decreases. See Milton Friedman and L. J. Savage, "The Utility Analysis of Choices Involving Risk," *Journal of Political Economy*, LVI (August, 1948), 279–304.
[30] A celebrated economist once observed that the "chance of gain is by every man more or less over-valued, and the chance of loss is by most men under valued, and by scarcely any man, who is in tolerable health and spirits, valued more than it is worth." Adam Smith, *The Wealth of Nations* (New York: The Modern Library, 1937), p. 107.

about reducing his economic status may cause the person considerable fear and worry. This anxiety may be present even if (1) the person's probability estimates are perfect and (2) his marginal utility does not diminish with increasing wealth. Indeed, the effect of this anxiety may be so great as to offset the countereffects of increasing marginal utility and optimistic probability estimates. On the other hand, the gambling instinct, the desire for success, the pleasure of placing small bets, or some other psychological drive may work in the opposite direction. For most of the population on most occasions fear and worry are more likely to predominate.[31]

The second cost of uncertainty is its tendency to cause inefficiencies in the utilization of existing capital and to retard the development of new capital. As a result, production is decreased. Again it is useful to turn to concepts employed by economists to explain this result. First assume that the amount of capital is fixed. Other things being equal, the marginal productivity of capital (the output made possible by the last unit of capital) in each industry tends to decrease as the amount of capital committed to that industry increases. Consequently, capital is apportioned in an optimum fashion when the marginal productivity in each industry is the same, for otherwise total production could be increased by transferring a unit of capital from an industry where the marginal productivity is least to the one where it is greatest. Uncertainty disturbs this balance, for relatively too many resources tend to flow into the safe industries, and society may even have to forgo the products of a very risky industry.[32] The fear and worry usually associated with uncertain undertakings plus diminishing marginal utility and overpessimistic probability estimates account for this result. Investors hesitate to invest their own capital in risky industries, and they can with difficulty get others either to extend them credit or to join them as partners or stockholders. In addition to reducing total production, the existence of uncertainty tends to increase the prices of products in the more hazardous industries and decrease the prices in the less hazardous industries. This effect on price structures is made even more unsatisfactory by the possible errors in the estimates of the relative hazards.

Within an industry, the existence of uncertainty may affect the apportionment of capital among firms, and within a firm, it may affect the selection of methods of production and distribution. For example, delegation of authority may be considered an efficient move in a particular firm, but the uncertainty involved may prevent its adoption.

Uncertainty may retard the accumulation of capital in all uses, thus

---

[31] For some excellent comments on the material discussed in the last two paragraphs, see Irving Pfeffer, *Insurance and Economic Theory* (Homewood, Ill.: Richard D. Irwin, Inc., 1956), pp. 132–144.
[32] The following newspaper headline illustrates the point. "Lack of Insurance Curbs Private Atom Projects," *Minneapolis Star*, March 14, 1956.

further reducing production compared with that in a riskless economy. Potential investors generally hesitate to commit capital to any use; their planning periods are shortened; less credit is extended than if there were no uncertainty, and certain resources are "hoarded" in liquid or quasi-liquid form in order that funds will be readily available when a loss occurs.

In summary, the costs of uncertainty, in addition to the unexpected actual losses, are generally (1) a reduction in total satisfaction simply because of the existence of uncertainty, and (2) less than optimum production, price levels, and price structures.

Although uncertainty is thus generally admitted to be costly, in many instances it also provides opportunities for improving the economic positions of families, firms, and societies. The existence of the uncertainties associated with pure risks, however, is *universally* agreed to be costly, because they involve only a chance of loss, and men have an intense desire to manage these risks successfully.

REVIEW QUESTIONS

1. Distinguish among chance of loss, risk, uncertainty, and reaction to risk.
2. Each of two business firms owns 50 automobiles. One firm is very much concerned about collision losses sustained by its automobiles; the other is not. How do you explain this difference?
3. A risk manager estimates that the probability that his employer's home office building will be seriously damaged during the next year is $\frac{1}{50}$.
   a. Is $\frac{1}{50}$ an objective or subjective probability?
   b. Is his uncertainty $\frac{1}{50}$?
4. A business believes that it can determine a risk manager's attitudes toward risk by his age, sex, intelligence, and scores on various psychological tests. How would you advise them?
5. Distinguish among pure risks, static risks, social risks, and particular risks. Give two illustrations of each type.
6. One of the most important classifications of risk is made according to the type of potential loss associated with the risk. What is the nature of these potential losses?
7. What two major types of economic costs are caused by uncertainty? Illustrate each type.
8. You are offered the following choice: (*a*) $1,000 or (*b*) a 50 per cent chance to receive $2,000 and a 50 per cent chance to receive nothing. Which would you choose? Why?
9. What are the economic costs of uncertainty itself to a business firm? to a family? to society? Illustrate each type.
10. Is all uncertainty undesirable? Illustrate your answer.

SUGGESTIONS FOR ADDITIONAL READING

Hammond, J. D. (ed.): *Essays in the Theory of Risk and Insurance* (Glenview, Ill.: Scott, Foresman and Company, 1968).

Hardy, C. O.: *Risk and Risk-bearing* (Chicago: The University of Chicago Press, 1923).

Knight, Frank: *Risk, Uncertainty and Profit* (London: London School of Economics and Political Science, 1933).

Kulp, C. A., and Hall, J. W.: *Casualty Insurance* (4th ed., New York: The Ronald Press Company, 1968), chap. 1.

Mowbray, A. H., Blanchard, R. H., and Williams, C. A., Jr.: *Insurance* (6th ed., New York: McGraw-Hill Book Company, 1969), chap. 1.

Pfeffer, Irving: *Insurance and Economic Theory* (Homewood, Ill.: Richard D. Irwin, Inc., 1956).

Willett, A. H.: *The Economic Theory of Risk and Insurance* (Philadelphia: University of Pennsylvania Press, 1951).

2

the risk management concept

Because of the pervasiveness of risk and its significant adverse economic effects, man is constantly searching for ways in which he can manage risk to his advantage. In a broad sense *risk management* may be defined as the minimization of the adverse effects of risk at minimum cost through its identification, measurement, and control. All business and family decision makers are risk managers.

This text, however, is not able to treat adequately all classes of risks or risk decisions. Although many of the concepts and tools to be presented are applicable to other types of risk, this text will discuss only the types of risks that are typically handled by the insurance or risk management departments of large business firms. Because these divisions increasingly use tools other than insurance to handle risk, a growing body of literature refers to their work as "risk management" instead of "insurance management." Because the persons engaged in this work are not the only risk managers in a business, most firms have been understandably reluctant to call their insurance managers "risk managers," but some businesses now use this title. This chapter discusses in more detail the types of risk handled by risk managers, the four steps in risk management decision making, whether risk management is a science or an art, the management aspects of risk management, and the contributions of risk management to the economic life of a firm or family.

Types of Risks Handled by Risk Managers

Defining the types of risks handled by risk managers is not an easy task. Five methods of classifying risks have been described in Chapter 1 under "Classes of Economic Risks," but none of the classes under any of these five methods describes exactly the types of risks with which the risk manager is typically concerned. The Willett concept of static risk as opposed to dynamic risk and the Mowbray concept of pure risk as opposed to speculative risk come closest to indicating the scope of the risk manager's interest and the major content of this text. All the classes included under the other three methods of classifying risks—property, liability, or personnel; economic, social, or physical; and fundamental or particular—include some risks that are within the risk manager's domain and others that are not.

The risk manager (as the term is used in this text) is responsible for *most* but not all static risks. The prospect of certain losses to the firm's own product as a result of faulty processing by employees is an example of a static risk for which the firm looks to other departments for correction. The risk manager may, on the other hand, be also concerned with a few dynamic risks, such as the inability to collect accounts receivable because of a business decline.

The risk manager is concerned with most pure risks. He is not typically concerned with speculative risks except to the extent that the creation of speculative risks forces him to face certain pure risks; for example, the acquisition of a new plant creates a potential fire loss. On the other hand, some pure risks are not ordinarily handled by risk managers, such as the probability that a strike will curtail business operations[1] or the possibility that some technological change will put the firm out of business.

In Chapter 11, it will be observed that insurers for the most part restrict their coverages to certain types of pure risks. Perhaps the best way to describe the risks handled by risk managers is to say that they include all insurable and quasi-insurable risks. It is, however, much more simple and, with a few exceptions, as correct to say that the risk manager is concerned with pure risks. Our text will follow this common practice. Consequently, our concern will be *potential property, liability, or personnel losses of economic, social, or physical origin where the risk is pure, not speculative.*

---

[1] This example is not as apt as it used to be. Strike insurance is now available on a limited scale, and the risk manager may be asked to arrange for this coverage.

The Four Steps in Risk Management Decision Making

Most authorities agree that decisions on the handling of risk should ordinarily be made by following four specific steps:

1. Procedures and communications should be established throughout the organization to allow for a complete inventory and discovery of the potential (pure) risks that may arise in the activities of the business firm or family. Risk discovery is the first and perhaps the most difficult function that the risk manager or administrator must perform. Failure to identify all of the risks faced by the firm or family means that the risk manager will have no opportunity to deal with these unknown risks intelligently.

2. After identification of risks, the next important step is the proper measurement of the losses associated with these risks. This measurement includes a determination of (a) the probability or chance that the losses will occur, (b) the impact the losses would have upon the financial affairs of the firm, should they occur, and (c) the ability to predict the losses that will actually occur during the budget period. The measurement process is important because it indicates the risks that are most serious and consequently most in need of urgent attention. It also yields information that is needed in step 3.

3. Once the risk is identified and measured, the various alternative solutions or tools of risk management should be considered and a decision made with respect to the best combination of tools to be used in attacking the problem. These tools include (1) avoiding the risk, (2) reducing the chance that the loss will occur or its magnitude if it does occur, (3) retaining or bearing the risk internally, (4) combination, or increasing the number of units exposed to loss, and (5) transferring the risk to some other party. The fifth alternative includes, but is not limited to, the purchase of insurance. In selecting the proper tool the risk manager must establish the costs and possible consequences of handling his potential losses through alternative methods. He must also consider the present financial position of his firm or family, its overall policy with reference to risk management, and its specific objectives. A new and growing company may wish to assume the consequences of certain possible losses simply because it needs to employ limited capital in the entrepreneurial functions of the firm. A mature business organization may be considerably more conservative in its approach to risk assumption or transfer or it may possibly be more venturesome. Families vary in a similar way.

4. After deciding among the alternative methods of risk treatment, the risk administrator and perhaps the appropriate management group must establish means for effective implementation of the decisions made. If insur-

ance is to be purchased, for example, the problems of establishing proper coverage, shopping the market for adequate and reasonable rates, and the selection of the insurer are part of the implementation process.

Each step will be discussed in greater detail in subsequent chapters.

The Science of Risk Management

One of the early exponents for the use of the scientific method in the solution of business management problems was Frederick W. Taylor, often referred to as the "father of scientific management." By the use of controlled experiments, Taylor attempted to hold all the elements constant and uniform except the one variable which was under investigation, "and as one variable was changed its effect on the problem was noted."[2]

Since the publication of the Taylor paper, scientific management and its modern counterpart, operations research, have come a long way in introducing quantifying, analytical procedures to business management problems. Not only has the application of mathematical and statistical tools given a new direction to the solution of business problems, but the development of electronic computers and data-processing machines has revolutionized the whole structure of business organization. The modern business manager must become aware of this new technology and its possible applications to his firm in order to survive in the new competitive environment into which he has been suddenly thrust.

But any new approach to a problem produces delay, and business managers have taken some comfort in the lag experienced between the formulation of these various analytical tools and their practical application. Furthermore, the applications and solutions which, according to their proposers, have broad implications in regard to management problems have been found of limited value in certain types of decisions or decision processes current in the business world.

As is true of management in general, risk management may be described as *both an art and a science*. In fact, scientific risk management is still in its infancy. Risk managers must instead rely almost entirely upon nonquantitative techniques which depend upon deduction and intuitive judgments. Yet certain broad principles of risk management have been developed. These principles and some of the early developments in scientific risk management will be presented at various points in this text. In time these guides to risk management will be improved and new ones will be created, but sound judgment will continue to play an important role.

[2] Frederick Winslow Taylor, "Testimony before the Special House Committee," *Scientific Management* (New York: Harper & Row, Publishers, Incorporated, 1911), p. 31.

A Management Function

Risk management involves the application of general management concepts to a specialized area. A sample of general management writings will reveal these concepts and the relationship of risk management to other management functions.

One of the most famous French authorities in the general management area, Henri Fayol, defined *management* as follows:

> To manage is to forecast and plan, to organize, to command, to coordinate and to control. To foresee and provide means examining the future and drawing up the plan of action. To organize means building up the dual structure, material and human, of the undertaking. To command means maintaining activity among the personnel. To coordinate means binding together, unifying and harmonizing all activity and effort. To control means seeing that everything occurs in conformity with established rule and expressed command.[3]

Risk management likewise requires the drawing up of plans with regard to future action, the organizing of material and individuals for the undertaking, the maintaining of activity among personnel for the objectives involved, the binding together and unifying of all the activities and efforts, and finally the controlling of this activity and seeing that everything occurs in conformity with established rules and objectives.

According to a leading current management textbook, a "highly useful way of dividing up the total task of management is organizing, planning, leading, and controlling."[4] This classification is basically the same as the one suggested by Fayol. Of these four tasks, risk managers spend most of their time planning, which consists of clarifying objectives, setting goals, and developing programs, strategies, and schedules to achieve these objectives. Planning involves decision making, and the four stages of decision making are described as follows: (1) diagnose the problem, (2) find good alternative solutions to this problem, (3) compare the results of these alternative courses of action, and (4) choose among them. These four stages correspond to the first three steps of risk management decision making on the handling of risk.[5]

Henri Fayol has contributed another very important concept to the field of management in general and to risk management in particular. In

[3] Reprinted with permission from Henri Fayol, *General and Industrial Management* (New York: Pitman Publishing Corporation, 1949), pp. 5–6. This book is an English translation of a work originally published in French in 1916.
[4] W. H. Newman, C. E. Summer, and E. K. Warren, *The Process of Management* (2d ed., Englewood Cliffs, N.J.: Prentice-Hall, Inc.), p. 10.
[5] *Ibid.*, chaps. 13 through 16.

his book *General and Industrial Management,* originally published in 1916, Fayol suggests that all activities to which industrial undertakings give rise can be divided into six basic functions:

1. Technical activities (production, manufacture, adaptation)
2. Commercial activities (buying, selling, exchange)
3. Financial activities (search for an optimum use of capital)
4. Security activities (protection of property and persons)
5. Accounting activities (stock taking, financial statements, costs, statistics)
6. Managerial activities (planning, organization, command, coordination, control)[6]

Thus at an early date Fayol identified risk management (i.e., the security function) as one of the prime functions of management. Fayol's perspicacity in this respect is even more noteworthy when we remember that at the time he wrote his famous book, the security function was much more limited in its scope than it is today. According to Fayol,

> The object of this (security activity) is to safeguard property and persons against theft, fire and flood, to ward off strikes and felonies and broadly all social disturbances or natural disturbances liable to endanger the progress and even the life of the business. It is the master's eye, the watch-dog of the one-man business, the police or the army in the case of the State. *It is, generally speaking, all measures conferring security upon the undertaking and requisite peace of mind upon the personnel.*[7] [Emphasis supplied by authors.]

Except for the last sentence, Fayol appears to be emphasizing the loss-prevention aspects of the modern risk management function; the security function would be more broadly conceived today.

Contribution of Risk Management to a Firm or Family

Because risk management, as defined in this text, is concerned with the management of pure risks, it may be regarded by some as the true "dismal science." The objective may be paraphrased as "making the best out of a bad situation." Pure risks can only hurt a firm or family, and the purpose of risk management is to minimize the hurt at minimum cost. Consequently the task of risk management may at first glance appear less glamorous and less important to a firm or family than those management functions dealing with speculative risks.

Risk management, however, is a fascinating field because it is con-

[6] Fayol, *op. cit.,* pp. 3–6.
[7] *Ibid.,* p. 4.

stantly concerned with uncertainty and change. Because profits can be improved by reducing expenses as well as by increasing income,[8] risk management should be regarded as an important contributor to company or family "profits." Risk management may lower expenses through preventing or reducing losses as the result of certain low-cost measures, through transferring potentially serious losses to others at the most attractive transfer fee possible, through electing to take a chance on small losses unless the transfer fee is a bargain, and through preparing the firm or family to meet most economically those losses that it has decided to retain.[9]

Risk management should also contribute indirectly to firm or family profits by freeing the business or family from an important class of economic uncertainties. This freedom enables them to assume speculative risks that they might otherwise have to avoid and, because of their greater peace of mind, to handle speculative risks more wisely and more efficiently. A family may assume greater risks in the stock market because they have adequate insurance protection against the death or poor health of the breadwinner, the destruction, damage, or disappearance of their property, or a liability suit. A business may develop its product lines more aggressively if it knows that it is adequately protected against suits by persons who may be harmed by these products. Creditors, customers, and suppliers also prefer to do business with a firm or family that has sound protection against pure risks.

In addition to increasing profits by reducing expenses or by removing barriers to the assumption of speculative risks, risk management should reduce the fluctuations in annual profits. Keeping these fluctuations within reasonable bounds aids planning and is a desirable goal in itself.

Finally, when a catastrophic loss occasioned by a pure risk does strike a firm or family, proper advance preparation for such an event through sound risk management may make the difference between survival and failure. Even if risk management did not contribute to the economic health of firms and families in any other way, this one benefit would make it a critical function of business or family management.

REVIEW QUESTIONS

1. The president of a large manufacturing firm objected when he discovered that the "insurance" department of his firm was called the "risk manage-

---

[8] Indeed, because families cannot deduct many of their expenses in calculating their income taxes, to paraphrase Benjamin Franklin, a penny saved may be better than a penny earned.
[9] For a more complete treatment of ways to increase profits, see Marshall W. Reavis, "The Corporate Risk Manager's Contribution to Profit," *Journal of Risk and Insurance*, XXXVI, No. 4 (September, 1969), 473–479.

ment" department. Can you explain the probable reason for his objection? Can you answer his objection?

2. How would you define the class of risks typically handled by risk managers?
3. According to a famous saying, a problem well defined is half solved. How is this statement relevant to risk management?
4. a. Is risk management a function of management?
   b. Does Henri Fayol's security function adequately describe the modern risk management function?
5. Compare the steps involved in general management decision making with the four steps in risk management decision making on how to handle risks.
6. "Risk management is not and never will be a science." Do you agree? Why or why not?
7. How can proper risk management increase a business's or an individual's "profitability"?
8. Besides increasing "profits," what contributions can proper risk management make to a firm or family?

SUGGESTIONS FOR ADDITIONAL READING

Fayol, Henri: *General and Industrial Management* (New York: Pitman Publishing Corporation, 1949).

MacDonald, Donald L.: *Corporate Risk Control* (New York: The Ronald Press Company, 1966), chap. 1.

Mehr, R. I., and Hedges, B. A.: *Risk Management in the Business Enterprise* (Homewood, Ill.: Richard D. Irwin, Inc., 1963), chap. 1.

Newman, W. H., Summer, C. E., and Warren, E. K.: *The Process of Management* (2d ed.; Englewood Cliffs, N.J.: Prentice-Hall, Inc., 1967).

Principles of Risk Management—Supplementary Readings (Bryn Mawr, Pa.: Insurance Institute of America), Topic 1.

part 2
business risk
management

Part 2 deals with the risk management problems facing a business firm; it also develops some tools and concepts, many of which are equally applicable to family risk management.

Our plan in this section is as follows: (1) We explore the nature of the risk management function in business and its relationship to other management functions; (2) we identify and measure the major potential property, liability, and personnel losses facing a typical business firm; (3) we describe and evaluate the noninsurance and insurance tools that can be used to handle these risks; (4) we suggest some approaches to selecting the proper tools; and (5) we present a framework for analyzing insurance contracts and apply this framework to some important examples. Finally (6) we discuss some supplementary insurance decisions, such as the choice of an insurer, a producer, and a pricing method and the proper preparation for loss adjustments following a loss.

Relatively few readers will be charged directly with the risk management function in a firm, but many will be asked to evaluate the risk manager's work and make policy decisions, and others will be involved in activities which affect or are affected by the work of the risk manager. Furthermore, as we noted above, many of the concepts important in business risk management are equally applicable to family risk management.

A. The business risk manager: his function and relationship to other business management functions

3

the risk management function in business

The organization and management of a business involve a variety of decisions involving risk. In creating a business enterprise, investors must decide the nature and scope of the operations to be undertaken. Capital must be accumulated and put to work in the most opportune and efficient manner. Once the business is in existence, investors or their managers must make new judgments and revise former ones as the competitive environment changes.

The contributions of the (pure) risk management function to the maximization of long-run profits has been discussed in the preceding chapter. The current chapter deals with the duties and organizational structure of the risk management function in modern business, and the interrelationship of this function and other business management activities.

Security Function a Responsibility of All Levels of Management

Writers in the field of business management have described the performance of general management functions as neither the exclusive privilege nor the particular responsibility of the head or senior members of the business. All management functions must be carried on at all levels of activity by both the head and members of the body corporate. The workman on the assembly line, the departmental manager, and others on up to the general manager must exercise relative skills and abilities in six areas of business

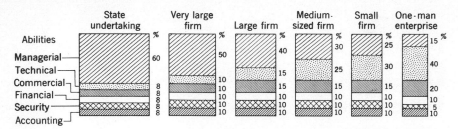

Figure 3.1. Requisite abilities for heads of industrial concerns of all sizes. [Reprinted with permission from Henri Fayol, *General and Industrial Management* (New York: Pitman Publishing Corporation, 1949), Table IV, p. 12.]

activity: managerial, technical, commercial, financial, security, and accounting.

Henri Fayol indicates, as shown in Figure 3.1, the relative importance of these six functions for the heads of industrial concerns of all sizes. As we pointed out in Chapter 1, Fayol's concept of the security function pre-supposes a more limited activity than the modern risk management function, and he therefore tends to understate the importance of the security ability.

Fayol also has discussed the relative importance of these six functions for the various personnel in each major department of a large firm.[1] The head of the security department, for example, must possess all six types of abilities in varying degrees. As one moves down the line in that department, the security ability becomes relatively more important. Conversely, personnel in other divisions must possess some security abilities. To illustrate: In Fayol's analysis the shop foreman in the production department must possess certain skills and knowledge in the area of *security* because he is responsible for the protection of personnel under his direction. Even the workman in the performance of his routine duties must be aware of safety precautions necessary for himself and for other personnel.

The need for some fundamental knowledge concerning the handling of risks and the reduction of their financial consequences to the business is clearly recognized and demonstrated by current business practices. More and more it is recognized that accountants, finance officers, production managers, personnel managers, and marketing people must be made aware of the security problems which arise out of their activities and responsibilities in their own management areas. Specific illustrations of these problems are provided later in this chapter.

The growing importance of the pure risk management function in busi-

[1] Henri Fayol, *General and Industrial Management* (New York: Pitman Publishing Corporation, 1949), Table V, p. 12.

ness is likewise recognized in our system of jurisprudence. The legal responsibilities of officers to stockholders or owners of the business clearly include the proper management of pure risks and concern for the security of the assets and personnel entrusted to them. Several recent court decisions emphasize the possibility that directors and officers may be held legally responsible for breach of these duties and for failure to take reasonable precautions in minimizing the dangers or consequences of catastrophic loss. From the decisions it appears that while a director may have no independent legal duty to insure corporate property or to prevent loss or to employ other specific security activities, he has an overall legal duty and a specific obligation to use care and to be diligent in the administration of the affairs of the corporation and in the use and preservation of its assets.[2]

In other words, the courts have recognized that the failure to effect proper insurance coverage, to pay premiums when due, to keep coverage in force and to carry out the security function may well be the basis for personal liability suits against the officers or directors of a business. The legal standard of performance, as announced by several courts, is that officers and directors must exercise the care that an ordinary prudent man would have exercised under similar circumstances.

Modern Management's Approach to Pure Risk and the Security Function

Just as it is impossible to center all entrepreneurial decisions in a large-scale business in a single department, so it is impossible to center all pure risk or security decisions in a single department or functional division. Nevertheless, the technical advice and counsel concerning pure risks must be left whenever possible in the hands of persons technically competent to perform the security function.

The complex decision processes relating to pure risks, particularly in the large-scale business enterprise, have prompted modern management to develop specialized technical skills and to assign specific pure risk responsibilities to individuals or departments in the business. As one corporate executive has expressed it:

> Forward looking management has long since come to look upon insurance (pure risk management) as a specialized field beyond the routine purchase of policies of indemnification. The concept of assigning the function of insurance management to an already over-burdened company official such as a secretary-treasurer or controller is today just as far fetched as would be the assigning of the legal or operating functions of the company to the

---

[2] Gaylord A. Jentz, "Are Corporate Directors Liable to the Corporation for Failure to Insure the Corporate Assets?" unpublished paper, University of Wisconsin, 1957.

same officials. Today we thus have full-time insurance executives or risk managers heading a separate department in the corporate structure—a specialist to whom management can look for an analysis of risks to which its company's physical plant is exposed, the selection of the methods by which these risks may be reduced or eliminated and the procurement of such insurance contracts as will provide proper indemnification in the event these risks result in financial loss.[3]

RISK MANAGEMENT IN THE LARGE BUSINESS FIRM

The effective division of labor, as first recognized by Adam Smith, has been the foundation of the mass-production processes in modern business. In the risk management field such division of labor and specialization has allowed large business firms to meet more effectively their pure risk exposures. The result has been a slow and gradual evolution of a special management position referred to as risk or insurance manager. One of the first associations, the Insurance Buyers of New York, was organized in 1932 with the purpose of developing camaraderie and exchanging technical information among the persons responsible for purchasing insurance for larger businesses. This organization later gave way to the Risk Research Institute, a national organization which spear-headed a drive to organize buyers of insurance on a national basis and to develop chapters at local levels. Through the exchange of information and ideas, through meetings and publications, the active members organized what is referred to today as the American Society of Insurance Management. This organization is currently composed of over 1,700 risk managers throughout the country.

In 1931 the American Management Association recognized the importance of the pure risk management function in business affairs by the establishment of the insurance section of their organization. Its membership has increased substantially, and each year the AMA holds regional conferences in various parts of the country on many subjects relating to the discharge of the pure risk management function. In addition, the association has published a series of insurance bulletins dealing with insurance and risk management. This insurance series serves as a valuable resource for students and practitioners alike in analyzing the technical and policy-formulation problems.

The scope of the risk manager's duties   In 1968 a consulting firm retained by the American Society of Insurance Management studied the role of the risk manager.[4] Questionnaires were mailed to 1,689 ASIM members in the

[3] Reprinted with permission from H. P. Liversidge, "What Management Expects from an Insurance Department," *The Growing Job of Risk Management*, AMA Management Report No. 70 (New York: American Management Association, 1962), p. 42.
[4] *American Society of Insurance Management Study of the Risk Manager and ASIM* (New York: Woodward and Fondiller, Inc., March, 1969).

United States and Canada. About 43 per cent (713 members) completed and returned the rather complex questionnaire. Most respondents worked for large businesses. Less than 10 per cent worked for companies with less than 500 employees; over 50 per cent were in companies with 5,000 or more employees. All types of industries were included in the sample, including some conglomerates. Almost half of the companies had overseas operations.

Table 3.1 shows what fraction of the respondents claimed full or shared responsibility for each of several risk management functions listed in the order of the frequency that some responsibility was reported.

Almost half of the respondents had some responsibility in each of these areas. These risk managers most often were solely responsible for handling property and liability insurance claims, identifying and evaluating the risks faced by the business, designing the insurance program, insurance accounting, and administering self-insurance plans. The most frequently shared re-

Table 3.1 Proportion of risk managers reporting full or shared responsibility for common risk management functions

Responsibility	Full	Shared	Shared most commonly with
Risk determination and evaluation	68%	30%	Financial executive
Insurance selection	55	41	Financial executive
Claims handling—property and liability insurance other than workmen's compensation	76	18	Not specified
Insurance accounting	49	36	Financial executive
Loss prevention	24	58	Safety engineer
Self-insurance administration	46	19	Financial executive
Claims handling—workmen's compensation	37	27	Personnel manager, safety engineer
Safety administration	19	44	Safety engineer
Design of group insurance plans and negotiations with carriers	25	38	Personnel manager
Group insurance administration	32	22	Personnel manager
Design and installation of other employee benefit plans	12	42	Personnel manager
Administration of other employee benefit plans	16	31	Personnel manager
Claims handling—group insurance	26	21	Personnel manager

Source: Derived from *American Society of Insurance Management Study of the Risk Manager and ASIM* (New York: Woodward and Fondiller, Inc., March, 1969), Table 9.

sponsibilities were loss prevention and safety work, which they shared most often with safety engineers outside the risk management department; the design and installation of employee benefit plans other than group insurance, shared with personnel managers; and insurance selection, shared with financial vice-presidents, treasurers, or other financial executives.

Because this text treats risk management as the identification, measurement, and treatment of property, liability, and personnel losses, the reader may be surprised to find that the design, installation, and administration of group insurance and other employee benefit plans were reported as full or shared responsibilities by less than two-thirds of the respondents. Personnel risk management is considered such a highly specialized topic and so closely related to personnel management that the task is often assigned exclusively to specialists in the personnel department or shared by the risk management and personnel management departments.[5] When the responsibility is shared, risk managers and related financial personnel are more likely than personnel departments to select the insurer and negotiate concerning the insurance. Personnel departments are more likely to take the lead in collective bargaining, establishing the eligibility requirements and benefits, and administering the daily operations.[6]

About one-third of the respondents reported that their most time-consuming responsibility, among those listed in Table 3.1, was risk determination and evaluation; for another 23 per cent this was the second most time-consuming task.[7] About 19 per cent said that selecting insurance contracts took more time than any other responsibility; another 14 per cent ranked this responsibility second, according to this criterion. Other functions were mentioned much less frequently as time-consuming responsibilities.

The authority possessed by risk managers in making fourteen specific key decisions is reported in Table 3.2. For each of these decisions at least 90 per cent of the respondents had full or shared authority. At least half had full authority for selecting the insurer, approving insurance contract renewals, deciding when to negotiate rates, seeking competitive bids[8] (including the preparation of specifications), reviewing the amount of insurance necessary, selecting the type of rating plan (see Chapter 25), determining

---

[5] For a 1965 study that treats the responsibility of risk managers toward employee benefit plans in more detail, see David A. Ivry, "The Corporate Insurance Manager and Employee Benefit Plans," *Journal of Risk and Insurance*, XXXIII, No. 1 (March, 1966), 1–17.

[6] Albert A. Blum, *Company Organization of Insurance Management*, American Management Association Research Study 49 (New York: American Management Association, 1961). This monograph also contains a detailed analysis of how businesses of various size organize their risk management departments.

[7] *ASIM Study, op. cit.*, p. 17.

[8] See end of Chap. 24 for a discussion of competitive bidding in insurance. About three-fourths of the ASIM respondents request competitive proposals irregularly; more than 20 per cent seek such proposals on policy renewals. *Ibid.*, p. 23.

Table 3.2 Proportions of risk managers reporting full or shared authority to make common risk management decisions

Decision	Full	Shared
Whether to retain	27%	68%
Whether to insure	32	65
Selection of agent or broker	35	54
Selection of insurer	53	40
Approval of insurance contract renewals	72	25
When to negotiate rates	76	19
When to seek competitive bids	72	22
What specifications to set up for bids	74	22
Which bid to select	42	52
Review of amounts of insurance necessary	66	33
Type of rating plan	59	35
Whether to buy a deductible or excess plan	41	55
Whether to file a claim for small insured losses	85	12
Liability loss settlements recommended by insurer	58	35

Source: Derived from *American Society of Insurance Management Study of the Risk Manager and ASIM* (New York: Woodward and Fondiller, Inc., March, 1969), Table 12 .

whether a claim should be filed for small insured losses, and reviewing liability loss settlements recommended by an insurer. Some basic risk management decisions that are usually shared with some financial executive include whether a risk should be retained, whether insurance should be purchased, and, if insurance is purchased, whether it should include a deductible provision (explained under "Deductible Clauses" in Chapter 16).

Policy statements   Many large businesses have policy statements that give the risk manager authority directly from the board of directors of the company. An example of such a statement is presented in Table 3.3. The preparation and review of these policy statements improve top management's understanding and appreciation of the risk management function. In addition these statements enable top management to control risk management decisions without constantly supervising the risk manager's activities. They also strengthen the risk manager's position in dealing with others and in reporting to top management on matters covered by the guidelines. On the other hand, the statement may be phrased in such general terms that it provides no guidance; it may be so specific that it ties the risk manager's hands and destroys his initiative.[9] Striking an appropriate balance is not easy. Further-

[9] Donald L. MacDonald, *Corporate Risk Control* (New York: The Ronald Press Company, 1966), pp. 27–28.

Table 3.3   General Mills, Inc., insurance policy statement

The Company's general corporate insurance policy is

1. To eliminate or reduce as far as practicable the conditions and practices which cause insurable losses
2. When these risks cannot be eliminated or reduced to workable levels,
    a. To purchase commercial insurance or operate formal self-insurance programs— in such amounts and in such areas as will provide assurance against catastrophe loss, and
    b. To either insure or assume—whichever judgment indicates to be in the Company's best interest—those risks not considered individually to be of major importance to the operating or financial position of the Company,

but, in any event, to retain whatever portion of the risk for General Mills' account that premium reductions make economically attractive.

The Insurance Department's responsibility for implementing this policy includes:

1. For reducing risks:
    a. Assisting the divisions and subsidiaries to design and operate fire control and loss prevention programs
    b. Reviewing new construction and facility alteration plans to assure risk control features and insurance acceptability
2. For protecting against risks that cannot be eliminated:
    a. Developing insurance coverage policy and programs, keeping them up to date, and assuring their effectiveness
    b. Administering insurance programs of domestic units of the Company and distributing premium costs as appropriate
    c. Controlling and reviewing foreign insurance programs to assure adequacy
    d. Negotiating and placing (or otherwise approving) all insurance contracts and bonds to assure conformity with established programs
    e. Approving insurance provisions in leases and other contracts prior to signature
    f. Reporting and adjusting all claims
    g. Maintaining such records as necessary to establish insurable value
    h. Developing and administering a corporate appraisal program, using commercial appraisals as appropriate
    i. Administering and operating the Company's captive insurance company, Gold Medal Insurance Co.

In carrying out these responsibilities, the Insurance Department will require the cooperation of people throughout the subsidiaries, divisions, and departments, for information and coordinated action. The development of this, in order to provide the full benefits of an effective risk management program to the units and corporation, is an important element of the Insurance Department's overall task.

---

more, once such a statement is d.afted, top management may be reluctant to keep it up to date. In short, policy statements can be highly useful but they should be carefully prepared and be reviewed periodically.

Records and reports[10]   Risk managers in large firms keep records of various sorts. Among the most important are lists of insurance contracts, including their expiration dates, valuation records showing the value and location of all property in which the firm has a financial interest, personnel records on the firm's employees, comprehensive analyses of the different types of losses faced by the firm (see Chapter 4), and data on past losses. Loss data are useful in determining potential future loss frequency and severity (scc Chapters 4 through 8), selecting the proper tool of risk management (see Chapters 9 through 13), obtaining the lowest possible prices from insurers (see Chapter 25), and designing loss-prevention programs (see Chapter 10).

Many risk managers have compiled manuals that contain the firm's policy statement, present in summary form the total risk management program, and describe the obligations of the risk management department and other divisions under this program. Such manuals are useful as a reference and educational device. Their preparation also forces a comprehensive review of the total program and emphasizes department interrelationships. These interrelationships necessitate many reports among the various departments dealing with risk management. For example, if the firm plans to purchase a new plant, ideally the risk manager should be informed and involved in the decision. In turn the risk manager should report periodically on the performance of the total risk management program.

Title and qualifications of the risk manager   The administration of the risk management program is usually assigned to a top financial officer of the firm.[11] About 60 per cent of the respondents in the ASIM survey cited earlier had a title of insurance manager (50 per cent), director of insurance (8 per cent), or risk manager (only 2 per cent). Over 20 per cent were chief executives, vice-presidents, or assistant executives.

Thirty-one per cent of the respondents considered themselves to be members of top management; almost all of the remainder were in middle management.[12] Almost half reported directly to a financial vice-president, secretary, or treasurer; 17 per cent reported directly to the chief executive officer or a senior vice-president.

[10] Based largely on papers by James Cristy and C. H. Austin in *The Growing Job of Risk Management*, American Management Association Report 70 (New York: American Management Association, 1962).
[11] *ASIM Study, op. cit.*, p. 14.
[12] *Ibid.*, p. 21.

About 86 per cent of the ASIM respondents attended college; 9 per cent have master's degrees.[13] Other qualifications of risk managers are not discussed in the ASIM report, but in an earlier study by the National Industrial Conference Board a broad general education was favored, plus a working knowledge in these special areas:

Insurance principles and practices, coverages, markets, and rate-making procedures

Commercial law, including liability and contract law

Safety engineering and construction practices

Accounting principles and practices

Economic and operating problems of the particular industry and company

Personal qualities rated most important were:

Sound judgment and an ability to think objectively

Ability to work well with others and obtain their active cooperation and help

Organizational and planning ability

Initiative and leadership in developing and selling new ideas

Willingness to ask and take advice from experts in and outside the company

Tact, patience, and an infinite capacity for the accurate and efficient handling of detail[14]

RISK MANAGEMENT IN THE MEDIUM- OR SMALL-SIZED BUSINESS FIRM

Whereas the principles of risk management are the same, regardless of the size of the business, many important differences exist in the application of these principles to risk management problems in business firms of different sizes. In the small sole proprietorship, where the owner may operate the business himself, it goes without saying that the decisions in the insurance and pure risk areas must be made by this one person and implemented by him. In this situation division of labor is not possible. The small sole proprietor must to the best of his ability perform all the functions of business management, including accounting, finance, and marketing. Usually he must rely upon an outside adviser or expert to give him the technical information necessary for the conduct of his business affairs. In the insurance area he will often rely upon local insurance agents and brokers, his banker, or his public accountant to advise him as to which insurance coverages he should carry. In addition, his attorney often will give him

---

[13] *Ibid.*, p. 23.
[14] *Company Insurance Administration,* Study No. 81 (New York: National Industrial Conference Board, 1956), pp. 17–18.

information which will be helpful to him in dealing with the various legal exposures that his risk-reduction program may encounter. The one important distinctive character of this form of business risk management is that the person who makes the decisions in this area also carries the full responsibilities and consequences of his decisions. The sole proprietor has no one but himself to blame if he has made errors in judgment.

As businesses increase in size, there is more division of labor among the specific affairs of the firm, including the risk management function. Small- and medium-sized firms, however, are at best likely to have a part-time risk manager on their staffs.

The Relationship of Risk Management to the Accounting Function

The discussion now turns to specific relationships between risk management and other management functions. *Accounting,* the first such function to be discussed, has been described as "the art of recording, classifying, and summarizing in a significant manner and in terms of money transactions, those events which are, in part at least, of a financial character, and interpreting the results thereof."[15]

INTERNAL CONTROLS

Internal control procedures involve accountants directly in risk management. These procedures are directed at safeguarding the assets of the company, proving and checking the accuracy and reliability of its accounting information, promoting increased operational efficiency, and encouraging strict adherence to prescribed management policies.[16]

The process of internal control involves a system and related procedures whereby the work of one employee is automatically verified and checked by another employee performing his individual task in such a way as to identify improper and ineffective operations of either party. It is important in this process that the different persons arrive at the same result and operate independently of each other to prevent fraud and to eliminate errors in the informational or accounting system.

The tremendous volume of individual transactions and recordings which must be made in the conduct of normal business affairs in most firms makes the use of certain control devices imperative in order to minimize errors or fraudulent activities. For example, comparison of total sales or cash receipts through the postings made to customer accounts by different persons and from different media is implicit in any system of control over

[15] Accounting Terminology Bulletin No. 1, "Review and Résumé," *Accounting Research and Terminology Bulletin* (final ed., New York: American Institute of Certified Public Accountants, 1961), p. 9.
[16] *Internal Control,* Special Report by the Committee on Auditing Procedure (New York: American Institute of Certified Public Accountants, 1949).

cash and accounts receivable. Similarly, the checking of prices, extensions, and footings of invoices, the comparison of invoices with purchase orders, receiving reports, and checking disbursements for plant additions, maintenance, and other expenses for proper authorizations are very important in minimizing fraudulent dissipation of resources.

The accounting department also normally establishes and maintains detailed and specific ledgers on inventories and property assets. A typical property plant ledger sheet indicates the original value of the asset, its location and use, and subsequent improvements and modifications. Insurable values are also entered in this basic record in order that the loss, if sustained, can be quickly and easily established.

Normally the responsibility for a system of internal control lies with the controller, who is the chief accountant and sometimes the chief financial executive of the firm. In addition, the independent certified public accountant in the course of his examination makes certain that a system of control is in operation and is effective in minimizing errors or fraudulent practices.

BUDGETARY CONTROLS

The controller or accountant is interested not only in minimizing loss to exsting assets, but also in controlling future expenditures. The preparation and use of budgets form an integral part of the total financial control process. The use of requisitions for purchase orders, and a preaudit of all expense vouchers by the accounting office are means to implement this type of budgetary control. Refinements of any system of budgeting, however, are completely dependent upon the total risk management program of the business firm, for any major loss or catastrophic occurrence may easily upset the best-laid plans of expense control or projected future income.

VALUATION ACCOUNTS

In the preparation of statements the accountant performs another important risk management function by establishing certain valuation accounts. For example, an *allowance for doubtful accounts* is an offset to the accounts receivable account for identifying those losses that may arise from credit extended to customers. A *reserve for contingencies* is a reservation of retained earnings to meet possible losses in the future.[17]

COST CONTROLS

The establishment of cost-control centers and the allocation of costs, both fixed and variable, to each of these divisions in a firm has the ultimate objective of controlling costs and assisting management to price its products.

[17] For the relationship of entries of this type to self-insurance, see Chap. 9.

Cost accounting can do much to identify spoilage problems, poor workmanship and damaged goods, excessive overtime and poor utilization of equipment, wasteful productive techniques, and overall poor management.

FINANCIAL-STATEMENT CONTROLS

The interpretation and use of accounting statements is both an accounting function and a financial function. The ratios of liabilities to surplus (or owners' equity), current assets to current liabilities, and merchandise inventory to sales tend to identify possible weaknesses in the firm's affairs. In addition, financial-statement analysis is necessary to determine the degree to which a business could withstand, for example, a major fire in its key productive unit or a substantial liability judgment arising from negligent operation of one of the firm's vehicles. The ultimate question to be decided by management is how large a maximum loss the firm could or should withstand without insurance. Such amounts may be expressed in terms of the relative profit position of the firm. For example, the board of directors may establish that up to 5 per cent of the firm's three-year average profit would be the maximum loss the firm should suffer in a given year.

THE INSURANCE REGISTER AND INSURANCE CONTROLS

While the accounting department may not be concerned with the actual safe-keeping of the policies of insurance which the business firm may purchase, it nevertheless keeps the important records relating to these insurance policies. The prepaid insurance and insurance expense accounts reflect the costs of professional protection during a given accounting period. The assignment of these costs to the respective functional and operating departments enables management to appraise the value and worth of such coverages in relation to the protection which is provided and also to assess each department with its proportionate share of the cost of safeguarding and minimizing financial loss. Businesses that favor the allocation of risk management costs to departments argue that this practice encourages loss prevention. Various bases are used to allocate these costs, such as actual losses or the insurance premiums that would be paid if each department purchased its own insurance.

A typical insurance register maintained in the accounting department lists the types of coverage provided, the assets protected, and the insurer and premium relating to each specific policy.[18]

The accounting department must also be concerned with special types

---

[18] For a sample form, see Russell B. Gallagher, *Buying and Administering Corporate Insurance*, AMA Research Report No. 15 (New York: American Management Association, 1949), p. 56.

of insurance requiring accounting information. For example, some reporting forms require periodic statements that indicate the values at specific locations. Assigning payroll to proper job classifications may have a significant effect upon the cost of workmen's compensation insurance since the rates for this coverage depend upon payroll classifications. The accountant is likewise concerned with insurable values for the purchase of business interruption insurance. Determination of these values involves projecting net profits and continuing expenses that would be lost in case of a shutdown.

Relationship of Risk Management to Financial Management

The chief financial officer of the business may carry the title of treasurer or controller, depending upon the particular nomenclature used and duties assigned. As has already been indicated, the risk manager often reports directly to this individual, and for this reason, risk management is often considered to be one phase of financial management. We are concerned here, however, with the relationship of risk management to those aspects of financial management that have not already been discussed in connection with the risk management function.

CAPITAL STRUCTURING

Perhaps one of the most important single functions which the chief financial officer must perform is planning the basic capital structure of the firm. Striking the proper balance between debt and equity financing, maintaining adequate working capital, and planning long-range capital fund needs are some of his primary problems. Capital structuring also implies basic planning to anticipate losses to some or all of the business assets. An adequate insurance program, coupled with other features of risk management, is the first line of defense against these losses. One common solution, in addition to insurance, is to establish lines of credit which may be used to furnish any additional short-term capital needed to meet such losses.

PROTECTION OF PROPERTY USED TO SECURE A DEBT

If the business chooses to issue mortgage bonds on its real estate, the financial officer must assure the bondholder that insurance has been properly executed to protect this collateral. Similar requirements are imposed on persons or organizations that issue equipment trust certificates and any other form of debt security where physical property is used to secure the debt. Typical first-mortgage bonds contain specific reference to the requirements for insurance on the property and are part of the guarantee given the bondholder when he makes the investment. Such provisions are also found in leasing arrangements.

TAX PLANNING

An important part of financial planning is legitimate tax minimization. Decisions with regard to credit costs in relation to the issuance of debt versus equity securities is part of this planning. Another concern is the impact that accidental property and liability losses may have upon taxes. There is also the problem of financing the firm's pension and welfare programs and measuring the impact of tax laws on different methods of funding.

APPROVAL OF INSURANCE PURCHASES

Approval of purchase requisitions for insurance likewise may be required from the controller or in some cases from the treasurer of the firm. The risk manager, if independent or separate from the controller, must first normally submit his proposal for coverage to the board of directors for authorization and then to either the controller or another officer who is assigned responsibility for approving such expenditures.

Relationship of Marketing Activities to the Risk Management Function

The officers in charge of the marketing or distributive function of the business firm are also concerned with risk management problems. Every customer may be a potential claimant against the firm for losses occasioned by defective or unsafe conditions in the products or services. The law of sales imposes upon sellers specific obligations which are discussed in Chapter 7. The proper conduct of the marketing activity to avoid such claims or losses is an important part of the overall risk management program.

HOLD-HARMLESS AGREEMENTS ON PURCHASE AND SALE ORDERS

In both the purchasing and sale of goods or services, it is customary in modern business practice to incorporate hold-harmless agreements to avoid liability claims. These are usually found on the purchase order or sales invoice and are executed as part of the transaction. Basically, these agreements require that when the purchaser buys the goods or services, he agrees to hold the seller harmless for any loss which may develop from its use.[19]

Similarly, hold-harmless agreements are used which require the seller to indemnify the buyer for any claims which the buyer subsequently may be forced to pay because of defects in quality of the purchased article.

[19] See under "The Imputed Liability of Others," in Chap. 7, for an example.

These hold-harmless agreements are passed back and forth between buyer and seller in practically all business transactions today, and their net legal effect is virtually impossible to measure. It is shocking to discover that many such hold-harmless agreements are executed without prior knowledge or restraint. They have become such a normal procedure in many business transactions that they are virtually ignored.

TRANSIT EXPOSURES

The selling department of most business firms is normally charged with the responsibility for transporting goods sold in the most expeditious and reasonably safe manner. These transit exposures, if not properly handled, bring about serious problems with regard to customer relations and can result in serious financial loss to the business.

COMPETITION AND COSTS

Marketing functions usually involve advertising and the making of statements concerning the performance of the product involved. Vigorous competition normally will encourage the seller to make many statements about the product. Such statements, however, may lead to endless trouble and litigation if the product does not meet the claims made for it. For example, a claim that a certain antifreeze will not rust a radiator may actually bring hundreds or thousands of lawsuits or claims against the business firm, should such a defect actually occur.

The proper service and installation of any product by the sales or marketing division is equally important to risk management and control. Losses that may result from improper installation of a piece of equipment can be very serious. A business firm recently had to replace the entire flooring in an extensive housing project because the glue used to cement the tile failed to hold properly. The faulty workmanship cost the firm the price of the tile and the glue as well as the rents lost during the reinstallation.

Relationship of the Risk Management Function to Personnel Department Functions

The typical personnel officer is charged with responsibility not only for recruiting, training, and placing of personnel in the various positions in the business firm, but also for employee benefit and welfare programs.

DESIGN, INSTALLATION, AND ADMINISTRATION OF EMPLOYEE WELFARE PROGRAMS

As noted earlier in this chapter, under "The scope of the risk manager's duties," most employee benefit and welfare programs are administered directly by the personnel department rather than by the full- or part-time risk manager. The reason for this assignment of duties is that employment relations, hiring practices, supervision, and the overall problem of employee morale are tied to these programs. The personnel officer often represents the employer on the pension or retirement administration board, since he has ready access to all employment records and the history of personnel necessary in the administration of the programs. In addition, the personnel department must supervise the enrollment of new employees in the group life program and disability insurance programs.

SAFETY AND LOSS PREVENTION

The personnel department, in cooperation with the maintenance and engineering department, has the responsibility of seeing that the proper work rules are developed and enforced for maintaining safety, and that the physical environment is conducive to the minimization of accidents and disabilities. Training programs geared to making employees safety-conscious, adequate supervision to assure safe processes, and facilities for providing prompt attention and medical assistance when injuries occur usually are responsibilities assigned to the personnel department. Standard hiring practices may include the administration of an extensive medical examination to the prospective employee by the plant doctor.

SUPERVISION OF NONOCCUPATIONAL DISABILITY PROGRAMS, REHABILITATION OF INJURED WORKERS, AND RELATED COVERAGES FOR DEPENDENTS

The personnel division is usually responsible for minimizing absenteeism among the work force and encouraging prompt rehabilitation of workers who may have been injured on or off the job. These functions are most important in controlling the costs of fringe benefit programs as well as the costs of workmen's compensation insurance, which is frequently rated at least in part on the basis of the firm's own experience. Insurers often work with the personnel department on rehabilitation programs for workers injured while working.

Many modern fringe benefit programs include also benefits for dependents. Here, again, the personnel department may have the responsibility for seeing that such claims are promptly processed and handled by the insuring organization.

Risk Management as Performed by the Production Department

In the modern manufacturing firm which undertakes production processes, many of the important responsibilities of risk management and minimization of loss are assigned to the production departments. Here the persons in charge of production, including supervisors and foremen, are responsible for seeing that the work is conducted in an efficient manner as well as in a safe physical environment.

PRODUCTION SCHEDULING

The speed of the assembly line and the requirements for output may be related specifically to the number of accidents. Time and motion studies designed to set standards for production goals must be prepared in such a way as to minimize personal injury as well as destruction of the plant's property and equipment.

DESIGN OF PLANT LAYOUT

The ventilation, lighting, heating, and location of equipment have a great effect upon lost-time accidents. Even the location of the rest-room facilities and other physical services, such as water fountains and safety aisles, may greatly affect the speed and safety with which the work may be performed.

OTHER RISK MANAGEMENT RESPONSIBILITIES

The handling of materials, the maintenance of equipment, and the overall housekeeping of the production facility may have similar effects upon safety, morale, and accident frequency and severity. Control of spoiled work and quality-control standards impose additional limitations upon the work force as it performs its functions. The establishment of safe working standards and proper supervision is vital to the discharge of these responsibilities in a typical manufacturing production operation.

The production department must have continuous contact with the plant maintenance department for the location of fire extinguishers and other medical and first-aid equipment in the event of injury or loss. Adequate marking of exits, the use of safety devices on doors to elevator shaftways and stairways, proper safeguards on machinery and equipment, and periodic inspection of plants and processes should all be a part of performing the risk management function.

Relationship of the Risk Management Function to the Legal Department

Not only should the legal department be intimately involved in the review of the insurance programs of the business firm, but it should also be deeply cognizant of all the exposures to liability and loss which result from the firm's activities. For example, the leasing of property may impose responsibilities for its care and maintenance. Proper provisions in the lease arrangement will establish these responsibilities either upon the lessor or lessee or both. In addition, all contracts which are negotiated by the firm should be reviewed in relation to insurance coverage, particularly in the matter of contractual liability. The legal department should handle any disputes involving responsibility for loss by insurers and see to it that purchase orders, leases, and liabilities which may arise from company activities are properly covered by insurance or other risk-meeting devices. Needless to say, the risk manager must work intimately with the legal counsel in designing coverages to fit specific exposures and in making certain that the contracts meet the minimum needs with regard to protecting the insured's rights.

Relationship of the Risk Management Function to Outside Services and Consultants

Where the business firm is not of sufficient size to warrant any full-time or even part-time risk manager on its staff, much of the technical administration must be performed by outside technicians. In the matter of insurance administration, the relationships between the firm and the insurance agent or broker must be very close in order to assure that all the operations and activities of the firm are properly reviewed and considered.

Even firms that use full-time or part-time risk managers must rely upon the services of agents or brokers to see that coverage is properly placed in the insurance market. If the coverage must be underwritten by several insurers, it may be necessary to rely upon several agents or brokers who specialize in various exposures.

Similarly, the use of outside legal services, accounting services, and management consulting services would imply relationships as intimate as those with the insurance agent or broker. Consultants in these areas normally provide a review function, passing upon the decisions which management may make in their respective areas. These services usually require special fees and/or retainer arrangements, which are based upon the scope and nature of the work performed. Questions often arise as to what may be the legal responsibility of these outside consultants in the event that they give improper or incorrect professional advice. For attorneys and accountants, the exposure to professional liability is always present. Upon demonstrating that the work or service was not performed according to the usual standards of the profession, the client may recover for damages suffered.

Many business firms also use outside consultants for appraisal of property for insurance, credit, tax, or selling purposes. The fees for appraisal services vary considerably according to the type of appraisal performed as well as the area and section of the country involved. For many firms, the appraisal fee will prove a wise investment because (1) an outside appraisal may provide a much more accurate basis for determining the proper amount of insurance than would otherwise be possible,[20] and (2) it may simplify the preparation for loss adjustments.

Under retention programs, the risk manager may have to work with consulting actuaries, investment advisers, loss-prevention engineers, and loss adjusters. Their services are discussed in more detail in Chapter 9.

The risk manager must also concern himself with outside services performed for other decisions of the firm because the use of these services may create additional risks for the firm. For example, the use of independent contract labor, independent contract hauling, the renting of property, or the use of rented equipment including data-processing machines may result in substantial liability. Here, again, it is important that the risk manager obtain the services of the legal department or of outside legal representatives to examine the nature of such contracts in order to see that the interests of the firm are properly protected, either by insurance or by hold-harmless clauses in these arrangements.

REVIEW QUESTIONS

1. "Even if risk management is defined in the narrow sense to mean the management of pure risks only, this function is not confined to one department of the firm." Comment on this statement.
2. Smith is a member of the board of directors of a medium-sized corporation, whose stock is publicly traded. What personal interest does Smith have in the proposals of the risk manager?
3. Prepare a job description for the risk manager of a large department store.
4. a. Do risk management policy statements serve a useful purpose?
   b. What types of records do risk managers usually keep?
5. Bill Brown, a college junior, has some interest in becoming a professional risk manager for a large firm. He wonders what personal characteristics and education he should possess to be a successful risk manager. How would you advise him?
6. In what respects does the risk management function in the small- or medium-sized firm differ from the same function in a large corporation?

[20] Under some insurance policies, failure to carry insurance equal to a specified per cent of the value of the property at the time of a loss causes the insured to bear part of the loss. (See the description of the coinsurance clause in Chap. 16.) The importance of a proper valuation in this case, by appraisal or otherwise, is obvious.

7. The accounting department serves risk management in two ways: (1) It provides information which the risk manager needs in order to perform his function, and (2) it applies some of the tools of risk management itself. Cite several illustrations of each of these two forms of service.
8. The chief financial officer of a business has reason to be interested in the activities of the risk manager and vice versa. Support this statement with illustrations.
9. The marketing division of the firm may create many risks about which the risk manager should be informed. Cite some examples of these risks.
10. In many firms the personnel department is almost as deeply involved in risk management as in the risk management department. Explain this statement.
11. The production department is actively concerned with the application of one tool of risk management. What is this tool?
12. What is the relationship of the legal department to the risk management function?
13. What outside services might the risk manager use in his work?
14. Why should the risk manager be concerned about outside services used by other divisions in the firm?

SUGGESTIONS FOR ADDITIONAL READING

American Society of Insurance Management Study of the Risk Manager and ASIM (New York: Woodward and Fondiller, Inc., March, 1969).

Blum, Albert A.: *Company Organization of Insurance Management,* AMA Research Study 49 (New York: American Management Association, 1961).

Company Insurance Administration, Study No. 81 (New York: National Industrial Conference Board, 1956).

Dillavou, E. R., Howard, C. G., Roberts, P. C., and Robert, W. J.: *Principles of Business Law* (7th ed., Englewood Cliffs, N.J.: Prentice-Hall, Inc., 1962).

Flippo, Edwin B.: *Principles of Personnel Management* (2d ed., New York: McGraw-Hill Book Company, 1966).

Fayol, Henri: *General and Industrial Management* (New York: Pitman Publishing Corporation, 1949).

The Growing Job of Risk Management, AMA Management Report No. 70 (New York: American Management Association, 1962), Parts II and VI.

Johnson, Robert W.: *Financial Management* (3d ed., Boston: Allyn and Bacon, Inc, 1966).

Mayer, R. R.: *Production Management* (2d ed., New York: McGraw-Hill Book Company, 1968).

McCarthy, E. J.: *Basic Marketing: A Managerial Approach* (3d ed., Homewood, Ill.: Richard D. Irwin, Inc., 1968).

Meigs, Walter B., and Johnson, Charles E.: *Accounting: The Basis for Business Decisions* (2d ed., New York: McGraw-Hill Book Company, 1967).

Practices in Risk Management—Selected Readings (Bryn Mawr, Pa.: Insurance Institute of America), Topics 1, 2, and 13.

Principles of Risk Management—Supplementary Readings (Bryn Mawr, Pa.: Insurance Institute of America), Topics 1 and 5.

B. Risk identification and measurement fundamentals and applications

4
risk identification and measurement fundamentals

The first step in business risk management is to identify the various types of potential losses confronting the firm; the second step is to measure the potential losses that are identified with respect to such matters as their likelihood of occurrence, their severity, and their predictability. This chapter and the next chapter discuss certain approaches and yardsticks that might be used to identify and measure risks; Chapters 6, 7, and 8 will identify and analyze the property, liability, and personnel losses faced by a typical business.

Risk Identification

Unless the risk manager identifies all the potential losses confronting his firm, he will not have any opportunity to determine the best way to handle the undiscovered risks. The business will unconsciously retain these risks, and this may not be the best or even a good thing to do. To identify all the potential losses the risk manager needs first a checklist of all the losses that could occur to any business. Second, he needs a systematic approach to discover which of the potential losses included in the checklist are faced by his own business. The risk manager may conduct this two-step procedure himself or he may rely upon the services of an insurance agent, broker, or consultant.

CHECKLIST OF POTENTIAL LOSSES

Checklists of potential losses are published by (1) individual insurers, (2) insurance publishing houses, and (3) the Insurance Division of the American Management Association. The American Management Association encourages free and open use of its "risk analysis questionnaire," which is probably the most detailed published checklist available. Like most checklists prepared by insurers or insurance publishing houses, the 43-page AMA questionnaire is designed to do more than suggest the types of potential losses that the firm may face. The questionnaire also seeks information that is required (1) to measure the risks identified and (2) to underwrite, price, and prepare insurance policies that will cover these risks. Existing insurance protection, loss-prevention measures, and other risk management devices are other topics included in the questionnaire.

The basic nature of the questionnaire is indicated by the following summary of the major headings:

General I: Name, Officers, History, and Locations
General II: Financial Organization
General III: Plant Management
Building and Location Schedule
Contents Schedule
Fire Underwriting Schedule
Automobile Exposure Schedule
Plate Glass
Elevators
Boiler and Machinery Schedule
Crime Section
Fidelity Schedule
Business Interruption Schedule and Work Sheet
Extra Expense Insurance Guide
Transportation Schedule
Boat and Aircraft Exposure Schedule
Claim and Loss Schedule
Key Man—Welfare Schedule
Receipt for Policies and Documents

In order to illustrate the detailed nature of the inquiry, the questions in the contents schedule are reproduced in Table 4.1.

Instead of using published checklists, the risk manager or insurance representative may wish to develop one of his own. This is a time-consuming task, but if he develops his own checklist, his imagination may add risks that are not included in the published checklists. Some published checklists are limited to insurable risks (sometimes readily insurable and sometimes insurable by a single insurer). Risk management requires a wider horizon. By comparing the new checklist with published checklists, he should be able to avoid omitting any of the more common types of risks. A second reason for constructing a new checklist is that the questions can be arranged in a manner that is most meaningful to the risk manager. Published questionnaires tend to organize the questions on potential losses into sections dictated by the types of insurance available, such as fire insurance, auto-

Table 4.1   American Management Association Risk Analysis Questionnaire

Schedule number_____
Location number_____
Building number_____

CONTENTS SCHEDULE

1. Machinery, equipment, tools, and dies:
   a. Replacement cost new_____
   b. Actual cash value_____
   c. Basis for (b); obtain appraisal if available_____

   d. Any chattel mortgage_____
      Name_____
      Address_____
2. Furniture & fixtures, equipment & supplies:
   a. Replacement cost new_____
   b. Actual cash value_____
   c. Basis for (b); obtain appraisal if available_____

   d. Any chattel mortgage_____
      Name_____
      Address_____
3. Improvements & betterments:
   a. Date installed_____
   b. Original cost_____
   c. Replacement cost_____
   d. Actual cash value_____
   e. Describe_____
   f. Obtain appraisal if available_____
4. Stock (raw, in process, and finished):
   a. Maximum—at cost_____ at selling price_____
   b. Minimum—at cost_____ at selling price_____
   c. Average at cost_____ at selling price_____
   d. Present—at cost_____ at selling price_____
   e. How and when inventoried?_____
   f. Any fluctuations between buildings_____
5. Property of others for repair, processing, or other purpose
   (including goods held on consignment)_____

6. Is there any agreement covering your responsibilities for these values?_____

7. Property of concessionaires_____Consignors_____
8. Employees' belongings_____
9. Valuable papers or drawings:_____
   a. Value_____Reproduction cost_____
   b. Where kept_____
   c. Description_____
10. Value of exhibits—sales office_____
11. Describe type, size, and value of signs:_____
    a. On premises_____
    b. At other locations_____

12. Care, custody, or control problems_____

13. Water damage and sprinkler leakage exposure and percentage of contents value subject to
    loss_____
14. Any unusual cameras, scientific equipment, or valuable instruments_____

15. Any fine arts in office_____
16. Any electronic computers, calculators, or similar "electronic brains"_____

    a. Who owns them?_____
    b. If leased, who is responsible for damage or destruction?_____
    c. Cost to replace data stored in destroyed unit_____
    d. Potential business interruption exposure_____
    e. Any use by others_____
    f. Liability for loss or destruction of data_____
17. Is stock subject to:
    a. Consequential loss?_____
    b. Crime loss?_____
    c. Damage by heat or cold?_____

mobile insurance, and transportation insurance. One alternative consumer-oriented classification system is the following:

A. Property and liability losses
   1. Property losses
      a. Direct losses associated with the need to replace or repair damaged or missing property.
      b. Consequential losses, such as an interruption of business, that are caused by the direct loss
   2. Liability losses arising out of damage to or destruction of others' property or personal injuries to others
B. Personnel losses
   1. Losses to the firm itself as a result of death, disability, or old age of employees, customers, or owners.
   2. Losses to the families of personnel or to the personnel themselves as a result of their death, disability, old age, or unemployment.[1]

In Chapters 6, 7, and 8 the major property, liability, and personnel risks faced by a business will be analyzed according to this outline. This analysis can be the basis either for creating a new checklist or for better understanding some published checklist.

Some analysts use insurance *policy* checklists to determine potential losses. The most useful policy checklists are those that group policies according to the types of exposures to which they apply (for example, banks, families, or department stores).[2] If the person reading the list knows the types of losses covered under each contract, he is alerted to the most important types of risks faced by businesses of this sort. This, however, is an awkward, inefficient way to identify the relevant potential losses. Furthermore, it identifies, at best, only all insurable risks. On the other hand, these checklists provide an extremely useful listing of the insurance contracts to be considered in selecting the proper tool.

APPLICATION OF CHECKLIST

The second step in risk identification is to use the checklist developed in step 1 to discover and describe the types of losses faced by a particular business. In some instances the person applying the checklist is so familiar with the property, operations, and personnel of the business that he can identify its risks by taking each item in the checklist and reflecting on the ways in which the business is exposed to that potential loss. However,

---

[1] As will be explained in Chap. 8, businesses are deeply concerned with personnel risks faced by their employees. Employee benefit plans covering these risks are commonplace. Employee benefit plans covering property and liability risks are still in their infancy, but the infant is extremely active.

[2] See, for example, R. C. McCormick, *Coverages Applicable* (1970 ed., Indianapolis: The Rough Notes Company, 1970).

because most businesses are complex, diversified, dynamic operations, a more systematic method of exploring all facets of the specific firm is highly desirable. Two methods that have been suggested are (1) the financial statement method and (2) the flow-chart method.

The financial-statement method   One systematic procedure for determining which of these potential losses apply to a particular firm has been proposed by A. H. Criddle.[3] The Criddle method is based on the various financial records and statements which are produced as part of the usual management reports of the business firm. The assumption underlying this method is that financial account titles serve as reminders of the various exposures to loss. Although the risk manager may often need to go beyond what is recorded in the balance sheet, operating statement, or supplementary financial reports in order to determine the complete picture, he will find that proceeding systematically through these statements is an excellent way to review the firm's properties and activities and to discover what additional investigations may be necessary. The financial-statement analysis may in fact reveal some potential losses which the risk manager omitted in his supposedly comprehensive list of risks. Criddle's analysis with respect to the inventory item in the balance sheet illustrates how account titles, coupled with some appreciation of the various losses which could occur, can help to identify potential losses:

> Inventory:
> The exposure represented by this item relates to inventory owned by and in the possession or under the control of the corporation at the date of the financial statement. It probably consists of raw materials and supplies and finished products. Inventory may be in the company's own manufacturing premises or in private or public warehouses or in the custody of processors or suppliers or in due course of transit. All such property is subject to physical damage, destruction or loss of possession. If this occurs, there is a possible consequential risk because of business interruption or other loss-causing conditions which were set in motion by the property destruction. There is also the risk of liability being incurred for injuries to persons or damage to property of others arising out of the ownership, existence or use of this property. Another characteristic is that such property customarily moves from place to place while still completely owned by the corporation; thus, there is a possible transit and location risk which may be significant with respect to high valued inventory items, especially when being transported by the corporation's own delivery equipment.
> Risk investigation of these items begins at the point the corporation takes title, and embraces all possible loss, exposures in transit, while in the company's own plant, or in storage, or in the hands of processors or others,

---

[3] A. Hawthorne Criddle, "A Theory of Risk Discovery," *National Insurance Buyer*, VI, No. 1 (January, 1959), 8, 14–18, 31, 35, 39. It is interesting to note that this improvement on the traditional insurance survey was suggested by a leading insurance broker.

or in inter-plant transit, until incorporated into final form and sold, delivered to and accepted by others. Values are necessary by locations and modes of transit. Because "inventory" is an item known to fluctuate, the investigation of values at risk should include maximum and minimum ranges.[4]

The flow-chart method   Another systematic procedure for identifying the potential losses facing a particular firm is the flow-chart approach. The flow-chart method can be used independently, but a combined financial-statement and flow-chart approach would be the best way to identify the risks facing a particular firm. In the words of one experienced risk manager,

> At the top of the chart, you put the raw materials at your suppliers' plants and your purchased utilities; at the bottom, the ultimate consumer of your product. There should be enough blank paper between that you can trace your operation through its entirety—your plants, processes, warehouses, common carriers, and occupational diseases—remembering such offshoots as research, advertising, and airplanes, that are not directly in this flow but certainly have a part in the panorama. If yours is a multiple-plant operation, you may well need a flow chart for each plant, or at least one for each group of similar plants.
>
> Now, with this simple—or complex—picture completed, you consider what might be the result if something of an insurable nature went wrong somewhere in this chain. . . .[5]

In applying either of these two methods two sources of information that are helpful, but which have not been specifically mentioned in the above descriptions, are (1) statistical records of past losses and (2) regular reports from other departments that reveal changes in kinds and amounts of exposure. Past losses or near-losses might be repeated, and other departments are constantly creating or becoming aware of risks that might otherwise escape the risk manager's notice.

USE OF OUTSIDERS TO APPLY CHECKLISTS

A risk manager may rely on insurance agents or brokers[6] to do the detailed work of risk identification. Bringing insurance representatives into the picture

---

[4] *Ibid.,* p. 16. Reprinted with permission.

[5] Reprinted with permission from A. J. Ingley, "Problems of Risk Analysis," *The Growing Job of Risk Management,* AMA Management Report No. 70 (New York: American Management Association, 1962), pp. 137–38. Mr. Ingley then goes on to state that the "question is not simply what *could* happen but how often and to what extent. You also want to know what effect it would have on your company's health." This is the task of risk measurement.

[5] See Chap. 23 for a discussion of insurance agents, brokers, and consultants. Consultants differ from insurance agents and brokers in that they sell advice on a fee basis only; they do not place insurance or receive commissions. In a sense they are a temporary or part-time addition to the risk manager's staff.

has the advantage of presenting to the risk manager the best thinking and informed opinion of a professional risk analyst. An insurance agent or broker may handle as many as 100 to 200 accounts, and the experience he gains in working with them is invaluable. Another advantage is that these services may be obtained normally at little or no direct cost but are paid indirectly through the commissions earned on the sale from the insurer.

Relying completely on insurance representatives, however, has also some important disadvantages. First, although some insurance representatives have demonstrated far more imagination than most risk managers in uncovering risks, most limit their analysis to insurable risks. Second, because of the time and energy which must be expended in preparing a comprehensive survey, particularly for a large firm, many insurance representatives will be understandably reluctant to undertake this task unless they have a reasonable chance of providing at least part of the insurance suggested by the survey. Until the risk manager has had an opportunity to do some informed thinking about his potential losses and the ways in which they might be handled, he may not be prepared to limit his access to insurers in any way.

A more satisfactory approach, where it is possible, is for the risk manager to prepare his own analysis first and to check this analysis with an insurance survey which is solicited after the risk manager is better acquainted with his needs and the possible solutions. Preparation of an independent survey is time-consuming, difficult work, but there is no better way to capitalize on the risk manager's intimate knowledge of his firm's or family's property, operations, and management philosophy. The preparation of a survey will also give the risk manager a much better appreciation of the potential losses facing his firm or family than any survey by an outsider; he will be much better able to notice changes in his potential losses, and he should be able to make more intelligent decisions with respect to possible solutions.

THE BEST METHOD

While no single method or procedure of risk identification is free of weaknesses or can be called foolproof, certain methods or procedures do have advantages over others. The strategy of management must be to employ that method or combination of methods that best fits the situation at hand. This option may imply a greater use of published checklists and outsiders by the smaller firms that cannot afford to have the task done by specialists in their own management structure. Larger firms with a more sophisticated risk management department may show more originality in identification procedures and in the use of financial records or deductive approaches of risk classification and analysis.

Risk Measurement

After the risk manager has identified the various types of potential losses faced by his firm, he must measure these losses in order (1) to determine their relative importance and (2) to obtain information that will help him to decide upon the most desirable combination of risk management tools.

DIMENSIONS TO BE MEASURED

Information is needed concerning three dimensions of each potential loss: (1) loss frequency or the probability that losses will occur, (2) the severity of the losses that may occur, and (3) the degree of variation in the losses experienced from one budget period to the next. The next chapter will investigate how probability distributions might be used to measure these potential losses; the present chapter tells why each of these dimensions is important and describes how one practicing risk manager measures loss frequency and loss severity.

IMPORTANCE OF EACH DIMENSION

The relative importance of a type of potential loss depends upon the loss frequency and the loss severity. Contrary to the views of most persons, the more important factor is loss severity. A risk with catastrophic possibilities, although infrequent, is far more serious than a risk associated with frequent small losses and no large losses. On the other hand, loss frequency cannot be ignored. If two losses are characterized by the same severity, the loss whose frequency is greater should be ranked higher. A loss associated with a certain severity may be ranked above a loss with a slightly higher severity because the frequency of the first loss is much greater than that of the second. There is no formula for ordering the losses in order of importance, and different persons may develop different rankings. The rational approach, however, is to place more emphasis on loss severity.

An example may clarify the point. The chance of an automobile collision loss may be greater than the chance of being sued as a result of the collision, but the potential severity of the liability loss is so much greater than the damage to the owned automobile that there should be no hesitation in ranking the liability loss over the property loss.

A particular type of loss may also be subdivided into two or more kinds of losses depending upon whether the loss exceeds a specified dollar amount. For example, consider the collision loss cited in the preceding paragraph. This loss may be subdivided into two kinds of losses: (1) collision losses of $100 (or some other figure) or less and (2) losses over $100. Losses in the second category are the more important although they are less frequent. Another illustration would be the losses associated with relatively small medical expenses as contrasted with extremely large bills. Such a breakdown by size of loss shows clearly the desirability of assigning more weight to loss severity than to loss frequency.

In determining loss severity the risk manager must be careful to include all the types of losses that might occur as a result of a given event as well as their ultimate financial impact upon the firm. Often, while the less important types of losses are obvious to the risk manager, the more important types are much more difficult to identify. Chapter 6 will discuss, for example, the recognition and measurement of direct and indirect or consequential property losses. The potential direct property losses are rather generally appreciated in advance of any loss, but the potential indirect losses (such as the interruption of business while the property is being repaired) are commonly ignored until the loss occurs.

The ultimate financial impact of the loss is even more likely to be ignored in evaluating the dollar value of any loss. Relatively small losses cause only minor problems because the firm can meet these losses fairly easily out of liquid assets. Somewhat larger losses, however, may force the firm to borrow funds, and the cost of borrowing must be added to what otherwise would be the dollar loss. Finally, very large losses may have serious adverse effects upon the firm's financial planning,[7] and their dollar impact may be much greater than it would be for a firm which could more easily absorb these losses. Ultimately the loss could be the ruin of the business as a going concern.

To illustrate, a fire could destroy a building and its contents valued at $100,000; the ensuing shutdown of the firm for six months might cause another $120,000 loss. This $220,000 loss might force the firm to shut its doors, an action that would result in an ultimate loss of the difference between the going-concern value of the business, say $800,000, and the value for which the remaining assets could be sold, say $400,000.

Finally, in estimating loss severity, it is important to recognize the timing of any losses as well as their total dollar amount. For example, a loss of $1,000 a year for 20 years is not as severe as an immediate loss of $20,000 because of (1) the time value of money, which can be recognized by discounting future dollar losses at some assumed interest

[7] Professor Bob A. Hedges, who suggested this threefold classification of losses, points out that large losses may disarrange cash flows and exhaust credit lines. Bob A. Hedges, "'Proper' Limits in Liability Insurance," *Journal of Insurance*, XXVIII, No. 2 (June, 1961), 73.

rate, and (2) the ability of the firm to spread the cash outlay over a longer period.

It may seem strange that the third dimension—the estimated variation or risk—has been ignored in determining the importance of the various losses. The reason is that inability to predict the losses in any budget period is not nearly as critical a factor in this regard as loss frequency or severity. In fact, a loss for which the degree of risk and uncertainty is very high (for example, 1 exposure unit subject to a total loss of $5 for which the chance of loss is 0.50) *may* be relatively unimportant.

In determining the best way or ways to handle the loss, however, all three dimensions are important. The loss-frequency and loss-severity data, for example, enable the risk manager to determine the losses that will be experienced in an average year, which is an important cost factor. The loss-severity data will also indicate, among other things, the maximum loss that the firm may have to absorb if it does not transfer the loss to some other party. The estimated risk will reflect the ability of the firm to predict its own losses and thus to handle these losses itself. These thoughts are developed further in Chapters 12 and 13, which deal with the selection of the proper risk management tools.

THE PROUTY APPROACH

One interesting qualitative measurement of loss frequency has been suggested by Richard Prouty, the risk manager for a large business firm.[8] Mr. Prouty suggests that for each potential loss-cause combination (destruction of a building by fire, for example), the risk manager should indicate whether the probability of loss is "almost nil" (meaning that in the opinion of the risk manager the event could not happen), "slight" (meaning that, though possible, the event has not happened to the present time), "moderate" (meaning that it happens once in a while), or "definite" (meaning that it happens regularly). These probabilities are influenced by the probability that any particular unit will suffer a loss and by the number of units exposed to loss. For example, the probability of a fire loss to one building could be "slight," but if the firm owns many buildings, the probability that the firm will incur a fire loss somewhere is "moderate."[9]

Mr. Prouty also suggests that loss severity may be measured by the maximum possible loss, the maximum probable loss, and the annual expected

---

[8] Richard Prouty, *Industrial Insurance: A Formal Approach to Risk Analysis and Evaluation* (Washington, D.C.: Machinery and Allied Products Institute, Jan. 19, 1960). For comments on this approach, see Robert Rennie, "The Measurement of Risk," *Journal of Insurance*, XXVIII, No. 1 (March, 1961), 87–91.
[9] For a very large firm, the loss could be definite.

loss. The maximum possible loss is the worst loss that could possibly happen; the maximum probable loss is the worst loss that is *likely* to happen. A worse loss could occur, but the chance of its occurrence is less than some percentage selected by the risk manager, such as once every forty years. The annual expected loss is the average annual loss the firm expects in the long run if the risk environment remains unchanged. It is affected by loss frequency as well as by the severity of individual losses.

It should be emphasized that a loss judged severe according to one of these three standards may not be judged severe according to one of the others. For example, the maximum possible loss may be large while the maximum probable loss is small, or the maximum probable loss may be large while the average loss is very small. Mr. Prouty observes that the maximum probable loss is the most difficult to evaluate but the most important to have correct.[10]

Although these three measures are extremely useful, they do not present the complete picture. One can construct many different probability distributions having the same maximum possible loss, maximum probable loss, and expected loss. For this reason the next chapter deals with probability distributions.

REVIEW QUESTIONS

1. "In a sense the most vital task in the performance of the risk management function is the establishment of a careful and systematic method of risk identification."
   a. Why is risk identification so important?
   b. Explain briefly the two steps in risk identification.
2. A business firm relies upon a local insurance broker to identify the risks faced by the firm. What are the possible advantages and disadvantages of this approach?
3. The risk manager of a firm decides that before consulting any insurer he will attempt himself to identify the risks faced by the firm.
   a. Would you recommend a standard "analysis form" for this purpose? Which one?
   b. Would you recommend an insurance policy checklist for this purpose?
4. Compare the financial-statement and flow-chart methods for relating the classification of losses to a particular firm or family.
5. a. For what reasons should a risk manager measure potential losses?
   b. What dimensions should be measured?

[10] Prouty, *op. cit.*, p. 6.

6. "Potential losses should be ordered in importance according to their loss severity." To what extent is this statement true? false?

7. In determining loss severity it is important to recognize (1) all types of losses, (2) their ultimate impact, and (3) their timing. Explain.

8. If risk is ignored in determining the importance of potential losses, why is it useful to measure the risk associated with potential losses?

9. As defined by Prouty, for which of the following firms is the loss frequency the highest: firm A, with one warehouse for which the probability of loss is $\frac{1}{20}$, or firm B, with fifty warehouses for each of which the probability of loss is $\frac{1}{20}$?

10. a. Distinguish among Prouty's three measures of loss severity.

    b. Is annual expected loss strictly a measure of loss severity? Illustrate your answer.

11. The risk manager of a firm maintains that the dollar value of the maximum probable loss to a building as a result of a steam-boiler explosion is $150,000, while his assistant estimates it to be $100,000. Both agree that the maximum possible loss is the complete destruction of the building.

    a. Why do their estimates of the dollar value of the loss differ?

    b. Do the dollar values provide an adequate measure of the amount of this loss relative to a $10,000 loss?

SUGGESTIONS FOR ADDITIONAL READING

The Growing Job of Risk Management, AMA Management Report No. 70 (New York: American Management Association, 1962), pp. 97–150.

MacDonald, Donald L.: *Corporate Risk Control* (New York: The Ronald Press Company, 1966), chaps. 3 and 4.

McCormick, Roy C.: *Coverages Applicable* (1970 ed., Indianapolis: The Rough Notes Company, 1970).

Mehr, Robert, and Hedges, B. A.: *Risk Management in the Business Enterprise* (Homewood, Ill.: Richard D. Irwin, Inc., 1963), chap. 6.

Mielke, R. G.: *Insurance Surveys: Business—Personal* (5th ed., Indianapolis: The Rough Notes Company, 1962).

Practices in Risk Management—Selected Readings (Bryn Mawr, Pa.: Insurance Institute of America).

Principles of Risk Management—Supplementary Readings (Bryn Mawr, Pa.: Insurance Institute of America).

Prouty, Richard: *Industrial Insurance: A Formal Approach to Risk Analysis and Evaluation* (Washington, D.C.: Machinery and Allied Products Institute, 1960).

Risk Analysis Questionnaire (New York: American Management Association).

5

probability distributions and risk measurement

A more sophisticated way to measure potential losses than the Prouty and related approaches discussed in the preceding chapter involves probability distributions. Unfortunately this method is more difficult to explain and the data needed to construct the required probability distributions are commonly not available. Nevertheless, probability distributions make possible more comprehensive risk measurements than the techniques discussed earlier; also, they are becoming a more common tool of modern management, and data sources are improving. Furthermore, probability distributions improve one's understanding of the more popular risk measurements and are extremely useful in determining which risk management devices would be best in a given situation.

Three types of probability distributions will be analyzed in this chapter: (1) distributions of total dollar losses per year (or some other period, such as a month or a calendar quarter), (2) distributions of the number of accidents per year, and (3) distributions of the dollar losses per accident. The analysis will indicate (1) the useful measurements that can be made with the help of these distributions and (2) how these distributions can be constructed.

Total Dollar Losses per Year

The probability distribution of total losses per year shows each of the total dollar losses of a given type[1] that the business may experience in the coming year and the probability that each of these losses might occur. For example, assume that the business has a fleet of five cars, each of which is valued at $3,000 and is subject to both partial and total physical damage losses. A hypothetical probability distribution that might apply in this situation is shown in Table 5.1.[2] In real life the number of outcomes in a similar situation would be considerably larger, but in order to emphasize the principles involved the hypothetical distribution has been intentionally oversimplified.

Each of the dollar losses per year could be produced by many combinations of the number of accidents per year and the average dollar losses per accident. For example, the $100 loss could result from one accident involving a $100 loss, two accidents involving an average loss of $50 each, or in many other ways. The $3,000 loss could result from one car being

Table 5.1 Hypothetical probability distribution of total physical damage losses per year to a fleet of five cars

Dollar losses per year	Probability
$ 0	.600
100	.300
1,000	.090
3,000	.006
6,000	.003
9,000	.001
12,000	{Almost 0
15,000	
	1.000

[1] No attempt will be made in this discussion to analyze the probability distribution of total losses of all types in a given year. Instead attention will be concentrated on losses of a given sort, such as physical damage to a fleet of cars, liability suits arising out of automobile ownership and operation, and physical damage to buildings and contents. In practice risk managers usually handle these separate exposures independently instead of jointly. However, there are dangers in doing so, because a business may suffer serious losses of various sorts in the same year.

[2] For a chart presentation of a different situation, see Figure 1.1.

totally destroyed, three cars suffering an average loss of $1,000 each, or some other combination of accidents and average loss. If a car can be damaged more than once a year, even the $15,000 loss could result from several combinations.

USEFUL MEASUREMENTS

From probability distributions of total dollar losses per year one can obtain useful information concerning (1) the probability that his business will incur some loss, (2) the probability that "severe" losses will occur, and (3) the risk or variation in the possible results. The measurement of each of these dimensions will be illustrated using the probability distribution in Table 5.1.

Given this distribution, the probability that the business will suffer no dollar loss is .60. Because the business must either suffer no loss or some loss, the sum of the probabilities of no loss and of some loss must equal 1.0. Consequently the probability of some loss is equal to 1.0 − .60, or .40. If the business suffers some loss during the year, the total dollar value of the losses must equal one and only one of the dollar values in Table 5.1. For this reason, an alternative way to determine the probability of some loss is to sum the probabilities for each of the possible total dollar losses; i.e., .300 + .090 + .006 + .003 + .001, or 40.

The potential severity of the total dollar losses can be measured by stating the probability that the total losses will exceed various values. For example, the risk manager may be interested in the probability that the dollar losses will equal or exceed $3,000. He can calculate these probabilities for each of the values in which he is interested and for all higher values. For example, the probability that the dollar losses will exceed $3,000 is equal to .006 + .003 + .001, or .01. Table 5.2 shows the probability that the dollar losses will equal or exceed each of the values in Table 5.1.

Two possible uses of this table would be to determine (1) the probability that the dollar loss would exceed the insurance premium that might be required to purchase complete financial protection against this risk and (2) the probability that the dollar losses would cripple the firm financially if the risk is retained. In terms of the Prouty analysis, the maximum possible loss is $15,000. If the risk manager is willing to ignore events that have less than a 1 per cent chance of occurring, the maximum probable loss is $3,000.

Another extremely useful measure that reflects both loss frequency and severity is the expected total dollar losses or the average annual dollar loss in the long run. Because the probabilities in Table 5.1 represent the proportion of times each dollar loss is expected to occur in the long run, the

Table 5.2 Probability that total dollar losses in the Table 5.1 distribution will equal or exceed certain specified values

Specified value	Probability
$ 100	.400
1,000	.100
3,000	.010
6,000	.004
9,000	.001
12,000	Almost 0
15,000	Almost 0

expected value can be obtained by summing the products formed by multiplying each possible outcome by the probability of its occurrence; i.e., $0(.600) + $100(.300) + $1,000(.090) + $3,000(.006) + $6,000(.003) + $9,000(.001) + $12,000(Almost 0) + $15,000(Almost 0), or slightly more than $165. This value is useful because it indicates to the business the average annual loss it will sustain if it retains the risk. If an insurer uses the same probability distribution, it will have to collect this much in annual premium just to pay its losses. The actual premium, however, must be higher to cover in addition the insurer's expenses and provide some allowance for profits and contingencies. The risk manager must decide whether he is willing to pay this additional amount in order, among other things,[3] to rid himself of the uncertainty concerning the timing of the losses, which is the next dimension to be measured.

Two probability distributions may have the same expected value but differ greatly with respect to risk or the variation in the possible results. For example, an expected value of $165 may be produced by the distribution in Table 5.1 or by a $165 loss every year. Considerable risk is present in the first instance, but there is no risk when one knows what will happen each year. The greater the variation in the possible results, the greater the risk. If the risk is small, the annual losses are fairly predictable and the business may be well advised to treat these losses as an operating expense. If the risk is large and some of the unpredictable losses could be serious, it may be wise to shift these potential losses to someone else.

Up to this point, no yardstick has been suggested for measuring risk, but its relationship to the variation in the probability distribution has been noted. Statisticians measure this variation in several ways. One of the most popular yardsticks for measuring the dispersion around the expected value

[3] For these other considerations, see Chap. 9.

is the standard deviation.[4] When there is much doubt about what will happen because there are many outcomes with some reasonable chance of occurrence, the standard deviation will be large; when there is little doubt about what will happen because one of a few possible outcomes is almost certain to occur, the standard deviation will be small. These observations suggest that the standard deviation of the probability distribution could serve as a measure of the risk associated with that distribution. However, statisticians have also suggested that for many purposes the coefficient of variation is a better measure of dispersion.

The coefficient of variation is calculated by dividing the standard deviation by the expected value. In other words, the standard deviation is expressed as a per cent of the average value in the long run. Because a standard deviation of $20 is much more significant if the expected value is $10 than if it is $2,000, the coefficient of variation has more appeal as a measure of economic risk than the standard deviation. Many writers, however, prefer to relate the standard deviation to the maximum amount exposed, their reasoning being that a standard deviation of $20 is much more important if the maximum amount that can be lost is $100 instead of $10,000. The best procedure is to relate the standard deviation to both of these bases and to others that may be of interest in a particular problem.

These measures of risk, unlike the probability of loss, have no simple interpretation and are not bounded by zero and 1. However, by comparing any of these measures for two or more distributions, one can determine the relative degrees of risk inherent in those distributions.

HOW TO CONSTRUCT THE PROBABILITY DISTRIBUTION

Unfortunately risk management science has not reached the stage where historical data or statistical theories permit one to do more than sketch rough approximations of probability distributions of total losses per year.

[4] The standard deviation is obtained by subtracting the average value from each possible value of the variable, squaring the difference, multiplying each difference by the probability that the variable will assume the value involved, summing the resulting products, and taking the square root of the sum. For example, if the probability distribution were as follows,

Value	Probability
0	.25
$1,000	.50
$2,000	.25

the average value would be $1,000 and the standard deviation would be the square root of $.25(0 - \$1,000)^2 + .50(\$1,000 - \$1,000)^2 + 25(\$2,000 - \$1,000)^2$, which is $\sqrt{\$500,000}$, or about $707.

The standard deviation for the probability distribution in Table 5.1 is about $556.

Probability estimates based upon historical data   By observing the proportion of times the various potential dollar losses have occurred over a long period of time under essentially the same conditions, one can estimate the probability of each possible outcome. But seldom, if ever, does one have the experience required to construct a reliable probability distribution in this fashion. Changes are occurring constantly in the risk environment that shorten the relevant experience period. For instance, if only the experience during the past five years is relevant, the risk manager would have only five observations. Five observations do not provide enough information to sketch a probability distribution unless the five observations are approximately the same and there is good reason to believe that the risk or variation in the possible results is extremely small. By using monthly instead of annual observations, the risk manager would have sixty observations instead of five, but the variation in monthly data is likely to be greater than the variation in annual data. In any event, few businesses are likely to experience anything approaching the full range of their possible losses in five years. Consequently, except in a few situations (e.g., a business making many shipments, all of approximately the same value, or a business with many employees exposed to industrial injuries), a business cannot rely upon its own historical data to construct a probability distribution of total dollar losses per year, per month, or during some other period of time.

Trade associations, private insurers, and government agencies may be able to provide supplementary information, but (1) data from these sources are commonly limited to average losses—not frequency distributions—and (2) the data combine the loss experience of many firms that may differ from a particular firm in many significant ways.

At best the risk manager can generalize on the basis of a sample of information. His estimated distribution of losses, which is necessarily subjective, will be influenced by the information at his disposal, by whether he tends to be an optimist or a pessimist, and by other factors.

Probability estimates based upon theoretical considerations   Instead of relying on data of his own or on those provided by others, the risk manager may be able to supplement this information with some probability distributions based on theoretical considerations. Statisticians have used this approach to develop useful estimates of the probability distributions in other fields. For example, the most important theoretical probability distribution is the normal distribution. The nature of this distribution is indicated by the bell-shaped curves in Figure 5.1. The exact location and shape of this curve is determined by a formula described in most elementary statistics texts. The curve is a function of only two variables—the expected value and the standard deviation. The peak of the curve always occurs at the

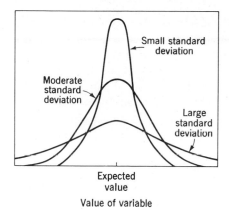

Figure 5.1 Normal probability distributions.

expected value. As is demonstrated in Figure 5.1, the smaller the standard deviation, the more clustered the outcomes will be around the expected value.

According to one classic text on statistical methods, for assumptions underlie this distribution:

1. The causal forces must be numerous and of approximately equal weight.
2. These forces must be the same over the universe from which the observations are drawn (although their incidence will vary from event to event . . .).
3. The forces affecting individual events must be independent of one another.
4. The operation of the causal forces must be such that deviations above the population mean of the combined results are balanced as to magnitude and number by deviations below the mean. . . ."[5]

The normal distribution has been used with considerable success to describe the probability distributions of errors in measuring a line, the neck sizes of college males, the annual message use of telephone subscribers, and the acidity of liquid dyes. Various statistical methods can be used to determine the adaptability or "goodness of fit" to available data.

The normal distribution is a particularly attractive probability distribution because it is relatively simple to determine the probability that the

[5] F. C. Mills, *Introduction to Statistics* (New York: Holt, Rinehart and Winston, Inc., 1956), p. 155.

variable will fall within a certain range of values.[6] For example, the probability is 68.27 per cent that the variable will fall within the range bounded by the expected value plus or minus 1 standard deviation; 95.45 per cent that the variable will fall within the plus or minus 2 standard deviation range; and 99.73 per cent that the variable will fall within the plus or minus 3 standard deviation range. With the aid of tables of the area under the normal curve found in almost all introductory statistics texts, one can make similar computations for other multiples of the standard deviation. For example, the probability is 98.76 per cent that the variable will fall within the plus or minus 2.5 standard deviation range about the expected value. Because the distribution is symmetrical with respect to the expected value, the probability that the variable will fall between the expected value and the expected value plus 2.5 standard deviations is one-half of 98.76 per cent, or 49.38 per cent. The probability that the variable will exceed the expected value plus 2.5 standard deviations is 50 per cent minus 49.38 per cent, or .62 per cent. The probability that the variable will exceed the expected value plus 1 standard deviation is 50 per cent less one-half of 68.27 per cent, or 15.86 per cent.

Even if one were correct in assuming that the probability distribution of total losses was normal, the distribution that the risk manager would construct would still be an estimate because he would have to estimate the expected value and the standard deviation. It is much easier to estimate these two parameters, however, than to estimate the entire probability distribution. Even a small sample of data may provide reasonably reliable estimates. In addition, the risk manager can supplement his own experience with the experience of others—insurers, trade associations, statistical agencies, and other firms. If, for example, a trade association reports that firms similar to his suffer annual losses of $500 per year and his own data indicate a $300 loss, he may want to estimate his average loss as some weighted average of these two figures. The more confidence he has in his own data, the heavier the weight he will assign to the $300. Some of the supplementary sources that the risk manager might wish to consult will be cited in Chapters 6, 7, and 8, which deal with property, liability, and personnel losses.

In determining his average loss, the risk manager should consider (1) the variability in the annual losses used to estimate the average annual loss and (2) any trends in the annual losses. If, for example, the annual

---

[6] The reader may have observed that the vertical axis in Figure 5.1 has not been labeled. That axis does not represent the probability that the event will occur. Unlike the distributions in Figure 1.1 which were discrete distributions dealing with a limited number of outcomes, the normal distribution is continuous, covering all values from $+\infty$ to $-\infty$. The area under this curve is the probability measure. The total area under the curve is 1, and the area encompassed by any range of values and the curve is the probability that some value in that range will occur.

losses have been steadily increasing each year, the average annual loss over the period may not be the best estimate to use.

Unfortunately, estimating a few parameters is not the only problem. It is clear that the normal distribution would not provide a suitable approximation to the distribution in Table 5.1, which is not an unlikely distribution for a business with a few exposure units. If the business had many more cars exposed to loss, it is true that the most likely outcome would be losses of some amount and the curve would be more nearly bell-shaped. Research has indicated, however, that the normal distribution is not in most instances a satisfactory approximation. Other theoretical probability distributions are being investigated, but much work remains to be done.[7] Most risk managers will have to rely for some time upon rough approximations to the probability distributions of total dollar losses per year.

Number of Accidents per Year

Researchers have been much more successful in their studies of the probability distribution of the number of accidents per year, although much remains to be done in this area. If each accident produces the same dollar loss, the distribution of the number of accidents per year can be transformed into a distribution of the total dollar losses per year by multiplying each possible number of accidents by the uniform loss per accident; e.g., 1($1,000), 2($1,000), 3($1,000), etc. If the dollar loss per accident varies within a small range, the distribution of the total dollar losses per year can be approximated by multiplying each possible number of accidents by the average dollar losses per accident. If the dollar losses per accident can vary widely, one needs the probability distributions of the dollar losses per accident and the number of accidents per year to develop information about the total dollar losses per year. However, even if information concerning the losses per accident is lacking, the risk manager will improve his understanding of the risk situation if he knows the probability distribution of the number of accidents per year.

Three theoretical probability distributions that are particularly useful in estimating the probability that a business will suffer a specified number of accidents during the next year are the following: (1) the binomial distribution, (2) the normal distribution, and (3) the Poisson distribution.

The binomial distribution   If (1) a firm or family has n units independently exposed to loss, (2) each unit can experience at most one accident during

---

[7] For a highly useful summary of the research in this area, see O. D. Dickerson with S. K. Katti and A. E. Hofflander, "Loss Distributions in Non-life Insurance," *Journal of Insurance*, XXVIII, No. 3 (September, 1961), 45–54. See also Robert Rennie, "The Measurement of Risk," *Journal of Insurance*, XXVIII, No. 1 (March, 1961), 87–89 and recent issues of the *Proceedings of the Casualty Actuarial Society*.

the year, and (3) the probability that any particular unit will suffer an accident during the year is p, the probability that the firm or family will suffer r accidents during the year is:[8]

$$\frac{n!}{r!(n - r)!}\, p^r(1 - p)^{n-r}$$

The term $p^r(1 - p)^{n-r}$ is the probability that r particular units will suffer an accident while the other $n - r$ units do not experience an accident. The term $n!/[r!(n - r)!]$ is the number of ways in which the r units which are to experience an accident can be selected from the n units.[9] To illustrate, consider the fleet of five cars for which the probability distribution of total losses per year was presented in Table 5.1. If one is interested in the probability that there will be exactly one accident, there are five ways in which this accident could happen, and the probability that it could happen in any one of these ways would be $p(1 - p)^4$. The formula yields the same result:

$$\frac{5!}{1!(5 - 1)!}\, p(1 - p)^{5-1} = 5p(1 - p)^4$$

If $p = \frac{1}{10}$, the answer is $5(\frac{1}{10})(\frac{9}{10})^4 = .328$, or almost one-third. The sum of the probabilities for no accidents, one accident, two accidents, three accidents, four accidents, and five accidents would be 1.

The probability that at least one of the five units will suffer a loss is the sum of the probabilities of one accident, two accidents, three accidents, four accidents, and five accidents. It can also be viewed as 1 minus the probability of no accidents, or $1 - (\frac{9}{10})^5 = 1 - .59 = .41$.

Statisticians have demonstrated that the expected value of this probability distribution is n times p, while the standard deviation is $\sqrt{np(1 - p)}$. Therefore, if $n = 5$ and $p = \frac{1}{10}$, as was assumed in the above example, the expected number of accidents during the year is $5 \times \frac{1}{10}$, or .5. In other words, on the average the business will suffer one accident every two years. The standard deviation of the distribution is

$$\sqrt{5 \times \tfrac{1}{10} \times \tfrac{9}{10}} \qquad \text{or} \qquad \sqrt{\tfrac{45}{100}} = .67$$

Risk relative to the mean is $.67/.5$, or 1.34. Risk relative to the maximum exposure is $.67/5$, or .134.

[8] $n!$, called *factorial* n, is equal to $n(n - 1)(n - 2) \ldots 1$.
[9] For example, assume that there are three units—A, B, and C. If two of these units are to experience an accident, the two units could be A and B, A and C, or B and C. The formula also indicates that three combinations are possible. For more details, see the discussion on permutations and combinations in most college algebra or statistics texts.

In practice, although it is very helpful to know that the probability distribution of the number of accidents may be described by the binomial distribution, one must still estimate p. Two risk managers faced with exactly the same situation may form different estimates. For example, one manager may estimate the probability of an automobile accident as .15, while the other estimates it as .05. The "true" unknown value may be .10. It should be clear that an error in the estimate of p affects the validity of the entire probability distribution. Even crude distributions, however, are better than no information at all if their limitations are duly recognized. Values of p can be estimated by a careful analysis of the firm's historical experience and by using supplementary information in the manner described earlier In this chapter.

It is instructive to analyze the formula for risk according to the binomial distribution in more detail. According to the formula relating risk to the maximum exposure [risk $= \sqrt{np(1 - p)/n} = \sqrt{p(1 - p)/n}$], risk is zero when the chance of loss is zero or 1. This result is in accord with the definitions of the chance of loss and risk. Furthermore, risk is at its maximum when the chance of loss is .50. This result, which has intuitive appeal, says that a person has the most doubt concerning the outcome when there are two out comes—a loss or no loss—and the odds are 50:50. However, if risk is defined as the standard deviation relative to the mean, i.e., $\sqrt{np(1 - p)}/np = \sqrt{(1 - p)/np}$, risk approaches its maximum value as p approaches zero. This relationship exists because the expected value approaches zero faster than the standard deviation. When p is close to zero, an extremely small standard deviation may still be a large percentage of the expected value.

For both risk measures, the risk decreases as the number of exposure units increases, but the decrease is not proportional to the increase in the number of units. For example, as the number of exposure units increases from n_1 to n_2, other things remaining equal, risk defined relative to n decreases from $\sqrt{p(1 - p)/n_1}$ to $\sqrt{p(1 - p)/n_2}$. In other words, the risk associated with n_1 exposure units relative to risk associated with n_2 exposure units is

$$\frac{\sqrt{p(1 - p)/n_1}}{\sqrt{p(1 - p)/n_2}} = \sqrt{n_2/n_1}$$

If $n_1 = 4$ and $n_2 = 16$, $\sqrt{n_2/n_1} = 2$. This result may be checked by computing the risk of each of the two values and comparing the results. Thus risk decreases as the number of exposure units increases but only in relation to the square root of the relative increase. An increase of n from 100 to 10,000, therefore, is more effective in reducing risk than an increase from 10,000 to 100,000, although the absolute increase in the number of exposure units is much greater in the second case. Moreover, since the existing risk with 100 exposure units is much greater than the existing risk with 10,000 units, the *absolute* decrease in risk in the second case is much smaller. In other words, risk decreases with each unit increase in the number of exposure units, other things being equal. Each unit increase, however, cuts the risk less than the preceding unit increase.

The normal distribution   As the number of exposure units increases, the binomial distribution approaches the normal distribution with an expected value of np and a standard deviation of $\sqrt{np(1-p)}$. The closer p is to $\frac{1}{2}$ and the larger the number of exposure units, the better the approximation,[10] but if p is more than $\frac{1}{10}$, the approximation is a fair one, even if the insured has as few as 25 units. As was indicated earlier in this chapter, with a table of areas under the normal curve it is a relatively simple matter to determine the probability that the number of losses will fall within a certain range of values. To illustrate: If a firm has 100 units independently exposed to loss for which the probability of an accident with respect to any single unit is $\frac{1}{10}$, the expected number of accidents is $100 \times \frac{1}{10}$, or 10. The standard deviation of the number of accidents is:

$$\sqrt{np(1-p)} = \sqrt{100 \times \tfrac{1}{10} \times \tfrac{9}{10}} \quad \text{or} \quad 3$$

Consequently the probability is 95.45 per cent[11] that the number of accidents will be no less than $10 - 2(3)$, or 4, and no more than $10 + 2(3)$, or 16. The probability is approximately 2.3 per cent that the number of accidents will exceed 16.[12]

Number of exposure units required to predict the future with a specified degree of accuracy   An important risk management problem is the determination of the number of exposure units the risk manager must have under observation in order for the probability to be a certain amount, say, 95.45 per cent, that the actual number of accidents during the period will fall within some range around the expected number. For example, assume that the chance of an accident is $\frac{1}{10}$. What number of exposure units must the risk manager possess for the probability to be 95.45 per cent that the actual number of accidents will fall within the range whose boundaries are the expected number of accidents plus or minus 10 per cent? From

[10] If p is small, less than $\frac{1}{10}$, the Poisson distribution to be described shortly is a better approximation.

[11] Because the number of accidents can only assume integral values, the probability that the number of accidents will fall between 4 and 16 is greater than 95.45 per cent. The correct probability is the chance that the number of accidents will fall between 3.5 and 16.5, which is a range of plus or minus $(10 - 3.5)/3$, or 2.2 standard deviations. This probability is 97.22 per cent. This correction becomes less important as the number of exposure units increases.

[12] With the correction noted in footnote 11, the probability is 1.4 per cent.

what was said in the preceding paragraph, if the normal distribution describes the probability distribution of the number of accidents,[13] the problem can be restated as follows: 10 per cent of the expected number of accidents must equal 2 standard deviations. The solution then is as follows:

$$0.10(n \times \tfrac{1}{10}) = 2\sqrt{n \times \tfrac{1}{10} \times \tfrac{9}{10}}$$

$$\frac{n}{100} = 2\sqrt{\frac{9n}{100}}$$

$$\left(\frac{n}{100}\right)^2 = 4\left(\frac{9n}{100}\right)$$

(after squaring both sides)

$$n = 3,600$$

This number is much larger than most risk managers would expect, but the requirements are also rather severe. For example, in this case the expected number of accidents would be $3,600 \times \tfrac{1}{10}$, or 360. The range is $360 - 36$, or 324, to $360 + 36$, or 396. Relative to the number of objects exposed (which was the basis used earlier to determine whether the risk decreased as the number of objects exposed increased), the per cent of maximum error permitted under this requirement was 36/3,600, or 1 per cent. If the risk manager prefers to state the margin of error relative to the total number exposed, a 10 per cent requirement can be restated as follows: 10 per cent of the *number exposed* must equal 2 standard deviations. The solution then is as follows:

$$0.10n = 2\sqrt{n \times \tfrac{1}{10} \times \tfrac{9}{10}}$$

$$\frac{n}{10} = 2\sqrt{\frac{9n}{100}}$$

$$\left(\frac{n}{10}\right)^2 = 4\left(\frac{9n}{100}\right)$$

$$n = 36$$

The expected number would be 3.6, rounded to 4, and the .9545 probability range would be $3.6 - 2(1.8)$ or 0 to $3.6 + 2(1.8)$ or, after rounding, 7.

The Poisson distribution   The binomial and normal distributions may not provide as good a description of the probability distribution of the number of accidents as some other common distributions. For example, if the chance that a particular unit will be involved in an accident is less than $\tfrac{1}{10}$, the

---

[13] If the nature of the probability distribution is not known, other techniques can be used to estimate the required number of exposure units for a given degree of accuracy. These techniques, being very conservative, suggest an even larger number of units than does the approach illustrated here.

Poisson distribution provides a better approximation to the binomial distribution than does the normal distribution. According to this distribution, the
probability that there will be r accidents is

$$\frac{(np)^r e^{-np}}{r!}$$

where e is always 2.71828. . . . The mean of this distribution is np; the
standard deviation, $\sqrt{np}$. For example, if $n = 100$ and $p = .02$, the probability of three accidents is [14]

$$\frac{(100 \times .02)^3 e^{-(100 \times .02)}}{3!} = \frac{(2)^3 e^{-2}}{3!}$$

$$= \frac{8 \times .135}{6} = .18$$

The mean of this distribution is 2; the standard deviation, $\sqrt{2}$.

The Poisson distribution is also more appropriate than the binomial
distribution if the exposure units can suffer more than one loss during
the exposure period.[15] This is a common situation in risk management problems. Given the expected number of accidents during the exposure period,
it is possible to compute the probability that there will be r accidents according to the formula presented in the previous paragraph. For example, assume
that the fleet of five cars whose probability distribution of total losses per
year was presented in Table 5.1 has been experiencing about one accident
every two years. Each of the cars in the fleet could be involved in more
than one accident each year. Consequently the Poisson distribution is applicable with a mean of .5. The probability of no accidents, therefore, is
$(.5)^0 e^{-.5}/0! = .607$.

Similar calculations can be made for the probability of any specified
number of accidents. The maximum possible number of accidents is unlimited (not 5 as was true for the binomial distribution), but the probability of
more than four accidents is negligible (less than .001).

If the probability of an accident is not the same for each of the buildings, cars, lives, or other independent exposure units, the negative binomial
distribution, whose characteristics will not be discussed in this text, may
provide a more satisfactory description of the probability distribution.[16]

[14] Tables of e raised to various negative integral exponents and of $r!$ make this calculation
easier than it first appears. In addition, the Poisson probabilities themselves have been
tabulated for various pairs of the mean and r.
[15] In this case it is necessary to consider each day, hour, or minute as a separate independent exposure, during which the probability of an accident is very small.
[16] An even more sophisticated and complicated analysis would recognize that the units
may not be independently exposed to loss. For example, a fleet of cars may be housed
every night in the same garage.

Dollar Losses per Accident

Researchers have also had some success describing the probability distribution of the dollar losses per accident. This distribution would state the probabilities that the dollar losses in an accident would assume various values. For example, for the fleet of five cars that has served as an illustration throughout this chapter, the possible losses per accident might be $100, $1,000, or $3,000 with probabilities of .80, .17, and .03 respectively. The log-normal curve, which will not be explained here except to state that it is a normal distribution applied to the logarithms of the values instead of to the values themselves, appears to describe adequately the distribution of the losses per accident for many types of losses.

With a distribution of this sort one can calculate, among other things, the probability that the dollar losses per accident would exceed some specified amount. Because the total dollar losses in a year is the product of the number of accidents per year and the average loss per accident, one can make some statements about the total losses per year if he has probability distributions for the number of accidents and for the losses per accident. For example, the expected total dollar losses per year is equal to the expected number of accidents times the expected dollar loss per accident. For the fleet of five cars, the expected number of accidents is $\frac{1}{2}$, the expected dollar loss per accident $340, and the expected total dollar losses over $165.

REVIEW QUESTIONS

1. Given the following probability distribution of total physical damage losses per year for a business with a warehouse valued at $50,000:

Loss value	Probability
$ 0	.800
500	.150
1,000	.030
5,000	.010
10,000	.007
25,000	.002
50,000	.001
	1.0

a. What is the probability that the business will suffer some dollar loss in the next year? (.200)[17]

b. What is the probability that the business will suffer losses totaling $5,000 or more? (.020)

c. What is the expected total dollar loss? ($325)

d. If the standard deviation is $2,200, how would you measure the risk? (7 per cent or 0.04 per cent depending upon the base)

e. If the expected number of losses is .5, what is the average loss size? ($650)

f. What is (1) the maximum probable loss and (2) the maximum possible loss?

2. a. How can the risk manager estimate the probability distribution of total dollar losses per year?

b. If a theoretical probability distribution is discovered that adequately describes the general shape of the probability distribution of total losses, does this mean that the risk manager will have an accurate picture of the probability distribution of total losses?

3. Distinguish among those situations in which the probability distribution of the number of losses is adequately described by (a) a binomial distribution, (b) a normal distribution, and (c) a Poisson distribution.

4. The risk, according to a binomial probability distribution, is a function of the chance of loss and the number of exposure units.

a. How does risk vary with the chance of loss?

b. How does risk vary with the number of exposure units?

5. In a given situation, where the only possible outcomes affecting each exposure unit are either a total loss or no loss, the probability of loss is .10.

a. If the risk manager has only 1 unit exposed, what is the risk relative to the maximum number of exposure units? ($3/10$)

b. If he has 4 units exposed, what is the risk? ($3/20$)

c. If he has 16 units exposed, what is the risk? ($3/40$)

d. If he has 16 exposure units and the chance of loss is .20, what is the risk? ($1/10$)

e. Is the risk manager able to predict the number of losses better when he has 4 exposure units or when he has 40 exposure units?

6. The Ajax Corporation has a fleet of 100 automobiles. According to the best estimate available, the chance that any particular automobile will suffer a collision loss during the year is $1/10$. The automobiles are independently exposed to loss and no automobile can suffer more than one loss per year.

a. What is the expected number of collision losses for the firm during the year? (10)

b. The actual losses during the year may exceed or be less than this expected number. The risk manager wants to know the range around the expected losses for which the probability is about .95 that it will contain the actual losses in a given year. (14 to 26)

c. What is the risk expressed as a fraction of the expected losses? ($\frac{3}{10}$) of the number of exposure units? ($\frac{3}{100}$)

d. How many automobiles would the Ajax Corporation have to own for the .95 probability range to be bounded by (1) the expected losses plus or minus 20 per cent of the expected losses? (900) (2) the expected losses plus or minus 20 per cent of the number of automobiles to be exposed? (9, but is the normal approximation a good assumption?)

e. How would you answer d if the probability of loss were $\frac{1}{5}$ instead of $\frac{1}{10}$? (400 and 16)

7. The Beacon Corporation has 500 employees. Industrial injuries during the past 15 years averaged about 5 a year. An employee can be injured more than once a year.

   a. Explain how you would calculate the probability that next year industrial injuries will total 10 or more. The actual calculation need not be performed.

   b. How would your calculation be affected if you discovered that although industrial injuries averaged 5 a year, there were no losses during each of the first five years, 5 losses during each of the second five years, and 10 losses during each of the last five years?

8. What theoretical probability distribution describes the distribution of the losses per accident for many types of losses?

SUGGESTIONS FOR ADDITIONAL READING

Dickerson, O. D., with Katti, S. K., and Hofflander, A. E.: "Loss Distributions in Non-life Insurance," *Journal of Insurance*, XXVIII, No. 3 (September, 1961), 45–54.

Greene, Mark: *Risk and Insurance* (2d ed., Cincinnati: South-Western Publishing Company, 1968), chap. 2.

Mehr, Robert, and Hedges, B. A.: *Risk Management in the Business Enterprise* (Homewood, Ill.: Richard D. Irwin, Inc., 1963), appendix to chap. 4.

Neter, John, and Wasserman, William: *Fundamental Statistics for Business and Economics* (3d ed., Boston: Allyn and Bacon, Inc., 1966).

Proceedings of the Casualty Actuarial Society, various recent issues.

Schlaifer, Robert: *Probability and Statistics for Business Decisions* (New York: McGraw-Hill Book Company, 1959).

6

property risk identification and measurement

Businesses are subject to property, liability, and personnel risks. Among these risks, perhaps the most well-known are those associated with possible losses to property. Most risk managers are well aware of possible losses to physical plant, equipment, inventories, and other tangible assets caused by the perils of nature, human error, or dishonesty. The concept of property loss, however, is far more subtle and involved than may be suspected by the novice in this field. Concern for tangible property losses is merely one and perhaps the easiest phase of property-risk recognition and measurement.

From legal definitions we realize that *property* refers to a bundle of rights which may flow from or be a part of the tangible physical assets, but which independently possess certain economic values.[1] For example, these rights may include mineral rights, patents, easements, leasehold interests, rights of possession, the holding of property which has been pledged or conditionally given, or even expectations of future use or benefit.

In this chapter we give special attention to the identification of property losses in the broad sense, to the measurement of those losses, and to some loss-frequency and severity data.

[1] The following definition is illustrative: "The word is also commonly used to denote anything which is the subject of ownership, corporeal or incorporeal, tangible or intangible, visible or invisible, real or personal; everything that has an exchangeable value or which goes to make up wealth or estate. It extends to every species of valuable right and interest, and includes real and personal property, easements, franchises and incorporeal hereditaments." *Samat v. Farmers' & Merchants' Nat'l Bank of Baltimore*, 247 Fed. 669, 671 (4th Cir. 1917).

Property Loss Identification

WHAT IS PROPERTY

As we have indicated in preceding paragraphs, property has a much broader meaning than the mere physical or tangible assets. Basically these rights in property may be divided into two broad classifications: (1) rights or interests in real estate or land and its appurtenant structures or attachments and (2) rights in personal property or property not attached to land.

INTEREST IN REAL ESTATE

The institution of private property, that is, the right of private citizens to own, possess, and use land for their own purposes within a framework of zoning, licensing, and permissive regulations, is one of the primary attributes of a free society. Private rights to own and use land and buildings for personal or business activities are firmly embedded in the law of real property and a part of our traditions of Anglo-American jurisprudence.

Interests in land may be identified in various ways. Some of the more common methods of identification include the following:

Fee-simple estate This is the highest estate known and encompasses the greatest number of rights for the holder; subject only to the limitations imposed by the state, it represents an absolute right to real property. The owner of an unencumbered fee-simple estate may use it as he sees fit in such manner as not to run counter to any statutes or limitations placed upon it by the state. The holder of a fee-simple estate may acquire or dispose of it by will, gift, purchase or sale, or in any other manner that pleases him. The fee-simple rights are independent of time limitations, since the owner and his heirs may enjoy its use forever.

Losses may occur to a fee-simple estate by the discovery, first, of imperfections in the chain of title and by the subsequent discovery of interests which have not been fully alienated or sold or conveyed in prior real estate transactions. These reversionary interests many times crop up to plague the holder of the fee-simple estate.

Life estate The conventional life estate gives the tenant full use of the land and buildings during his lifetime. Since this interest is completely nullified at his death, the length of the estate interest is indeterminate in time. Upon termination of the life estate, interests in the property normally pass to "remaindermen," who are entitled to a full fee simple upon the demise of the life tenant. The remaindermen, or persons entitled to the reversionary interest of the life tenant, ordinarily have a vested interest in the property prior to the death of the life tenant, and therefore may obtain protection, such as insurance or other means to conserve the property even though present use and enjoyment are denied them. Similarly, the life tenant may wish to protect and possibly to insure the property for the value of its use during the continuance of his life. In this way it is possible that several interests may arise out of a single estate or property and several interests be properly indemnified in the event of its destruction.

Dower and curtesy interests   The dower interests of the wife may exist in all real estate owned by the husband at any time during their married life, but the degree of enforcement of this interest varies by individual states as to whether or not the wife may assert this dower interest in property which was sold or alienated prior to the death of her husband. A dower interest is usually equal to one-third of the value of the property held by the husband.

Similarly, some states give the husband the right of curtesy equivalent to the wife's dower right in property. The right of curtesy is acquired during the marriage or held at the wife's death. Many states have allowed the wife to transfer property without her husband's consent during her lifetime, since the curtesy interest matures only at death and is based upon the birth of a child entitled to inherit the wife's property. Many states have completely abolished the curtesy interest.

Community property   In several states all other property acquired after the marriage is presumed to be the joint effort of the husband and wife and therefore is classified as community property. If either spouse dies, the other has a valid right to claim his or her half of the community property.

Homestead rights   Statutes in many states have provided a homestead exemption to prevent the loss of a home by the levy of creditors against the property to satisfy the debts of the owner. Generally homestead rights give life tenancy to the surviving spouse but do not apply to real estate used for commercial purposes or any other purpose than a home. Homestead rights may also be alienated or disposed of by sale, mortgage, or release, unless the law prohibits such alienation.

Leaseholds or limited tenancies   In most situations, these estates arise when the relationship is that of landlord and tenant, namely, when the landlord who holds the greater estate gives possession or use to another for a period of time.

Other interests in land may include "tenancies at sufferance," which may be terminated at any time by the holder of the fee, or "tenancies at will," namely, terminable at the option or will of the landlord.

Incorporeal interests   Incorporeal interests in real estate are found in easements and franchises which may be held on the property. An easement may give to someone other than the owner of the land the right to use it for a specified purpose which does not ordinarily exclude the owner from using the land for a similar purpose. Adjoining lots, for example, may have a common driveway, and each party grants the easement to the other for a specified strip of land for this use. Easements are acquired by either express or implied grants. Where property is possessed and used over a long period of time, the easement may be obtained through prescription.

Licenses to use property may be granted in writing for a limited period of time, and are normally revocable at the will of the owner of the property. The licensee may have permission to spend considerable money in the process of improving his license, and therefore the owner may not in some cases easily revoke this privilege granted to him.

A secured creditor may have a legal or equitable interest in land, depending on which method of security financing is used (land contract or mortgage) and on which theory of real estate law the particular jurisdiction subscribes to.

With regard to secured creditors, it is important to note that the law clearly establishes their right to obtain and maintain insurance on the specific property securing the debt to their benefit. On the other hand, courts have disallowed unsecured creditors the right to collect on property insurance policies maintained on the debtor's property.

Each of the above legally enforceable interests often have certain economic value to the owner, depending on the values derived by exercising the right in the future. Possible loss or destruction of these interests by human or natural causes becomes the basic challenge to the risk manager in his efforts to protect his firm's basic economic position.

INTERESTS IN PERSONAL PROPERTY

Personal property, or as it is called in the law, *personalty*, refers to that property which is movable and not attached to land or buildings. The distinction between real property and personalty causes many problems in the law. For example, when the owner of a building purchases fixtures and improvements on conditional sale, the question arises as to whether these fixtures and improvements (such as a furnace) are a part of the real property and therefore used to satisfy the claims of the mortgagee, or whether they are still personal property, or personalty, and used to satisfy the claims of the seller of these items. The courts have resolved this conflict between the vendor on conditional sales and the mortgagee by suggesting that the conditional vendor may repossess the articles only if this can be done without serious injury to the larger unit.

When losses occur to personal property by theft, fire, wind, riot, or other perils, the questions often arise: Who owns the property? and who is the party who must bear that loss? The answers to these questions are often dependent on when and how the respective interests in the property were acquired in the first place.

1. The property may be purchased from a seller as *a bona fide purchaser for value*. Such a bona fide purchaser for value takes superior title to the property under most conditions, even if the seller may not have perfect title at the time of the sale. Of course, sales may be made according to conditional sales where title does not pass until after the last payment has been made. In general, the risk of loss follows those who may have title. This fact is true of ordinary sales, where the vendor or vendee has to bear loss depending upon which had title at the time the loss occurred. The conditional sales transaction, however, places the risk of loss squarely upon the vendee since he has possession and beneficial use of the property. The vendor merely has a security title for the purchase price, and the vendee therefore must assume all the risks of loss during his possession and use of the property. Where the loss may threaten repayment of the debt, certainly the vendor is likewise concerned with possible loss.

In transactions where the terms of sale are not clear as to when title passes, the courts have relied upon the method of billing and shipment as an expression of intent. Some states have enacted the Uniform Commercial Code which clarifies some of these questions, whereas other states still operate under the Uniform Sales Act. In general, the rules are as follows: (*a*) Goods shipped f.o.b. point of shipment places title in the buyer when goods are delivered to the common carrier, since the buyer is paying the costs of freight and the common carrier therefore is his agent. (*b*) Goods shipped f.o.b. point of destination transfers title to the buyer when goods are received from the common carrier, since the common carrier is the agent for purposes of shipment of the seller. (*c*) Goods shipped f.a.s. (or free alongside) passes the title to the goods when they are delivered intact alongside the conveyancing equipment, and therefore loss or damage during the course of shipment must normally fall upon the buyer. (*d*) Goods shipped c.o.d. (or collect on delivery) normally does not affect the passing of title. Such a provision in the bill of lading merely indicates that the shipper is retaining the right of possession in the goods until payment is made. Title passes to the buyer if he is to pay transportation charges at the time the goods are received by the carrier, but the seller reserves a lien on the property until payment has been made. (*e*) Goods shipped c.i.f. (or cost, insurance, freight) normally passes title at the time the goods are delivered to the common carrier at the point of shipment, and the insurance documents and title papers are given to the common carrier at that time.

Under the Uniform Sales Act, goods which are ascertained and identifiable and sold normally pass title immediately to the buyer. Where the ascertained goods must be placed in a deliverable condition, however, title does not pass until they are appropriated to the contract and placed in a deliverable state. For goods not identifiable or ascertainable, title normally does not pass until the goods become specifically identifiable and appropriated to the contract.

2. Interests in personal property may be obtained by gift, either *unconditional* or *conditional*. The law imposes the following requirements to make an effective gift: (*a*) The subject matter must be capable of legal transfer; (*b*) the donor must be competent; (*c*) the donor must have a donative or giving intent; (*d*) the actual or constructive delivery of the item given must be protected or completed; (*e*) delivery and acceptance by the donee are necessary; (*f*) the donor must be solvent and capable of such gift; (*g*) title in the donor is implicit or implied in a legal gift. Failure to complete any one of the seven requirements may eventually upset interests in property obtained by gift.

3. Still another way of obtaining an interest in property is through a *bailment relationship*, which is a legal transaction involving the surrender of possession to one person called the "bailee" and the retention of title or interest by another called "bailor." The typical bailment therefore involves some contractual relationship or implied understanding between the bailee and bailor that upon the completion of certain conditions or upon demand, property must be resurrendered to the bailor. As will be observed in Chapter 7, in the section on Bailee Liability Exposures, the obligation of the bailee is normally dependent upon the nature of the bailment, but in general a bailee is responsible for damage to the bailed property only if he is negligent.

4. Still another way of obtaining interests in personalty is by *lease*, which may convey to the leaseholder interests in use and possession of the property subject to contractual limitations and restrictions.

5. In addition to lease arrangements, interests may be obtained through *liens*, which are asserted for the benefit of obtaining satisfaction of other indebtedness. For example, an innkeeper normally has a lien on the property of the guests of the inn to the extent of the bill which is owned. Mechanics' liens are also privileged to the extent of the value of work performed on the property.

Valuation of Potential Property Losses

Once the risk manager has identified the various property interests that may be exposed to loss, he must move on to the equally important problem of establishing the value of those interests. In valuing losses he may need to call upon outside consultants who have expertise in valuing special kinds of real or personal property as well as to rely on talent within the firm itself.

Property-loss valuation must be approached from two different vantage points. First, the risk manager must set some dollar or financial figure on the economic loss incurred by the destruction of the tangible asset itself. For example, a fire loss to a company building will impose certain costs to the business firm in obtaining new space in another building or in rebuilding the existing structure. This loss of the intrinsic value of the property is referred to as direct loss. The second problem is to establish the destruction of economic value resulting from the destruction of the building in terms of loss of operation, interruption of processes, and additional costs to continue operations imposed by the fire until new facilities can be obtained. This type of loss is referred to as indirect loss.

The following discussion approaches the loss-valuation problem primarily from the point of view of the owner and possessor or user of the property. The risk manager must be aware of the loss-valuation problems surrounding the holders of other than fee-simple titles to real estate, such as life tenants and leaseholders as well as bailees, secured creditors, and other persons whose interests are reflected either in real estate or personalty. For example, a life tenant enjoying the use of property faces a potential loss that decreases as he grows older because his life expectancy decreases.

METHODS OF VALUING DIRECT LOSS TO PROPERTY INTERESTS

Whether the property be real estate or personalty, several basic measures of value are recognized by appraisers and others working professionally in this field. It is important to note that each method of property-loss valuation has certain advantages and disadvantages, depending on the purpose or emphasis of the valuation. For example, an appraisal of plant property for credit purposes may be quite different from a similar appraisal for insurance purposes. Each of the methods may be employed separately or in combination to arrive at that measure of value which suits the immediate purposes of the firm.

Original cost   Most business firms keep their asset ledgers and financial information relating to property on an original-cost basis. This figure is important for depreciation purposes, as well as for establishing the historical financial basis for the investment in the first place. Original cost is simply the amount of money paid for the property at its acquisition by the business firm. For purposes of potential loss valuation, however, original cost has many weaknesses. First of all, the value arrived at is completely dependent upon the price level and bargaining position of the business firm at the time of acquisition. Secondly, original cost takes no account of obsolescence or depreciation which has occurred during the period of use since acquisition. A building built to manufacture horse-drawn buggies may have little value today in the manufacture of modern automobiles. If the building is especially designed for a particular process or use, although it may possess an unusually high value for its owner, its special design also increases the possibility of technological or economic obsolescence. In conclusion, original cost is merely an historical figure of value which the accounting department and tax people must use in their calculations, but as far as the risk manager is concerned, it is in most cases a poor measure of actual loss arising from the destruction of the assets.

Original cost less depreciation Similarly, original cost, less accounting or even physical depreciation, has many deficiencies as a measure of value. The accountants depreciate the asset on the basis of spreading its cost over its useful life and reflecting this cost in each period of operations against the income earned during that period. Therefore, accounting depreciation may have little or no relationship to actual engineering or physical depreciation. Similarly, since original cost less depreciation begins with an historical figure in the first instance, a subtraction for depreciation may produce an equally artificial measure of value for the risk manager.

Market value In the case of real estate, the market value established by obtaining offers to purchase is an additional indication of value to the risk manager. The difficulty with this approach, however, is that market value is closely linked to the supply-and-demand function for real estate of the particular kind involved (what a willing seller or buyer will pay or accept for a particular piece of property) and the lot value, which usually is not destroyed by most contingent events. Here again market value also may vary with the economic conditions surrounding the investment, the level of interest rates, and the zoning or other limitations placed upon the use of the property. Market value is also somewhat difficult to establish, since each building is unique, and completely duplicate facilities seldom exist for most forms of real estate. Location of the lot and the economic use to which the building may be put are further factors or variables which may greatly influence the current market value of a piece of real property.

Personal property which is readily obtainable in established markets may be valued according to current purchase or invoice prices from these market sources. A typewriter can be valued quite easily by obtaining the purchase price of similar typewriters either in the new or used market and thereby determining the cost of such property in the market. On the other hand, market value for personalty in certain situations may be too low. A new car, one week old, may have a lower market value than its true value.

Tax-appraised value   The value placed upon the property both real or personal for tax purposes has been suggested by some as a way of establishing potential loss to property interests; but these values have many deficiencies. For example, tax values are based upon a given level of assessed valuation in the community or locality of the property. The extent to which these values are kept current and the very basis of establishing the value itself may thoroughly discredit it for potential-loss-valuation purposes. Tax-appraised value may at best be used as additional evidence of value.

The economic or use value of the building or personal property   Still another way of valuing property loss is by measuring the present value of the income it produces. For example, if a property produces a gross income of $50,000 at the end of each year for three years, the present value of this income stream is the sum of the present values of each of the three $50,000 incomes. The present value of each $50,000 is the lump-sum equivalent value at the present time. A sum of $50,000 payable one year from now is worth less than $50,000 right now because of the ability to earn some interest on the lump-sum equivalent during the year and because of some uncertainty concerning the receipt of the $50,000 at the end of the year. In the example cited, allowance must also be made for the fact that expenses must be deducted from gross income, but it would be possible and usually more exact to subtract these expenses from the gross income in advance and determine the present value of the net income. If the person appraising the property assumes a 10 per cent discount, each dollar payable at the end of the year is worth $1/1.10 or about $0.91 at the present time. In other words, $0.91 accumulated at 10 per cent for one year will yield $1 at the end of the year. The present lump-sum equivalent of $50,000 payable at the end of one year is about $50,000 (.091) or $45,500. The same procedure is followed with the other incomes except that the discount must be applied more than once. The $50,000 payable at the end of the second year, for example, must be discounted first to the end of the first year and then to the present. This second discounting process yields [$50,000 (0.91)] (0.91) = $45,500 (0.91), or about $41,400. The $50,000 payable at the end of the third year has a lump-sum equivalent of $41,400 (0.91), or about $37,700. The approximate present value of the three incomes, therefore, is $45,500 + $41,400 + $37,700 = $124,600. In practice this computation can be performed much more simply. Tables are available which show the present value of $1 payable at the end (or the beginning) of each year for n years. For example, if the interest rate is 10 per cent, the present value of $1 payable at the end of each year for three years is $2.4868. The present value of $50,000 payable at the end of each year for three years is, therefore, $50,000 (2.4868), or $124,340, which is close to the approximate answer developed earlier.

As the number of periodic payments increases, the present value gets closer and closer to the periodic payment divided by the assumed interest rate. Consequently, the present value of a long series of payments of $50,000, assuming 10 per cent interest, can be closely approximated as $50,000/0.10, or $500,000. Since a long series of payments is usually assumed in appraising property, this much more simple formula can be used.

This capitalization procedure is often used when the property is rented or peculiarly designed and the income and profit position of the firm would be directly affected by its destruction. The major disadvantage associated with using this approach to determine direct losses is that the value also reflects indirect losses, which should be measured separately. Furthermore, the value may be greatly affected by the location of a building and the skill of the management. And finally, the valuation method is very subjective.

Reproduction value   Reproduction cost operates on the assumption that the existing building would be replaced in the same design and construction at current prices. The underlying assumption under this method is that if a property is worth what it costs to reproduce at current prices, then this is the potential loss that would be suffered by the firm by its destruction. Several objections to this procedure have been expressed. If the property is of any age at all, few would wish to have the building reproduced as it currently exists. Changes in style and arrangement or even in the building's purpose would more likely be desired. The business firm would most probably not choose to reproduce the building exactly as it stands but would want to modify it in many ways in view of changing construction technology and changes in the internal operations of the company. While reproduction costs may not be the answer to valuing potential loss, they nevertheless often serve as an upper limit on value to the risk manager.

Replacement cost   Instead of visualizing the exact or even approximate reproduction of a given property, the interested persons may determine what it would cost to replace a building by another equivalent in terms of space or volume at the same or another location but of reasonable and current design and innovation. Unquestionably this method is extremely useful in measuring the value of any specific property. The basic problem here again, however, is that the business firm would be getting a new building for an old one; its cost may be an unfair amount to impose upon any potential-loss estimate. On the other hand, the argument can be effectively made that so long as the old building stands it can be used in its present design and construction. As soon as it is destroyed, however, these additional costs will be imposed on the business firm and therefore should be considered in any risk manager's appraisal of potential loss. The fact that a roof is ten years old does not in any way diminish the cost of replacing it with a new roof, and it is argued that the cost of the new roof should be the potential loss planned for in the loss-control program. These same observations would apply with equal validity to damage or destruction to personal property.

Replacement cost less physical depreciation and obsolescence   The recognition of actual physical depreciation as a valid subtraction from replacement cost can be justified in most potential property-loss-valuation calculations. According to many authorities, the cash position of the business should be such as to obtain adequate financing for innovations and improvements when the building is replaced. The risk manager, therefore, should plan only for the actual replacement loss of the physically depreciated or obsolescent property and leave to the finance or accounting department of the firm all capital budget planning for innovations and improvements. At most, the depreciation loss should be viewed as a consequential loss, not part of the direct loss. This practice is followed in this text.

   Risk managers may avail themselves of various appraisal-information services which publish the change in construction price indices for various types of buildings in various localities of the country. This appraisal information is of invaluable assistance to anyone who attempts to keep appraisal costs current in view of changing economic conditions. One word of caution is necessary: In using these indices one should note that they fail to take into account economic obsolescence, physical depreciation, or functional obsolescence that may be occurring in the particular property involved.

METHODS OF VALUING INDIRECT LOSS TO PROPERTY INTERESTS

When a building or item of personal property is destroyed, not only does the owner or user suffer the cost of its replacement, but he also usually suffers an interruption of the income or production from that destroyed unit. The risk manager must carefully appraise this additional loss in establishing and measuring potential property losses; it is most often ignored in potential loss calculations.

   Since indirect loss usually refers to economic loss resulting from inability to use or possess a piece of property, its determination is linked closely to a capitalization of income approach. For example, if the business firm were located on a particularly strategic corner in the community and relied heavily on walk-in business, the inability to occupy the premises over any period of time could result in a serious interruption in the flow of income to the company. The loss would be the present value of the interrupted income less noncontinuing expenses. Since this interruption would presum-ably not continue much beyond the repair period, the present value is the sum of the interrupted income each week or month discounted for interest. For example, if the interrupted income less noncontinuing expenses was $1,000 payable at the end of each of the next three months, the present value of this loss at 12 per cent interest compounded monthly would be $1,000/1.01 + $1,000/(1.01)^2 + $1,000/(1.01)^3 = \$990 + \$980 + \$971$, or $2,941.

If the property were leased, the lease would probably contain the usual fire clause terminating rights in a lease in the event of destruction by fire. If the fair rental value exceeds the contract rent, the loss of the lease may impose additional hardships on the business firm if a fire loss should occur to the property. For example, if the lease has ten years to run when it is canceled and the fair monthly rental value exceeds the contract rent by $1,000, the loss by cancellation would be $1,000 a month for ten years. The lump-sum value of the loss is the present value of $1,000 a month for ten years. This loss decreases with the passage of time. Looking at the transaction from the other side, the owner of the building or leased property would suffer an interruption in his rental income if the building were destroyed or made uninhabitable during the period of reconstruction and renovation.

Newspaper publishers, dairies, and other businesses which must have daily production capacity to preserve their relationships with customers could suffer irreparable damage if losses interrupted their production and market-ing activities. The extra expenses of obtaining other facilities to continue operations is an important indirect loss, which should be recognized.

Some indirect losses do not result from the inability to use or possess a piece of property and must be valued in some other way. For example, the difference between the replacement cost and the replacement cost less depreciation may be viewed as an indirect loss. The nature of this loss has already been described in an earlier section. Another example of an indirect loss not involving the loss of use of the property is the cost of removing the debris following a loss. Still another example is the additional cost of tearing down a structure and replacing it with a more expensive building; it occurs when a city ordinance requires that if a building not meeting current construction standards is damaged by more than a specified per cent, it be demolished. Some of these ordinances also apply to certain repairs to a building such as a new roof.

A more complete listing of the indirect losses facing a business than has been possible in the preceding paragraphs is presented below.

A. Indirect losses involving the loss of use of the property
  1. Loss of the rental value of owner-occupied property which is rendered untenantable by a direct loss
  2. Loss of rent on a property rendered untenantable by a direct loss
     a. To a landlord
     b. To a tenant, when the lease or common law requires that he continue to pay the rent even if the property is untenantable
  3. Loss to a tenant of the excess of the rental value over the rent when the property is rendered untenantable by a direct loss
  4. Loss to a tenant of the excess of the rental value over the rent for the remainder of a valuable lease which can be canceled by the landlord if the direct damage exceeds a certain per cent
  5. Loss by the landlord of the amount by which the rent exceeds the rental value for the remainder of a lease which is valuable to him but which can be canceled by the tenant if the direct damage exceeds a certain per cent
  6. Loss of net profits and continuing expenses caused by the interruption of sales by a mercantile operation or the production process of a manufacturing operation by direct damage to the premises
  7. Loss of profits on finished manufactured goods suffering a direct loss[2]
  8. Extra expenses incurred in order to continue operations following direct damage to the premises
  9. Increased collection expenses and bad debts as a result of direct damage to accounts receivable records
  10. Decreased sales or attendance as a result of inclement weather causing decreased profits or loss of investment
B. Other indirect losses
  1. Debris-removal costs
  2. Depreciation costs arising out of the fact that in many cases old damaged property must be replaced with new property even when the old property was performing satisfactorily
  3. Demolition costs and increased reconstruction costs as a result of city ordinances forbidding reconstruction of buildings not meeting certain standards if direct damage exceeds a certain per cent

---

[2] The reason for separating this seventh type of loss from business interruption losses will become apparent from the discussion in Chap. 17, in "Section I—Forms and Endorsements," under "Property Insurance."

4. Loss in value of the remaining part of a matched set or of machinery when the other part is damaged

Most of the serious indirect losses are associated with direct damage to real property because this type of property cannot be replaced as quickly as personal property. Furthermore, a used market exists with respect to many types of personal property.

Property Loss Frequency and Severity Data

The value of property destroyed by fire in 1969 totaled $2,415,000,000—an increase of $260 million over the previous year's total, according to the National Fire Protection Association Reports.[3] Of the property loss total, $1,940,000,000 represents damage to buildings and contents. Nonbuilding fires—those involving aircraft, ships, motor vehicles, and similar equipment, as well as forests—cost about $475 million. The worst property loss fire of 1969 in the United States was the $45 million fire at the United States Atomic Energy Commission's plant, operated by Dow Chemical Company at Golden, Colorado, on May 11.

In recent years, robbers, burglars, embezzlers, and other thieves have been making off with stolen property in excess of $3.5 billion a year—more than $9.5 million, on the average, a day.[4] While about 50 per cent of the stolen property is recovered—particularly is this true of stolen automobiles, of which 85 per cent are recovered—insured losses run into many millions of dollars annually.

According to the Federal Bureau of Investigation's *Uniform Crime Reports*, in 1968 the number of crimes per 100,000 inhabitants in the United States was 2,235, almost twice the crime rate in 1960. Crimes involving property losses numbered 1,940 per 100,000 inhabitants. Almost half of these crimes were burglaries (breaking and entering). The crime rates ranged from 389 per 100,000 inhabitants in North Dakota to 3,764 per 100,000 inhabitants in California.

While the FBI's annual *Uniform Crime Reports* does not include embezzlement losses, other authoritative sources estimate that losses due to embezzlers and other persons who misappropriate property of their employers exceed $5 million a day, or more than $1.8 billion a year.

Statistical plans filed by insurers with state insurance departments are another valuable source of accident data on fire, theft, and other property losses.

[3] See also *Insurance Facts* (New York: Insurance Information Institute, annual).
[4] See *Uniform Crime Reports* (Washington, D.C.: Federal Bureau of Investigation, annual).

REVIEW QUESTIONS

1. a. When a person says he *owns* a building, what could this mean in a legal sense?
   b. How would you estimate the value of a life estate to the person who holds it?
   c. Why should the risk manager of a business be acquainted with the various types of estates?
2. Two or more persons may have a property interest in the same real estate. Use three examples to illustrate the truth of this statement.
3. A firm purchases goods f.o.b. point of destination. At what point does the title pass to the firm? What other terms of shipment are possible and what is their effect upon the passing of title?
4. In what ways other than through a purchase may a firm obtain an interest in property?
5. Twenty years ago a firm purchased a building, which was then five years old, for $100,000. The price was generally considered a bargain. The firm's current balance sheet states that the building is worth $100,000 less depreciation of $60,000. What would be the direct loss if the building were totally destroyed by fire?
6. According to one construction index, the cost of building the structure described in question 5 has increased 50 per cent over the past twenty years. The risk manager decides, therefore, to value the building at $150,000. Criticize this valuation.
7. Describe briefly four types of indirect losses which a firm may suffer because it loses the use of property through a direct loss, and indicate how you would determine the potential dollar losses.
8. Describe briefly two types of indirect losses not involving a loss of use, and indicate how you would determine the potential dollar losses.
9. Cite some sources of information concerning the frequency of property losses of various types.

SUGGESTIONS FOR ADDITIONAL READING

Dillavou, E. R., Howard, C. G., Roberts, P. C., and Robert, W. J.: *Principles of Business Law* (7th ed., Englewood Cliffs, N.J.: Prentice-Hall, Inc., 1962).

Hoagland, Henry E.: *Real Estate Principles* (3d ed., New York: McGraw-Hill Book Company, 1955), chaps. 2–13.

Insurance Facts (New York: Insurance Information Institute, annual).

Mehr, R. I., and Hedges, B. A.: *Risk Management in the Business Enterprise* (Homewood, Ill.: Richard D. Irwin, Inc., 1963), chaps. 6, 8, and 9.

7

liability risk identification and measurement

In his treatise on the common law, the noted jurist Oliver Wendell Holmes, Jr., discusses very interestingly the history of the early forms and concepts of legal liability.[1] After examining various writings, both legal and literary, on ancient civilizations, Justice Holmes concludes that the early forms of legal redress were in fact grounded in the passion for obtaining vengeance. For example, in Jewish law as reported in the well-known passage in the Bible, revenge is taken against the thing causing the loss:

> If an ox gore a man or woman, that they die: then the ox shall be surely stoned and his flesh shall not be eaten; but the owner of the ox shall be quit. But if the ox were wont to push with his horn in time past and it had been testified to his owner, and he had not kept him in, but that he had killed a man or woman; the ox shall be stoned and his owner shall also be put to death.[2]

Similarly, the Greeks made provisions in their law for satisfaction of revenge when an intentional harm or injury had occurred. Plato wrote that slaves who had killed other men had to be given to a relative of the deceased.

[1] Oliver Wendell Holmes, Jr., *The Common Law* (Boston: Little, Brown and Company, 1923), pp. 1–38.
[2] Exod. 21: 28–29. This early Jewish law was a forerunner of the principles of *scienter*, relating to liability for keeping dangerous animals, found in our modern law. If the animal is known to be dangerous because of past acts, liability of the possessor or keeper is clearly established for the consequences of the animal's acts.

When an oxcart ran over a man, the oxen had to be surrendered to the injured party or his relatives. Justice Holmes states that these principles of liability in ancient law established the modern concepts of restitution and of punishment for the wrongdoer. The early legal concepts and others have gradually changed over the years to meet the needs of a more advanced, complex civilization. The fact that our modern law has extended legal responsibility to cover the consequences of unintentional or accidental acts or omissions greatly expands the liability risk for firms and families.

After defining legal liability and discussing its kinds and types, this chapter examines in some detail the concept of tort liability, which is the major concern of the risk manager. The chapter explores the components of a successful tort action and discusses the magnitude of the losses that could occur as a result of that action. The discussion then turns to some specific liability exposures and problems, including bailee exposures and those that involve motor vehicles, premises, employment relationships, business operations, and professional services.

Some Principles of Legal Liability

The term *liability* is used in various ways in our present language. A general definition is: the state of being exposed to damage, danger, expense, etc.; responsible; answerable. In general usage, the term has become synonymous with "responsibility" and involves the concept of penalty when perhaps a responsibility may not have been met. In the business world, accountants use liability to describe "the obligations (financial) of the firm outside of the equities represented by proprietary accounts which may require expression in definite financial terms. The amounts involved may be either due or accrued, or they may represent fixed or variable claims payable at a future date or dates."[3]

These general usages of the term "liability" must be distinguished from the use ascribed to the term "legal liability." A person may be generally obligated to another, because of moral or other reasons, to do or not to do something; the law, however, does not recognize moral responsibility alone as legally enforceable. *Legal* liability has been defined as "that liability which courts recognize and enforce as between parties litigant."[4] Thus the term "legal liability" is narrower than moral obligation, since the courts and the law determine what a person may be legally liable for. On the other

---

[3] *The Accountants' Handbook* (3d ed., New York: The Ronald Press Company, 1947), p. 883.
[4] *Abbott v. Aetna Cas. & Sur. Co.*, 42 F. Supp. 793, 806 (D. Md. 1942).

hand, the term is broader than the word "debt" or "indebtedness" and "includes in addition existing obligations which may or may not in the future eventuate into an indebtedness."[5] The word is not synonymous with loss or damage since a liability insurance policy may provide recovery to the third party claimant without actual formal litigation of the facts of the case.[6]

In conclusion, the term "legal liability" describes specific limited responsibilities and obligations, enforceable at law, which are independent of moral obligations and other feelings of responsibility. Only where such obligations and liabilities are found by a court or clearly established from prior court decisions does the individual or business firm find itself subject to possible enforceable financial losses or claims.[7]

VARIOUS KINDS AND TYPES OF LEGAL LIABILITY

An individual or a business firm may be held legally responsible in various ways. The two major classes of general legal liability are (1) civil liability and (2) criminal liability. Civil liability is distinguished from criminal liability by the nature and form of the action as well as by the penalties imposed. In the criminal action, the actual legal procedure is begun by the law-enforcement officer in behalf of society or the state. For example, the district attorney or attorney general of either the Federal or state government normally initiates the criminal action against the individual or business firm. Criminal liability must be clearly established by statute or administrative rule, whereas in civil liability, the statutes, administrative rules, and prior court decisions announce the rights of the parties as opposed to each other.

A civil liability action is brought normally by one party against another party for the wrongs alleged. Penalties consist of indemnity for the loss or punitive damages imposed by the courts, restitution of the property or loss, injunctive relief precluding future conduct or action, and other remedies, including possession of the property or an accounting of the property entrusted. These civil actions are brought by the litigants at their own expense and in the event of successful prosecution may impose the costs of the action on the losing party. In criminal liability cases, when it is clearly shown that the defendant is unable to hire counsel, the state will provide such counsel at its own expense.

[5] *Daniels v. Goff*, 192 Ky. 15, 232 S.W. 66, 67 (1921).
[6] *Ducommun v. Strong*, 193 Wis. 179, 214 N.W. 616 (1927).
[7] Another concept which is often misunderstood in discussing liability insurance and the concepts of legal liability involves the situation where the insurance company may deny liability but not deny coverage under the policy. The denial of liability to a third party under the policy may be based upon the substantive law relating to the peculiar facts of the case, whereas the insurance company may still assert coverage for the insured, should legal liability be found by a court of record. To deny liability to a third party under a policy is not the same as denying coverage to the insured—a fact often confused by claimants and insureds alike.

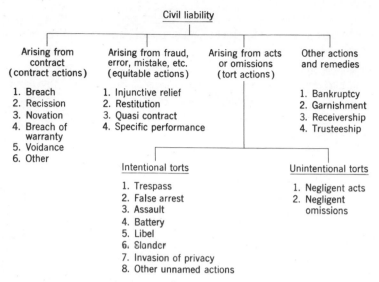

Figure 7.1   Civil liability analysis. [Equitable actions are actions or suits seeking equal and impartial justice, based on the spirit of fairness, justness, and right, as distinguished from the common law, which may not have afforded an adequate remedy. See *Black's Law Dictionary* (4th ed.; St. Paul, Minn.: West Publishing Co., 1951), p. 632.]

The discussions in this chapter are not geared to the problems of meeting possible criminal liability. While avoidance of criminal liability is important as far as business or individual conduct is concerned, generally the risk manager confines his activities to meeting the civil liability exposures, leaving these other problems to legal counsel and the conscience of those involved.

The concept of civil liability may be further classified into the varying kinds of sources of legal actions that may be brought to establish civil liability. For example, in Figure 7.1 the sources of civil liability are classified into those arising from contract or similar agreements, those arising from fraud, error, mistake, etc., referred to generally as equitable actions, and those arising from acts or omissions which are called "torts."

It should be clearly understood that in order to bring a civil action it is not necessary that the type of action be named as such but merely that the theory of recovery be established for deciding the rights of the parties. For example, breach of contract may in fact be accomplished by the commission of a tort. The plaintiff's attorney may decide to bring the action in contract law to recover damages suffered by the breach rather than to bring the action in tort law because of problems in establishing proof. It may be more difficult to show actual negligent conduct and legal duty of the defendant than to show nonperformance of the contract obligation. It is important to note that the figure does not attempt to catalog all the various types of actions that may be brought and their specific remedies, but merely to reflect generally on the more important theories of recovery which may be espoused in a legal civil liability action.

HOW CIVIL LEGAL LIABILITIES ARE ESTABLISHED

It has been stated in various writings that the law protects only those persons who can afford it. Although the statement is, of course, an oversimplification of the actual administration of the law, it makes an important point. Anglo-American jurisprudence is built upon the principles of advocacy and trial by combat; that is, the parties present their cases before the bar, outlining all the facts of the case as well as the law involved. The magistrate or judge must make the final determination from the written and oral presentations made to the court. This process of law requires that the litigant must either in his own behalf or with a professionally skilled attorney present his case as forcefully and as accurately as possible in order to arrive at the desired decision by the judge or jury. This process of administration has proved effective over the years in that justice and fair play generally have prevailed. On the other hand, it should be emphasized that the law does not profess to give justice specifically but to give each party the opportunity to have "his day in court." Having that day in court may be dependent upon the financial ability of the individual to obtain proper legal counsel.

Another important point which must be made in the discussion of the legal process is that the rights of a party are not protected in a civil case unless he himself takes the initiative to assert them. In other words, the law does not protect those who sleep on their rights. Most states have what are referred to as statutes of limitations, which impose time requirements upon the bringing of a legal action against another in a civil liability case. Failure to bring the legal action within the period of limitations will bar forever the injured party's right to recovery.

In addition to the statutes of limitations, other important provisions of the law must be met; for example, all the statutes relating to legal process must be complied with as well as statutes governing rules of evidence and methods of obtaining evidence. Generally speaking, the plaintiff in a civil liability case must carry the burden of proof by "the preponderance of the evidence." Some jurisdictions in negligence actions shift these burdens of proof during the course of the trial; such action depends upon the facts of the case and the legal principles involved. For example, under the doctrine of *res ipsa loquitur* the burden of proof may shift to the defendant. If so, he must show the absence of specific involvement with the facts alleged by the plaintiff.[8] The entire process of litigation is very technical and normally requires the skill and services of a competent attorney. It has been said that "he who attempts to litigate his own case has a fool for a client."

HOW AWARDS ARE DETERMINED

Historically, the role of the judge (or judges) in litigation is not only to supervise the conduct of the trial by ruling upon proper procedures and admissibility of evidence, but also to hold the opposing attorneys, as officers of the court, directly accountable for their conduct to the court as well as to their clients. The judge may impose serious penalties for improper conduct or procedure engaged in by either opposing counsel. In the absence of a jury trial (usually optional with either the defendant or plaintiff in most civil cases in most jurisdictions) the court performs the function of "trier of fact" as well as determiner and interpreter of the law involved. The jury role is traditionally limited to finding the facts of a case upon instructions from the judge as to the law.

Hence the question of damages may be an issue of fact as to their nature and extent, determined by the jury (or the judge, if no jury), or it may be an issue of law determined by the judge. Evidence as to the exact amount and nature of damage suffered by the plaintiff is introduced, and the kind of evidence admitted and the use of evidence is ruled upon by the judge as a matter of law. The use of demonstrative evidence, such as colored slides showing especially gruesome, bloody scenes of the plaintiff's injuries may be excluded from the trial on the ground that they shock the conscience of court as to what is fair and reasonable in the conduct of a trial. Several associations, including the American Trial Lawyers' Association, have been quite successful in encouraging the use of demonstrative evidence in personal injury litigation. Similar associations have been formed by defense attorneys to counteract these developments.

Damages may be special, general, or punitive. Special damages are usually the out-of-pocket expenses incurred by the plaintiff, such as medical

---

[8] The term *res ipsa loquitur* means "the thing speaks for itself," namely, for the fact that the plaintiff was injured under circumstances clearly establishing the possible negligence of the defendant. For example, if a flowerpot falls from the window ledge of a building, and the person below is injured, the facts and circumstances of the injury attest the negligence of the person dropping the flowerpot. The conditions usually stated as necessary for application of the doctrine of *res ipsa loquitur* are three: (1) The accident must be of the kind which ordinarily does not occur in the absence of negligence; (2) it must be caused by an agency within the exclusive control of the defendant; and (3) it must not have been due to any voluntary action or contribution on the part of the defendant. See W. L. Prosser, *Prosser on Torts* (St. Paul, Minn.: West Publishing Company, 1941), pp. 291, 295.

bills, loss of earnings,[9] property-repair costs, and legal fees. General damages may be allowed for those losses which may not be directly measurable, such as pain and suffering. Punitive damages may be allowed where the conduct of the defendant is grossly negligent, reckless, and done without regard to life or property.

Jury awards, once determined, may be reduced by the court where they are held to be "unreasonable" for the injury sustained.

The Concept of Tort Liability

The word "tort" is derived from the Latin *tortus* meaning twisted. Tortious conduct is indeed twisted or crooked. In general common use in the English language, the word "tort" means wrong. Legally speaking, however, a *tort* is a civil wrong other than breach of a contract for which the court will provide a remedy in the form of an action for damages.[10] On the other hand, Prosser indicates that there is no satisfactory definition for the word "tort" and that it might be better to define a tort action by enumerating the things that it is not. Prosser says that a tort is not a crime; it is not a breach of contract; it is not necessarily concerned with property rights or problems of government. Tort occupies a large residual field of other types of legal actions. In this sense, tort is a sort of a legal garbage can to hold what cannot be put elsewhere in the law. The field of tort law is based upon the entire legal structure and is so interlocked at every point with property, contract, and other accepted classifications, that any specific arbitrary classification becomes meaningless.

It is likewise important to note that not every tort must have a name. New and nameless torts are being recognized continuously. For example, the denial of the right to vote, the conveyance of land to defeat a title, and other unusual misconducts have been recognized by the courts as being tortious in character.

One of the often-quoted decisions phrases the definition of a tort as follows:

> . . . a legal wrong committed upon a person or property independent of contract. It may be either (1) a direct invasion of some legal right of the individual; (2) the infraction of some public duty by which special damage accrues to the individual; or (3) the violation of some private obligation by which like damage accrues to the individual. In the former case, no special damage is necessary to entitle the party to recover. In the two latter cases, such damage is necessary.[11]

[9] This loss alone can be very large. See Chap. 8 for a method of estimating this loss.
[10] Prosser, *op cit.*, p. 3.
[11] *Hayes v. Massachusetts Mut. Life Ins. Co.*, 125 Ill. 626, 18 N.E. 322 (1888).

Basically there are two kinds of torts: (1) intentional torts, involving conduct which may be by intention or design (but not necessarily with the intention that the resulting consequences should occur) and (2) unintentional torts, involving the failure to act or not as a reasonably prudent person would have done under similar circumstances.

INTENTIONAL TORTS

The intentional-tort field includes that type of conduct which can be identified as premeditated or planned but whose consequences are not necessarily anticipated. Various specific kinds of intentional torts have been recognized by the courts. They include the following:

Trespass   Trespass consists of the entry of a person or a thing upon the land in the possession of another without permission. This action is designed to protect the exclusive possession of land and its physical status or condition. Any person who may be in actual or exclusive possession of property can maintain the action although he may not have legal title or is himself in a wrongful occupation. Recent problems have arisen in the intentional-tort field involving the extent of vertical possession of the air space above land. A recent decision by the United States Supreme Court recognized the possible tort liability of municipalities to owners of properties surrounding airports for the disturbance, noise, and inconvenience to these landowners resulting in devaluation of their property.

Conversion   Conversion is the act of interference or dominion over personal property. It may be committed by acquiring possession of the goods or intangibles with the intent to assert a right in them which is adverse to the owner, or by transferring them in a manner which deprives the owner of control. Any serious damaging or misusing of personalty in defiance of the owner's rights has likewise been viewed as conversion.

Assault   When the plaintiff is placed in apprehension of immediate harmful or offensive contact with the defendant, the threatening acts which cause him to fear for his person or property give rise to the intentional tort of an assault. Generally speaking, mere words, however violent, are not sufficient to amount to an assault. In order to have the essentials of an assault, there must be a clear and present danger evident to the plaintiff and the apparent ability by the defendant to execute the threatened act.

Battery   Battery is an unpermitted and unprivileged contact with another caused by acts intended to result in the possible effect of harm or apprehension as the result of the contact. The least touching of another in anger has been held to be a battery.[12] The gist of the action for battery is not the hostile intent to execute the touching but rather the absence of consent of the innocent party.

False imprisonment   False imprisonment or arrest is the illegal and unlawful confinement of another within boundaries fixed by the defendant without legal justification and with the intention that the act or breach of duty shall result in such confinement. The restraint may be by means of physical barriers or by threat of force, either or both of which intimidate the plaintiff into compliance with the orders. The restraint upon the plaintiff's freedom may also be imposed by the assertion of legal authority which the defendant contends he possesses. The duty not to confine another or restrict his freedom is the basis for the action, and recovery has been allowed even though the detainment was caused by innocent acts of the defendant. For example, in *Talcott v. National Exhibition Co.*, 144 App. Div. 337, 128 N.Y. Supp. 1059 (1911), the baseball park was held liable for failing to inform a business visitor of the exit after the main entrance closed because of the crowd.

Libel and slander (defamation of character)   Libel and slander are tort actions which involve the invasion of the interest, reputation, and good name of a person by communicating to others information which diminishes the esteem in which the plaintiff was held, or excites adverse feelings or opinions against him. Defamation is usually made up of the twin torts of libel and slander, the first being written, the other, oral. The courts have held that an allegation of insanity, an assertion that a woman has been raped, or other language which holds the plaintiff up to hatred, contempt, or ridicule or would cause him to be shunned or avoided is a proper action for defamation. The courts similarly have held that to allege that the plaintiff has attempted suicide, refused to pay his just debts, is immoral or unchaste, is a coward, a drunkard, a hypocrite, a liar or a crook, or to make any other oppressive, insulting, or dishonorable accusation is defamation. Ridiculing and making fun of the plaintiff have also been held to be defamatory in nature. In the case of libel and slander, of course, truth is always a defense, and the failure to prove the falsity of the charge would defeat the action.

Normally, proof of special damages is required; mere hurt feelings are not sufficient. On the other hand, the courts very early have established certain specific exceptions to the showing of special damages; these include the allegation that specific crimes have been committed by the plaintiff, that he possesses a loathsome disease, that he is held up to ridicule in his business, trade, profession, or office, and possibly that he is given to unchastity.

---

[12] *Cole v. Turner*, Holt K. B. 108, 90 Eng. Rep. 958 (1704).

In suits involving defamation of character, the courts have held that certain forms of privileged communications will not invoke liability under the tort of defamation. Absolute immunity from defamation suits has been granted, for example, to judges and members of grand or petit juries, members of the legislature, and certain executive officers of government in the discharge of their duties. Qualified or conditional privilege is extended to other interests in society, such as publishers or newspapers and magazines and commercial credit agencies. Newspaper accounts must be limited to the facts, and suits of defamation may not be brought if the facts are fairly and honestly presented, without any intent to do injury to the person's character. Commercial credit agencies investigating a person's character or financial reputation must have some specific objective in regard to a business or commercial interest and must make their inquiries honestly and carefully.

Other intentional torts   In addition to the above intentional torts, many others have been recognized by the courts under varying circumstances. For example, invasion of privacy, malicious and unlawful prosecution, interference with family relations, and interference with contractual relations are some of the other so-named torts. One of the more interesting intentional torts recognized by the law as imposing strict liability involves persons who keep animals which are likely to do harm to the land or person of others; the escape of such animals, whether by wrongful intent or negligence, usually imposes strict liability upon the owner. Keepers of animals of dangerous species which are known (or can be reasonably supposed) to have dangerous propensities are liable for the damage which such animals may cause, regardless of the care and safety used in maintaining them. On the other hand, with respect to domesticated animals, which are not known to possess dangerous propensities to do damage or injury to others, such as dogs, cats, and other household pets, the court requires that the plaintiff, in alleging the possible negligence or liability of the owner, prove that the owner knew (the law refers to this as "scienter") of the dangerous propensities of the animal. This is referred to as the "first bite doctrine." If the domesticated animal is known to have bitten someone else, the second bite will impose liability upon the owner. Some states have statutes which place a heavier responsibility upon dog owners by abolishing the scienter rule with respect to these pets.

THE UNINTENTIONAL TORT: NEGLIGENCE

It is estimated by legal authorities that approximately 90 per cent of the cases brought for personal injury or property damage involve the unintentional tort of negligence. The dividing line between an intentional tort and an unintentional tort is made in terms of the conduct of the defendant. The attorney bringing the case for the plaintiff must choose that theory of recovery which he is best able to prove. For example, a recent case involved a salesman who attempted to demonstrate a fly spray by spraying the product profusely around a grocery store. The wife of the grocer, who was allergic to this particular product, developed a very serious personal injury as a result of inhalation of the fumes. The plaintiff's attorney in this case could have brought the action on a theory of negligence, namely, that the salesman did not act as a reasonably prudent person would have acted in failing to discover whether or not any possible injuries might result to the people who inhale such fumes. In the particular case, however, the action was brought on a battery charge, namely, that the spraying of the fly spray was intentional, and that the touching of the plaintiff by this product was a battery committed on the grocer's wife, causing her great bodily harm. The plaintiff's attorney may choose various theories of recovery, depending upon the nature of the evidence and the ease with which he may prove his case under the theory he chooses.

Ingredients for a cause of action   An action for negligence requires showing of the following ingredients to make out a cause of action:

1. Legal duty to act or not act. Legal duty implies that the plaintiff can show that the defendant should have used a legal duty of care in acting or failing to act in the manner involved. A legal duty of care is the normal basis of proving or showing existence of negligence.

2. The breach of legal duty. Similarly the plaintiff must prove that the defendant clearly breached the legal duty to act or not act as a reasonably prudent person would have done under similar circumstances.

3. Proximate cause between the breach of duty and the injury suffered. The plaintiff must show that the breach of legal duty by the defendant was the *proximate or closest cause* in producing the injury to the plaintiff. Showing that the defendant's negligence truly caused the injuries complained of is, of course, a very troublesome area in law. The facts are often very complex and involve possible other intervening forces. For example, in one case, the plaintiff was severely injured in an automobile accident, and his wife was uninjured. An ambulance was called to the scene of the accident, and the plaintiff and his uninjured wife were placed in the ambulance. While returning to the hospital the ambulance was struck by another car, and the wife subsequently died of injuries sustained. The question of proximate cause raised in the trial was whether the injury caused by the first driver to the husband was the causal negligence resulting in the injury to the wife in the second accident. Had the accident not occurred in the first

place, the ambulance ride would not have been necessary. On the other hand, the ambulance driver's negligence or the negligence of the other third party hitting the ambulance might be a separate intervening negligence factor which would cut off the liability of the first accident driver.

The doctrine of proximate cause draws a circle around the scope of responsibility of the negligent offender and attempts to cut off those liabilities which he in fact and according to public policy should not be responsible for. The courts use language and phrases to express the doctrine and policy questions concerning the extent and duration of a negligent act. For example, the courts inquire as to whether or not the defendant could have forseen the consequences of his act when he engaged in it, whether he created an unreasonable risk of harm to others, and whether the injuries were within the foreseeable consequences of his negligent acts. In addition, the plaintiff's interest must be in the *zone of risk*, namely, sufficiently close to the actual commission of the negligence in the first place, in order to make it foreseeable; there must be no separate intervening cause; and the physical forces unleashed by the plaintiff must bear some relationship to the ultimate injury which the plaintiff suffers.

4. Injuries sustained. In the showing of injuries in a negligence action, the plaintiff may allege actual bodily injury or damage to his property. In addition, the courts are allowing recovery for mental suffering and pain or emotional distress caused by the alleged shock imposed as a result of the defendant's conduct. In a recent case involving the invasion of the right of privacy (which happens to be an intentional tort) the court allowed recovery to a mother who was making delivery of her child when the doctor allowed a nonmedical person in the delivery room to watch the actual birth. The mother sustained humiliation and mental suffering as a result of such conduct, and the court allowed recovery to her for her mental distress. Another recent court case allowed recovery to a woman who was almost hit by an oncoming vehicle. The mental anxiety resulting from such a near miss produced shock and mental injury to the plaintiff for which the court allowed recovery.

DEFENSES

Various defenses are privileged and often are successfully asserted if the facts of the case fit the defenses.

Assumption of risk   The defense of assumption of risk enables the defendant to show that the plaintiff consented to the clear and present danger of the possible negligent conduct of the defendant and failed clearly to establish his objections to such conduct. The assumption of risk defense is often used in host-guest cases in the operation of vehicles, where the driver's conduct is sufficiently bad and is known to the plaintiff-guest. The driver in defense may allege that the guest in the vehicle did not remove himself from the vehicle or clearly establish his objections to his negligent driving.

Contributory negligence Another defense, contributory negligence of the plaintiff, may remove any claims against the defendant for his alleged negligent conduct. The contributory negligence defense is usually asserted in those states where it is allowed on the theory that both parties were at fault and that neither should recover from the other.

Numerous statutes have been enacted in the United States to overcome the much-discussed evils of the contributory negligence doctrine. For example, the Federal Employers' Liability Act, the Merchant Marine Act, and the State Railway Labor Acts all provide that the contributory negligence of an injured workman shall not bar his recovery but that his damages shall be reduced in proportion to his negligence. Wisconsin, Minnesota, Mississippi, and Nebraska, as well as four Canadian provinces, have adopted more general provisions applicable to all negligent actions. Under these statutes, if the plaintiff's fault is found to be less than the defendant's, recovery is allowed.[13]

Another offsetting doctrine to the contributory negligence defense is that of *last clear chance.* Many states contend that this theory indicates the proper way to mitigate the evils of the contributory negligence defense. Under this doctrine, if the plaintiff can clearly show that the defendant's negligence has been spent and that the plaintiff has a last clear chance to avoid the injury, then recovery will be granted. One such case involved the negligent conduct of an elevator operator in leaving the gate open. The plaintiff negligently walked into the open elevator shaft and grabbed a protruding cable. The elevator operator heard the screams of the plaintiff (who

---

[13] In Wisconsin and Minnesota the plaintiff's negligence must be less than the defendant's negligence, and money is granted for 100 per cent of his injuries, less his own percentage of negligence. This is a partial comparative negligence statute. In Mississippi, which has a complete comparative negligence statute, each party receives 100 per cent of his damages diminished by his own percentage of negligence. The following example illustrates the difference between these two statutes:

| | | | Recovery | |
	Damages	Per cent of negligence	Wisconsin	Mississippi
Mr. A	$10,000	25	$7,500	$7,500 ⎱ net of
Mr. B	5,000	75	0	1,250 ⎰ $6,250 to A

had spent his negligence) and proceeded to drop the car, further injuring the plaintiff. In this situation, because the elevator operator had a last clear chance to avoid the injury and failed to do so, the plaintiff recovered.

Charitable and governmental immunity defenses   In the development of the common law concept of liability, the courts at various times have granted immunity to certain activities and institutions. Among others, immunity has been granted to charitable institutions and the government itself. These concepts of immunity, however, have been undergoing a rapid change in the last decade, and many states have virtually lifted the immunity.

In the case of charitable institutions, the theory of immunity from liability is based upon the concept that a charitable institution is a trust and that the trustees of the funds could not pay, and the property of a charity could not be used to pay judgments. This concept would permit hospitals, old-age homes, and other charitable activities to be conducted without fear of legal liability for their negligence.

The common law rule of nonliability has given way, however, to a more modern concept that the charitable institution is liable (1) to persons receiving benefit from its activities for injury caused by the negligence in the selection of employees, and (2) to anyone else for injury caused by negligent acts or omissions of their employees. In most states a charity patient in a hospital could sue for injuries sustained even though he paid nothing for the services rendered.[14]

Governmental immunity is based upon the concept that the king can do no wrong. The courts have held generally that immunity applies to governmental activities in which the functions of governing are carried on. These would include legislative activities and such other administrative duties as the conduct of education, law enforcement, and fire protection. On the other hand, governmental immunity has been removed in recent cases for those functions referred to as *proprietary*. These would include the operation of municipal light and power plants, maintenance of streets, and the operation of parks and playgrounds. Here again the tendency has been continually to narrow the area of immunity, and more and more decisions have been rendered holding municipalities and other branches of government liable for the negligent conduct of their employees and for negligence generally.[15] It is also important to note that officers of the law who falsely arrest individuals, even in the course of their official capacity, may be held personally liable for such conduct, and that immunity does not extend to the employees

---

[14] *Cashman v. Meriden Hospital,* 117 Conn. 585, 169 Atl. 915 (1934). *Kojis v. Doctors Hospital,* 12 Wis. 2d 367, 107 N.W.2d 131 (1961).
[15] *Krantz v. City of Hutchinson,* 165 Kan. 449, 196 P.2d 227 (1946) defined proprietary and governmental functions. *Molitor v. Kaneland Community Unit Dist. #302,* 163 N.E.2d 89 (Ill.) totally abolishd immunity of school districts in Illinois.

in these cases. The legislature has also seen fit, in many jurisdictions, specifically to waive the common law immunity with regard to the operation of government vehicles and tort liability in general.[16] The Federal government has waived immunity under the Federal Tort Claims Act.

WRONGFUL DEATH AND SURVIVORSHIP STATUTES

At common law, death of the tort-feasor or the claimant means death of the tort action. Statutes in most states have abrogated this common law defense. The estate of the deceased claimant as well as his surviving dependents may sue for damages. The estate of a deceased tort-feasor remains responsible for his negligent acts. Many state laws limit recoveries for wrongful death to a stated dollar amount. Other states, such as New York, do not place dollar limits on the recovery but restrict it to loss of earnings, expenses incurred prior to death, and funeral expenses.[17]

THE IMPUTED LIABILITY OF OTHERS

Various doctrines in the law hold people responsible for the negligent conduct of others. For example, the doctrine of *respondeat superior* holds that the employer is responsible for the tortious acts of his employee or agent while such agent or employee is acting in the course and scope of employment or agency relationship. Other examples are discussed below.

Liability arising from activities of independent contractors, joint venturers, or joint tort-feasors   One of the more troublesome areas of liability law relates to the contingent liability of a firm or individual for the negligence of persons or firms hired as independent contractors. Initially, the law adopted the general rule that the employer was not liable for the tortious conduct of an independent contractor, whereas he would assume liability for the activities of his own employees. The basic reason for the nonliability rule was that an employer was deemed to have no right of control over the manner in which the work is to be done, it being regarded as the contractor's own responsibility; the latter is the proper party to be charged with the responsibility of preventing the risk.

Opposed to this reasoning is the argument that the employer is the person primarily benefiting from the work; he selects the contractor and

---

[16] A 1963 Minnesota law subjects cities, villages, counties, public authorities, and public corporations to tort liability for proprietary and governmental functions, subject to certain exceptions and within specified dollar limits. A 1963 Wisconsin law set a $25,000 limit on lawsuits against counties and municipalities after the Supreme Court of Wisconsin had overturned the doctrine of governmental immunity.

[17] For an extensive discussion of this complicated subject and liability losses in general, see James H. Donaldson, *Casualty Claims Practice* (rev. ed., Homewood, Ill.: Richard D. Irwin, Inc., 1969).

is obligated to pick someone who is financially responsible for the consequences of his acts. If the contractor has been unwisely chosen, then the employer should be held responsible.

The general rule of nonliability of the employer has been whittled away by court decisions to the point where one can say that very little still remains. In the first place, the employer has been held liable for his own negligence in connection with the work to be done. So far as he gives directions, furnishes equipment, retains any control whatever, he is held responsible. He must interfere with and stop any unnecessarily dangerous practices, as well as inspect the work after it is completed to see that it is safe. Furthermore, certain duties are held to be "nondelegable"; that is, the employer must take certain safety measures, such as fencing off operations which may cause an unreasonable risk of harm to others.

Beyond these exceptions, the courts have also recognized imputed liability for independent contractors where the operation to be performed is "inherently dangerous." In these cases, such as blasting, clearing land by fire, tearing down walls and chimneys, the courts have held that a high degree of risk is created, and the employer is held to be strictly liable for injuries or damage suffered by third persons caused by the independent contractor's activities.

In many commercial and personal activities several persons or firms are apt to engage in a joint undertaking. Here again the law recognizes the right of a third party to bring an action for recovery of damages caused by any or all of the joint venturers. Each or all may be sued for the total damages suffered, and in that sense the negligence of one is imputed to the other.

Assumption of liability by contract   Contracts specifically requiring one party to assume liability for the other's conduct raise serious problems for businessmen in many of their commercial activities. Those contracts which shift one party's liability to another are often referred to as "hold-harmless" or "save-harmless" agreements. Common examples of such contracts are:

1. Railroad switch-track agreements. If the firm desires to have a railroad sidetrack or spur leading to its property from the main railroad track, the railroad company invariably requires that the firm must hold the railroad harmless for any loss or expense for injury or property damage due to the use or existence of the siding. Therefore, any person injured because of the spur or its use could sue the railroad, but in turn, the business firm requesting the spur, having signed the sidetrack agreement, will be obligated to pay the judgment and all related costs.

2. Leases. Landlords will often insert in their leases hold-harmless agreements which shift the liability of the landlord to the tenant, for defects in the building or for any act or neglect by any tenant or occupant of the building or by any other person, including the landlord. These hold-harmless agreements may also be used in reverse, when the tenant requests that the landlord hold him harmless for his negligence in causing damage to the premises or persons.

3. Contracts to supply goods or services. As we have indicated in the discussion of independent contractors, one business firm doing work for another may execute hold-harmless agreements as a condition of doing the work or furnishing the services. For example, a subcontractor may be required to sign a hold-harmless agreement in favor of the primary contractor in order to be awarded the job.

In addition, hold-harmless agreements are often contained in purchase and sales orders, shifting potential liability arising from defects in the product either to the purchaser or seller. An example of hold-harmless conditions used by one drug company on all purchase orders which they execute is presented below:

General Conditions of Purchase Order
Seller agrees to defend, indemnify and keep harmless the Buyer, its agents and employees, from any and all liability, loss, damage and expense, including attorneys' fees, which may or might be sustained or incurred because of the infringement by the goods supplied by the Seller under this purchase order of any patent, trademark or copyright, or claim thereof or because of any claim or action against the Buyer, its agents or employees, on account of any adulteration or other defective condition or any claim thereof, in any manner involving the goods hereby sold and purchased or any part thereof, or on account of any act or failure to act by Seller arising out of the services performed by Seller or any claim thereof, in any manner involving the goods hereby sold and purchased or any part thereof, except such claims and actions as arise by reason of unauthorized express warranties on the part of the Buyer, its agents and employees, and except such claims and actions as are alleged by claimant to be due to the sole negligence of the Buyer, its agents or employees; provided prompt written notice be given to the Seller of the bringing of any such claim or action and an opportunity be given the Seller to settle or defend same as the Seller may see fit. In case any apparatus, or any part thereof, furnished under this contract is held to constitute infringement of any patent and the use of said apparatus or part is enjoined, the Seller shall, at its own expense, either procure for the Buyer the right to continue using said apparatus or part; or replace same with non-infringing apparatus, or modify it so it becomes non-infringing, or remove said ap-

paratus and refund the purchase price and the Transportation and Installation costs thereof. Nothing herein shall prevent Buyer from providing its own representation at its own expense in the event of litigation against Buyer.

4. Bonds and permits from governing units. Often municipalities will allow a person or business firm to obstruct the street or sidewalk to carry on certain operations. In nearly all these situations, however, the permittee must assume all liability for any accidents which may happen as a result of this obstruction. In addition, many municipalites require that the permittee post a bond guaranteeing payment of any damages that may be awarded. Hold-harmless clauses are used, for example, for the construction of driveways, canopies, street signs, basement space under sidewalks, tunnels, and other overhangs.

Statutory liability   The legislatures of several states have seen fit to impose statutory liability for certain types of business activities. Two of the most notable of these laws are described briefly below:

1. Dram shop laws. Dram shop laws hold the tavern or place of business where liquor is dispensed not only liable for all resulting injuries which an intoxicant may receive, but also liable for injuries he may inflict upon others, and for such consequential losses as his family's loss of financial support. Approximately twenty-five states have variations of this law which impose liability upon a tavern owner or operator for damages sustained as a result of the dispensing of alcoholic beverages.

2. Parent liability for torts of children. The common law rule historically has been that parents are not liable for the tortious conduct of their children. Because of the imputed general breakdown in parental discipline, many legislatures have now enacted laws which change this common law rule. One such law, enacted in Wisconsin, holds the parent liable for up to $300 in damages caused by the negligent conduct.

Other examples of imputed liability will be discussed in the later sections of this chapter dealing with automobile liability.

Specific Liability Exposures and Problems

In the following discussion, special activities and circumstances under which liability may be imposed will be carefully examined. The discussion is not intended to be exhaustive or fully descriptive of all the areas of potential legal liability. Rather it will emphasize the special problems in certain areas of business and personal activity which are most apt to impose possible legal responsibility and for which special risk control measures are necessary.

BAILEE LIABILITY EXPOSURES

In many commercial and noncommercial activities, personal property is surrendered to another for a temporary period of time. The person taking possession may perform some service pertaining to the property, borrow it for his own use, or keep it for the owner's benefit, after which time he must return the property to the owner or lawful possessor. These transactions where possession of personal property is vested in one person, and eventual lawful right of possession vests in another are called "bailments." The owner or original possessor of the goods is called the *bailor;* the person receiving possession for the temporary period of time is called the *bailee.* In order to have a bailment relation, three distinguishing characteristics must normally be present in the contractual relationship: (1) The title to the property or the ultimate right to possess it must be retained by the bailor; (2) the possession and temporary control of the property must be surrendered to the bailee; and (3) ultimate possession of the property must revert to the bailor unless he orders the transfer to some other designated person.

Important liability questions arise concerning the rights and duties of the bailee for any possible claims which the bailor may make for damages while the property was in the custody and care of the bailee. In establishing the legal duty of care to be exercised by the bailee, the law has classified bailments into three general categories: (1) bailments for the benefit of the bailor (where property is left with the bailee without any compensation for care and safekeeping); (2) bailments for the benefit of the bailee (in which cases the bailee often borrows or uses the property involved for a period of time, usually without compensation to the rightful owner); and (3) bailments for the mutual benefit of the bailor and bailee (where both parties benefit from the bailment, which may involve the repair, carriage, storage, or safekeeping of the property). Each party to the last-mentioned transaction receives some benefit; the bailor receives the service rendered by the bailee, for which he usually pays a fee to the bailee. The interests of both parties are served by the transaction.

In establishing these three classes of bailment relationships, the courts clearly recognize different degrees of care required of the bailee. In a transaction for the exclusive benefit of the bailor, the bailee is required to exercise only slight care. In transactions for the exclusive benefit of the bailee, extraordinary care is essential. In other words, the law looks behind the purpose of the transaction and demands that the degree of care vary according to the respective benefits conferred on the parties involved. In a bailment for the mutual benefit of the parties, the law normally demands ordinary care on the part of the bailee, in other words, that degree of care which an average individual or company would usually exercise over his or its own property.

In addition, the courts recognize that the amount of care expected of the bailee varies with the nature and substance of the bailment. For example, the degree of ordinary care normally required to protect a very valuable negotiable security would be much greater than the amount of care required to protect an ordinary piece of paper; the higher the value of the article bailed, the higher the standards of protection. Where property is bailed for mutual benefit, the bailor is usually held liable for any defects in the property rented or bailed about which he may or should have known. The bailor is ordinarily responsible for any damage suffered by the bailee as the result of such defects unless he notifies the bailee prior to the injury or damage.

Under some circumstances, either the bailee or bailor may change the degree of care required by a written statement in the contract itself. For example, the parking ticket issued to a person parking a vehicle in a commercial parking lot may state, as one of the terms of the bailment relationship of the automobile, that the owner of the lot is not responsible for loss by theft of personal property inside the vehicle unless the property is placed in the possession of the parking attendant. Such restrictions upon liability are normally recognized by the law, provided that the agreement meets all the tests of a valid legal contract, including the presence of adequate consideration. In addition, many courts have held that a bailee, regardless of the nature of the bailment, may be held absolutely liable for misdelivery of the goods or property bailed. Consequently, the bailee must make certain that repossession is granted only to the rightful party, namely the bailor, or to someone the bailor may select.

One of the more obvious commercial relationships involving bailment is the transport of goods by common carrier.[18] The common carrier in receiving the goods performs the acts of a bailee and assumes certain duties of care with reference to the handling of such goods. The written contract for carriage, called a *bill of lading*,[19] sets forth the terms and conditions

---

[18] *Common carriers* are carriers engaged in the transport of goods for the public according to regular time schedules, defined routes, and for established rates. It has long been a general rule of law that the common carrier is responsible for the safe delivery of goods. This was further established by statute with the passage of the Interstate Commerce Act of 1887 and subsequent amendments of 1915 and 1935 regulating interstate carrier operations. Each state likewise passed statutes regulating intrastate operations. *Contract carriers* haul under a specific contract; *private carriers* carry their own goods in their own equipment.

[19] A bill of lading is a written document given by the carrier to the shipper which acknowledges receipt of the goods by the carrier and sets forth the contract for carrying the property. If the bill of lading limits the liability of the carrier to a maximum amount in the event of loss or damage, it is called a "released bill of lading."

of the bailment. The amount of care required of the common carrier, however, greatly exceeds that of ordinary care by statute. Under the various bills of lading acts, for motortruck carriers[20] as well as railroads and aircraft, the common carrier is liable for all loss of goods with the following exceptions: (1) an act of God; (2) action of an enemy alien; (3) exercise of public authority; (4) any inherent defects in the nature of the goods themselves; (5) any negligence or fault of the shipper, including misaddressing the package or mislabeling the merchandise. Thus the common carrier becomes virtually an insurer of goods, unless the loss or damage falls within the exceptions thus stated. Acts of God normally are those acts of nature which are neither preventable nor controllable by the common carrier, and about which it has no reasonable warning or opportunity to avoid damage. In a recent flood which occurred in the Missouri River Valley, a Federal court held that the damage to goods located in flooded railway cars was caused 40 per cent by an act of God and 60 per cent by the negligence of the railway compainies in failing to place the boxcars on higher ground. Litigation established the percentage of responsibility of the common carriers' liability policies, in paying the damage for the freight loss.

Many other commercial transactions involve bailments. Automobile repair agencies exercise physical control over automobiles being worked upon and have a duty to use ordinary care in the protection of such property. In the case of *Parry v. Maryland Cas. Co.*, 228 App. Div. 343, 240 N.Y. Supp. 105 (1930), the garage tow truck, operated by an employee of the garage, was pulling a vehicle which was being steered and braked by an employee of the customer; the automobile subsequently collided with a pole. The court held that the automobile was not in the actual physical control of the garage but in the control of the customer and that no liability existed for the garage under the bailment law. Questions arise as to the actual surrendering of control of the property to the bailee, and the bailee's responsibilities arise only where such actual physical control has been surrendered.

Some very interesting cases have developed in regard to the parking of cars in parking lots. Where the business establishment provides an attendant to park the vehicle for the customer, courts have held that a bailment has occurred and that care arising from a mutual benefit bailment must be exercised. On the other hand, where the business establishment merely provides space for the customer to park his own car, the courts have held that a lease arrangement exists which does not impose the same

---

[20] Under the Motor Carrier Liability Act of 1935, Congress required that interstate trucking operations provide adequate "security for the protection of the public." The Interstate Commerce Commission under this section specifies that each trucker provide insurance of $1,000 for the loss or damage to the contents of any one vehicle and $2,000 for aggregate losses or damages at any one time and place. Self-insurance may be permitted if the financial stability of the carrier warrants the permission.

kinds of duties of care as would be imposed in the usual bailment situation. The same would hold true with reference to restaurants and night clubs where facilities are provided for checking of coats and other personal articles. If facilities are merely provided with no attendant in charge, usually no bailment is found. However, where the attendant actually gives a receipt for the goods checked, the bailment relationship is established, and all the duties of care and the liabilities for misdelivery arise.

AUTOMOBILE, BOAT, AND AIRCRAFT LIABILITY EXPOSURES

Perhaps the most complicated area of potential liability in business or personal activity surrounds the use of automobiles, boats, aircraft, and other vehicles. This is due in part to the large number of accidents involving these vehicles, the wide variety of circumstances surrounding these accidents, and the speed with which they occur. Indeed, this complexity is one reason some persons favor the automobile compensation plans described in Chapter 33.

The finding of negligence and liability   The finding of negligence relating to the use of vehicles normally depends upon a jury's decision as to certain questions of fact: (1) Did the defendant fail to have the vehicle under proper control? (2) Did the defendant fail to exercise proper lookout? (3) Did the defendant operate the vehicle at an excessive speed? An affirmative answer to any one or all of the three above questions will result in conviction and judgment against the wrongdoer. The owner of a vehicle, however, cannot be concerned only about his own driving habits and his ability to meet the above negligence tests. Liability may also exist under certain conditions in the use of the owned automobile when it is operated by someone other than the owner.

The *law of agency* may impute the negligent conduct of the operator to the owner when the operator is acting as an agent of the owner. For example, if A asked B to go to the grocery store and purchase some articles, B, while on such an errand, would be operating either his own car or someone else's car in A's behalf and would subject A to possible suit resulting from B's negligent operation of the vehicle. Questions often arise concerning the responsibility of the owner of the family car for the tortious driving of his children. Many states have recognized liability of the parent for their children's driving through court decision by what is referred to as the *family car doctrine*. Since the parent is responsible for the provision of food, clothing, shelter, and transportation for his family, the use of the car by any member of the family for these purposes has been held to make the parent legally responsible. Some states have enacted laws to reinforce the court decisions, holding the owner of the vehicle responsible for the operator's negligence.[21] These laws, referred to as *vicarious liability* statutes, make the owner liable for personal injuries or property damage caused by the negligence of the operator. In addition, many states have made the signer of the license application for a minor responsible for the operation of all vehicles by the minor, not only the vehicle owned by the parent. Some states, like Wisconsin, still cling to the agency principle and require that the showing of this relationship between the parent and the child must first exist in order to impute the negligence of the child back to the parent.

Another variation of the agency problem relates to liability arising from nonowned automobiles. For example, in an important court decision in California, *Malloy v. Fong*, 37 Cal. 2d 356, 232 P.2d 241 (1951), a church was held liable for the negligent operation of a vehicle by a volunteer who had agreed to transport children to a public playground for a church function. In the particular case, the child, who was riding on the outside of the vehicle, was involved in an accident. As a result, the suit was brought against both the driver of the car and the church for this tortious conduct. Since the operator of the vehicle did not have any assets and did not carry insurance, the ultimate loss fell upon the church organization, which had to pay the judgment for $41,500 for such conduct. It is important to note that many vehicles are used in behalf of commercial establishments or individuals without their specific knowledge but with their general authorization. Under these conditions, this authorization may impose serious and important legal exposures upon the authorizing agency or individual.

Joint venture situations arise where two or more parties use the vehicle in a particular pursuit for a common objective, such as a business trip or some other commercial activity. When injury is sustained by a third party as a result of this type of activity, the third party may sue any member of the joint venture even though no one of the joint venturers may be operating the vehicle; the negligence of the operator is imputed to all the other members of the joint venture. The courts in most states have circumscribed this theory of recovery and have limited it only to those situations where a business or commercial purpose is in fact involved. Mere social relationships ordinarily do not impute negligence under the joint venture theory.

Joint control usually arises where the operator of the vehicle and the guest jointly look for road signs or in some other way control the vehicle together. When the vehicle is under such joint control, the negligence of one may be imputed to the other in a suit by a third party.

In order to avoid suits brought by guests who may be injured in an automobile as the result of the driver's negligent operation, many states have enacted what are referred to as *guest* statutes. These statutes will

[21] California, Connecticut, District of Columbia, Florida, Idaho, Iowa, Massachusetts, Michigan, Minnesota, New York, North Carolina, Rhode Island, and Tennessee.

exempt the owner or the operator of the vehicle from liability to a guest in the vehicle unless the conduct of the driver is viewed as willful, wanton, and grossly negligent or is proved to be done with an intent to do bodily injury to the guest. The purpose of these statutes is to preclude hitchhikers and other social guests from suing the owner of the vehicle and thereby taking advantage of what otherwise might be friendly conduct. Still other states have not enacted guest statutes, but require that the driver with guests in his vehicle only exercise that degree of skill and care that he would normally exercise in his own behalf. If he normally drives recklessly, then his guest would have no suit against him, since this is his normal and usual conduct exercised in his own behalf.

Recognizing that there is a need for immediate medical attention at the time and scene of an automobile accident, many states have enacted what is referred to as the Good Samaritan law. In the absence of such a statute, physicians and surgeons could be held personally liable for any malpractice which might result from their voluntarily assisting or aiding injured persons on a public highway. As a result, members of the medical profession have avoided becoming involved in accidents because of potential personal liability. The Good Samaritan law encourages a physician to render aid at the time and scene of the accident by barring all tort liability claims arising from these activities.

Accident frequency and severity data   According to the National Safety Council, there were approximately 15 million motor vehicle accidents in 1969, which resulted in over 56,000 deaths and 5 million injuries. The total estimated economic loss suffered from this appalling situation in property damage, legal, medical, hospital, loss of income, and insurance administrative costs has been placed at $16.5 billion or approximately $80 per person.[22] Because of inflation, particularly as it affects medical and auto repair costs and increased accident frequency and severity, the yearly loss has been rising about 15 per cent per year. Chapter 33, "Automobile Insurance Problems and Issues," analyzes these accident costs in more detail.

The chance of being involved in an accident appears much higher for youthful drivers, according to the statistics. Drivers under 25 accounted for about 21 per cent of all drivers but were involved in 34 per cent of all accidents. Contrary to popular belief, drivers over 65 constituted about 8.5 per cent of all drivers and accounted for only 6 per cent of all accidents.

Probability estimates of the likelihood of having an accident vary substantially, according to the characteristics of the exposure. For example,

[22] *Insurance Facts* (New York: Insurance Information Institute, 1970), pp. 49–55.

insurance company studies report that the chances of having an accident are five times greater if the driver has had three or more traffic violations than if the driver has not. Similarly, drivers of the "hot" car (super-horse-powered) are recognized to be the cause of over 40 per cent more dollar loss to their insurers than they would account for under their proportionate share. Accident frequency also is a function of vehicle saturation, with urban areas having a much higher proportion of accidents than rural areas. A good measure of accident frequency and severity probability for a given risk is to obtain several rate quotations from insurers. High rates or even unacceptability would indicate the vehicle use or driver characteristics indicative of high accident probabilities.

LIABILITY ARISING OUT OF OWNERSHIP, USE, AND POSSESSION OF LAND

The ownership, use, and possession of land may impose very serious possible liabilities. The life tenant, for example, has a certain duty to preserve and protect the property from future loss which might entail liability to the remaindermen for waste. In the excavation of land, the adjoining property owners are entitled to lateral support and are privileged to use drainage established by the natural terrain. Any interruption of either of these two rights may invoke liability. The following discussion, however, will deal more exclusively with the liability exposures of a property owner or possessor to visitors on his property.

The legal liability of a landowner to individual visitors upon his property depends on the status which they occupy at the time of the visitation. The law has placed visitors to land into three classifications:

> 1. *Trespassers:* "A trespasser may be defined as one who unauthorizedly goes upon the private premises of another without invitation or inducement, express or implied, but purely for his own purposes or convenience and where no mutuality of interest exists between him and the owner or occupant."[23]
>
> 2. *Licensees:* "A licensee is defined as one who stands in no contractual relationship to the owner or occupier of the premises, but is permitted or tolerated thereon, expressly or impliedly, or inferentially, merely for his own interest, convenience or pleasure, or for that of a third person."[24] A licensee differs from a trespasser in that he is permitted to go onto the land with the possessor's consent; however, he is there for his own purpose and not for any benefit or business advantage to the possessor.

[23] See *Keesecker v. G. M. McKelvey Co.*, 141 Ohio St. 162, 47 N.E.2d 211 (1943).
[24] *Ibid.*

3. *Invitees:* "The invitee, also called a business visitor—is a person invited, expressly or impliedly, to come onto the land of the possessor for the business advantage of the possessor."[25]

In establishing the liability of the owner, occupier, or user of the land in relation to visitors, it is necessary that the visitor be classified in one of the three above categories of visitation. The duty of care which must be exercised to each of these kinds of visitors is as follows:

Liability to trespassers   The owner of the land is normally not bound to anticipate the presence of a trespasser, for the law assumes that he has the right to enjoy the safe and peaceful possession of his land without interference. A trespasser thus enters land without specific permission, express or implied, and must assume the unsafe conditions of the premises as they exist. The owner of the land is under no duty to provide the intruder with a safe place on which to trespass, and the general rule is that there is no liability to an undiscovered trespasser who is injured because of the unsafe premises. Responsibility is increased slightly with regard to known trespassers, since the lawful possessor has a duty not to use the property as a trap or to alter it in any way so as to create a hidden peril of injury to the unwary, known trespasser. The owner of the land or lawful possessor must refrain from doing anything intentionally to injure the uninvited visitor, and in some jurisdictions he must use reasonable care for his safety.[26]

A very notable exception in the law relating to trespassers is found in the *attractive nuisance doctrine* which imposes a special duty of care upon a person maintaining an artificial condition on land which attracts children. Generally speaking, trespassing children occupy the same position before the law as trespassing adults; but, because of their lack of judgment, many jurisdictions have placed special legal responsibility for injuries to such trespassing children where the injuries result from conditions of land which are highly dangerous to them. Under the attractive nuisance doctrine, children enjoy the status and protection of invitees, and in some cases the landowner has been held absolutely liable even though they were trespassers. Certain limitations of the doctrine have been expressed by various courts. In *Morse v. Douglas*, 107 Cal. App. 196, 290 Pac. 465 (1930), the court said: "The contrivance must be artificial and uncommon as well as dangerous, and capable of being rendered safe with ease and without

[25] *Restatement of Torts* (St. Paul, Minn.: The American Law Institute, 1934), sec. 332. "A business visitor is a person who is invited or permitted to enter or remain on the land in possession of another for the purpose directly or indirectly connected with the business dealings between them."
[26] See *Frederick v. Philadelphia Rapid Transit Co.*, 337 Pa. 136, 10 Atl. 2d 576 (1940). "When the owner-operator is on guard as to the presence of a trespasser, the latter immediately acquires the right to proper protection under the circumstances."

destroying its usefulness, and of such a nature as to virtually constitute a trap into which children would be led on account of their ignorance and inexperience." Section 339 of the *Restatement of Torts* defines the doctrine of attractive nuisance as follows:

> (*a*) The place where the condition is maintained is one upon which the possessor knows or should know that such children are likely to trespass, and (*b*) the condition is one of which the possessor knows or should know and which he realizes or should realize as involving an unreasonable risk of death or serious bodily harm to such children, and (*c*) the children because of their youth do not discover the condition or realize the risk involved in intermeddling in it or in coming within the area made dangerous by it, and (*d*) the utility to the possessor of maintaining the condition is slight in comparison to the risk of young children involved therein.

The courts have found in addition that some enticement or entrapment should be present in most of the circumstances in order to encourage children to enter on the land. The condition normally must be artificial; that is, not a natural cliff or a tree or natural vegetation.The child must be below an age of reason, which in some jurisdictions is as high as sixteen years. Generally speaking, the age of seven to nine is the highest age at which an individual is still considered a child not possessing sufficient intelligence or awareness to appreciate his peril.

The following have been held in various cases to be attractive nuisances and have been classified by the courts as such, finding liability to the children for injuries sustained: artificial bodies of water, swimming pools, sewers, electric power lines, construction work of all kinds, gasoline, oil tanks, ladders, cyclone fences, chemical refuse, ash hoists, dumps, railroad turntables, parked cars, junk yards, lumber piles, lawn mowers, unsteady mailboxes, snow piles, muddy basement floors, parking lots with merry-go-rounds, and others.

Liability to licensees   The common law holds that the possessor of land owes a licensee no duty to make the premises safe for his reception. On the other hand, the licensee is entitled to the same obligations as are owed to a discovered trespasser; that is, the landowner must use reasonable care for his protection to avoid injuring him by any active negligence and must warn him of known concealed dangerous conditions. While the licensee is required to accept the premises as the possessor uses them, he is entitled to know the dangers which the possessor knows. In one interesting case, *Shock v. Ringling Bros., etc., Combined Shows,* 5 Wash. 2d 419, 105 P.2d 838 (1940), children were injured while watching the circus unload at the railroad yard. The court held that there was no mutuality of interest as between the children and the circus company, and that the children were licensees permitted on the property as spectators. Typical licensees include policemen and firemen who enter upon the premises under license given by law. On the other hand, postmen, garbage collectors, and meter readers have been held to be invitees. Generally speaking, a visitor to a restaurant or a lunchroom is in the position of an invitee, but in the particular case of *Sheridan v. Ravn,* 91 Cal. App. 2d 112, 204 P.2d, 644 (1944), a customer went behind the counter and by so doing ceased to be an invitee. Since he was not where he belonged, the court held that the proprietor owed him no duty other than that of warning him of known defects in the premises and of refraining from any willful injury. In another case, a customer who had visited a store and purchased certain articles, decided on her way out to go back and use the telephone. She went to a hallway, reached out to turn on the light, and fell down a stairway. The court held that a person visiting a store for transacting business is normally an invitee, and the store owner must use reasonable care to see that the premises are in a reasonably safe condition. On the other hand, in this case the customer was held to be a licensee, since the business which she was to perform at the time of the injury was not of any benefit to the defendant.[27]

Liability to invitees   An invitee is a visitor to the premises for the benefit of the owner or occupier of the premises as well as of himself. The common law generally imposes the duty of reasonable care to make the premises safe for anyone accepting an invitation to do business thereon—a duty to inspect and to warn of dangers. The typical cases in this area of law have involved business visitors who engaged in specific transactions with the owner or occupier of the premises. The court held in a recent food-market case that a business invitation includes also the use of the parking lot, since parking is a part of the business transaction. Therefore the premises include not only the building but also any other property used in the business venture.[28]

In some states, safe place statutes have reinforced the duties of care required of landowners or possessors of land open to the public. In Wisconsin, a safe place statute makes the owner of the property absolutely liable for injuries caused by frequenters or business visitors to his property where the injury is due to some unsafe condition. In bringing an action under the statute, the plaintiff does not have to show specific negligence with reference to the care or maintenance of the premises, but merely to show that the injury was caused by a defect.

[27] *Westbrock v. Colby Inc.,* 315 Ill. App. 494 (1942).
[28] See *Tschumy v. Brooks Mkt.,* 60 Cal. App. 2d 158, 140 P.2d 431 (1943).

EXPOSURES TO FINANCIAL LOSS ARISING FROM EMPLOYMENT RELATIONSHIPS

In our modern industrial society the creation of the employment relationship brings into play many risks of serious financial losses to both employers and employees. The employee, when accepting employment, has the responsibility under the common law to render service faithfully and loyally to his employer and to discharge his responsibilities to the best of his ability. Failure to serve loyally and to follow the directions and work rules of his employer may result in a personal liability judgment. In addition, employment relationships often produce many accidents resulting in death or disability to the worker, extracting a heavy toll in physical pain and financial loss.

The employer, on the other hand, when offering employment must be prepared to comply with numerous Federal and state laws which govern such relationships, such as the wage and hour laws, fair labor standards acts, unemployment compensation and old-age and survivors' insurance tax laws, and safety statutes governing working conditions. Violation of these laws may impose civil as well as criminal liability for unintentional or intentional violations. In addition, employers must meet their legal obligations under workmen's compensation statutes and common law or statutory concepts of employers' liability. These obligations will be emphasized in the following discussion.

Common law liability for employers   Prior to 1837 there were few, if any, cases in which an employee sued an employer. In that year occurred a famous English case, *Priestley v. Fowler,* in which the judge, Lord Abinger, made it clear that an employee would find it more difficult to collect from his employer under the law of negligence than would a complete stranger.[29] This inferior position of the employee was in part a reflection of the laissez-faire attitude of the Industrial Revolution.

This process of social and financial justice imposed many hardships on the employee. The employee, like the stranger, was forced to prove negligence on the part of his employer, had to share his recovery with his legal counsel, and often was forced to wait many years for recovery because of crowded court calendars and difficulties of proof. Verdicts often bore little relationship to the merits of the employee's case. The employee's plight was worse than that of the stranger, however, because fellow employees were often unwilling to testify for fear of losing their jobs. In addition, the courts allowed the employer to plead certain defenses to these actions

---

[29] This case involved a butcher's helper and a boy helper who were delivering meat. The wagon was overloaded by the butcher's helper and fell over on the boy, causing injury. See *Priestley v. Fowler,* 3 M. & W. 1, 150 Eng. Rep. 1030 (Ex. 1837).

which were quite effective in defeating the worker's claim. These defenses were the following:

1. Fellow-servant defense. If the injury was caused by the negligence of a fellow servant, then the employer was relieved from liability. Since many industrial processes involved cooperative work, many injuries fell within this category.

2. Assumption of risk. In the absence of statutory rules or provisions in the employment contract, the employer was not liable for injury caused by unsafe conditions of work if the worker knew of such conditions and voluntarily entered or continued in the employment.

3. Contributory negligence. If the worker's own negligence in the performance of the work was a contributing cause of the injury, the employer was held not liable.

4. Injuries resulting in death. The remedies of the employee were considered personal and expired upon his death (prior to the enactment of the wrongful death and survivors' statutes).

Only the last two defenses could have been raised to counter the claim of a stranger.

Nevertheless, courts slowly began to recognize a special duty owed to the "servant" by the "master," distinct from those owed to the general public or to those not his servants. While they held that the master was not an insurer of his servant's safety, they maintained that he owed a duty to provide working conditions which were reasonably safe, considering the nature of the employment, or to warn him of unsafe conditions that the servant might not discover by the exercise of due care. This duty was gradually extended to include inspection, maintenance, and repair of the premises within the master's control and of the tools which the worker used. If an injury was due to the employer's violation of these duties, the employee could bring his action for recovery of damages sustained. In addition, the courts began to chip away at the employer's defenses. For example, the employer could not plead the fellow-servant rule if the negligent employee was a foreman or one with whom the injured employee normally had little contact. Some courts substituted a comparative negligence doctrine for contributory negligence.

By the early 1900s, employers' liability statutes, which also favored the employees, were enacted in most jurisdictions, and the Federal government had enacted the Federal Employers' Liability Act, applying to interstate railroad employees, and the Jones Act, applying to merchant seamen. These laws, like the courts, tended to modify and limit the employer's use of fellow-servant, assumption of risk, and contributory negligence defenses. Specific safety statutes were enacted to prescribe minimum safety appliances and working conditions, making it easier for the worker to show negligence of the employer by violation of the law. However, the basic defects of a system dependent upon negligence claims remained, and the early 1900s were years of social agitation and reform.

Workmen's compensation   As a result of this agitation and reform, workmen's compensation laws were enacted which completely changed the concepts of employer responsibility for accidents and injuries "arising out of or in the course of employment." The revolutionary changes introduced by this legislation were as follows:

> 1. The concept of negligence and fault on the part of the worker or employer was abandoned as the basis of financial responsibility. Rather, all accidents or injuries related to "industrial causation" or arising out of the employment were to be compensated. The cost of injuries was determined to be a cost of manufacture and therefore passed on to the consumer through higher prices.
> 2. The amounts or levels of benefits were scheduled by statute rather than awarded by juries.
> 3. Administration was in most cases given to an administrative agency of the state which had authority to make rules and regulations concerning interpretations of the law, subject to judicial review.

These laws were enacted as early as 1902, but the first state law not declared unconstitutional became effective in Wisconsin in early 1911. Several other states followed, and by 1925 twenty-four jurisdictions had this legislation. In addition, the Federal government in 1908 enacted a law covering civilian Federal employees. Some current workmen's compensation legislation still shows the effects of the 1911 decision of the New York Court of Appeals in *Ives v. South Buffalo Ry. Co.,* 201 N.Y. 271, 94 N.E. 431 (1911), that a *compulsory* workmen's compensation law violated the Fourteenth Amendment because it takes property away from the employer without due process of law. Today, all jurisdictions have workmen's compensation laws covering industrial injuries. All jurisdictions also cover occupational diseases, but about one-third of the laws cover only specifically designated diseases.

Although the state laws vary considerably, the following summary of the coverage, injuries and diseases covered, benefits, and funding requirements will indicate the basic approach.[30]

[30] For current detailed information on these laws, see the bulletins on *State Workmen's Compensation Laws* published by the U.S. Department of Labor, and *Analysis of Workmmen's Compensation Laws* prepared periodically by the Chamber of Commerce of the United States.

Most workmen's compensation laws cover all employments which are not specifically excluded, but a few cover only hazardous or extra-hazardous employments. The most commonly excluded employments are domestic service, casual work, and agricultural employment. Railroad workers engaged in interstate commerce are excluded under all state laws because they are covered under the Federal Employers' Liability Act. Almost one-half of the states exclude employers with less than a certain number of employees. Another factor reducing coverage under the workmen's compensation laws is the fact that over twenty jurisdictions permit the employer to determine whether he will bring his employees under the law. However, if he elects not to be covered, he loses the assumption of risk, fellow-servant, and contributory negligence defenses in any employers' liability suits. Employees also have the right to reject workmen's compensation in these states and one other, but they seldom do so. In the compulsory states, workmen's compensation is ordinarily the exclusive remedy of the employee with respect to the employer; he cannot elect to sue the employer under employer's liability.[31] He can elect to sue third parties, however, which in many states means that he may even sue fellow employees. Recent estimates by the Social Security Administration indicate that about 80 per cent of the wage and salary workers in the United States are covered under workmen's compensation. The others must rely upon employers' liability suits.

The laws are fairly uniform in language but have been interpreted differently as to what injuries "arise out of and in the course of employment." The principal question is whether the injury is job-related. Otherwise, the only two defenses available to the employer are that the injury was intentionally inflicted or that, subject to certain exceptions, the employee was intoxicated at the time of the injury. Examples of some troublesome claims are heart attacks on the job, injuries during a coffee break or on the way to work, and injuries resulting from horseplay.

The laws provide four types of benefits: (1) medical benefits, (2) disability income benefits, (3) death benefits, and (4) rehabilitation benefits. Most jurisdictions will pay all the injured worker's medical expenses incurred as a result of his injury or disease, but some jurisdictions limit these payments in time or amount.

The disability benefits are related to the worker's wage at the time he was disabled. Most of the disability claims involve temporary total disability, for which a typical benefit is two-thirds of the weekly wage but in no case more than $60 a week, beginning with the eighth day of disability and continuing until the claimant has recovered or until a stated period such as 360 weeks has expired. The maximum payments, which vary widely

---

[31] Exceptions to this rule are injuries deliberately inflicted by the employer and certain serious violations of safety statutes.

among the states, have been subject to extensive criticism by many observers because they have not kept pace with rising wages and as a result the maximum payment is the benefit for too many workers. Permanent total disability benefits are determined in the same way except that in most, but not all, states they are continued for the lifetime of the worker. Permanent partial disability benefits are also determined in the same way, except that if the permanent partial disability involves the loss of an arm, the loss of a foot, the loss of sight, or some other scheduled injury, payments are made for a specified number of weeks following the convalescent period, regardless of the effect the injury may have on the worker's actual earnings. The other disability benefits are based on "the actual wage" loss; scheduled permanent partial disability benefits are based supposedly upon the presumed wage loss in order to encourage rehabilitation. However, if this is true, the variation among the states in the number of weeks' wages payable for the same injury is disturbing. For example, for the loss of a leg a Minnesota worker would receive a lump sum payment equal to 220 weeks of benefits; the award in Wisconsin for the same injury would be 500 weeks of benefits.

The death benefits include a limited funeral expense benefit and an income for dependents which is usually expressed as a percentage of the deceased worker's weekly wage, subject to a specified maximum. Usually a widow with children receives a higher percentage, say $66\frac{2}{3}$ per cent, than a widow without children, who receives, say 40 per cent. In some states, widows receive benefits until they die or remarry, but most states limit the benefits to some total dollar amount or some specified number of weeks.

Five jurisdictions operate their own rehabilitation centers, and over twenty other jurisdictions provide some maintenance and similar benefits for persons undergoing rehabilitation. Unfortunately, more has been done on paper than in practice; but there are some significant accomplishments.

Another measure designed to help handicapped workers is the second-injury fund, which exists in all but four states. The fund is designed to encourage the employment of handicapped workers by transferring to the fund, which is administered by the state, all responsibility for the extra workmen's compensation benefits, if any, associated with the handicap. Some second-injury funds apply only to certain handicaps, such as the loss of sight or a dismemberment, but some of the funds provide very broad coverage. Many methods are used to finance these funds, the most common method being special payments in death cases where there are no dependents to receive compensation benefits.

In addition to prescribing the benefits to be paid, legislators have been concerned, from the beginning of workmen's compensation legislation, about the ability of employers to make these payments when the occasion arises. The table given here shows the present situation with respect to the funding of benefits. It is interesting to observe that although workmen's compensation is clearly social legislation, most states have not established state funds. The heavy reliance on private insurers can be explained by the fact that when workmen's compensation was introduced, private insurers were already experienced writers of employer's liability insurance and workmen's collective insurance (a form of health insurance); the British had adopted this approach; there was much opposition to "government in business"; and competition among insurers was considered necessary to stimulate the loss-prevention and reduction activities which at that time were so sorely needed. The principal counterarguments in favor of state funds were that workmen's compensation insurance, being social insurance, should be written by non-profit public insurers; public insurers should be able to operate with lower expense loadings; and competitive state funds provide a yardstick for measuring the performance of private insurers.

Funding medium	Number of states
Monopolistic state fund	4
Monopolistic state fund or self-insurance	2
State fund, private insurer, or self-insurance	12
Private insurer or self-insurance	31
Insurance not required	1
Total	50

Accident frequency and severity data   For comparative industry information on work injury frequency and severity rates, the reader can consult the United States Department of Labor's annual report on *Injury Rates by Industry*. These data indicate that in 1968 manufacturing industries suffered 14.0 injuries on the average for each 1 million employee hours worked, with an average 49 days of disability per case. The disparity in experience among industries is dramatized by comparing coal mining, with 40.8 injuries per 1 million employee hours, with finance, insurance, and real estate experiencing 2.0 injuries on the same basis. State industrial commissions also report extensive injury-disability experience by industry and worker classifications.

LIABILITY ARISING FROM BUSINESS OPERATIONS

Business firms must be aware of serious exposures to loss arising from their various activities. Some of these exposures will be examined in detail.

Maintaining a nuisance   A business firm may be sued for maintaining either a public or private nuisance in relation to the use and enjoyment of its premises. These nuisance actions require that the claimant show substantial harm as the result of activity and indicate that the value gained by the user of the land is much less in proportion to the harm or risk which it creates. Public nuisance actions normally involve possible criminal liability for interference with the rights of the community at large. They may involve, for example, the construction of an unsafe roadway or the performance of business transactions corrupting the morals of the community.

Private nuisances, on the other hand, may include such highly dangerous activities as blasting, storing explosives, drilling oil wells or laying pipelines, which generate risk of harm to others. They may also involve such things as keeping vicious animals, shooting fireworks in the streets, ringing bells or blowing whistles, or making disturbances which may invade the quiet and solitude of others. An unpleasant odor, a whiff of smoke, or an increased fire hazard due to the presence of certain types of buildings may also be viewed as the basis of suit.

Patent and copyright infringement, unfair trade practices, etc.   Civil liability may also exist for patent or copyright infringements which may seriously hurt or harm the economic affairs of competitors. Civil actions may also be brought for unfair trade practices, including conspiracies to restrain trade. Treble damage suits have been allowed in cases where such practices by the business firm seriously impair the market position of competitors.[32]

Liability arising from the sale, manufacture, and distribution of products or services   Special liability problems exist for the businessman in relation to the manufacture, sale, or distribution of goods and services. Special legal problems arise out of the sales contract itself, involving promises and obligations concerning the performance of the products sold. In addition, the product itself may be defective or manufactured and designed in a negligent manner so as to produce serious harm to those using it. Tied to the product itself may be the necessary services of delivery, installation, and maintenance, which may be negligently performed. Serious liability problems may arise from faulty installation and service of the product rather than from defects in the product itself.[33]

---

[32] See *Hopkins Chem. Co. v. Read Drug & Chem. Co.,* 124 Md. 210, 92 Atl. 478 (1914). See also *American Waltham Watch Co. v. United States Watch Co.,* 173 Mass. 85, 53 N.E. 141 (1899).

[33] It should be noted at this point that the subject of professional liability—namely, the liability arising out of the performance of special services such as the practice of medicine, law, public accounting, pharmacy, and related skills—involves special concepts of legal liability. These problems will be discussed later in this chapter.

1. Breach of warranty actions arising from sales contract. Breach of warranty actions arising from the sales of goods or services may be based upon either express or implied warranties. The *express* warranty has been defined as "an affirmation of fact or a promise by the seller relating to the goods which may serve as an inducement for the buyer to purchase the goods." If the purchaser relies upon the statement of the seller and the product does not meet these expressed guarantees or promises, then liability for the purchase price and the property damages resulting from the breach may be established by a suit based on breach of express warranty. It is important therefore in the sale of products that the retailer or seller does not make statements that go beyond the normal effective capacity of the product performance to induce the purchase.

In addition to the express warranty actions, the common law has established certain *implied* warranties attached to most sales contracts, the breach of which may give rise to liability. They are: (1) implied warranty of title, (2) implied warranty of fitness for a particular purpose, and (3) implied warranty that the goods are of merchantable quality.

In the sale of goods the seller makes the implied warranty that he has title to the goods and may convey them free and clear of other claims in the absence of any expressed reservations. If it subsequently develops that the seller does not have this title, then he is liable to subsequent buyers for the purchase price and any other damage suffered as a result of breach of this warranty.

Where goods are purchased by description or catalog number, the buyer may specify that the article ordered must be used to fit or fulfill a particular purpose. Where the buyer specifically indicates to the seller that the article must be suitable for a particular purpose as a condition of purchase, and where he relies on the skill and judgment of the seller concerning the capcaity of the goods to fulfill this purpose, then failure of the product to perform accordingly may also result in legal liability. For example, if a heating man installs a particular type of furnace to heat your home properly and you rely on his skill and judgment concerning the size and type of furnace required, then failure of the product to heat your home may involve the seller in a liability resulting from breach of the implied warranty of fitness.

The third warranty of merchantability governs situations involving food or other products which must maintain a certain minimum quality. Goods are said to be merchantable when they are free from hidden defects and are fit for the use for which they are ordinarily intended. When the goods may be inspected by the buyer, normally this implied warranty against defects does not apply, since examination would reveal such defects. A recent action brought under this warranty is illustrative. The Cutter Laboratories manufactured polio vaccine which subsequently caused patients who had been vaccinated to contract the disease. In the actions brought against the Cutter Laboratories, the theory of the action was tied to the warranty of merchantability or fitness for the purpose. Even though the manufacturer offered evidence to show it used great care and skill in manufacturing the vaccine, the court allowed recovery for breach of warranty of fitness.[34]

It is important to note that in many states, suits for breach of warranty are not allowed unless the party is a member of the contract relationship. This is referred to in the law as the *privity of contract* requirement. Actions brought in Alabama, Arkansas, Connecticut, the District of Columbia, Maine, Maryland, Massachusetts, Montana, New Hampshire, New Jersey, New York, North Carolina, South Dakota, Tennessee, Virginia, West Virginia, and Wisconsin have been denied when the plaintiff was not in privity of contract with the defendant. In these states the action on breach of warranty rests on the notion that the warranty is a part of the sales contract to which it is attached, and unless the plaintiff is the actual purchaser, no recoveries are allowed. On the other hand, California, Florida, Illinois, Iowa, Kansas, Louisiana, Mississippi, Pennsylvania, Oklahoma, Texas, and Washington have rejected the privity requirement and do allow direct action against the retailer even though the party injured was not an actual buyer in the sales contract.

2. Liability arising out of negligent manufacture of goods or products. Because of the problems of establishing privity of contract where the goods may be purchased from a person at the retail level but the actual defect is caused by the manufacturer, who is far removed from the specific sales transaction, many actions have been brought against the manufacturer directly for the tort of negligence.[35] This action must be based upon proof that the articles manufactured affect human life, and that they are eminently dangerous in their natural state or in their defective condition. The problem for the plaintiff in these actions is to show that the specific plaintiff's injuries are directly traceable to the negligence of the manufacturer, that the defect is not common to the product, and that an identifiable error in design or manufacture threatens human life in its defective condition. If liability for manufacture is to be successfully proved, it must rest upon the fact that the defendant either created the condition or refrained from removing it and that creation or nonremoval was the result of his carelessness. The defense which the manufacturer can use is that he maintained an establishment which has adopted all reasonable precautions of manufacture and that the plaintiff was injured by other means. Many court actions have been

---

[34] The Uniform Sales Act, which has been enacted in most states, makes special reference to these implied warranties. For example, the warranties of fitness and merchantability are contained in secs. 15.1 and 15.2.

[35] *MacPherson v. Buick Motor Co.*, 217 N.Y. 282, 111 N.E. 1050 (1916). Also see John L. Hill, "How Strict Is Strict?" *Insurance Law Journal*, No. 564 (January, 1970), 18–28.

brought against manufacturers of food when foreign objects have been found in sealed containers. Recent deaths traceable to canned tuna fish were reported in the press. In these cases plaintiffs have had little difficulty in tracing their injuries to defendant manufacturers and over the years have enjoyed a high degree of success in recovery. Many of the interesting cases surround the soft-drink manufacturers and the finding of deleterious substances in bottled soft drinks.

Under certain circumstances, courts have found *absolute liability* of a manufacturer without regard to negligence. The finding of absolute liability raises serious problems for the defendant manufacturer, since he cannot defend himself by showing that he used proper and reasonable care. In the vending of pharmaceutical prescriptions and drugs, the courts have found for plaintiffs on the theory of *absolute liability*. The same applies to the dispensing of poisons and other deleterious substances.

Because of the public interest involved, special liability exposures exist for those retailers and manufacturers who dispense food or drugs which greatly affect the public interest. The Coca-Cola Company, for example, is a target for many such claims, and over the years has paid millions of dollars for either alleged, actual, or possible side effects from breach of the sales warranty relating to the soft drink or negligence in manufacture. In these circumstances, the amount of recovery has not been large, but the number of suits has been very great. The problems are particularly serious for manufacturers of parts or equipment to be used on other expensive, assembled equipment or machinery. For example, the manufacturer of a particular part for a jet airliner may be held liable for defects in its manufacture if it caused the crash of a plane. Much of the investigation of airplane crashes is conducted for the purpose of placing the ultimate legal liability upon the manufacturer or supplier of particular defective parts involved. Under this theory of law, it is possible for a manufacturer to furnish a part valued at 10 cents which may give rise to a liability judgment running into millions of dollars. Needless to say, such exposures require careful handling and strict control in the modern business world.

Another particular example of exposure relates to services involving subcontractors who may be performing specific work on large construction or development projects. One recent situation involved an individual who had agreed to dig a sewer ditch into a particular building for a fee under $1,000. In the process of digging the ditch, the subcontractor hit a gas main, and the resulting explosion destroyed the entire building beyond repair. In assuming the responsibility for digging the ditch the subcontractor laid himself open to exposures many, many times the amount of profit that he could expect to earn from performing the work.

It is important to note that the legal liability to which one may be subject is not related in any way to the amount of profit he may expect from the transaction; in many circumstances the liability exposures may far exceed the value of the product or service to be furnished. Evidently these risks or exposures should be properly met with insurance or other devices, in order that the businessman may receive the proper fruits of his labors instead of ruining his entire future financial state as the result of unavoidable negligence or carelessness.

PROFESSIONAL LIABILITY EXPOSURES

Special liability problems confront persons who engage in professional pursuits, or perform services requiring special care and skill. Courts have defined the term *profession* as follows: "The word implies professed attainment in special knowledge as distinguished from mere skill. A practical dealing with affairs as distinguished from mere study or investigation, and an application of such knowledge to uses for others as a vocation, as distinguished from its pursuit for its own purposes."[36] In surveying the common law, however, one becomes thoroughly confused in an attempt to formulate any generalized legal definitions of the term. Courts have held in specific cases that the following are professional servants:

1. Operator of a pool hall[37]
2. Private detective[38]
3. Insurance agent[39]
4. Minister of the Gospel[40]
5. Operator of a school bus[41]
6. Teacher of singing and music[42]
7. Pharmacist[43]
8. Physician[44]
9. Optometrist[45]
10. Architect[46]
11. Chemist[47]

[36] James A. Ballentine, *Law Dictionary* (Rochester, N.Y.: Lawyers' Cooperative Publishing Company, 1948), p. 1028.
[37] *Harris v. Todd*, 158 S.W. 1189 (Tex. Civ. App. 1913).
[38] *State v. Pendleton*, 9 La. App. 100, 119 So. 73 (1928).
[39] *Betz v. Maier*, 12 Tex. Civ. App. 219, 33 S.W. 710; Insurance agents have also been held not to be professional. See *Recht v. Graves*, 257 App. Div. 889, 12 N.Y.S.2d 158 (1939).
[40] *Miller v. Kirkpatrick*, 29 Pa. 226 (1857).
[41] *Hamner and Co. v. Johnson*, 16 La. App. 580, 135 So. 77 (1931).
[42] *People ex rel. Fullam v. Kelly*, 255 N.Y. 396, 175 N.E. 108 (1931).
[43] *Lee v. Gaddy*, 133 Fla. 749, 183 So. 4 (1938).
[44] *Village of Dodge v. Guidinger*, 87 Neb. 349, 127 N.W. 122 (1910).
[45] *Babcock v. Nudelman*, 367 Ill. 626, 12 N.E.2nd 635 (1937).
[46] *Georgia Bd. of Optometry v. Friedman*, 183 Ga. 669, 189 S.E. 238 (1936).
[47] *Wright v. Borthwick*, 34 Hawaii 245 (1937).

12. Newspaper editor[48]
13. Journalist[49]
14. Landscape gardener[50]
15. Certified shorthand reporter[51]
16. Engineers, including surveyor,[52] consulting engineer,[53] civil engineer,[54] and industrial designer[55]
17. Lawyer[56]
18. Dentist[57]
19. Accountant[58]
20. Veterinarian[59]

On the other hand, the application of the test for professional status by the courts has resulted in numerous activities being held not to be professions, including beauty culture,[60] brokerage,[61] undertaking and embalming,[62] furniture designing,[63] and management consulting.[64]

The rise of professionalism in the United States has produced interesting developments in the civil law. The attainment of professional status by certain types of activity, including law, medicine, pharmacy, and accounting, has produced certain legal consequences which may or may not have been contemplated by the professions during their evolutionary rise.[65] The individual practitioner has discovered, sometimes after painful and expensive litigation, that his conduct is not measured by the common law tests of quality used in the ordinary relationships among individuals.[66] On the con-

[48] *Id.* at 252.
[49] *Geiffert v. Mealey,* 293 N.Y. 383, 59 N.E.2d 414 (1944).
[50] *Ibid.*
[51] *Ibid.*
[52] *Wright v. Borthwick, supra,* note 47, 34 Hawaii at 254.
[53] *Ericsson v. Brown,* 38 Barb. 390 (N.Y. Sup. Ct. 1862).
[54] *Teague v. Graves,* 261 App. Div. 652, 27 N.Y.S.2d 762 (1949).
[55] *Wright v. Borthwick, ubi cit. supra,* note 52.
[56] *Lanier v. Macon,* 59 Ga. 187 (1877).
[57] *Geiffert v. Mealey, supra,* note 49.
[58] *Ibid.*
[59] *Ibid.*
[60] *People v. Maggi,* 310 Ill. App. 101, 33 N.E.2d 925 (1941).
[61] *Jones v. Robertson,* 79 Cal. App. 2d 813, 180 P.2d 929 (1947) (real estate broker).
[62] *Babcock v. Laidlaw,* 113 N.J. Eq. 318, 166 Atl. 632 (1933).
[63] Application of *De Vries,* 266 App. Div. 1030, 44 N.Y.S.2d 535 (1943).
[64] *Pennicke v. Mealey,* 266 App. Div. 888, 42 N.Y.S.2d 884 (1943).
[65] Whether contemplated or not, neither the growth in numbers nor the quality of services can be shown to have been adversely affected by these legal developments. In fact it may be argued that the very success in attaining or preserving professional status is attributable to the established legal framework within which the professional servant is required to operate. See John Carey, *Professional Ethics of Public Accounting* (New York: The American Institute of Accountants, 1946).
[66] In cases involving ordinary negligence, the usual test applied is whether or not the defendant acted as an ordinarily reasonable, prudent man would have acted. See *Restatement of Torts, supra,* note 25, at sec. 283.

trary, the law has recognized that the professional calling places responsibilities far above those imposed upon persons engaged in less skilled or intellectual pursuits:[67]

> The relation between a physician and his patient is predicated on the proposition that the physician has a *special knowledge and skill* in diagnosing and treating diseases and injuries, and that the patient has sought and obtained the services of the physician because of such knowledge and skill. A physician will be held to the exercise of an *amount of skill common to his profession, without which he would not have taken a case, and a degree of care commensurate with his position.* [Italics supplied by the authors.]

This same test of "special knowledge and skill common to the profession" has been enunciated time and again in litigation involving the conduct of other professional activities including law,[68] pharmacy,[69] dentistry,[70] nursing,[71] optometry,[72] accounting,[73] osteopathy,[74] and chiropractic.[75]

The malpractice problem facing the professions   The necessity and desirability of imposing fairly rigid controls over professional conduct to safeguard the public interest is certainly not denied by the patients or clients and least of all by the professions themselves. Professional status, as we have indicated, is dependent upon the quality and sophistication of the services rendered by all practicing members. It is for that very reason that the individual professions have not looked only to legal censure to preserve the quality and stature of their services, but have imposed in every case very strict and rigid rules of self-control and self-policing as a matter of self-preservation. Actions to bring about disbarment, loss of certification or license, and finally expulsion from the organized profession are usually brought in the name of the professional organizations against the individual violating member. Codes of professional ethics, which carefully summarize the moral responsibilities of the individual members are promulgated and enforced by every professional group. State practice and licensing laws are usually sponsored by the individual profession. Control and regulation are thus an indispensable part of the total picture of professional activity and are welcomed by patient, client, and practitioner alike.

[67] *Tvedt v. Haugen*, 70 N.D. 338, 294 N.W. 183 (1940).
[68] *Hampel-Lawson Mercantile Co. v. Poe*, 169 Ark. 840, 277 S.W. 29 (1925).
[69] *Corona Coal Co. v. Sexton*, 21 Ala. App. 51, 105 So. 716, *cert. denied*, 213 Ala. 554, 105 So. 718 (1925).
[70] *Phillips v. Stillwell*, 55 Ariz. 147, 99 P.2d 104 (1940).
[71] *Ales v. Ryan*, 8 Cal.2d 82, 64 P.2d 409 (1937).
[72] *Hampton v. Brackin's Jewelry & Optical Co.*, 237 Ala. 212, 186 So. 173 (1939).
[73] *Ultra Mares Corp. v. Touch*, 229 App. Div. 581, 243 N.Y. Supp. 179 (1930).
[74] *Josselyn v. Dearborn*, 143 Me. 328, 62 A.2d 174 (1948).
[75] *Janssen v. Mulder*, 232 Mich. 183, 205 N.W. 150 (1925).

A problem arises for the professional practitioner, however, when the control and regulation takes the form of litigation by the client or patient concerning the particular standards and qualities of the individual's conduct. It is in these situations and with this type of legal control that the professional servant faces the severe test which may bring about complete failure and economic ruin.

The malpractice or liability action strikes at the very heart of the practitioner's greatest and most cherished asset, his professional reputation. The bad publicity arising from such a suit, even in situations where the defendant is entirely innocent and the eventual outcome is entirely favorable, may spell complete ruin of a professional career which took a lifetime to build.

Loss of reputation and professional standing are not the only consequences of malpractice litigation. Final judgment may be rendered against the practitioner for tremendous sums for the injury caused by careless, unexpected, unpredictable, or unintentional blunders. The loss in terms of trial time in testifying in the defense of one's actions, the legal and court costs which are usually assessed to the loser, to say nothing of the emotional and physical strain of enduring the whole ordeal, are some of the other losses suffered as a consequence of litigation.

Several factors make the malpractice problem extremely difficult to meet and solve. First of all, the common law regulations of standards of conduct are not easily identified and defined. The legal test of performance is vague and impossible of accurate interpretation in any given set of facts outside the courtroom walls. Second, the rapid advance in the technology of professions makes the practitioner extremely vulnerable to suit because of failure to possess knowledge of the advancements or changes in his field and to exercise skill and care in its application. Also, this rapid change in the underlying technical knowledge of the professions makes older legal requirements of performance outmoded and obsolete. As an example, a doctor using penicillin for the first time could not be sure that he would be absolved from prosecution for experimentation if the drug produced unfavorable results in his patient. On the other hand, he could be prosecuted for lack of skill and care if he failed to use the drug when the conditions called for its use according to the technical information common to the profession at the time. Just as technology changes, so does the law. Today the legal standard would probably absolve the user of the wonder drug, whereas ten years ago the doctor might have been prosecuted for experimentation.

The current impact of the malpractice problem   In appraising the current status of the malpractice problem in the various professions, several important facts are clear. Greater numbers of malpractice claims and suits are being brought every year, larger verdicts are being awarded, and education and technology are constantly raising the standards of performance expected of the practitioners. Legal rights, which have existed for a long period of time, are currently being exercised with greater intensity by injured plaintiffs and their legal counsel.

This upsurge in professional liability claims and suits has been explained in several ways. One explanation is that a general weakening of the nonprofessional ties between the professional servant and his patient or client has taken place. The country doctor, considered not only a professional servant, but also a close personal friend by his patients, has been gradually replaced by specialists residing in metropolitan centers. Patients today travel many miles from their social circles for medical care and attention. Consequently, they do not usually hesitate to sue the stranger for his malpractice, whereas no thought of suit would arise from similar misconduct of the honored and respected country doctor. Comparable statements can be made about the legal, accounting, and pharmaceutical professions.

Another reason which has been advanced for the increased frequency of suits has been the general "claims consciousness" of the public as a whole. This claims consciousness has developed in the area of automobile liability and has spread to other types of tortious conduct, including professional malpractice.[76]

REVIEW QUESTIONS

1. Distinguish between:
   a. Liability and legal liability
   b. Criminal and civil liability
2. a. What are the various kinds or sources of legal actions which may be brought to establish civil liability?
   b. Is it possible for more than one source of legal action to exist in the same situation?
3. "Law does not protect those who sleep on their rights." What does this statement mean?
4. a. What is an intentional tort?
   b. Cite some examples of intentional torts.
5. Comment on the legal liability status of the following:
   a. A man whose dog bites a neighbor
   b. A newspaper columnist who accuses a government official of being a liar

[76] Virtually every profession is currently conducting research on the problem. Committees at work include the Committee on Law and Medicine of the American Medical Association, the Committee on Accountants' Liability and Liability Insurance of the American Institute of Accountants, the Professional Ethics Committee of the American Bar Association and others.

    c. A congressman who, on the floor of the House of Representatives, calls a newspaper columnist a liar

    d. A department store which by mistake causes a man to be arrested

6. Can an intentional tort and an unintentional tort exist simultaneously?

7. In order to make out a cause of action for negligence, what must the plaintiff demonstrate?

8. a. In what way can the burden of proof be shifted from the plaintiff to the defendant?

    b. Why would this be an important shift?

9. The plaintiff in a particular case was totally and permanently disabled in an automobile accident. At the time of the accident he was thirty years of age and was earning $6,000 a year. His automobile was completely destroyed in the accident. What factors will be considered in determining how much the defendant will have to pay this plaintiff?

10. What defenses might be asserted by the defendant in a case involving negligence?

11. In a particular case, it is agreed that both the plaintiff and the defendant were negligent. The plaintiff was responsible for 25 per cent of the negligence involved and the defendant for 75 per cent. The plaintiff suffered losses of $60,000 in the accident, while the defendant's losses were $30,000.

    a. How would this case probably be settled in a contributory negligence state? in a comparative negligence state?

    b. Comment on the fairness of these various settlements.

12. John Smith is a partner in a construction firm. Comment on John's liability for negligent actions by each of the following parties:

    a. John's partner

    b. An employee of the partnership

    c. An employee of another construction firm participating with John's firm in a joint venture

    d. A plumber hired to install some new pipes in the partnership's home office building

13. Comment on the liability of each of the following:

    a. A laundry for customers' goods

    b. A parking lot for cars stored on the premises

    c. A firm for a hired car

    d. A tenant for the building he occupies

14. The liability of a trucking firm or a railroad as a common carrier continues for 48 hours beginning at 7 A.M. after written notice of arrival has been sent or given to the consignee. After that time, the legal responsibility of the carrier is that of a warehouseman only. Why is this information important to the consignee?

15. Comment on the legal responsibility of Bill Brown, a sole proprietor, for negligent actions by each of the following parties:
    a. His son, while driving the firm's one automobile
    b. An employee, while driving that automobile
    c. A friend who borrows that automobile for his own personal purposes

16. What is the responsibility of the owner of a manufacturing plant for injuries to each of the following persons:
    a. A curious adult who enters the premises despite signs forbidding him to enter
    b. A mailman
    c. A salesman
    d. A customer

17. Children receive a favored position under the attractive nuisance doctrine.
    a. What is the attractive nuisance doctrine?
    b. Cite several examples of items which some courts have considered to be attractive nuisances.

18. Employers' liability statutes improved the legal position of the employee, but his position remained unsatisfactory.
    a. What was the legal position of the employee under the common law?
    b. How did employers' liability statutes improve the position of the employee?
    c. In what sense did the employee's position remain unsatisfactory?

19. a. How does the workmen's compensation approach differ from the employers' liability approach?
    b. Is workmen's compensation the exclusive approach to industrial injuries today?

20. Discuss workmen's compensation statutes with respect to:
    a. Eligibility requirements
    b. Injuries and diseases covered
    c. Benefits
    d. Administration
    e. Insurance requirements

21. What sources of legal actions are likely to be brought to establish legal liability in each of the following cases?
    a. The casing on a power mower broke and injured the person mowing the lawn.
    b. A man became ill as a result of some impurities contained in a seasoning purchased by his wife.
    c. Some soft-drink bottles which a retailer had placed near a radiator exploded, causing serious injuries to some customers.
    d. A customer requested a refrigerator with a true freezer compartment. The store sold him instead a refrigerator with a section which, though

colder than the rest of the refrigerator, was not a true freezer. The customer became ill as a result of eating some food which would have been kept fresh in a true freezer but was not preserved in his refrigerator.

    e. The steering wheel of a car suddenly failed to work, and an accident resulted.

22. Many retailers believe that they do not have to be concerned about product liability because this is the manufacturer's responsibility. Do you agree?

23. a. What are the special problems associated with professional liability?

    b. Construct one illustrative professional liability case for each of the following professions: law, medicine, accounting, and engineering.

24. Do current trends in matters affecting liability exposures favor plaintiffs or defendants? Illustrate your answer.

SUGGESTIONS FOR ADDITIONAL READING

Baylor, John: "The Ghetto's Need for Liability Insurance," *Insurance Law Journal* (November, 1969), 666ff.

Cheit, E. F.: *Injury and Recovery in the Course of Employment* (New York: John Wiley & Sons, Inc., 1961)

Condon, W. J.: "Products Liability Cases," *Insurance Law Journal* (September, 1958), 615ff.

Donaldson, James H.: *Casualty Claims Practice* (rev. ed., Homewood, Ill.: Richard D. Irwin, Inc., 1969).

Heins, R. M.: "Incurred vs. Discovered Losses in Malpractice Insurance," *Insurance Law Journal* (June, 1955), 399–405.

Hill, John L.: "How Strict Is Strict? Have the Walls of the Citadel Really Crumbled?" *Insurance Law Journal* (January, 1970) 16ff.

Holmes, Oliver Wendell, Jr.: *The Common Law* (Boston: Little, Brown and Company, 1923).

Kulp, C. A., and Hall, J.: *Casualty Insurance* (4th ed., New York: The Ronald Press Company, 1968).

Liability (Corpus Juris Secundum, LIII) (New York: The American Law Book Co. and St. Paul, Minn.: West Publishing Company, 1948), pp. 16–21.

Negligence (Corpus Juris Secundum, LVA) (New York: The American Law Book Co. and St. Paul, Minn.: West Publishing Company, 1966), pp. 1–1077.

Prosser, W. L.: *Handbook of the Law of Torts* (3d ed., St. Paul, Minn.: West Publishing Company, 1964).

Somers, H. M., and Somers, A. R.: *Workmen's Compensation* (New York: John Wiley & Sons, Inc., 1954), chaps. 3–8.

Spell, R. V.: *Public Liability Hazards* (3d ed., Indianapolis: The Rough Notes Company, 1955).

8

personnel risk identi~~~
and measurement

The discussion now turns from property and liability losses to personnel losses—the financial losses that occur when one or more people (usually employees in whom the firm has some direct interest) die, reach an advanced age, become ill, or lose their jobs for some reason other than illness or old age.[1] Both the individual employees and the firm itself face these losses, and the risk manager has good reason to be interested in the losses to the employees as well as those to the firm. This chapter describes the nature and frequency of both types of losses.

Losses Facing Individual Employees

The firm's employees obviously have reason to plan against the potential financial losses to themselves and their families associated with their death, superannuation, accidental injury or sickness, or unemployment. The risk manager of the firm is also interested in these potential losses to the individual employees for less obvious but very important reasons. Because of this interest, business risk management of personnel risks includes some family risk management.[2]

[1] It is more common to refer to these risks as personal risks, but the term "personal" has also been used to distinguish family risks from business risks. "Personnel" avoids this problem.
[2] Business risk management of property and liability risks may also include some family risk management, but this is still the exception rather than the rule. For an explanation of the slower growth of employee benefit plans covering property and liability losses, see end of Chap. 22.

is concerned with these potential financial losses to indi-
s for the following reasons: He wishes (1) to improve relation-
sh ployees and to increase their productivity, (2) to satisfy a
se mployer responsibility, (3) to create and maintain good public
re and (4) to prevent what is considered an unwarranted expansion
su insurance programs.[3]

Employer-employee relationships A business firm may be concerned about
the potential financial losses to its personnel primarily because it wishes
to improve relationships between the employer and the employee. It believes
that its interest will attract high-grade new employees, increase employee
loyalty to the firm, and reduce turnover and strikes. The firm may also
believe that it will increase the productivity of its workers by freeing them
from some of their worries and by replacing workers whose productivity
has suffered through superannuation or disability. Whether the firm will
accomplish all these results is debatable, but the beliefs undoubtedly have
some basis.

The firm may itself provide some of the necessary protection for the
employees, in which case the firm must make the final decisions. Instead
of actually providing the protection (or in addition to such protection), the
firm may offer to advise the employee concerning his personal protection
program. Although the responsibility for the final decision in this case rests
with the employee, the risk manager must act as if he were choosing the
form of protection.

Many firms are forced to take an interest in the risks to their employees
because of collective bargaining demands for fringe benefits or the threat
of such demands. Prior to 1949, very few employee benefit plans were
the result of collective bargaining. Unions were more interested in pressing
for wage increases than for fringe benefits. Some union leaders, in fact,
mistrusted employer protection plans because they feared the plans would
weaken the employees' loyalty to the union. The 1940s changed this climate
because (1) wage controls during World War II directed attention to fringe
benefits as a valuable condition of employment; (2) prices leveled off in
1949, thus reducing the strength of the case for the unions' demand for
direct wage increases; (3) high income tax rates increased the attractiveness
of fringe benefits to employees (for reasons explained in Chapter 22) and
decreased the real cost of these benefits to employers; and (4) two important

---

[3] Reasons why risk managers may prefer to avoid or limit this concern are the costs involved, a possible negative effect on initiative and incentive, and possible misinterpre-
tation of the motive as objectionable paternalism.

court decisions in 1949 established without question the legal right of unions to bargain with employers with respect to insurance and pension benefits.[4] Since the late forties, collective bargaining has resulted in the establishment of many new insurance and retirement plans and in the modification of many plans established earlier.

Tax considerations are responsible for a special interest in protection plans for executives in the firm. These officials are likely to be in such high income tax brackets that an increase in salary or profits may not be so attractive as one might expect. For example, assume that the president of the firm receives a salary of $80,000 and has other income amounting to $20,000. Further assume that instead of increasing the president's salary by $20,000, the firm sets that amount aside each year to provide the president with an income after he retires (probably subject to restrictions upon his activities during retirement). Because the money set aside is not considered taxable income, the president's income tax is not increased by this action. Under current tax regulations, if the president has a wife and a dependent son, and if his total deductions for charitable contributions, taxes, medical expenses, and the like are $20,000, his Federal income tax will be about $32,300 and his disposable income about $67,700. The income received during retirement will be subject to tax, but the probability is high that the retired president will at that time be in a much lower tax bracket. If instead of funding a retirement income, the firm decided to pay the president a $100,000 salary, his tax would be about $44,100 and his disposable income about $75,900. Plans for deferring compensation, therefore, may be a more effective way to improve executive compensation than direct salary increases and consequently a better way to attract and retain key personnel. Executive compensation may also be improved by making available life and health insurance protection which the executive could not purchase himself at any cost or, in any event, only at a much higher cost.

Sense of employer responsibility   Employers may be interested in the welfare of their employees because they feel responsible for their well-being. The employer may take pride in an insurance and retirement program which is the best in the industry, or he may simply believe that it is his duty to provide a good program.

Public relations   Some employers may not have any sense of responsibility, but they know that the vast majority of the general public attribute some

[4] *Inland Steel Co. v. National Labor Relations Bd.*, 170 F.2d 247 (7th Cir. 1949), *affirmed sub nom. American Communications Ass'n v. Douds*, 339 U.S. 382 (1950) and *W. W. Cross & Co. v. National Labor Relations Bd.*, 174 F.2d 875 (1st Cir. 1949).

responsibility to the employer, and they recognize the value of good public relations.

Threat of extended social insurance benefits   Most business firms are probably opposed at present to the extension of social insurance programs much beyond the current level and types of protection because they fear that government intervention in any area of private enterprise is a forerunner of entry into their own industry. Many of these firms realize that the most effective way to prevent the extension of existing social insurance programs is to demonstrate that individuals are already adequately protected.

NATURE AND IMPORTANCE OF LOSSES TO THE EMPLOYEES

Employees face a potential loss of earning power and unexpected expenses as the result of death, accidental injury, sickness, unemployment, or old age.

Death   The major loss faced by most families as a result of death is a *loss of earning power*. This loss to the family may be estimated by (1) forecasting the income after taxes which the individual would have received each year until his retirement but which he will not receive if he dies, (2) subtracting from each year's expected income the portion that would be used to maintain the individual, and (3) discounting each of these differences to its present value. The last step is necessary because if money can be invested at a certain rate of interest, each dollar available at the present time is worth more than a dollar at some future date.

Applying this concept to a particular case may serve to clarify the preceding paragraph. Assume that an individual, aged 30, earns a salary of $10,000 a year after taxes. Further assume that this is the individual's only income, that it will be his income for the remainder of his working career, that he will retire after 35 more years of employment, that about one-fifth of his income, or $2,000, is needed for his own maintenance costs, and that a reasonable interest rate would be 5 per cent. Under these assumptions, the estimate of the earning power loss would be computed as shown in the table at the top of page 151.[5]

If the annual income had been $20,000 and the maintenance cost $4,000, the loss of earning power would have been twice this amount, or $262,000. If the worker had been aged 60, only the first five present values

---

[5] The estimate is low because it is also assumed that the income is paid annually at the end of the year. Almost without exception, income is payable throughout the year, and the discount to the present time will be less.

would have to be summed, which would produce an earning power loss of slightly over $34,636.

Year	Income	Maintenance cost	Differ- ence	Discount factor	Present value of loss*
1	$10,000	$2,000	$8,000	$(1.05)^{-1}$	$ 7,619
2	10,000	2,000	8,000	$(1.05)^{-1}$	7,256
3	10,000	2,000	8,000	$(1.05)^{-3}$	6,911
. . . .	. . . .	. . . .	. . . .	. . . .	. . . .
33	10,000	2,000	8,000	$(1.05)^{-33}$	1,599
34	10,000	2,000	8,000	$(1.05)^{-34}$	1,523
35	10,000	2,000	8,000	$(1.05)^{-35}$	1,450
					$131,000 (approximately)

*If the difference is assumed to be constant, as it is in this case, the answer can be obtained by multiplying this difference by the present value of $1 a year for the remainder of the working career. For example, $8,000(16.3742) = $130,994. The present values of $1 for selected periods and interest rates are tabled in most college algebra and mathematics of finance textbooks.

Because the estimates of future income, maintenance costs, and interest rates are crude at best and because the indicated loss at the younger ages will usually be far greater than the protection the person can afford to purchase, the dollar value obtained in this way is of limited practical value. However, the estimate is instructive because it emphasizes the magnitude of the earning power loss and demonstrates that the earning power loss tends to diminish with age. As is demonstrated above, if an employee dies at a young age, the loss to his family will be greater than if he dies at a more advanced age.[6]

A more realistic way of determining the amount of protection which the individual's family should have against the loss of earning power is

[6] Steady inflation plus normal salary progressions usually results in an increasing income over time. If this progress is rapid enough, the earning power may increase slightly with age at the younger ages because of the reduction in the sizable interest discounts applied to the larger later incomes. Eventually, however, this effect will disappear.

For a set of tables expressing the "human life value" (discounted for interest and all factors other than mortality that might stop the person from working) as a multiple of gross earnings for selected occupations and ages based on average career expectations, see Alfred E. Hofflander, Jr., *Human Life Value Concepts*, unpublished doctoral dissertation, University of Pennsylvania, 1964. For example, the multiple for an engineer, aged 25, is 36.

For a comparison between the net loss of earning power as calculated in this text and the human life value discounted for all factors that might interfere with future earning power, see Juan B. Aponte and H. S. Denenberg, "A New Concept of the Economics of Life Value and Human Life Value," *Journal of Risk and Insurance*, XXXV, No. 3 (September, 1958), 337–56.

to assess the minimum needs of the family after death. If the family is to maintain the same standard of living after the breadwinner's death as before, the two approaches produce the same answers, but the needs approach is more realistic in that it recognizes that such a standard is impossibly high. Besides minimum needs can be more accurately (though far from perfectly) estimated.

The needs approach generally recognizes the following types of needs:

1. A readjustment income close to the actual loss of income for a short period during which the family is expected to readjust their needs and desires to their new circumstances
2. A reduced but still substantial income following the readjustment period and continuing until the children are self-sufficient (normally to age 18)
3. A further reduced but adequate lifetime income for the widow beginning after the end of the dependency period

For example, the individual for whose family the earning loss was computed might develop the following needs:

1. $600 a month during a two-year readjustment period following his death
2. $500 a month during the next 13 years until his one child, now aged 3, attains age 18
3. $400 a month for the rest of his widow's life beginning after his child reaches age 18

The needs approach depends upon the individual's desires as much as (and perhaps more than) upon his needs. Consequently, two persons in approximately the same financial and family situation may develop a different needs pattern. The above needs, however, are generally recognized as the most important.

The second type of loss that a family suffers when the breadwinner dies is *additional expenses*. Funeral expenses, including the cost of the funeral itself, the cemetery lot, and the headstone, will affect all families and will probably run well in excess of $1,000. Probate costs and the fees of executors and administrators will be an additional cost, and for large estates these costs will be sizable. Finally the Federal estate tax and the state inheritance and estate taxes will demand a sizable amount of cash even from the moderate-sized estate. For large estates, these taxes may make the loss caused by additional expenses far greater than the loss of earning power. If other assets in the estate must be sold at forced liquidation prices in order to provide the cash for these taxes, the additional expenses will be even greater.

For selected ages between ages 0 and 60, inclusive, Table 8.1 shows (1) the probability in 1959 to 1961 that a person of a certain age would die within a year, (2) the probability that a person that age would die prior to attaining age 45, and (3) the probability that a person of that age would die prior to attaining age 65. The probabilities are based upon the mortality rates reported for the entire United States population during these years.

Table 8.1 Probabilities of death within a year following birthday and prior to ages 45 and 65

	Probability of death				Probability of death		
Age	Within a year	Prior to age 45	Prior to age 65	Age	Within a year	Prior to age 45	Prior to age 65
0	.0259	.086	.29	35	.0019	.029	.24
5	.0006	.058	.27	40	.0030	.024	.24
10	.0004	.056	.26	45	.0048	. . . .	.22
15	.0007	.054	.26	50	.0077	. . . .	.20
20	.0012	.049	.26	55	.0116	. . . .	.16
25	.0013	.043	.26	60	.0176	. . . .	.10
30	.0014	.037	.25				

Source: U.S. Department of Health, Education, and Welfare, Public Health Service, *United States Life Tables: 1959–61* (December, 1964), pp. 8–9.

The probability of death within the next year is very small during the age span shown. The probability of death prior to age 45 is much larger but still small. The probability of death prior to age 65 is substantial. More than one out of four persons between ages 20 and 30 will die before reaching age 65. When this probability is considered together with the magnitude of the potential loss, the case for some active protection measures is clear.

The total population, of course, may be divided into subgroups with varying mortality rates. For example, the probabilities of death are lower for the white population than for the nonwhite population and for females than for males.

The leading causes of death are major cardiovascular-renal diseases and malignant neoplasms. In 1959–61 the probability at birth that a white male would eventually die from the first of these two diseases was .59 and from the other .15.[7]

[7] U.S. Department of Health, Education, and Welfare, Public Health Service, *United States Life Tables by Causes of Death: 1959–61* (May, 1968), p. 7.

Poor health   Poor health, like death, may cause two types of losses: (1) loss of earning power through disability and (2) extra expenses.

If a person is totally and permanently disabled to the extent that he cannot work, the loss of earning power may be computed as it is in the case of premature death, but there is no deduction for the disabled person's maintenance cost except for any expenses involved in going to work or engaging in other activities which may have to be discontinued. The loss of earning power caused by this degree of permanent and total disability is therefore greater than the loss caused by death. For the example presented in the section on Death, if the reduction in expenses is assumed to be negligible, the estimated earning-power loss would be over $160,000.

If the work-loss disability is temporary instead of permanent, the loss of earning power is computed in the same fashion, but the loss period is shorter. To illustrate: If the person whose situation was described earlier was prevented from working for 5 years, the loss of earning power would be about $43,000. If the disability is such that the person can do some but not all of his work and that his wage is reduced, the analysis is the same, except that the reduction in wages is used instead of the total wage. For example, if the reduction in wages is 50 per cent, the earning-power losses in the examples used to illustrate the total permanent work-loss disability and the total temporary work-loss disability would be one-half of the losses computed earlier.

Unexpected extra expenses accompanying an injury, a sickness, or an impairment take the form of hospital bills, surgical fees, charges for physicians' care (nonsurgical) in the hospital, at the doctor's office, or at the patient's home, dental bills, charges for nursing services, costs of artificial limbs and the like, and other medical expenses.

Estimating the probability that a person will suffer a "morbidity condition" and the extent to which that condition will be disabling is extremely difficult because (1) morbidity, unlike mortality, cannot be defined exactly,[8] (2) morbidity varies in seriousness as well as frequency, and (3) morbidity conditions are not reported on a regular basis to public authorities.

Because of the paucity of data on morbidity conditions, in 1956 Congress authorized a continuing National Health Survey to secure information about health conditions in the United States. Some recent data on the number of disability days per person derived from this survey are presented in Table 8.2 for various age and sex groups. Survey data do not reveal the probability of becoming disabled or the average number of days that elapse before a disabled person recovers. The average number of disability days

---

[8] For example, two persons in exactly the same state of health may disagree as to whether they are ill or have an impairment. If they agree that they have a morbidity condition, they may disagree as to whether this condition is disabling.

depends upon the proportion of the population that is disabled during the year and the average length of their disabilities.

Insurance data reveal that out of 10,000 insured persons aged 27, 66 will be disabled for three months or longer within the next year. For groups of 10,000 aged 37, 47, and 57, the numbers who will be disabled in this way are 98, 168, and 311, respectively. The chance that a person in his twenties will suffer a disability lasting three months or more prior to age 65 is about $\frac{2}{3}$.[9] The chance of a serious disability, therefore, is substantially greater than the chance of death, particularly at the younger ages.

Table 8.2 Disability days per person per year, by sex and age, United States, 1968

	Restricted-activity days		Bed-disability days		Work-loss days	
	Male	Female	Male	Female	Male	Female
Under 17 years	10.0	9.9	4.4	4.6	—	—
17–24 years	9.8	11.7	3.9	5.5	4.6	5.1
15–44 years	11.1	14.5	4.5	6.1	4.3	6.0
45–64 years	20.6	20.9	7.1	8.1	6.4	6.2
65 years and over	32.5	36.9	13.5	15.2	5.5	6.5

Source: *Current Estimates from the National Health Survey, United States—1968,* Series 10, Number 60 (Washington, D.C.: United States Public Health Service, 1970), p. 20.

According to the National Health Survey, almost 46 per cent of the civilian, noninstitutional population had some chronic condition during the period July, 1963–June, 1965. About 12 per cent had their activity limited in some degree by these chronic conditions; over 2 per cent were unable to carry on their major activity as a worker, homemaker, or student. The aged and the poor were even more likely to have a chronic condition, to have their activity limited by this chronic condition, and to be unable to carry on their major activity.[10] In a special 1966 survey of the noninstitutional population aged 18 to 64, the Social Security Administration estimated that almost 18 per cent of the population were limited in their ability to work (including keeping house) because of chronic health conditions or impairments. The higher estimate was explained in terms of survey techniques.[11]

[9] Health Insurance Association of America, *1964 Commissioners Disability Table,* Vol. III, p. 13.
[10] National Center for Health Statistics, U.S. Department of Health, Education, and Welfare, Public Health Service, *Chronic Conditions Causing Activity Limitation, United States, July, 1963–June, 1965* (Series 10, No. 51), p. 19.
[11] Lawrence D. Haber, "Disability, Work, and Income Maintenance: Prevalence of Disability, 1966," *Social Security Bulletin,* XXXI, No. 5 (May, 1968), 14–15.

Acute conditions—those lasting less than three months—accounted for about half of the restricted-activity days in 1968. Respiratory ailments alone accounted for over one-fourth of these less active days. Injuries were responsible for slightly more than 10 per cent. Of the chronic conditions causing activity limitations, heart conditions were the most common, accounting for 16 per cent of the total. Arthritis and rheumatism were a close second at 15 per cent of the total.[12]

Personal consumption expenditures for medical care in 1968 were $37.6 billion, of which 34 per cent was spent for hospital services, 27 per cent for physicians' services, 20 per cent for medicines and appliances, 10 per cent for dentists' services, 5 per cent for the net cost of health insurance, and 5 per cent for all other medical care.[13] The medical care expenditures were 7 per cent of the amount consumers spent to meet all their personal needs. The per capita expenditure was $190, but for some persons suffering serious illnesses, the outlay was many times this amount.

According to the American Hospital Association, hospital admissions during 1968 totaled 138 per 1,000 population.[14] The average stay was about 10 days.

National Health Survey data reveal that in 1968 the average person visited a physician between four and five times. Females visited their doctors more often than males, and older persons were more frequent visitors than younger persons.[15]

A most disturbing fact is the recent rapid rise in the cost of medical services. In September, 1970 the Consumer Price Index for all items was 136.6, the base years being 1957–1959. The medical care index was 167.6.

Unemployment   Involuntary unemployment caused by economic factors—not mortality, morbidity, or superannuation—is another threat to a person's earning power. The potential loss can be computed in the manner described in the previous section, total unemployment being analogous to total disability, and partial unemployment to partial disability.

Unemployment may be classified as (1) aggregate unemployment affecting the entire economy, (2) selective or structural unemployment affecting particular firms, industries, employee groups, or regions, and (3) personal unemployment affecting workers individually. Other concepts are "disguised" unemployment—employment in a job which underutilizes a person's capacity—and "involuntary-voluntary" unemployment—voluntary unemployment because job seeking has become burdensome. Aggregate unemployment is

[12] National Center for Health Statistics, *Current Estimates from the National Health Survey, United States, 1968*, p. 9, and *op. cit.*, p. 3.
[13] *1969 Source Book of Health Insurance Data*, p. 51.
[14] *Ibid.*, p. 54.
[15] National Center for Health Statistics, *Estimates from the National Health Survey, United States, 1968*, p. 22.

caused by secular or cyclical factors acting upon most industries. Structural unemployment may result from seasonal fluctuations, technological changes, strikes, acts of God, changes in demand, and the like. Personal unemployment may occur because of difficulties in locating a job or in obtaining or holding a job for a variety of reasons.

In 1969 the total labor force of the United States was about 61 per cent of the total noninstitutional population and the average monthly unemployment rate for the civilian labor force was about 3.5 per cent.[16] Data for the past twenty years show that the highest annual average monthly unemployment rate was 6.8 per cent in 1958. In 1933 about one-quarter of the labor force was unemployed in an average month. These data indicate the prevalence of unemployment on specified dates rather than the "probability" of unemployment.[17] The data also do not reveal the extent of partial unemployment, but it is known that many persons do work less than 35 hours a week.

One measure of the magnitude of the unemployment loss is the duration of the unemployment. As one would expect, the average duration is related to the general state of the economy, but particular industries, areas, or persons can suffer substantial losses even when the economy is performing satisfactorily by most standards.

Unemployment data may also be analyzed by regions, occupation, industry, age, sex, and color, but such analysis would be beyond the scope of this text.[18]

Superannuation   Even though many persons may not appreciate fully the seriousness of the potential financial losses associated with premature deaths, serious accidental injuries or sicknesses, and extended unemployment, the vast majority do fear these contingencies and recognize that some financial losses accompany them. Old age is much less often recognized as a source of financial problems.

At advanced ages, while a person's earning power usually stops or is considerably reduced, his expenses continue. The person may prepare for this retirement period by saving and investing during his earning career, but (1) saving is neither painless nor automatic, and the amounts needed may be very great, and (2) the necessary amount is indefinite because it depends upon the length of the retirement period.

---

[16] *Monthly Labor Review*, XCIII, No. 11 (November, 1970), p. 77. The September, 1970, rate was 5.5 per cent.

[17] Because unemployment is much less clearly a chance phenomenon than mortality or morbidity, the word "probability" is placed in quotes. The annual frequency of unemployment, which would provide a better estimate of the "probability," would be greater than the prevalence of unemployment because the number unemployed during the year would exceed the number unemployed during the survey week in an average month.

[18] See the latest issue of the *Monthly Labor Review*.

The probabilities that persons at selected ages will survive to age 65 are presented in Table 8.3. The table also indicates the average number of years that a person at each age will live beyond age 65. Consider the plight of a person now aged 35. The chances are about 3 out of 4 that he will live beyond age 65, his probable retirement age. The average person age 35 will live 8.5 years beyond age 65. Therefore, if the 35-year-old is willing to consider himself average, he will have to accumulate a sum which, invested at a reasonable rate of return, will produce enough to meet his expenses over a period of 8.5 years. If his expenses are $4,000 a year and a reasonable rate of return is 5 per cent after taxes, the amount needed is over $27,000.

Table 8.3 Probability of survival to age 65 and average remaining lifetime

Age	Probability of survival to age 65	Average remaining lifetime, years	Average remaining lifetime beyond age 65, years
0	.71	69.9	4.9
10	.74	62.2	7.2
20	.74	52.6	7.6
30	.75	43.2	8.2
35	.76	38.5	8.5
40	.76	33.9	8.9
45	.78	29.5	9.5
50	.80	25.3	10.3
55	.84	21.4	11.4
60	.90	17.7	12.7

Source: Same as Table 8.1.

As the person grows older, however, the average number of years that he can expect to live beyond age 65 increases. If a person knew that he would live to be 100 years old and that his earning power would end completely at age 65, he would have to accumulate over $65,000 by his retirement age, assuming expenses of $4,000 a year and a 5 per cent return after taxes on the balance of the accumulated sum. Few persons will live this long, but some will, and their identity is unknown.

Unlike the probabilities associated with the other perils which have been declining over time, the probabilities associated with superannuation have been increasing. Much more attention has been devoted to this peril in the past two decades than previously, partly because of the increasing proportion of aged persons in the total population. In 1920, 40 per cent of the population was under 20 years of age, 54 per cent was between

20 and 64, and 5 per cent was aged 65 or more. In 1960, the corresponding percentages were 38 per cent, 53 per cent, and 9 per cent. Estimates for 1980 vary according to fertility assumptions, but the range for people 65 years of age and over is 9 to 11 per cent. The trend may then be reversed because birth rates increased following the Great Depression of the thirties until the sixties.

That the present financial position of the aged is inadequate is indicated by the fact that in 1966 about 22 per cent of the families headed by a person aged 65 or over had incomes below the Social Security Administration poverty level.[19]

Possible explanations of this disturbing financial picture are the relatively low income status of much of our population, the Great Depression, the inflationary postwar period, high income taxes, the importance to Americans of "keeping up with the Joneses," restrictive employment practices with respect to the aged, personal misfortunes, the weakening of family ties, and a human tendency to postpone preparation for retirement. Fortunately, private and public programs are already in progress that will improve the financial status of the aged, but much remains to be done. Individual families, however, must be expected to do some of this advance planning on their own initiative.

Losses Facing the Firm Itself

In addition to his concern with potential losses to individual employees, the risk manager must deal with the potential losses to the firm itself as the result of the death or disability of an employee, a customer, or an owner. These losses may be classified as follows: (1) key-man losses, (2) credit losses, and (3) business-liquidation losses.

KEY-MAN LOSSES

Certain workers in a firm stand out because of their skill and knowledge or because they are an important source of business or of credit for the firm. The death or disability of these key men may result in a serious loss to the firm by reducing sales, increasing costs, or restricting credit.

In some cases, the firm will suffer a reduction in its annual profit which it will never be able to recover. For example, assume that a key executive, aged 45, is expected to retire at age 65 and that his death or permanent and total disability would reduce the annual earnings of the firm by $20,000 a year. His immediate economic death, therefore, would cost

---

[19] Carolyn Jackson and Terri Velten, "Residence, Race, and Age of Poor Families in 1966," *Social Security Bulletin*, XXXII, No. 6 (June, 1969), 6.

the firm the present value of $20,000 a year for the next 20 years. At a 5 per cent rate of interest, the present value is approximately $250,000. If, as assumed, the annual loss to the firm does not change over time, the potential loss to the firm will decrease each year. Under the conditions assumed, the potential losses to the firm 5, 10, 15, and 20 years hence are about $208,000, $154,000, $86,000, and zero. In other cases, the firm may have made an investment in a project which will be abandoned because only the key man could have completed it. In still other cases, the services of the individual can be replaced at least in part, but the cost of replacement may be high, and the replacement may be delayed.

Creditors of the firm (including banks, trade creditors, corporate bond purchasers, and the like) are also concerned about key men because their death or disability may affect significantly the ability of the firm to repay its borrowings. Hence, if the risk manager does not take steps to protect the firm against this risk, the credit rating of the firm may suffer even if the key men do not actually die or become disabled. As a result, credit and credit terms may be restricted.

The potential loss to the firm caused by the death or disability of key men may also affect the attitude of the employees. They may wonder what effect the death or disability of some key workers would have on them personally, and their uncertainty will affect their attitude toward their work.

CREDIT LOSSES

Many firms extend credit to their customers. For example, financial institutions make loans to customers, and vendors of various types assume a creditor position as a result of the sale of securities, real estate, merchandise, and other types of property. It is important for the risk manager to recognize that the death, extended disability, or unemployment of a customer may either reduce the chance that the loan will be repaid or create a public relations problem if it is necessary to force repayment.

BUSINESS-LIQUIDATION LOSSES

Business-liquidation losses are very likely to occur when a person with an ownership interest in a sole proprietorship, a partnership, or a *close* corporation dies or is disabled for a long period of time. Each of these forms of business organization is characterized by the fact that the owners are usually also active in the management of the firm. Hence their death or extended disability may have severe effects upon the future of the business enterprise.

Although some of the problems arising when an owner-manager dies are peculiar to each form of business organization, certain problems for the firm and for the heirs are common to all modes of organization. In order to avoid repetition, therefore, and to emphasize the applicability of these losses to all small businesses, the discussion which follows, unless otherwise noted, will apply to all three organizational forms.

The nature of the problem   When an owner-manager dies, his heirs will no longer receive that portion of the income from the business which was attributable to the owner's active participation and association with the firm. In a sole proprietorship, this portion is equal to a reasonable compensation for the personal services of the owner-manager, including recognition of his personal and nontransferable contribution to the goodwill of the firm. The loss for the heirs of partners and close corporation stockholders is the present value of the compensation of the deceased plus the deceased's share of his personal contribution to goodwill. The surviving partners and stockholders also suffer a loss equal to their share of the deceased's contribution to goodwill.

An alternative way of viewing these losses in the case of a partnership or sole corporation is to regard the loss with respect to goodwill as a key-man loss to the firm, the loss being shared by the heirs and any surviving owners. The heirs of the deceased also suffer a loss equal to the present value of his salary.

These losses, however, are not the business-liquidation losses to be discussed in this section. These losses, which would occur even when the business is continued, are in fact examples of losses of earning power and of key-men losses discussed in earlier sections. Business-liquidation losses, on the other hand, occur only if the firm goes out of business, and this is a very likely result for reasons to be developed in succeeding paragraphs. The remaining goodwill value may be completely lost because the assets may have to be sold piecemeal or at sacrifice prices.

The threat of these business losses may affect the firm adversely even if they never come to pass. The firm's credit rating may be reduced because its future is uncertain. Employee morale may suffer because prospective earnings are dependent upon the continuance of the firm. In order (1) to avoid the death of the firm with attendant liquidation losses, when an owner-manager dies and (2) to improve the credit rating of the firm and employee morale even if such death does not occur, the risk manager should recognize these losses in his planning.

Similar arguments may be made in the case of permanent and total disability and superannuation, although liquidation under these circumstances is not so probable. The partners or close corporation stockholders should note especially that they are likely to continue the salary of a disabled or aged co-owner even when he contributes no services.

Special problems for sole proprietorships and partnerships   Liquidation of a sole proprietorship or a partnership is especially likely in case of death. In most states, the executor or administrator of the owner's estate must take immediate steps to liquidate the business assets unless the owner has expressly authorized the continuation of the business or unless all heirs are adults and they consent to the continuation of the business. Even if the executor or administrator is authorized to continue the business (1) until conditions for disposing of the business are more favorable, (2) as a long-term source of income for the family, or (3) until some heirs take over,[20] the return to the heirs is likely to be relatively low, and a shortage of working capital or other business problems may force the executor into a liquidation of the firm. A quick sale may also be necessary if a large portion of the personal estate plus the business estate[21] must be converted into cash in order to pay outstanding expenses, such as the costs of the owner's last illness, funeral expenses, taxes, and probate costs.[22] Even if some heirs take over, they may not succeed, and in the early years, at least, they will probably not be so successful as the deceased proprietor. Moreover, it might be necessary to liquidate some of the business assets in order to distribute equitable shares of the total estate to the other heirs.

Special problems for partnerships   In addition to these difficulties, the death of a partner poses a problem that is not present in the case of a sole proprietorship. Under the Uniform Partnership Act, which is in effect in about three-quarters of the states, if a partner dies, the partnership is dissolved, and the surviving partners must liquidate the business as soon as possible. The reason for this legislation is that each partner has the power to bind the partnership so long as he acts ostensibly in the interest of the partnership. Moreover, each partner has unlimited liability for the debts of the partnership. Consequently, the choice of one's partners is extremely important and is reserved for the partners themselves.

After a partner dies, the heirs may not want to continue as partners, or the surviving partners may not be willing to accept the heirs as partners. If the heirs and the surviving partners do continue the business, it may not be successful, and liquidation may be necessary at a later date. If the heirs intend to sell their interest to someone else, this person will have to be acceptable to the surviving partners before the business will be continued.

---

[20] The executor or administrator remains personally liable to the heirs and the creditors unless they all consent to the continuance.

[21] The personal and business estates of a sole proprietor are not separated as are the estates of partners or stockholders in a close corporation. If the liquidation value of the business assets is less than business debts, the family estate will also shrink.

[22] It is estimated that on the average about one-third of the gross estate value is needed to meet these costs.

Special problems for close corporations   The liquidation problem in a close corporation is somewhat different and less obvious. Under this form of business organization, the owners hold stock in the corporation, and this stock is transferable to other persons. However, because the stock is closely held, it is not so marketable as the stock of public corporations. Under forced sale conditions, the heirs or surviving stockholders will probably suffer a sizable loss on the sale of the stock; a minority stockholder will suffer disproportionately.

Regardless of whether the deceased was a majority or minority stockholder, the best (although unsatisfactory) solution for the heirs and for the other stockholders may be to dispose of their stock in the business or to liquidate the business itself. The surviving stockholders, for example, will have to accept a successor to the deceased, who, if he is a majority stockholder, may run the business to their disadvantage or, if he is a minority stockholder, may constantly challenge the majority. The heirs of a majority stockholder may not be capable of exercising their power to run the business, and in spite of their majority stockholdings, the effective management may fall into the hands of the minority. This contingency could be to their detriment. The heirs of a minority stockholder (especially when they are not willing or able to be active in the firm) are at the mercy of the majority. If the deceased stockholder shared the ownership with the survivor, the close working relationship that is necessary for a firm of this type may disappear. Even if no financial losses result in any of the above circumstances, life for the heirs and the survivors could be far from pleasant.

REVIEW QUESTIONS

1. Business risk management of personnel risks includes some family risk management.
   a. Explain this statement.
   b. Why are business risk managers concerned about personnel losses to individual employees?
2. One employee, aged 30, earns $10,000 a year after taxes. Another employee, aged 62, earns $30,000.
   a. How would you compute the loss of earning power if each of these employees were to die today?
   b. For which employee would the loss of earning power be greater?
3. Distinguish between the human-life-value and the needs approach in determining the losses caused by death.

4. a. What types of unexpected expenses are associated with death?
   b. For what persons would these unexpected expenses be the major financial loss associated with death?
5. Compare the following probabilities:
   a. That a man, aged 35, will die before age 65
   b. That a man, aged 35, will reach age 65
   c. That a man, aged 35, will become disabled for a period of at least three months before reaching age 65
6. a. How would you compute the loss of earning power if the two employees in question 2 became totally and permanently disabled today?
   b. For which employee would the loss of earning power be greater?
7. Compare the importance of unexpected expenses associated with poor health with those associated with death.
8. a. Published unemployment rates tend to underestimate the probability of becoming unemployed during the year. Why?
   b. What are the different types of unemployment?
9. a. What types of financial problems are associated with superannuation?
   b. Why is society more concerned about these problems than it was in the past?
10. a. What types of employees might be key men in the business firm?
    b. How would you compute the potential loss caused by the death or disability of a key man?
11. Jones and Smith are equal active partners in a thriving business. What is the nature of the potential losses to:
    a. Jones's heirs?
    b. Smith, if Jones should die tomorrow?
12. The majority stockholder in a small manufacturing corporation believes that his heirs are immune from business-liquidation losses because of their majority position. Do you agree?

SUGGESTIONS FOR ADDITIONAL READING

Current Estimates from the National Health Survey, issued periodically by the National Center for Health Statistics, Public Health Service, U.S. Department of Health, Education, and Welfare.

Dickerson, O. D.: *Health Insurance* (3d ed., Homewood, Ill.: Richard D. Irwin, Inc., 1968), chap. 1.

Dublin, L. I., and Lotka, A. J.: *The Money Value of a Man* (rev. ed., New York: The Ronald Press Company, 1946).

Gregg, D. W. (ed.): *Life and Health Insurance Handbook* (2d ed., Homewood, Ill.: Richard D. Irwin, Inc., 1964), chaps. 1–3, 47–51, 55, and 61–64.

Hofflander, Alfred E., Jr.: *Human Life Value Concepts,* unpublished doctoral dissertation, University of Pennsylvania, 1964.

Huebner, S. S., and Black, K.: *Life Insurance* (7th ed., New York: Appleton-Century-Crofts, 1969), chaps. 2–4.

McGill, Dan M.: *Life Insurance* (rev. ed., Homewood, Ill.: Richard D. Irwin, Inc., 1967), chap. 1.

Mehr, R. I.: *Life Insurance: Theory and Practice* (Austin: Business Publications, Inc., 1970), chaps. 20, 22.

Turnbull, J. G., Williams, C. A., Jr., and Cheit, E. F.: *Economic and Social Security* (3d ed., New York: The Ronald Press Company, 1968), chaps. 2, 6, and 11.

U.S. Department of Health, Education, and Welfare, Public Health Service: *United States Life Tables: 1959–61* (Washington, D.C.: U.S. Government Printing Office, 1964).

White, E. H.: *Business Life Insurance* (3d ed., Englewood Cliffs, N.J.: Prentice-Hall, Inc., 1963).

C. Tools of risk management: their nature and selection

9

tools of risk management: avoidance and retention

After the risk manager has identified and measured the risks facing the firm, he must decide how best to handle them. The five basic tools of risk management are (1) avoidance, (2) retention (including self-insurance), (3) loss prevention and reduction, (4) combination or increasing the number of units exposed to the loss, and (5) transfer to others (including the purchase of insurance). This chapter explains the avoidance and retention tools and the factors to be considered when deciding whether to use them. Chapter 10 is concerned with the other noninsurance tools and Chapter 11 with insurance. Chapters 12 and 13 provide a framework for processing information about these tools in order to select among them.

Avoidance

One way to handle a particular pure risk is to avoid the property, person, or activity with which the risk is associated by refusing to assume it even momentarily. To illustrate, if a business does not want to be concerned about the risk of property losses to a building or to a fleet of cars, it can avoid these risks by never acquiring *any* interest in a building or a fleet of cars. Alternatively, the ownership risk, but not all the pure risk, can be avoided by leasing the building or fleet of cars instead of owning it. Similarly, subcontracting part of a manufacturing, contracting, or distribution task before the job is accepted may enable a business to avoid some but not all of the risks associated with that job.

A leading chemical firm once planned to conduct a series of experiments in a rural area containing one small town. While preparing for the experiments, the researchers discovered that the venture might possibility cause extensive property damage to the town. The risk manager was asked to purchase insurance against this possibility, but only a few insurers were willing to provide the protection and the premiums for the insurance were much greater than the firm wished to pay. Finally the firm decided to abandon the experiments.

A firm which marketed household goods considered entering the drug field. Shortly thereafter it was discovered that defective polio vaccine was responsible for some cases of poliomyelitis. As a result, the firm revised upward its evaluation of the probability of a product liability claim arising out of the manufacture of drugs and decided to defer any expansion plans.

Many firms have discovered that by lending their names to a softball team or by allowing a Cub Scout pack to meet on their premises, they have created additional sources of liability. Some of these firms have decided to avoid the risks involved by refusing all such requests.

Avoidance, therefore, is a useful and common approach to the handling of risk. Often, however, it is impossible or clearly impractical to use this approach. For example, most businesses would not be able to operate unless they either owned or rented a fleet of cars. In other cases the potential benefits to be gained from employing certain persons, owning a piece of property, or engaging in some activity may so far outweigh the potential losses and the risks involved that the decision maker gives little consideration to avoiding the associated risks. In still other cases the decision is less clear, and the risk manager must compare carefully the relative merits of avoidance and other methods. The comparison may yield different results during one period in the history of the firm from those it would yield during some other period.

Retention

The most common method of handling risk is retention by the firm itself. This retention may be passive or active. Active retention may or may not be self-insurance.

The retention is *passive* when the risk manager is not aware that the risk exists and consequently does not attempt to handle it. By default, therefore, the firm has elected to retain the risk. For example, some persons believe that the only type of potential liability is automobile liability. They have done nothing about the other types of liability risks; they are not even aware of them. A related form of passive retention occurs when the risk manager has properly recognized the risk but has underestimated the magnitude of the potential losses. Automobile liability exposures exemplify the type of potential loss that is often underestimated. In other cases, the individual, although aware of the risk, may continually postpone making a decision on how to handle it. To illustrate, a firm is often aware of the financial risks associated with the death of a key technician but fails to take any action designed to handle this risk.

A risk manager *actively* retains the risk when he considers other methods of handling it and consciously decides to pay the potential losses out of his own resources.

Passive retention may by chance be the best approach to a particular risk, but it is never a rational way of handling the matter. Whether active retention is rational or irrational depends upon the circumstances surrounding the decision to retain the risk. Sometimes risks are retained that most persons would agree should not be retained, whereas other risks are not retained when they should be. For example, some individuals retain the risk of being sued on account of an automobile accident, when a transfer of this risk is possible and highly desirable. Other individuals transfer the risk associated with small losses when these losses could rather easily be retained.

Self-insurance is a special case of active retention. It is distinguished from the other type of retention usually referred to as *noninsurance* in that the firm or family can predict fairly accurately the losses it will suffer during some period because it has a large number of widely scattered and fairly homogeneous exposure units. Self-insurance is not insurance, because there is no transfer of the risk to an outsider. Self-insurers and insurers, however, share the ability, though in different degrees, to predict their future loss experience. Some writers would not consider a retention program to be self-insurance unless earmarked funds are accumulated in advance of any losses.

WHEN ACTIVE RETENTION SHOULD BE CONSIDERED

Active retention should be considered only when at least one of the following conditions exists:

1. It is impossible to transfer the risk to someone else or to prevent the loss from occurring. The only possible alternative—avoidance—may be undesirable for various reasons. For example, firms with plants located in

a river valley may find that no other method of handling the flood risk is available. Other firms will find that they are exposed to larger potential liability losses than they can prevent or transfer.[1]

2. The maximum possible loss or, if conservatively valued, the maximum probable loss is so small that the firm can safely absorb it as a current operating expense or out of small reserve funds.

3. The chance of loss is so extremely low that it can be ignored or is so high that to transfer it would cost almost as much as the worst loss that could occur. In some areas the chance of a flood loss is so small that this peril can be safely ignored. The chance that a man, aged 95, will die within a year is so high that an insurer would demand a premium close to the amount it would pay upon his death.

Of the four conditions listed here, this third one will be encountered much less often than the other three. Fortunately the chance of loss is seldom so high that this condition applies. Unfortunately it is seldom so low that it can be ignored. One must be careful not to retain simply because the probability of loss is low; it must be *extremely* low and the other factors explained below should also be considered.

4. The firm controls so many independent, fairly homogeneous exposure units that it can predict fairly well what its loss experience will be; in other words, a retention program for this firm could properly be called "self-insurance." In this instance one of the principal reasons for transferring the risk to someone else does not exist.

In all four situations, top management must in addition be willing to accept the risk of some bad years and to have many administrative tasks performed by employees or some independent servicing agency.

OTHER FACTORS TO BE CONSIDERED

If the first of the above four conditions exists, the business has no choice. It must retain the risk. In the other three cases, there are other factors to be considered. Usually the business must choose between retention and insurance, with loss-prevention and reduction measures being employed in conjunction with either retention or insurance. The four major factors to be considered in making this choice are explained below. If the choice is between retention and some transfer device other than insurance, similar reasoning is involved.

---

[1] Most speculative risks fall into this category. The businessman does not want to avoid the venture, because there are potential profits; he cannot prevent the loss from occurring, although he may be able to reduce its likelihood; and he cannot transfer the chance of loss to someone else. Diversification through involvement in several ventures or markets might reduce the risk, but what remains must probably be retained.

Retention appeals to potential insureds for the following reasons:

1. By retaining the risk, the business or family can save part or all of the loading that insurers must add to their expected loss estimates to cover their expenses and provide some margin for profit and contingencies. These expenses include the cost of acquiring business (mainly selling expenses), adjusting claims, rendering loss-prevention and reduction services, and performing general administrative tasks.

The loading charged by the insurer varies among lines, among insurers, and among insureds. For instance, in many property and liability insurance lines, the average ratio is 35–45 per cent of the premiums charged. Life and health insurance written in connection with employee benefit plans usually has an expense ratio under 10 per cent. Different insurers charge different expense loadings because they do not all render the same services or operate with the same efficiency. Large insureds are commonly charged a lower-percentage expense loading than small insureds because in their pricing insurers usually recognize that their expenses do not increase proportionately with the size of the insured.[2]

In analyzing these potential savings, the risk manager must recognize that some of these expenses are incurred for services rendered to insureds, and that, if he chooses not to purchase insurance, he must either forego these services, provide them himself, or purchase them elsewhere. Loss adjustment and loss-prevention and reduction services provide the clearest illustration of this consumer benefit in property and liability insurance, but risk-analysis services provided by the agent and the insurer must also be considered. If an employer self-insures a pension plan, he will probably have to engage a bank or trust company to invest the monies in the pension fund and a consulting actuary to determine how much money should be placed in the fund each year. In most instances, the employer will save some, but not all, of the money that he would pay to an insurer to cover its expense loading.

2. If the business believes that its expected losses are less than those assumed by the insurer in calculating its premium, it may reason that it can save the difference between the two expected-loss estimates. Even if the two expected-loss estimates are the same, the business may be willing to gamble that in the short run its experience will be better than it will average in the long run.

An understanding of insurance pricing, such as that provided in Chapter 25, is important in evaluating the potential saving available from differences in expected losses. Although small employers pay the same rate as other employers sharing a few major characteristics, large firms are rated under

[2] For more details, see Chap. 25, under "Modification Rating: Size-discount Plans."

procedures that pay considerable attention to their unique characteristics or their individual loss experience. Consequently larger employers are less likely to have a valid reason for doubting the insurer's estimate.

One must also remember that the loss experience in any single year may differ considerably from the expected loss. The variation of the actual losses around the expected losses has been studied in Chapter 5. If the business is able to sustain the maximum potential losses with relatively little strain, it may be well advised to retain the risk in the hope that in the short run the actual losses will be less than the expected losses. The ability to sustain these losses depends upon the magnitude of the potential losses and the economic status and liquidity position of the business. If the firm is not able to bear these losses without considerable strain, it may be willing to pay an insurer more than its expected-loss estimate to eliminate uncertainty in the short run. The extra amount it is willing to pay depends in part upon the severity of the potential losses and its ability to sustain these losses. It also depends upon the estimated variation in the potential losses and the attitude of the business toward bearing risk. Because a firm with many independent exposure units is more likely to experience each year actual losses close to its expected losses, it will be unwilling to pay an insurer much more than its expected losses to transfer the risk. Risk attitudes are a matter of management philosophy.

Insureds who are willing to assume substantial risks but wish to be protected against losses exceeding a specified amount can purchase excess insurance to protect themselves against large losses only.

Excess insurance usually protects the insured against individual losses in excess of some stated amount, but sometimes it covers excess total annual losses. Deductible clauses in insurance contracts permit an insured to retain only small losses.[3]

A quasi-self-insurance arrangement that may be an attractive alternative to self-insurance for large insureds is to purchase insurance but to have the premium retrospectively rated. Under retrospective rating the premium paid for insurance depends upon the insured's loss experience during the period the insurance is in effect, but it cannot be less than a specified minimum premium nor more than a specified maximum premium. The insured must pay the insurer to service the program and for the protection afforded by the maximum premium, but in exchange he avoids servicing responsibilities and knows that his annual outlay cannot exceed the maximum premium.

3. The opportunity costs involved in the timing of the premium payments relative to the alternative losses and expenses is another considera-

[3] For more on deductibles, see the last section of Chap. 11, "Use of Insurance with Other Tools."

tion. For example, even if the business reasons that the premium will be slightly less than the alternative losses and expenses, it might prefer to retain the risk if the time lag between the premium payment and the alternative loss and expense payments would permit it to earn an attractive rate of return on the declining balance of funds not yet spent for losses or expenses. To illustrate, assume that the premium is $11,500. The alternative loss and expense payments are $1,000 at the beginning of each month for the next twelve months. Funds invested in the business earn 12 per cent. Consequently if, instead of paying the $11,500 premium, the business pays its own losses and expense, the return on the unpaid balance would produce a "profit" of about $170.

4. Some firms believe that many of the services provided by insurers can be better performed internally or by some servicing agency. For example, some risk managers argue that if the firm pays its own claims, it will pay them more promptly and more equitably. They believe that the firm's own staff will resist unjustifiable claims which many insurers would pay. In addition, some managers are of the opinion that the firm gets more public relations value out of paying its own claims.

In response, insurers argue that instead of tightening up claims adjustments, the firm is often too lenient and less efficient than an insurer because of its lack of experience in this area and that it tends to be overgenerous, especially with claims involving employees. This is particularly true if the firm has many small, widely dispersed locations and as a result must assign this responsibility on a part-time basis to someone at each location. The public relations value may also be overestimated. In fact, dissatisfied claimants who may have been content to blame an insurer must now blame the business.

Supporters of retention reply that if these counterarguments are correct, an experienced independent servicing firm can be hired to adjust the losses under a retention program.

The relative quality of the loss-prevention and general-administration services under a retention program and an insured program is another bone of contention. Supporters of both retention and insurance claim superiority on this score. Insurers claim the advantage of experience gained by working with many firms over a long period of time; some can also claim the benefit of research staffs which are capable of studying specific problems. Yet the firm's own staff knows the firm, concentrates on its problems, and may receive better cooperation from its other employees than would an outsider. In certain lines, such as boiler and machinery insurance, the insurer does provide important, highly specialized inspection services; in other lines, the firm's employees may be the experts. With respect to some losses, such as dishonest acts by employees, the mere involvement of an insurer who is not so likely to be sympathetic with a dishonest employee may reduce the chance of loss.

In pension plans a key consideration is the investment performance of the pension fund. Consequently the business will want to compare carefully the investment advice and services available from insurers and from banks and trust companies which might service a self-insured plan.

Tax considerations   The impact of taxes on a retention decision can be complicated. Only a few major points will be noted here.[4] Contributions to a retention fund set up in advance to cover property and liability losses cannot be deducted in the calculation of a firm's Federal income tax liability, but property and liability insurance premiums are tax-deductible as a business expense. Losses incurred under a retention program are deductible; but because they may be spread irregularly over time, they may have less favorable tax consequences than regular distributions. Furthermore, property loss deductions are limited to the depreciated book value, which may be less than the actual cash value of the property. Finally, if the losses are spread irregularly over time and a large fund is accumulated to cover the losses in bad years, the firm may incur a tax penalty for the unlawful accumulation of surplus.

Employers who turn over funds to a bank or trust company in connection with a self-insured employee benefit plan, usually a pension plan, can deduct these contributions at the time they are made. Furthermore, the return on the invested funds is not taxable income to the employer. Income tax considerations, therefore, do not favor an insured pension plan over a self-insured plan or vice versa.

FUNDING ARRANGEMENTS

Most decisions to retain property and liability losses do not involve any formal advance funding. The business simply bears the losses when they occur. This approach cuts administrative detail to a minimum; but if the losses fluctuate widely from year to year, the business may have to borrow money or sell property on unfavorable terms in order to develop the cash required to meet the losses. Another disadvantage is that its operating statements are unduly influenced by chance results.

Fluctuations in the operating statements can be avoided by creating a liability account or earmarking some portion of the surplus that will be credited each year with an amount equal to the expected losses and debited

[4] For a more extensive discussion, see Frank A. O'Shaughnessy, "The Accounting and Tax Aspects of Risk Management," chap. 11, in H. W. Snider (ed.), *Risk Management* (Homewood, Ill.: Richard D. Irwin, Inc., 1964).

with the actual losses. This liability or earmarked-surplus account, however, is a paper entry that does not affect the liquidity problem.

A more conservative approach would, in addition to creating a liability or earmarked-surplus account, establish a corresponding earmarked asset account consisting of assets that could be turned into cash with little diffi- culty. If losses occur soon after the earmarked asset account is created, the liquidity problem will be only partially solved. The generally lower return on liquid assets will be a deterring consideration in the formation of such a fund.

Some businesses have funded their property and liability risk retention program by organizing an insurer whose sole (or major) customer is the business itself. Such insurers are captive insurers. The major attraction of this method of funding a retention program[5] is that the captive insurer can obtain certain covers from reinsurers, who deal only with insurers, that the business itself cannot obtain, at least without considerable effort, from insurers serving the public directly. By nature and tradition reinsurers are more flexible in their approach to insurance. In addition reinsurers are not subject to so many legal restrictions as are insurers servicing the general public.[6] Premiums paid to the captive insurer can also be deducted when determining the business' Federal income tax. Possible disadvantages include the capital and manpower requirements to organize and operate a cap- tive insurer, the special taxes that must be paid by insurers, and the legal obligation imposed in some states to participate in plans covering insureds who cannot secure insurance through normal channels.[7] On balance, interest in captive insurers appears to be increasing.

Pension plans and other self-employed benefit plans are usually funded by making periodic contributions to a trustee such as a bank or trust company.

Retention Practices

Professor Robert Goshay recently completed a comprehensive study of prop- erty and liability risk retention practices which sheds further light on the retention method. Further information on personnel risk retention programs is presented in Chapters 21 and 22. As part of his study[8] Professor Goshay

---

[5] See Robert Goshay, "Captive Insurance Companies," chap. 6 in Snider, *op. cit.*
[6] Because these legal restrictions also affect the coverage that the captive insurer can issue to the controlling firm, some firms favor locating the captive firm outside the United States. (Bermuda is a popular location.) There may also be tax advantages in this location.
[7] See Chap. 30.
[8] Goshay, *Corporate Self-insurance and Risk Retention Plans* (Homewood, Ill.: Richard D. Irwin, Inc., 1965): this entire section on self-insurance practices is based on the Goshay publication, particularly chaps. 6, 7, and 8.

surveyed 1,100 large firms of moderate to superior financial strength. Out of 650 respondents, 282 retained some fire losses, 100 retained some liability losses, and 148 retained some workmen's compensation losses. One hundred and fifty of these firms either purchased no insurance or retained losses of $10,000 or more per occurrence under deductible insurance policies. These 150 firms were resurveyed to obtain more detailed information. Out of the 100 firms that responded in some way to this second request for information, 52 per cent reported that they retained fire losses up to at least $10,000; 34 per cent retained liability losses; and 66 per cent retained workmen's compensation losses. Sixteen per cent reported that they retained all three types of losses; 2 per cent retained two of the three types; and 82 per cent retained only one type.

Loss experience   The experience under these retention programs over a three-year period is extremely interesting. In order to determine the stability of the loss experience, Professor Goshay computed the fluctuations in loss experience as a percentage of the average loss over this period. Less than one-tenth of the fire plans had fluctuations of less than 15 per cent, the standard which Professor Goshay suggests a retention program should satisfy to be considered self-insurance. In fact, 66 per cent of the fire programs had fluctuations in excess of 50 per cent. This result is not unexpected in view of the low-frequency rate for fire losses and the fact that among the fire plans reporting their number of locations, almost 40 per cent had fewer than 20 locations.

The loss experience under the liability retention plans was a bit more stable, but it still fluctuated a great deal. Only about one-fifth of the plans had fluctuations under 15 per cent; almost two-thirds experienced fluctuations in excess of 50 per cent.

The workmen's compensation plans ranked first in terms of stability. According to Professor Goshay, about one-half of the workmen's compensation plans deserved to be regarded as self-insurance plans because the fluctuations satisfied his 15 per cent criterion. Less than 10 per cent had losses in excess of 50 per cent. This result is again not too surprising, in view of the relatively high loss-frequency rate and the fact that almost all the workmen's compensation programs included more than 500 employees and that about 65 per cent included more than 3,250 employees.

Yet these programs seldom had serious financial consequences. Despite the unstable loss experience under most of the fire and liability programs, the fact that two-thirds of the fire programs and one-third of the liability programs experienced fewer than five losses over the three-year period lessened the financial impact. For all types of retention programs combined, less than one-tenth had average annual losses in excess of 1 per cent of their net working capital (current assets minus current liabilities). Net working capital was selected as the appropriate base for determining the financial consequences, because it represents the amount which could be converted to cash in a short period in excess of the amount needed to meet current liabilities. In addition, most of the firms purchased insurance against serious losses. The limiting effect of this catastrophe insurance upon the losses actually retained is not reflected in any of the statistics quoted earlier in this section.

Claims adjustments   The arrangements for adjusting claims are also of interest in view of the importance attached to this matter in the earlier discussion. Retained losses were adjusted by the firm's own staff under all the fire programs except when the losses approached or exceeded the deductible under a deductible fire insurance contract, in which case the insurer adjusted the loss. About 70 per cent of the respondents with automobile liability programs, about one-half of those with other liability programs, and over one-half of those with workmen's compensation programs adjusted their own claims. If the firm handled its own claims under the workmen's compensation program, this responsibility was usually assigned to the personnel department, not to the risk management department. If the firm did not handle its own claims under the workmen's compensation program, it usually hired an independent servicing agency, which received a percentage of what the insurance premium would have been. Automobile and general liability claims not handled by the firm itself were usually handled by independent adjusting firms on a fee basis, by insurers under a deductible insurance policy, or by intra-industry association services.

Financial arrangements   About two-thirds of the firms with fire programs, one-half of the firms with liability programs, and one-third of the firms with workmen's compensation programs did not maintain any reserves— either as earmarked assets, earmarked surplus, or a liability item. They preferred, instead, to regard these losses as current operating expenses, to be considered in budgeting cash flows or to be met when the occasion arose. The reserves which were maintained were usually only bookkeeping entries.

Those firms which maintained reserves established the amount most frequently by judgment estimates based on past experience. The average reserves over the three-year period for which data were available were less than 75 per cent of the average annual losses paid for about one-half of the fire and liability programs. On the other hand, three-fourths of the workmen's compensation programs had average reserves in excess of 100 per cent of the average losses paid. Professor Goshay concludes that the reserve arrangements under the workmen's compensation programs reflect a tendency of accounting practice to become conservative when the loss is stable and recognized.

Evaluation by risk managers   Professor Goshay presents evidence which indicates clearly that most decisions to retain losses have not been based upon a careful cost analysis of the sort described earlier. For example, only 35 per cent of the firms with fire programs had evaluated the expenses involved in servicing a self-insurance program. For liability programs, the proportion evaluating expenses was 20 per cent and for workmen's compensation programs, 53 per cent. Firms that did evaluate expenses often ignored expenses commonly associated with retention programs, such as the cost of loss prevention.

The savings associated with a retention program can be computed by subtracting from the costs of comparable insurance the cost of the retention program. All the firms evaluating the expenses of a retention program covering fire or liability losses also computed the savings, but some of the firms evaluating expenses under workmen's compensation retention programs did not evaluate the savings. Many firms obtained quotations from insurers for this purpose. Most firms, however, prepared their own estimates of the insurance costs as a supplement or a substitute for the insurer quotations.

Professor Goshay suggests five reasons why risk managers do not test the premise of financial gain under a retention program. First, the risk manager often performs a routine function; policies are established at higher management levels. At best there is often dual authority. Second, the necessary data are not always available. Many costs are joint costs, and risk management is not independent of other functions. Third, secondary goals, such as better employee or public relations, may be more important. Fourth, risk management costs are a relatively small part of the total costs of the firm. On the other hand, Professor Goshay argues, they are a much larger portion of controllable costs. Finally, there is a shortage of trained personnel.

REVIEW QUESTIONS

1. A risk manager argues that since avoidance always involves forgoing some activity, it is undesirable for his firm and for society.
   a. How would you answer him?
   b. Cite three situations in which avoidance might be desirable.
2. "Active retention may be irrational, passive retention is always irrational." Explain this statement.

3. Retention, according to the text, deserves consideration only when one or more of four conditions exist.
    a. What are these four conditions?
    b. What is the justification for each of these conditions?
    c. If one of these conditions exists, is retention the best solution to the risk?
4. A firm employs 1,000 workers. The risk manager of the firm believes that the firm should self-insure its workmen's compensation obligation.
    a. One reason the risk manager favors a self-insurance program is that he believes the firm can save all the expenses incurred by the insurer and included in the premium. Comment on this belief.
    b. A second reason for favoring a self-insurance program is that his firm has had very few losses during the last three years, while in his opinion, the workmen's compensation insurance premium is designed for the average firm. Comment on this reasoning.
    c. What other factors should influence his decision?
5. If the risk manager in question 4 decides to retain the risk, would you recommend that the firm form a captive insurer for this purpose? Support your reasoning.
6. A retention program can be funded in several ways. What are the advantages and disadvantages of each approach?
7. "Self-insurance is a special case of retention." Explain.
8. How does retention affect the risk or uncertainty in society?

SUGGESTIONS FOR ADDITIONAL READING

Goshay, Robert: *Corporate Self-Insurance and Risk Retention Plans* (Homewood, Ill.: Richard D. Irwin, Inc., 1964).

MacDonald, Donald L.: *Corporate Risk Control* (New York: The Ronald Press Company, 1966), chap. 9.

Mehr, R. I., and Hedges, B. A.: *Risk Management in the Business Enterprise* (Homewood, Ill.: Richard D. Irwin, Inc., 1963), chaps. 2 and 5.

Practices in Risk Management—Selected Readings (Bryn Mawr, Pa.: Insurance Institute of America).

Principles of Risk Management—Supplementary Readings (Bryn Mawr, Pa: Insurance Institute of America).

Snider, H. W. (ed.): *Risk Management* (Homewood, Ill.: Richard D. Irwin, Inc., 1964), chaps. 4, 6, and 11.

10

tools of risk management: loss prevention, combination, and transfer

The avoidance and retention tools of risk management were discussed in the previous chapter. This chapter describes the three remaining tools: loss prevention and reduction, combination, and transfer.

Loss Prevention and Reduction

Loss-prevention and reduction measures attack risk by lowering the chance that a loss will occur or by reducing its severity if it does occur. Loss prevention and reduction has the unique ability to prevent or reduce losses for both the individual firm and society. The transfer method discussed below eliminates the loss for the person transferring the risk, but someone else in society assumes the risk.

BASIC APPROACHES

There are basically two ways to approach loss prevention: by considering (1) engineering risks and (2) personnel administration or human relations.[1] It is, of course, possible to consider both mechanical and human problems simultaneously.

The engineering approach emphasizes mechanical causes of accidents such as defective wiring, improper disposal of waste products, poorly de-

[1] C. A. Kulp and J. W. Hall, *Casualty Insurance* (4th ed., New York: The Ronald Press Company, 1968), pp. 174–90.

signed highway intersections or automobiles, and unguarded machinery. The consideration of engineering hazards is an essential part of any loss-prevention and reduction program, but human failures are also extremely important. An examination of engineering hazards is supposed to be particularly pertinent to fire losses because tangible things, such as the construction of the building, the provisions for protection, the type of occupancy, and the external features, such as the quality of the surroundings, may contribute to fire hazard; even so, personnel failures have been blamed for at least 40 per cent of the losses by fire.[2] H. W. Heinrich, a pioneer in the human relations approach, has claimed unsafe acts of persons (operating or working at unsafe speed, using unsafe equipment or using any equipment unsafely, distracting or teasing workers, abusing equipment, making safety devices inoperative, etc.) are the major causes of 88 per cent of the industrial accidents resulting in personal injuries to workers.[3] The emphasis on human relations and consequently on the personal causes of risk became important during the thirties when the engineering approach, despite its dramatic achievements, was seen to be an inconclusive answer. According to Somers and Somers, just as the development of safety engineering around 1910 coincided with the development of scientific management by Frederick Taylor and others who argued that safety equals efficiency, so the development of the human relations approach to loss prevention, with its emphasis on safety education, safety contests, rest periods, and the like, coincided with the development of interest in the human relations field in industry.[4] In more recent years, the emphasis on human relations has been expanded to include special attention to the psychological problems of the accident-prone individual. Some trucking firms, for example, use psychological tests of driver attitudes in selecting personnel and in trying to locate trouble spots. This development also coincides with the general awakening of interest in mental health.

[2] The Factory Mutual Insurance Companies (see Chap. 23, for more details on this group of insurers) based an estimate of 40 per cent on a study of all their losses since 1913 exceeding $1 million. The results of this study plus two others which assigned human errors even greater importance are reported in C. H. Martin, "The Human Element: A Broader Concept of Fire Prevention," *The Growing Job of Risk Management,* AMA Management Report No. 70 (New York: American Management Association, 1962), pp. 191–92.

[3] H. W. Heinrich, *Industrial Accident Prevention* (4th ed., New York: McGraw-Hill Book Company, 1959), pp. 19–34. Heinrich also states that only 2 per cent of these accidents are unpreventable. About one-half are practically preventable.

One of the most interesting and controversial aspects of Heinrich's approach to loss prevention is that accidents, not injuries, should be the point of attack. According to Heinrich, out of 330 accidents of a similar type, 300 will produce no injury, 29 minor injuries, and 1 a major injury. Too often, he claims safety engineers ignore accidents that do not cause injury; moreover they concentrate on those that produce major injuries. Yet whether accidents result in injuries is largely a matter of chance.

[4] H. M. Somers and A. R. Somers, *Workmen's Compensation* (New York: John Wiley & Sons, Inc., 1954), pp. 201–04.

This increased attention to human errors has been criticized on several grounds. First, it is argued, the effect of mechanical causes has been underestimated. For example, using unsafe equipment probably should not be considered solely a human error; it might be possible to make this equipment more nearly foolproof. Second, industry may devote so much of its resources to the more glamorous human relations preoccupations that engineering will be insufficiently considered. Third, blaming the worker for the industrial accident is not in accord with the principle of workmen's compensation, which does not blame management or labor for industrial accidents.

In conclusion, both the engineering and the human relations approach to loss prevention and reduction have their advantages and limitations. Neither should be used to the exclusion of the other. The most difficult task is to determine the proper blend.

OTHER CLASSIFICATIONS OF PROGRAMS

Loss-prevention and reduction methods can also be classified in other useful ways. The most obvious distinction is that between (1) loss-prevention programs which seek to reduce or eliminate the chance of loss and (2) loss-reduction programs which seek to reduce the potential severity of the loss. Some programs are both loss-prevention and loss-reduction programs.

The variety of loss-prevention programs is illustrated by the following examples: The chance of a fire loss can be reduced by fire-resistive construction, building in an area where there are few external dangers, and having many suppliers in order that a fire loss suffered by one supplier will not halt the firm's operations. The chance of a product liability suit can be reduced by tightening the quality-control limits, choosing distributors more carefully, and checking on statements made by salesmen or the advertising department which may lead to a suit based on an implied or express warranty. The chance of an industrial accident can be reduced by safety meetings, providing safety goggles, and checking the ventilation in the plant. Employers can reduce the chance that their workers will be unemployed by stabilizing the demand for their products and services through diversification, market research, and advertising and by producing for stock during slack seasons. (Market and product research are examples of loss-prevention measures used to handle speculative risks.)

Loss-reduction programs can be subclassified as minimization or salvage programs. Both try to limit the amount of the loss, the distinction between the two being that minimization programs take effect in advance of the loss or while it is occurring, whereas salvage programs become effective after the loss is over. Automatic sprinklers, for example, are designed to minimize a fire loss by spraying water or some other substance upon a fire soon after it starts in order to confine the damage to a limited area. The restoration of the damaged property to the highest possible degree of usefulness would constitute a salvage operation. For example, a recently reported loss involved a few thousand mildewed, waterlogged shoes which might easily have been discarded as useless. Instead, the shoes were matched in pairs, treated with driers and buffing machines, and sold to a wholesaler. Raising a ship from the bottom of the ocean and restoring it to economic usefulness is another illustration of a salvage operation.

Other examples of loss-reduction programs include alternate facilities to reduce the indirect losses arising out of direct losses to the original facilities, periodic physical examinations for employees, reducing the dependency of the firm upon one or a few key employees, immediate first aid for persons injured on the premises, medical-care and rehabilitation programs for injured workmen, fire alarms, internal accounting controls, actions against persons responsible for losses suffered by the firm, and speed limits for motor vehicles.

Another classification of the loss-prevention and reduction efforts groups the approaches according to their timing. Timing has already been used as the criterion to distinguish between minimization and salvage programs, but the classification now under discussion applies to both loss prevention and loss reduction. The three phases are (1) the planning phase, (2) the safety-maintenance phase, and (3) the emergency-organization phase.[5] The planning phase includes those measures which precede the erection of a new building, the purchase of new machinery, or some other major change in the firm's operations requiring considerable advance planning. This is usually the most economical time to make any changes which seem desirable from the viewpoint of loss prevention or loss reduction. The fire walls, for example, may be thickened at small expense and without disturbing the utility of the building. Machines which are as foolproof as possible may be purchased nearly as cheaply as equipment which is no more productive but considerably less safe. The safety-maintenance phase includes all programs following the advance-planning stage, excluding the emergency phase. For the most part they consist of measures which check on the implementation and desirable modifications of the original decisions. To illustrate: The quality of the watchman service and the alarm systems can be checked as can the quality of the first-aid facilities and safety classes. The emergency phase includes those programs which become effective in an emergency—the fire-fighting facilities, emergency watchmen, and the like.

[5] W. T. Brightman, Jr., "What the Underwriting Company Can Offer," *Insurance Costs and Controls: A Reappraisal*, AMA Management Report No. 19 (New York: American Management Association, 1958), pp. 36–37. Mr. Brightman was referring to fire loss prevention and reduction in his paper, but the classification is more generally applicable.

THE RESPONSIBILITY FOR LOSS PREVENTION AND REDUCTION

The responsibility for loss prevention and reduction in industry is shared by (1) the government, (2) private organizations specializing in loss prevention and reduction, and (3) the individual firm.

The government is involved in loss prevention and reduction because (1) only the government can require all industries to provide information, meet certain standards, and stop undesirable practices, and (2) the government can provide certain services such as those of fire departments more economically and efficiently than can scattered private firms. The government exercises this responsibility through a variety of educational efforts (pamphlets, posters, and conferences); through statutes and codes regulating building construction, working conditions, safety equipment and safety clothing, maximum occupancy of rooms and elevators, sewage-disposal facilities, the operation of motor vehicles, and many other activities; by means of inspections designed to enforce the statutes and codes; by police and fire departments, rehabilitation programs, and the assembling and dissemination of statistical data related to loss prevention and reduction; and by the conduct and encouragement of research activities.

The private groups active in this area are too numerous to list, but a partial listing will indicate the range of activities. The National Safety Council is perhaps the most famous of these groups. The Council includes among its members individuals, business firms, schools, government departments, labor organizations, insurers, and others. It assembles and disseminates information concerning all types of accidents, cooperates with public officials in safety campaigns, encourages the establishment of local safety councils, and helps members to solve their own safety problems. Other examples are one division of the American Insurance Association, an organization of insurers, which publicizes the extent and causes of fire losses, investigates suspected cases of arson, grades municipalities according to the quality of their exposures to fire and their protection against fire loss, and suggests codes of various sorts; the Underwriters Laboratories, another insurance-sponsored organization, which tests equipment (television sets, electric wiring, safes, etc.) to determine whether it meets certain high safety standards; the National Fire Protection Association, which establishes numerous standards and codes, stimulates local prevention activities, and in numerous other ways tries to promote the service of fire prevention, educate the public, and encourage its members, including public officials, to adopt its suggestions; the Insurance Institute for Highway Safety, which provides financial assistance for other organizations engaged in traffic safety work and direct assistance in selected states; the National Automobile Theft Bureau, whose name indicates its concern; and the Jewelers' Security Alliance, a jewelers' trade association, which seeks ways to prevent theft, apprehend jewel thieves, and recover stolen property. Individual insurers maintain engineering departments that study the risks faced by their insureds, suggest ways in which these risks might be reduced, provide posters, films, pamphlets, and other educational materials, and conduct safety classes.

The ultimate and major responsibility for loss prevention and reduction rests with the firm itself. This activity is properly regarded as a risk management function, but the risk management department of the firm may be only one of the divisions involved in this activity, and its position may be simply one of advice and counsel. For example, in one large corporation a safety committee including the works manager, the facilities manager, the safety manager, the medical director, the fire chief, and the risk manager establishes loss-prevention policies. It is clear from the composition of the committee that the risk manager in this company is not charged with the implementation of many loss-prevention and reduction policies; but, as was demonstrated in Chapter 3, in some firms the risk manager is more directly involved in loss-prevention work. According to one risk manager, no matter what the risk manager's supervisory responsibilities are with respect to loss prevention work, the following should be his minimum responsibilities in this area:

1. To extend the loss-control concept to include all exposures.
2. To inform himself of and advise others about the insurance-cost implications of various safety and loss-prevention measures.
3. To make sure that the company's insurance costs reflect the results of its safety and loss-control efforts.
4. To see that good or bad safety and loss-prevention experience is brought to the attention of management, and that effective loss- or cost-reduction measures are made known throughout the organization.[6]

DETERMINING ECONOMIC FEASIBILITY

Although the prevention of all losses would be desirable, it is not always possible or economically feasible. The potential gains from any loss-prevention activity must be weighed against the costs involved. Unless the gains equal or exceed the costs, the firm would be better off not to engage in that activity. (Of course if human suffering is involved, society may benefit greatly from expenditures that, from a selfish point of view, a firm would be ill-advised to make.) The firm, however, must be certain to consider all the gains (a reduction in both insurable and noninsurable losses, and improved public, customer, and employee relations) and all the costs.

[6] T. V. Murphy, "A Company-wide Approach to Loss Prevention and Control," *Corporate Insurance: Management and Markets*, AMA Management Report No. 38 (New York: American Management Association, 1959), p. 41.

The costs fall into three categories:

1. Capital expenditures and depreciation on special construction features such as fire walls, and equipment such as sprinklers and hose extinguishers.
2. Expenses (salaries, fringe benefits, clothing, and training costs, for example) for watchmen, safety supervisors, firemen, consultants, engineers, and others directly involved in safety work.
3. Program expenses such as the cost of manuals and other training aids, employee time in training periods, extra packing and special cases, inspections, and preventive maintenance.[7]

In determining the cost of any loss-prevention program, the risk manager must determine the most efficient way to conduct the program. For example, it may be possible to cut the number of watchmen, produce black-and-white movies instead of color films, or use less elaborate safety manuals without reducing the effectiveness of the program. If the firm is insured, the risk manager should make certain that the firm is receiving all the services to which it is entitled. Some risk managers have found that they can save money in the long run by hiring a consulting loss-prevention engineering service to evaluate the recommendations made by the firm's insurers and to prepare the detailed plans and specifications for implementing these recommendations or modified recommendations.[8] If the firm is not insured, this consulting service may profitably supplement the firm's own staff.

Combination

The fourth tool of risk management is pooling or combination. Risks are pooled or combined when the number of independent exposure units under observation is increased. Other things being equal, because of the law of large numbers, this increase reduces the risk or uncertainty concerning the proportion of the units that will suffer a loss.

One way in which a firm can combine risks is to expand through internal growth. For example, a taxicab company may increase its fleet of automobiles. Combination also occurs when two firms merge or one acquires another. The new firm probably has more buildings, more automobiles, and more employees than either of the original companies. Combination can also be achieved by spreading the firm's exposures to loss instead of concen-

---

[7] R. J. Ruppel, "Controlling the Cost of Loss Prevention," *Insurance Costs and Controls: A Reappraisal*, AMA Management Report No. 19 (New York: American Management Association, 1958), pp. 56–57.
[8] Frank H. Gage, "Special Engineering Services and Their Value," *Insurance Costs and Controls: A Reappraisal*, AMA Management Report No. 19 (New York: American Management Association, 1958), pp. 42–49.

trating them at one location where they might all be involved in the same loss. (Spreading the risk in this way is also an example of loss prevention and reduction.)

Pooling or combination of pure risks is not generally the major reason why a firm expands its operations, but this combination may be an important by-product of merger or growth. (An example of pooling with respect to speculative risks, which may be a *primary* objective of a merger or expansion, is the diversification of products by a business.) Insurers, on the other hand, combine pure risks purposefully; they insure a large number of persons in order to improve their ability to predict their losses.

Transfer

Transfer, the final basic tool to be discussed, may be accomplished in two ways. First, the property or activity responsible for the risks may be transferred to some other person or group of persons. For example, a firm that sells one of its buildings transfers the risks associated with ownership of the building to the new owner. A contractor who is concerned about possible increases in the cost of labor and materials needed for the electrical work on a job to which he is already committed can transfer the risk by hiring a subcontractor for this portion of the project. This type of transfer is closely related to avoidance. The difference is that to transfer a risk, a firm must already possess it and want to pass it to someone else. If the firm avoids the risk, it will never possess it. Second, the risk, but not the property or activity, may be transferred. One example of this second type of transfer is a contractual provision holding someone else responsible for a loss. Since hold-harmless agreements have already been described in detail in Chapter 7, all that need be said here is that the firm can use these provisions to transfer risks either (1) by inserting a provision holding the other party responsible for the loss or (2) by having provisions removed that would make the firm responsible.

A second example is a surety bond under which a person, called a "surety," guarantees that another person, called a "principal," will carry out some express obligation to some third person, called an "obligee." Illustrative obligations are paying off a debt, supplying a certain quantity of products within a specified period, and constructing a factory by a stated date. If the principal does not fulfill his obligation, the surety must either satisfy the obligation or pay some penalty stated in the bond. The surety can then try to recover his loss from the principal. In some instances the surety can claim cash or government securities that it required the principal to deposit as collateral at the time the bond was issued. Through the bond the obligee transfers the risk that the obligation will not be met to the surety. Even though the principal receives no protection, he obtains the bond because he wishes some advantage, such as a loan, a supply contract, or a construction contract that the obligee will not grant without a bond.[9] Although there are some significant differences between an insurance contract and a surety bond that will be explained in the next chapter, the surety under most bonds is an insurer. The most common types of bonds written by insurers will be described in Chapter 11, under "Distinction between Insurance and Bonding," in Chapter 18, under "Surety Bonds," and in Chapter 28, under "Fidelity and Security Bonds."

The final example of the second type of transfer is the purchase of an insurance contract. Insurance transfers are the subject of the next chapter.

Neutralization   Neutralization, which is very closely related to transfer, is the process of balancing a chance of loss against a chance of gain. For example, a person who has bet that a certain team will win the World Series may neutralize the risk involved by also placing a bet on the opposing team. In other words, he transfers his risk to the person who accepts the second bet. Because there is no chance of gain associated with pure risks, neutralization is not a tool of pure-risk management. However, because it is an important way to handle speculative risks, it is treated briefly here. A commercial example of neutralization is hedging by manufacturers who are concerned about changes in raw material prices or by exporters who would be affected by changes in foreign exchange rates. The following highly simplified and idealistic example illustrates the principle involved: Suppose that a flour manufacturer buys some wheat for $1,000 on October 1. He expects to convert this wheat into flour and have it on the market by February 1. He estimates that he will be able to sell the flour for $1,800, which will cover the cost of the labor and materials and provide him with a reasonable profit. However, a change in the price of wheat (other than the addition of small carrying charges which are ignored here in order to simplify the example) will affect the price of flour, it will be assumed, by the same amount.[10] Hence the manufacturer's profit depends upon the uncertain state of the wheat market, and he does not want to retain this risk. The risk may be neutralized if he agrees on October 1 to sell the same amount

---

[9] When 100 per cent collateral is required, the principal may question the need for a bond. The answer is that the surety is merely extending credit like a bank, and some collateral may be necessary. The obligee may prefer a bond because he receives also the benefit of the surety's investigation and avoids the task and risk of handling the collateral. The principal can often recover this collateral more rapidly from a surety, and the obligee may charge more for handling collateral than the bond premium. This is particularly true with respect to bonds required by courts in connection with litigation.
[10] The reader is correct if he questions this assumption; but there will be a rough correspondence between the movements in these two prices.

of wheat for February delivery at the October 1 price. If the price changes, the gain or loss on the sale of the flour is offset by the gain or loss on the sale of the wheat, which must be purchased by the manufacturer at the current price. For example, if the wheat price on February 1 is $1,200, the flour sells for $2,000, producing an unexpected gain of $200; but it costs the manufacturer $1,200 to purchase the wheat which he must sell for $1,000. In practice, this method is applicable only to certain risks and, where applicable, cannot be expected to work nearly as ideally as it does in the example cited.

REVIEW QUESTIONS

1. Two safety engineers are engaged in a heated debate concerning the relative merits of the engineering and the human relations approach to loss prevention and reduction.
   a. What claims are probably being made by each engineer?
   b. Which method is the better?
2. Three methods of classifying loss-prevention and reduction methods are discussed in the text. Classify each of the following loss-prevention and reduction measures according to each of the three methods of classification.
   a. Oily rags and paper are cleaned up each day.
   b. Nonslip treads are placed on each stairway.
   c. Brakes on motor vehicles are checked weekly.
   d. Safety meetings are held monthly.
   e. Machines are equipped with safety guards.
   f. A private detective agency is equipped to respond quickly to a burglar alarm.
   g. All key employees are required to take an annual physical examination.
   h. A new product is manufactured during slack periods.
3. Safety in industry is the responsibility of many groups.
   a. What contributions to safety within the individual firm are made by outside agencies?
   b. Who within the firm is responsible for loss-prevention and reduction measures?
4. Determining whether a particular loss-prevention measure is desirable is often a complex process.
   a. What types of costs are involved in a loss-prevention and reduction program?
   b. What is the fundamental principle upon which the decision should be made?

5. Would combination make retention more or less attractive? Why?
6. In what ways can a business transfer a risk but not the property, person, or activity responsible for the risk?
7. What effect does a transfer of risk have upon the uncertainty in society?
8. Why is neutralization not applicable to pure risks?

SUGGESTIONS FOR ADDITIONAL READING

Building Codes—Their Scope and Aims (New York: American Insurance Association, 1969).

Denenberg, H. S., et al.: *Risk and Insurance* (Englewood Cliffs, N. J.: Prentice-Hall, Inc., 1964), chaps. 8–9.

Factory Mutual Engineering Division: *Handbook of Industrial Loss Prevention* (New York: McGraw-Hill Book Company, 1959).

Heinrich, H. W.: *Industrial Accident Prevention* (4th ed., New York: McGraw-Hill Book Company, 1959).

MacDonald, Donald L.: *Corporate Risk Control* (New York: The Ronald Press Company, 1966), chaps. 10, 11, 14, 15, and 18 and pp. 228–31.

Mehr, R. I., and Hedges, B. A.: *Risk Management in the Business Enterprise* (Homewood, Ill.: Richard D. Irwin, Inc., 1963), chap. 2.

Practices in Risk Management—Selected Readings (Bryn Mawr, Pa.: Insurance Institute of America).

Principles of Risk Management—Supplementary Readings (Bryn Mawr, Pa.: Insurance Institute of America).

Simonds, R. H., and Grimaldi, J. V.: *Safety Management* (rev. ed., Homewood, Ill.: Richard D. Irwin, Inc., 1963).

Snider, H. W. (ed.): *Risk Management* (Homewood, Ill.: Richard D. Irwin, Inc., 1964), chap. 3.

11

tools of risk management: insurance

Insurance is not one of the five basic tools of risk management, but it is easily the most important illustration of the transfer technique and the keystone of most risk management programs. This chapter defines insurance, compares insurance with gambling and with bonding, examines its benefits and costs, describes its limitations, traces its growth, and explains how it might be used with other tools.

Insurance Defined

Insurance can be defined from two points of view. First, insurance is the protection against financial loss provided by an insurer. Second, insurance is a device by means of which the risks of two or more persons or firms are combined through actual or promised contributions to a fund out of which claimants are paid. From the viewpoint of the insured, insurance is a transfer device. From the viewpoint of the insurer, insurance is a retention and combination device. The distinctive feature of insurance as a transfer device is that there is some pooling of risks; i.e., the insurer combines the risks of many insureds. Through this combination the insurer improves its ability to predict its expected losses. Although most insurers collect in advance premiums that will be sufficient to pay all of their expected losses, some rely at least in part on assessments levied on all insureds after losses occur.

Insurance Not Gambling

The purchase of insurance is sometimes confused with gambling. Both acts do share one characteristic. Both the insured and the gambler may collect more dollars than they pay out, the outcome being determined by some chance event. However, through the purchase of insurance, the insured transfers an existing pure risk. A gambler creates a speculative risk.

Distinction between Insurance and Bonding

From the viewpoint of the obligee, the protection provided by the surety bonds described under "Transfer" in Chapter 10 resembles insurance. Furthermore, corporate sureties are considered insurers under state laws, and most major property insurers have bonding departments. However, there are at least five major differences between a typical property insurance contract and a typical surety bond:

1. A surety bond has three parties to the contract—the principal, the obligee, and the insured. Two parties normally enter into an insurance contract—the insured and the insurer.

2. Under a surety bond, the principal obtains the bond and pays the premium but the obligee receives the protection. An insured usually purchases an insurance contract to protect himself.

3. A loss under a surety bond may be caused intentionally by the principal. An insurance loss should be accidental from the viewpoint of the insured.

4. Ideally, there would be no losses under a surety bond because the surety would not write the bond if there were any chance of loss and the surety would discover any potential losses in its investigation. An insurer expects some losses among the insured group. Ideally, therefore, a surety bond premium would not have to contain any expected-loss allowance. The premium would cover only the surety's investigation and other expenses and provide some margin for profit and contingencies. An insurance premium must provide for expected losses. In practice, sureties do incur some losses because their investigations are not completely effective, but losses are a much smaller proportion of surety bond premiums than of insurance premiums. Surety bond loss ratios also tend to fluctuate more widely over time because of lower loss frequencies and the sensitivity of much bond experience to economic cycles and natural catastrophes.

5. If a loss does occur, the surety can turn to the principal for reimbursement. An insurer does not have this right against an insured.

Not all property insurance contracts nor all surety bonds share the characteristics contained in the above list. Some surety bonds more closely resemble insurance than others. Nevertheless this distinction between typical property insurance contracts and surety bonds is valid and useful.

One type of surety bonding—fidelity bonding—differs so much from the other types that, instead of including it under surety bonding, it is usually considered a separate class. Fidelity bonding protects an employer against dishonest acts by his employees. Most fidelity bonds so closely resemble insurance that they are commonly called "dishonesty insurance." Originally fidelity bonds were written on the same basis as surety bonds. Some still are. Under these less common fidelity bonds, there are three parties to the contract—the employer, the employee, and the insurer or surety. The employee applies for the contract and pays the premium, but the employer has the protection. The insurer will investigate the employee carefully before writing the bond. Finally, although this right is not too valuable, the surety becomes a creditor of the employee if it makes any payment. One major difference between this fidelity bond and a surety bond is that the fidelity bond covers only the implied obligation of honesty, not ability. Surety bonds cover any nonexcluded failure to carry out the expressed obligation.

Most dishonesty insurance, however, is not written on this basis. An insurer protects the employer against losses caused by dishonest acts of his employee(s). The employer pays the premium. Although it is customary to require an application from each employee to provide underwriting information, the employee is not otherwise a party to the contract. The investigation of the employee's character is often at best perfunctory. Sometimes the insurer does not even have his name. Losses are expected and recognized in the premium. The right to collect from the principal is no different from the right to collect from any thief. It is clear, therefore, that bonds written in this way more clearly resemble insurance than surety bonds.

Benefits and Costs of Insurance

Insurance, like most institutions, presents society with both benefits and costs. The advantages will be discussed first.

BENEFITS

Indemnification   The direct advantage of insurance is indemnification for those who suffer unexpected losses. The unfortunate businesses and families are restored or at least moved closer to their former economic position. The advantage to these individuals is obvious. Society also gains because these persons are restored to production, tax revenues are increased, and welfare payments are reduced.

Reduction of uncertainty   The more significant but less obvious advantages of insurance arise from the fact that (1) it eliminates the insured's risk, uncertainty, and adverse reaction to risk and (2) it reduces the total risk, uncertainty, and adverse reaction to this risk in society. How it accomplishes this result is so important that it is worth repeating: prior to the purchase of insurance, each potential insured is subject to considerable risk, he knows it (consequently his uncertainty is high), and he is worried about whether he will suffer any financial losses. Through the purchase of insurance, each insured transfers his risk to an insurer. His uncertainty is eliminated and he no longer is concerned about the financial loss.[1] The insurer is subject to some risk, but, because it depends upon the experience of many insureds, this risk is small. The insurer, being aware of the law of large numbers, knows this. His uncertainty, therefore, is also small. Being a risk-bearer by profession, he should not be bothered much by the small risk that remains. Consequently the risk, uncertainty, and adverse reaction to risk in society have been reduced substantially through the purchase of insurance.

Several benefits result from this reduction of risk for insureds and for society. First, if the insurance premium is not excessive, a person—or a firm—can purchase insurance protection and improve his utility position.[2] For example, assume that a person with $10,000 is told that in the next minute he may lose $5,000 and that the chance this will happen is $\frac{1}{2}$. Given these facts, an insurer would reason that the expected loss or average loss for all persons under the same circumstances would be $2,500. Merely because of the principle of diminishing marginal utility of money, the person could improve his utility position by paying $2,500 to have the chance of loss removed since the loss in satisfaction caused by a $5,000 loss is more than twice the loss caused by a $2,500 premium. In fact he could improve his position even if he had to pay slightly more than $2,500. How much more depends upon his utility curve, but for most persons in many situations the extra amount would be more than enough to cover the expenses and profit of the insurer.[3] This argument is more persuasive when one remembers that (1) many persons tend to be pessimistic concerning the chance of loss and that (2) fear and worry further reduce the satisfaction associated with uncertain positions. In fact, in the opinion of the authors, the elimination of fear and worry, rather than the principle of diminishing

[1] If the insurer reserves the right to levy an assessment or promises to return a dividend if the premiums exceed its needs, the insured assumes some risk concerning the dividend or an assessment. This risk should be small because it depends upon the combined experience of the insurer.

[2] See Chap. 1, under "Costs of uncertainty itself," for a definition of utility.

[3] Milton Friedman and L. J. Savage, "The Utility Analysis of Choices Involving Risk," *Journal of Political Economy,* LVI (August, 1948), 279–304. See also pp. 16–18 in Chap. 1 and the section on the "Expected Utility Model" in Chap. 13.

marginal utility of money, is the major reason why insurance improves utility positions and why persons become interested in buying insurance.

Second, because insurance reduces individual and social risk and uncertainty, it also reduces in society, as well as within an industry and within a firm, inefficiencies in the utilization of existing capital and labor. The reduction of uncertainty will also encourage the accumulation of new capital because potential investors are less likely to hesitate, their planning periods are lengthened, credit is more generally extended, and fewer resources are hoarded. Insurance, therefore, results in more nearly optimum production, price levels, and price structures. The price structures are further improved by the fact that the insurer's estimate of the chance of loss for each insured is generally superior to that of the individual unit. The importance of insurance in this regard has been recently expressed by Peter F. Drucker: "One of the greatest achievements of the mercantile age was the conversion of many of these physical risks into something that could be predicted and provided against. It is no exaggeration to say that without insurance an industrial economy could not function at all."[4]

Funds for investment   Insurers can make more funds available for investment than insureds who "save for a rainy day" not only because their risk is small but also because a constant inflow of new money makes it generally unnecessary for them to liquidate existing assets to pay claims. In fact, insurers are the most important sources of long-term funds in the United States money and capital markets. As indicated in Table 11.1, in 1969 life insurers provided about 8.6 per cent of the funds used in the United States money and capital markets. Only commercial banks supply more funds, and they tend to specialize in short-term funds. Indeed, as indicated in Table 11.2, life insurers supply 10.7 per cent of long-term funds raised in these markets. Property and liability insurers play a much less important role than life insurers mainly because their contracts cover a shorter period and as a result they accumulate less premium dollars in advance of loss payments. Nevertheless their contribution is considerable, particularly to investment funds. Self-insured private pension plans, which are insurance from the viewpoint of the covered employees and which closely resemble insured pension plans in their objective and operation, have provided an increasing proportion of the funds for these markets. The same is true of public pension plans covering the employees of state and local governments. All of these insurers combined provided 22.3 per cent of the total funds and 34.7 per cent of the investment funds. Not included in this total are government insurers, such as the Social Security Administra-

[4] Peter F. Drucker, *The New Society* (New York: Harper & Row, Publishers, Incorporated, 1950), p. 57.

Table 11.1 Sources and uses of funds (Amounts in billions of dollars)

	1961		1969	
	Amount	Per cent	Amount	Per cent
Uses (funds raised)				
Investment funds	30.6	63.5	61.9	58.0
Short-term funds	11.5	23.9	38.6	36.1
U.S. government and agency securities,				
publicly held	6.1	12.7	6.3	5.9
Total uses	48.2	100.0	106.8	100.0
Sources (funds supplied)				
Savings institutions:				
Life insurers	5.6	11.6	9.2	8.6
Property and liability insurers	1.3	2.7	2.7	2.5
Private self-insured pension plans	3.7	7.7	6.3	5.9
State and local government retirement				
funds	2.3	4.8	5.6	5.2
Contractual-type savings institutions	12.9	26.8	23.8	22.3
Savings and loan associations	9.4	19.5	9.4	8.8
Mutual savings banks	2.1	4.4	2.8	2.6
Credit unions	.4	.8	1.5	1.4
Deposit-type savings institutions	11.9	24.7	13.7	12.8
Investment companies (mutual funds)	1.4	2.9	3.0	2.8
Total savings institutions	26.2	54.4	40.5	37.9
Commercial banks	15.8	32.8	10.0	9.4
Business corporations	3.5	7.3	25.8	24.2
Others	2.7	5.6	30.4	28.5
Total sources	48.2	100.0	106.8	100.0

Source: Derived from *The Investment Outlook for 1970* (New York: Bankers Trust Company, 1970), Table 1.

tion, that operate social insurance programs and that are important buyers of United States government bonds.

At the close of 1969 life insurers controlled assets worth more than $197 billion. At year-end, 1961, they owned slightly more than half this amount. During 1969 life insurers increased their net assets by $10.2 billion. New investments totaled $53 billion.[5] New investments exceeded the net increase in assets because of reinvestments, exchanges, replacements, and short-term security purchases. At present life insurers hold over one-fifth of the nation's mortgage debt and a substantial portion of the private corporate bonds outstanding. Recently they have increased significantly their purchases of common stocks.

[5] *Life Insurance Fact Book.*

Table 11.2 Sources and uses of investment funds (amounts in billions of dollars)

	1961		1969	
	Amount	Per cent	Amount	Per cent
Uses				
Real estate mortgages	16.9	55.3	27.2	44.0
Corporate bonds	5.2	17.0	14.2	22.9
Corporate stocks	2.6	8.5	4.3	6.9
Total corporate securities	7.8	25.5	18.5	29.9
State and local government securities	5.2	17.0	9.3	15.0
Other uses	.6	2.1	6.9	11.1
Total uses	30.6	100.0	61.9	100.0
Sources				
Savings institutions				
Life insurers	5.6	18.3	6.6	10.7
Property and liability insurers	1.2	3.9	3.2	5.2
Private self-insured pension plans	3.7	12.1	5.8	9.4
State and local government retirement funds	2.2	7.2	5.9	9.5
Contractual-type savings Institutions	12.7	41.5	21.5	34.7
Savings and loan associations	8.8	28.8	9.5	15.3
Mutual savings banks	2.1	6.9	3.1	5.0
Credit unions	.1	.3	.1	.1
Deposit-type savings institutions	11.0	35.9	12.7	20.5
Investment companies (mutual funds)	1.4	4.6	2.3	3.7
Total savings institutions	25.0	81.7	36.5	59.0
Commercial banks	4.0	13.1	11.6	18.7
Business corporations	0.4	1.3	2.6	4.2
Others	1.2	3.9	11.2	18.1
Total sources	30.6	100.0	61.9	100.0

Source: Derived from *The Investment Outlook for 1970* (New York: Bankers Trust Company, 1970), Table 2.

In late 1967 life insurers agreed to divert $1 billion from their normal investments to projects involving above-average risks in urban core areas. Most of this money was invested in housing for low- or moderate-income families, but substantial amounts were also invested in job-creating and service facilities, such as hospitals, retail stores, and factories. In 1969 a second $1 billion was committed to this type of investment.

At the close of 1969 property and liability insurers had assets valued at $51 billion compared with $33 billion at year-end 1961. Because these insurers have invested more heavily in common stocks than life insurers have, their asset values are more subject to market fluctuations.[6]

[6] More information on insurer investment portfolios is presented in Chap. 24.

Loss prevention   Although loss prevention is not an inherent part of the insurance concept, the insurance industry is a leader in loss-prevention work at the levels of both individual insurers and trade associations. A sample of these activities has been discussed under "Loss Prevention and Reduction" in Chapter 10. While recognizing the present contributions of insurers in this area, some observers believe that they should do much more.

Aid to small business   Insurance encourages competition because without an insurance industry, small business would be a less effective competitor against big business. Big business may safely retain some of the risks which, if they resulted in loss, would destroy most small businesses. Without insurance, small business would involve more risks and would be a less attractive outlet for funds and energies.

Summary of benefits   In summary, insurance (1) indemnifies those who suffer unexpected losses, (2) improves total satisfaction for the individual and society, (3) results in more nearly optimum production, price levels, and price structures, (4) releases funds for investment,[7] and (5) improves the competitive position of small business. In addition, the insurance industry in practice engages in some important loss-prevention activities.

COSTS

Although the advantages arising out of the existence of an insurance industry are sizable, insurance is not without its costs.

Operating expenses   Insurers incur expenses such as loss-adjustment expenses, expenses involved in acquiring insureds, state premium taxes, and general administrative expenses. These expenses, plus a reasonable amount for profit and contingencies, must be covered by the premium charged. In real terms, manpower and other resources that might have been committed to other uses are required by the insurance industry.[8] The following data illustrate the magnitude of these expenses, excluding the amounts for profits and contingencies. Life insurers in 1969 used about 17 per cent of their total income to pay expenses, excluding taxes.[9] This percentage varies greatly among industrial, group, and ordinary insurance, between health insurance and life insurance, among insurers, and according to many other

[7] An advantage of life insurance, which is not included in the above list because of its specialized nature, is the systematic savings plan provided by some types of life insurance. The advantages of this systematic saving for the individual are presented in Chap. 19. Society gains to the extent that additional funds are made available for investment.
[8] On the other hand, the insurance industry may be viewed as a creator of jobs within industry. Over 1.4 million persons were employed in some type of insurance activity in 1969.
[9] For more detailed information, see the latest edition of *Life Insurance Fact Book* (New York: Institute of Life Insurance, annual). Taxes were 4.5 per cent of the total income.

factors. In terms of premium income, these expenses were about 22 per cent; but the income base is more representative in this case because the nonpremium income is sizable and, as is shown in Chapter 25, investment income is directly recognized in premium computations. Property and liability insurers use almost 40 per cent of their premium income to pay expenses, excluding Federal income taxes. These percentages, like those in life insurance, vary greatly according to several factors, as well as among individual insurers. The higher expense ratio in this case largely represents differences in the nature of the protection sold. These differences are clarified in later chapters.[10]

Moral hazard   A second cost of the insurance industry is the creation of moral hazards. A moral hazard is a condition which increases the chance that some person will intentionally cause a loss. Some unscrupulous persons can make, or believe that they can make, a profit by bringing about a loss. Others abuse the insurance protection by (1) making claims which are not warranted, thus spreading through the insurance system losses which they should bear themselves (e.g., claiming automobile liability when there is no negligence on the part of the defendant), (2) overutilizing the services (e.g., staying in a hospital beyond the period required for treatment), (3) charging excessive fees for services rendered insureds, as is done by some doctors and garages, and (4) granting larger awards in liability cases merely because the defendant is insured. Some of these abuses are fraudulent; others indicate a different (and indefensible) code of ethics where insurance is involved.

Morale hazard   Another related cost is the creation of morale hazards. A morale hazard is a condition which causes persons to be less careful than they would otherwise be. Some persons do not consciously seek to bring about a loss, but the fact that they have insurance causes them to take more chances than they would if they had no insurance.

Opinions differ on the degree to which moral and morale hazards are created by insurance, but all agree that some persons are affected in each way and that morale hazards are more common than moral hazards.

Reduction of costs   These costs created by the existence of an insurance industry are far outweighed by the sizable advantages described earlier. The proper course of action is to reduce these costs. Insurers are constantly trying to reduce their costs through innovations in such matters as administrative procedures and marketing methods. Selling insurance to groups of persons instead of to individuals is a prime example. The creation of moral

[10] For more detailed information, see the latest edition of *Best's Fire and Casualty Aggregates and Averages* (New York: Alfred M. Best Company, Inc., annual).

hazard and morale hazard itself is offset, at least in part, by the loss-prevention activities of insurers. Moral hazard is specifically attacked through such measures as reporting services on suspicious fires, a systematic index of automobile personal-injury claims against all member insurers (which helps to reveal fraudulent claims), and close investigations of suicide claims. Morale hazard is most effectively handled by pointing out the direct relationship between premiums and losses and the sizable indirect losses and inconveniences that are not covered by insurance.[11]

Limitations of Insurance

Insurance is clearly a useful device for handling risk; but some risks cannot safely be handled by insurance. Because a public body can provide protection without issuing a legal contract and because such a body has taxing power, certain risks not safely insurable by private enterprise may be handled under a public system. The following discussion refers principally to private insurance, but some references will be made to the greater potential scope of public insurance.

LIMITATION TO PURE RISKS

Insurance has been applied only to certain pure risks. Speculative risks have not been insured, either because the risks involved do not meet the characteristics specified in the following paragraphs or because there is no reason for applying it to the problem at hand.[12] For example, insuring against a speculative risk may involve a premium which would offset any advantages associated with the chance of gain. Insurance is not a static concept, however, and it may be extended in the future to cover speculative risks.[13]

CHARACTERISTICS OF AN IDEALLY INSURABLE RISK

Among pure risks, the following conditions should be satisfied before the risk is *ideally* insurable:

1. There should be a large number of independent units, all of approximately the same value, exposed to the risk and controlled by persons inter-

---

[11] For example, one leading loss-prevention authority has pointed out that the uninsured costs of an industrial accident are four times the insured costs. Examples of uninsured losses are interruptions in the production schedule and overcautiousness on the part of fellow workers immediately following the injury. See H. W. Heinrich, *Industrial Accident Prevention* (4th ed., New York: McGraw-Hill Book Company, 1959), pp. 50–65.

[12] There may also be legal obstacles.

[13] For a possible approach, see Orieon M. Spaid, "Insured Chronological Stabilization Plans," *National Insurance Buyer* (September, 1957). Reprinted in H. Wayne Snider, *Readings in Property and Casualty Insurance* (Homewood, Ill.: Richard D. Irwin, Inc.,

ested in insurance protection. This requirement follows from the law of large numbers, since an insurance operation is safe only when the insurer is able to predict fairly accurately what proportion of its exposure units will suffer losses. Enough units must have been exposed in the past to provide some reasonable estimate of the probability of loss; enough units must be insured in the future for future experience to approach that same probability.

A large number of insured units should be exposed to the risk because risk varies inversely with the square root of the number of units exposed. The units should be exposed independently, for otherwise what happens to one unit will determine what happens to other units and the effect will be the same as if there were many fewer units. All units should be of approximately the same value, since otherwise the loss of a high-valued unit will be as costly as the loss of several low-valued units.

In order to make certain that the owners of a large number of units will be interested in insurance protection, two subrequirements must be satisfied. First, the potential loss must be serious enough in terms of its probability and its severity to cause many people to seek protection through insurance. On the other hand, the chance of loss must not be so great that the size of the premium will discourage the purchase of insurance.

2. The loss should be definite or determinate in time, place, cause, and amount; otherwise, loss-adjustment problems are created. Another problem related to the next desirable characteristic is that the accumulation of loss experience becomes much more difficult when the loss is indefinite.

3. The expected loss over some reasonable operating period should be calculable. This condition is necessary if the premiums are to be set at the level necessary to produce with some certainty a reasonable, but not excessive, profit or operating margin for the insurer. Conditions 1 and 2 must exist before condition 3 can be satisfied, but in addition, the expected loss should either be fairly stable over time or otherwise be predictable.

4. The loss should be accidental from the viewpoint of the insured. From a business viewpoint, it is clearly unwise to insure a person against an intentional loss.

INSURABLE RISKS NOT ALWAYS IDEAL

Ideal insurable risks should meet all four requirements, but few risks (if any) currently insured by one or more insurers do possess all these characteristics. Most risks that are considered insurable, however, come close

---

1959), pp. 47–52. In 1968 one insurer announced its intent to insure investors against declines in the value of mutual fund shares. "Want to Insure Against Stock Loss?," *Business Week* (December 28, 1968), p. 70. This protection is now available.

to being insurable risks either inherently or because certain safeguards have been introduced. Some risks whose insurability is questionable by these standards have nevertheless been insured because of the importance to the public of providing protection against a given peril, because of social pressures, because the risk is expected to become insurable in the future, or for some other reason. Insurers differ widely in their appraisal of many risks. Some insurers are anxious to insure risks that others flatly reject as uninsurable. Some insure risks to which only a few units are exposed because they seek predictability only for their total writings. The following illustrations may clarify these points.

The risk of a fire loss is an insurable risk. A large number of units owned by persons interested in insurance protection are exposed to fire; although many units may be adjacent to one another, independence can be achieved to a satisfactory degree for practical purposes by insuring only widely scattered units or by reinsuring adjacent units with other insurers; the loss is fairly definite in time, place, and amount; the expected loss is calculable; and the insured loss is accidental from the viewpoint of the insured since the insurance protection does not cover intentional losses.

The risk of death affects a large number of persons who are independently exposed for practical purposes and who are interested in insurance protection. The loss is definite in time and place, and since the amount payable is specified in the contract, it is definite in amount. The chance of loss is calculable. If suicide is excluded, the loss is accidental from the viewpoint of the insured. Suicide is excluded during the early years of the contract but is covered after that time on the grounds that (1) society benefits from payments to the beneficiaries and (2) life insurance contracts are not likely to be purchased in contemplation of suicide one or two years later. This is an instance of a justifiable slight departure from ideal practice.

Another example is sickness insurance. Sickness is not definite in time and place, and some insurers question whether the sickness risk is insurable. On the other hand, insurance covering the costs of sickness is one of the most rapidly growing forms of insurance. At least three reasons can be advanced for this growth in spite of the questionable insurability. First, the sickness risk is one of the most important risks facing mankind, and if at all possible, protection should be made available. Second, the market is great, and if underwriting safeguards can be successfully introduced, sickness insurance can contribute a great deal to the growth of an insurer. Third, if private enterprise does not make sickness protection available, the government almost certainly will, and private insurers are opposed to government activity in areas which they believe they can service.

Aviation in its early days presented many risks which insurers hesitated to insure largely because they had no basis for determining the premium. But the infant aviation industry needed the protection, and insurance was written. Since loss experience has now been accumulated, the situation of aviation insurers has improved, although aviation insurance is still risky, particularly with respect to jumbo jets and "hijacking." This example illustrates the writing of an uninsurable risk which was expected to become insurable. Many new kinds of insurance originate in the same way.

RISKS NOT INSURABLE BY PRIVATE INSURERS

Examples of pure risks which are generally considered to be uninsurable by private insurers through normal channels are those associated with flood losses to real estate (except under very special circumstances), bank insolvencies, and unemployment. The major problem associated with flood insurance is that the persons who would be interested in the protection would no doubt find the price too high. Furthermore, a single flood usually affects many persons. Because flood threatens many families and businesses, and because private insurance is not generally available, Congress passed the National Flood Insurance Act of 1968, under which the Federal government will subsidize the cost of protection written by a pool of private insurers.[14] Bank insolvencies are unpredictable and present catastrophic possibilities. The same is true of unemployment.[15]

RISK INSURABLE BY GOVERNMENT INSURERS ONLY

Government insurers can insure risks that private insurers cannot because they can make the insurance compulsory. This compulsion enables them to spread the cost of the program over exposures of varying quality. It also enables them to vary premium rates over time as their needs dictate without fear of losing any insureds. It can even make up in this way losses suffered in the past. For these reasons government insurance is available to protect bank depositors against bank failures and to protect persons against unemployment. Through its taxing power, the government may also subsidize voluntary public or public-private programs of the sort described in Chapter 30. Even government insurers, however, would prefer the more stable operations made possible when the risk approximates the ideal insurable risk.

INSURABLE RISKS NOT STATIC

In conclusion, it should be noted that a risk that is generally uninsurable today may be considered insurable at some future date because of some

[14] For more details, see Chap. 30, in "Flood insurance," under "Some Current Problems in Regulation."
[15] Employers, however, self-insure supplementary unemployment benefits. See "Supplementary Unemployment Compensation" in Chap. 22. Also, at least one insurer has experimented with a policy that would continue an owner's mortgage payments if he died, was disabled, or became unemployed.

change in the risk itself, because of improvements in the technical knowledge or other abilities of insurers, or because some more compelling reasons are introduced for insuring the risk.

Growth and Importance of Insurance

The recent growth and importance of insurance as a method for handling risks can be indicated by the measures in Table 11.3 for the years 1950 and 1969. Because the figures speak for themselves, they are presented without further comment except to note that several less important operations have been omitted from the table. More detailed information on the opera-tions of particular types of insurers is given at other points throughout the text.

Another measure of the importance of the insurance business is the number of employees. In 1969 over 1.4 million persons were employed by private insurers. Contrary to common belief, only about one-third were en-gaged directly in selling activities.

Use of Insurance with Other Tools

As was pointed out earlier, insurance, from the insured's point of view, is an example of transfer of risk. Just as the five basic tools may be applied singly or in some combination, so insurance may be applied as the sole method of handling the risk or in combination with some other method. Loss prevention may of course always be practiced at the same time that insurance is purchased, but the advantages of, and possibilities for, combin-ing insurance with retention are less fully appreciated.

Deductibles and excess insurance are examples of insurance devices which make this useful combination possible. Deductibles make it possible for the insured to bear all or certain types of losses up to a specified amount, while the insurer assumes the losses in excess of this amount up to the policy limits. Normally the insured may choose one of several deductible amounts.

Regardless of the form of the deductible,[16] the obvious effect is a reduction in the premiums for a given amount of insurance protection. This is especially noticeable when the losses which are not insured because of the deductible are relatively quite numerous. Loss-adjustment expenses are also reduced for the insurer, and if the noninsured losses are small, the effect of excluding loss-adjustment expenses may even exceed the effect of excluding the losses themselves. These two reasons explain why deducti-

[16] For a description of the forms available, see Chap. 16, under "Deductible Clauses."

Table 11.3 Major insurance operations in the United States: estimated assets and premiums (in billions)*

Operation	Assets			Premiums or taxes		
	1950	1969	Per cent increase	1950	1969	Per cent increase
Private insurers:						
Property and liability insurance	$13.5	$ 51.0	277	$ 4.0	$27.0	575
Life insurance	64.0	197.2	208	7.2	24.3	237
Health insurance†				2.0	17.3	765
Total	$77.5	$248.2	220	$13.2	$68.6	420
Public insurers:						
Old-age, survivors, disability, and health insurance	$13.7	$ 36.9	169	$ 2.7	$37.9	1,304
Veterans Administration	6.9	8.4	22	.5	.6	20
Railroad Retirement Board	2.6	4.6	77	.5	.9	80
Unemployment compensation funds	7.7	13.2	71	1.4	3.3	136
Total	$30.9	$ 63.1	104	$ 5.1	$42.7	737

* Intentionally omitted are self-insured pension funds, the civil service retirement system, and state and local government retirement systems because the employer does not transfer the risk. From the viewpoint of the employee, however, these operations are insurance. They have expanded rapidly. For example, the assets of private self-insured pension funds increased from $6.5 billion in 1950 to over $80 billion at year-end 1968.

† Health insurance is written for the most part by insurers also selling life insurance or property and liability insurance.

Sources: Insurance Facts 1970 (New York: Insurance Information Institute, 1970), pp. 10, 27. *Life Insurance Fact Book, 1970* (New York: Institute of Life Insurance, 1970), pp. 57, 70. Data for life insurance premiums and assets do not include the relatively small operations of fraternals, mutual savings banks, and assessment associations.

Source Book of Health Insurance Data, 1970 (New York: Health Insurance Institute, 1970).

Social Security Bulletin, monthly.

Social Security Bulletin, Annual Statistical Supplement, 1960, pp. 7–9.

Statistical Supplement to Annual Report, Administration of Veterans' Affairs, 1969 (Washington, D.C.: U.S. Government Printing Office, 1969), pp. 19–20.

Annual Report, Administration of Veterans' Affairs, 1951 (Washington, D.C.: U.S. Government Printing Office, 1951), pp. 240–241.

1969 Annual Report, Railroad Retirement Board (Washington, D.C.: U.S. Government Printing Office, 1969), pp. 13–14.

bles are most frequently used when small losses are relatively more important than large losses and loss frequency is fairly high. Another reason why the premium may be reduced is that the insured must bear part of every loss and as a result has reason to be more careful.

An insured may choose a deductible because the maximum retained loss is small and may safely (and in the long run, economically) be met out of operating income or emergency funds. On the other hand, the insured may decide that he can safely self-insure losses, up to a certain amount, even though that amount may be large, because he can predict with a fair degree of accuracy what his losses within the range up to the deductible are likely to be. In either case, the risks which cannot with safety be retained are transferred to the insurer. The premium savings may be used to pay the losses which have been retained, increase the amount of insurance protection against sizable losses, or both. Normally each dollar saved because of the deductible will purchase considerably more insurance protection against sizable losses than is lost against nonserious losses, because of the predominance of small losses and the relatively high loss-adjustment expenses associated with small losses.

Excess insurance is a form of deductible insurance; often the two terms are used interchangeably whenever the potential loss to be borne by the insured is sizable. Excess insurance, however, has acquired a more specialized meaning. The minimum amount borne by the insured under excess insurance is usually established by negotiations between the insurer and the insured and commonly equals the maximum probable loss. The amount retained under deductible insurance is usually much smaller than the maximum probable loss. Moreover, instead of establishing the deductible amount through special negotiations, the insurer usually presents the insured with a choice of several specified deductible amounts. Another difference between deductible insurance and excess insurance is that under deductible insurance the insurer usually provides safety-engineering and claims-adjustment services for the entire loss, while under excess insurance the insured must arrange for outside services or provide them himself. Consequently excess insurance is much less common than deductible insurance and is useful only to large businesses. The advantages of deductible insurance and excess insurance differ primarily in degree.

REVIEW QUESTIONS

1. a. Define insurance.
   b. Which of the five tools of risk management does it illustrate?

2. Distinguish between insurance, gambling, and bonding.
3. "Insurance makes possible the substitution of certainty for uncertainty." To what extent is this statement true? false?
4. One of the advantages of an insurance institution is that it reduces the risk, the uncertainty, and the adverse reaction to risk in society. How does insurance attain these objectives?
5. What advantages do business firms, families, and society obtain from the fact that insurers indemnify insureds who suffer losses? From the fact that insurers reduce risk, uncertainty, and adverse reactions to risk?
6. Describe the role of insurers as financial intermediaries.
7. The existence of insurers also presents certain costs.
   a. What is the nature of these costs?
   b. How can these costs be reduced?
8. Insurance is almost exclusively concerned with pure risks. Why is this true? Will it always be true?
9. a. What are the characteristics of an ideal insurable risk?
   b. Do all risks covered by private insurers satisfy these characteristics? Use two types of insurance to illustrate your answer.
   c. Why might private insurers insure a risk whose characteristics differ considerably from those of an ideal insurable risk? Use two examples to illustrate your point.
   d. Why might government insurers be able to write certain risks which all or most private insurers would decline to write?
10. The risks that are considered insurable vary among insurers and over time. Comment on this statement.
11. Insurance is most useful when the chance of loss is high. Comment on this statement.
12. The deductible is an extremely useful insurance device.
    a. What forms may the deductible take?
    b. Under what conditions are deductibles useful?
    c. How does the deductible cut insurance premiums?

SUGGESTIONS FOR ADDITIONAL READING

Athearn, J. L.: *Risk and Insurance* (2d ed., New York: Appleton-Century-Crofts, Inc., 1969), chaps. 1 and 4.

Bickelhaupt, D. L., and Magee, J. H.: *General Insurance* (8th ed., Homewood, Ill.: Richard D. Irwin, Inc., 1970), chap. 2.

Denenberg, H. S., et al.: *Risk and Insurance* (Englewood Cliffs, N.J.: Prentice-Hall, Inc., 1964), chap. 12.

Greene, Mark: *Risk and Insurance* (2d ed., Cincinnati: South-western Publishing Co., 1968), chap. 3.

Mehr, Robert, and Hedges, B. A.: *Risk Management in the Business Enterprise* (Homewood, Ill.: Richard D. Irwin, Inc., 1963), chap. 5.

———— and Cammack, E.: *Principles of Insurance* (4th ed., Homewood, Ill.: Richard D. Irwin, Inc., 1966), chaps. 1 and 2.

Mowbray, A. H., Blanchard, R. H., and Williams, C. A., Jr.: *Insurance* (4th ed., New York: McGraw-Hill Book Company, 1969), chap. 5.

Riegel, Robert, and Miller, J.: *Insurance Principles and Practices* (5th ed., Englewood Cliffs, N.J.: Prentice-Hall, Inc., 1966), chaps. 1 and 2.

Willett, A. H.: *The Economic Theory of Risk and Insurance* (Philadelphia: University of Pennsylvania Press, 1951).

12

selecting the proper tools:
a conventional approach

Preceding chapters have described in some detail the nature, advantages, and limitations of the basic tools of risk management. Attention has also been paid to the factors to be considered in deciding whether to use each of these tools. In practice, because of the rapidly changing risk environment, the need for quick responses to immediate problems, and human and institutional limitations, risk managers often deal with one part of their total risk management program at a time. For example, they may concentrate their attention on industrial injuries or on losses to mail shipments. In making these decisions, they tend to follow the reasoning presented in the earlier discussions of the basic tools.

Periodically, however, the risk manager should broaden his perspective and review at one time, on his own or with the aid of insurer representatives, the firm's total risk management program. In other areas of business management the systems approach is forcing businessmen to consider simultaneously more and more aspects of their operations; risk management should increasingly move in the same direction. One reason for a total review of risk management philosophy and procedures is the need to develop a statement of company policy that is consistent with the business's overall objectives and that recognizes the interrelationships among the various individual risk management areas and decisions. Without such a policy to guide individual decisions the risk manager may fail to recognize such interrelationships. For example, he may not realize that retaining the first $5,000 of losses per accident with respect to two or more types of losses (e.g., industrial accidents and physical damage losses to a fleet of cars) may expose the firm to more than a $5,000 loss per accident if a single accident involves these two or more types of losses. Without a policy statement the risk manager may also be inconsistent in his decision making over time or in his treatment of different risks. For example, a risk manager may without good reason use different standards to determine in January and in June what losses the firm should be willing to retain. He may also apply different standards to retention decisions involving potential automobile physical damage losses and building losses.

Periodic reviews of the total risk management program are desirable to revise the initial statement of company policy and to check compliance with the policy statement.

This chapter describes how procedures and principles in common use might be employed to design a total risk management program. The next chapter will explain and illustrate three quantitative methods that are not in common use but which could prove helpful in designing a total risk management program or parts of that program.

A Two-step Approach

The conventional approach to total risk planning is a two-step procedure. Insurance coverages serve as the focal point of the analysis. After the risk manager has identified and measured the potential losses, he first prepares a listing of the insurance coverages that would best cover these losses. The coverages in the list are divided into three groups primarily on the basis of the severity of the potential losses they cover. He then reviews the insurance contracts in each group to determine which of these losses might be more satisfactorily handled in other ways. Each of these two steps is explained in more detail below.

THE INITIAL LISTING

In step one the risk manager must determine first what combination of insurance coverages would provide the best protection against the losses to which the business is exposed, on the assumption that the business would prefer to buy insurance whenever it is available. To make this determination the risk manager must understand insurance contracts and insurance pricing. His objective is to provide the most complete protection at minimum cost. Because some of the risks faced by the firm may not be insurable, the risk manager is alerted through this analysis to the fact that these risks will have to be handled by some tool other than insurance.

In addition to selecting the proper combination of coverages, the risk manager must select policy limits that provide as complete protection as possible. Generally the policy limits in this initial listing should equal the maximum possible loss, but sometimes this loss may exceed the maximum coverage available. Losses in excess of the maximum amount available will have to be dealt with in some other way.

After the risk manager has determined the best combination of coverages and policy limits, he divides the insurance contracts in this combination into three groups: (1) essential coverages, (2) desirable coverages, and (3) available coverages.

The *essential* contracts include those that are compulsory or that rate top priority on other grounds. Insurance protection may be compulsory because it is required by law (e.g., automobile liability insurance in some cases and workmen's compensation insurance in most cases) or by contract (e.g., a group life insurance contract required under a union contract or property insurance required under a mortgage). The other insurance protection in this category is coverage against *high-severity* losses which could result in a financial catastrophe for the firm. Liability losses are an example of this type.

The *desirable* contracts provide protection against losses which could seriously impair the operations of the firm but which probably would not put it out of business. Automobile physical damage insurance might be an example of this type.

The *available* contracts include all the types of protection which have not been included in the first two classes. These contracts protect against types of losses that would inconvenience the firm but would not seriously impair its operations unless several of them occurred within one year. Insurance against breakage of glass might be considered an available coverage.

REVISED LISTING

After the initial listing has been completed, the risk manager then reviews the contracts in each group to determine which of these losses might be more satisfactorily handled in other ways. For example, contracts which might be dropped from the essential category would include contracts covering:

1. Losses that can be transferred to someone other than an insurer at a smaller cost than the insurance premium
2. Losses that can be prevented or reduced to such an extent that they are no longer severe
3. Losses that happen so infrequently that they can be safely ignored (There will be few such cases and the risk manager should be careful not to ignore a loss merely because the chance of loss is fairly low.)

4. Losses that happen so frequently that they are fairly predictable, thus making self-insurance an attractive alternative because of expense savings

In making these decisions the risk manager can weigh the advantages and disadvantages of each tool presented in the three preceding chapters or he can apply the quantitative approaches explained in the next chapter.

The discussion up to this point has been in terms of types of losses, but as we pointed out under "Risk Measurement" in Chapter 4, it may also be possible to divide any particular type of loss into two (or more) subtypes, depending upon the amount of the potential loss. For example, although the maximum possible loss of a given type is $1 million and the coverage against this loss is therefore an essential coverage, losses of $500 or less may be either so predictable or so unimportant that the risk manager would regard this type of insurance on the first $500 of loss as at best available insurance with only the excess being essential. The types of deductibles and excess insurance available from insurers would limit what could be done along these lines.

The risk manager then subjects the desirable coverages to the same type of analysis. The case for noninsurance methods is stronger with respect to these coverages because the consequences of not insuring are not so severe. Still, this insurance is desirable, and unless some other method of handling the loss is at least as attractive, insurance should be purchased. As in dealing with essential coverages, the risk manager may decide to buy the insurance with a deductible provision.

The available contracts rate the lowest priority. Some available contracts will be attractive to a particular risk manager because the insurer will perform certain services that he values highly. For example, although he can predict small workmen's compensation losses fairly well, he may elect to buy insurance because the premium is not too high, considering the loss-prevention and loss-adjustment services rendered by the insurer. Although potential glass damage may be limited in its severity, the risk manager may believe that the rapid replacement service provided by the insurer justifies payment of the premium. Insurance against some relatively unimportant property losses may become attractive if the premium is, in the eyes of the risk manager, a bargain price. With respect to many of the available coverages, however, other risk management tools will appear more convenient, will cost less to apply, or will have some other relative net advantages.

This threefold classification does not tell the risk manager the point at which he should draw the line with respect to insurance purchases, particularly if the line must be drawn within one of the three classes, but it does give him some priorities with respect to the use of funds he has available for insurance premiums. It also focuses his attention on the consequences of not insuring. The essential and desirable insurance contracts that have not been eliminated in the second listing should be purchased unless the other demands for the premium dollars are very great. What insurance these two classes will contain depends upon a host of factors, including the economic status of the firm, the nature of its exposures, its aversion to risk, and the accuracy of the measurements of its potential losses.

The risk manager must also decide what the business should do about those potential losses not included in the first listing because insurance was not available.

As a result of this analysis of the initial listing of insurance coverages and the uninsurable potential losses, the risk manager should produce a revised list that shows how each risk management tool should be used to handle each of the risks faced by the business. An *abbreviated* example of such a listing is presented below:

A. Avoidance (not possible)
B. Loss prevention and reduction
   1. Safety inspections of premises
   2. Annual physical examination for key employees.
C. Retention
   1. Losses up to $500 of any type
   2. Liability losses in excess of limits available from insurers
D. Noninsurance transfers
   1. Hold-harmless agreement in lease of premises
E. Insurance
   1. First priority (essential)
      a. Workmen's compensation insurance
      b. Liability insurance
   2. Second priority (desirable)
      a. Automobile physical damage insurance
      b. Disability insurance on key men
   3. Third priority (available)
      a. Glass insurance
      b. Sprinkler leakage insurance

Sample Application

In Chapter 27 this conventional method is applied to a specific business situation. Chapters 28 and 29 apply the method to a specific family situation, but because family risk management is less complex, the first step in the two-step process is omitted. Furthermore, personnel insurance planning and property and liability insurance have been separated in these two chapters because personnel insurance planning for families involves many additional considerations.

Implementing the Decision

Choosing insurance or some other tool as the proper way to handle any particular risk does not, of course, end the decision-making process. If insurance is chosen, for example, a particular type of contract must be selected,[1] an insurance producer and insurer must be chosen, and decisions may have to be made with respect to the portion of the administrative work to be handled by the insured and with respect to the pricing method. If a loss occurs, more decisions will be necessary. If some noninsurance method is selected, usually it can be applied in various ways, and further decisions are therefore necessary. In some instances the choice of tools may involve such close discrimination that some of these supplementary decisions may have to accompany the basic decision. For example, the risk manager may need to know the exact insurance premium, not an approximation, before he selects the proper tool. Each of these decisions must, of course, be executed, or the preliminary effort has been wasted. Unfortunately, a good decision maker is not always a good executor, and vice versa.

REVIEW QUESTIONS

1. Under the conventional approach for selecting the best combination of risk management tools, what criteria determine whether an insurance contract covering a particular type of loss is "essential," "desirable," or "available"?
2. Would the risk manager automatically buy all essential and desirable coverages and reject all available coverages? Explain your answer.
3. Prepare an abbreviated revised listing showing how each risk management tool might be used by a hypothetical department store.
4. After the risk manager has decided which tool he will use, has he completed his assignment? Explain your answer.

SUGGESTIONS FOR ADDITIONAL READING

MacDonald, Donald L.: *Corporate Cost Control* (New York: The Ronald Press Company, 1966).

---

[1] While it might be uneconomic to insure against some potential losses separately, the same losses might become attractive candidates for insurance when the coverage is included with a contract covering other potential losses. For example, protection against windstorm becomes much more attractive when it is packaged with protection against fire and several allied perils and sold at an attractive price.

Mehr, R. I., and Cammack, E.: *Principles of Insurance* (4th ed., Homewood, Ill.: Richard D. Irwin, Inc., 1966), chaps. 21 and 22.

————, and Hedges, B. A.: *Risk Management in the Business Enterprise* (Homewood, Ill.: Richard D. Irwin, Inc., 1963).

Mielke, R. G.: *Insurance Surveys: Business—Personal* (5th ed.; Indianapolis: The Rough Notes Company, 1962).

Practices in Risk Management—Selected Readings (Bryn Mawr, Pa.: Insurance Institute of America).

Principles of Risk Management—Supplementary Readings (Bryn Mawr, Pa.: Insurance Institute of America).

13*

selecting the proper tools: quantitative methods

Quantitative approaches to selecting the proper tool will be illustrated by three approaches: (1) the expected utility model, (2) the worry factor model, and (3) the critical probability–paired comparison approach. The first of these approaches has been suggested by decision theory as a general model for making decisions under risk or uncertainty. The second and third models have thus far been applied only to pure-risk management problems, but with some minor changes they could be applied in more general risk situations. These models are useful for at least two reasons: (1) They can be used to make risk management decisions and (2) they make explicit assumptions that are implicit in conventional methods.

The discussion of these three methods is designed for readers with no previous acquaintance with these methods and employs no advanced mathematics.

The rationale underlying each method and the steps in its application will first be described. Then, in order to clarify the discussion, the method will be applied to a sample problem which will be the same for all three methods. In the sample problem a risk manager of a medium-sized business

* This chapter is based largely upon instructional materials developed for an experiment reported by John Neter and C. A. Williams, Jr., in two papers on the relative acceptability of the expected utility method and two other approaches to making decisions under uncertainty, which have been submitted for publication. In that experiment the utility method was less acceptable to a group of insurance agents and risk managers for making insurance decisions than the other two methods.

will be required to decide which, if any, of four types of insurance he should buy to protect his business against losses to a building valued at $100,000. The balance sheet of the business reveals assets of $1,000,000, liabilities of $600,000, and capital and retained earnings of $400,000. According to its operating statement last year its sales were $500,000, its expenses $450,000, and its net income before taxes $50,000.

The best estimate of the probability distribution of possible losses to the building during the coming year is as follows:

Potential losses	Probability
$ 0	.800
500	.100
1,000	.080
10,000	.017
50,000	.002
100,000	.001
	1.0

In real life, of course, the number of possible outcomes would be much larger, but using a small number reduces the calculations, thus permitting greater concentration on the principles involved in each method.

Similarly, the number of possible insurance decisions has been limited to five—no insurance plus the four following insurance amounts:

Insurance amount		
Policy limit	Deductible	Premium
$ 10,000	$ 0	$470
50,000	0	640
100,000	1,000	500
100,000	0	710

For each possible decision the total dollar loss to the business will be the sum of the premium and the uninsured loss to the building. For example, with $10,000 insurance and a $100,000 loss to the building, the total dollar loss will be $470 + $90,000 = $90,470.

The possible decisions, the possible building losses, and the total dollar loss to the firm associated with each possible insurance decision—building loss combination can be summarized in the following matrix form:

		Building loss					
Decision	Amount Probability	$0 .800	$500 .100	$1,000 .080	$10,000 .017	$50,000 .002	$100,000 .001
No insurance		$ 0	$ 500	$1,000	$10,000	$50,000	$100,000
$10,000 insurance		470	470	470	470	40,470	90,470
$50,000 insurance		640	640	640	640	640	50,640
$100,000 insurance, $1,000 deductible		500	1,000	1,500	1,500	1,500	1,500
$100,000 insurance		710	710	710	710	710	710

Expected Utility Model

Under the expected utility model, the objective is to minimize the expected loss in utility. The expected dollar loss has been explained in Chapter 5. The expected loss in utility associated with a given decision is calculated in the same way except that a utility index number is substituted for each of the dollar losses associated with that decision. This utility concept is more complicated than that explained in Chapter 1, because it reflects risk attitudes as well as one's satisfaction with certain increases or decreases in wealth. In the words of one authority, this utility reflects "an indecomposable mixture of attitude toward risk, profit, and loss in a particular kind of situation."[1]

A person's attitude toward risk is in fact the major determinant of the shape of his utility function. If the function is graphed, as in Figure 13-1, with the potential dollar loss along the horizontal axis and the loss of utility along the vertical axis, a concave-upward curve indicates that the person is a risk averter; i.e., he is willing to pay something more than the expected dollar loss to avoid the risk. For example, for the person with the concave-upward curve in Figure 13-1 (a risk averter), if the probability is .5 that there will be a $20,000 loss and .5 that there will be no loss, the expected dollar loss is $10,000. The expected utility loss is calculated as follows:

.5 (loss of utility for $0 loss) + .5 (loss of utility for $20,000 loss)

$$= .5(0) + .5(.63)$$
$$= .315$$

[1] Robert Schlaifer, *Probability and Statistics for Business Decisions* (New York: McGraw-Hill Book Company, 1959), p. 42.

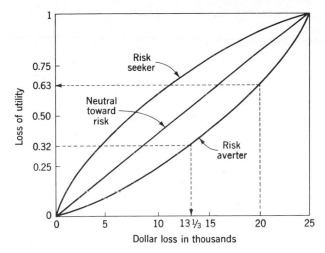

Figure 13.1 Hypothetical utility functions.

This loss of utility corresponds to a dollar loss of $13,333. Thus, according to this model, the person's uncertain position is equivalent to a certain dollar loss of $13,333. Consequently he should be willing to incur any certain dollar loss equal to or less than $13,333 in order to eliminate his uncertainty. In other words he should be willing to pay up to $3,333 in excess of the expected dollar loss to transfer the risk to some other party. A person with a linear utility function (a person who is neutral toward risk) should be willing to pay the expected dollar loss to eliminate his uncertainty, but no more; a person with a concave-downward function (a risk seeker) should prefer to retain his uncertainty unless the transfer cost is less than the equivalent certain value, which will be some value less than the expected dollar loss. Actual utility functions may be more complex than the three shown here with both concave-upward and concave-downward sections.

To apply this method using the "reference contract" approach, one would proceed as follows:[2]

1. Derive the person's (dis) utility function in the following way:
    a. Assign a (dis)[3] utility index of 1 to the worst loss that can happen, regardless of the decision.

---

[2] Instead of keeping $p = .5$ and reducing the potential loss, as in the example below, one can hold the potential loss constant and change p. For example, the utility index of $35,000 would be .25 if this is the maximum amount the person is willing to pay to avoid a .25 probability that he will lose $100,000, the worst possible loss. For an extensive discussion of the reference-contract approach, see Robert Schlaifer, *Analysis of Decisions under Uncertainty*, Vol. I (New York: McGraw-Hill Book Company, 1967).
[3] In order to conserve space, (dis) will be dropped in the remainder of this discussion, but the reader should remember that the utility index being derived is actually a loss of utility index.

b. Assign a utility index of zero to the best thing that can happen, namely no loss, regardless of the decision.

c. Ask the person the maximum amount he is willing to pay to relieve himself of a .5 probability that the worst thing will happen, the only alternate outcome being no loss. Because this certain payment has the same utility index as the expected value of his uncertain position, its utility index is .5 (Utility of the worst loss) + .5 (Utility of no loss) = .5(1) + .5(0) = .5.

d. Ask the person the maximum amount he is willing to pay to relieve himself of a .5 probability that he will lose the amount he answered in step c, the only alternate outcome being no loss. This value has a utility index of .5(.5) + .5(0) = .25.

e. Ask the person the maximum amount he is willing to pay to relieve himself of a .5 probability that he will lose the amount he answered in step d, the only alternate outcome being no loss. This value has an index of .5(.25) + .5(0) = .125.

f. Continue this procedure until the person has provided enough points to describe his utility function. Generally the last amount mentioned should be close to the lowest premium amount or dollar loss.

g. Chart the points.

2. For each decision under investigation list the possible dollar losses and associated probabilities.

3. Using the chart developed in step 1, convert the possible dollar losses for each decision into utility index values.

4. Calculate the expected loss of utility.

5. Select that decision for which the expected loss of utility is the smallest.

APPLICATION

Applied to the sample problem described above, this method produces the following results:

1. Utility function derivation:

a. Let the utility index for a $100,000 loss be 1.

b. Let the utility index for a $0 loss be zero.

c. Ask the person the maximum amount he is willing to pay to avoid a .5 probability that a $100,000 loss will occur. Assume an answer of $60,000. The utility index for $60,000 is thus .5.

d. Ask the person the maximum amount he is willing to pay to avoid a .5 probability that a $60,000 loss will occur. Assume an answer of $35,000. The utility index for $35,000 is thus .25.

e. Ask the person the maximum amount he is willing to pay to avoid a .5

probability that a $35,000 loss will occur. Assume an answer of $20,000. The utility index for $20,000 is thus .125.

f. Assume that continuing this process produces the following results:

(1)	(2)	(3)	(4)
			Utility index
		Maximum	of maximum
Potential loss	Probability	transfer fee	transfer fee
$100,000	.5	$60,000	.5
60,000	.5	35,000	.25
35,000	.5	20,000	.125
20,000	.5	11,000	.0625
11,000	.5	6,000	.0312
6,000	.5	3,500	.0156
3,500	.5	2,000	.0078
2,000	.5	1,100	.0039
1,100	.5	600	.0020
600	.5	350	.0010

g. The utility function derived from columns (3) and (4) is shown in Figure 13.2.

2, 3, and 4. For each decision, list the possible dollar loss. Using the above utility function [graphically, by using a mathematical formula that describes the curve, or by linear interpolation between two values for which index values were derived—linear interpolation is used in this example. For example, the utility index for $500 is the utility index for $350 plus

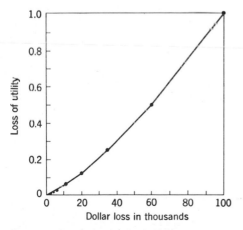

Figure 13.2 Sample problem utility function.

$15/25$ of the difference between the index for \$350 and \$600 or .0010 plus $15/25$ (.0020 − .0010 = .0016.)] convert these dollar losses into utility index values and calculate the expected loss of utility for each possible decision. For the decision to buy no insurance:

Potential dollar loss	Potential utility index	Probability	Expected utility loss	Expected dollar loss
$ 0	.0000	.800	.00000	$ 0
500	.0016	.100	.00016	50
1,000	.0035	.080	.00028	80
10,000	.0563	.017	.00957	170
50,000	.4000	.002	.00080	100
100,000	1.0000	.001	.00100	100
			.01181	$500

For the decision to buy \$10,000 insurance:

Potential dollar loss	Utility index	Probability	Expected utility loss	Expected dollar loss
$470	.0015	.997	.00150	$469
$470 + ($50,000 − $10,000)	.3057	.002	.00061	81
$470 + ($100,000 − $10,000)	.8808	.001	.00088	90
			.00299	$640

For the decision to buy \$50,000 insurance:

Potential dollar loss	Utility index	Probability	Expected utility loss	Expected dollar loss
$640	.0022	.999	.00220	$640
$640 + ($100,000 − $50,000)	.4064	.001	.00041	51
			.00261	$691

For the decision to buy $100,000 insurance, $1,000 deductible:

Potential dollar loss	Utility index	Probability	Expected utility loss	Expected dollar loss
$500	.0016	.800	.00128	$400
$500 + $500	.0035	.100	.00035	100
$500 + $1,000	.0056	.100	.00056	150
			.00219	$650

For the decision to buy $100,000 insurance:

Potential dollar loss	Utility index	Probability	Expected utility loss	Expected dollar loss
$710	.0024	1.0	.00240	$710

5. Select that decision for which the expected loss of utility is the smallest. In this case, according to this criterion, the $100,000 policy with the $1,000 deductible is the best decision.

　　Note that this is not the decision that produces the lowest expected dollar loss. According to that criterion, the individual should buy no insurance. This is not surprising, because an insurer must add an expense and profit loading to its estimate of the insured expected losses. The expected utility model recognizes that the insured may be willing to pay some amount in addition to the insurer's expected loss estimate for three reasons:

a. The risk manager may estimate the insured expected losses to be higher than the insurer's estimate.

b. The risk manager's dissatisfaction with various dollar losses may increase more rapidly than the dollar losses; i.e., the dissatisfaction associated with a $100,000 loss may be more than ten times as great as the dissatisfaction associated with a $10,000 loss.

c. The risk manager may worry about the risk associated with a retained exposure and be willing to pay something to rid himself of this worry.

　　Because utility functions cannot be developed with great accuracy, a risk manager should not rely too heavily upon this approach when the differences in the expected utility loss are small. He may also wish to determine whether small changes in the utility values produce different decisions—he can do this by fitting several curves to the points given and making the necessary calculations for each curve.

Many factors have been ignored in this analysis that might have been included. For example, no attention has been paid to the possibility that the firm may incur some consequential losses (including inconvenience) not covered under any of the insurance decisions that would change the values in the loss matrix and affect the expected utility values. For example, if each possible direct loss to the building is increased 20 per cent by consequential losses not covered under any of the insurance contracts, the total dollar loss associated with each insurance decision—building loss combination is increased by 20 per cent of the building loss. To illustrate, the total dollar loss for the $100,000 insurance—$100,000 building loss combination in the lower right-hand corner of the loss matrix would become $20,710. The analysis has also failed to recognize that a $100,000 uninsured loss that must be paid out of current income or retained earnings may develop into a larger loss because of borrowing costs, because of delays in securing the financing necessary to make repairs, or because of forced liquidation of the business.

With respect to expense savings, it has been assumed that all of the expenses incurred by the insurer can be saved. If some of these expenses cannot be saved, each of the potential losses can be increased to reflect this fact. Similarly, differences in tax treatment and opportunity costs can be incorporated in the model. If the relative effectiveness of the insurer's loss-prevention and loss-adjustment services in reducing losses is known, this too can be recognized in the model, but some quality differentials (e.g., public relations impact) are best judged independently as supplementary information. The reader is encouraged to investigate the effect these additional considerations would have in the example under study for persons with differently shaped utility functions.

This model is not limited to insurance-retention decisions. Loss-prevention and noninsurance transfers can be included as possible decisions with their attendant costs and effects upon losses. Finally, decisions to use a combination of tools, such as loss prevention and retention or loss prevention and insurance, can be considered.

The Worry Factor Model

Under the worry factor model, the objective is to minimize the sum of (1) the premium payment, if any, (2) the expected dollar value of any losses that are still uncovered if the insurance does not provide complete financial protection against this risk, and (3) the dollar value assigned by the risk manager to the risk or uncertainty associated with the uncovered dollar losses. Given the probability distribution of potential losses and the schedule of insurance premiums for each of the possible insurance decisions, the calculation of the premium and the expected uncovered loss is a mechanical matter. The dollar amount assigned to the worry value, on the other hand, is a subjective value that varies with the risk manager's reaction to risk. Consequently one would expect this value to be a function of the potential uncovered losses associated with each decision, the premium associated with that decision, the economic status of the risk manager's business, and the risk attitudes of the management. Other things being equal, one would expect a risk manager to assign higher worry values to a decision that will still expose him to financially crippling losses than to one that may cause him inconvenience losses. Like the utility model, the worry factor model introduces risk aversion into the decision-making process, but it does so explicitly.

The procedure is as follows:

1. For each decision, list the premium, the probability distribution of uncovered losses, and the expected uncovered loss. The risk manager should realize that, with each decision, in the long run his *average* annual loss will be the premium plus the expected uncovered loss.

2. For each decision ask the risk manager the maximum amount he would be willing to pay in addition to the premium, if any, and the average uncovered loss to eliminate the annual fluctuations in his loss experience. His answer is the dollar value he assigns to the worry factor. The value for one risk manager may be zero while for another person it could be a large sum.

3. For each decision add the premium, the expected uncovered loss, and the dollar value of the worry factor provided in step 2.

4. Select that decision for which the sum calculated in step 3 is the smallest.

APPLICATION

The first three steps in the worry factor approach are applied to the sample problem on page 228. The dollar values assigned to the different worry factors are assumed to be the answers given by the risk manager in step 2. With complete insurance the worry value was assumed to be $0 because there is no uncertainty; the highest value was assigned to a no-insurance

decision because this decision involves the most uncertainty and exposes
the business to the greatest potential loss.

	No insurance	$10,000 insurance	$50,000 insurance	$100,000 insurance, $1,000 deductible	$100,000 insurance
1. Premium	$ 0	$ 470	$ 640	$ 500	$710
2. Potential	0 .800	0 .997	0 .999	0 .800	0 1.0
uncovered	500 .100	40,000 .002	50,000 .001	500 .100	
losses	1,000 .080	90,000 .001		1,000 .100	
and	10,000 .017				
associated	50,000 .002				
probabilities	100,000 .001				
3. Expected uncovered loss	500	170	50	150	0
4. Worry factor value	500	200	50	30	0
Sum of 1, 3, and 4	$ 1,000	$ 840	$ 740	$ 680	$710

According to the worry factor model, this risk manager should select
the $100,000 insurance policy with the $1,000 deductible because the sum
of the premium, the expected uncovered loss, and the worry value is smaller
for this decision than for any other. One advantage of this approach is
that the table presented above displays the data in a manner that facilitates
sensitivity analysis. For example, the risk manager can see that he could
raise the $30 value he assigned to worry with the $1,000 deductible policy
as high as $60 before he would choose to eliminate the deductible. He
would prefer complete insurance to no insurance unless the worry factor
value for no insurance were reduced from $500 to below $210. He can
also experiment with the effect of different probability distributions, but
this would require a new calculation of the expected uncovered losses.

Like the utility model application, this application of the worry factor
model has been purposely oversimplified. The application need not be limited
to probability distributions with only a few outcomes. Consequential losses[4]
that are not insurable and the extra losses that might occur if there is
no insurance can be considered, as well as insurer expenses that are not
saved, tax implications, and opportunity costs. Finally, tools other than insurance and retention can be included in the analysis.

A simplified version of this model may prove extremely useful in deciding how much insurance to purchase. For example, assume that the risk

---

[4] See Chap. 6, under "Methods of Valuing Indirect Loss." If such consequential losses
exist, the worry value for $100,000 insurance would not be $0 for all persons.

manager must choose between no insurance or complete insurance involving a premium of $100. If the insurer's expenses and profit for this line of insurance are about 35 per cent of its premiums, the insurer must be estimating that the insured's expected losses are about $65. Unless the insured has reason to question this estimate, he may accept it. The question then becomes whether the insured is willing to pay at least $35 to rid himself of the worry and uncertainty associated with retention. If there is a reasonable chance that serious losses might occur (e.g., this would be the situation in liability insurance), the answer would normally be yes. Similarly, if the difference in premiums for a policy with and without a $100 deductible is $20, the expected uncovered loss, assuming a 35 per cent expense ratio, is $13. If the insured is unwilling to pay at least $7 to rid himself of the uncertainty associated with the deductible, he should buy the policy with a deductible.

Critical Probability—Paired Comparison Approach

Under the critical probability—paired comparison approach, the possible decisions are compared systematically in pairs until one decision emerges as the preferred action. Under this method it is assumed that if the risk manager prefers decision A to decision B and decision B to decision C, he prefers decision A to decision C. Each paired comparison involves two decisions, one of which would enable the insured to pay a smaller premium. He is then asked whether in exchange for the premium savings associated with the less expensive policy he is willing to assume the calculated probability that the additional uncovered losses under the less expensive approach will equal or exceed the premium savings. Presumably his decision will depend upon such factors as how large the additional uncovered losses can be, the firm's ability to handle these losses, and his own risk attitudes. Instead of or in addition to calculating the probability that the additional uncovered losses will equal or exceed the premium savings, the risk manager may wish to calculate the probability that the losses will equal or exceed some other critical values. To simplify this discussion, however, only the probability that the additional uncovered losses will equal or exceed the premium savings will be calculated.

The procedure is as follows:

Round 1 Compare each possible decision with the decision involving the highest premium cost. Eliminate all those decisions for which the risk manager is unwilling to accept the probability that the additional uncovered losses will equal or exceed the premium savings.

If the risk manager is unwilling to accept any of the calculated probabilities, he should make the decision involving the highest premium cost. If in one instance he prefers to take the premium savings but in the other comparisons he rejects them, he should make the decision that provides the preferred savings. If he prefers to take the premium savings made possible by two or more less-than-complete insurance decisions, he must compare these preferred alternatives in a second round of paired comparisons.

Round 2   Compare each of the remaining decisions with that decision among the remainder that involves the highest premium cost. The comparisons are conducted in the same manner as in Round 1. The results will determine whether it is necessary to compare the remaining preferred alternatives in a third round of paired comparisons.

This process is continued until only one decision remains among the preferred alternatives.

APPLICATION

A set of preferences requiring two rounds of comparisons will be assumed in applying this method to the sample problem:

Round 1

	Premium saving	Additional uncovered losses	Probability	Probability that additional uncovered loss will equal or exceed premium savings	Accept this probability?
No insurance vs. $100,000 insurance	$710 − 0 $710	$ 0 500 1,000 10,000 50,000 100,000	.800 .100 .080 .017 .002 .001	.100	No
$10,000 insurance vs. $100,000 insurance	$710 − 470 $240	$ 0 40,000 90,000	.997 .002 .001	.003	No
$50,000 insurance vs. $100,000 insurance	$710 − 640 $ 70	$ 0 50,000	.999 .001	.001	Yes
$100,000 insurance, $1,000 deductible, vs. $100,000 insurance	$710 − 500 $210	$ 0 500 1,000	.800 .100 .100	.200	Yes

Round 1 produces two preferred alternatives to $100,000 insurance. Fifty thousand dollars insurance is assumed to be preferred because of the extremely low probability that any loss will occur in excess of $50,000. One hundred thousand dollars insurance with a $1,000 deductible is preferred because the worst loss that can occur is not a serious one. Because there are two preferred alternatives, they must be compared in Round 2.

Round 2

	Premium saving	Additional uncovered losses	Prob- ability	Probability that additional uncovered loss will equal or exceed premium savings	Accept this probability?
$100,000 insurance,	$640	−$49,000	.001		
$1,000 deductible, vs.	− 500	0	.800		
$50,000 insurance	$140	1,000	.199}	.199	Yes

Because the risk manager is assumed to prefer the $140 premium savings associated with the $100,000 insurance, $1,000 deductible policy, and there are no other comparisons to be made, he should purchase this policy. The reason for the negative additional uncovered loss is that if there is a $100,000 loss, the risk manager will lose $50,000 with a $50,000 insurance policy but only $1,000 with the base contract.

Like the other two methods, this approach can be altered to include other considerations in insurance-retention decisions and other tools of risk management. The student should apply these methods to more complex problems after he understands thoroughly the principles underlying each approach.[5]

An Admission

The reader can with good reason be skeptical of the fact that all three methods applied to the sample problem dictated the same decision. The authors admit that this result is no accident. The subjective values assumed in the example were chosen to produce this result. On the other hand, they are reasonable values that might have been supplied by a risk manager. In practice each of the three methods may produce a different answer to the same problem. In this case the risk manager should reconsider the subjective values that he supplied under each approach to determine whether

[5] For a more complicated application of the worry factor approach, see the first edition of this text, pp. 61–66, but assume linear utility in that example.

he might want to make some changes. If the methods still produce conflicting results, he must decide in which method, coupled with supplementary information, he has the most confidence.

REVIEW QUESTIONS

1. For the firm whose balance sheet and operating statement data are presented in Chapter 27, assume the following probability distribution of liability losses arising out of its premises and operations.

Potential loss	Probability
$ 0	.8500
1,000	.1200
10,000	.0250
50,000	.0045
500,000	.0005

Further assume that there are four possible insurance decisions:

Insurance amount		
Policy limit	Deductible	Premium
No insurance		$ 0
$ 10,000	$ 0	600
500,000	1,000	1,000
500,000	0	1,200

a. Prepare a matrix summary of the problem.

b. Assume that you are the risk manager for this business and use the expected utility model to decide what insurance decision the business should make.

c. Use the worry factor model to make your decision.

d. Use the critical probability–paired comparison approach to make your decision.

e. Do all three decisions produce the same result? If not, why not?

f. Which method do you prefer? Why?

g. From your answers to the questions asked under the three methods, can you say whether you are a risk averter or a risk seeker?

h. How much would your worry factor have to change to alter your decision using that method?

2. Suppose that, in addition to the four insurance acts listed above, you could retain the risk, spend $200 annually on some loss-prevention measure, and as a result eliminate the .0005 chance that a $500,000 loss would occur. In other words, the chance of no liability loss would become .8505 and the probabilities for losses of $1,000, $10,000, and $50,000 would remain unchanged. How would you incorporate this additional choice into your answer to question 1?

3. A workmen's compensation insurer will protect a firm against industrial injuries to its 50 employees for a premium of $500. It will cover all losses in excess of $1,000 per accident for a premium of $200.

a. What is the insurer's probable estimate of the insured's expected loss if he purchases no insurance? ($300–$350)

b. What is the insurer's probable estimate of the insured's expected uncovered losses if he purchases the deductible policy? ($180–$210)

c. If the business has only a vague idea of the probability distribution of its workmen's compensation losses, can it use any of the three methods discussed in this chapter to determine what insurance it should purchase? How?

d. If the firm had 5,000 employees and the premiums for complete and deductible coverage were $50,000 and $20,000, respectively, how would this affect the firm's decision under each method?

SUGGESTIONS FOR ADDITIONAL READING

Bros, Irwin D. J.: *Design for Decision* (New York: The Macmillan Company, 1953).

Greene, Mark: *Risk and Insurance* (2d ed., Cincinnati: South-Western Publishing Company, 1968), chap. 2.

Hammond, J. D. (ed.): *Essays in the Theory of Risk and Insurance* (Glenview, Ill.: Scott, Foresman, and Company, 1968).

Mehr, R. I., and Hedges, B. A.: *Risk Management in the Business Enterprise* (Homewood, Ill: Richard D. Irwin, Inc., 1963), chaps. 3 and 11.

Raiffa, Howard: *Decision Analysis* (Reading, Mass.: Addison-Wesley, 1968).

Schlaifer, Robert: *Analysis of Decisions under Uncertainty* (Vol. I, New York: McGraw-Hill Book Company, 1967).

D. Insurance contracts and their uses

14

some legal aspects of insurance contracts

A risk manager has several reasons for understanding the fundamentals of insurance contracts—their construction and their interpretation. For example, in deciding whether to use insurance or some other tool, he should know what the insurer promises to do under its contract. Either at this decision level or later, he may prefer to participate in the drafting of a tailor-made insurance contract instead of accepting the printed forms normally sold by the insurer. Even if he decides to purchase one of the insurer's conventional products, he must have some basis for selecting among these various forms. Finally, after a contract is in effect, an insured should know his rights and responsibilities under the contract.

Chapters 14 through 22 deal with insurance contract fundamentals. After a discussion of some legal aspects of insurance contracts, two chapters are devoted to a framework for analyzing insurance contracts and concepts common to all contracts. The remaining six chapters are devoted to some leading property, liability, and personnel insurance contracts, their major provisions, and their uses.

This chapter on some legal aspects of insurance first discusses what contracts the law considers to be insurance contracts and the reasons why this is important. Other topics include the unique characteristics of insurance contracts, the requirements for a valid insurance contract, some rules on the disclosure of information by the insured, the doctrines of waiver and estoppel, how mistakes in an insurance contract can be corrected, and the extent and nature of insurance contract standardization.

A Legal Definition of Insurance[1]

The significance of whether a particular contract is or is not *legally* insurance is not solely a question of semantics; it becomes important in a variety of ways. First of all, the fact that an insurance business is being transacted by a particular individual or firm raises the question as to whether state laws and regulations governing the business are being complied with. The state may raise such an issue by *quo warranto* proceedings (action to discontinue illegal exercise of powers), criminal prosecution, action for statutory penalty, or upon answer to a company's petition for mandamus or injunctive relief.

Second, this issue of whether a transaction is or is not insurance may be raised in a civil action whereby one party alleges certain rights which flow from insurance contracts. These actions may include suit to recover a promised benefit under the alleged policy, a return of premiums paid, or a money judgment for damages suffered by the claimant because of insurance coverages promised. The courts in these cases have tended to favor the theory that the claimant should recover from organizations holding themselves out as providing such benefits. It should be remembered that what may be determined to be insurance in such civil actions may not be held to be "doing a business of insurance" as related to state regulation.

The issue also is raised in bankruptcy proceedings since Section 4 of the Bankruptcy Act excludes insurance corporations from the operation of the act. The exclusion has had the effect of shifting defunct insurers to an elaborate procedure and process of liquidation under state insurance laws and administration.

The courts have also been asked to rule on what is or is not insurance under the administration of our tax laws. Insurance companies are entitled to special treatment regarding deductions for reserves, investment income, and accounting treatment of expenses. The United States Supreme Court has announced the general rule that the state's classification of a company will serve as a basis for making the decision for tax administration and treatment unless there has been a gross misuse of the name to hide the real purposes of the business enterprise.

Case law shows clearly that there is no single legal definition of insurance. Instead, the courts use a definition or test which relates to the method

---

[1] The legal definition of insurance may differ considerably from the economic definition presented in Chap. 11 because, as will be apparent from the following discussion, it serves a different purpose. For a comprehensive study of legal definitions, see H. S. Denenberg, "The Legal Definition of Insurance," *Journal of Insurance*, XXX, No. 3 (September, 1963), 319–43.

of raising the issue.[2] Certain tests which are often applied to the business or transaction in question are:

1. Is there a risk of economic loss to the beneficiary or insured?
   a. Independent of the contract itself
   b. Outside the control of either party
   c. A kind of loss that may be distributed among those who are subject to loss
2. Is this risk assumed by the insurer or promisor?
3. Does the contract incorporate a plan to distribute the cost of the loss among a group exposed to risk?

The case law and commentary on the subject contain the following examples of what the courts have held to be or not to be insurance:[3]

Insurance	*Not insurance*
Indemnity for loss by theft	Lightning-rod salesman's guarantee
Indemnity for loss by death of cattle	Bicycle repair contract issued by a bicycle association
Contracts guaranteeing the performance of, or indemnifying against the nonperformance of, certain contracts	Agreement to protect employee from striking employees
Comprehensive guarantee of auto tires	Tire warranty promising indemnity against defects in the tire
Contracts for replacement of plate glass, if broken	Provision in lease making the lessor responsible for replacement of a chattel injured by fire
Newspaper promise to pay a stated amount to a person killed in an accident if at the time he had a copy of the newspaper on his person	Contract entitling members of groups to medical services free or at reduced rates

Unique Characteristics of Insurance Contracts

When a person buys private insurance, he is entering into a contract with the insurer which entitles him to certain advantages but which also imposes upon him certain responsibilities. Although the contract may be one of the most important to which the person will be a party during his lifetime, he may never read it. As a matter of fact few insureds read the contract

[2] In certain states, such as Kentucky, the legislature has defined insurance. Courts sometimes cite these statutory definitions.
[3] See *American Jurisprudence* (Rochester, N.Y.: Lawyers' Cooperative Publishing Co., 1960), XXIX, pp. 430–45.

carefully before (or after) they purchase the insurance. Some do not even realize that an insurance contract is a legal document.

Insurance contracts are subject to the same basic law that governs all types of contracts. On the other hand, one can be an expert in the general law of contracts and know very little about the application of this law to an insurance contract; it is a unique type of contract, and a special body of law has developed to handle the legal problems associated with insurance. The unique nature of insurance contracts is best indicated by the following list of their prevailing characteristics:

Personal contract   Insurance contracts are personal contracts. Although the subject of a property insurance contract, for example, is a piece of property, the insurance contract insures a person or persons, not the property. Suppose the insured is the owner. If the owner sells the property to someone else, the new owner is not insured under that contract unless the insurer agrees to an assignment of the contract to the new owner; the identity of the insured is an important factor in the insurer's decision to insure the property. On the other hand, an insurance contract may create rights for persons other than the insured such as a mortgagee under a standard mortgagee clause or the beneficiary under a life insurance contract. Life insurance contracts are personal contracts in the sense that the insurer is interested in the identity of the person purchasing the contract; but after the contract is issued, it can be assigned to anyone without the consent of the insurer.

Unilateral contract   Insurance contracts are commonly unilateral contracts. After the insured has paid his premium or premium installment and the contract has gone into effect, only the insurer can be forced to perform, because the insured has fulfilled his promise to pay the premium. On the other hand, if the insured does not pay his complete premium on the due date (as in the case of an assessable contract or an order placed on the phone) but promises to do so in the future, both parties have made promises to perform in the future, and the insurance contract is bilateral.

Conditional contract   Insurance contracts are conditional contracts. Although only the insurer can be forced to perform after the contract is effective, the insurer can refuse to perform if the insured does not satisfy certain conditions contained in the contract. For example, the insurer need not pay a claim if the insured has increased the chance of loss in some manner prohibited under the contract, or if he has failed to submit a proof of loss within a specified period.

Aleatory contract   Insurance contracts are aleatory contracts; i.e., the obligation of at least one of the parties to perform is dependent upon chance. If the event insured against occurs, the insurer will probably pay the insured a sum of money much larger than the premium. If the event does not occur, the insurer will pay nothing.

Contract of adhesion   Insurance contracts are usually contracts of adhesion. The insured seldom participates in the drafting of the contract although risk managers of large firms may occasionally do so and this practice is apparently becoming more common. Usually the insurer offers the insured a printed document on a take-it-or-leave-it basis. Courts frequently refer to this characteristic of insurance contracts when they interpret ambiguous provisions in favor of the insured.[4]

Contract *uberrimae fidei*   Insurance contracts are contracts of the utmost good faith. Both parties to the contract are bound to disclose all the facts relevant to the transaction. Neither party is to take advantage of the other's lack of information. The legal questions involving this characteristic usually center on the disclosure of information by the insured. These legal questions are important enough to merit the separate treatment given in the section on Disclosure of Information later in this chapter.

Contract of indemnity   Property and liability insurance contracts are, subject to certain exceptions, contracts of indemnity. The person insured under these contracts should not benefit financially from the happening of the event insured against. Life and frequently health insurance contracts are not contracts of indemnity. For an extended discussion of this important subject, see Chapter 16.

Requirements for a Valid Contract

According to the law of contracts, a contract must satisfy four conditions before it is legally enforceable. These four conditions and their special application to insurance are:

1. The contract must serve a legal purpose. It must not be contrary to public policy. An insurance contract, for example, cannot protect a person against damages awarded as a result of harm he intentionally causes to the person or property of some other person.

---

[4] This is true in spite of the fact that in some instances the state, not the insurer, drafts the contract. See the section on Standardization in this chapter.

2. There must be a definite offer by one party and an acceptance of that offer by the other party. If the person to whom the offer has been made refuses to accept the offer without some modifications, he is considered to have made a counteroffer, which must be accepted by the other person before the agreement is effective. In property and liability insurance, technically the applicant makes an offer to the insurer which accepts the offer, rejects it, or makes a counteroffer. The insurance agent usually has the power to accept the offer on behalf of the insurer he represents, and the contract is effective as soon as he agrees to bind the coverage.

In personnel insurance, prospective insureds complete a written application for insurance. Usually the applicant does not pay the premium at the time, and the application is considered an invitation to the insurer to make an offer. Not until the applicant has accepted the policy and paid or promised to pay the first premium, has he accepted unconditionally a definite offer. Furthermore, the insurer sometimes conditions its offer upon the continued good health of the applicant until the date of delivery.

Even if the premium is paid with the application, the coverage is not immediately binding because the insurer's agent lacks the authority to make it so. Customarily, however, he issues a binding receipt which makes the coverage effective on (1) the date of application or (2) the date of the application or (if required) the medical examination, if later, provided that the prospective insured was acceptable on that date.[5] In this instance there has been an offer by the applicant and a conditional acceptance by the insurer. To illustrate the effect of the receipt, consider the following: A person applies for life insurance on February 10, pays the first premium with his application and obtains a binding receipt of the first type, and is killed in an automobile accident on February 12. If this person was insurable on February 10 according to the underwriting standards of the insurer, the coverage is effective even if the insurer does not receive the application from its agent until February 14.

Sometimes the insurer will reject the applicant's offer and make a counteroffer based on a different type of coverage or rate. Usually this counteroffer will delay the effective date until the insured accepts the counteroffer.

3. Each party to the contract must be required to make some consideration on behalf of the other party. The contract is not enforceable unless one party gives up a right, power, or privilege which he already has in exchange for an equivalent renouncement by the other. The contract is enforceable, however, even if one person promises to do much more than

---

[5] A few insurers issue life insurance binding receipts, which provide temporary protection similar to that given by property and liability insurance binders.

the other.[6] Under an insurance contract, the insured must pay or promise to pay a premium and meet certain conditions stipulated in the contract. The insurer must promise to make certain payments or provide certain services in case of loss.

4. The parties to the contract must be legally competent. Insane or intoxicated persons are not considered competent. Minors (persons under eighteen in some states and under twenty-one in others) may void a contract to which they are a party, except a contract for "necessities" (food, clothing, and shelter, for example), if they do so during their infancy. Only the minor has the option, however, and if he chooses not to void the contract, it is valid.

An insurer is competent if it meets certain statutory requirements described in Chapter 23. Insureds are generally considered to be competent unless they are insane or intoxicated. Insurance is not considered a necessity, but the rule with respect to minors has been modified in some states to permit infants to enter into legally enforceable life insurance contracts as early as age fourteen. The courts of a few states deny the rights of minors to void an insurance contract, on the ground that since the insurer has fulfilled its promise, the contract has been executed.

Disclosure of Information by the Insured

An insurance contract, as was noted earlier, is a contract *uberrimae fidei*. Consequently, an insurer is entitled to rely upon information provided by the insured and to seek some relief if this information is incorrect. The doctrines that will be introduced by the insurer in any court case involving this issue will be the doctrines of concealment, misrepresentation, or breach of warranty. In the following discussion of these three doctrines we shall assume first that there are no special statutes modifying the common law doctrines, and then describe the effect of the statutes upon these doctrines.

Concealment   Concealment is the failure to reveal certain facts known to the insured which are not such common information that the insurer should also know them. The common law doctrine of concealment is much more harsh with respect to ocean marine insurance than with respect to other kinds of insurance, because at the time ocean marine insurance law was being developed, the courts believed that insurers needed protection. Communications were very poor, and insurers were often asked to insure vessels thousands of miles away. In fact the vessels were insured "lost or not lost," and some had already been sunk or damaged. Consequently an ocean marine insurer can successfully plead concealment if it can show that the

[6] Contracts that require the government to pay a prominent person $1 a year in return for some valuable services illustrate this principle.

fact concealed was material. A fact is considered to be material if previous cognizance of it would have caused the insurer to refuse the insured's proposal or make a counteroffer. The practices of other insurers in similar situations may be introduced as evidence and in some states become the standard to be applied.[7] The reasoning here is that if the insurer had not accepted the offer, it would have had no obligation with respect to the loss. Note that the fact misrepresented need not have actually contributed to the loss that the insurer refused to pay. An insurer could claim that some information the insured concealed with respect to some cargo was material even if a loss to the cargo had nothing to do with the fact concealed.

The ocean marine insurer need not prove that the concealment was intentional; in fact it is sufficient for the insurer to show that the applicant should have had the information. Other types of insurers, however, must prove that the applicant *intentionally* concealed some facts that he knew to be material and which would not be apparent from an inspection of the exposure. This additional requirement reduces substantially the insurer's reliance upon the doctrine of concealment, because fraud is difficult to prove and failure to prove intent may result in a countersuit.[8] The definition of materiality is the same as for ocean marine insurance. The following situation illustrates the application of this rule: Suppose that at the time the risk manager applied for fire insurance the building next door was on fire and that he did not report this fact to the insurer. This fire did not reach the insured building, but three weeks later a fire in the basement caused extensive damage. The insurer could probably successfully deny the insured's claim if it could prove that the risk manager knew about the fire next door and intentionally did not report the danger to the insurer. The materiality of the concealed fact would be evident. The fact that the claim that is being denied did not arise out of the unreported fire is inconsequential. On the other hand, if the risk manager did not know about the fire next door, the insurer would not be able to deny the claim.

Misrepresentation   A *representation* is a statement made by the applicant in response to a question by the insurer. The statement may express a fact or an opinion. Under common law an insurer can successfully plead misrepresentation of a *fact* if it can demonstrate that the factual information is (1) incorrect and (2) material. A fact is material if it meets the condition prescribed earlier. If an *opinion* is involved instead of a fact, the insurer

[7] E. W. Patterson, *Essentials of Insurance Law* (2d ed., New York: McGraw-Hill Book Company, 1957), pp. 408–28 and 461.
[8] According to Prof. Edwin Patterson, a noted authority on insurance law, the application of the law of concealment has not been so harsh in ocean marine insurance as the above discussion implies. In most cases in which the insurer has raised the issue of concealment, the insured knew that the ship was lost, stranded, or long overdue. *Ibid.*, p. 452.

must also show that the misrepresentation was intentional. The following cases illustrate these concepts: Assume that a property insurer includes in its application a question concerning the existence of other insurance and that the applicant answers the question incorrectly. To deny a claim later, the insurer must prove that the incorrect answer affected its underwriting decision. The insurer need not prove that the insured intended to deceive. If an applicant for a life insurance contract responds affirmatively to a question asking whether his health is good, his answer is considered an opinion. To contest a claim on the ground that this opinion is a misrepresentation, the insurer must prove that the answer was incorrect, material, and fraudulent.

According to Prof. Edwin Patterson, the common law doctrine of misrepresentation is confined in practice for the most part to cases involving life insurance. In most kinds of property and liability insurance, the insurer converts most representations by the insured into warranties (a concept described in the next paragraph) by incorporating the insured's statements in the contract.[9]

Breach of warranty A warranty is a condition in an insurance contract. A representation achieves the status of a warranty if it becomes a condition of the insurer's promise. Courts are not likely to give it this status unless the contract clearly indicates that the insured's answer is a contract condition. A question may also arise as to whether the warranty is affirmative or promissory. An affirmative warranty states a condition which is supposed to exist on the date the statement is made; a promissory warranty states a condition which is to exist throughout part or all of the policy period. For example, an automobile insurance policy contains an affirmative warranty which states that no insurer has canceled an automobile insurance policy covering the insured during the past three years. A burglary policy contains a promissory warranty which states that during the policy period the burglar-alarm system described in the policy will be maintained in proper working order.

In order to void a contract on the ground that there has been a breach of warranty under common law, an insurer must simply prove that the condition has been breached. Unlike the situation with respect to misrepresentations, the insurer need not prove materiality of the condition. Furthermore, the courts are more likely to require more nearly literal compliance with a warranty than with a representation.

Statutory modifications The common law doctrines described above, particularly the breach of warranty doctrine, were harshly applied during the

[9] *Ibid.,* p. 382.

eighteenth and early nineteenth centuries, and many insurers took advantage of insureds by denying claims on the basis of breaches which were clearly not material. As a result, many state legislatures have enacted statutes modifying the common law. These state statutes can be grouped into four classes:

1. Statutes declaring that all statements by the insured shall, in the absence of fraud, be deemed representations and not warranties. These statutes are limited for the most part to life and health insurance. All states in the case of life insurance, and most states in the case of health insurance, have statutes of this sort.

2. Statutes permitting the insured to recover unless the breach of warranty or, in most of the states with these laws, the fact misrepresented actually contributed to the loss. Very few states have legislation that modifies the common law this radically.

3. Statutes permitting the insured to recover unless the breach of warranty or, in some instances, the fact misrepresented either (a) increased the "risk" (meaning chance or severity of loss) or (b) materially affected the hazard assumed by the insurer. The type (a) statute seems to imply that the materially will be determined by using the standard of a prudent insurer instead of the standard of the individual insurer in question. These "increase-the-risk" statutes, which are not "contribute-to-the-loss" statutes, are the most common modification of the case law affecting property and liability insurance.

4. One statute (New Hampshire) providing for a reduction in the amount paid under a fire insurance contract if the insured makes a nonfraudulent misrepresentation which does not contribute to the loss. The reduction depends upon the premium paid relative to the premium which would have been paid if the fact had not been misrepresented.[10]

Even such a distinguished scholar as Professor Patterson admits that "it is often well-nigh impossible to determine" the meaning of these statutes.[11]

Among the variables to be considered are the type of insurance to which the statute applies, the type of insurer, the type of warranty (affirmative or promissory, for example), the type of hazard (physical or moral), the effect of fraud, and several others.

In practice, insurers should have little difficulty in proving the materiality of almost all statements by the insured which in current contracts are made conditions of the insurer's promise. As a result, despite academic and legal interest in the distinction between the doctrines of misrepresenta-

[10] *Ibid.*, pp. 349–77, 428–33, and 461.
[11] *Ibid.*, p. 352.

tion and breach of warranty, relatively few court decisions depend on this difference.[12]

The most important difference between personnel insurance and the other lines with respect to disclosure of information by the insured is the presence of an incontestable clause in personnel insurance contracts. In life insurance these clauses vary somewhat among insurers, but their basic effect is to render the policy incontestable on the grounds of concealment or misrepresentation one or two years after the inception of the contract. This is true even if fraud (with a few rare exceptions) is involved. In health insurance, the same situation prevails after two or three years from the date of issue but, except for noncancelable and guaranteed renewable policies explained in Chapter 20, fraudulent misstatements usually still provide a basis for a contest.

Another relevant provision found in most personnel insurance contracts is the entire contract provision which states that the policy, including the endorsements and attached papers, constitutes the entire contract. Because of this provision, an insurer wishing to void a policy or contest a claim on the basis of misstatements by the insured, must refer to statements contained in a written application attached to the policy.

Waiver and Estoppel

In denying the right of the insurer to void a contract on the grounds that the insured violated some condition in the contract, concealed some information, or misrepresented some fact, the insured may cite the doctrines of waiver and estoppel. Legal scholars and some courts distinguish between these two doctrines as follows. A *waiver* is the voluntary relinquishment of a *known* right, whereas *estoppel* prevents a person from asserting a right because he has acted previously in such a way as to deny any interest in that right. A waiver usually involves a statement to the insured that he need not worry about compliance with some condition in the contract or disclosing certain information. Most courts appear to use the doctrines interchangeably. For example, it is common to read that the insurer waived this right and is, therefore, estopped from asserting this right at a later date. This practice will be followed in this text.

Whether the insured will be successful in his claim depends in part upon the time when the waiver was supposed to have occurred. The court decisions can be divided into three categories depending upon when the

[12] The major effects of making a representation a warranty are to make a deeper impression on the insured and to ease the job of the lawyer for the insurer. Courts are also prone to require closer compliance with a warranty.

waiver supposedly took place:

1. Before the contract becomes effective. Waivers by the insurer during this period are likely to result in a valid contract because, the courts reason, the insured is in a vulnerable position since he has not received his contract. For example, if the insured has already breached a condition in the contract on the date it is issued and the insurer or its agent knows about this breach, the courts will usually hold that the insurer has waived the condition with respect to the breach.

2. After the contract is issued but before any loss. This period is the most difficult to discuss because of the tremendous variance in the court decisions. It is possible to state, however, that the insured is less likely to be successful in claiming a waiver during this period than in either of the other two. It is also possible to state that courts in reaching their decisions consider (a) the degree of ambiguity in the breached condition, (b) the authority of the insurance representative who is supposed to have been aware of the breach, (c) the kind of action which is supposed to have constituted a waiver, and (d) the seriousness of the breach.

3. After the loss. This third period offers the best opportunity for the insured to claim a waiver. Insurance adjusters must be careful not to require too much of the insured before they admit their liability; if they do, they may be held to have waived any breached conditions. Insurance adjusters, by first denying liability, have also been held on occasion to have waived postloss requirements such as the submission of a proof of loss within a specified time.

Correction of Mistakes

Sometimes the insurance contract does not express the actual agreement between the insured and the insurer. If (1) an oral contract was made, (2) it was intended that this oral contract be reduced to writing, and (3) a mistake in incorporating the oral agreement in the written document was the result of a mutual mistake or a mistake on one side of which the other was aware, the aggrieved party may seek an equitable remedy of reformation of the contract; i.e., he may ask the court to reform the contract to represent the true agreement. Otherwise the parole evidence rule applies, and testimony concerning oral agreements before or at the time of the written agreement cannot alter the written agreement. In other words, the courts will absolve the insured from reading the written agreement only within certain limitations.

Sometimes the mistake is an obvious one such as writing an address 1856 Larpenter Avenue instead of 1856 Larpenteur Avenue, the first spelling being clearly incorrect. An example of a more troublesome error is the transposition (1865 for 1856) of the numbers in the address because the two properties may not be equally attractive to the insurer.

Standardization

Fortunately for the consumer, insurance contracts are highly standardized as a result of statutory or administrative directives, voluntary agreement, or customary practice. Otherwise choosing among the policies issued by thousands of insurers would be extremely difficult.

In most states the standard fire policy, which is the foundation for all fire insurance contracts, is prescribed word for word by statute.[13] All insurers, domestic or foreign, writing fire insurance in those states must use the prescribed policy. Consequently, (1) the insured need not consider differences in policy language when selecting an insurer, (2) all insureds are subject to the same treatment, (3) policy conflicts do not arise when two or more insurers are required to provide the necessary protection or become involved in the same loss, (4) court interpretations of the contract become more meaningful, (5) insureds and insurance agents save time and energy in contract analysis, and (6) loss experience can be pooled for rate-making purposes. On the other hand, (1) desirable changes may be delayed because these can be accomplished only by revising a statute, (2) a contract that survives the legislative process may not be the best one, (3) the policy designed to meet the needs of the average insured may not meet the needs of many insureds, and (4) the advantages of experimentation and competition are lost.

In some states use of a standard fire policy is made compulsory because of a directive from the state insurance department. The effect in practice is about the same as if there were a statutory policy.

A less restrictive statutory approach is the use of statutory standard provisions under which the state prescribes certain important provisions but insurers can change the wording so long as the revised provision is at least as liberal as the statutory provision. This approach is best illustrated by life insurance and health insurance standard provisions. For example, all state laws prescribe clauses dealing with such matters as the period following the effective date within which any misstatements by the insured must be contested, the grace period following premium due dates within which premiums must be paid, and the minimum values to which the insured is entitled if he stops paying premiums. However, some important provisions, such as those describing the ways in which the insurers will pay out the

---

[13] The fire insurance contract always includes this statutory policy plus at least one form which varies with the type of property insured. The forms are not prescribed by statute. Forms for most types of property may be standardized for insurers using the services of a rating bureau or by a state insurance department directive.

proceeds, are not included among the standard provisions.[14] State laws also prohibit certain types of provisions. For example, life insurers can only exclude certain causes of death, such as suicide, during the first two years or military service during wartime. A similar situation exists in health insurance, most states having adopted the 1950 Uniform Individual Accident and Sickness Policy Provisions Law, which prescribes twelve required provisions (covering such matters as the entire contract, the time limit on certain defenses, reinstatement, and claims notices and proofs of loss) and eleven optional provisions (such as those regarding a change of occupation, other insurance, and cancellation). The provisions in health insurance that are not covered by standard provisions are more numerous and important than those in life insurance.

Most insurance contracts must be approved by the state insurance department before they can be used. Except in the rare case where this authority results in a directive that all insurers use the same form, the effect of this requirement is difficult to measure.

Voluntary standardization is common in many property and liability insurance lines. To some extent, such as in workmen's compensation insurance and automobile insurance, one of the original incentives for voluntary agreement was to make statutory or administrative action unnecessary. The voluntary products are generally known as "standard-provisions" contracts. All insurers using these contracts provide the same basic protection, but they have some flexibility with respect to the exact language and the arrangement of the provisions. These contract provisions are usually developed by rating bureaus,[15] which may also develop a common price for the product. In only one instance—workmen's compensation—has this method produced complete standardization. In the past there was a high degree of standardization in automobile insurance, but increased competition in recent years has resulted in a more diversified set of products.

Other forces favoring standardization are the tendency of businessmen to produce a product that is not too different from that of their competitors and a hesitancy to experiment with new phraseology that may expose them to new risks of interpretation. On the other hand, competition also favors some product differentiation, and insurance contracts are seldom completely standardized. The degree of standardization varies among lines, with workmen's compensation insurance being the most highly standardized field and marine insurance the least standardized. Normally the insurance buyer can expect some product differentiation, but his understanding of the contract issued by one insurer will have a high transfer value in understanding the contracts issued by other insurers.

[14] State laws do require that the policy contain tables describing the options available.
[15] See under "Rating Bureaus" in Chap. 25.

REVIEW QUESTIONS

1. A tire manufacturer offers to repair or replace any tire which for any reason fails to give trouble-free service for eighteen months. Is this an insurance transaction?

2. Which characteristic of an insurance contract probably led to the following court decisions?
   a. An ambiguous provision in the contract was interpreted in favor of the insured.
   b. A contract covering the former owner of a building was held not to protect a new owner because the insurer had not consented to an assignment of the contract.
   c. The insurer was held not responsible for a loss because the insured failed to submit a proof of loss within the proper time period.

3. An agent asks a risk manager to purchase an insurance policy. The risk manager agrees, and the agent binds the coverage.
   a. Who made the offer in this case?
   b. When was the offer accepted?
      Why is the time important?
   c. If the agent does not have the power to bind the coverage, when is the transaction completed?

4. A sixteen-year-old boy purchases an automobile insurance contract. At the end of the policy year, he demands the return of his insurance premium.
   a. On what basis does he make this request?
   b. Will he be successful?
   c. What other insureds may be legally incompetent to purchase insurance?

5. An employee signed an application for individual life insurance on January 10. He did not pay any premium at that time. The underwriter at the home office of the insurer accepted the application on January 17 and mailed the contract to the agent that afternoon for delivery to the employee. When the agent called at the employee's home with the policy, he discovered that the employee had died. Is the insurer liable if the employee died on January 12? on January 18?

6. How would you answer question 5 if the employee paid the first premium with his application and received a binding receipt from the agent?

7. In its application for fire insurance, a firm failed to reveal that a disgruntled stockholder had threatened to set the building on fire if the president did not grant him an interview by the end of the week. The following week the building burned to the ground as the result of an accidental explosion.
   a. Was the concealed fact material?
   b. Can the insurer successfully deny liability in this instance?

8. An automobile insurer customarily asks an applicant whether any insurer

has canceled his automobile insurance during the past three years. The new risk manager of a firm answers in the negative because he believes no cancellation has occurred; but actually a contract was canceled eighteen months ago. The insurer issues the contract, and two months later there is a collision loss.

a. Was this misrepresentation material?

b. Can the insurer successfully deny liability?

9. a. What is the nature of the statutory modifications of the common law doctrine of warranties?

b. How important is the warranty doctrine today?

10. a. At the time an automobile insurance contract was being negotiated, the risk manager told the insurance agent that the firm's two automobiles were encumbered under a conditional sales agreement, but the agent did not note this fact in the application. Since this information is important to the insurer, it refused to pay a loss under the contract when it discovered the omission. Will the insurer be successful in its denial of the claim?

b. A risk manager informed his agent during the policy period that a building would be unoccupied beyond the period permitted under a fire insurance contract. The agent assured him that the period of non-occupation would make no difference, but the insurer reacted differently following a loss. What is the probable outcome?

11. In his application for individual life insurance, an employee stated in reply to a direct question that he had not visited a doctor in the past three years. The employee's answer appears on a written application attached to the contract. Five years after purchasing the contract, the employee died, and the insurer discovered for the first time that the employee had visited a doctor several times in connection with a pain in his chest.

a. Will the statement made by the insured be considered a warranty?

b. Is the insurer liable for the face amount of the contract?

12. How does the incontestable clause in life insurance differ from the incontestable clause in health insurance?

13. Since automobile liability insurance is required or highly encouraged in all states, it has been suggested that each state legislature enact a statutory automobile liability insurance policy. What would be the advantages and disadvantages of such action?

14. a. To what extent have property and liability insurance contracts been standardized?

b. What is the current trend with respect to standardization?

15. Compare the degree of standardization in:

a. Life insurance

b. Health insurance

c. Fire insurance

d. Automobile insurance

SUGGESTIONS FOR ADDITIONAL READING

Freedman, Warren: *Richards on the Law of Insurance* (5th ed., New York: Baker, Voorhis, & Company, Inc., 1952).

Greider, J. E., and Beadles, W. T.: *Law and the Life Insurance Contract* (rev. ed., Homewood, Ill.: Richard D. Irwin, Inc., 1968).

Patterson, Edwin W., and Young, W. F., Jr.: *Cases and Materials on the Law of Insurance* (4th ed., Brooklyn: The Foundation Press, Inc., 1961).

————: *Essentials of Insurance Law* (2d ed., New York: McGraw-Hill Book Company, 1957).

Vance, W. R., and Anderson, B. M.: *Handbook on the Law of Insurance* (5th ed., St. Paul, Minn.: West Publishing Company, 1951).

15

contract analysis: events covered

Analyzing an insurance contract can be a complex, difficult task. The sentences are sometimes arranged in seemingly random fashion; the langauge is often highly technical; and interpretation of the language may require references outside the contract to court decisions, statutes, custom, and negotiations with the insurer. Most risk managers must learn how to analyze insurance contracts in order to comprehend contracts drafted by insurers. The risk managers of some large businesses require this knowledge to participate in the drafting of tailor-made manuscript contracts.

This chapter describes first the structure of a typical insurance contract. The remainder of the chapter suggests a logical approach for determining what events are covered under the contract. The next chapter deals with the provisions affecting the amount the insured can recover if the loss is covered. The steps the insured must take following a loss and other postloss provisions are covered in Chapter 26.

Structure of the Contract

In some lines of insurance the terms "policy" and "contract" are used interchangeably because the contract consists only of the policy plus perhaps some riders or endorsements that extend, limit, or modify the policy. Automobile insurance contracts and life insurance contracts belong in this category. Other contracts always consist of a basic policy plus a form that adapts the policy either (1) to a particular kind of insurance (for example, an inland transit policy plus a merchandise form produces a contract that protects a person shipping goods via common carriers against property losses in transit) or (2) to the needs and desires of particular insureds (for example, a grain elevator form is added to the standard fire policy to adapt that policy to the special characteristics of fire insurance on this type of property). Endorsements that alter the basic contract may be attached.

The provisions in an insurance contract can be classified as (1) declarations, (2) insuring agreements, (3) exclusions, and (4) conditions. In many property and liability insurance contracts the provisions are grouped into these four categories and labeled accordingly, but in other lines the provisions must be rearranged to achieve this grouping.

DECLARATIONS

The declarations identify the insured; describe the property, activity, or life being insured; state the types of coverage purchased, the applicable policy limits, and the term of the coverage; and indicate the premium paid for each separate coverage purchased. The purpose of the declarations made by the insured is to give the insurer sufficient information to enable it, with information from other sources, to issue the desired contract at a proper price. These declarations are subject to the legal doctrines of concealment, misrepresentation, and breach of warranty discussed in Chapter 14 under "Disclosure of Information by the Insured." The insured should check his declarations to make certain that they are complete and correct and that the contract provides the coverages he requested.

INSURING AGREEMENTS

The insuring agreements state what the insurer promises to do. The insuring agreements describe the characteristics of the events covered under the contract. A section of the insuring agreements may also define certain terms used in the contract.

EXCLUSIONS

The exclusions limit the coverage provided under the insuring agreements. They may exclude certain perils, property, sources of liability, persons, losses, locations, or time periods. The exclusions usually serve one or more of the following purposes:

1. To except losses that the insurer considers to be uninsurable because one or more of the characteristics of an ideal insurable risk outlined

in Chapter 11 under "Limitations of Insurance" is seriously violated. For example, wars may affect many persons at the same time, thus violating the independent-exposure condition. Some losses occur so frequently that to include them would raise the premium to such unrealistically high levels that there would be insufficient demand for the contract to permit the law of large numbers to operate effectively. Other losses may be too indefinite as to cause, time, place, or amount, or the expected loss may be too difficult to determine in the short run. Intentionally caused losses are excluded not only because they violate the accidental-loss standard but also because public policy requires such an exclusion.

2. To reduce the morale hazard. For example, freezing of an automobile radiator is not covered under an automobile insurance contract because an insured can easily prevent this loss with antifreeze.

3. To exclude losses that are traditionally covered under other contracts or that require some special underwriting or rating. For example, liability for injuries to employees is generally excluded under liability insurance covering the premises because this liability is usually covered under workmen's compensation or employers' liability insurance, and the extent of exposure is measured by payroll units, which may not be an appropriate measure of other liability exposures.

4. To exclude losses that are incurred by relatively few people, thus removing the cost of these accidents from the premium paid by most insureds. Automobile liability insurance, for example, excludes trips outside the United States and Canada because most people do not travel by car outside this area.

5. To eliminate losses that are the result of ordinary wear and tear and should consequently be expected.

6. To produce a limited coverage that can be sold at an attractive rate. An insurer is more likely to seek this objective through a narrow insuring agreement. Limited health insurance contracts described in Chapter 20, under "Branches of Health Insurance," illustrate the point.

Some exclusions merely clarify what should be apparent from the insuring agreement. For example, the fire insurance policy excludes losses caused by riot unless fire ensues, in which case it covers the fire loss only. If this exclusion were omitted, the coverage would not be any greater, because a riot is not a fire, and fire and lightning are the only perils specified in the insuring agreement.

CONDITIONS

The conditions define terms used in the other parts of the contract, prescribe certain conditions that must be satisfied before the insurer is liable, and may describe the basis for computing the premium. Most conditions describe the rights and obligations of the insured and the insurer following a loss.

A Framework for Analysis

In analyzing an insurance contract for the first time, one should first read quickly the entire contract to gain some understanding of the format and the content. During the second reading the analyst should slowly and carefully seek answers to the following questions from all portions of the contract:[1]

1. Under what circumstances would the insurer be responsible for tho loss? What events are covered?
   a. What perils are covered?
   b. What property or source of liability, or whose life or health, is covered?
   c. What persons are covered?
   d. What losses are covered?
   e. What locations are covered?
   f. What time period is covered?
   g. Are there any special conditions that do not fall into any of the other six categories that may suspend or terminate the coverage?
2. If the insurer is responsible for the loss, how much will he pay?
3. What steps must the insured take following a loss?

The remainder of this chapter will be devoted to the analysis of the event covered. The amount of recovery is the subject of the next chapter and postloss provisions are discussed in Chapter 26.

Events Covered

A particular event is covered only if it possesses characteristics that are covered under the seven-question analysis in the above outline. If the peril, property, loss, time, and location are covered under a property insurance contract but the person seeking payment is not, the insurer is not liable. Consequently a clear understanding of the information sought through each of the seven questions is extremely important.

PERILS COVERED

Relevant considerations in determining what perils are covered are (1) whether the contract is a named-perils or an all risks contract, (2) how the

---

[1] This method of analysis is adapted from the method introduced in Robert Mehr and Emerson Cammack, *Principles of Insurance* (Homewood, Ill.: Richard D. Irwin, Inc., 1952), chaps. 7–11.

covered or excluded perils are defined, (3) the excluded perils, and (4) the chain-of-causation concept.

Named-perils or all risks contracts Named-perils contracts specify the perils covered. Loss by any perils not included in the list is not covered. The exclusions may except losses caused by the named peril on some occasions (e.g., a fire caused by war).

All risks contracts cover all perils not otherwise excluded. In other words, a named-perils contract lists the included perils; an all risks contract names the excluded perils. All risks contracts sometimes cover losses beyond one's wildest imagination because the insurer has not excluded the particular cause of loss. For example, insurers have paid claims because a policeman's horse licked paint off a car.

All risks contracts (1) generally provide broader coverage[2] than named-perils contracts and (2) permit the insured to consider explicitly all of the perils to which he might still be exposed if he buys the contract. In some instances the all risks contract replaces two or more named-perils contracts that would require more effort to administer and that might provide overlapping coverage. On the other hand, the all risks contract may cost more than the insured is willing to pay. Furthermore, he may not want or need protection against some of the perils, known or unknown, included in the all risks contract.

A life insurance contract and many of the newer property insurance contracts are all risks contracts. Fire insurance and theft insurance contracts illustrate the named-perils approach.

Perils defined A few contracts define the covered perils. For example, burglary is commonly defined as "the felonious abstraction of insured property from within the premises by a person making felonious entry therein by actual force and violence, of which force and violence there are visible marks" on the exterior of the premises. Sometimes the peril is defined in a statute. For example, most states have statutes that define a riot as (1) a violent or tumultuous act against the person or property of another by (2) three or more persons. The first part of this definition is important in distinguishing between a riot and an act of vandalism.

Most contracts leave the interpretation of the covered perils to the courts. Courts, for example, have defined the following: windstorm, explosion, accident, collision, and fires. Their interpretation of "fire" is particularly important because it adds so much meaning to the statutory policy and

[2] Sometimes with respect to particular losses named-perils coverage is more liberal. The comparison depends upon the exclusions and the provisions determining the amount of recovery.

because fires are experienced by so many insureds. According to the courts a fire has not occurred unless there has been a visible flame or glow. Scorching and consequent blackening, for example, may not have involved any fire. The courts have also held that the fire must be a "hostile" fire, not a "friendly" fire. A hostile fire is one that has escaped from its proper container. If an object is accidentally thrown into a furnace or oven, the loss is not a fire loss because there has been no hostile fire. Some courts, however, also consider a fire raging out of control to be a hostile fire even if the fire remains in the proper container.[3]

The courts' interpretation of accident as a sudden, unexpected event is also important because some liability contracts cover accidents for which the named insured is legally responsible. Others are written on an "occurrence" rather than on an "accident" basis. Some courts argue that an event is not an accident unless it is sudden. An occurrence, on the other hand, need not meet this requirement. Consequently the gradual pollution of a stream with industrial wastes *might* not be covered under an accident policy but would be covered under an occurrence policy. Some courts also argue that deliberate acts which have unintentional and unexpected results are not accidents, but they would be occurrences.

Excluded perils   Whether the contract is written on a named-perils or an all risks basis, the exclusions in the contract pertaining to perils affect what perils are covered under the contract. Sometimes the courts add exclusions not mentioned in the contract. For example, fires are excluded under the fire contract if they are caused by war or are intentionally set by public authorities (except to prevent the spread of fire). The contract does not exclude fires set intentionally by the insured, but the courts have held that to cover them would be contrary to public policy. Automobile comprehensive insurance covers all perils except collision, wear and tear, mechanical or electrical breakdowns, freezing, war, and confiscation by duly constituted public authorities. Losses caused intentionally by the insured are excluded by the courts. Liability policies written on an occurrence basis specifically exclude losses caused intentionally by the insured. Life insurance contracts may exclude deaths caused by suicide the first two years the contract is in force.

Chain-of-causation   Courts have also contributed to the interpretation of the covered perils through the proximate-cause or chain-of-causation doctrines. According to the proximate-cause doctrine, a policy covering a named peril covers not only losses caused directly by that peril but also

[3] *L. L. Freeberg Pie Co. v. St. Paul Mutual Insurance Co.,* 10 CCH (Fire and Casualty) 255.

losses caused by other perils set in motion by that named peril. To illustrate, a fire insurance contract covers not only hostile fire losses but also losses caused by smoke and water damage resulting from the fire. In fact a business can collect under its fire insurance policy for damage from smoke or water occasioned by a hostile fire next door even if there is no hostile fire on the insured premises.[4] A health insurer is held responsible not only for disability income losses or medical expenses caused by an accidental injury but also for losses caused by a disease contracted as a result of the accident.

Decisions on whether a specified peril is the proximate cause of some other peril depends upon how much space or time elapses between the two perils and whether there was some intervening cause. For example, the walls of a building left standing after a fire may collapse many days later and damage an adjoining building. To determine whether the fire was the proximate cause of the collapse of the wall the court will consider the elapsed time and whether there were any strong winds in the meantime.

Insurers are in fact held responsible for many losses for which the named peril is not the proximate cause. For example, after a windstorm has damaged a property, a fire may ensue and cause smoke damage; the fire insurer must pay the fire and the smoke damage even though the windstorm is the proximate cause.

A more complete explanation than the proximate-cause doctrine is the chain-of-causation concept, which works as follows:

1. Construct a chronological chain of the perils involved. In the illustration cited above, this chain is as follows:

Windstorm $\rightarrow$ Fire $\rightarrow$ Smoke

2. Identify the peril (or perils) covered under the contract. In the illustration, this is fire.

3. The loss caused by all perils to the right of the specified perils are covered so long as they are a consequence of that specific peril and are not specifically excluded. In the illustration, this means that the policy covers the loss caused by fire and by smoke. On the other hand, a theft loss following a fire is specifically excluded under the contract. Many courts, however, prefer to overlook this exclusion, thus demonstrating the force of the chain-of-causation concept.

PROPERTY, SOURCES OF LIABILITY, OR LIVES COVERED

The *property* covered under a property insurance contract may be either real property or personal property. If it is personal property, it may consist

---

[4] The fire insurer may be able to recover its payment from the owner or tenant of the building next door if it can prove negligence on his part.

of a specific item (e.g., a machine, an automobile, or a watch), a specific type of property (e.g., machinery, equipment, or jewelry), or simply all personal property or contents not specifically excluded. The latter approach (1) provides broader coverage, (2) enables the insured to check explicitly the property that is not covered, and (3) may include new types of property acquired while the contract is in force. On the other hand, for a given amount of insurance insurers usually charge higher premiums for this broad coverage than for more specific insurance.

If the contract covers a business building, the building item typically includes machinery used for the service of the building, such as plumbing, air-conditioning and heating apparatus, and elevators. It also includes ovens, kilns, furnaces, and the like, under most conditions. Awnings, screens, storm doors, window shades, and the like, if owned by the building owner, are considered part of the building. Finally, personal property such as janitors' supplies, fuel, and the like, which is used solely in the service of the building is covered under the building item. Commonly excluded under the building item are excavations, underground flues and drains, and foundations below the surface of the ground.

Policies covering all personal property or contents commonly exclude automobiles, airplanes, animals, money, and securities. Policies covering specific types of property may exclude specific subtypes of items (for example, a policy may cover a contractor's equipment but not his trucks).

Liability insurance may be written on a selective or a comprehensive basis. Selective liability insurance contracts cover named *sources of liability*, such as the ownership, maintenance, or use of premises; the manufacture or distribution of products or services; the practice of accounting; or the ownership, maintenance, or use of an owned automobile. These stated sources may be further limited through exclusions. For example, premises liability insurance may exclude liability for elevator accidents. Automobile liability insurance may exclude situations in which the automobile is used as a taxi or a bus.

Comprehensive liability insurance covers all sources of liability not specifically excluded. For example, a comprehensive general liability insurance policy covers all sources other than the ownership, maintenance, or use of an automobile or an airplane and some other specified sources. The advantages and disadvantages of comprehensive liability insurance, compared with selective liability insurance, are basically the same as those stated above in comparing broad personal property coverage with more specific coverage.

A contract occupying an intermediate position between selective and comprehensive liability insurance is illustrated by comprehensive automobile liability insurance. This contract covers only the ownership, maintenance, or use of automobiles, but, unlike selective automobile liability insurance, it applies to any automobiles not specifically excluded.

The *person whose life or health is insured* is named in a personnel insurance contract. Life insurance contracts usually insure one person; health insurance contracts commonly pay medical expenses occasioned by the poor health of the named insured or his family.

PERSONS INSURED

Property insurance contracts may protect only the named insured against losses to property in which he has some financial interest. He may be a sole or part owner, a bailee with a liability interest in property in his care, custody, or control, or a secured creditor. Other persons whose property interests may be covered include such varied groups as the named insured's family, his guests, his legal representatives, his secured creditors, his customers, or his employees. These other persons may be protected against losses to their own property or their liability to the named insured for damage to his property. They may be covered automatically or only at the option of the named insured.

Secured creditors, such as a bank-mortgagee (or an automobile finance company), may receive special treatment under the contract. The usual procedure is to include in the owner's contract a standard mortgage clause (or a standard loss payable clause in automobile insurance) under which the insurer obligates itself to pay the mortgagee even if the owner violates the contract, so long as the breach was not within the control or knowledge of the mortgagee. Under these clauses, the insurer must also give the mortgagee separate notice of cancellation. The mortgagee can also sue the insurer in his own name. If the owner has violated the contract, the insurer has no obligation to the owner but must pay the mortgagee. In return for this payment the mortgagee must surrender to the insurer an equivalent amount of his claim against the owner. The insurer may, if it wishes, avoid sharing a claim against the owner by paying the mortgagee the total amount of the mortgage. If the insurer and the mortgagee share the claim, the mortgagee recovers his uninsured loss first if a foreclosure becomes necessary. If the owner has not violated the contract, the insurer usually makes the check payable jointly to the owner and the mortgagee. The mortgagee usually releases the money to the owner for repairs. The mortgagee could, however, claim this money and reduce the mortgage by an equivalent amount.

A property or liability insurance contract can be assigned by the named insured to some other party, such as a secured creditor, but the insurer must consent to the assignment. The insurer's consent is necessary because the hazard may be changed by the assignment. Life and health insurance contracts are assignable without the consent of the insurer but the insurer is not bound to recognize the assignment until it has been filed with the insurer. In either case the assignee does not become a party to the contract and can collect only what the named insured would have collected except for the assignment. Following a loss an insured can assign any claim he may have against the insurer to some other person.

Liability insurance contracts, like property insurance contracts, may be limited to the named insured or extended to include other persons. Other possibilities are his family, his legal representatives, his employees, friends he permits to drive his car, tenants who occupy a building he owns, and distributors who market a product he manufactures.

The beneficiaries of a life insurance contract are named in the contract. Health insurance contracts usually provide benefits for the person whose health is insured.

LOSSES COVERED

Property insurance contracts cover direct losses or certain types of consequential losses. Direct losses occur because the insured has to replace or repair property that has been damaged or destroyed or that has disappeared. Consequential loss insurance specifies the type of indirect loss that is covered, such as the loss of rent from a property rendered untenantable for a specified period, the loss of net profits and the expenses that continue while a business is shut down for repairs following a covered accident, or the loss of a valuable lease that can be canceled in the event of a major loss to the property.

In addition to paying settlements or court or statutory awards to the claimant, liability insurance contracts provide certain supplementary services such as investigation of the claim; negotiation and, hopefully, settlement with the claimant; defense of the suit, if this proves necessary; payment of premiums on bonds and of court costs that may be incurred in connection with the claim; and payment of expenses incurred by the insured in cooperating with the insurer. Some contracts include a medical payments section under which medical expenses incurred by certain persons are paid without regard to the insured's liability.

Health insurance contracts cover either a loss of income caused by the insured's disability or medical expenses. Contracts may limit the types of medical expenses covered. Life insurance contracts simply pay a specified amount upon the death of the insured.

TIME PERIOD COVERED

The starting and expiration times of the coverage must be stated in the contract. So long as the peril commences before the expiration time, the entire loss resulting from that peril is covered.

Of particular interest are the hours at which the coverage begins and terminates (for example, noon or midnight) and the basis for determining the hour at the time of the loss (for example, (1) standard time or daylight saving time and (2) the time at the address of the named insured or the time at the place of loss). Sometimes the coverage does not begin until some event occurs, such as the departure of a ship or the award of a contract to a successful bidder.

The policy term for most property and liability insurance contracts is usually one year, but it may be some fraction of a year (for example, six months) or some multiple of a year (for example, three years). Some surety bonds run until canceled. Life and health insurance contracts may be written for a specified number of years or for the lifetime of the insured.

Cancellation Insurance contracts may be canceled only by mutual agreement, based upon a new consideration, of the parties to the contract unless the contract contains a provision to the contrary. Most property and liability insurance contracts contain a cancellation provision that gives both the insured and the insurer the right to cancel the contract prior to the expiration date. Neither need give any reason for requesting the cancellation. If the insurer cancels the contract, the cancellation is effective a stated number of days after the insurer notifies the insured, and the insurer must return a pro rata portion of the premium to the insured. The required period of advance notice runs from midnight of the day on which notice is given. In many contracts "notice" means mailing of the notice, in which case the insured may receive less effective advance notice than the number of days stated in the contract.

If the insured cancels the contract, the cancellation is effective as soon as he notifies the insurer. The insurer must return a short-rate portion of the premium. The short-rate return is less than a pro rata return because the insurer is permitted to recognize that most of the expenses other than losses have already been incurred. For example, the short-rate return after 180 days on a one-year contract is 40 per cent. The short-rate cancellation also discourages the purchase of insurance to cover only the more hazardous parts of the policy period.

Automobile liability insurance contracts usually prohibit the insurer from canceling the contract except for a few specified reasons, such as nonpayment of premiums or revocation of the insured's drivers' license or motor vehicle registration. A restricted cancellation provision is required by law in many states and is used in some areas in other property and liability insurance contracts.[5]

---

[5] See Chap. 33.

Life insurance contracts cannot be canceled by the insurer; the insured can stop paying premiums but he cannot recover premiums already paid. Health insurance contracts include a wide variety of cancellation provisions.[6] At one extreme they permit the insurer to cancel the contract at any time after a stated number of days' notice. Noncancelable contracts require the insurer to continue the coverage until the insured attains some advanced age.

LOCATIONS COVERED

Insurance contracts may be written (1) on a specified locations basis or (2) as a floater or floating insurance, in which case they cover losses anywhere within a specified area that is not excluded. To illustrate, some contracts provide protection only if the loss occurs at one specified location; others cover all locations anywhere in the world that are not specifically excluded. Between these two extreme treatments of the locations covered there are numerous other possibilities. For example, policies may cover losses at any one of a number of specified locations, at specified locations plus any new locations acquired by the insured, or anywhere within the United States and Canada that is not specifically excluded. Sometimes the coverage is more restricted as to perils, property, persons, or other features at certain locations.

SPECIAL CONDITIONS

After analyzing the six features of an insurance contract described above, the risk manager may find some conditions that do not fit easily into any of these six categories. For convenience they may be considered extra special conditions. For example, a fire insurance contract may suspend the coverage while there is any increase in the hazard within the knowledge or control of the insured, such as a change in occupancy from a retail store to paper manufacturing, without notification to the insurer. Automobiles insured as private passenger cars under an automobile property insurance contract are not covered when they are used as a taxi or a bus because the expected losses are much greater for vehicles used for public transportation. Instead of being considered a special condition, this automobile example might be considered to be a restriction on property covered. Personal preference will dictate where to include it; the important point is not to omit this factor in the analysis.

[6] For more details see Chap. 20, end of article "Commercial Policies" under "Disability Income Contracts."

REVIEW QUESTIONS

1. The provisions in an insurance contract can be classified as (1) declarations, (2) insuring agreements, (3) exclusions, and (4) conditions.
   a. Describe briefly each of these sets of provisions.
   b. Are contract provisions always grouped into these categories?
2. Do contract exclusions ever benefit the insured?
3. Summarize briefly the framework suggested in the text for analyzing insurance contracts with respect to events covered.
4. Would you prefer a named-perils or an all risks contract? Why?
5. An explosion in building A is followed by fire and smoke damage. Wind carries smoke from the fire into building B, causing further damage.
   a. Are "explosion," "fire," "windstorm," and "smoke" defined in insurance contracts? If not, where are they defined?
   b. What portion of the damage in building A would be covered under a fire insurance contract on building A?
   c. What portion of the damage in building B would be covered under a fire insurance contract on building B?
6. Which of the following losses would be covered under a fire insurance contract?
   a. Wallpaper turns brown as a result of the overheating of an oven.
   b. A plastic container melts when placed on the filaments of an electric stove.
   c. Some valuable heat-measuring equipment is lost when it falls into a kiln.
7. a. Would you prefer comprehensive liability insurance or one covering the ownership, maintenance, or use of premises? Why?
   b. If a property insurance contract covers a department store but not its contents, what property is typically covered?
8. a. The Smith Manufacturing Company owns a $100,000 building on which the First National Bank holds a $50,000 mortgage. The Smith Manufacturing Company has a $100,000 fire insurance contract covering the building. If the building is vacant for over four months (a breach of a contract condition) when a fire occurs causing $60,000 damage, what is the responsibility of the insurer if the contract:
      (1) Has been assigned to the First National Bank?
      (2) Contains a standard mortgage clause?
   b. If the Smith Manufacturing Company had not breached a condition in the contract, how would the loss be settled if the contract contains a standard mortgage clause?
9. In analyzing a contract with respect to the losses covered, what questions would you ask if the contract is:
   a. A property insurance contract?

b. A liability insurance contract?

c. A health insurance contract?

d. A life insurance contract?

10. Discuss the cancellation rights of insurers in:

a. Property and liability insurance

b. Life insurance

11. A property insurance contract covers contents located at three different addresses. Is this contract a floater?

12. In addition to those provisions dealing with the events covered, what two other major sets of provisions remain to be analyzed?

SUGGESTIONS FOR ADDITIONAL READING

Denenberg, H. S., et al.: *Risk and Insurance* (Englewood Cliffs, N.J.: Prentice-Hall, Inc., 1964), chap. 17.

Greene, Mark R.: *Risk and Insurance* (2d ed., Cincinnati: South-Western Publishing Company, 1968), chap. 9.

Mehr, R. I., and Cammack, E.: *Principles of Insurance* (4th ed., Homewood, Ill.: Richard D. Irwin, Inc., 1966), chaps. 8 and 9.

Mowbray, A. H., Blanchard, R. H., and Williams, C. A., Jr.: *Insurance* (6th ed., New York: McGraw-Hill Book Company, 1969), chaps. 10 and 11.

16

contract analysis: amount of recovery

After the risk manager has determined what events are covered under the contract, he must determine how much the insurer will contribute toward his loss. The contract provisions affecting the amount of recovery include (1) those related to the concept of indemnity, (2) the policy limits, (3) coinsurance provisions, and (4) deductible clauses.

Concept of Indemnity

As noted in Chapter 14, under "Unique Characteristics of Insurance Contracts," most property and liability insurance contracts are contracts of indemnity. The insured will not benefit from an event against which he has insured himself. Life contracts are not contracts of indemnity; health insurance contracts are sometimes, but not always, contracts of indemnity.

PROPERTY AND LIABILITY INSURANCE

Four characteristics make property and liability insurance contracts contracts of indemnity: (1) the way in which they measure the loss, (2) the insurable interest requirement, (3) provisions dealing with duplicate insurance, and (4) subrogation rights.

Measure of loss Property insurance contracts insuring against direct loss generally promise to pay no more than the actual cash value of the loss.

Usually the actual cash value is interpreted to mean the cost of repair or replacement less an allowance for physical depreciation and economic obsolescence.[1] Since this concept of actual cash value was used in Chapter 6 to measure the direct loss, it is clear that these contracts do not (if properly applied) result in overpayments to the insured. More than twenty states, however, require insurers to issue *valued* contracts on real estate under which the insurer must pay the face value of the contract if there is a total loss.[2] The purpose of this legislation is to encourage insurers to inspect property before they insure it, because insureds who overinsure in states without this legislation are wasting premium dollars. Although insurers generally have elected to take a chance on overinsurance in these states, the effect of this legislation upon the principle of indemnity is probably slight, because in order for an overpayment to occur, there must be (1) a total loss and (2) overinsurance, both of which are infrequent events. Valued policies are also common in connection with insurance on rare articles because these articles are more easily and accurately valued before a loss than later. Finally, valued policies are common in marine insurance, but the values are commonly based on invoice cost or some other objective measure and seldom violate the principle of indemnity.

Property insurance policies covering indirect losses usually limit recovery to the actual loss sustained[3] and value the loss in the manner in which they were measured in Chapter 6. Some valued policies also exist in this field, however, but the values are usually fixed at reasonable levels. Finally, liability insurance contracts provide the insured with defense services and promise to pay up to the policy limits whatever the court or statutes award the injured party. Although it is true that the insurer may pay more than the insured would have been able to pay,[4] the insured does not benefit from the suit.

Insurable interest   Property insurance contracts also promise to pay the insured no more than his insurable interest at the time of the loss. An insured possesses an insurable interest if he would lose financially if the loss occurred. The extent of his possible financial loss measures the amount of his insurable interest. A sole owner's insurable interest is measured by the possible loss to the insured property, whereas a part owner's insurable interest is limited to his share of the loss. A secured creditor such as a mortgagee has an insurable interest equal to the debt plus the cost to

[1] For exceptions in court cases, see Walter Williams, "Principle of Indemnity: A Critical Analysis," *Insurance Law Journal*, No. 471 (August, 1960), 471–80, and three sequels in the January, February, and May, 1961, issues of the same journal.
[2] In a few states the statutes also apply to partial losses.
[3] A possible exception is depreciation or replacement cost insurance.
[4] For example, the insurer promises to pay up to the policy limits, regardless of the bankruptcy or the insolvency of the insured.

the creditor, if any, of the insurance protection. Other examples of insurable interests are the liability interest of a bailee in property in his care, custody, or control; the interest of a bailee or of some representative of the owner who acts as an agent for the owner, and of persons holding judgments against the owner. Although the interest of a general creditor is considered to be too distant to justify an insurable interest, he achieves an insurable interest when and if he obtains a judgment against the owner.

The insurable interest need not exist at the time the insurance is purchased. A bailee, for example, may purchase insurance on all the customers' property which he expects to come under his control within the next year. The interest must exist, however, at the time of the loss. Thus the principle of indemnity is preserved.

Avoidance of duplicate coverage   Limiting the insured's recovery under the contract to his interest in the actual loss may not be enough, however, to make the insurance contract one of indemnity. The insured could still purchase several contracts and collect under each unless there were provisions preventing this duplicate coverage. Property and liability insurance contracts contain three types of provisions dealing with this problem.

The most common provision prorates the liability for the loss among the insurers involved. For example, if an insured who has purchased a $5,000 property insurance contract from insurer A, a $10,000 contract from insurer B, and a $15,000 contract from insurer C suffers a loss of $18,000, insurer A must pay $5/30 \times $18,000$, or $3,000, insurer B, $6,000, and insurer C, $9,000.

Some contracts provide that the coverage is to be excess over other insurance covering the loss. For example, most automobile insurance contracts state that the insured is protected while driving automobiles he does not own but that the insured must exhaust first any protection he obtains from the insurance on the nonowned automobile. Finally, other insurance is sometimes prohibited, and the purchase of other insurance would constitute a breach of warranty.

Subrogation   The principle of indemnity could still be violated if the insured could collect (1) from the insurer and (2) from some third party who might be responsible for the loss. Common law, however, states that after paying the insured, a property and liability insurer is subrogated to the insured's rights of recovery from anyone causing the loss. The insurer's right, however, is limited to the extent of its payment, and the insurer can recover only after the insured has been fully indemnified. For example, if a $20,000 property, insured for $15,000, is totally destroyed by some tort-feasor, the insurer will pay the insured $15,000. If the insured and the insurer sue the feasor jointly and recover $18,000 net of costs, the insured will receive $5,000 and the insurer the remainder.

Although this right of the insurer is a common law right, property and liability insurance contracts contain subrogation clauses to remind insureds that this right exists and that any interference with this right may result in a denial of liability by the insurer. Sometimes the insurer will waive this right. For example, in a policy protecting a landlord, the insurer may agree to waive subrogation rights against a tenant.

In addition to preventing the insured from collecting twice, the subrogation principle increases the probability that tort-feasors will be punished for their misdoings.

PERSONNEL INSURANCE

Unlike property and liability insurance contracts, personnel insurance contracts are not usually contracts of indemnity. Insurers do attempt, however, to prevent insureds or their beneficiaries from gaining in economic terms from death or from accidental injury or sickness. To understand these statements, we must study with respect to personnel insurance the four principles that make the property or liability insurance contract a contract of indemnity.

Measure of loss   Policies providing protection against medical expenses commonly promise to pay expenses incurred up to a specified amount, but most personnel insurance policies are valued policies. Upon the happening of the event insured against, the policy pays a stated number of dollars even if this sum exceeds the financial loss to the recipient.[5] This procedure has been adopted because of the practical difficulties involved in measuring personnel losses other than medical expenses. Insurers attempt to reduce the moral and morale hazards involved by requiring some reasonable relation between the value and the probable loss at the inception of the contract.

Insurable interest   In personnel insurance, with the exception of medical expense insurance, which probably resembles property and liability insurance in this respect, the beneficiary must have an insurable interest in the life or continued health of the insured person at the inception of the policy, but, with some exceptions, this interest need not exist at the date of the loss. In other words, the situation is the reverse of that in property and liability insurance. Because the insurable interest need not exist at the time of the loss, it is possible for the beneficiary to benefit from the loss.

[5] Some long term disability-income contracts relate the benefit to the insured's average monthly earnings for the two years preceding the commencement of his disability. See Chap. 20, article "Noncancelable and Guaranteed Renewable Policies," under the heading "Disability Income Contracts."

The insurable interest may, as in the case of property and liability insurance, arise out of some financial relationship, but it may also be based solely on *love and affection*, i.e., close blood relationships and marriage. If the person taking out the policy is the person whose life is being insured (and this is the usual situation), the irrebuttable presumption is that the beneficiary has an unlimited insurable interest in the insured's continued life and health.

Avoidance of duplicate insurance   Life insurance policies and annuities make no reference to other insurance covering the loss. The same is true of most individual health insurance contracts, but an increasing number of these contracts provide, under certain conditions, for a prorating of the losses with other policies covering the same loss.[6] The problems created by ignoring other contracts are attacked by requiring the insured to disclose his other insurance contracts at the inception of the contract. Health insurance contracts issued in connection with employee benefit plans usually have provisions dealing with duplicate insurance.

Subrogation   Life insurers do not possess subrogation rights, the theory being that because the value of a human life is unlimited, the insured's beneficiaries should be able to collect additional monies from persons who caused the insured's death. Until recently the same principle applied to health insurance, but medical expense insurance contracts increasingly give insurers subrogation rights.

Policy Limits

Insurance contracts also contain policy limits that state the maximum amount the insurer will pay. These limits may reduce the recovery below the amount indicated by the provisions and concepts discussed above.

PROPERTY INSURANCE

Property insurance policy limits may be stated in a variety of ways. These limits may be classified according to (1) whether there is an explicit dollar limit, (2) whether the limits provide specific coverage or blanket coverage, (3) whether they are subject to special internal limits, and (4) whether the limits are responsive to changes in the values of the property covered. Most contracts cover losses up to a stated number of dollars, but some contracts, illustrated by most automobile physical damage insurance,

---

[6] See Chap. 20, end of article "Commercial Policies" under heading "Disability Income Contracts."

do not include a dollar limit. In these contracts the policy limit is in effect the maximum possible loss to the property.

If a single policy limit applies to many types of property at one location or property at two or more locations, this insurance is called *blanket* coverage. If different limits apply to narrowly defined types of property or to the same type of property at different locations, the insurance is called *divided* or *specific* coverage. For example, one limit may apply to a building, another to machinery, and still another to contents, or one limit may apply to contents at one location with a different limit applying to contents at another location. The effect is the same as if a separate contract had been written on each division of property, each having its own policy limit. A distinction might also be made between limits applying separately to a scheduled property item such as machine A and limits applying to a fairly specific type of property. The major attraction of blanket coverage over specific coverage is the flexibility it provides by making the face amount of insurance available to cover losses to any item covered under the contract. On the other hand, blanket insurance may cost more and be subject to more severe coinsurance (see below) and other restrictive provisions.

Another approach places a limit on a certain type of property but some subclass is subject to a lower *internal* limit. For example, one limit may apply to personal property but money losses may be limited to $100. This approach differs from the preceding case in that the internal limits are not separate, independent limits. In the above example a $100 recovery against a money loss is charged against the overall policy limit.

Separate limits can also be applied under the specific-coverage or the internal-limit approach to different perils, losses, or persons.

Most property insurance limits are fixed at the beginning of the policy period, but some limits vary according to actual or expected changes in the value of the property covered. All contracts without specific dollar limits fall in this latter category. Some, such as automobile physical damage insurance, cover specific items (or their replacements) and thus adjust only in response to changes in the value of those specific items. Others apply to a class of property, in which case new items may be substituted for or added to the original items, some of the original items may be removed but not replaced, and both the new and remaining old items may change in value. To illustrate, take the case of insurance on the contents of mercantile or manufacturing premises where the stock fluctuates in quantity and value. The fixed-amount approach would make it necessary for the insured to carry continuously an amount of insurance equal to the maximum value of his stock and pay premiums for more insurance than he needs at other times, or to take less and run the chance of a loss exceeding the insurance, or continuously to watch his stock and his insurance and add or cancel insurance (at the higher short rates) to keep it in step with his stock. These alternatives entail excessive expense, risk, or labor, or all of them. Hence, *reporting forms* have been developed. These forms provide for a provisional amount of insurance, or a stated percentage of the total concurrent insurance, with maximum limits set for property in each location. Provisional values and a provisional premium are agreed upon. The insured makes monthly reports of values exposed to loss at each location. At the expiration of the contract term the values in excess of those covered by specific insurance are averaged, appropriate rates applied, and the premium adjusted by the insurer. The insured either pays additional premium on coverage in excess of the provisional amounts or receives a refund on amounts by which the provisional amounts exceed the actual. The principal advantage of these forms is that the insured is never overinsured or underinsured. For a large insured with multiple locations, the price is also usually more attractive than for equivalent nonreporting insurance. The principal disadvantage is the effort involved in making the periodic reports. A final example of variable limits is a recent innovation under which the policy limit increases at a stated per cent per month reflecting a specified assumed rate of increase in property values.

Most property insurance contracts provide for reinstatement of the policy limits to their original amount following a loss. A pro rata additional premium which covers the cost of the restored amount is sometimes payable.

LIABILITY INSURANCE

Liability insurance contracts usually contain separate limits applicable to awards or settlements (1) for bodily injuries and (2) for property damage. The bodily-injury limits state, first, the maximum amount payable on account of the injuries sustained by one person and, second, the maximum amount payable per occurrence. For example, under a $25,000/$50,000 contract the insurer will pay no more than $25,000 for claims arising out of injuries to one person. If two or more persons are injured in the occurrence, the insurer is not responsible for more than $50,000 of their combined claims, each individual claim being subject first to the per person limit. If two injured persons have claims of $40,000 and $20,000, respectively, the insurer will pay $25,000 plus $20,000, or $45,000. If three injured persons each have claims of $20,000, the insurer would pay $50,000. The property-damage limit is usually a stated amount per occurrence.

Single-limit liability insurance contracts are becoming more common. A maximum amount is payable per occurrence, regardless of the number of persons involved and the mix of bodily injuries and property damage. Because of this flexibility, a $25,000 single-limit contract is more liberal than a policy with $10,000/$20,000 bodily-injury limits and a $5,000 property-damage limit.

Most liability insurance contracts provide the same protection for each occurrence during the policy period, but sometimes aggregate limits state the insurer's maximum liability for all such events.

The defense and investigation costs and other supplementary benefits are not subject to any limits (except for some internal limits on some items) and are provided in addition to the limits applicable to awards or settlements.

Medical payments coverage, often written in conjunction with liability insurance, is usually subject to a specified dollar limit per person. The medical expenses must also be incurred within a specified period of time following the accident. Sometimes there is also a limit per accident.

Workmen's compensation policies do not place any dollar limit on compensation benefits other than those prescribed by statute.

PERSONNEL INSURANCE

Life insurance contracts pay a stated amount upon death. This stated amount may increase or decrease during the lifetime of the insured. If death is caused by accidental means and the contract contains a multiple-indemnity rider, the insurer may pay some multiple—usually double—of the amount otherwise paid.

Health insurance contracts limit the amount paid in various ways. Disability income contracts usually state the amount paid per week or per month and the maximum number of weeks or months the benefit will be paid. Medical expense benefits of all types may be subject to a single amount or time limit, or separate limits may apply to each type of medical expense, such as hospital bills or doctors' fees. Internal limits may apply to such items as daily room-and-board charges and surgical fees. The limits may be doubled if the person is injured in certain specified types of accidents.

Coinsurance and Pro Rata Distribution Clauses

Two important clauses affecting the amount of recovery under many business property insurance contracts are (1) coinsurance clauses and (2) pro rata distribution clauses.

COINSURANCE CLAUSE

The usual coinsurance clause states that if the insured fails to carry insurance equal to some specified percentage of the value of the property at the time of the loss, the insurer is responsible only for that portion of the loss that the amount of insurance bears to the amount required to escape any penalty. For example, assume that an insured six months ago purchased $100,000 of insurance on property with an actual cash value of $150,000. Assume further that the insurance contract contained an 80 per cent coinsurance clause. If the property is worth $200,000 today, the amount the insurer would pay toward a loss today would be computed as follows:

$$\frac{\text{Amount of insurance}}{\text{(Coinsurance }\%)\left(\begin{array}{c}\text{value at}\\\text{time of loss}\end{array}\right)} \times \text{loss}$$

but not to exceed the loss or the amount of insurance, or

$$\frac{\$100,000}{0.80\,(\$200,000)} \times \text{loss} = \frac{5}{8} \times \text{loss}$$

If the loss were $80,000, the insurer would pay $50,000. If the loss were $170,000, the insurer would pay $100,000, the amount of insurance. The answer will always be the amount of insurance when the loss exceeds the required insurance. The answer will be the loss only when the amount of insurance exceeds the required insurance and equals or exceeds the value of the loss.

If the insured purchases insurance from two or more insurers, each of which issues a contract containing the same coinsurance clause, each insurer will follow the same procedure in determining its liability. For example, if the insured whose situation was analyzed in the preceding paragraph had also purchased $60,000 from some other insurer and the loss was $80,000, that insurer would pay $\frac{3}{8}$ of $80,000, or $30,000. The insured would suffer no coinsurance penalty because the total amount of insurance would equal the amount required. If the total amount of insurance in all insurers exceeds the amount required, the liability of the insurer depends (usually) only upon a pro rata liability clause. For example, if the same insured carried $100,000 with the first insurer and $80,000 with the second, the first insurer would be responsible for $\frac{5}{9}$ of the loss, or $44,444, and the second insurer for $\frac{4}{9}$, or $35,556.

Some property insurance contracts always contain a coinsurance clause. For example, blanket forms and reporting forms are available only if the insured accepts some coinsurance condition. In other instances the insured can elect to buy insurance on a "flat" (no coinsurance) or some coinsurance basis. The incentive for accepting a coinsurance clause is a reduced rate. For example, one fire insurance rating jurisdiction offers discounts from the flat rate on buildings as shown in the table in the middle of page 277. The reasons for the different discounts will be explained shortly, but the reader should note the sizable discounts available under certain circumstances.

The purpose of coinsurance is to encourage large amounts of insurance relative to the value of the property. Because most property losses are small, the cost of providing insurance protection without any coinsurance on property of a specified value does not increase proportionately with the amount of insurance. For example, it does not cost twice as much to provide $80,000 of insurance on a $100,000 building as to provide $40,000 of protection. For the same reason, if all insureds with $100,000 buildings purchased $80,000 insurance contracts, the insurance premium rate (price per $100 of insurance) could be considerably less than if they all purchased $40,000 of protection. Consequently, it would be unfair to charge the same premium rate for $40,000 and $80,000 contracts. To state the matter more generally, the premium rate should depend upon the relation between the insurance and the value of the property.

	Coinsurance per cent		
	50	80	90
Type of property and location	Discounts per cent		
Fire-resistant building			
Highly protected community	56	70	73
Poorly protected community	45	60	64
Frame building			
Highly protected community		10	15
Poorly protected community			

One solution would be to prepare a table of rates that decrease as the ratio of insurance to value increases. Each property to be insured would have to be appraised and the relation of the desired amount of insurance to the value calculated. The proper rate could then be obtained from the table. This solution has usually been rejected because the insurer would incur considerable expense in appraising each property presented for insurance. This solution would also be inadequate from the insurer's viewpoint if the property values fluctuated widely during the policy period.

An alternative solution is the coinsurance clause. Each of the coinsurance discounts should produce a rate corresponding to the calculable graded rate for the corresponding relation between the insurance and the property value. For example, the discount for an 80 per cent coinsurance clause should be related to the graded rate for insurance equal to 80 per cent of the property value. The coinsurance discounts should vary (as they do in some jurisdictions) with the type of property and the grade of community protection, because smaller losses are relatively more important with respect to high-grade properties in well-protected communities. The insureds who carry insurance equal to 80 per cent or more of the value can select an 80 per cent coinsurance clause, get the rate discount, and yet avoid any coinsurance penalty. Insureds who carry less insurance but elect the 80 per cent clause will find that when a loss occurs, the insurer will assume that the insured has total insurance equal to 80 per cent of the property value and determine its own liability on a pro rata basis. This approach is less costly for the insurer to administer because it needs only to check carefully the value of the relatively few properties involved in a loss.

Basing the coinsurance on the value at the time of the loss can be troublesome for the insured, however, because he may wonder whether he has purchased enough insurance to avoid a coinsurance penalty. This difficulty is especially evident with respect to personal property which fluctuates widely in value. One solution is an agreed amount endorsement, under which the insured and the insurer agree in advance upon the valuation for coinsurance purposes. Another solution with respect to personal property is the reporting form noted under "Policy Limits—Property Insurance" in this chapter, which is always written on a full-reporting (100 per cent coinsurance) basis but in which the insurance always equals the amount exposed.

If a loss is small, the cost of appraising the entire property following a loss in order to determine its value for coinsurance purposes may exceed or almost equal the loss. Under a waiver of inventory clause, the insurer agrees to waive the requirement of a separate inventory if the loss is less than, say, 2 per cent of the insurance amount.

An interesting variant of the typical coinsurance clause is used in burglary insurance covering merchandise, furniture, and fixtures. Under this clause the insurer states that it shall not be liable for a greater proportion of the loss on merchandise than the policy limit bears to the *lesser* of two values: (1) a coinsurance percentage times the actual cash value of the merchandise[7] or (2) a coinsurance limit. All policies contain coinsurance percentages and coinsurance limits. The coinsurance percentage varies by territory; it is higher in those territories where burglaries are more common. The coinsurance limit varies by trade group; it is higher for those trades with high-value, lightweight items. The coinsurance limit approximates the maximum probable burglary for each trade group, regardless of the value exposed.

The following example illustrates the application of this clause. Assume that the insured purchases a $2,000 contract with a 40 per cent coinsurance percentage and a $4,000 coinsurance limit. The following table illustrates

---

[7] Other than jewelry or property held by the insured as a pledge or collateral which is subject to certain internal limits.

how the amount the insurer will contribute to a $1,000 loss varies as the value increases.

Value	Insurance payment			
$ 2,000	$\dfrac{2{,}000}{0.40\,(2{,}000)}$	×	1,000	(Pays $1,000 loss)
4,000	$\dfrac{2{,}000}{0.40\,(4{,}000)}$	×	1,000	(Pays $1,000 loss)
6,000	$\dfrac{2{,}000}{0.40\,(6{,}000)}$	×	1,000	= $833
8,000	$\dfrac{2{,}000}{0.40\,(8{,}000)}$	×	1,000	= $625
10,000	$\dfrac{2{,}000}{0.40\,(10{,}000)}$	×	1,000	= $500
12,000	$\dfrac{2{,}000}{4{,}000}$	×	1,000	= $500

Note that the answer for all values in excess of $10,000 would be $500 because the coinsurance limit of $4,000 will always appear in the denominator of the fraction. Note also that, regardless of the value, the insured can always avoid a coinsurance penalty by carrying insurance equal to or greater than the coinsurance limit.

Up to the point where the coinsurance limit applies, the coinsurance practice and the justification for the practice are the same as in most property insurance lines. Beyond that point, the mercantile burglary policy imposes a lower penalty upon the insured. The justification for this difference is the difference between, say, fire and burglary losses on large values. A fire loss of $5,000, or 10 per cent on $50,000 worth of contents, is about as likely as a $1,000, or 10 per cent loss to $10,000 worth of contents. On the other hand, a burglary loss of 10 per cent of $50,000 worth of contents is much less likely than a loss of 10 per cent on $10,000 worth of contents. In fact, the chance that any burglar, regardless of the values exposed, would be able to take more than the coinsurance limit is extremely small.

PRO RATA DISTRIBUTION CLAUSE

A pro rata distribution clause may be used in connection with blanket insurance on property at two or more locations. The clause states that the insurance applicable at each location is to be determined by prorating the insurance according to the values at each location at the time of the loss. For example, if four locations are covered under a $40,000 blanket insurance contract and a loss occurs at a location where one-half of the values are located, the maximum liability of the insurer is $20,000.

Without coinsurance or pro rata distribution clauses, the full amount of blanket insurance is available to cover losses to any of the items or locations covered under the contract. For example, a $50,000 contract covering contents at three locations would provide up to $50,000 of protection at each location. Consequently, an insured with $50,000 at each of three widely scattered locations would have complete protection if he purchased $50,000 blanket insurance.[8] In order to eliminate this possibility, blanket fire insurance is usually sold only with a 90 per cent coinsurance clause, an 80 per cent coinsurance clause, or an 80 per cent coinsurance clause and a pro rata distribution clause.

Coinsurance clauses force the insured to carry insurance equal to the stated percentage of the *total* value at all locations if he wishes to avoid a coinsurance penalty; the pro rata distribution clause limits the maximum responsibility of the insurer for losses at each location. When a contract contains both a coinsurance clause and a pro rata distribution clause, the insurer's liability for any loss is determined first by calculating the insurance applicable at the location where the loss occurred according to the pro rata distribution clause. This insurance amount and the value at that location at the time of the loss then become the data for a conventional coinsurance calculation.

Deductible Clauses

The purpose and general nature of deductible clauses have already been discussed in Chapter 11 under "Use of Insurance with Other Tools." Attention will be focused here on the different forms that deductibles can assume. The examples are taken primarily from property insurance and health insurance, where they are most common, but deductibles are also found in liability insurance contracts. Life insurance contracts do not contain deductible clauses; all losses are total.

The first way to classify deductibles is according to whether they apply to each item damaged, each person insured, each accident or illness, or the total losses in a stated period. Deductibles applicable to the total losses in a year are usually called "aggregate deductibles." Both the frequency and the severity of his losses determine whether an insured will have a claim in excess of an aggregate deductible.

Second, the deductible may be a specified amount, a percentage of

---

[8] The chance that the same fire would affect two or more locations is assumed to be zero.

the loss, a percentage of the face amount of insurance, or a waiting period before disability income losses are paid, or it may be determined in some other way. Expressing the deductible as a percentage of the loss differs from the other practices described above in that the deductible amount in dollars increases as the size of the loss increases. Sometimes a percentage deductible applies to losses after first subtracting a stated deductible amount; in other cases a percentage deductible is not permitted to exceed a stated dollar amount. Sometimes the deductible amount decreases as the loss size increases—for example, the insurer may agree to pay 125 per cent of the losses in excess of $100 or more until the deductible amount is reduced to zero, after which the entire loss is paid. The result is a $100 deductible for losses of $100 or less, a $75 deductible for a $200 loss, a $25 deductible for a $400 loss, and no deductible for losses of $500 or more. A related concept in some disability income insurance contracts (mainly workmen's compensation insurance) is a retroactive waiting period under which the waiting period is waived if the disability extends beyond a certain period. Still another type of deductible is a flat amount that decreases as the number of claim-free years increases.

Third, the deductible may apply to all losses covered under the contract or only to certain losses. For example, under an all risks contract the deductible may not apply to losses caused by fire and several other specified perils.

Fourth, the deductible may be a franchise, in which case the insurer pays all losses in excess of the franchise amount. For example, if the franchise is 3 per cent of the amount of insurance, the insurer under a $10,000 contract would pay nothing on losses of less than $300 but would pay the total amount of larger losses. This approach is used primarily in marine insurance.

REVIEW QUESTIONS

1. Describe briefly the four sets of contract provisions affecting the amount of recovery.
2. a. Are property and liability insurance contracts contracts of indemnity? Why or why not?
   b. Are life and health insurance contracts contracts of indemnity? Why or why not?
3. Compare the concepts of insurable interest in (a) property insurance and (b) life insurance.
4. A $50,000 building, insured for $40,000, is totally destroyed by a fire

caused by the negligent act of a neighbor. The insurer pays $40,000 and the insured and the insurer sue the tort-feasor jointly. If the recovery is $33,000 net of costs, how much will the insured recover? ($10,000)

5. Under what conditions would a risk manager select each of the following?
   a. Specific coverage
   b. Blanket coverage
   c. A reporting form

6. An insured suffers an insured loss during a policy period. How will the insured's recovery for this loss affect the policy limits applicable to future losses in
   a. Property insurance?
   b. Liability insurance?
   c. Health insurance?

7. From the viewpoint of the insured, which of the following liability limits is more liberal—a single limit of $50,000 or a $20,000/$40,000 bodily-injury limit and a $10,000 property damage limit? Why?

8. An insured purchases a three-year $90,000 fire insurance contract containing an 80 per cent coinsurance clause on a building valued at $100,000. Two years later, when a $40,000 loss occurs, the building is valued at $150,000. How much will the insurer pay? ($30,000) How much would the insurer pay if the loss had been $130,000? ($90,000)

9. Why should an insured receive a larger coinsurance discount from the flat rate
   a. For an 80 per cent coinsurance clause than for a 60 per cent coinsurance clause?
   b. If he has a fire-resistant building than if he has a frame building?

10. a. Instead of using coinsurance clauses, fire insurers could have graded rates according to the relation (expressed in per cents) of insurance to value. Why was this approach rejected?
    b. What problem arises under the coinsurance approach which would not arise under the graded-premium approach? What solutions are available?

11. Smith believes that the coinsurance clause will not be applicable to small losses his firm may incur because his contract contains a waiver of inventory clause. Is he correct?

12. a. A firm purchases a $2,000 mercantile burglary policy. The coinsurance per cent is 40 per cent, while the coinsurance limit is $3,000. If the firm suffers a loss of $1,000 in merchandise other than jewelry, how much will the insurer pay if the value of this merchandise at the time of the loss is $2,000? If the value is $4,000? $6,000? $8,000? $9,736? (1,000, $1,000, $833, $667, $667)
    b. What is the justification for the difference between the coinsurance provision in this policy and the coinsurance provision in fire insurance?

13. A firm has merchandise at three locations valued as follows:

    Location A: $20,000
    Location B: 30,000
    Location C: 50,000

The firm purchases a $60,000 blanket fire insurance contract with a 90 per cent coinsurance clause attached. At the time a fire caused an $18,000 loss at location A, the property was distributed as follows:

    Location A: $50,000
    Location B: 30,000
    Location C: 20,000

    a. How much will the insurer pay? ($12,000)
    b. How much would the insurer pay if the loss had been $48,000? ($32,000)
    c. How much would the insurer contribute to each of these losses if the firm had purchased instead a contract with an 80 per cent coinsurance clause and a pro rata distribution clause? ($13,500; $30,000)

14. Deductibles can be classified in at least four ways. Explain each of these four classifications.

15. a. If an insurer agrees to pay 111 per cent of losses in excess of $50, what deductible amount applies to a $350 loss? ($17)
    b. If an insurance contract contains a $50 franchise clause, how much will the insurer contribute toward a $30 loss? ($0) a $75 loss? ($75)

SUGGESTIONS FOR ADDITIONAL READING

Greene, Mark R.: *Risk and Insurance* (2d ed., Cincinnati: South-Western Publishing Company, 1968), chap. 9.

Mehr, R. I., and Cammack, E.: *Principles of Insurance* (4th ed., Homewood, Ill.: Richard D. Irwin, Inc., 1966), chaps. 8 and 9.

Mowbray, A. H., Blanchard, R. H., and Williams, C. A., Jr.: *Insurance* (6th ed., New York: McGraw-Hill Book Company, 1969), chaps. 10 and 11.

17

property and liability insurance contracts: I

Insurers have developed a multitude of business property and liability insurance contracts. Instead of presenting an extensive catalog of these contracts with an abbreviated description of each one, we will describe in some detail a few popular contracts. With these few contracts most businesses can secure fairly complete protection against property and liability risks.

This chapter concentrates on the special multi-peril policy program which is the standard version of a variety of package programs developed to provide basic property and liability insurance. It closes with a discussion of several separate contracts that some businesses, particularly large ones, often prefer to the package approach.

The next chapter summarizes some important contracts not included in the package programs: automobile insurance, workmen's compensation insurance, cargo insurance, and surety bonds.

Special Multi-peril Policy Program

HISTORICAL BACKGROUND

Despite its popularity, the package approach, incorporated in the special multi-peril (SMP) policy program, is a fairly recent development.

Until the late 1940s property and liability insurers in most states were authorized to write fire and marine insurance or casualty insurance but not both. Fire and marine insurers could write fire insurance; miscellaneous specified-perils property insurance, such as windstorm and explosion insurance, water damage insurance, and automobile collision insurance, and marine or transportation insurance. Many fire insurers, however, were not legally qualified to write marine insurance nor could many marine insurers write fire insurance. Casualty insurers could issue health insurance, glass insurance, theft insurance, boiler and machinery insurance, elevator insurance, animal insurance, automobile collision insurance, general liability insurance, automobile liability insurance, workmen's compensation and employer's liability insurance, and surety bonds. Furthermore, only the kinds of insurance included in the preceding lists could be underwritten by either type of insurer. Property and liability insurance packages could not exist in this legal environment.

This "compartmentalization" of insurance dated back to colonial times, when the first insurers organized in the United States elected to specialize in narrowly defined lines of insurance.[1] Later this concept of limited underwriting authority was perpetuated by charters and by the insurance laws of most states.[2] Insurers were forced to specialize and new kinds of insurance could be written only if state legislatures agreed to add additional lines of insurance to the authorized list. At first fire and marine insurers were the only property and liability insurers, but in the nineteenth century a new type of insurer, the casualty insurer, was assigned responsibility for most of the newer forms of insurance developed after the Civil War. The New York law was particularly influential because the large population and business market of that state attracted many insurers, and under the so-called "Appleton rule" insurers domiciled in other states but operating in New York had to obey nationally the New York law on compartmentalization.

The arguments supporting compartmentalization were that (1) it contributed to insurer solvency, (2) it promoted equity among policyholders by segregating the assets accumulated from each type of insurance written, (3) insurers could render better service if they specialized, and (4) new kinds of insurance were not written until their potential and their problems had been explored in sufficient depth to convince legislators that the law should be amended. For many years this approach was sufficient to meet the relatively simple demands for insurance.

[1] For example, the Philadelphia Contributorship, of which Benjamin Franklin was one of the organizers in 1752, insured against fire losses only brick or stone buildings in the Philadelphia area with nonhazardous occupancies. Later it decided not to insure houses with trees on the premises, which led to the formation of a new insurer, the Mutual Assurance Company, often called the "Green Tree Mutual."

[2] See R. M. Heins, "Multiple Line Underwriting and Wisconsin Insurer Laws," *Wisconsin Law Review*, 1957, No. 4 (July, 1957), 567–68.

Great Britain, on the other hand, had adopted a completely different approach. In that nation the first chartered insurers were ocean marine insurers, which insured vessels and their cargoes against property losses at sea. Later they added liability insurance on the vessels. Ocean marine insurance contracts were characterized by (1) a broad perils clause which covered at the minimum fire and perils of the sea,[3] (2) property insurance in an amount equal to the value of the property insured, and (3) frequent use of deductibles or franchises. Because of this early marine influence, insurers in Great Britain, unlike their United States counterparts, have always had broad underwriting authority.

Marine insurers were also the first to challenge compartmentalization in the United States. While fire insurance and casualty insurance were rigidly defined and in some states were subject to strict rate regulation, marine insurance was loosely defined and its rates were loosely regulated because of the importance of international competition in this field. Because of their historical development and the many unusual exposures they encountered, marine insurers also tended to be less conservative in their underwriting, particularly in comparison with fire insurers. Consequently, when there arose in the twenties a demand for new, broad forms of protection—e.g., all risks protection on a jeweler's stock of merchandise—insurers writing marine insurance were the only ones able and willing to provide the desired protection. Inland marine insurers also began to write slight variations of traditional fire and casualty insurance at lower rates. Fire and casualty insurers, being prevented by law from meeting this new competition, appealed for some relief. On the assumption that it was not logical to permit this unrestrained development of marine insurance at the same time that fire and marine insurers were closely regulated, the National Convention of Insurance Commissioners had two options—to tighten the reins on marine insurers or to relax the regulations on fire and casualty insurers. They chose the first approach. In 1933 they agreed upon a "nationwide definition and interpretation of the insuring powers of marine and transportation underwriters." This definition, which was extended somewhat in 1953, limited the scope of marine insurance. In principle, a considerable transportation element had to be present before a coverage qualified as marine insurance, but some coverages were included because marine insurers were already deeply involved in this form of protection at the time the definition was presented. Most state legislatures enacted the definition into law.

As the insurance industry matured and as the demand for broader insurance coverages increased, the compartmentalization of insurance became undesirable and unnecessary. By the late 1940s most states had enacted "multiple line" legislation under which state regulating bodies could

[3] See Chap. 18, "Ocean Marine Insurance," under "Cargo Insurance."

permit one insurer to write all types of property and liability insurance plus health insurance, including lines which had not formerly been listed as fire insurance, marine insurance, or casualty insurance. By 1955 such legislation had been enacted by all jurisdictions.[4] About one-quarter of the states now permit an insurer to write *all* kinds of insurance; but life insurance is usually treated separately because of the distinctive features of the life insurance contract—principally its long-term and investment characteristics. Health insurance can be written by life insurers or other insurers because, although from a functional point of view health insurance is personnel insurance, the first health insurance policy was written in 1864 by a casualty insurer, and health insurance is still a sizable portion of the business of many nonlife insurers.[5]

Because the exercise of multiple line underwriting authority involved new risks, new institutional arrangements, many changes in attitudes and practices that had developed over decades, and, in some instances, additional capital, insurers moved cautiously into the new areas now open to them. At first they merely included some traditional fire and casualty perils in one contract. Next they issued some all risks contracts on certain types of property that had not been eligible for marine insurance. The first package contract combining property and liability insurance was the homeowner's contract, described in Chapter 28. Developed first by one insurer in 1950, insurers using standard contracts soon had a program of their own. Because business exposures are more complex than family exposures, insurers were much more hesitant about issuing business package policies. In the late fifties, however, a few insurers introduced some business packages that were highly successful. The first standard package contract was designed for motel owners. Subsequently, similar standard programs were created for hotels, apartment houses, office buildings, mercantile (retail or wholesale) establishments, institutional buildings (e.g., hospitals, churches, colleges, and community buildings), processing or service enterprises (e.g., breweries, laundries, furniture warehouses, and beauty parlors), and industrial buildings used principally for manufacturing purposes. In late 1966 a new special multi-peril (SMP) policy program introduced a common basic contract for all types of exposures. Some businesses, such as public utilities and mines, are still not eligible for the SMP policy program, but they are few in number.

Although all multiple line property insurance (all the combinations of lines and all of the kinds of insurance which were not possible prior to

---

[4] For a more comprehensive development of multiple line legislation than has been possible here, see Heins, *op. cit.*, pp. 563–85, and David L. Bickelhaupt, *Transition to Multiple-Line Insurance Companies* (Homewood, Ill.: Richard D. Irwin, Inc., 1961).
[5] Through the formation of holding companies and the acquisition of subsidiaries, insurers moved rapidly during the late sixties into financial services other than insurance. See Chap. 23 under "Financial Services Combinations."

multiple line legislation) is relatively new, it relies heavily upon three concepts introduced by marine insurers—a broad list of perils, insurance equal to or close to the value of the property insured, and frequent use of deductibles. The premiums for multiple line property and liability insurance are attractive as compared with the premiums for equivalent separate coverages because of reduced selling and administrative expenses, better-quality insureds, and higher insurance-to-value ratios.

STRUCTURE OF THE CONTRACT

The SMP contract always includes (1) a policy, (2) a property form, and (3) a liability insurance form. Endorsements may be attached to either of the two forms. The same policy is used for all insureds. The policy contains (1) a declarations section, (2) conditions applicable to the entire contract (e.g., a war risk exclusion, a right to inspect the insured's property at any time, and a subrogation clause), (3) conditions applicable only to Section I—the property insurance (e.g., a nuclear reaction or radiation exclusion, a formula for sharing losses with other insurers, and a requirement that the insured notify the police promptly if loss is caused by a law violation), (4) conditions applicable only to Section II—the liability insurance (e.g., the insured's duty to report occurrences as soon as practicable, a different formula for sharing losses with other insurers, and a special nuclear exclusion), and (5) some definitions applicable to Section II. The policy also contains the wording that is contained in the standard fire policy that is generally required by state law.

The property form is usually a general property form, but another form may be substituted if the business wants all risks coverage. The liability form is always the same but it may be endorsed in various ways.

The most important aspects of the property insurance and the liability insurance provided under an SMP contract will be discussed below. In each case an analysis of the basic coverage will be followed by a brief discussion of the alternative forms and endorsements that can be included.

PROPERTY INSURANCE

Property insurance is provided under three sections of the contract—Section I, which is the basic property coverage; Section III, termed "crime coverage"; and Section IV, which is boiler and machinery coverage. Section I is compulsory; the other two sections are optional. Only Section I is considered in the first part of this analysis.

Events covered   The basic form provides named-perils coverage. The *perils* included are fire, lightning, windstorm and hail, explosion, riot, riot attending a strike, civil commotion, aircraft, vehicles, and smoke. Excluded are losses resulting from or aggravated by earth movements, floods, and water backing up through sewers or drains unless fire or explosion ensues, in which case the ensuing loss is covered. All war losses are excluded. Limitations are also imposed by the definition of the perils. For example, vehicles must have direct physical contact with the property they damage and must not be owned or operated by the insured or any occupant of the described premises.

The *property* covered includes (1) the building, which is defined to include any permanent fixtures, machinery, and equipment pertaining to the service of the building and other related property and (2) business personal property belonging to the insured or held by him but belonging to others. Business personal property also includes any improvements or betterments made by an insured tenant. Excluded are such items as automobiles, aircraft, watercraft (except rowboats and canoes out of water on the described premises), money and securities, outdoor swimming pools, outdoor signs, and growing crops and lawns.

Newly acquired buildings are covered for 30 days, within which time they should be reported to the insurer if the business wants the protection to continue. Trees, shrubs, and plants are covered but only against losses by fire, lightning, explosion, riots, civil commotion, or aircraft. Personal effects of others in the care, custody, or control of the insured are covered at the option of the insured, but the maximum amount of recovery is small.

The *persons* insured are the named insured and his legal representatives. As noted under the property description, the property of others held by the insured is also covered. A standard mortgagee clause that applies if the mortgagee is named in the declarations is part of the form. Assignments are not valid without the written consent of the insurer.

The *losses* covered are primarily direct property losses, but the contract specifically mentions some consequential losses. The first is the expense incurred in removing debris following a direct property loss. Second, if valuable papers and records are destroyed, the contract covers the cost of research and other expense required to reproduce the original business records, including such recording media as film and tapes.[6] Third, the insurer promises to pay the necessary extra expense incurred by the insured in order to continue as nearly normal operations as possible following a direct property loss to an insured building or contents. Finally, if the full cost of repairing or replacing a building structure new is less than $1,000 and if the insurance on that structure is at least equal to the coinsurance percentage specified in the policy multiplied by the structure's actual cash value, the insurer will pay that full cost. However, this amount will

[6] Without this extension only the cost of blank materials would be covered.

not be paid unless and until the property is actually repaired or replaced on the same premises.

The *locations* of the insured buildings are specified in the contract. The business personal property is covered while in the described buildings or in the open on the premises or within 100 feet thereof. Newly acquired buildings or personal property at newly acquired locations are covered automatically for 30 days. A limited amount of insurance can be applied to cover losses to property (but not merchandise or stocks) while temporarily removed from the premises for the purposes of cleaning, repairing, reconstruction, or restoration. This off-premises extension, however, does not apply to property in transit or while located at premises owned, leased, operated, or controlled by the insured. If property is removed with good cause from premises that are endangered by one of the insured perils, that property is insured for five days while in transit and at their new location. This five-day coverage gives the insured time to arrange permanent protection. The newly acquired property and off-premises coverages apply only to property located within the fifty states of the United States and the District of Columbia.

The *term* of the contract is usually three years, starting at noon standard time at the location of the property involved. The contract contains a typical cancellation clause requiring 10 days' notice to the insured.

Special conditions state that the insurance is suspended—not terminated—(1) while the hazard is increased by any means within the control or knowledge of the insured or (2) while an insured building is vacant (no people or personal property) or unoccupied for more than 60 consecutive days. Specific permission is granted, however, to make alterations and repairs that might increase the hazard and for such unoccupancy, but not vacancy, as is usual to the described occupancy.

Amount of recovery   The SMP contract is a *contract of indemnity*. Direct property losses are generally valued at their actual cash value. Damage to property of others is further limited to the amount for which the insured could be held liable. Losses to improvements and betterments are valued (1) at their actual cash value if repaired or replaced by the insured or (2), if not repaired or replaced, at that proportion of the original cost that the unexpired term of the lease or rental agreement bears to the period from the time such improvements were made to the expiration date of the lease. Valuable papers and records are valued at the cost of blank materials or forms except for the special extension noted above. The limited replacement cost coverage may violate the indemnity concept to some degree. Extra expense recoveries are limited to necessary expenditures in excess of normal costs.

Insureds can recover only to the extent of their insurable interest in any loss. If the insured has other SMP contracts, these contracts prorate the loss according to the policy limits. If the loss is subject to a deductible the insurer is responsible only for its pro rata share of the losses in excess of the deductible. If other contracts cover the loss, the SMP contract does not apply until the other insurance is exhausted. Finally, the contract contains a subrogation clause, but the insured is granted specific permission (1) to release others in writing from liability for potential losses to property on the insured premises and (2) to accept bills of lading that limit the amount for which transportation carriers can be held responsible. Neither of these two exceptions permit the insured to recover more than he loses and he often encounters requests for such releases.

If written on a specific basis, the *policy limits* are stated dollar amounts per occurrence for each described building and for the personal property at each location. The policy, however, may be written on a blanket basis to cover property at two or more locations. Internal limits that may further limit the recovery are the following:

Coverage	Policy limits
Newly acquired buildings	10% of the sum of the limits on described buildings, but not exceeding $25,000
Personal property at newly acquired locations	10% of the sum of the limits on personal property at described locations, but not exceeding $10,000
Off-premises losses to property temporarily removed for cleaning, repairing, reconstruction, or restoration	2% of the limit on personal property at the location from which it was removed, but not exceeding $5,000
Personal effects of others	$500 but no more than $100 for property belonging to any one person. Nothing if loss is covered by other insurance.
Valuable papers and records, reproduction costs	$500
Trees, shrubs, and plants	$1,000 but no more than $250 on any one tree, shrub, or plant
Extra expenses	$1,000

If the policy is written on a specific basis, it must include a *coinsurance* clause containing an 80 per cent or higher coinsurance percentage. This clause applies separately to the property covered under each limit of liability. Blanket insurance must contain a 90 per cent or higher coinsurance percentage. In determining the actual cash value of the property under this clause, debris removal costs, the value of others' personal effects or of trees, shrubs, or plants, and the cost of replacing trees, shrubs, and plants are not considered.

Two disappearing deductible clauses are part of the general property form. Both make the insurer responsible for 111 per cent of the loss in excess of $50. The deductible does not apply to losses in excess of $500. Loss deductible clause 1, which is mandatory in most jurisdictions, applies only to windstorm or hail losses to buildings or to personal property in the open. Optional loss deductible clause 2 applies to losses not involving clause 1 and not caused by fire or lightning.

Section I—forms and endorsements   The basic property insurance provided under Section I can be modified in many ways, of which only a few of the more important examples can be noted here.

Many of the alternative forms and endorsements increase the number of perils covered. One endorsement adds *vandalism and malicious mischief;* another adds *sprinkler leakage;* a third protects the business against *burglary of its merchandise, furniture, fixtures, and equipment.* This third endorsement includes a coinsurance clause of the type explained in Chapter 16, "Coinsurance clause," under "Coinsurance and Pro Rata Distribution Clauses," for burglary insurance. A fourth endorsement covers burglary losses and, for a separate limit, *theft* losses not caused by burglary. An *optional perils endorsement* not available to mercantile insureds except on their buildings or to institutional insureds adds several perils: glass breakage; falling objects; weight of snow, ice, or sleet; water damage (but not sprinkler leakage); and collapse. Mercantile insureds can purchase an *additional coverage endorsement* on their business personal property that adds the perils of vandalism; sprinkler leakage; falling objects; weight or snow, ice, or sleet; collapse; and on-premises burglary or robbery. It also extends the coverage under the contract to include (1), up to $1,000, losses to personal property while temporarily away from the described premises and (2), up to $1,000, losses to property (not in the control of salesmen) while being transported in motor vehicles owned, leased, or operated by the insured. This transportation coverage, however, applies only to losses caused by fire, lightning, windstorm and hail, explosion, riot, smoke, vandalism, and collision or by overturning or upset of the vehicle.

Insureds preferring all risks coverage on their buildings may request a *special building form.* Mercantile insureds can also purchase one of two *special commercial property coverage forms* that provide all risks coverage on their business personal property. One of these two forms is a reporting form under which the insurance amount is adjusted automatically in accordance with changes in property values. The other is a nonreporting form. In addition to covering property at specifically declared locations, the insured may also elect under this form to include property in transit or at locations not owned, leased, operated, or regularly used by the insured. A *special office personal property form* provides all risks protection on property usual to an office occupancy. One of two *special institutional property forms* can be purchased by institutions desiring all risks coverage on buildings or personal property.

Accounts receivable and valuable papers and records can be insured against "all risks" under separate endorsements.

A *reporting endorsement* converts insurance written under the basic form to a reporting basis. An alternative approach is a *peak season endorsement* that increases the amount of insurance during stated monthly periods.

Under a *replacement cost endorsement* buildings and certain types of personal property are insured under a replacement-cost basis instead of an actual cash value basis. The insured, however, must maintain insurance equal to at least 80 per cent of the replacement cost of the insured property.

A *disappearing deductible endorsement* applicable to all losses other than fire and lightning can be used to increase the deductible above the $50 in the basic contract.

Several endorsements relate to consequential losses involving the loss of use of insured property. An *extra expense endorsement* increases the insurer's responsibility for losses of this sort to 40 per cent of a stated dollar amount for a one-month restoration period, 80 per cent for a period exceeding one month but not two, and 100 per cent for longer periods. A *loss of rents endorsement* covers rents lost by the insured because all or a portion of an insured building is untenantable. A coinsurance clause is included, the coinsurance base being one year's rent.

Two endorsements cover business interruption losses. Under a *gross earnings endorsement* the insurer promises to pay the gross earnings that the firm could have made while the business is shut down because of damage caused by an insured peril less those expenses that do not continue. Gross earnings for a *nonmanufacturing* firm are in most cases net sales (gross sales less returns and allowances) less the cost of goods sold. Gross earnings for a *manufacturing* firm are the net sales value of production less the cost of raw materials and supplies used in converting these raw materials into finished stock. The distinction is important because the mercantile firm is protected against interruption to the *selling* process, whereas a manufacturing firm is protected against interruption to the *manufacturing* process. A manufacturing firm which had voluntarily ceased manufacturing in order to concentrate on selling finished goods in its warehouse would collect nothing under business interruption insurance if a fire damaged the manufacturing plant and warehouse, but the damage would have been repaired before the firm would have voluntarily resumed its manufacturing operations.

Because the loss of gross earnings less the noncontinuing expenses equals the net profit loss plus the continuing expenses, the loss which is covered can be computed either way. The reader should note that even a firm operating at a slight loss would suffer a business interruption loss if its operation would have enabled it to meet some of the continuing expenses.

The gross earnings form must contain a 50 per cent, 60 per cent, 70 per cent, or 80 per cent coinsurance clause. The value to which the coinsurance percentage is applied is the loss of gross earnings which would probably have occurred during the one-year period following the commencement of the shutdown. Note that noncontinuing expenses are not deducted from this figure because these expenses would be difficult to estimate, especially at the time the contract is purchased. Since one factor affecting the amount of insurance to be purchased is the value to which the coinsurance percentage will be applied in case of a loss, the drafters of the form decided to ignore the difficult-to-estimate noncontinuing expenses in calculating the value. The insured will therefore have to purchase more insurance to avoid a coinsurance penalty, but this disadvantage is supposed to have been offset by lower premium rates.[7]

The method for determining the amount the insurer will pay can be summarized in the following formula:

$$\frac{\text{Insurance amount}}{[\text{Coinsurance \%}] \begin{bmatrix} \text{probable loss of gross} \\ \text{earnings during year} \\ \text{following commence-} \\ \text{ment of shutdown} \end{bmatrix}} \begin{bmatrix} \text{probable loss of gross} \\ \text{earnings less noncon-} \\ \text{tinuing expenses dur-} \\ \text{ing shutdown} \end{bmatrix}$$

To illustrate the application of this formula, assume that the following abbreviated financial statement summarizes the annual operations of a small manufacturing firm whose operations are not seasonal and have not changed over time:

Net sales value of production	$800,000
Cost of raw materials	400,000
Payroll	200,000
Other expenses	150,000

Assume further that the firm is shut down for three months as a result of a fire and that one-half of the other expenses are discontinued but that

---

[7] Note that in case of a year's shutdown, the insured will collect less than the value for coinsurance purposes unless there are no noncontinuing expenses. He can, however, continue to collect, if the shutdown exceeds one year, until he exhausts the proceeds.

the entire payroll is continued. Under a 50 per cent coinsurance gross earnings form for $200,000, the firm will collect the following amount:

$$\frac{\$200,000}{0.50 \, (\$800,000 - \$400,000)} \, [\tfrac{1}{4} \, (\$800,000 - \$400,000) - \tfrac{1}{4} \, (\$75,000)]$$

$$= \frac{\$200,000}{0.50 \, (\$400,000)} \, (\$100,000 - \$18,750)$$

$$= \$81,250$$

If an insured who selects a 50 per cent coinsurance clause, as in the above example, purchases insurance equal to 50 per cent of the value for coinsurance purposes, he will be protected against total shutdowns for *at least* six months if his business is normally stable throughout the year. How much longer he will be protected depends upon how many of his expenses can be discontinued. If the business is seasonal and the shutdown occurs during the busy season, insurance equal to 50 per cent of the value for coinsurance purposes might not provide protection for even a half-year. It is clear that the amount of insurance to be purchased depends upon the probable period of shutdown, the seasonal characteristics of the business, the expenses which can be discontinued if absolutely necessary, and the premium discounts for higher coinsurance percentages.

One other provision in the gross earnings form should be noted briefly. If the insured incurs extra expenses in order to resume operations at an earlier date than would otherwise be possible, the insurer will reimburse him for these expenses to the extent that his efforts actually reduce the business interruption loss.

If the business is almost certain that it will lay off some of its employees almost immediately after a shutdown, it can exclude a portion of its payroll from coverage under an *ordinary payroll exclusion endorsement*. "Ordinary payroll" is defined as the payroll for all employees of the insured except officers, executives, department managers, employees under contract, and other "important" employees. "Important" employees are those whom employers are likely to continue on the payroll for some time following a shutdown. The attraction of this endorsement is that ordinary payroll is subtracted from the annual gross earnings base to which the coinsurance percentage is applied. If ordinary payroll is a substantial expense item for the firm, this subtraction may reduce greatly the amount of insurance the business must buy to avoid a coinsurance penalty. However, the excluded payroll is not covered even if the insured elects with good reason to retain some of these employees. Furthermore, the minimum coinsurance percentage is 80 per cent. A decision to use this endorsement depends upon the ratio of ordinary payroll to gross earnings, the insured's desire to decide later whether he should continue part of this payroll, the effect of different coin-surance percentages, and relative premium costs. Instead of excluding or-dinary payroll completely, the business may, under an *ordinary payroll limited coverage endorsement,* cover ordinary payroll for a maximum of 90 consecutive days. This endorsement reduces the coinsurance base by the ordinary payroll for a year less 90 days.

An alternative, simpler approach to business interruption insurance than a gross earnings endorsement is a *loss of earnings endorsement.* Like the gross earnings form, this endorsement covers the loss of profits and continuing expenses during a business shutdown. The difference is that there is no coinsurance provision. Instead, for each 30 days the business is suspended, the insured recovers some fraction (one-third, one-fourth, or one-sixth, depending upon his choice at the time he buys the insurance) of a specified total limit of liability.

Section III—crime coverage   If the insured purchases Section III coverage, either a comprehensive crime coverage endorsement or, where applicable, a public employees' blanket coverage endorsement is attached. Only the first of these two endorsements will be described here.

Under this endorsement the insured can select one or more of five insuring agreements:

1. Employee dishonesty
2. Loss inside the premises
3. Loss outside the premises
4. Money orders and counterfeit paper currency
5. Depositors' forgery

Different limits can apply to each coverage purchased.

The employee dishonesty coverage is either a commercial blanket or a blanket position bond. Both bonds protect the employer against dishonest acts by any of his employees. Despite a common belief that fidelity bonds cover only the loss of money and securities, this insuring agreement covers any type of property. Unlike bonds covering only specific individuals or specified positions, blanket bonds do not require the insured to identify the specific employees involved in any loss. A disadvantage of the blanket approach is that each employee is bonded for the same amount while the loss potential is greater for certain employees. An excess indemnity endorse-ment can be used to provide increased coverage on one or more named positions. Related endorsements can be used to exclude certain employees or to apply deductibles to either specified positions or any employee.

The major difference between a commercial blanket bond and a blanket position bond is the statement of the policy limits. The commercial blanket bond limits the insurer's liability to a stated amount per loss; the blanket position bond limits the insurer's liability to a stated amount per person involved in the loss. To illustrate, assume a $10,000 commercial blanket bond and a $5,000 blanket position bond. If one employee is involved in an $8,000 loss, the first bond pays $8,000, the second $5,000. If three employees are involved in a $14,000 loss, the first bond pays $10,000, the second $14,000. In most businesses, fidelity losses involve only one employee, and for this reason commercial blanket forms are the more popular.

The second and third coverages are designed primarily to cover losses to money and securities, but they also provide substantial theft protection on other property. The second covers on-premises losses; the third, off-premises losses. The on-premises insurance covers the destruction, disappearance, or wrongful abstraction of money and securities while the property is on the premises or within any recognized safe depository, from any cause which is not specifically excluded. In other words, the protection not only extends beyond burglary and robbery into theft but is all risks protection. It covers fire, windstorm, explosion, and numerous other perils in addition to any form of theft. The only excluded perils are war, infidelity losses by any employee or authorized representative (but this exclusion does not apply to an employee burglary or robbery), accounting errors, or the giving or surrendering of money or securities in any exchange or purchase. This broad coverage of money and securities is important because most property insurance contracts provide limited, if any, protection on this valuable property. Property other than money and securities is protected against safe burglary and robbery. Burglary of property other than money and securities is not covered under Section III but, as noted in "Section I—Forms and endorsements," can be covered under an endorsement to Section I.

The off-premises insurance also covers money and securities on an all risks basis. The property is protected while it is being conveyed by a messenger or any armored motor vehicle company or is within the home of any messenger. Property other than money and securities is covered against robbery only.

The fourth coverage covers loss due to the acceptance in good faith of illegal or counterfeit money orders, or United States or Canadian paper currency in exchange for merchandise, services, or money. The final coverage protects the insured against forgery losses on outgoing instruments. Outgoing instruments include checks, drafts, promissory notes, bills of exchange, or similar written promises, where the insured makes the promise or is supposed to have made the promise. The forgery may consist of an impersonation of a real payee, a fictitious payee, or some alteration in the amount of an otherwise valid instrument. This coverage protects the insured's bank as well as the insured. Section III can be endorsed to cover incoming instruments.

If the insured elects blanket position fidelity coverage, losses are covered if they are discovered within two years after this coverage expires. Note that this discovery period does not start with the loss but with the expiration of the coverage. If the bond is continued in force for several years, it may cover a loss incurred ten years ago as a result of an act by an employee who left the employer three years ago. This discovery period is important because fidelity losses are often not discovered until some time after they occur. The discovery period under the commercial blanket bond and the other four coverages is one year.

Section IV—boiler and machinery coverage The boiler and machinery coverage that may be added through the purchase of Section IV is principally property insurance, but it also includes some liability insurance. The insurer promises to pay first direct losses to property of the insured damaged by an "accident" involving certain "objects." An "accident" is defined as a sudden and accidental breakdown of the object that manifests itself at the time of its occurrence by physical damage to the object that necessitates its repair or replacement. "Objects" are defined as any boiler, pressure vessel, or other apparatus, but these objects are divided into three groups with special provisions applying to each group. Loss to the property of the insured from an accident is not covered if it is caused by fire or explosions outside the object, even if these perils follow an accident as defined in the contract. Direct property losses are usually paid on an actual cash value basis, but the insured can elect to have the coverage written on a replacement cost new basis.

If the policy limit per accident is not exhausted by the loss to the property of the insured, the insurer will pay, up to $1,000, the reasonable extra cost of temporary repair or of expediting the repair of the insured's damaged property.

If the direct property loss and the expediting expense are less than the policy limit, the insurer will pay any amount the insured becomes legally obligated to pay for damage to the property of others. The insurer also promises to provide the usual defense and investigation services at no cost to the insured.

All property and liability losses caused by war, nuclear reaction, nuclear radiation, or nuclear contamination are excluded.

If other insurance covers the loss, the insurer pays that fraction of the loss that the amount it would pay if there had been no other insurance bears to the sum of the amounts payable by each of the insurers if there had been no other insurance.

One unique feature of boiler and machinery insurance is the emphasis upon loss prevention. Over one-third of the premium is used to pay for inspections by highly skilled engineering staffs. In fact, many insureds purchase this insurance primarily because of the inspection service for which the relatively few insurers writing this line of insurance have become famous. In states requiring inspections of boilers and similar equipment, the insurance inspection is generally considered more than adequate.

The contract, however, does not bind the insurer to make inspections; it permits him to make them. In his selection of an insurer, the risk manager should be very much concerned about the quality and extent of the inspection service likely to be provided. If the insurer does inspect the equipment and discovers a dangerous condition, it can suspend the insurance immediately by mailing or delivering written notice to the insured.

Endorsements are used primarily (1) to add additional objects for which the definition of an accident may differ and (2) to add consequential loss insurance. Illustrative of the first type are the additional unfired vessels endorsement, the machinery endorsement, and the refrigerating and air conditioning vessels and piping endorsement. Illustrative of the second type are the extra expense endorsement and the use and occupancy endorsement. The use and occupancy endorsement provides business interruption insurance but, unlike the forms described on pages 293–296, the endorsement provides a specified amount of daily or weekly indemnity for each day or week the business is prevented from operating. Part of the daily or weekly indemnity is paid if the production or business volume is only partially reduced.

LIABILITY INSURANCE

Liability insurance is provided almost entirely under Section II of the contract. To the extent that property insurance covers the property of others it provides protection against the business' responsibility as a bailee. Section IV includes property damage liability insurance as a residual coverage. The discussion here is limited to Coverage C—Bodily Injury and Property Damage Liability under Section II.

Events covered   The *peril* under Coverage C is an occurrence for which the insured is legally responsible. An *occurrence* is defined as an accident, including injurious exposure to conditions, which results in bodily injury or property damage neither expected nor intended from the standpoint of the insured. Some courts argue that an event is not an accident unless it is sudden, but the inclusion in this definition of injurious exposure to conditions eliminates that possible limitation. The last part of the definition excludes those occurrences that are fortuitous from the viewpoint of the claimant but not for the insured.

The *sources of liability* are the ownership, maintenance, or use of the insured premises and all operations necessary or incidental to the business of the named insured conducted at or from insured premises. This insuring agreement covers all sources of liability not specifically excluded that are associated with the designated premises and operations conducted at or from those premises. Coverage of new premises and operations at or from those premises are covered for only 30 days unless the insured reports his intention to insure these new premises.

Several important sources of liability are specifically excluded. Liability assumed under any contract is not covered, but incidental contracts are an exception. Incidental contracts are defined as any written (1) lease of premises, (2) easement agreement, except in connection with construction or demolition operations on or adjacent to a railroad, (3) agreement to indemnify a municipality except in connection with work for the municipality, (4) sidetrack agreement, or (5) elevator maintenance agreement.

The ownership, maintenance, operation, use, loading, or unloading of most automobiles, aircraft, and watercraft is also excluded.[8] Because courts do not agree on the meaning of "loading and unloading," it is often not clear whether an automobile liability insurer, say, or the SMP insurer is responsible. One way to avoid the delay and trouble experienced in resolving this issue is to purchase both forms of insurance from the same insurer.

Bodily injury to an employee of the insured arising out of his employment is excluded. Workmen's compensation insurance covers this exposure.

The policy covers bodily injuries or property damage arising out of defective products or work completed, but it does not cover (1) claims arising out of the failure of the product or work to serve its intended purpose, (2) liability for replacing any defective product or work, or (3) the cost of withdrawing, inspecting, repairing, replacement, or loss of use due to known or suspected defects in the product or work.

An important property damage exclusion applies to (1) property owned by, occupied by, or rented to the insured, (2) property used by the insured, or (3) property in the care, custody, or control of the insured, or as to which the insured is for any purpose exercising physical control.[9] The third part of this exclusion does not apply to occurrences involving elevators.

---

[8] Liability arising out of the parking of an insured automobile on the premises is covered if the automobile is not owned by, rented to, or loaned to the named insured. The named insured is also protected if for some reason he is held responsible for the negligent operation of an automobile by an independent contractor, such as a plumber, hired by the named insured.

[9] The addition of physical control was designed to counter a court decision that required the insurer to pay for damage to an airplane that an insured was operating without the owner's consent or knowledge. See *Great American Indemnity Company v. Saltzman,* 213 Fed. (2nd) 743.

It is often difficult to determine in advance what property is technically in the insured's care, custody, or control. Because the insurance contract is a contract of adhesion, the courts will lean toward a liberal interpretation of this exclusion, but in doubtful situations the insured should obtain, where possible, an understanding with his insurer in advance of any loss.

Also excluded are liability under "dram shop" laws for manufacturing, distributing, selling, or serving alcoholic beverages; liability for property damage to premises transferred to someone else and arising out of those premises; and liability arising out of demolition operations performed by or on behalf of the insured.

The *persons* protected under this section are the named insured (including partners if a partnership); if a corporation, an executive officer, director, or stockholder while acting in his physical capacity; and any organization or person managing real estate for the named insured. Employees of the named insured, other than executive officers, are not protected by the policy except when operating, for the purpose of locomotion upon a public highway, "mobile equipment" registered under any motor vehicle registration law. "Mobile equipment" includes vehicles designed for use principally off public roads or for the sole purpose of moving such equipment as power cranes, shovels, air compressors, and generators that are an integral part of the vehicle. Indeed, any person operating this equipment with the permission of the named insured is covered.[10]

Several kinds of *losses* are covered under the contract. First, the insurer promises to pay all sums that the insured becomes legally obligated to pay as a result of bodily injury or property damage. "Bodily injury" is defined as bodily injury, sickness, or disease sustained by any person. It does not include personal injuries such as libel, slander, false arrest, and invasion of privacy. "Property damage" is defined as injury to or destruction of tangible property. It does not include damage to intangible interests such as an infringement of patents or copyrights or unfair trade competition.

Second, the insurer will pay expenses incurred by the insured in order to provide necessary immediate medical and surgical relief at the scene of the accident. This relief includes such items as first aid and transportation to a hospital in an ambulance. The insurer pays these costs even if the insured is not liable, but if some other party is responsible, the insurer has the right through subrogation to collect from that party.

Third, the insurer promises to defend at its expense any suit against

---

[10] No employee or other person is covered with respect to bodily injuries to any fellow employees. Although workmen's compensation is the exclusive remedy of an injured employee against his employer, several states permit the injured employee to sue a negligent fellow employee. This exclusion removes the insurer from such a suit.

the insured coming within the scope of the policy even if the suit is ground-less, false, or fraudulent. However, the insurer need not defend the insured in court if it decides that a negotiated settlement would be a better solution. If the case goes to court, the insurer promises to pay the premiums on release of attachment and appeal bonds. It will pay all costs levied against the insured and *all* interest accruing after the judgment has been entered until it has paid its share of that judgment. Finally, it promises to reimburse the insured for all reasonable expenses incurred at the insurer's request, including loss of wages not to exceed $25 per day because he attends hearings or trials.

The bodily injury or damage must occur at *locations* within the following territory: the United States, its territories or possessions, or Canada; interna-tional waters or air space (but the injury or damage cannot occur in the course of transportation to or from any country other than Canada); and anywhere in the world if the injury or damage arises out of a product sold for use within the United States or Canada.

The *time* period is the same as for property insurance.

Amount of recovery   The insurer's maximum responsibility with respect to negotiated settlements or judgments is a stated amount per occurrence. All injury or damage arising out of continuous or repeated exposure to substantially the same general conditions is considered to arise out of one occurrence. In addition three types of claims are subject separately to an aggregate limit applicable to all claims paid during each annual period the policy is in force. The three types of claims are (1) property damage arising out of the premises or operations of most manufacturers and contractors, (2) property damage arising out of the operations of independent contractors, and (3) bodily injury and property damage associated with the product or com-pleted operations hazard. However, the second type of claim does not include maintenance of or repairs to premises owned by or rented to the named insured or structural alterations at such premises that do not involve chang-ing the size of or moving buildings. The products hazard is limited to injuries or damage occurring (1) away from premises owned by or rented to the named insured and (2) after the insured has relinquished possession of the property. Other occurrences involving products are not subject to an ag-gregate limit. The completed operations hazard is a similar concept. The injury or damage must occur away from the insured's premises and after the operation has been supposedly completed or abandoned. It is further agreed that accidents involving tools, uninstalled equipment, and abandoned or unused materials do not fall in this category.

If this insurance and other insurance apply to a loss on the same basis, and if all other valid and collectible insurance provides for contribution by equal shares, the insurer will contribute on that basis. Each insurer pays an equal share until the share of each insurer equals the lowest applicable limit or until the full amount of the loss is paid; the remaining insurers then contribute equal shares of the remaining loss on the same basis until each insurer has paid its limit or the full amount of the loss has been paid. For example, if the SMP limit is $50,000 per occurrence and another policy exists with a single limit of $25,000, the SMP insurer will pay $10,000 on a $20,000 claim and $35,000 on a $60,000 claim. If any of the other insurance does not provide for contribution by equal shares, the insurer pays that fraction of the loss that its limit bears to the total applicable limits. In the example used to illustrate the contribution-by-shares formula, the SMP insurer would pay two-thirds of both claims.

The insurer is subrogated to the insured's rights of recovery against other parties.

Endorsements   Important endorsements modify either the perils or the sources of liability covered. Under a *personal injury liability insurance endorsement* the insured may add one or more of the following types of offenses: false arrest, detention or imprisonment, or malicious prosecution; libel, slander, defamation, or violation of the right of privacy; and wrongful entry, eviction, or other invasion of the right of private occupancy. A *comprehensive general liability insurance endorsement* provides automatic coverage of new premises and operations. *An employer's non-ownership automobile liability insurance endorsement* adds coverage for (1) the use by any person, other than the insured, of a non-owned private passenger automobile in the business of the insured or (2) the occasional use by an employee of the insured of a non-owned commercial automobile in the insured's business. An *exclusion endorsement* is available that will exclude the products and completed operations hazard.

HEALTH INSURANCE

Coverage D—Premises Medical Payments under Section II is neither property insurance nor liability insurance. The insurer promises to pay, regardless of liability, all reasonable medical expenses incurred within one year by a person who sustains bodily injury caused by an accident arising out of (1) the premises or (2) operations with respect to which the insured has liability coverage under Coverage C. This, then, is a special form of health insurance.

Medical payments insurance may be purchased as goodwill insurance. From the viewpoint of the insurer, this insurance may also reduce the insured's temptation to admit legal responsibility when it did not exist but when he felt some moral responsibility or when the injured party was a friend. Medical payments insurance reduces this temptation because the insured knows that at least the injured party's medical expenses will be paid. Voluntary payment of medical expenses may also avert a claim by the injured party. On the other hand, because the medical payments coverage is independent of the liability coverage, the injured party could also collect twice for the same medical expenses when negligence is involved—once under the medical payments section and once as the result of a suit.

In addition to the exclusions applicable to the liability coverage, this insurance does not apply to bodily injury (1) associated with the products hazard or the completed operations hazard, (2) arising out of the operations of independent contractors other than maintenance, repair, or minor structural alterations of the insured premises, or (3) sustained by the named insured, any tenant, employee, or any independent contractor engaged in maintenance, repairs, or structural alterations or demolition at the insured premises.

The policy states a maximum amount the insurer will contribute toward the medical expenses incurred by each person as the result of one accident. A separate dollar limit applies to the total expenses incurred by two or more persons as a result of one accident.

There is no provision dealing with duplicate insurance, but the insurer is subrogated to the insured's right of recovery against other persons.

Separate Property Insurance

Some businesses are ineligible for the SMP package or the equivalent protection issued by independent insurers. Others, particularly the larger firms, prefer to purchase each type of insurance from the insurer offering the best combination of coverage, service, and price for that type of insurance. Large businesses develop so much premium in one line of insurance that they may be able to obtain special concessions on each type of coverage. Tailor-made manuscript policies may be drafted to meet their needs. The discussion here, however, is limited to a brief description of the leading conventional separate property contracts that may serve as an alternative to the package contracts. Some insurers sell a portfolio of these contracts placed in a folder with the entire account being subject to one rating plan.

FIRE, EXTENDED COVERAGE, AND VANDALISM INSURANCE

Businesses may purchase fire insurance contracts covering their building, its contents, or both against the perils of fire and lightning. The contract may include an extended coverage endorsement that adds windstorm, hail, explosion, riot, riot attending a strike, civil commotion, aircraft damage, vehicle damage, and smoke. A vandalism endorsement adds the vandalism peril. With respect to these perils the coverage closely resembles the basic protection provided under the SMP package policy. Business interruption insurance, extra expense insurance, and other consequential losses can be added by endorsement.

COMMERCIAL PROPERTY FORM

The commercial property form, attached to a fire policy, provides "all risk" coverage for most retailers and wholesalers. War, infidelity of employees, flood, and earthquakes are among the excluded perils. The property insured is the insured's stock of goods, wares, and merchandise and, if he so desires, his furniture, fixtures, and equipment (other than machinery in a manufacturing plant). Important excluded property is money, securities, and automobiles. The policy covers property anywhere within the continental United States or in transit in Canada. There is no coverage, however, on shipments by mail or by boat.

Separate policy limits apply to losses at various locations. The form can be written on a nonreporting basis with an 80, 90, or 100 per cent coinsurance clause or on a reporting basis. A $50 deductible applies to all losses except those caused by certain specified perils.

MANUFACTURER'S OUTPUT POLICY

Most manufacturers are not eligible for the commercial property form but a special manufacturer's output policy providing similar "all risks" protection has been designed for large firms in this group. The policy does not cover property on the insured's manufacturing premises unless there is an endorsement, which is in common use, covering this location. This form is always written on a reporting basis and runs until canceled. Although no deductible clause is mandatory, most insurers encourage a minimum deductible of $50. The maximum deductible is $5,000.

OFFICE CONTENTS FORM

An office contents form has been developed for many businesses with office exposures that are separated from the fire hazards associated with a mercantile or manufacturing occupancy. The form provides "all risk" coverage on office contents consisting principally of furniture, fixtures, equipment, and supplies. Ten per cent of the insurance at all locations, but not in excess of $10,000, is available for off-premises losses.

MARINE PROPERTY FLOATERS

As mentioned at the beginning of the present chapter, inland marine insurers wrote some broad-coverage floater contracts that included a considerable transportation element prior to multiple line legislation. They also wrote some contracts prior to the Nationwide Definition that involve little transportation insurance but which they were permitted to continue under a grandfather clause. Four important types of marine business floaters that cover exposures similar to those under the SMP Policy are (1) equipment floaters, (2) merchandise or stock floaters in the hands of others, (3) bailee's customers contracts covering property in the hands of the insured, and (4) block policies.

Equipment floaters   Equipment floaters cover movable property which is being used by the insured in his business, but they exclude merchandise on sale or consignment or in course of manufacture. Illustrations of equipment floaters which indicate the type of property covered are (1) a contractor's equipment floater covering power shovels, air compressors, concrete mixers, pumps, boilers, bulldozers, caterpillar tractors, scaffolding, and the like, (2) a farm equipment floater, (3) an oil-well-drilling equipment floater, and (4) a physician's, surgeon's, and scientific-instrument floater. Some of these contracts are written on an all risks basis, but most of them contain a long list of specified perils. Most of these floaters do not protect property on the insured's premises. Some of the contracts, however, do provide coverage when the location of the property at the insured's premises is incidental to its frequent use off the premises.

Merchandise or stock floaters covering property in the hands of others   For many reasons, a business may have placed its property in the hands of others, and this property is subject to transportation perils. A partial listing of the business floaters which will protect the insured in such cases is given below.

Processing risk contracts protect an owner against loss to his goods while they are en route to or from or in the hands of some other person for some type of processing. For example, a garment contractor's floater provides a clothing manufacturer with all risk protection on his property while it is being sent to, in the hands of, or being returned by, contractors or subcontractors who insert shoulder pads, make buttonholes, embroider the material, or process the clothing in some other way.

Consignment floaters cover property consigned to a factor or agent for various purposes. The consignment may be for exhibit, trial, auction, approval, distribution, or sale. These floaters, in addition to covering the property in transit, provide coverage at the consignee's premises.

Bailee's customers' insurance   Bailee liability insurance protects a bailee against liability for damage to property in his care, custody, or control.

Bailee's customers' insurance enables the bailee to protect his customers' goods, regardless of his liability for the damage. Bailees may purchase this insurance in order to improve relationships with their customers. Although bailee's customers' insurance is not limited to inland marine insurance, it has been most fully developed by marine insurers. The most common purchasers of inland marine bailee's customers' insurance are laundries, dry cleaners, tailors, cold-storage companies, and furriers. Other processors and consignees may also be interested in this insurance, which protects the property from the time the bailee accepts the goods until they are returned to the customer. Policies issued to laundries, dry cleaners, and tailors exclude damage to property that is stored, but stored property is the principal subject of insurance issued to cold-storage companies and furriers. Since the insurance is usually written on a full reporting basis, most contracts contain no coinsurance clause.

Most bailee's customers' contracts are specified-perils contracts, but furrier's customers' insurance is all risks insurance. Typical perils under the specified-perils contracts are fire; the extended coverage perils; vandalism; earthquake; sprinkler leakage; flood; theft; collapse of structure, bridges, or culverts; collision, upset, or overturn of transporting conveyance; and stranding, sinking, burning, or collision of a regular ferry. Inability to identify goods because of the attendant confusion is also covered. Losses caused by war or infidelity of the insured's employees are excluded.

Block policies Inland marine insurers are permitted to issue block policies resembling the commercial property form only to jewelers, musical-instrument dealers, camera dealers, fur dealers, and heavy agricultural- and construction-equipment dealers. Until the development of multiple line contracts, most merchants could not obtain the comprehensive protection afforded by the block policies, which served as the models for many multiple line contracts.

THEFT AND DISHONESTY INSURANCE

Theft insurance contracts may be divided into two basic coverages: (1) limited and (2) comprehensive or broad-form contracts. The limited contracts protect the business against particular types of theft, such as burglary, safe burglary, and robbery. Comprehensive contracts cover any form of theft. The two contracts that best illustrate this group are (1) the comprehensive destruction, disappearance, and dishonesty policy, which is equivalent to Section III of the SMP package, and (2) the money and securities broad form, which is the equivalent of the on-premises and off-premises insuring agreements under Section III. The 3-D contract can be endorsed to provide mercantile burglary insurance, mercantile theft insurance, burglary coverage on office equipment, theft coverage on office equipment, and forgery insurance on incoming instruments.

BOILER AND MACHINERY INSURANCE

Boiler and machinery insurance similar to that provided under Section IV of the SMP contract is often purchased separately. The principal reason for buying this insurance individually instead of on a package basis is that some insurers are noted for their inspection services.

Separate Liability Insurance

The liability insurance provided under an SMP contract is general liability insurance. General liability insurance that can be purchased separately includes (1) comprehensive general liability insurance, (2) owner's, landlord's, and tenant's liability insurance, (3) manufacturer's and contractor's liability insurance, (4) professional liability insurance, and (5) umbrella liability insurance. The last two types of insurance will be described in greater detail than the first three because they may be purchased in addition to an SMP policy.

COMPREHENSIVE GENERAL LIABILITY INSURANCE

Comprehensive general liability insurance provides basically the same coverage as the SMP contract with a comprehensive general liability endorsement attached to Section II. All sources of liability not excluded are covered. However, bodily injury payments are limited to stated amounts per person and per occurrence. An aggregate limit applies to payments on account of the completed operations—product hazard. Property damage payments are subject to a separate limit per occurrence, with aggregate limits also applying to some insureds, to certain operations by independent contractors, and to the completed operations—products hazard.

OWNER'S, LANDLORD'S, AND TENANT'S LIABILITY INSURANCE

O. L. & T. insurance resembles the SMP Section II basic coverage in that it covers the ownership, maintenance, or use of the insured premises and all operations necessary or incidental thereto. However, the contract specifically excludes (1) the completed operations—products hazard and (2) injury or damage arising out of structural alterations that involve changing the size of or moving buildings, new construction, or demolition operations. The second exclusion can be deleted if the insured is willing to pay an extra premium. The completed operations–products liability exclusion cannot be removed. Separate completed operations–products liability insurance is available for firms that wish to insure only this hazard. Persons who seek this type of protection plus O. L. & T. liability insurance should buy comprehensive general liability insurance. Unlike the SMP coverage, O. L. & T. insurance has separate limits for bodily-injury payments and property damage payments.

MANUFACTURER'S AND CONTRACTOR'S LIABILITY INSURANCE

The M. & C. coverage closely resembles O. L. & T. insurance except that it is designed for a different type of insured whose premiums are determined on a different basis. Because contractors in particular may be engaged in many projects involving structural alterations, construction, and demolition, the exclusion of these sources of liability would greatly reduce the usefulness of this insurance. Consequently this exclusion is replaced by one that excludes operations performed for the named insured by independent contractors except maintenance and repairs at premises owned by or rented to the named insured or minor structural alterations at such premises. An *independent-contractor's liability insurance coverage part* is available to cover this exposure.

PROFESSIONAL LIABILITY INSURANCE

Professional liability is usually excluded by endorsement under the policies heretofore described, when the insured has a significant exposure of this sort. To fill this gap, a wide variety of professional liability policies has been developed. Illustrative of these contracts are a druggist's liability policy; a hospital professional liability policy; a physician's, surgeon's, and dentist's professional liability policy, a lawyer's professional liability policy, and an insurance agent's and broker's errors and omissions liability policy. Many of these coverages can be written as endorsements to other liability insurance contracts. In each case the insurer agrees essentially to pay all sums which the insured becomes legally obligated to pay because of damages arising out of malpractice, error, or mistakes in rendering or failing to render the appropriate professional services. A detailed analysis of these contracts would reveal some significant differences that we cannot consider in this text. It is important, however, to indicate some important differences between the typical professional liability insurance policy and most other general liability insurance policies.

1. Most professional liability policies limit the insurer's liability to a stated amount per claim and a stated amount per occurrence. Several claims may be associated with injury to a single person. No distinction is made between injuries to persons and injuries to property.

2. Except with respect to some product liability losses, professional liability policies exclude the kinds of losses which are covered under other general liability insurance contracts. A hospital or a druggist, for example, still has need for other types of general liability insurance.

3. Professional liability insurance applies to claims arising out of services which were performed or should have been performed during the policy term, even if the accident, such as the taking of a drug, occurs later.

4. Under many professional liability insurance policies, the insurer does not have the right to settle a claim in the manner it deems most expedient. Because the insured's professional reputation and his livelihood may be at stake, the insurer may not be permitted to negotiate a settlement with the plaintiff without the insured's consent.

UMBRELLA LIABILITY INSURANCE

"Umbrella" liability insurance, which until recently was available only from insurers domiciled abroad, provides two types of protection. First, umbrella insurance is excess insurance over the insured's traditional liability insurance policies of all sorts—general liability, automobile liability, aviation liability, workmen's compensation, and others. Second, umbrella insurance covers sources of liability not covered under the insured's other liability policies, usually subject to a minimum deductible of $25,000 per occurrence. Illustrations might be contractual liability not covered under the primary insurance, non-owned aircraft liability insurance, and liability for invasion of privacy in an advertisement. The maximum limit of liability under the umbrella insurance is usually at least $100,000 per occurrence and may range as high as $25 million or more per occurrence.

To obtain umbrella liability insurance, a business must have certain basic liability insurance protection. For example, the bodily-injury–liability limits must be at least $100,000 per person and $300,000 per accident. The underlying general liability insurance contract must be a comprehensive general liability insurance policy. If this underlying contract does not protect the insured against product liability or liability for personal injuries arising out of false arrest, libel and slander, or invasion of privacy, the deductible with respect to these losses is usually raised to $100,000 per occurrence.

REVIEW QUESTIONS

1. Could the special multi-peril policy program have been developed in 1940 if insurers had wanted to do so? Explain your answer.
2. a. What characteristics do multiple line property insurance and marine insurance share?

   b. Why is an SMP contract less expensive than equivalent separate coverages?
3. What are the (a) mandatory and (b) optional parts of an SMP contract?
4. Which of the following property losses would be covered under Section I of an SMP contract issued to a department store occupying a rented building? Explain your answers.

   a. Fire destroys some merchandise held for sale.

   b. Fire destroys $200 in cash belonging to the store.

   c. A burglar steals some merchandise held for sale.

   d. A windstorm damages some permanent improvements the store has made to the real estate.

   e. Vandals cause some damage to desks and chairs owned by the store.

   f. Some merchandise being delivered to a customer In a truck owned by the store is destroyed in a collision.

   g. A steam boiler explodes, causing damage to the boiler itself, the building, some furniture and equipment, and some merchandise.

   h. A fire causes the store to cease operations for two months. As a result the store loses $30,000 in profits and continuing expenses.

   i. A windstorm causes damage to merchandise located in a warehouse acquired 15 days earlier but not reported to the insurer.

   j. An explosion damages some customers' goods being repaired at the store.
5. An SMP contract has the following Section I policy limits:

Building at location 1	$100,000
Personal property at locations 1 and 2	60,000

   a. What internal limits affect the recovery under this policy?

   b. What are the minimum coinsurance percentages possible under the building and the contents coverages?

   c. What deductible clause is compulsory under this form?
6. In question 4 which losses would be covered if the department store had a special commercial property coverage form attached to Section I of the SMP contract?

7. Assume the following annual data for a department store with an SMP contract and stable operations from month to month:

Net sales	$750,000
Cost of goods sold	350,000
Payroll	200,000
Other expenses	140,000

a. If the SMP contract has a gross earnings endorsement with a face amount of $100,000 and a 60 per cent coinsurance clause, how much will the insurer pay if the store must cease operations for three months because of explosion damage? Assume that during these three months half of the payroll and other expenses continue.

b. How much insurance would the store need to recover this loss in full?

8. Contrast the crime coverage available under Section III of the SMP contract with that available through endorsements to Section I.

9. Describe briefly the protection provided under Section IV of the SMP contract.

10. Which of the following liability losses is covered under Section II of an SMP contract issued to a department store occupying rented premises?

a. An employee trips a customer with an extension cord.

b. A customer is injured in a defective revolving door.

c. A customer slips on a greasy substance on an escalator.

d. Employees of a contractor hired to build an addition to the building drop a plank on a bystander's leg.

e. A customer who has bought a power mower is injured, while cutting his grass, when the blade comes loose from the shaft.

f. A customer trying out a ladder in the store is injured when one of the steps breaks under his weight.

g. A customer is embarrassed when he is falsely accused of shoplifting and arrested.

h. An employee is injured while riding in an elevator.

i. A fire caused by an employee damages some customers' property in the repair department.

j. An employee assaults a customer.

k. A bystander is injured while watching store employees unload a refrigerator at the home of a customer.

11. Does a claim under the liability section of the SMP contract affect the coverage available for further accidents during the policy period?

12. Describe the purpose of the following SMP Section II endorsements:

a. Comprehensive general liability insurance endorsement

b. Employer's non-ownership automobile liability insurance endorsement

13. "Premises medical payments coverage is health insurance, not liability insurance. It permits double recovery of medical expenses by the insured." Do you agree? Why or why not?

14. a. What property insurance contracts are common alternatives to an SMP contract?

   b. Why might a business prefer one or more of these alternatives?

15. a. How does professional liability insurance differ from most other general liability insurance contracts?

   b. How does umbrella liability insurance supplement basic general liability insurance?

SUGGESTIONS FOR ADDITIONAL READING

Bickelhaupt, D. L.: *Transition of Multiple-line Insurance Companies* (Homewood, Ill.: Richard D. Irwin, Inc., 1961).

————, and Magee, J. H.: *General Insurance* (8th ed, Homewood, Ill.: Richard D. Irwin, Inc., 1970).

Fire, Casualty, and Surety Bulletins (Cincinnati: The National Underwriter Co.), monthly reporting service.

Gordis, P.: *Property and Casualty Insurance* (17th ed., Indianapolis: The Rough Notes Company, 1970).

Huebner, S. S., Black, K., and Kline, R.: *Property and Liability Insurance* (5th ed., New York: Appleton-Century-Crofts, 1968).

Kulp, C. A., and Hall, J. W.: *Casualty Insurance* (4th ed., New York: Ronald Press Company, 1968).

Long, J. D., and Gregg, D W.: *Property and Liability Insurance Handbook* (Homewood, Ill.: Richard D. Irwin, Inc., 1965).

MacDonald, Donald L.: *Corporate Risk Control* (New York: The Ronald Press Company, 1966).

Magee, J. H., and Serbein, O. N.: *Property and Liability Insurance* (4th ed., Homewood, Ill.: Richard D. Irwin, Inc., 1967).

1967 Special Multi-peril Guide (Indianapolis: The Rough Notes Company, 1967).

Ratcliffe, D.: *General Liability Insurance Handbook* (Philadelphia: McCombs & Co., 1954).

Riegel, R., and Miller, J.: *Insurance Principles and Practices* (5th ed., Englewood Cliffs, N.J.: Prentice-Hall, Inc., 1966).

18

property and liability insurance contracts: II

Four important kinds of business property and liability insurance not covered under the SMP or most equivalent package contracts are automobile insurance, workmen's compensation insurance, cargo insurance, and surety bonds. A detailed description of these four types of insurance is the major purpose of this chapter, but a brief description of some other contracts not covered under the SMP program is also included.

Automobile Insurance

Automobile insurance is the second most commonly held type of property and liability insurance, but it ranks first in terms of premium volume. Most automobile insurance contracts are schedule contracts that permit the insured to purchase both his property and liability insurance under one policy. The contract can be divided, however, into two separate contracts—one providing insurance against physical damage to his automobiles and the other protecting him against his potential liability arising out of the ownership, maintenance, or use of a car. Some automobile insurance contracts, notably those issued by insurers associated with automobile finance companies, cover only physical damage insurance.

Types of Contracts

Unlike the standard fire insurance policy, automobile insurance contracts are not prescribed by statute. Many insurers use the same contracts by

voluntary agreement, but others, including the four largest writers of automobile insurance, have designed their own. They are so similar, however,
that an analysis of the standard contracts will enable the reader to understand the most important provisions in most, if not all, automobile insurance
contracts.[1]

Three standard automobile insurance contracts can be used by business
risk managers. The first is the basic automobile policy (BAP), which until
1956 was the only standard contract available. Because this contract was
used to insure all types of automobiles—private passenger cars owned by
families or corporations, delivery sedans, household moving vans, taxis,
buses, and others—it is a fairly complicated document, many parts of which
are not applicable to any particular type of vehicle. In 1956 the second
contract, the family automobile policy (FAP), was introduced. This contract
can be purchased only by individuals insuring private passenger vehicles,
including station wagons and jeeps; trailers designed for use with private
passenger vehicles; and small farm trucks.[2] Trucks of the pick-up–body,
sedan-delivery, or panel type with a load capacity of 1,500 pounds or less
can be insured under the FAP only if they are not used in business. Because
of the special characteristics of the groups served, this contract is more
concise, easier to read, and more liberal than the BAP. Two more standard
contracts were introduced as economy versions of the FAP in 1959 and
combined into a special package automobile (SPAP) policy in 1963. Although
the eligibility requirements for the SPAP are the same as for the FAP, individual insurers tend to be more selective with respect to the SPAP in other
ways. For example, they may not issue the SPAP to a sole proprietor who
has in his household a young male driver.

Business risk managers, then, may purchase the FAP or the SPAP
if the insured is a sole proprietor insuring a private passenger automobile
or the other vehicles mentioned in the preceding paragraph. They must
purchase the BAP if the insured vehicle is not one of those mentioned
above or, regardless of the kind of vehicle, if the insured is a partnership
or a corporation.

Because (1) most business insureds are sole proprietors or partnerships
insuring private passenger cars and (2) families, like these businesses, buy
the FAP or the SPAP, we will analyze only the FAP in detail. We will then
describe the major differences between the SPAP and the FAP and between
the BAP and the FAP. We will also discuss briefly three other types of
automobile insurance: (1) comprehensive automobile liability insurance, (2)

[1] Minor differences may be important in particular cases, and the analyst must look for
these differences. The nonstandard contracts may be more liberal in some respects and
less liberal in others.
[2] Individuals purchasing insurance through the assigned risk plan (see Chap. 33) obtain
a BAP.

garage liability insurance, and (3) special physical damage insurance for automobile dealers.

THE FAMILY AUTOMOBILE POLICY

The family automobile policy is divided into four parts: (1) Part I—Liability, (2) Part II—Expenses for Medical Services, (3) Part III—Physical Damage, and (4) Part IV—Protection against Uninsured Motorists.

Property insurance   Property insurance is provided under Part III. The insured may choose the perils against which he wishes to be insured. The perils against which he may obtain protection are:

1. Fire, lightning, and transportation, which includes fire, lightning, smoke, and the stranding, sinking, burning, collision, or derailment of any conveyance transporting the automobile.
2. Theft.
3. Combined additional perils (windstorm, hail, earthquake, explosion, riot or civil commotion, aircraft damage, flood, vandalism, external discharge or leakage of water except loss from rain, snow, or sleet).
4. "Comprehensive" perils. This comprehensive insurance protects the insured against all risks or perils other than collision or upset and the excluded perils discussed below. It is expressly agreed *in connection with this coverage* that losses caused by the following perils shall not be considered collision losses and are, therefore, covered: missiles, falling objects, collision with birds or animals, fire, theft, explosion, earthquake, windstorm, hail, water, flood, vandalism, and riot or civil commotion. Breakage of glass, however caused, is also not considered to be a collision loss under this coverage.

The insured who elects comprehensive insurance need not purchase any of the three preceding coverages, because comprehensive insurance includes all the perils mentioned plus many more. It would, for example, cover paint damage caused by a road-tarring machine.

5. Collision or upset. Losses that would not be considered collision losses in connection with comprehensive coverage might still be considered collision losses under the collision coverage. Damage caused by a falling brick, for example, could be either a comprehensive loss or a collision loss. If the insured has only comprehensive insurance, he should claim a comprehensive loss; if he has only collision insurance he should claim a collision loss. If he has both coverages, he can collect under either coverage but not both. Since collision insurance is almost always written with a deductible, while comprehensive insurance is usually written on a full coverage basis, the insured should usually claim a comprehensive loss.

6. Disablement of the automobile from any cause resulting in towing costs and costs for labor performed at the place of disablement. This coverage would pay, for example, for towing costs incurred if an automobile cannot be moved under its own power because of deep snow. Because the maximum possible loss covered by this insurance is relatively small, this is not an important kind of insurance. Furthermore, it permits adverse selection against the insurer.

The excluded perils include wear and tear, mechanical or electrical breakdown, and freezing, unless the damage results from a theft covered under the policy. Perils set in motion by these excluded perils, such as a collision resulting from a mechanical breakdown, are not excluded. Other excluded perils are war and radioactive contamination.

Property insured includes the automobiles named in the contract and owned by the named insured (including his spouse), temporary substitute automobiles, replacement automobiles, and additionally acquired automobiles. A temporary substitute automobile is an automobile not owned by the named insured or spouse which is used as a substitute when the named automobile is temporarily removed from service because it breaks down, is being repaired, or is lost. A replacement automobile is a newly purchased automobile that replaces the named automobile. An additionally acquired automobile is a newly purchased automobile that is not a replacement for one of the automobiles owned by the named insured or spouse when the contract is written. This additional automobile is not insured unless the same insurer insures all the automobiles owned on the delivery date and unless the insured notifies the insurer within 30 days of his intent to insure the new vehicle.

The policy also covers non-owned private passenger automobiles not owned or furnished for the regular use of either the named insured or any relative who is a resident of the same household. Consequently if a non-owned automobile borrowed by an insured is damaged in a collision or a fire, the insurer will pay the loss, assuming the contract covers these perils. This coverage does not apply, however, to an insured while engaged in the business or occupation of selling, servicing, storing, or parking automobiles.

An automobile is defined to include permanently attached equipment. Losses to robes, wearing apparel, and other personal effects belonging to the named insured or a resident relative and carried in the automobile are covered only if damaged by fire or lightning unless the contract is endorsed to cover more perils.

Tires must be damaged by fire or vandals or stolen before the loss is covered, unless other parts of the automobile are damaged at the same time. The primary purpose of this exclusion is to exclude such losses as blowouts when a wheel hits a curb, but if strictly enforced, its impact would be much greater. Trailers other than home, office, store, display, and passenger trailers are considered automobiles under this part if they are designed for use with a private passenger automobile. Owned trailers, however, must be specifically insured.

Persons insured with respect to owned automobiles are the named insured and any person or organization (other than a bailee for hire or a person selling, servicing, storing, or parking automobiles) having custody of the automobile with the permission of the named insured or spouse. The insurer, therefore, cannot exercise any subrogation rights against a stranger using an owned car with the owner's permission. The named insured and resident relatives are insured while using non-owned private passenger automobiles with the permission of their owners.

The protection is restricted to direct *losses* with one exception—theft. It is assumed (perhaps naively) that in all other circumstances the automobile can be quickly repaired or replaced and consequential losses held to a minimum. The reason for excepting theft is to give the insurer time to recover the automobile. The contract states that the insured is entitled to $10 a day for transportation expenses commencing 48 hours after the insurer and the police have been notified concerning the theft and ending when the automobile has been returned to use or the insurer pays for the loss. The total recovery under this consequential coverage is limited to $300.

An interesting feature of the contract, which reveals its marine heritage, is a promise to pay general average and salvage charges if the policy covers the transportation peril.[3]

The *place* where the car will be principally garaged is stated in the declarations. The automobile is covered, however, so long as it is being used in the United States or Canada. The notable omission is Mexico, where the driving conditions and repair facilities are considered significantly different. Some insurers will add Mexican coverage by endorsement, but insureds commonly purchase this insurance from a Mexican insurer at the border.

The contract, which usually has a *term* of one year, is effective at 12:01 A.M., standard time, at the place of principal garaging on the commencement date and terminates at the same hour on the expiration date. The contract may contain a typical cancellation clause, but in many jurisdictions on all renewals, and 60 days after the effective date of a contract issued to a new insured, the insurer may cancel only for two reasons. The first is nonpayment of a premium or premium installment. The second is the suspension or revocation of the driver's license or motor vehicle registration of the named insured or any other operator who resides in the same

---

[3] General average charges are discussed under "Cargo Insurance" later in this chapter.

household or customarily operates an automobile insured under the contract. The insurer must also give the insured 20 days' notice if it intends not to renew the contract.[4]

One *other condition* is worthy of note. The coverage is suspended while the automobile is being used as a public or livery conveyance (for example, as a taxi or a bus) unless it is insured as such, because the chance of loss and the severity of the potential loss are then both considerably increased. Sharing-expense arrangements and car pools do not ordinarily violate this condition.[5]

Several conditions affect the *amount of recovery*. The contract can be written on an actual cash value or a stated-amount basis. Under actual cash value contracts, which are much more common, no dollar limits are stated in the contract, but each insured automobile is covered up to its actual cash value. Under stated-amount contracts, losses are also adjusted on an actual cash value basis, but the contract states the maximum dollar liability of the insurer.

Loss of personal effects in any one occurrence is limited to $100 and loss of non-owned trailers to $500. Collision insurance is usually, if not always, written with some deductible provision. Comprehensive insurance is being increasingly written on this basis. The deductible does not apply to a loss caused by a collision with another car insured by the same insurer. The most common type of deductible is the straight deductible, under which the insurer deducts a stated amount, say $50 or $100, from each separate loss.

The most important provision dealing with other insurance makes the policy excess over other insurance on temporary substitute automobiles and non-owned automobiles.

Liability insurance. Part I of the FAP is liability insurance. The *peril* is an occurrence for which the insured is legally liable. Injury or damage caused intentionally by or at the direction of the insured is specifically excluded.

The *source of liability* is the operation, maintenance, or use of the automobiles or trailers described in the declarations—trailers are defined more broadly than under Part III to include home, office, store, display, and passenger trailers—a temporary substitute automobile not owned by the named insured or spouse, or a newly acquired automobile. If the newly acquired automobile replaces the described automobile, no notice need be given to the insurer during the policy period. If the newly acquired automobile is an additional automobile, there is no protection unless the same insurer

[4] See under "Availability of Insurance" in Chap. 33 for a discussion of state laws regarding cancellation and renewal restrictions.
[5] In order to violate the condition, the owner would have to charge so much that he was in effect running a taxi or bus service.

insures all automobiles owned by the named insured and the insurer is notified within 30 days after the acquisition. The contract also covers the operation, maintenance, or use of automobiles or trailers not owned or furnished for the regular use of either the named insured or any resident relative. This is an important extension of coverage.

The FAP offers no protection (1) while the automobile is being used as a public or livery conveyance unless this is the declared use,[6] (2) against liability for injuries, disease, or deaths of employees (other than domestic employees not covered under workmen's compensation statutes) of the insured arising out of and in the course of employment, (3) against liability for damage to property transported by the insured or property rented to or in charge of the insured other than a residence or private garage, or (4) against liability with respect to which the insured is covered under a nuclear energy liability insurance policy.

The following *persons* are considered insureds with respect to owned and described automobiles: (1) the named insured (including his spouse), (2) any person using the automobile with the permission of the named insured or spouse, and (3) any person legally responsible for the use of the automobile. For example, if an employer instructs an employee to drive a company car in behalf of some other person or firm, all three parties—the employer, the employee, and the other person or firm—are considered insureds.

The protection with respect to insureds other than the named insured, however, does not apply to any person operating an automobile sales agency, garage, service station, or public parking lot or to any of his employees. For example, if a parking attendant damages another car while parking the named insured's car, the insurer will not defend the parking attendant or his employer. It will defend the named insured with respect to this accident, but he is probably not liable.[7]

Employees are not insured with respect to liability for the injury, disease, or death of another employee caused by an accident arising out of employment. This exclusion is necessary because although workmen's compensation is the exclusive remedy of an injured employee against his employer, several states permit the injured employee to sue a negligent fellow employee.

With respect to non-owned automobiles, the persons insured are the named insured and resident relatives. However, resident relatives are covered only if the non-owned car is a private passenger automobile or trailer being

---

[6] This exclusion does not apply to losses resulting from the named insured occupying, but not operating, a non-owned automobile, e.g., riding as a guest in a taxi.
[7] This exclusion, however, does not apply to a person who resides in the insured's household, a partnership in which such a resident or the named insured is a partner, or to any partner, agent, or employee of such a partnership.

used with the permission of the owner. Business use of non-owned vehicles is excluded except that the named insured, his private chauffeur, or his domestic servant is covered while operating or occupying a private passenger car in any business other than selling, servicing, storing, or parking automobiles. Because of the extensive use of non-owned cars in modern business, a clear understanding of this non-owned car coverage is important.

The *losses* covered are essentially the same as those noted earlier in the analysis of Section II of the SMP policy. The insured may elect protection against either bodily-injury liability or property damage liability or against both types of liability. The contract provides the usual defense and investigation services.

The *geographic limits* on covered accidents are the same as those under the physical damage section. The *time limitation* is also the same.

The *amount of recovery* is determined by several factors. The bodily-injury—liability limits on judgments or negotiated settlements are a stated amount per injured person and a stated amount per accident. The property damage limit is a specified amount per accident. There are no aggregate limits applicable to either bodily-injury or property damage claims. Defense, settlement, and first-aid costs are not subject to these limits. The insurer will pay all reasonable expenses incurred by the insured at the insurer's request but it will not reimburse him for loss of earnings.

Deductibles are not common but are available for firms with a fleet of cars.

The most important other insurance provision states that the insurance with respect to a temporary substitute automobile or a non-owned automobile is excess insurance over other valid and collectible insurance. Thus if an insured is involved in an accident while driving a non-owned vehicle, the insurance on that car will protect him first as a person driving with the owner's permission. The FAP insurer pays if the loss exceeds the limits in the policy on the non-owned car.

Health insurance   Part II, covering expenses for medical services, is a form of health insurance. The legal liability of the insured for these expenses is not an issue. The insurer promises to pay all reasonable medical and funeral expenses incurred within one year following an accident by the named insured or a resident relative who was injured while entering, occupying, or alighting from an owned or non-owned automobile, as defined in Part I, or who was struck by an automobile or trailer. Other persons receive similar protection against accidents when entering, occupying, or leaving an owned automobile or if they incur expenses arising out of the operation or occupancy of (1) a non-owned car by the named insured (or operation on his behalf by a private chauffeur or domestic servant) or (2) a non-owned private passenger car by a named insured's resident relative. This promise is subject to exclusions closely resembling the Part I exclusions.

Medical expenses paid under this part do not reduce the insurer's responsibility under liability insurance. Thus, if an insured is legally responsible for medical expenses incurred by a passenger, that passenger could collect twice from the insurer for the same medical expenses. The only other insurance affecting the injured person's recovery under this part is other automobile medical expense insurance. If the accident involves a non-owned car, any medical payments insurance on that car is primary. If some person other than an insured is legally responsible for the loss, the insurer has no subrogation rights under medical payments insurance.

The policy limit under this part is a stated amount per injured person.

Protection against uninsured motorists   One problem that has disturbed many insureds and many state legislatures is that a person may be injured by another driver who is clearly negligent but who does not have sufficient financial resources to compensate the injured victim. This problem of the uncompensated automobile accident victim is discussed at length in Chapter 33. In order to provide protection against such uninsured motorists and against hit-and-run drivers, insurers have developed uninsured motorist's insurance, which is Part IV of the FAP. Under this insurance, the insured victim can collect from his own insurer, which will act as if it represented the negligent uninsured driver or hit-and-run driver.

It should be noted that the insured cannot collect under this coverage unless the uninsured motorist (or the hit-and-run driver) was negligent. On the other hand, it is not necessary for the insured to obtain a judgment before he seeks or obtains reimbursement from his insurer. Instead, the insured and his insurer must decide through negotiations whether the uninsured motorist was negligent. If they disagree, the matter is to be settled by arbitration in accordance with the rules of the American Arbitration Association. Although the insurer is forced under this section to assume a position counter to that of the insured, settling these claims has not been nearly so awkward as might be assumed, and relatively few cases have had to be arbitrated. If the insurer pays the insured, it possesses subrogation rights against the uninsured motorist. If the uninsured motorist is financially responsible even though he has no insurance, the insurer will probably sue him in order to recover the money it has paid out.

The persons insured under this coverage are the named insured and any relative sharing the same residence. Also covered is any other person injured while occupying an automobile insured under the contract. Insured automobiles include non-owned automobiles being operated by the named insured.

The policy limits are usually the limits of the financial responsibility law of the state, although higher limits are now becoming available. Any workmen's compensation benefits are deducted from what would otherwise be paid under this endorsement before the application of the policy limits.

SPECIAL PACKAGE AUTOMOBILE POLICY

The special package automobile policy (SPAP) is an economy version of the family automobile policy. It was conceived in response to price competition from independent insurers, but it contains several features that can be justified on other grounds, such as avoidance of duplication of benefits. The principal features that distinguish the SPAP from the FAP are the following:

1. The special package policy is written for a maximum term of six months.

2. The insured has less choice with respect to the covers to be included in the package and the policy limits. For example, the liability insurance must include liability insurance, medical payments, accidental-death benefits for the named insured or spouse, and uninsured motorist's protection. The insured may select his own liability-insurance and medical-payments-insurance limits, subject to minimum limits of $25,000 per occurrence and $1,000 per person, respectively, but the insurer limits accidental-death benefits to $1,000 per person and the uninsured motorist's coverage to $20,000 per occurrence.

3. Comprehensive property insurance automatically includes $200 personal effects coverage and $25 towing and labor charges protection. The personal effects coverage includes several perils in addition to fire and lightning.

4. There is no property insurance on trailers, and the liability insurance is much more restricted. For example, the only non-owned trailers that can be used without a suspension of the liability coverage are utility-type trailers.

5. The liability insurance is subject to a single limit per occurrence.

6. Resident relatives who own a private passenger automobile are not covered under the policy when they drive non-owned cars. This affects both the property and the liability insurance. These relatives are expected to insure their own cars and in this way insure themselves when they drive non-owned cars. When they drive cars owned by the named insured, however, they are covered under his policy, whether or not they have insurance on their own cars.

7. The liability coverage provides no protection for the insured with respect to bodily injury to (1) his spouse, parent, son, or daughter, or (2) the named insured (including his spouse).

8. The insured's loss of wages or salary because of his requested attendance at hearings or trials is covered up to $25 per day.

9. Numerous provisions are included to prevent duplication of benefits. For example, a claimant receiving medical-payments benefits must agree in writing that these benefits will reduce the amount of any liability settlement. The medical payments insurance is excess insurance over most other forms of medical expense insurance. Finally, the insurer has subrogation rights with respect to these payments.

BASIC AUTOMOBILE POLICY

Persons not eligible for the FAP or the SPAP must purchase the basic automobile policy (BAP). The BAP provides basically the same protection as the FAP, but it is less liberal in several respects. For example,

1. The injuries or damage for which the insured has liability protection must be caused by an "accident," not an occurrence.

2. Except for individuals insuring a private passenger car under this policy (an unusual situation except when the individual is insured under an assigned-risk plan), there is no protection with respect to the use of non-owned automobiles.

3. The liability protection for the use of trailers and the coverage for damage to trailers are more limited.

COMPREHENSIVE AUTOMOBILE LIABILITY POLICY

Businesses or individuals purchasing the BAP face a major gap in their coverage because of the lack of protection with respect to non-owned cars, such as hired cars, borrowed cars, or employee cars used in the business of the insured. One way to fill this gap with respect to liability exposures is to purchase a comprehensive automobile liability policy which covers occurrences arising out of the ownership, maintenance, or use of any automobile not excluded. If written in combination with comprehensive general liability insurance, the result is a rather broad liability insurance contract.

An alternative approach would be to purchase a *schedule liability insurance policy*. Under this policy the insured can choose to include one or more of the following sources of liability: (1) owned automobiles, (2) hired (and borrowed) automobiles, and (3) other non-owned automobiles. This third division is designed primarily to protect employers against their liability for the use by employees of their own private passenger cars on company business. The comprehensive automobile liability insurance contract provides at least as much protection.

GARAGE LIABILITY INSURANCE

Designed for automobile dealers, repair shops, service stations, and the like, garage liability insurance combines automobile liability insurance with general liability insurance. The general liability insurance covers the premises-operations hazard and the completed operations—products hazard. The automobile liability insurance may be limited to automobiles not owned or hired, or it may cover all automobiles—owned, hired, customers', and others not specifically excluded.

Elevator liability insurance and garagekeepers' legal liability insurance can also be included. The latter cover protects the insured against his liability for damage to automobiles in his care or control if this damage is caused by certain specified perils.

SPECIAL PHYSICAL DAMAGE INSURANCE FOR AUTOMOBILE DEALERS

Because automobile dealers have some unique exposures, some special physical damage insurance policies have been designed for them. One contract permits the dealer to purchase insurance against certain perils on new and used cars consigned to or owned by him. Fire and the extended-coverage perils are much more important threats to the dealer than to other automobile owners because of the stationary nature of much of the exposure.

When a customer buys insurance on the installment plan, he is usually required to purchase physical damage insurance, including a loss-payable clause that protects the dealer in the same way that the standard mortgagee clause in the fire insurance contract protects the mortgagee. Sometimes, however, the dealer protects himself against failure of the purchaser to buy insurance through single interest insurance that covers only his own interest.

Workmen's Compensation Insurance

Although state funds write workmen's compensation insurance in eighteen jurisdictions and many firms elect to self-insure their workmen's compensation obligation because they have numerous exposure units, private insurers currently make over 60 per cent of the workmen's compensation payments. All this private insurance is provided under a standard workmen's compensation and employer's liability insurance policy. The standardization is voluntary except in a few states and with respect to certain provisions which are often required under state law. This voluntary action reflects, in part, the fear that otherwise the states might respond with standard policies of their own. It also reflects the fact that once the basic promise to pay workmen's compensation benefits has been made, it is extremely difficult, if not impossible, to design a competitive contract with additional benefits. If this last statement is not immediately clear to the reader, it should become more evident after reading the following contract analysis.

EVENTS COVERED

The standard workmen's compensation and employer's liability policy is really two policies in one—workmen's compensation insurance and employer's liability insurance. Consequently, in certain sections of this analysis we shall have to distinguish between the two coverages.

Perils and sources of liability   Under the workmen's compensation section, the policy covers accidental bodily injuries and diseases for which the insured may be legally responsible under the workmen's compensation law, including any amendments made during the policy period. The policy does, however, exclude any nonoccupational disability benefits provided under any workmen's compensation law.[8] Under the employer's liability section, the peril is an accidental bodily injury or disease sustained by an employee, arising out of and in the course of his employment by the insured, which is not covered under the workmen's compensation law but for which the insured is legally liable. This second section is particularly useful in states without any occupational disease act or with limited occupational disease provisions. Even if the occupational disease provisions do not limit the protection to scheduled diseases, it is possible that certain illnesses such as the common cold, which may lead to pneumonia, might not be considered occupational diseases even if the employer were responsible for the illness. Employer's liability insurance may also be helpful to a business that employs different types of workers, some of whom are not included under the workmen's compensation act. Finally, under certain special circumstances, an injured employee may sue and recover from some third party on the ground that the third party's negligence caused the accident. The third party may in turn be able to sue the employer, something which the employee could not do. Employer's liability insurance would provide the necessary protection unless, as is usually true, the third party's right to sue the employer arises out of a hold-harmless agreement with the employer. Despite these numerous possibilities, almost all claims under the standard policy are paid under the workmen's compensation section.

Neither section of the policy applies to domestic or farm employees unless these employees are covered under the workmen's compensation act or are listed in the declarations. In those states which permit noncovered employees of various sorts to be brought under the workmen's compensation

[8] New York is the only state where this exclusion is important at present. See Chap. 31.

act voluntarily, a *voluntary compensation* endorsement can be attached for this purpose.

Under the employers liability section, there is no coverage with respect to any employee hired in violation of the law with the knowledge of any executive officer.

Persons The person insured under the contract is the employer. If he should die, his legal representatives are insured if the insurer receives written notice of the insured's death within 30 days after it occurs. Assignment of the policy without the insurer's consent is not binding on the insurer.

Although the employees are not insureds, they receive certain valuable rights under the workmen's compensation section—not under the employer's liability section—which improve their status compared with that of the usual liability claimant. For example, the employee can proceed directly against the insurer, instead of indirectly through the employer. Furthermore, if the employee tells the employer about an injury and the employer fails to pass on the information to the insurer, the insurer must still pay the claim.

Losses The workmen's compensation section protects the insured against his obligations under the workmen's compensation act, but the employer must reimburse the insurer for any excess payments arising out of the insured's serious and willful misconduct or out of his employment of any person in violation of law with the knowledge of any executive officer. The employer's liability policy does not cover punitive or exemplary damages added because the employee was hired in violation of the law.

Location The workmen's compensation section applies to the workmen's compensation laws of each of the states listed in the contract by the insured. An *all states* endorsement provides automatic coverage in those states where exposures may develop during the policy period which do not exist when the policy is purchased.

The workplaces of the insured are listed in the contract, but nonlisted workplaces are also included under both sections of the contract unless the insured has other workmen's compensation insurance for these operations or is a qualified self-insurer.

The employer's liability section applies only to injuries sustained in the United States of America, its territories or possessions, or Canada.

Time The policy starts at 12:01 A.M. and usually runs for a term of one year. The cancellation provision is typical, except that it is to be amended to conform to any provisions in the state workmen's compensation law.

Many of these state laws require separate notification to state industrial commissions.

The contract covers accidental injuries occurring during the policy period. Diseases are covered if the last day to which the insured was exposed to this disease while working for the employer occurs during the policy period.

AMOUNT OF RECOVERY

There is no policy limit with respect to the workmen's compensation section. The insurer must pay whatever the law provides, even if a large number of employees are involved.

The employer's liability promise, however, is limited to $100,000 per accident unless this limit is increased in return for a slight extra premium. The defense and other supplementary benefits are not subject to this limit.

STATE FUND CONTRACTS

The workmen's compensation insurance contracts provided by state funds are essentially the same as the standard private contracts except that there is often no employer's liability coverage. In addition, state funds provide no out-of-state coverage for multistate employers.

SEPARATE EMPLOYER'S LIABILITY INSURANCE

Employer's liability insurance is also occasionally written as a separate policy for employers not subject to the workmen's compensation act. The protection is essentially the same as that provided under the employer's liability sections of the standard workmen's compensation and employer's liability policy except that the basic limit is $5,000 per person and $10,000 per accident.

EXCESS WORKMEN'S COMPENSATION INSURANCE

As we have noted earlier, many large firms prefer to self-insure their workmen's compensation obligation. Some states, such as New York, require self-insurers to protect themselves against unusual losses through excess workmen's compensation insurance. As was indicated in Chapter 9, most firms that retain workmen's compensation loss purchase some form of excess insurance. This insurance usually assumes one of two forms: (1) specific excess insurance and (2) stop-loss aggregate or aggregate excess insurance. Under the first form, the insurer agrees to pay losses in excess of a stated amount, such as $25,000, per accident. Under the second form, the insurer must pay total losses during the year in excess of some stated amount, such as 75 percent of the customary workmen's compensation premium. This latter form is commonly sold as part of a package plan providing safety and claims service with respect to all losses. For example, one plan charges 25 per cent of what would have been the premium for a standard policy in return for safety and claims service and aggregate excess insurance. The business retains the other 75 per cent for paying claims and saves whatever is not needed for paying losses. Under both forms the insurer may limit its maximum liability to some stated number of dollars. The risk manager should realize that the firm is exposed to losses beyond this point.

Cargo Insurance

Although the SMP policy with a special commercial property coverage form attached and some of the other contracts analyzed in Chapter 17 provide some protection on property in transit, most insurance on shipments is provided separately under marine insurance contracts.

OCEAN MARINE INSURANCE

Contracts concerned primarily with water transportation are considered to be ocean marine insurance. For a considerable time ocean marine insurance was the only kind of modern insurance. Prior to the fourteenth century it was customary for money lenders to make *respondentia* loans under which they agreed that if the cargo failed to arrive at its destination, the loan was canceled and no repayment was necessary. Modern ocean marine insurance was born in the Mediterranean area when the twin functions of lending and insuring were separated and a separate insurance contract was issued. Until the seventeenth century or later, people were generally not insurance-conscious because of the feudal system and the modest accumulations of most families. There was also a strong religious sentiment against thwarting the "will of God." Merchants, however, were risking substantial sums at sea, and they feared the perils of the sea. It took the London Fire of 1666 to create a similar awareness of the fire peril and to inspire the formation of the first fire insurers.

In order to take advantage of an extensive body of court interpretations, and because of the rich tradition of marine insurance, cargo insurance contracts covering water transportation are often phrased in antiquated language (e.g., "Touching the Adventures and Perils which we, . . . , are contented to bear"). In addition the contracts are often a hodgepodge of unrelated provisions. Consequently these contracts are among the most difficult to analyze. On the other hand, they are notable for the broad protection they afford.

Events covered With respect to perils the minimum coverage is fire and perils of the sea. Although "perils of the sea" are not defined, they are understood to include all perils arising out of water transportation, such as collisions with other vessels, grounding on a sandbar, and heavy weather. Fire and theft are perils *on* the sea, not *of* the sea. Other perils that may be added include theft, explosion, onshore risks, accidents involving machinery, and barratry (or roughly, embezzlement by the master or the crew). Sometimes the contract is written on an all risks basis.

The property covered is the cargo being shipped. Freight charges are usually included if the person shipping the cargo suffers the loss.

Cargo insurance contracts usually cover the named insured "for account of whom it may concern," the loss, if any, being payable to the insured or order. In other words, the contract is freely assignable to any person. Insurers grant this right because neither the named insured nor any assignee has any physical control over the exposed cargo.

Because the cargo is usually insured for the amount of the invoice, including all charges therein, plus any prepaid, advanced, or guaranteed freight, the insurance covers loss of profits and freight charges, if any, in addition to direct losses. Although a delay clause excludes loss of markets or any other loss resulting from any delay for any reason, losses of this sort can be covered for an additional premium.

Ocean marine insurance contracts also contain some special terms applicable to losses. Losses may be divided, first, according to whether they affect only the insured or some other person. The first group may in turn be divided into total losses or particular average losses,[9] the last category including all partial losses to a particular interest. Losses that involve persons other than the insured are called "general average" losses.

In order to be considered a general average loss, (1) there must be a voluntary loss for the purpose of saving a joint venture and (2) the voluntary act must be successful. For example, if a vessel, valued at $1 million and carrying two sets of cargo, cargo A valued at $200,000 and cargo B at $300,000, starts to sink because of heavy seas, the captain may decide to jettison half of cargo A in order to reach his destination. In such a case, the loss of $100,000 worth of cargo A is considered a general average loss. It is a rule of the sea, dating back to the days before Christ when the city of Rhodes in Greece was a commercial power, that general average losses are to be shared by all the interests who benefit from a general average loss on the basis of the value of their interests at the time the loss occurred. Since the value of all interests at the time of the loss totaled $1,500,000, the vessel owner must pay the owner of cargo A $\frac{2}{3} \times$

---

[9] Since the term "average" means loss in maritime insurance, it is sufficient to refer to these losses as particular averages.

$100,000, or $66,667. The owner of cargo B must pay $\frac{3}{15} \times$ $100,000, or $20,000, and the owner of cargo A must bear the remainder of the loss, or $13,333. Marine insurers will pay these general average charges on behalf of their insureds.

The contract usually insures the cargo or the hull "at and from" ports or places within a designated geographical area. The at-and-from wording means that the coverage is effective while the vessel is in port as well as at sea. Most policies also contain a warehouse-to-warehouse clause, which extends the coverage from the point of origin, which may be an inland location, to the final destination, which may also be an inland location.

Cargo policies written on a voyage basis cover that single voyage, but open policies usually cover all shipments made on and after a certain date. Either party may cancel an open policy by giving thirty days' written notice to the other; otherwise the insurance is continuous. If the policy is canceled, the coverage continues on shipments made prior to the cancellation date. Some open policies, however, are written for a specific period.

Amount of recovery   Because cargoes can fluctuate greatly in value during an ocean voyage, it is customary to insure cargoes on a valued basis. If the cargo is totally destroyed, the insurer must pay the face value. The valuation in the contract, however, is expected to be realistic. Instead of specifying a stated number of dollars, the contract customarily states that the value shall be the amount of the invoice plus any prepaid, advanced, or guaranteed freight.

If the cargo is only partially damaged, the insured and the insurer must agree on the percentage of damage. If they cannot agree, the damaged cargo is to be sold for the account of the owner and the amount received compared with what would have been received had the cargo been in sound condition. In either case, the liability of the insurer is determined by applying the percentage of damage to the amount of insurance. For example, assume that a cargo insured for $4,000 could have been sold for $6,000 in sound condition but is worth only $4,500 in damaged condition. Since the damage is 25 per cent, the insurer must pay 25 per cent of $4,000, or $1,000. Note that if the amount of insurance is less than the value of the cargo in sound condition, the amount of the insurance payment is equal to the amount under a 100 per cent coinsurance clause.

Because marine insurance contracts cover so many perils, they would be very expensive unless they excluded relatively small losses. Marine insurers recognized from the beginning that it was wiser to omit coverage on small losses than to narrow the scope of the perils clause. Small losses are omitted through one or more franchise or deductible clauses, the franchise principle being the most common.

If the insured has two or more contracts, the contracts apply to any loss in the order in which they were written.

INLAND MARINE INSURANCE

Inland marine cargo insurance covers shipments primarily by land or by air. Although the trucker, railroad, or airline may be a common carrier with the extensive liability described in Chapter 7 in the section "Bailee Liability Exposures," the shipper may still be interested in cargo insurance because (1) it is usually more convenient to collect from an insurer than a carrier, (2) a common carrier is not responsible for perils such as an act of God, an act of war, exercise of public authority, or inherent defects in the cargo, and (3) the carrier may have issued a released bill of lading. Unless the insured makes only a few shipments each year, it is generally less expensive to buy cargo insurance than to increase the limits under the bill of lading.

No one cargo insurance contract exists. Instead, different insurers may issue different contracts, and a given insurer will tailor the contract to the insured's needs. A convenient way to classify the contracts is according to the type of transportation covered. One or more of the following modes of transportation may be covered—railroad, motor truck, or air. Incidental water transportation may or may not be included. Shipments by mail are covered under separate first-class mail, parcel post, or registered mail insurance. Special contracts have also been designed to handle shipments on the insured's own trucks, by railway express, or by an armored-car operator. Another classification of these contracts would group them according to the perils covered. Most provide protection against a broad list of specified perils, but some, especially those covering air transportation of high-value items, are written on an all risks basis. Finally, some contracts cover one trip, while others cover all shipments during the term of the policy.

Inland marine transit policies covering shipments by mail are especially interesting because similar insurance is sold by the U.S. Post Office, but for persons who make enough shipments to pay more than the minimum premiums for the private insurance, the cost of the private protection will actually be less. Furthermore, the private protection may be more convenient because it is not necessary for the insured to leave his premises to effect the coverage.

Surety Bonds

Since the essential characteristics of surety bonds and the ways in which they differ from insurance were analyzed in Chapters 10 and 11, the discussion will be limited here to the expressed obligations commonly guaranteed through surety bonds. Although any expressed obligation could be the subject of a surety bond and new types of surety bonds are constantly being written, the more common surety bonds can be grouped into the following classes: (1) contract bonds, (2) court bonds, and (3) license and permit bonds. Illustrations of the many other bonds available are *lost instrument* bonds, which protect the issuer of a lost instrument such as a stock or bond if it issues a replacement to the owner and some other party appears later with the original document and a valid claim against the issuer; *self-insurance* bonds, which a firm may have to post before it will be permitted to self-insure its workmen's compensation obligation; and *financial responsibility* bonds, which a car owner may have to file in lieu of an automobile liability insurance policy if he wishes to retain his right to drive after an accident.

CONTRACT BONDS

Under contract bonds, the surety guarantees the promise the principal has made to the obligee under some contract. Usually the contract covers construction, supply, or maintenance. Some of these bonds promise that the surety will carry out the contract if the principal fails to do so; others promise to pay damages.

Construction contracts   Construction contract bonds can in turn be divided into bid bonds and final or performance bonds. *Bid* bonds guarantee that if the bidder wins the award, he will sign the contract and post a performance bond. The *performance* bond guarantees that the contractor will complete his work in accordance with the agreement between him and the owner. In addition, the surety usually guarantees that the contractor will pay all labor and material bills incurred, but the unpaid laborers and material men have no right to proceed directly against the surety. Finally, the performance bond may guarantee that the obligee will not suffer any loss for some specified period through defects in the construction.

COURT BONDS

Court bonds include all those bonds which may be filed in connection with judicial proceedings. They fall into two general classes: (1) litigation bonds and (2) fiduciary bonds.

Litigation bonds   Litigation bonds may be required by the court whenever the plaintiff or the defendant asks the court to take some action on his behalf which may injure the other party to the suit. A few examples will illustrate the numerous bonds in this category. Perhaps the best-known surety bond is a *bail* bond which stipulates a penalty to be paid if a defendant does not appear in court at the time of the trial. An *attachment* bond guarantees that if the plaintiff asks the court to attach certain property of the defendant to prevent him from disposing of that property to avoid paying the judgment and the plaintiff loses the case, the plaintiff will pay the defendant any damages he sustained as a result of the temporary attachment. An *appeal* bond guarantees that if an appeal to a higher court sustains the judgment of the lower court, the person making the appeal will pay the original judgment, interest on the judgment, and the court costs.

Fiduciary bonds   Fiduciary bonds guarantee that persons entrusted through court order with the management of property for the benefit of some other person will perform their duties honestly and capably. The principals under these bonds include the following fiduciaries: executors or administrators of estates, guardians of minors or the mentally incompetent, receivers or trustees of a bankrupt business, or assignees for the benefit of creditors.

LICENSE AND PERMIT BONDS

License and permit bonds are often required by Federal, state, or local law when a person applies for a license to engage in a particular occupation or business or for a permit to engage in a specific activity. These bonds can be divided into two major classes: (1) those which guarantee the licensing authority that the licensee will be responsible for losses to the government or to the public caused by violations of certain regulations or in some cases from the activity itself, and (2) those which guarantee the payment of certain taxes on products processed or sold.

Some of the bonds in the first group give injured third parties the right to proceed directly against the surety, while others protect only the public authority against damages to its own property or suits by private persons. Some of these bonds, which could be considered to constitute a third category, also provide for the forfeiture of the bond penalty if the licensee violates certain regulations even if no damage results.

Miscellaneous Property and Liability Insurance

Private and public insurers issue many kinds of insurance in addition to those described to this point. Some of these contracts are described briefly below:

Glass insurance covers damage to glass and to any lettering or ornamentation caused by breakage of the glass or by chemicals accidentally or maliciously applied. The only exclusions are fire, war, and nuclear reaction. Under most property insurance contracts the insurer rarely exercises its right to repair or replace the damaged property, but glass insurers compete primarily on the basis of their replacement service. Prompt replacement cuts consequential losses, and insurers can take advantage of quantity discounts.

Credit insurance protects the insured business against abnormal losses on accounts receivable. Credit insurance differs from *accounts receivable insurance,* which covers abnormal bad debts losses suffered by an insured because his records are damaged or destroyed. Where credit insurance applies, the records are not destroyed but one or more debtors for some reason (e.g., bad luck, a recession, or poor management) fail to pay what they owe by the due date. Only firms such as manufacturers and wholesalers who sell to other businesses are eligible for this insurance.

Export credit insurance protects exporters against credit risks (insolvency of the buyer) and political risks (inconvertibility of a foreign currency to dollars and cancellation or restriction of export or import licenses) on sales to buyers in friendly foreign countries. The credit risk is underwritten by the Foreign Credit Insurance Association, an unincorporated association of over fifty-five stock insurers. The Export-Import Bank underwrites the political risks.

Title insurance reimburses the insured for any losses he may incur if his title to real estate proves to be defective. Title insurers search records in their own offices and other sources and protect the insured against existing defects that they fail to discover. Only one premium is paid at the commencement of the insurance, which continues until the insured's interest in the property ceases. Some states and counties operate a Torrens system, under which a hearing is held in order to discover defects. If no defects are discovered, the title is registered, and the owner is, except under certain circumstances, assured of a clear title. The registration fee includes a contribution to a fund that is used to indemnify persons who can prove later that they have some right that existed prior to the registration.

Aviation insurance, a rapidly growing field, includes a wide variety of contracts. Like automobile insurance, aviation insurance includes both property insurance on the planes and liability insurance.

Nuclear energy insurance also includes both property insurance and liability insurance. Nuclear energy property insurance protects the operator of a nuclear reactor against damage to the reactor itself and his other property on the described premises as the result of a nuclear explosion or *any other peril not specifically excluded.* Because of the large values exposed to loss and the catastrophic possibilities, this insurance is underwritten only by a stock insurer pool and a mutual insurer pool. Individual insurers write radioactive contamination insurance for firms with nuclear hazards less than those faced by firms eligible for nuclear energy insurance. Nuclear energy liability insurance protects the insured and *any* other person who may be held liable for the loss (e.g., a negligent motorist who collides with the facility) against liability arising out of a nuclear incident.

Crop insurance is sold by private insurers and by the Federal Crop Insurance Corporation. Three major classes of private insurance exist: (1) crop-hail insurance, whose name signifies its function, (2) insurance on fruit and vegetable crops against frost and freezes, and (3) insurance covering hail, drought, excessive heat, flood, excessive moisture, and many other perils. The Federal program covers all natural perils. Both the Federal coverage and the broad private form are written only in selected areas.

Errors and omissions insurance protects mortgagees against their failure through an error or omission to obtain the insurance protection they normally require on the property that serves as security for the loan.

Computer insurance covers the cost of reproducing computer tapes that are destroyed by a covered peril plus the loss of valuable computer time when a computer is damaged.

Motor truck cargo legal liability insurance obligates the insurer to pay any loss to cargo for which the trucking concern, as a common carrier, is liable if the cause of the loss is one of a stated number of perils. As a common carrier, the trucker has the responsibility discussed on pages 120–121 and the Interstate Commerce Commission requires motor carriers engaged in interstate commerce to purchase this insurance unless they can demonstrate their ability to self-insure this obligation. Under the contract the insurer does not pay unless the carrier is legally responsible for the loss, but the carrier can be legally responsible without the insurer incurring any liability because the cause is not one of the specified perils. Covered perils are typically fire and lightning, windstorm, perils of the seas, lakes, and rivers, collisions, collapse of bridges, and flood. In order to satisfy the Interstate Commerce Commission, the contract must be endorsed to extend the insurer's liability to all perils, but the extension of liability is limited to $1,000 per truck and $2,000 per loss at any one time and place. If a loss involves a peril not covered under the basic policy but covered under the endorsement, the insurer can recover any payment it makes from the insured.

Unusual coverages are illustrated by *all risks business interruption insurance, all risks worldwide blanket protection* covering direct and consequential losses to both real and personal property anywhere in the world, and *cast insurance* protecting the insured against the failure of an actress to appear on a movie set, a theater stage, or a television program.

REVIEW QUESTIONS

1. Which of the standard automobile insurance contracts would be applicable in each of the following cases?

   a. A sole proprietor insures a private passenger automobile for business and personal use.

   b. A partnership insures two private passenger automobiles for business and personal use.

   c. A corporation insures a 2-ton truck and two private passenger automobiles.

   d. A corporation insures a panel-type truck with a load capacity of 1,200 pounds.

   e. A sole proprietor insures a taxicab.

2. A firm purchases protection against the "comprehensive" perils and collision. A $50 deductible applies to collision losses. A cornice falls off a building and lands on the roof of the insured vehicle, causing $300 damage. How much will the insurer pay?

3. Which of the following losses is covered under the comprehensive coverage?

   a. A cold snap damages the insured's car radiator.

   b. A thief steals a $50 typewriter from the back seat of a salesman's car.

   c. An insured truck is swept away in a flood.

   d. The insured's brakes fail, and he collides with a brick wall.

   e. The insured's car, which is being shipped by rail, is completely destroyed when the train is derailed.

4. a. A private passenger car belonging to a sole proprietor is destroyed in a fire. Before the vehicle can be replaced, the firm must spend $15 a day for taxi fares for 20 days. If the car is insured against the losses, will the insurer contribute to the cost of the taxi fares?

   b. Would your answer be different if the car was stolen and was insured against theft? How?

   c. What is the reason why insurers will pay one of these consequential losses but not the other?

5. In what ways does the cancellation provision in the family automobile policy differ from the cancellation provision in the fire insurance policy?

6. Automobile physical damage insurance contracts contain no coinsurance clauses. Why?

7. a. A sole proprietor has a private passenger car insured under a family automobile policy. An employee is instructed to drive a private passenger car belonging to a neighboring firm on company business. The borrowed car is damaged in a collision. Is the collision damage to the borrowed car covered under the sole proprietor's family automobile policy if the car is insured under the neighboring firm's policy? if it is uninsured?

   b. Would your answer be different if the employee was the sole proprietor's son?

8. a. Mr. Jones, a sole proprietor, has a special package automobile insurance contract covering the family automobile. His son, Tom, owns an unin-

sured automobile. If Tom drives a friend's uninsured automobile and causes collision damage valued at $550, what is the obligation of Mr. Jones's insurer?

b. How would you answer (a) if Mr. Jones had purchased instead a family automobile policy?

9. A business has a family automobile liability insurance policy covering a fleet of three private passenger automobiles. Which of the following losses are covered under the liability sections? Assume that negligence is involved in each case.

a. An employee driving a company car on company business injures a pedestrian.

b. An employee driving his own car on company business injures a pedestrian.

c. An employee driving a company car with the permission of his employer on an errand for the Red Cross injures a pedestrian.

d. A company car that was carrying some merchandise belonging to another firm is demolished in a collision.

e. Two employees are injured when the employee driving a company car tries to pass on a hill.

f. An attendant in a parking lot drives one of the corporation private passenger cars into another car parked in the same lot.

g. A salesman collides with another automobile while driving a hired automobile.

h. The son of the corporation president has an accident while driving a friend's uninsured car.

i. The corporation president has an accident while driving one of the private passenger cars on vacation in Mexico.

10. Explain the difference between the medical payments coverages in automobile liability insurance and general liability insurance with respect to:

a. The coverage of the insured and his family.

b. The events covered under the liability section of the contract.

11. The president of the firm collides with a parked car when he takes his eyes off the road to stare into the window of a competitor. The damages are as follows:

President	Medical expenses	$ 100
Guest in the firm's car	Medical expenses	300
	Loss of wages	2,000
Occupant in the parked car	Emergency first aid	100
	Other medical expenses	2,000
	Loss of wages	12,000
Parked car		1,000
Firm's car		500

The firm has a basic automobile policy with the following limits:
  Bodily injury liability: $10,000 per person; $20,000 per accident
  Property damage liability: $5,000 per accident
  Medical payments: $250 per person
How much will the insurer pay
a. If the president is considered negligent?
b. If the president is not considered negligent?
c. If the president is considered negligent and at the time was driving his personal uninsured car?

12. a. What social problem gave rise to uninsured motorist coverage?
   b. Must the uninsured motorist be financially irresponsible before the insured can collect under this coverage?
   c. How are disputes handled between the insured and his insurer?

13. a. Mr. Jones, a sole proprietor, has a special package automobile liability insurance policy. What is the insurer's responsibility in each of the following cases?
     (1) Tom Jones, the son, has an automobile of his own which is not insured. Tom has an accident while driving the family automobile.
     (2) Mr. Jones has to miss work for two weeks while appearing in court and otherwise helping the insurer to defend a case in which Mr. Jones is the defendant.
     (3) A guest in the Jones's car is injured when Mr. Jones collides with another car at an intersection. Mr. Jones is negligent. The guest suffers a loss of $3,000, including $500 in medical expenses.
     (4) In question (3), assume that the other driver was negligent and that Mr. Jones also suffered a loss of $200 in medical expenses.
     (5) Mr. Jones is injured while a friend who was driving Mr. Jones's car collides with another automobile. The friend was negligent. Mr. Jones suffers a loss of $8,000, including $3,000 in medical expenses.
   b. How would you answer each of these questions if Mr. Jones had purchased instead a family automobile insurance policy?
   c. What are the other major differences between the liability sections of the special package automobile policy and the family automobile policy?

14. Why might a business with either (a) a family automobile policy or (b) a basic automobile policy be interested in comprehensive automobile insurance?

15. The risk manager of a local garage cannot decide whether to buy a basic automobile liability policy or a garage liability policy. What are the major differences in the protection afforded by these two policies?

16. a. In what sense is the standard workmen's compensation insurance contract two policies in one?
   b. Cite an example to illustrate why employers in your state might need the employer's liability protection in this contract.

17. An employer purchases workmen's compensation insurance in late October. The following month the weekly benefits under the workmen's compensation law are increased, effective June 1. What steps, if any, must the employer take as a result of the amendment to the state statute?

18. Compare the rights of the employee under the workmen's compensation and employer's liability sections of the standard contract.

19. A sole proprietor purchases a standard workmen's compensation and employer's liability insurance contract with an all states endorsement attached. Which of the following losses is covered?
   a. An employee is injured while driving a company car on company business.
   b. The sole proprietor is injured while inspecting a machine at his plant.
   c. A clerical employee contracts pneumonia because the temperature in the office where he worked was too low.
   d. A child below the legal working age is injured on the job. The sole proprietor knew about this violation of the law. In addition to the regular workmen's compensation benefits, the employer is also responsible for some penalty payments.
   e. An employee hired three months ago is disabled by silicosis. He was exposed to this disease during these three months and also during the twenty years he worked for his former employer.

20. A risk manager has decided that he wishes to self-insure his workmen's compensation losses. He is concerned, however, about sizable losses arising out of a single accident or an unusually large number of accidents in any single year. How would you advise him?

21. "Ocean marine insurance contracts are all risks contracts." Do you agree with this statement? Why or why not?

22. Cargo insurance contracts are usually open policies.
   a. What are open policies?
   b. Explain the special features of the cancellation provision under open policies.

23. a. A cargo insured for $10,000 is damaged by fire. In sound condition it would have sold for $8,000 at its destination. In damaged condition it sells for $2,000. How much will the insurer pay?
   b. How much will the insurer pay if the property would have sold for $12,000 in sound condition but sells for $3,000 in damaged condition?
   c. Do either or both of these loss settlements seem illogical? Why or why not?

24. A vessel, valued at $1,500,000, is carrying three cargoes belonging to A, B, and C, each cargo valued at $500,000. In heavy weather the ship is in danger of sinking unless the load is lightened, and the captain orders half of A's cargo thrown overboard. As a result of this act, the ship is able to proceed to its destination.

a. If none of the parties are insured, how will the loss be settled?

b. If all the parties are insured, how will the loss be settled?

c. If the jettison is not successful and the ship sinks to the bottom of the ocean, how will the loss be settled if all parties are insured?

25. A person making extensive shipments argues that he does not need to insure these shipments because the transportation carrier is responsible for any losses which might occur. How would you advise him?

26. A school district asks for bids on the construction of a new school. What types of bonds might be used in connection with this construction project? For each bond, identify the obligee, the principal, and the expressed obligation.

27. a. Distinguish between litigation bonds and fiduciary bonds.

b. Give three illustrations of each type.

28. Boiler and machinery insurance, glass insurance, credit insurance, and title insurance have service features which may make them attractive to some risk managers who are not impressed by the indemnification they afford. What are these service features?

29. The Carry Transport Company has a motor truck cargo legal liability policy. Theft losses are not covered under the policy. Is the insurer responsible for the following losses to cargo in his custody?

a. A truck carrying cargo is completely destroyed in a collision with another truck.

b. Thieves hijack a truck carrying cargo.

c. A flash flood completely destroys a truck and its cargo.

d. A fire destroys completely four trucks in a terminal.

e. A fire destroys cargo which had been placed in a warehouse one week before, at which time the consignee was asked to pick it up.

SUGGESTIONS FOR ADDITIONAL READING

Bickelhaupt, D. L., and Magee, J. H.: *General Insurance* (8th ed., Homewood, Ill.: Richard D. Irwin, Inc., 1970).

Brainard, C.: *Automobile Insurance* (Homewood, Ill.: Richard D. Irwin, Inc., 1961).

Fire, Casualty and Surety Bulletins (Cincinnati: The National Underwriter Company), monthly reporting service.

Gordis, P.: *Property and Casualty Insurance* (17th ed., Indianapolis: The Rough Notes Company, 1970).

Huebner, S. S., Black, K, and Kline, R.: *Property and Liability Insurance* (5th ed., New York: Appleton-Century-Crofts, 1968), chaps. 19–22 and 24–27.

Kulp, C. A., and Hall, J. W.: *Casualty Insurance* (4th ed., New York: The Ronald Press Company, 1968).

Long, J. D., and Gregg, D. W.: *Property and Liability Insurance Handbook* (Homewood, Ill.: Richard D. Irwin, Inc., 1965).

MacDonald, Donald L.: *Corporate Risk Control* (New York: The Ronald Press Company, 1966).

Magee, J., and Serbein, O. N.: *Property Insurance* (4th ed., Homewood, Ill.: Richard D. Irwin, Inc., 1967).

Ratcliffe, D.: *Workmen's Compensation Insurance Handbook* (Philadelphia: McCombs & Co., 1954).

Riegel, R., and Miller, J.: *Insurance Principles and Practices* (5th ed., Englewood Cliffs, N.J.: Prentice-Hall, Inc., 1966).

Rodda, W. H.: *Inland Marine and Transportation Insurance* (2d ed., Englewood Cliffs, N.J.: Prentice-Hall, Inc., 1958).

Somers, H. M., and Somers, A. R.: *Workmen's Compensation* (New York: John Wiley & Sons, Inc., 1954).

Winter, W. D.: *Marine Insurance* (3d ed., New York: McGraw-Hill Book Company, 1952).

19

individual life insurance contracts

Life insurers issue many different types of individual contracts. This chapter describes the basic policy types and a few of their more important modifications and combinations. It also analyzes some major policy provisions, placing emphasis upon those that require the insured to make decisions.

Branches of Life Insurance

Life insurance can be classified according to whether it is underwritten by commercial insurers, fraternal insurers, or mutual savings banks. At the close of 1969, commercial insurers had issued over 97 per cent of the private life insurance in force and practically all the annuities. Fraternal life insurance in force was about 2 per cent of the total and mutual savings bank insurance less than 1 per cent.[1] Because of the dominant role of commercial insurers, this chapter will be devoted almost exclusively to their contracts. Much of the discussion, however, is applicable to the contracts of fraternal insurers and mutual savings bank insurers, whose important special characteristics will be discussed at the close of this chapter.

Commercial insurance in turn falls into two major classes—individual insurance and group insurance. *Individual* insurance differs from group insurance in that the contract covers a person or a family as opposed to a group of persons. Each contract covering a person or family is separately

[1] Life Insurance Fact Book, 1970, p. 100.

sold, underwritten, and administered. Individual insurance can be subclassified as ordinary insurance or industrial insurance.

Ordinary insurance is generally sold in amounts of at least $1,000; the premiums are quoted on an annual basis but may be paid on a semi-annual, quarterly, or monthly basis; and only the first premium is collected by the agent, the remainder of the payments being made directly to the insurer. As is demonstrated in Table 19.1, ordinary insurance is the most important branch of individual insurance. Unless otherwise specified, our discussion in this text will refer to this branch of insurance, although we shall describe other branches as well.

Industrial insurance is usually sold in amounts less than $1,000; the most common method of premium payment is weekly; and the premium is customarily collected at the home of the insured by a "debit agent." The face amount is usually adjusted to the size of the premium the insured wishes to pay. Industrial policies are very similar to ordinary policies, the principal differences being the absence of loan values, the prohibition of assignments, the requirement that the proceeds be paid in a lump sum, and the automatic inclusion of accidental death and dismemberment provisions. Although still a sizable proportion of the total insurance in force, industrial insurance is declining relatively in importance and since 1957 has also declined in absolute amount.

Group insurance covers a group of persons under one contract, the contract being sold, underwritten, and administered on a group basis. Group insurance, which is the most rapidly growing branch of insurance, is important enough to merit separate treatment in Chapter 22.

Credit life insurance is listed as a fourth branch of insurance in Table 19.1, but it is probably better described as a unique application of ordinary insurance or group insurance. The insurance in force devoted to this use has increased very markedly since 1945; group credit life insurance has increased more rapidly than individual insurance. At the close of 1969, *group* credit life insurance accounted for over 85 per cent of the total credit life insurance in force.

Credit life insurance policies are issued through (1) lending institutions, such as banks and credit unions, or (2) retailers, such as department stores and automobile dealers selling goods or services on a charge account or an installment basis. Under group credit insurance, the creditor is the policyholder and often pays the premiums. Under individual insurance (which in this field is characterized by group underwriting), the debtor is the policyholder and almost always pays the premiums. The insurance in either case is on the life of the debtor, and if he dies, the insurer pays the unpaid balance of his debt to his creditor thus canceling the debt. Under some individual policies, the protection does not decrease over time, and the

Table 19.1 Commercial life insurance in force in the United States, 1920–1969 (in billions of dollars)

Year	Ordinary	Industrial	Group	Credit	Total
1920	32.0	6.9	1.6	*	40.5
1925	52.9	12.3	4.2	*	69.5
1930	78.6	18.0	9.8	0.1	106.4
1935	70.7	17.5	10.2	0.1	98.5
1940	79.3	20.9	14.9	0.4	115.5
1945	101.6	27.7	22.2	0.4	151.8
1950	149.1	33.4	47.8	3.9	234.2
1955	216.6	39.7	101.3	14.8	372.3
1960	340.2	39.6	175.4	31.2	586.4
1965	497.6	39.8	306.1	57.0	900.6
1966	539.0	39.7	343.4	62.7	984.7
1967	582.6	39.2	391.1	67.0	1,079.8
1968	630.4	38.8	438.2	75.9	1,183.4
1969	678.9	38.6	483.2	83.8	1,284.5

* Less than 0.1.

Source: *Life Insurance Fact Book, 1970* (New York: Institute of Life Insurance, 1970), p. 22.

balance is paid to some other designated beneficiary. Several states have acted recently to correct important abuses in this field, such as unduly high commissions given by some insurers to creditors in connection with individual insurance and excessive premium rates for both individual and group insurance.

Types of Contracts

The basic types of contracts are (1) term insurance, (2) whole life insurance, (3) endowment insurance, and (4) annuities. Some important modifications and combinations are (1) modified life and graded premium contracts, (2) family policies, (3) family income policies, (4) family maintenance policies, (5) retirement income contracts, and (6) preferred risk policies or "specials." Guaranteed insurability riders, which are, strictly speaking, neither a modification nor a combination of the basic policy types, will also be discussed.

the term, the policy expires. In other words, term life insurance resembles automobile insurance, fire insurance, and the like, which are always term insurance. Common types of term life insurance are one-year term, five-year term, ten-year term, twenty-year term, and term to age 60 or 65. The term insurance is usually level over the policy period, but decreasing term insurance is also common.

Term insurance may be renewable, convertible, or both. If the policy is renewable, the insurer will renew the policy, regardless of the insurability of the insured, for the number of times specified in the contract—commonly to age 60 or 65. The premium paid upon renewal is the cost of a new policy issued to standard (as opposed to substandard) lives at the attained age. If the policy is convertible, the insured can convert the policy to nonterm insurance, either (1) as of the attained age or (2) as of the date of issue of the term policy. In the latter case, the premium paid is the premium which the insured would have been charged if he had been covered under the nonterm contract from the beginning. In addition, the insured will be asked to make a lump sum payment (which may be computed in various ways) to make up for the deficiency in premiums to the date of the conversion. These two rights are important because they make the term insurance more flexible.

Because of its nature, term insurance provides the maximum protection per premium dollar for a stated period of time. The relative protection provided by different types of contracts may be computed from Table 19.2, which presents the premium rates charged by one large nonparticipating insurer for some leading term insurance and nonterm insurance contracts. In order to avoid the complicating and nonguaranteed effect of dividends, the rates of a nonparticipating insurer were selected to illustrate the rates, although over 60 per cent of the life insurance in force is participating.

One common use of term insurance is to meet a need for protection that expires at the end of a specified period. For example, term insurance may be purchased to complete the payments under a mortgage or to reimburse a business if its key engineer should die before an important project is completed. Young husbands with high protection needs but little income may purchase renewable and convertible term insurance to protect their families in their early years. Others may purchase only renewable term insurance for the investment reasons cited in the next section.

Whole life insurance   Whole life insurance protects the beneficiary when the insured dies, since the contract can be continued in force as long as the insured lives. Whole life insurance contracts may be placed in two categories, depending upon the premium payment period: (1) straight life insur-

Table 19.2 Base premium rates* per $1,000 insurance charged by one leading non-participating insurer for contracts issued to men†

Age	Term 5-year‡	Term 10-year§	Straight life	Paid-up at 65	20-payment life	Endowment at 65	20-year endowment
20	$ 4.28	$ 3.99	$10.55	$11.66	$18.84	$ 14.68	$41.55
25	4.33	4.19	12.35	13.86	21.07	17.55	41.69
30	4.41	4.77	14.65	16.83	23.73	21.35	42.01
35	5.04	6.09	17.61	20.93	26.93	26.71	42.63
40	6.61	8.18	21.55	26.68	30.80	34.16	43.76
45	9.08	11.74	26.58	35.49	35.49	45.67	45.67
50	13.40	17.59	32.61	49.66	41.19	64.05	48.65
55	20.05	25.63	40.57	78.10	48.25	101.88	53.14
60	32.03		51.71		57.68		60.26
65			66.65				

* To obtain the premium, first calculate the base premium by multiplying the rate in the table by the amount of insurance in thousands. Next add to this base premium the policy fee. For policies of $2,000 or more on which the premium is paid annually, the policy fee is $10. To illustrate, the premium for a $10,000 straight life contract issued at age 35 is ($17.61 × 10) + $10, or $186.10, while the premium for a $20,000 policy would be ($17.61 × 20) + $10, or $362.20. The result is a decreasing rate per $1,000 insurance as the amount of insurance increases. (For straight life insurance the decrease is greater than shown here because the base premium rates are also lower ($16.29 at age 35) for policies of $25,000 or more.)

Some insurers, who grant premium discounts as the amount of insurance increases, do not use this policy-fee approach. Instead they establish size groups, such as policy amounts between $1,000 and $4,999, between $5,000 and $9,999, between $10,000 and $24,999 and $25,000 or more, and charge a different rate for each group. Under this approach, a person considering the purchase of, say, a $9,000 policy may find that for a small extra premium he can purchase a $10,000 contract. Some participating insurers grade dividends, not initial premiums.

† The base premium rates for women are less than those for men. For example, a female, aged 35, would pay the same rates for most of these contracts as a male, aged 32. The base premium rates would be $15.75 for a straight life insurance contract, $19.22 for a paid-up-at-65 contract, $24.94 for a 20-payment life contract, $25.92 for an endowment at 65 contract, and $42.21 for a 20-year endowment contract.

‡ Renewable to age 65 and convertible prior to age 60. Minimum issue amount, $5,000. Not issued after age 55.

§ Nonrenewable but convertible within 8 years. Minimum issue amount, $5,000.

ance and (2) limited payment life insurance. Under straight life insurance,[2] the premiums are payable for the remainder of the insured's lifetime. Under limited payment life insurance, the premiums are payable for the remainder of the insured's lifetime or until the expiration of a specified period, if

[2] Sometimes referred to as "continuous premium whole life insurance or as ordinary life insurance." The latter term is unfortunate because of the use of the term "ordinary" to denote a branch of insurance.

earlier. Some examples of limited payment contracts and the level premiums for some whole life contracts are presented in Table 19.2.

The level premium concept underlying these policies is extremely important, because (1) otherwise, permanent protection would be unavailable, since no insurer renews term insurance indefinitely, and (2) a savings or investment element is created, which may prove useful in emergencies or during retirement. To understand these two arguments, one must know how the level premium concept works. Assume that a person, aged 35, wants $1,000 of permanent protection against death. Two contracts that would provide this protection are a straight life insurance contract and a one-year term policy renewable for life. In practice, this second contract is not issued by any insurer because the insurance would be too costly to be salable at the advanced ages, especially since only persons in poor health would be likely to continue the protection. Conceptually, however, this comparison is revealing.

One clear difference between the two approaches would be the premium-payment pattern. The yearly renewable term would be much cheaper in the early years, but in the late fifties or early sixties, depending upon the table of premium rates selected, the annual yearly renewable term premium would exceed the level premium for the straight life contract. In the late seventies or early eighties, the total premiums paid for the term insurance would exceed the total premiums paid for the straight life contract. This eventuality will occur even if the loss of interest in the early years on the difference between the term premium and the straight life premium is acknowledged. Of course the persons who die in the early years will contribute much more in premiums if they purchase straight life insurance.

Because insureds with straight life contracts pay more than the cost of term protection in the early years, the insurer is able to use part of the premium in those years to establish a "savings account" or investment element.[3] This investment element is part of the face amount paid if the insured dies, and the cost of the "pure" insurance component, therefore, is actually less than the premium for a yearly renewable term contract of the same face amount as the straight life contract.

The investment element is credited with a guaranteed interest rate by the insurer and continues to grow throughout the policy period. During the early years of the contract, the growth is obvious, but as mortality rates increase, it takes place only because the interest on the savings account is more than adequate to make up for the deficiency in the level premium relative to the cost of the pure protection. With each increase in the invest-

---

[3] The following discussion illustrates the principle involved. For a more rigorous discussion, see Davis W. Gregg (ed.), *Life and Health Insurance Handbook* (2d ed., Homewood, Ill.: Richard D. Irwin, Inc., 1964), pp. 53–54.

ment element, the amount of pure protection decreases. Eventually, the fact that the amount of pure protection is decreasing more than offsets the increasing mortality rates, and as a result the cost of the pure protection decreases. Under the usual current mortality assumptions, a person, aged 99, is assumed to die within the next year. Therefore the insurer must be prepared to deliver the face amount to the insured when he reaches age 100. At age 100 the investment element must equal the face amount, and the cost of the pure protection the last year is zero.[4]

Straight life insurance, therefore, is a combination of decreasing term insurance (the pure-protection element) and an increasing investment element which equals the face amount at age 100.

The investment element is available to the insured at any time in the form of a cash value or some form of insurance. (The so-called nonforfeiture options are described later in this chapter in the section "Nonforfeiture Options.") In practice, the investment element will ordinarily be less than the preceding discussion would lead one to believe, because the insurer is permitted to give some recognition to its heavier expenses the first year (for example, the fee for a medical examination, the cost of preparing new policy records, and the agent's first-year commission, which is larger than the commission in succeeding years) before it diverts any of the premium into the investment element. Generally, therefore, there is *no* investment element the first year, the cash values usually becoming available during the second year.

Straight life insurance provides permanent insurance protection at the lowest cost. It may be used to leave a legacy to some person or organization, regardless of when the insured dies, or to pay probate costs and estate and inheritance taxes. It also permits an insured to accumulate some savings through life insurance without sacrificing too much protection against death at an early age. As will be explained in the section on nonforfeiture options, straight life insurance is a highly flexible contract.

Limited payment contracts also combine decreasing term insurance with an investment element, but the investment element is more important than in straight life insurance because of the higher limited payment premiums during the early years. The cash value patterns under the nonterm insurance contracts for which premium rates were presented in Table 19.2 are given in Table 19.3 for contracts issued at age 35. Figure 19.1 displays the same information in a different form. The reader's attention is directed particularly to (1) the absence of a cash value the first year under most contracts, (2) the cash values at age 100 under the whole life contracts, (3) the continued growth in the cash values under the limited payment

[4] Under policies issued prior to the late 1940s, the limiting age was assumed to be age 96 instead of age 100.

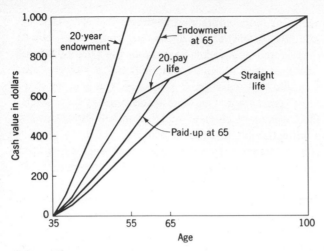

Figure 19.1   Cash values per $1,000 insurance provided under some representative contracts issued to an insured, aged 35.

contracts after the end of the premium-payment period, and (4) the comparison between the cash value patterns of the limited payment life contracts and the endowments.

Limited payment life insurance is attractive when an insured wishes to stop premiums after a specified period but wants the original face amount of protection to be continued for the rest of his life. For example,

Table 19.3   Cash values per $1,000 insurance provided by one leading non-participating insurer to an insured, aged 35

End of policy year	Straight life	Paid-up at 65	20-pay-ment life	Endowment at 65	20-year endowment
1					
2		$ 4	$ 12	$ 12	$ 35
3	$ 16	23	36	36	75
5	48	62	86	87	157
10	137	168	226	226	389
15	235	288	386	386	665
20	342	423	574	573	1,000
Age 65	522	690	690	1,000	
Age 100	1,000	1,000	1,000		

he may want to stop paying premiums at age 65, the normal retirement age, or twenty years from now, when his peak earning period as an actor or an athlete has passed. Limited payment contracts are often used as gifts because the donor can complete the premium payments within a specified period. These contracts also appeal to persons who wish to devote a larger portion of their premiums to savings than is possible under straight life insurance. Most young married persons considering a 20-payment life policy would be well advised to spend the same amount of premium to purchase a larger face amount of paid-up-at-65 or straight life insurance. Otherwise they are trading important additional protection for slightly higher cash values during the next twenty years and the cessation of premium payments in twenty years when these payments should be much easier to meet than when the purchasers are young.[5]

Endowment insurance   Endowment insurance protects the beneficiary if the insured dies within the endowment period, and in addition it provides for the payment of the face amount to the insured if he is living at the end of the endowment period. Endowment insurance may be regarded as a combination of term insurance for the endowment period and a pure endowment which would provide benefits only for those who survive. Endowment insurance, like all nonterm insurance contracts, may also be considered a combination of decreasing term insurance and an increasing investment element. The investment element, of course, is relatively more important for endowments than for whole life contracts. Some examples of endowment contracts and the level premiums for these contracts are shown in Table 19.2. The relative importance of the investment elements in these contracts is shown in Table 19.3.

Endowment insurance is a useful way for some persons to accumulate a specified sum over a stated period of time whether they live or die. The objective may be funds to finance a child's college education, to pay living expenses during retirement, or to retire a debt. Because a substantial portion of each annual premium is used to build up the investment element in the contract, the purchaser of an endowment should value savings much more than protection and should be convinced insurance is a good investment.

Life insurance as an investment   Some observers believe that insureds would always be better off to "buy term and invest the difference" between the premiums for a nonterm policy and for a term policy. Their argument is

---

[5] If unforeseen circumstances do make it desirable to terminate premium payments at that time, the nonforfeiture options described in "Nonforfeiture options" under "Option clauses" later in this chapter can be exercised to provide continuing protection under paid-up-at-65 or straight life insurance.

basically that insureds can obtain more attractive yields and capital appreciation from other investments, even from government bonds. A few comments are in order here. First, although this advice to buy term and invest the difference may be sound for some persons, it is far from being a universal truth. Second, in making any evaluation of insurance as an investment, an insured should clearly understand its major advantages and disadvantages. The advantages are as follows:

1. Life insurance is a secure investment. Although losses may be suffered, they are very few. Even during the Great Depression, the industry achieved an enviable record.

2. Insureds are reluctant to skip premium payments or to make withdrawals from their savings accounts (although the liquidity of this asset is also a valuable feature in emergencies). Consequently, the savings plan will very probably be carried out.

3. The insured does not have to concern himself with the investment decisions or details except as a decision may affect his initial choice of an insurer.

4. The cash values in the contract guarantee the insured a minimum rate of return that increases with the duration of the contract.

5. Actual interest returns compare favorably with returns on other investments of similar quality. Because a life insurance premium purchases a package of decreasing protection and increasing savings, the return on the savings element in a life insurance contract is a complicated concept. One widely used approach calculates the rate of return one would have to make on some alternative investment program to achieve the same results over a specified period at the same cost as the purchase of the nonterm insurance contract for which the rate of return is being sought. More specifically, assume that a person, aged 35, is considering the purchase of a $1,000 straight life insurance contract for which the cash value at the close of the twentieth policy year is about $365. Instead of buying this policy he could buy decreasing term insurance and invest the difference between the premium for the straight life insurance and the premium for the decreasing term insurance in a savings account, mutual fund shares, or some other medium. The face value of the decreasing term insurance must be such that, added to the increasing investment, it equals $1,000.[6] In this way, if the insured dies prior to the expiration of the twentieth year, his beneficiary receives the same amount whether he purchases the straight life insurance or the separate term-insurance–investment plan. The rate of return on the life insurance savings element is assumed to be the

[6] Determining this amount involves a trial-and-error procedure because the amount of term insurance determines the moneys available for investment, which in turn affect the amount of term insurance needed. There is one equilibrium solution.

rate of return one would have to make on the separate investment fund for it to equal the $365 cash value at the close of the twentieth year. Mr. Albert Linton, who developed this method, calculated a return of 4.78 per cent on straight life insurance contracts issued in 1963 by ten large mutual companies. At issue ages 25, 45, and 55, Linton calculated returns of 4.80 per cent, 5.17 per cent, and 6.37 per cent, respectively.[7]

The ten mutual insurers whose contracts were included in the Linton analysis provide their policyholders with a higher rate of return than the average insurer, but some insurers sell contracts with an even higher rate of return. In a study of $10,000 st aight life insurance contracts issued in 1962 to males, aged 35, by 148 insurers who account for approximately 85 per cent of the total life insurance in force, Professor Joseph Belth found an average rate of return of 4.11 per cent for 88 participating insurers (assuming 1962 nonguaranteed dividend rates) and 3.44 per cent for 60 nonparticipating insurers. Nine insurers had rates of return of over 5 per cent; 16 insurers had rates under 3 per cent.[8]

The principal reasons why this rate of return exceeds the 2½ or 3 per cent assumptions used by most participating insurers in their cash value computations are that (1) insurers have improved considerably their average net (of expenses) rate of return on invested assets in recent years (5.12 per cent in 1969) and (2) insurers experience higher mortality rates under separate term Insurance and charge accordingly.[9]

No Federal income taxes are payable until the person cashes in his contract, and only the excess of the cash value over the premiums paid less dividends) is taxable. As a result, most persons will pay less taxes than they otherwise would; some will pay no tax. This feature makes the investment returns mentioned above much more attractive.

As we shall explain shortly, the cash value can be converted into an annuity without any additional expense loading and with perhaps some favorable tax consequences.

6. In case of death, the investment passes to the beneficiaries directly, thus avoiding the expense and delays of probate action.

---

[7] M. A. Linton, "Life Insurance as an Investment," in Davis W. Gregg (ed.), *Life and Health Insurance Handbook* (2d ed., Homewood, Ill.: Richard D. Irwin, Inc., 1964), p. 242.

[8] J. M. Belth, "The Rate of Return on the Savings Element in Cash-Value Life Insurance," *Journal of Risk and Insurance*, XXXV, No. 4 (December, 1968), 573. For other comments on the Linton method and suggested modifications see J. R. Ferrari, "Investment Life Insurance versus Term Insurance and Separate Investment," *Journal of Risk and Insurance*, XXXV, No. 2 (June, 1968), 181–198, and Stuart Schwarzschild, "Rates of Return on the Investment Differentials between Life Insurance Policies," *Journal of Risk and Insurance*, XXXV, No. 4 (December, 1968), 583–595.

[9] The Linton rate of return is highly sensitive to the rates assumed for the separate decreasing term. In his calculation Linton assumed fairly low term insurance rates. See Belth, *op. cit.*, pp. 570–571, 577.

On the other hand, for a given issue age, the return one would have to make under an alternative investment combined with separate term insurance in order to accumulate the same amount as the cash value under a nonterm insurance contract is less under contracts such as endowments, which place more emphasis upon the investment element than does straight life insurance.[10] These contracts provide less pure protection, and consequently the insured saves fewer dollars than he would under straight life insurance by purchasing the pure insurance protection as part of the package contract instead of through higher-priced separate term insurance. Therefore, the second reason cited above to explain why the rate of return under a straight life insurance contract exceeds the return assumed in cash value calculations is less effective.

The reader should also remember that the equivalent investment return is much less in the short run; at the end of one or two years it is commonly negative. A person who is saving to meet short-term needs would be well advised to invest in some other media, such as bank savings accounts, savings and loan association deposits, or credit union shares.

The most common objection to life insurance as an investment is that it provides no protection against long-period inflation. Like other fixed-dollar investments, such as corporate bonds and bank savings accounts, life insurance does not provide any opportunity for capital appreciation. Equities have become an increasingly popular investment because they permit capital gains and because, in the long run, the value of a diversified portfolio of common stocks tends to rise when prices rise, thus preserving real purchasing power. Since 1945, consumer prices (as measured by the Consumer Price Index) and stock prices (as measured by Standard and Poor's Composite Stock Index) have risen as follows:

	Consumer prices, per cent	Stock prices, per cent
1950	34	21
1955	49	167
1960	64	268
1965	75	482
October, 1970	119	457

Equities, however, may decline in value and the investor may suffer capital losses instead of making capital gains. Persons differ in their willingness and their desire to assume the risks associated with investments in

[10] In an analysis of 20-payment life contracts issued by 93 insurers, Professor Belth calculated a return of only 2.9 per cent for participating insurers and 2.10 per cent for nonparticipating insurers. *Ibid.*, p. 574.

equities. Because it is impossible to predict with much confidence the future state of the economy (although the evidence suggests an upward trend with cyclical fluctuations), the best approach for most persons is some blend of fixed-dollar investments and equities, the exact proportion depending upon one's personal estimate of the future and his assessment of the risks associated with various proportions. Because life insurance has many advantages as a long-term fixed-dollar investment, risk managers should consider seriously the use of some nonterm life insurance as one of their fixed-dollar investments.

Mutual funds and life insurance   For the reasons cited above and because of improved and more widespread knowledge of stock investments, an increasing proportion of consumer savings has been directed toward equities. Particularly noteworthy is the increased share of mutual funds, which permit an investor to participate in a diversified, managed portfolio of securities. These securities may include corporate bonds as well as equities, but most mutual fund portfolios emphasize equities. Corporate bonds and life insurance, although still important outlets for consumer savings, have declined in importance.

Because they have been concerned about their diminishing share of consumer savings and because they have increasingly considered themselves to be financial service institutions, a large number of life insurers have in recent years established an organization to market and manage a new mutual fund, acquired an existing organization for this purpose, or have affiliated themselves with an independent mutual fund broker-dealership. Regardless of the technique employed, the result is that some or all of their agents can sell both life insurance and mutual funds. Consequently the agent should be able to meet the full range of investment needs and desires ranging from the wish to buy term and invest the difference to the need for life insurance policies with high cash values. Life insurer activity in this area is expected to increase.

Mutual funds have been commonly sold in conjunction with life insurance in two principal ways. Under one approach the insured purchases (1) decreasing term insurance or some nonterm insurance contract plus a decreasing term rider and (2) shares in a mutual fund that through annual purchases and capital appreciation are expected to increase in value over time. Under a second approach, the insured buys a nonterm insurance contract, borrows the full cash value, and invests the loan amount in mutual fund shares. Integrated packages of various sorts already exist and will become more commonplace in the future.

Annuity contracts   Annuity contracts differ considerably from the life insurance contracts we have been discussing. Under an annuity, the insurer promises to pay the insured an income for a specified period. The specified period may be a definite number of years, in which case the contract is called an *annuity certain*. Most annuities sold as separate contracts, however, provide payments conditioned in some way upon the continued survival of the annuitant.

These life-contingency contracts assume many forms. A straight life annuity will provide payments as long as the insured lives. Even if the annuitant dies after having received only a few payments, the insurer has fulfilled its obligation. On the other hand, even if the annuitant lives to a very advanced age, the insurer must continue to make the payments. Under some annuity contracts involving life contingencies, a minimum number of payments is guaranteed. For example, under a life annuity contract with ten years certain, the insurer promises to make payments for ten years, regardless of whether the annuitant lives, and after the ten-year period as long as the annuitant survives. Under an installment refund annuity, the guaranteed period is that necessary to refund the purchase price. A cash refund annuity differs from an installment refund annuity in that the excess, if any, of the purchase price over the annuity payments made to the date of death is refunded in cash instead of in installments. Table 19.4 demonstrates the effect of the different refund features upon the purchase price for a given monthly income, on the assumption that the purchase price is payable in one lump sum and that the annuity payments begin one month after the

Table 19.4 Premium rates charged by one leading nonparticipating insurer for immediate annuities issued to men, providing $10 monthly income*

Age†	Straight life annuity	Installment refund annuity	Cash refund annuity
45	$2,031	$2,092	$2,111
55	1,693	1,801	1,834
65	1,310	1,457	1,498
75	937	1,137	1,189

* If the state imposes a premium tax on annuities, these basic rates must be multiplied by a tax factor. In Iowa, for example, the tax factor is 1.02.

The rates for women are much higher. For example, for a woman, aged 65, the three rates are $1,481, $1,585, and $1,613.

† A pro rata allowance is made for each complete month elapsed since the insured's last birthday.

purchase. To understand how the insurer can promise to pay *at least* the purchase price to all annuitants and to explain the smaller payment under the cash refund annuity than under other contracts refunding the same number of dollars, one must remember that the insurer guarantees a specified rate of interest on the unpaid balance of the funds in its possession.

Annuities can also be classified according to other characteristics, and all characteristics must be considered if an annuity contract is to be described completely. First, annuities can be classified as immediate or deferred, depending upon whether the benefits are payable immediately after the purchase of the contract, as in Table 19.4.[11] Second, annuities may be paid for by a single premium as in Table 19.4 or by annual premiums. Third, annuities may cover one life or joint lives. If two or more lives are covered, the payments may stop at the death of the first annuitant or at the death of the last annuitant. Payments of the first type are provided under joint life annuities, of the second type, under joint life and survivorship annuities.

The final classification to be considered is of recent origin and depends upon whether the contract promises to deliver periodically (1) a fixed number of dollars or (2) a fixed number of units, the value of which will depend upon the market value of a portfolio of equity assets or, less commonly, upon changes in the Consumer Price Index. Contracts of the first type are called *fixed* or *conventional* annuities; contracts of the second type are termed *variable* annuities.

Variable annuities were introduced for the first time in 1952 by the Teachers Insurance and Annuity Association (TIAA), an insurer that restricts its contracts primarily to college educators. TIAA established a running mate, the College Retirement Equities Fund (CREF), to underwrite these new contracts. In brief, the dollar amount to be provided under the contracts at the retirement date depends upon the performance of the CREF portfolio to that date. At retirement, the annuitant is guaranteed a certain number of annuity units per month for the remainder of his life (a refund feature may be included), the units being revalued once a year upon the basis of the performance of the CREF portfolio. The variable annuity was introduced because of the failure of the fixed annuity to produce (1) an initial retirement income reflecting changes in the cost of living during the premium-payment period and (2) a constant purchasing power income during the retirement period. The variable annuity blends the characteristics of a mutual fund with those of an annuity. A variable annuity is superior to a mutual fund as a retirement vehicle because it provides a lifetime income. It is an inferior

---

[11] Under most individual deferred annuity contracts, the insured is entitled to a refund of his premiums or a cash value, if higher, if he should die or surrender the contract prior to the maturity date.

way to accumulate funds to meet short-term needs or to create an estate to be passed on to survivors.[12] Many life insurers sell both products.

TIAA-CREF studies revealed that over several selected periods in the past, equal annual contributions toward a fixed annuity and a variable annuity would have produced a retirement income satisfying (for practical purposes), over the long run, both of these criteria. The variable annuity alone produced payments that fluctuated more violently than the cost of living.

Although a few commercial insurers that specialize in variable annuities were formed during the 1950s, none of the major life insurers issued any contracts until 1964, when a few insurers began to write group annuity contracts for selected groups. This belated and relatively limited activity on the part of major insurers can be attributed to legal obstacles, strong differences of opinion within and outside the industry concerning the desirability of marketing variable annuities to the general public,[13] technical problems such as the nature of the separate fund, and a natural hesitancy to enter a new field without extensive advance preparation.

Legal obstacles occurred first at the state level because state insurance laws had to be changed to permit the writing of group and individual variable annuities. After a few states had made the necessary changes, the Supreme Court of the United States ruled in 1959 that insurers specializing in variable annuities are subject to regulation by the Securities and Exchange Commission under the Investment Company Act of 1940. In April, 1964, after considerable legal sparring, the SEC announced its intent to approve group variable annuities for insured pension plans on a fairly liberal basis. Shortly thereafter many insurers became active in this field. SEC requirements for writing individual variable annuities have been more restrictive, but by the late sixties many major insurers were selling this product, and their number has been increasing steadily.

MODIFICATIONS AND COMBINATIONS

In order to illustrate the ways in which the basic policy types can be modified and combined, several popular nonbasic insurance contracts (often called "special" contracts) are described very briefly below.

1. *Modified life* and *graded premium life* contracts are whole life contracts for which the premiums are not level over the premium-payment period. Under the modified life contract, the premium is lower than the

---

[12] The two products are also taxed differently. Which system is more favorable to the consumer depends upon the circumstances.

[13] For example, opponents argued that policyholders would lose faith in life insurance if the monthly income drops, that life insurance agents were not qualified to sell a contract providing a variable income, and that supporting the variable annuity was equivalent to surrendering to inflation.

level premium (but greater than the premium for term insurance) during the early years (generally the first three or five years), after which, in order to be actuarially equivalent, it increases to a higher amount than the level premium. Graded premium contracts resemble modified life contracts except that the premium increases gradually over the early years instead of remaining level over that period.

2. A *family* policy covers all members of the family under one contract. For example, the insurer whose rates were quoted in Table 19.2 issues a two-parent family policy which combines $5,000 of whole life insurance on the husband with $1,250 term insurance to age 65 on the wife,[14] $1,000 term insurance to age 21 on the children, including children born after the inception of the contract, and $1,250 term insurance on the husband, payable only if he dies after his wife and before age 65. The term insurance is usually convertible at the time it expires. A family may purchase more than one unit. Not all family policies contain the same combination of coverages, but they are based on the same general principles.

3. A *family income* policy combines whole life insurance with decreasing term insurance. The policy provides for (*a*) a monthly payment of 1 per cent (or 2 or 3 per cent) of the face amount of the whole life policy from the date of death until the expiration of the family income period (usually 10, 15, or 20 years, beginning at the date of issue of the contract) and (*b*) the payment of the face amount at the end of the family income period or the date of death, whichever comes later. For example, a 2 per cent $10,000 twenty-year family income policy issued at age 35 would make possible the following benefits.[15]

Date of death	Benefits
Policy Issue date	$200 a month for 20 years, $10,000 at end of 20 years
Ten years later	$200 a month for 10 years, $10,000 at end of 10 years
Fifteen years later	$200 a month for 5 years, $10,000 at end of 5 years
Twenty or more years later	$10,000 payable immediately

The purpose of this contract is to provide a large sum of money if the insured should die while his family is young. The sum decreases as his children become older but never drops below the basic policy amount.

[14] Adjustments are made in the term insurance amount if the wife is younger or older than the husband. For example, if the wife is five years younger, the amount is $1,750; if the wife is five years older, the amount is $900.
[15] Some contracts also provide for the immediate payment of a lump sum of $150 or $200 per $1,000 of whole life insurance.

The $10,000 is, of course, provided by the whole life contract. The $200 a month comes from two sources: the interest on the $10,000 being held by the insurer and decreasing term insurance.[16] Generally the decreasing term insurance is provided by a rider attached to a new whole life insurance contract. The decreasing term insurance is usually convertible if the insured acts prior to 5 years, say, before the expiration date. The converted policy cannot exceed some portion, say, 80 per cent, of the amount of the term insurance on the conversion date.

4. A *family maintenance* contract combines whole life insurance with *level* term insurance. The family maintenance contract differs from the family income contract only in that the payments are always made for the same number of years as the family maintenance period if death occurs during this period. For example, if the contract illustration used in the preceding paragraph had been a family maintenance contract, the payment, if death had occurred on the policy issue date, 10 years later, or 15 years later, would have been $200 a month for 20 years and $10,000 at the expiration of that time. If death occurred 20 or more years later, $10,000 would be payable immediately.

Some authorities prefer this contract to a family income contract because the family may continue to grow after the insurance is purchased. Even if the family does not grow, the level insurance may be required as a hedge against inflation.

5. A *retirement income* contract combines an annual premium deferred annuity contract with decreasing term insurance. Generally the contract provides a death benefit of $1,000 or the cash value, if greater, for each $10 of retirement income. In the early years of the contract, the cash value is much less than $1,000, and the term insurance provides most of the death benefit, but eventually the term insurance decreases to zero.

6. *Preferred risk* policies or *specials* are contracts (usually whole life contracts) sold at attractive rates for one or more of the following reasons: (*a*) superior underwriting requirements, (*b*) minimum amount requirements, such as $15,000, (*c*) reduced agent's commissions, (*d*) lower cash values, or (*e*) less liberal settlement options or policy services.

Until 1956, these contracts provided the only way for insurers to reflect in their rates expense savings on larger policies because antidiscrmination statutes that prohibited any discrimination between individuals of the same class and life expectancy were interpreted to mean that an insurer could not grade its premium rates in the manner shown in Table 19.2. An insurer could, however, issue a special policy for a certain minimum amount and reflect the resultant expense savings in its rates for that policy, because

---

[16] In this instance the term insurance decreases from about $30,000 to zero over the 20-year period.

the policy type sold as a special was not issued on any other basis.[17] In 1956, the interpretation of these statutes was changed, and most insurers now reduce their premium rates on all policies as the face amount increases. Consequently, specials have become less important in recent years.

7. The *guaranteed insurability* rider, when attached to a new life insurance policy, gives the insured the option to purchase at standard rates at certain specified ages additional amounts of insurance. The rider thus provides protection against uninsurability or insurability at substandard rates and forces the insured to make definite decisions at the option dates. The following contract is illustrative: Attached to a base policy of $10,000 issued at age 20, this rider guarantees the right of the insured to buy $10,000 additional protection at (1) each of the following ages: 25, 28, 31, 34, 37, and 40, (2) on his wedding date, and (3) at the birth of each child.

8. The eighth contract to be considered in this section is a life insurance contract with a *double indemnity* rider attached. The rider usually provides that if death results (*a*) solely from external, violent, and accidental means (*b*) independently and exclusively of all other causes and (*c*) within 90 days after the accident, double the face amount of the contract is to be paid the insured. The rider then proceeds to exclude certain types of deaths that would be covered even under this narrow definition.[18] The coverage usually terminates at age 60 or 65. Triple indemnity riders based on the same principles are also available.

The authors agree with many insurance authorities that the double indemnity rider should not be included in most insurance programs. There is no reason why the need for insurance proceeds should be greater in the case of a death caused by accidental means. Indeed the opposite may be true. The rider is most misused when it is purchased at the expense of protection against all causes of death.

9. *Variable life insurance* is the latest development in life insurance contracts. Several insurers have introduced contracts under which the face amount is adjusted according to some index such as the Consumer Price Index. Limits are usually placed on how high or low the face amount can be adjusted in a single year or over a stated period of time, and the face amount is not permitted to drop below the initial amount. In effect part of the premium is used to purchase one-year term insurance each year equal to the difference between the adjusted amount and the initial amount. Most of these contracts are term insurance that expires after a fixed period.[19]

---

[17] For example, the special policy might be a straight life policy while the closest regular policy was a paid-up-at-85 contract.
[18] For example, deaths resulting from the inhalation of gas may be excluded because of the possibility that suicide may be involved.
[19] For more details, see W. Lee Shield, "Looking Backward and Forward at the Same Time," *American Life Convention News Letter* (September 16, 1969), 4–5, 8–9.

Other variable contracts under development at this writing would adjust both the face amount and the cash value according to (1) some index or (2) the performance of some separate investment account. Variable life insurance is a natural development following the maturation of the variable annuity concept.

Major Policy Provisions

The major policy provisions may be divided into two groups: (1) the nonoption clauses, which do not require the insured or his beneficiary to make decisions, and (2) the option clauses, which require such decisions.

NONOPTION CLAUSES

Some important nonoption clauses are the grace period clause, the suicide clause, and aviation and war clauses. All these clauses, like the entire contract, assignment, and incontestable clauses described in Chapter 14, are required or permitted statutory standard provisions clauses in most states.

The *grace period* clause establishes a period of 1 month or 31 days after the premium-due date during which the premium may be paid without penalty. Under most laws, the insurer could charge interest following the due date, but this is seldom, if ever, done. The reinstatement clause gives the insured the right to reinstate a policy after lapse for nonpayment of premiums if the policy has not been surrendered for cash and if the reinstatement is effected within a certain period after the lapse, usually five years. Overdue premiums must be paid with interest, and the person must present evidence of insurability.[20] The *misstatement of age* clause provides for the adjustment of the amount payable to the amount the premium being paid would have purchased at the correct age at issue. The discovery of the misstatement is not limited by the incontestable clause. The clause may result in either an increase or a decrease in the face amount. The *suicide* clause excludes deaths by suicide, sane or insane, within one or two years from the date of issue. It is assumed that persons do not plan suicide thus far in advance and that the public interest is best served by making the proceeds available to the innocent beneficiaries where the policy has not been purchased with suicide in mind. *Aviation* clauses which limit the insurer's liability to the premiums paid plus interest if death occurs as a result of certain hazardous types of aviation (pilots of nonscheduled passenger flights, for example) are seldom used today, the preferred method

[20] Two reasons why the insured may be interested in reinstating his policy instead of purchasing a new one are that (1) the heavy first-year expenses in a new contract can be avoided and (2) older policies frequently have more liberal settlement options or some other attractive features.

of dealing with this extra hazard being by payment of an additional premium. *War* clauses, which limit the liability of the insurer if the death results from war or, in some cases, occurs while the insured is in service outside the home area, are generally used only when a war appears likely or already exists. After the war, the clauses are usually canceled.

OPTION CLAUSES

The option clauses deal with policy conversions, nonforfeiture options, loans, settlement options, and dividend options.

Statutory standard provisions usually (1) prescribe the minimum nonforfeiture values and require a cash value option and at least one insurance option, (2) demand a loan provision and limit the maximum interest charge, and (3) make mandatory the annual payment of dividends. Otherwise, the statutes require only that the insurer present tables showing the amounts available under the various options. Consequently, considerable variation is possible among insurers with respect to these options.

Policy conversions   The *policy change* clause permits the insured to convert his policy, without demonstrating evidence of insurability, to some other form requiring a higher premium. The conversion is retroactive, the insured usually making up the deficiency in the premiums already paid by a lump sum payment equal to the difference in the reserves under the two plans. Conversion to a lower premium plan, if permitted at all, generally requires proof of insurability.

Nonforfeiture options   As we have pointed out earlier in this chapter, nonterm insurance contracts combine decreasing term insurance with an increasing savings component.[21] This savings component, called the "nonforfeiture value," is available to the insured who wishes to surrender his policy. The cash values provided under several leading policies issued at age 35 were presented in Table 19.3.

Two other nonforfeiture options are also available. The *paid-up insurance* option permits the insured to exchange the cash value[22] at *net* rates[23] for a paid-up policy of the same type as the surrendered contract. The *extended term insurance* option permits the insured to continue the face amount of insurance[24] in force as term insurance for as long a period

---

[21] Some term insurance contracts of long duration also provide for nonforfeiture values.
[22] More exactly, the cash value less any policy loans plus any dividend accumulations or cash values on dividend additions.
[23] No expense loading.
[24] More exactly, the face amount plus any dividend accumulations or additions less any policy indebtedness.

as the cash value applied as a *net* single premium will provide.[25] However, if the original contract was an endowment contract and the cash value is sufficient to provide insurance for more than the remainder of the endowment period, the excess cash value is used to purchase a pure endowment payable to those insureds who survive to the end of the endowment period.

Specific illustrations of surrender value patterns for three popular types of policies issued at age 35 are presented in Table 19.5. If the insured does not pay a premium when it is due and does not select a nonforfeiture option within a specified period, such as 3 months, one of the insurance options, usually the extended term insurance option, becomes effective automatically.

Loan provisions   The *loan provision* permits the insured to borrow an amount which, accumulated at 5 or 6 per cent interest, will not exceed the cash value[26] on the date to which premiums have been paid. Interest accrues on the loan from day to day, and the policy terminates when the total indebtedness exceeds the cash value. The loan may be repaid in whole or in part at any time. In case of death, the indebtedness is subtracted from the proceeds.

The 5 or 6 per cent interest rate is charged to offset the loss of earnings because the money borrowed is not invested elsewhere by the insurer, and to meet the costs of administering the loan.

The *automatic premium loan provision,* which is not included by most insurers except upon request (and in this sense only is an option clause), provides that if the insured fails to pay any premium, the insured is assumed to have paid the premium by borrowing against the policy.

Settlement options   The settlement options make it possible to have the death proceeds and usually the cash value payable in some manner other than a lump sum. The insured may at any time select options which his beneficiary must accept, or he may permit the beneficiary after his death to change his selection. If the insured does not make any selection, this right is usually given to his beneficiary.

Although other options may be available upon request, the four most common options applicable to death proceeds are the following.

1. *Interest* option. The insurer holds the proceeds for some specified period, a guaranteed rate of interest being payable to the primary beneficiary.

---

[25] More exactly, the cash value less any policy loans plus any dividend accumulations or cash values on dividend additions.

[26] More exactly, the cash value plus dividend accumulations or the cash values of dividend accumulations.

At one time the 5 or 6 per cent interest rate was considered high, but currently these rates are attractive and policy loans have increased.

Table 19.5 Nonforfeiture values provided by one leading nonparticipating insurer to an insured, aged 35

End of policy year	Straight life				20-payment life				20-year endowment			
		Paid-up insur-	Extended term insurance			Paid-up insur-	Extended term insurance			Paid-up insur-	Extended term insurance*	
	Cash value	ance	Years	Days	Cash value	ance	Years	Days	Cash value	ance	Years	Days
5	$ 48	$127	9	9	$ 86	$227	14	89	$ 157	$258	15	$125
10	137	313	14	284	226	516	21	101	389	543	10	$481
15	235	468	16	116	386	768	24	185	665	788	5	$772
20	342	597	16	76	574	Fully paid			1,000			
Age 65	522	757	15	295	690	Fully paid						

* Extended term insurance never extends beyond the remainder of the endowment period. The remainder of cash value is used to purchase a promise that the number of dollars stated under "Days" will be paid to those persons who survive to the end of the endowment period.

The primary beneficiary may have the right of withdrawal in whole or in part. At the end of the specified period (for example, the death of the primary beneficiary), the proceeds are payable, perhaps according to some other option.

2. *Installment time* option. The proceeds are payable as a monthly income for a specified number of years. The monthly income is computed on the basis of a guaranteed interest rate on the unpaid balance.

3. *Installment amount* option. The proceeds are payable as a specified monthly income for such time as the proceeds will provide. The time is computed on the basis of a guaranteed interest rate on the unpaid balance.

4. *Life income* option. The proceeds are used as the purchase price for an annuity at net rates. The common annuity forms are the straight life annuity, an annuity with a specified number of years certain, a cash refund annuity, and an installment refund annuity. The monthly payments are based on guaranteed interest and mortality rates. Some insurers have recently added a variable annuity settlement option.

The policy specifies the guaranteed interest rate applicable to option 1 and the monthly benefits possible under options 2 and 4. A portion of a table of monthly values under options 2 and 4 is reproduced as Table

Table 19.6 Monthly installments per $1,000 proceeds provided by one leading nonparticipating insurer under the installment time and life income settlement options

Installment time option		Monthly life income option					
		Age of payee		Years certain			
Number of years	Monthly installment	Male	Female	5	10	15	20
2	$42.77	35	40	$3.59	$3.58	$3.56	$3.54
3	28.90	40	45	3.83	3.82	3.80	3.76
4	21.97	45	50	4.16	4.13	4.08	4.00
5	17.81	50	55	4.57	4.51	4.42	4.29
10	9.51	55	60	5.09	4.98	4.81	4.59
15	6.76	60	65	5.75	5.56	5.27	4.90
20	5.39	65	70	6.62	6.26	5.75	5.18

19.6. Option 3 values are computed on the same assumptions as option 2 values, and a rough estimate of the time over which they will be paid is obtainable from the same table.[27] For example, under a $10,000 policy, $100 a month would be payable for over 9 years but less than 10 years. In each case, the insurer may declare some excess interest each year that will increase the amount or the time of the monthly payments. For example, although the installment time option amounts in Table 19.6 are calculated on the basis of a $2\frac{3}{4}$ per cent interest return, this particular insurer is currently paying 4.65 per cent on the unpaid balance of the proceeds.

The insured may also elect to receive the cash value of the contract according to one of these options. In addition, the policy commonly permits the insured to purchase a joint and survivorship annuity at net rates. The insurer whose settlement option values were reproduced in Table 19.6 provides a guaranteed monthly income of $5.38 for a male, aged 65, and a wife, aged 60, per $1,000 of cash value applied under this option, two-thirds of this amount being continued for the lifetime of the survivor. For a husband and wife, both 65, the joint income would be $5.78.

The settlement options give the insured guaranteed interest and mortality rates, some tax advantages,[28] conversion rights at net cost, freedom from investment worries, and the ability to evaluate a lump sum payment in terms of the income it replaces. If the insured wishes to have the proceeds managed by some third party but wants more flexibility than that provided

[27] In practice, however, a separate exact computation is made for the value selected.
[28] For example, only the interest portions of the payments are taxable, and the spouse of a deceased person may receive $1,000 in interest of this sort tax-free under all options other than the interest option.

by the settlement options, a lump sum payment may be paid to a trustee under a trust agreement. The return on the trusted proceeds, however, is not guaranteed; it may be greater or less than if the proceeds had been retained by the insurer.

Dividend options   Participating policies provide dividends for policyholders when the premium charged exceeds the actual costs of the protection. Sizable dividends are probable under participating policies because the initial premiums include a substantial "cushioning" factor.

The usual dividend options in a participating contract permit the insured to receive his annual dividends as (1) a cash payment, (2) a reduction in the next premium, (3) paid-up additional life insurance, the additional insurance being purchased by the application of the dividend as a single premium at net rates, (4) a deposit with the insurer accumulating at not less than a guaranteed rate of interest, or (5) one-year term insurance, the dividend being used as a single premium to purchase the term insurance at net rates. The amount of term insurance under this fifth option may be limited to the cash value under the contract, in which case the remainder of the dividend is accumulated at interest for use in future years.

The dividends may be used to reduce the number of premiums by converting the policy to a paid-up contract when the cash value under the contract plus the cash value under dividend additions or the dividends accumulated at interest equal the cash value of a paid-up policy. The dividends may also be used to mature the policy as an endowment when these same values under the contract equal or exceed the face amount of the contract. Other options may also be permitted.

The paid-up additions option has the advantage of providing additional protection and, over a long period, will provide almost as much cash value as if the dividends were accumulated at interest.[29]

Flexibility provided by options   The four sets of options discussed in this section make the life insurance contract a highly flexible instrument. An example will serve to summarize the preceding discussion and to demonstrate this flexibility.

A man, aged 35, purchases a $10,000 straight life insurance contract. At any age, he may elect to convert this contract to a limited payment contract or an endowment contract. He may choose to receive his dividends according to one of the dividend options. At any age, he may elect to borrow on the policy or to surrender the contract and exercise the nonforfeiture options. For example, at age 65, he may decide that he wants to surrender

[29] Since the interest on the accumulations is taxable annually while the interest on the cash value may never be taxed, the effective return may actually be greater.

the contract, have it continued as paid-up insurance of a reduced amount, or have the insurance continued in the same face amount for some limited period. If he elects a cash value, he may ask to have the proceeds paid out according to one of the settlement options. Finally, in case of death before surrender of the policy for cash, the death proceeds may also be placed under one of the settlement options.

Special Characteristics of Fraternal Life Insurance and Savings Bank Life Insurance

Although most of the discussion of types of contracts and major policy provisions applies to the contracts issued by fraternal societies and by mutual savings banks in three states, these insurers have some special characteristics, a few of which are noted below.

FRATERNAL SOCIETIES

Fraternal societies include in their membership persons sharing a common occupation, religion, nationality, race, or sex. The societies are characterized by a system of lodges and a representative form of government. Fraternals first started to sell life insurance to members after the Civil War. Although many fraternals continue to emphasize the social and benevolent activities for members (picnics, lodge meetings, homes for the aged, orphanages, and the like) for which they were originally formed, some fraternals now concentrate most of their attention on the sale of life insurance. Although the practices of the leading fraternals closely resemble those of commercial insurers, some fraternals issue policies that are not quite so liberal. Similarly, the leading fraternals run a financially sound operation, but the financial condition of some fraternals is inferior to that of most commercial insurers.[30] The contracts of *all* fraternals differ from those of commercial insurers in that the fraternal policy is an "open" contract. The fraternal policy is assessable, and the contract includes, in addition to the policyholder's certificate and application, the articles of association or incorporation, the constitution and the by-laws, and all amendments to these documents. Leading fraternals claim that they do not need the assessment right any more than do the commercial insurers, which do not possess the right. Consequently they look upon the assessment right as a safeguard, not a drawback, for the insureds. The share of the market controlled by fraternals as a group is decreasing, but some of the leading fraternals, particularly those associated with religious groups, have been increasing their market share.

[30] Initially, fraternals attempted to underwrite life insurance on a pure assessment basis and because of inadequate assessments encountered financial difficulties. Some fraternals are still attempting to eliminate the deficits on old contracts.

MUTUAL SAVINGS BANKS

Mutual savings banks in Connecticut, Massachusetts, and New York are authorized under certain conditions to issue to residents life insurance policies which are very similar to those sold by commercial insurers. The amounts, however, are limited. In New York, for example, a person cannot usually own more than $30,000 of this type of insurance. No agents are employed, the insurance being sold over the counter at the bank. For this and other reasons, the premiums are attractive. An interesting feature of this savings-bank operation is the "unification" in each state of the mortality experience of the participating banks, which produces for each bank through a pooling operation the same ratio of actual to expected mortality.

REVIEW QUESTIONS

1. Five years ago an insured, now aged 35, purchased a ten-year renewable and convertible term insurance contract from the insurer whose rates were presented in Table 19.2.
   a. What annual premium does he pay for a $5,000 policy?
   b. If he wishes to renew the term insurance policy five years from now, what annual premium will he pay?
   c. If he wishes to convert the term insurance policy to a straight life insurance policy five years from now, what annual premium will he pay?
2. "A straight life insurance contract combines an increasing savings account with decreasing term insurance." Do you agree with this statement?
3. Construct a chart similar to Figure 19.1 for the following contracts issued to (a) a person, aged 20, and (b) a person, aged 45:
   Straight life insurance
   10-payment life
   20-payment life
   Paid-up at 65
   20-payment endowment
   Endowment at 65
4. An executive in the firm argues that he sees no reason to purchase life insurance other than term insurance because (a) he is self-disciplined enough to save regularly and (b) he can earn a large return on a savings account. Is he correct? Why or why not?
5. Some people refer to annuities as an upside-down application of life insurance. What do they probably mean by this reference?
6. Smith purchases an annual premium-deferred installment refund annuity. What benefits are provided under this contract?

7. Life insurers have been concerned about their decreasing share of consumer savings and the increased share of mutual funds.
   a. Why has the share of life insurers decreased?
   b. What changes have life insurers made as a result?
8. a. "Purchasing a conventional annuity with half of your premium and a variable annuity with the other half will provide a life income at retirement which will rise and fall with the cost of living." Is this statement correct?
   b. Are variable annuities generally available?
   c. Compare and contrast a variable annuity with a mutual fund.
9. Compare the benefits provided under the following contracts:
   a. A 20-year 1 per cent $10,000 family income policy and a 20-year 1 per cent $10,000 family maintenance policy
   b. $10,000 renewable and convertible term insurance and $5,000 straight life insurance with a guaranteed insurability rider
10. Bill Brown purchased a $30,000 20-payment life insurance contract at age 35. Bill is now 50 and is unable to continue his premium payments. What can he do?
11. Suppose that Bill (see question 10) had used the same premium to purchase a straight life insurance contract.
    a. How much insurance would he have been able to purchase? Assume that the rates in Table 19.2 apply.
    b. What could Bill do under this contract if at age 50 he was unable to continue his premium payments?
12. An insured dies leaving a wife, aged 60. If the insured had a $20,000 insurance policy, how much monthly income would his widow receive if all the proceeds were applied under each of the four most common settlement options? Assume that the insured's life insurance policy contains a table of settlement options similar to Table 19.6.
13. How much insurance would an insured, aged 45, need to accomplish each of the following objectives if he died today?
    a. $200 a month to his widow for 15 years.
    b. $200 a month for the remainder of his widow's life, the income to be paid during the first 15 years, regardless of whether she lives or dies. His wife is 45 years of age.
14. a. Compare the additional paid-up insurance dividend option with the one-year term insurance dividend option.
    b. How can the insured through dividends convert a straight life insurance contract into a limited payment life insurance contract?
15. Describe briefly:
    a. The "open" contracts of fraternals
    b. The role of mutual savings bank life insurance

SUGGESTIONS FOR ADDITIONAL READING

Gregg, Davis W. (ed.): *Life and Health Insurance Handbook* (2d ed., Homewood, Ill.: Richard D. Irwin, Inc., 1964), chaps. 4–9, 14–16, 19, 20, 42, 56–59.

Greider, J. E., and Beadles, W. T.: *Law and the Life Insurance Contract* (rev. ed., Homewood, Ill.: Richard D. Irwin, Inc., 1968).

Huebner, S. S., and Black, K.: *Life Insurance* (7th ed., New York: Appleton-Century-Crofts, 1969), chaps. 5–15.

McGill, D. M.: *Life Insurance* (rev. ed., Homewood, Ill.: Richard D. Irwin, Inc., 1966), chaps. 3–7 and 22–34.

Mehr, R. I.: *Life Insurance: Theory and Practice* (4th ed., Austin: Business Publications, Inc., 1970), chaps. 4–8, 10, and 11.

20

individual health insurance contracts

Health insurance can be divided into two major categories: (1) disability income insurance, which provides a periodic income for a person who is disabled according to some specific standard, and (2) medical expense insurance. After describing the branches of health insurance and indicating the scope and growth of this line of insurance, this chapter will describe the basic policy types and some major provisions.

Branches of Health Insurance

Health insurance can be classified according to whether it is underwritten by commercial insurers, Blue Cross and Blue Shield associations, or other insurers known as "independent" plans because they are not associated with the other two types of insurers. Some measure of the relative importance of each of these types of insurers is provided in Table 20.1, which presents the number of persons protected against loss of income and medical expenses at the close of 1968.

Disability income insurance is underwritten almost exclusively by commercial insurers. The only other important type of income protection is formal paid sick leave, which, though it may be insurance from the viewpoint of the employee, is self-insurance to the employer. The 55 million persons protected against short-term disability income loss at the close of 1968

Table 20.1 Number of persons protected by private insurance against disability income loss and medical expenses, end of 1968

	Number insured, millions	
Type of protection	Short-term	Long-term
Disability income loss:		
Commercial insurance:		
Group insurance	30.8	4.7
Individual insurance	13.8	3.0
Net total corrected for duplication	40.1	7.7
Formal paid sick leave*	13.8	
Other	1.1	
Net total	55.0	7.7

Medical expenses	Hospital expense	Surgical fees	Charges for physicians' care	Major medical expense†
Commercial insurance:				
Group insurance	76.1	77.4	61.4	61.7
Individual insurance	39.7	28.2	12.2	5.1
Net total corrected for duplication	104.4	96.1	68.4	66.9
Blue Cross, Blue Shield, and medical society plans	71.3	63.0	59.2	
Independent plans	7.7	8.8	8.9	
All insurers—net total	169.5	155.7	129.1	66.9

* Net figures after adjustment for duplication of other coverage
† Major medical expense insurance data available only for commercial insurers.

Source: Source Book of Health Insurance Data, 1969 (New York: Health Insurance Institute, 1969), pp. 20–26. .

are a substantially higher figure than the 40 million protected a decade earlier, but the proportion covered at year-end 1968 was still only about one-quarter of the population.

Medical expense insurance, unlike the other types of insurance discussed earlier in this text, is underwritten to a considerable extent by insurers other than commercial insurers. As indicated in Table 20.1, Blue Cross, Blue Shield, and medical society plans are also important underwriters of medical expense insurance. Independent plans do not cover nearly as many persons as the other two groups, but they are an important source of new ideas in health care. In 1958 the numbers covered against hospital expenses, surgical fees, and charges for physicians' care were about 120 million, 100 million, and 75 million, respectively. The persons covered at year-end 1968 against each of the three types of medical expenses were about 85 per cent of the population, 80 per cent, and 65 per cent, respectively.

As is true of life insurance, health insurance written by commercial insurers (and by Blue Cross and Blue Shield associations) can be classified as *individual* insurance or *group* insurance. Group insurance is treated in depth in Chapter 22. Individual insurance can be subclassified according to whether it is (1) commercial insurance, guaranteed renewable insurance, or noncancelable insurance, (2) industrial insurance, (3) special risk insurance, or (4) limited insurance. Disability riders attached to life insurance contracts can be considered a fifth class of individual health insurance.

The first class of individual insurance—commercial insurance, guaranteed renewable insurance, or noncancelable insurance—corresponds to ordinary insurance in life insurance. The three components of this class vary according to the insurer's right to cancel or to refuse to renew the contract. Because these contracts are easily the most important individual contracts, they will be described at length later in this chapter.

Industrial policies are marketed on the same basis as industrial life insurance and bear essentially the same relationship to commercial insurance that industrial life insurance bears to ordinary life insurance. *Special risk* policies are specially designed contracts providing substantial benefits, protection against unusual hazards, or both. For example, the contract might indemnify a motion-picture corporation if sickness prevents a movie actress from performing on schedule, or it might promise to provide a certain income if a person is disabled while in a war area or while engaged in some scientific experiment, such as a flight into space. *Limited* policies include a heterogeneous group of contracts which provide protection only against specified types of accidental injuries or diseases or which protect the insured only for a few days or weeks.[1] Popular examples include the ticket accident policy sold in railway stations, the aviation ticket policy sold in connection with flights by the insured, automobile accident policies, and dread disease contracts, most of which protect the insured against medical expenses associated with a specified list of important diseases. Although these policies can be used to fill gaps in broader-gauged coverage or to increase coverage amounts when the chance of loss is temporarily increased, they are dangerous in that they may mislead insureds into believing they provide more complete protection. Because of the relatively (and increasingly) less impor-

---

[1] For an interesting comprehensive discussion of limited policies, see O. D. Dickerson, *Health Insurance* (3d ed., Homewood, Ill.: Richard D. Irwin, Inc. 1968), chap. 14.

tant role of both industrial and limited policies and the restricted use of special policies, they will not be discussed further.[2]

Disability riders attached to life insurance policies are important enough to merit separate treatment with "ordinary" health insurance later.

Credit health insurance, like credit life insurance, is best described as a unique application of health insurance providing disability income protection. Lending institutions and merchants selling on a charge-account or an installment basis have used this insurance to protect themselves and the debtor against the debtor's failure to meet installment payments if he becomes disabled. Under this insurance, the insurer makes these payments during the debtor's disability, subject commonly to some maximum number of payments. As is true of credit life insurance, most of this insurance is written on a group basis.

Disability Income Contracts

Disability income contracts may in some instances also provide medical expense protection, but they are designed primarily to provide disability income coverage. Three major types of contracts will be described in some detail: (1) commercial policies, (2) noncancelable and guaranteed renewable policies, and (3) riders on life insurance policies.

COMMERCIAL POLICIES

Commercial policies derive their name from the market (white-collar workers) they were originally designed to serve; today they serve a considerably broader market. They differ from the other two types to be described in this chapter with respect to (1) the range of benefits offered and (2) the right of the insurer to refuse to renew the contract on the anniversary date.

Commercial policies usually cover either accidental injuries alone or both accidental injuries and sickness combined. In the latter type of policy, it is common practice to issue a separate contract covering each of the two perils because of the differences in the protection afforded against them.

The accident policy or the accident portions of a combined policy generally provide protection against loss "resulting *directly and independently*

---

[2] A type of group insurance which perhaps should be regarded as a type of limited insurance is blanket insurance. Like group insurance, it covers a group of persons under one contract, but unlike group insurance, it does not specify the individuals, whose identities are constantly changing. Like limited insurance, blanket insurance usually provides protection for the individuals only for short periods or against specified types of accidents and diseases. An example is blanket insurance providing death and dismemberment benefits for employees when their duties require them to travel by air. Such insurance can also be obtained on a group basis with the names of the employees specified.

of all causes from *accidental bodily injury* occurring while this policy is in force." Under this provision the result, but not the means, must be accidental. For example, an insured may strain his back while lifting a heavy object. The requirement that the loss result independently of all other causes is supposed to cut out claims where some preexisting impairment or sickness causes the accident and to reduce claims where the preexisting condition increases significantly the severity of the loss. In practice, the full loss is usually payable if the accident is the dominating cause even if it is not the sole cause.

Certain types of accidents are excluded, for example, losses caused by war, suicide and intentionally inflicted injuries, injuries while in military service during wartime, and injuries sustained while a crew member of an aircraft or a student pilot.

Most commercial policies are schedule policies permitting the insured to select the types of benefits he wishes to purchase. Sometimes, however, the contract provides only one or a few of the possible coverages; sometimes the contract is a package including all or most of the common coverages. The following discussion is directed toward the schedule policies.

The most important disability income benefits included in the schedule are the total disability income and the partial disability income benefits. The total disability income provision provides a stated weekly income for a specified number of weeks (for example, 24 months) if the injury within a short period following the accident (commonly 90 days) completely prevents the insured from engaging in his regular occupation. The requirement that the disability commence shortly after the accident eliminates the claims of doubtful origin which occur later, but it may also eliminate some legitimate claims. The payments will generally be continued after the expiration of the specified number of months for life or for some stated number of years as long as the insured is prevented from engaging in any gainful occupation for which he is reasonably fitted by education, training, and experience. A common proviso is that in no case is a person to be considered totally disabled if he engages in any occupation for remuneration or profit.

The partial disability provision provides a specified weekly income (commonly two-fifths or half of the monthly total disability income benefit) for a specified number of months (for example, six months) if the injury within a short period following the accident or immediately following a period of total disability renders the insured able to perform one or more but not all the duties of his occupation.

The determination of total or partial disability depends upon the physical capacity of the insured, not his loss of wages. The fact that his employer may continue his wages does not reduce his insurance benefit.

Another important disability benefit is provided by the dismemberment and loss-of-sight provision. A "capital sum" such as $10,000, or 208 times the total disability weekly indemnity, is payable for the loss of both hands, both feet, the sight of both eyes, one hand and one foot or either hand or foot, and the sight of one eye if the loss occurs within specified times (for example, 90 days or during a period of compensable total disability) following the accident. Lesser amounts are provided for other dismemberment and sight losses and a separate provision may provide similar benefits for various fractures and dislocations. This provision may be worded in several ways, some of which favor the insured while others actually restrict the benefits.[3] For example, the dismemberment benefits may be in addition to total disability income payments, or they may establish a minimum number of such payments. On the other hand, the dismemberment benefits may be in place of total disability income payments.[4]

The contracts also commonly contain an accidental death benefit, which is a limited kind of life insurance. Another provision doubles the amount payable under the benefits described to this point if the injuries result from *specified types* of accidents, such as those occurring while the insured is a passenger in or upon a public conveyance, except aircraft, or as a result of the collapse of the outer walls or the burning of a building if the insured is in the building at the time of its collapse or at the commencement of the fire. The comments made in the last chapter with respect to the double-indemnity clause in life insurance could be repeated here because the value of this clause is even more questionable than the double indemnity rider. Other "fringe" benefits may also be included.

The sickness policy generally provides protection against loss "resulting from sickness contracted and causing loss commencing after the first fourteen days from the date of this policy." Preexisting sicknesses, in other words, are excluded, and in addition there is a probationary period designed to reduce adverse selection against the insurer.

Usually the only disability income benefit under a sickness policy provides a total disability income.[5] If the insured is completely unable to engage in his regular occupation, the insurer will, usually after a waiting period of one or two weeks, pay him a specified weekly income for a stated period, generally two years or less. Longer-term benefits are available, but few policies pay benefits beyond age 65. When the maximum duration of benefits is more than one or two years, the test of disability is usually changed

---

[3] O. D. Dickerson, *op. cit.*, p. 207.
[4] This provision is restrictive only if the insured would have received more in total disability income payments.
[5] True partial disability benefits are rare. Sometimes a sickness contract is interpreted as providing partial in addition to total disability benefits if it pays a specified benefit while a disabled person is house-confined and a reduced benefit while the person is unable to work but is not house-confined. Such a contract is less liberal than the one described above and fortunately is becoming less common.

after one or two years to inability to engage in any occupation for which the insured is fitted by education, training, and experience.

The waiting period in sickness insurance contracts, which may be much longer than the one cited above, serves the same purpose as the deductible in property and liability insurance—to cut costs of unimportant losses and morale hazard. Accidental injury contracts may also contain waiting periods, but their use in those contracts is much less common.

The contract provisions discussed to this point are not covered under the 1950 Uniform Individual Accident and Sickness Policy Provisions Law mentioned in Chapter 14. Some of the twelve required uniform provisions (the entire contract clause and the time limit on the defense of misrepresentation) have already been described. The uniform provisions also prohibit the insurer from contesting a claim for loss commencing three years or later from the date of issue of the contract on the ground that the condition existed prior to that date unless the condition is specifically excluded in the contract. Other required provisions deal with reinstatement, a grace period, claims notices, claim forms, proofs of loss, claims payments, beneficiary changes, physical examinations and autopsies, and time limits on legal actions.

The most important optional provision is the cancellation provision, which permits the insured to cancel the contract at any time after a stated number of days' notice. The insured may cancel at any time *after* the expiration of the original term. The omission of this provision (and this practice is becoming common), however, does not guarantee the renewability of the contract. An increasing number of commercial contracts give the insurer the right to cancel the contract or refuse renewal only for reasons specified in the contract. They also declare that prior to some specified time the insurer will not cancel or refuse renewal merely because the insured's health deteriorates.

Other common optional provisions deal with the adjustments to be made in the amounts paid because of changes in occupation during the policy term or misstatements of age in the application. An optional provision dealing with duplicate insurance states that the insurer will pay only that proportion of the amount it would pay if there were no other insurance in force that the benefits provided by all policies of which the insurer had notice prior to the loss bear to the total of all benefits applicable to the loss. For example, an insurer providing a benefit of $300 a month would pay only half that amount if the insured had another $300-a-month policy in force and failed to tell the insurer about this duplicate insurance. Other optional provisions deal with the deductibility of unpaid premiums from claim payments, the necessity of conforming to state statutes, and the exclusion of losses caused by the commission of a felony, an illegal occupation, or the illegal use of intoxicants and narcotics.

For a given set of benefits, the prices for commercial policies vary primarily according to the sex and occupation of the insured. Usually, age is important only when the insured is in his fifties or sixties. One nonparticipating insurer charges a male lawyer (one of the safest occupations) under age 60 $2.20 for each $5 of lifetime weekly indemnity provided under an accidental injury contract. The charge under a sickness policy providing benefits for up to 104 weeks after a waiting period of 7 days is $6.80 if the lawyer is under 50 years of age, $10.20 if he is older. Increasing the waiting period to 14 days would reduce these two changes to $5.20 and $8.00, respectively. The corresponding rates for females are almost 50 per cent higher.

NONCANCELABLE AND GUARANTEED RENEWABLE POLICIES

Noncancelable policies are renewable at the option of the insured to some advanced age such as 60 or 65. Guaranteed renewable contracts differ from noncancelable policies in one important respect: The insurer reserves the right to change the table of premium rates applicable to oustanding policies in the same series but not with respect to a single insured. In other words, the insurer cannot raise the rate for a single insured merely because his attractiveness as an insured decreases unless it raises the rate for all insureds in the same class. Even this limited right to change the rate is much less common in the disability income field than in medical expense insurance, where increases in medical costs over time are a major problem and it is more important for the insurer to reserve this right.

In contrast to the practice in commercial insurance, protection against losses caused by accidental bodily injury and by sickness are usually provided in one contract. Like commercial contracts, however, the contracts usually provide different protection against each peril. The exclusions are also similar to those in commercial contracts.

The primary benefit is the total disability income benefit. With respect to injury-caused disability, a stated monthly indemnity is usually payable for some period such as 12 months or 60 months so long as the insured is completely unable to engage in his own occupation and as long thereafter as he is unable to engage in any gainful occupation for which he is reasonably fitted by education, training, and experience. Blindness and double dismemberment are generally conceded to cause total disability. With respect to sickness-incurred disability, the maximum duration of benefits is almost never the insured's lifetime. Noncancelable and guaranteed renewable contracts are commonly classified according to the maximum duration of these benefits as follows: short-term contracts (3 years or less), intermediate-term contracts (usually 5 years), long-term contracts (usually 10 years), and extra-long-term contracts (usually to age 65).[6] Some contracts provide a stated benefit for a limited number of years with some fraction such as one-half being continued to, say, age 65. Long waiting periods (90 days, for example) or "elimination periods," as they are called in this field, are usually written into the total disability income provision but are not generally applicable to losses caused by blindness or double dismemberment. Disabilities due to the same or related causes are considered to be different disabilities for the purpose of applying the maximum duration and the elimination period if the insured has returned to his work for at least six months or some other specified period.

Other disability income benefits may or may not be included in the contract. The short-term contracts tend to resemble the commercial policies with respect to the variety of benefits afforded; the variety is reduced under intermediate-term contracts; and the long-term contracts most often provide only partial disability income benefits in addition to total disability income benefits. On the other hand, a benefit rarely found in commercial contracts but usually found in long-term noncancelable and guaranteed renewable contracts is the waiver of premiums payable under the contract if the insured is totally disabled for more than a specified period of time.[7]

The required uniform provisions in noncancelable and guaranteed renewable contracts are essentially the same as those in commercial contracts except that an incontestable clause similar to that used in life insurance generally replaces the provision placing a time limit on the defense of fraudulent misrepresentation.

Among the optional clauses, the change of occupation clause is usually omitted, but the misstatement of age clause almost always appears. The other insurance clauses found in some commercial policies are seldom included, but there is commonly an average earnings clause not permitted in commercial contracts. Under this clause, if the total monthly income benefits payable under all valid coverages (not including workmen's compensation or employee benefit plans unless specified) exceed the greater of (1) the insured's monthly earnings at the time disability commenced or (2) his average monthly earnings for the two preceding years, the insurer is liable only for that proportionate part of the benefits under the policy that the higher earnings figure bears to the total of the valid coverages. This clause, however, cannot reduce the benefits under all valid coverages below $200 or, if less, the total benefits under all such coverages. The

---

[6] For more details, see Dickerson, *op. cit.*, pp. 433–434.
[7] The waiver may be limited to the time during which monthly income benefits are payable.

portion of the premium paid during the past two years for the benefits not paid because of this provision is returned to the insured. To illustrate: Assume that an insured's gross monthly earnings at the date of the disability were $400, while his average monthly earnings during the past two years were $300. A contract with an average earnings clause and benefits of $200 a month would pay only $160 if another contract provides benefits of $300. Such a clause is important in noncancelable and guaranteed renewable contracts because of the potential fluctuations in earnings over the long run.

Noncancelable and guaranteed renewable disability income premiums, like life insurance premiums, are usually level over the premium-paying period. The rates vary by age, occupation, and sex. One nonparticipating insurer which issues noncancelable contracts only to males in relatively safe occupational groups charges a male, aged 35, about $80 a year for each $100 of indemnity provided to age 65 following a 30-day waiting period. A 90-day waiting period would cut the cost to less than $70.

In recent years insurers have added some interesting benefits to traditional noncancelable and guaranteed renewable insurance. One applies the family-income concept developed by life insurers. The insurer promises to pay a monthly income to a totally disabled insured for the remainder of a stated period that commences when the policy is issued. Under a guaranteed insurability rider the insured can purchase certain additional disability income protection at specified option ages without providing his insurability. The insured may wish to increase his protection because his income increases, the cost of living rises, or he wishes more adequate protection.

RIDERS ON LIFE INSURANCE POLICIES

Two major disability benefits may be added to life insurance contracts: (1) a waiver of premium and (2) a disability income. Both benefits are commonly provided by means of riders attached to life insurance contracts, but the waiver of premium benefit is often included in the life insurance contract itself. All life insurers issue waiver of premium insurance, although not on all types of contracts. Many insurers also offer a total disability income rider. The waiver of premium benefit may be purchased without the disability income benefit, but the opposite is not possible.

The waiver of premium benefit provides that if the insured, as a result of either accidental bodily injury or disease, is totally and (presumably) permanently incapable of engaging in any occupation for wage or profit (interpreted by most courts to mean any occupation for which he is fitted), the insurer will waive the payment of premiums on the contract *during the continuance of the disability*. The disability must occur, however, prior to some advanced age such as 55 or 60 and must not have resulted from intentionally self-inflicted injury, war, or a violation of the law. Before the disability is presumed to be permanent, it must usually have lasted at least six months, but the waiver is retroactive. Blindness and double dismemberment, however, are considered immediately as having caused total and permanent disability.

The waiver of premium rider provides in effect a disability income benefit, but the insured has no freedom of choice with respect to the expenditure of the income. Instead, a very important expense, the policy premium, is paid in his behalf. The disability income rider, on the other hand, provides income which the insured may spend as he wishes.

This rider usually pays $10 a month per $1,000 to a totally and (presumably) permanently disabled person, as defined above in connection with the waiver of premium benefit.[8] The income is payable during the continuance of his disability until age 60 or 65, at which time the rider converts the life insurance contract into a matured endowment contract. Some riders provide only $5 a month, and in many cases the income is payable for life without any change in the life insurance contract. No payment is usually made, however, for the first five or six months of disability, the first payment being made at the end of the sixth or the seventh month.

The disability income rider is appealing because, on a guaranteed renewable basis[9] and for a relatively attractive price made possible by the packaging concept, the insurer promises to pay a disabled person an income to an advanced age or for life, regardless of whether the cause of the disability is accidental injury or sickness. The major drawback is the required relationship between the rider and a life insurance contract.

The premiums for life insurance waiver of premium and disability income riders are level over the premium-payment period of the life insurance contract or until the coverage under the rider ceases, whichever comes first. The rates for standard lives depend primarily upon the issue age and sex of the insured. Applicants rated substandard for reasons of occupation or health may be denied this coverage or charged a higher premium rate. One nonparticipating insurer charges a male, aged 35, $0.54 for a waiver of premium rider attached to $1,000 of straight life insurance and $4.20 for a rider providing waiver of premium and $10 a month disability income. The corresponding rates for females are about 50 per cent higher.

---

[8] Average earnings clauses similar to those used in noncancelable and guaranteed renewable contracts are seldom found. The most interesting and apparently successful attempt to reduce the overinsurance problem is the practice of one insurer which, in addition to an average earnings clause which provides only enough income to bring the benefits from all contracts up to 75 per cent of the former earned income, defines total disability as a reduction in earned income of at least 75 per cent.

[9] However, the disability income benefit and the waiver of premium benefit are usually excluded from the operation of the incontestable clause.

Medical Expense Contracts

Medical expense contracts are underwritten by commercial insurers, by Blue Cross or Blue Shield associations, or by independent plans. The contracts issued by each of these types of insurers will be discussed separately.

CONTRACTS ISSUED BY COMMERCIAL INSURERS

Commercial insurers issue (1) basic medical expense contracts, (2) major medical expense contracts, and (3) comprehensive contracts.

Basic medical expense contracts   Basic medical expense insurance may be included in commercial or, much less often, in guaranteed renewable disability income contracts by mention in the contract itself or by means of a rider. Usually, however, the basic medical expense benefits are provided under a separate contract.

Under a *hospital expense* policy the insurer usually promises to pay room and board charges up to a specified daily amount, say, $20 or $40, for not more than a stated number of days, such as 70 or 365. The insurer also promises to pay other miscellaneous operating expenses (including charges for such items as drugs and the use of the operating room) up to some multiple, say, 10 or 20, of the daily room-and-board limit. The protection is designed primarily for registered bed patients, but the contract may also cover, on a limited basis, emergency out-patient treatment necessitated by an accidental injury. Maternity benefits, if available, are also usually limited to some multiple, say, 10, of the daily room-and-board benefit. Furthermore, the hospitalization caused by pregnancy, childbirth, or miscarriage must occur 9 or 10 months after the effective date of the contract. On the other hand, the maternity coverage covers such confinements occurring during the 9 or 10 months following the expiration of the contract.

Exclusions are generally more extensive than those found in disability income contracts and often include, in addition to those mentioned earlier in this chapter, such things as appendicitis, tonsillitis, heart disease, female disorders, and others until the expiration of a qualification period; injuries or sickness for which workmen's compensation benefits are payable; and services provided in a Federal government hospital.

The contract may be written to cover a family as well as an individual. Dependent children are usually covered under a family contract from some minimum age such as 2 or 3 weeks to some maximum age such as 18 or 19 years.

A modified version of basic hospitalization insurance is one that provides stated weekly or monthly dollar benefits while the insured is hospitalized. This contract is, therefore, a valued contract that provides income for a hospitalized insured.

Hospitalization contracts generally include *surgical expense* coverage on an optional or compulsory basis. Separate surgical expense contracts are seldom issued. Under the surgical coverage, the insurer promises to pay surgical fees incurred up to the amount shown in a schedule. The schedule amounts vary according to the seriousness of the operation. Obstetrical benefits may or may not be included. If included, the probationary period and the extension period described in connection with maternity benefits in hospitalization insurance are made a part of the contract.

Charges for nonsurgical physician's care may be covered under a hospitalization contract or under a separate contract, perhaps a surgical expense contract. The coverage usually applies only to in-hospital calls, but it may apply to in-hospital calls, office calls, and home calls. In the latter case, it may or may not require that the insured be totally disabled. Generally a limit is specified per day or per call, and there is some maximum dollar amount or number of calls per illness. The first few visits may also be excluded.

Protection against private nurses' fees may also be included in the hospitalization contract or in conjunction with policies covering surgical or medical treatment only. Nurses' fees are generally paid up to some specified amount per day, for not more than a stated number of days.

Basic medical expense insurance contracts are usually guaranteed renewable, subject to adjustable class premiums, but a substantial volume is still renewable only with the consent of the insurer. The uniform provisions already noted with respect to disability income contracts are also part of the medical expense contracts.

The premiums for basic medical expense contracts are most closely related to the sex of the insured, especially when maternity and obstetrical benefits are provided. Age is important only at advanced ages. Because rates are necessarily responsive to changes in the cost of medical care, any sample quotations would probably rapidly be outdated.

Major medical expense insurance   The basic medical expense insurance contracts provide specific coverage of particular medical expenses up to certain stated limits. They are designed to provide first-dollar (or almost first-dollar) and fairly complete protection against those accidental injuries or sicknesses which are the least serious financially. Major medical expense insurance, on the other hand, generally provides blanket coverage against almost all types of medical expenses in excess of a certain relatively small amount, the liability of the insurer being set at a rather high amount. In other words, major medical expense contracts are designed to provide fairly complete protection against the financially serious illnesses and little or no protection against the less serious ones. This objective, of course, has much to recommend it for the reasons presented on pages 206 to 208 in favor of deductibles. Basic medical expense insurance, on the other hand, covers many losses which are predictable or relatively expensive to settle. It may also encourage overutilization of the services. Some observers, however, prefer to emphasize the encouragement of early treatment, which may prevent a minor illness from becoming a major one.

Major medical expense insurance was not introduced until the late forties and did not become common until the middle fifties, but its growth since that time has been rapid.

Major medical expense Insurance contracts vary greatly in details, but most of them share the following basic characteristics:

1. The insurer covers on a blanket basis a long list of medical expenses. The list usually includes such expenses as hospital bills, fees for surgical and nonsurgical care by a physician, and charges for drugs, iron lungs, and wheel chairs. Some contracts limit surgical fees and the daily hospital room-and-board charges to specified amounts. Customary exclusions are expenses incurred in connection with ordinary pregnancy and childbirth, cosmetic surgery (unless necessitated by an injury), alcoholism and narcotics, workmen's compensation claims, war, military service, and self-inflicted injuries.

2. The insurer pays none of the expenses up to a stated deductible amount. The deductible provision cuts the cost and the moral and morale hazards. Although the deductible is usually applied to the expenses associated with each accidental injury or sickness, other bases are possible.[10] If, however, two or more covered family members are involved in a common accident, usually only one deductible is applied to the family medical expenses arising out of that accident. The deductible amounts are commonly between $100 and $1,000 but deductibles as high as $10,000 are available.

3. The covered expenses must usually be incurred within a short period, say, two years, beginning on the date on which is incurred the first covered charge applied against the deductible.

4. The insurer pays most of the expenses in excess of the deductible amount but not more than a specified maximum amount. The insurer pays 75 or 80 per cent of the excess expenses; the insured pays the corresponding 25 to 20 per cent. The percentage participation of the insured cuts the cost and gives him an incentive to keep the expenses incurred within reasonable bounds. The maximum payment by the insurer is usually between

[10] For example, the deductible may apply to the expenses of an individual or a family in a calendar year or some other period.

$5,000 and $20,000, but at least one insurer issues a contract with no maximum limit. The maximum usually applies to each accident or sickness but sometimes applies to each person.

The nature of the coverage can be illustrated as follows: Assume a contract with a $500 deductible per accident or sickness, a 25 per cent participation clause, and a face amount of $20,000 per accident or sickness. The table presented below shows the amount the insurer will contribute toward the total covered medical expenses in each of five cases:

Total covered medical expenses	Insurance payment
$ 400	
4,500	$ 3,000
8,500	6,000
12,500	9,000
30,500	20,000

Like basic medical expense insurance, major medical expense contracts are usually guaranteed renewable, subject to adjustable class premiums. Rates depend primarily upon the age and sex of the insured.

Comprehensive medical expense insurance   Comprehensive medical expense insurance occupies a position midway between basic medical expense insurance and major medical expense insurance. Two versions are available. The first is essentially major medical expense insurance with a very low deductible, such as $25 or $50. The second is a blending of basic medical expense insurance and major medical expense insurance. For example, one common plan of this type provides basic hospitalization and surgical expense coverage up to $500. In addition, the insurer promises to pay a specified percentage of (1) the hospital and surgical expenses in excess of the basic coverage and (2) other medical expenses in excess of a specified deductible such as $100, until the insurer's contribution exceeds some amount such as $10,000. Although less justifiable theoretically for high- and middle-income groups than major medical expense insurance because it covers many relatively unimportant losses, comprehensive medical expense insurance is an efficient blending of basic and major medical expense insurance and has proved highly marketable.

As indicated in Table 20.1, 67 million persons now have insurance company major medical protection through major medical insurance or comprehensive insurance. Ten years ago the number was only 10 million.

CONTRACTS ISSUED BY BLUE CROSS AND BLUE SHIELD ASSOCIATIONS

Although most of the Blue Cross and Blue Shield contracts are sold to members of eligible groups, many contracts are issued to individuals. Blue Cross is more active in non-group insurance than is Blue Shield.

Blue Cross plans   A Blue Cross association plan is a voluntary nonprofit hospital expense prepayment plan[11] which has sought and received the approval of the American Hospital Association. Otherwise, each of the approximately eighty Blue Cross associations is essentially an independent operation and, except in North Carolina, is the exclusive agency within a given area. The associations were organized originally by the member hospitals in each area, but the public and the medical profession are also usually represented on each board of directors, and the boards are sometimes self-perpetuating.

Each association contracts with its subscribers and with its member hospitals. There is no one subscriber or member-hospital contract form. The contracts differ among the associations, and, in addition, over half of the associations offer more than one subscriber contract.

Despite such diversity, a summarization is useful. The most popular non-group subscriber contract (and the ideal one from the viewpoint of the associations) provides for a stated period such as 70 or 120 days'[12] full coverage of (1) room-and-board costs, usually on a semiprivate basis, and (2) charges for a long list of hospital extras if these services are provided by a member hospital in the plan area. Maternity benefits, however, are generally limited to 10 days' service or to a stated dollar amount.

This contract is a service contract because it provides the benefits prescribed regardless of the actual dollar charges by the hospital and because the association pays the hospital directly (although this practice is also possible under commercial insurance nonservice contracts).

If a subscriber wants better accommodations (say, a private room) than those provided under the plan, he receives a daily cash allowance for room and board which may be the same or less than the cost of the accommodations provided on a service basis under the contract. If the subscriber is hospitalized in a nonmember hospital, which is not likely because over 90 per cent of the hospital beds are in member hospitals, the plan usually provides a per diem amount which is commonly less liberal than the cash equivalent of the service benefits. Finally, if the subscriber is hos-

---

[11] The plan is nonprofit because no dividends are paid to the controlling hospitals. Profits are supposed to be used to reduce rates or improve contracts in the future. The hospitals do benefit from the plans indirectly. See the later section on Interest in Major Medical and Comprehensive Insurance.

All cooperative insurers are, of course, nonprofit in the sense that they pay no dividends to any stockholders.

[12] Contracts providing benefits for 365 days are becoming more common.

pitalized in a member hospital in a different plan area, an Inter-plan Service Benefit Bank arrangement usually makes it possible for the member to receive the benefits provided by the plan in that area for the period of time provided in the home area. When a person moves into a new area, an Inter-plan Transfer Agreement enables that person to maintain continuous coverage.

The most common and the most important variation from this typical contract covers room-and-board costs up to a specified daily allowance. Other common variations are dollar limitations on some of the hospital extras, small deductibles, and partial benefits for an additional specified period.

Common exclusions are workmen's compensation cases, cases for which hospitalization is provided by law, and hospitalization primarily for diagnostic studies and rest cures. Although some plans provide full benefits, the following are usually excluded or benefits are limited: tuberculosis, nervous and mental diseases, alcoholism, and drug addiction. Preexisting conditions are sometimes excluded entirely, but the usual procedure is to impose a waiting period of 6 to 24 months. Waiting periods may also apply to tonsillitis, adenoiditis, or appendicitis.

Dependents may be covered under the contract, the coverage for children usually commencing at birth and continuing to age 19.

The contracts usually give the Blue Cross association the right to cancel the contract, but this right is very seldom exercised.

The contracts between the associations and the member hospitals are primarily concerned with the method of determining the payment for services rendered to subscribers. Although the payment may be (1) a straight per diem (based on average charges) for each day of care or (2) all or part of the actual hospital bill, the usual procedure is to base the payment upon cost statements prepared by the hospital. Some plans have used average cost statements instead of individual cost statements in order to encourage efficient hospital administration. Costs are interpreted liberally to include obsolescence and depreciation, interest, and contingency allowances, but the Blue Cross association usually pays less than the charges to nonmembers. This differential has been justified on the ground that (1) billing costs are low, (2) there is no collection problem with Blue Cross subscribers, and (3) Blue Cross through its acceptance of many insureds who would be rejected by most other insurers makes paying patients out of many who would otherwise be charity cases. Because the payments to the hospitals under these contracts will no doubt be influenced by the financial condition of the association, the member hospitals are in fact, if not in name, the ultimate insurers.[13] Under some plans, the hospitals specifically guarantee the benefits.

[13] See Dickerson, *op. cit.*, p. 230.

Blue Cross rates for individual contracts are the same for all applicants, regardless of age, sex, or occupational classification. Family rates usually fall into two classes—(1) husband and wife and (2) husband, wife, and children.

Blue Shield plans   A Blue Shield association plan is a voluntary nonprofit surgical and nonsurgical physician's care plan[14] which has sought and qualified for membership in the National Association of Blue Shield Plans. The approximately eighty locally autonomous Blue Shield associations were organized originally by local medical societies, but the boards of directors commonly include some non-doctors. The daily operations of the plan are frequently handled by the staff of the local Blue Cross plan.

All Blue Shield contracts provide surgical benefits; most cover charges for in-hospital nonsurgical physician's care; and some include benefits applying as well to home and office calls by a doctor. The typical contract provides the service covered, regardless of the normal charge by the attending physician, if the doctor is a participating doctor in the area and if the income of the subscriber is below certain specified amounts; for example, $6,000 for a single subscriber and $9,000 for a family. For subscribers with incomes in excess of the stated amounts, the benefit is a reduction in the normal charges by the allowance in the contract. A small but increasing proportion of Blue Shield subscribers are covered under "usual and customary" contracts that pay the entire physician's fee for all income groups as long as that fee is within limits set by prevailing fees in the area.

If the subscriber is attended by a nonparticipating doctor, reduced allowances are usually payable. If the subscriber is treated by a participating physician in a different area, the full benefits are payable, and although no formal promise is made, the participating physician usually accepts the benefit as full payment for patients who would be entitled to service benefits at home.

Usually dependents may be covered under the contract, although the benefits may be less liberal. Coverage for children usually extends from birth to age 19.

The exclusions and limitations in Blue Shield contracts are similar to those in Blue Cross contracts but are often more restrictive.

The associations pay the participating physicians the allowances in the contracts, but the physicians would no doubt accept some modification of these payments if the Blue Shield association encountered financial difficulties. Most of the plans in fact are specifically underwritten by the partici-

---

[14] Some Blue Shield plans include hospital benefits, and some Blue Cross plans include surgical and physician's care benefits. In a few such instances, Blue Cross plans compete with Blue Shield plans.

pating physicians. Blue Shield rates and Blue Cross rates are arrived at in the same way.

Interest in major medical and comprehensive insurance   Blue Cross and Blue Shield plans have always emphasized first-dollar protection. In part, this emphasis may be traced to the origin of the Blue Cross associations during the early years of the Great Depression at a time when any loss was catastrophic to most families and when the hospitals were greatly concerned about the amount of free care they were providing. Hospitals are still concerned about the prompt payment of bills by patients. First-dollar coverage has also been preferred because a strong market has always existed for this protection, because the association leaders believe that first-dollar coverage serves an important social purpose which otherwise would have to be met through national health insurance, to certain forms of which they have been strongly opposed, and because this coverage has aided them in maintaining in most states that they are prepayment plans—not insurance plans—and consequently should not be subject to all the special insurance laws and taxes.

Nevertheless many Blue Cross associations and some Blue Shield associations provide major medical expense benefits to supplement those provided under their basic plans. The combination basic–major medical expense insurance coverage is probably best classified as a form of comprehensive insurance. Through these combination plans Blue Cross and Blue Shield have become important providers of coverage against financially catastrophic illnesses as well as the more common variety.

CONTRACTS ISSUED BY INDEPENDENT PLANS

Independent plans include a wide variety of insurers.[15] Most of the approximately 600 independent plans cover industrial groups whose members work for a single employer or belong to a single union. On the other hand, because some of the nonindustrial plans are sizable operations, the industrial plans insured only about 65 per cent of the enrollees for hospital care under independent plans in 1968. Most of the industrial plans are welfare funds covering members of a single union and are jointly managed by employers and employee representatives. An example of such a plan is the program of the United Mine Workers of America Welfare and Retirement Fund, which covers almost completely the services provided miners and their dependents by approved hospitals and physicians.

Industrial plans covering the employees of a single employer are much

---

[15] For more details than can be provided here, see Louis S. Reed and Willine Carr, *Independent Health Insurance Plans in the United States—1968 Survey* (Washington, D.C.: U.S. Government Printing Office, 1970).

less important. These plans are more properly regarded by the employer as retention instead of insurance, the employer's motive usually being a desire to avoid the expense loading of the insurer and to administer his own claims. In addition, many employers provide limited plant facilities, which consist usually of the services of an industrial nurse or first-aid attendant and of a full-time or part-time physician. The purpose of these facilities is generally to administer preliminary and other physical examinations, to render emergency treatment, and less commonly, to consult with the employees with respect to temporary minor illnesses. As a rule, the services and the facilities increase as the size of the firm increases.

The leading nonindustrial independent plans include plans sponsored by a community or a private group clinic. Community plans, which are open to most individuals or groups in the community, are usually sponsored by a community or a local consumer group. These plans account for only 8 per cent of the groups but for almost 35 per cent of the enrollees for hospital care. Private group-clinic plans are prepayment plans operating under the direction, control, and ownership of a group of doctors. Dental society plans are prepayment dental care plans resembling Blue Shield plans. An example of a large nonindustrial community plan is the Health Insurance Plan of Greater New York, which provides without additional cost (except for special service, such as late-night and early-morning calls) medical care by approved physicians and home-nursing service. The medical services include such items as physical examinations, immunizations, eye refractions, and care by a specialist. There is also a limited cash payment toward the cost of services provided by other physicians. Members are required to purchase hospital insurance from the New York Blue Cross association.

The benefits provided under these plans vary greatly, but most of them provide fairly complete protection for their members against most types of medical expenses. Physical examinations and immunication shots, for example, are often included among the benefits. Over half of the persons covered under independent plans are covered under programs that provide at least one type of medical service through salaried physicians, nurses, and others or through contractual arrangements with community hospitals or group-practice clinics. These service arrangements are the most controversial feature of the independent plans. Proponents believe that group-practice arrangements give the plan more control over the cost and quality of the services rendered. Opponents argue that they remove some freedom of choice from the consumer and interfere with traditional doctor-patient relationships. The frequent inclusion of physical examinations and similar items has also been questioned. Supporters argue that including these items encourages preventive medicine, lowers the cost of these services, and reduces the total cost of illness. Those opposed believe that predictable expenses, particularly those over which the insured has considerable control, should be borne by the insured out of current income or savings.

Impressed by the possible validity of the control and loss-prevention arguments, several Blue Cross associations and commercial insurers are currently experimenting in this area. Plans have been established in various cities across the country under which these insurers contract with groups of doctors or hospitals to provide comprehensive services to their insureds. Several of the plans involve university medical schools. The recent rapid rise in the cost of medical services and the threat of national health insurance described in the section "Issues" in Chapter 31 have intensified interest in these experiments. In the future some of these insurers may operate their own facilities instead of merely providing financial support.

MEDICAL INSURANCE FOR THE AGED

The Medicare program (Title XVIII of the Social Security Act, to be described in Chapter 31) includes a compulsory hospital expense plan for the aged and a voluntary supplemental plan covering primarily the cost of physicians' and surgeons' care. Although these public programs provide comprehensive protection for the aged, they do not cover all types of expenses (prescription drugs used at home, for example), they include deductibles, and they limit the number of days of hospital care and other services. Commercial insurers, Blue Cross and Blue Shield associations, and independent insurers have all developed plans designed to fill these gaps.

INSURANCE COVERING NURSING HOMES, DENTAL SERVICES, AND MENTAL ILLNESS

Insurers are constantly expanding their coverages to include new types of services or illnesses. Three areas which will probably be included in many more contracts in the next decade are nursing homes, dental services, and mental illness.

Many persons who are hospitalized could be adequately cared for at less cost in a skilled nursing home. Until the sixties insurers were reluctant to cover the cost of nursing home services because of the difficulties involved in defining acceptable facilities. When the Medicare program was established in 1965, it included services provided by extended care facilities as well as hospitals. Consequently the demand for nursing home services increased and their quality had to be improved to meet the eligibility requirements established by Medicare administrators. Many private contracts already cover the cost of post-hospitalization nursing home services. In a few years this practice should become commonplace.

Dental insurance covering the cost of examinations, fillings, extractions, and other dental care first attracted considerable attention in the sixties.

Some independent group-practice plans included dental services prior to that time, but it was not until the sixties that commercial insurers and some Blue Cross and Blue Shield associations became active in this field. Also formed in this decade were many dental service corporations sponsored by local dental societies and patterned after Blue Shield plans. Most of the protection provided to date has been written on a group basis, and its future growth appears to depend upon the extent to which it becomes a part of employee benefit plans.

Until recently mental and nervous diseases were almost always excluded under medical expense contracts. Many contracts still exclude these diseases, but a more common current practice is to provide more limited coverage for these conditions than for others. For example, a contract may provide up to 365 days of hospital room-and-board coverage but limit coverage for nervous or mental conditions to 70 days. Furthermore the treatment must be rendered in a general hospital, not in a special mental hospital. Some major medical and comprehensive contracts cover treatment for nervous and mental conditions but impose a larger deductible, a higher participation percentage, or a lower face amount. Treatment outside a hospital is much more subject to abuse than treatment in a hospital and may, therefore, be subject to more stringent restrictions. Some contracts make no distinction between nervous and mental diseases and other covered conditions. As people become more knowledgeable about and interested in mental health, broad mental disease coverage should become more popular.

REVIEW QUESTIONS

1. The typical disability income insurance contract provides less liberal benefits with respect to sickness than to accidental injuries. Illustrate this statement.
2. Design a checklist for comparing two disability income contracts.
3. Disability income contracts have been criticized on the ground that they provide benefits based on the extent of physical disability rather than on loss of earnings.
   a. What is meant by this criticism?
   b. Is the criticism justified?
4. a. Compare the cancellation provision under a health insurance contract with the cancellation provision under a fire insurance contract.
   b. Should insurers be prohibited from writing cancelable contracts? Why or why not?
5. a. What type of benefits are provided under noncancelable and guaranteed renewable contracts?

b. Is the guaranteed renewability feature rendered meaningless if the insurer reserves the right to change the premium rate?

6. What are the advantages and disadvantages associated with using riders to life insurance contracts to provide protection against disability income losses?

7. Health insurers have been severely criticized in the past for denying claims on the ground that the condition existed prior to the starting date of the contract. What is the current situation with respect to preexisting conditions?

8. a. Basic medical expense insurance has been called first-dollar coverage. Why?

   b. Major medical expense insurance has been called catastrophe insurance. Why?

9. a. What type of expenses are covered under a basic medical expense insurance contract issued by a commercial insurer?

   b. What type of expenses are covered under a major medical expense insurance contract issued by a commercial insurer?

10. An insured and his family are protected under a $250 per-illness deductible, 20 per cent participation, $15,000 per-illness medical expense insurance contract. How much will the insurer contribute toward each of the following events?

    a. The insured's wife has a serious abdominal ailment. The total medical expenses are $16,250.

    b. The insured's son has his tonsils removed. The total medical expenses are $225.

    c. The insured and his daughter are seriously injured in an automobile accident. The insured's total medical expenses are $10,000. His daughter's expenses are $8,250.

    d. The insured's son falls from a ladder and suffers serious internal injuries. The total medical expenses are $20,250.

11. Many people believe that major medical expense insurance and comprehensive insurance are designed to attain the same objective. Do you agree?

12. Blue Cross contracts have been distinguished from those issued by commercial insurers on the ground that they provide *prepaid service* benefits rather than *insured cash* benefits. Explain this distinction.

13. Compare the service features of Blue Cross plans and Blue Shield plans.

14. Many independent plans provide their service benefits through group-practice arrangements.

    a. Are Blue Cross or Blue Shield benefits provided in this way?

    b. What are the advantages and disadvantages of group-practice arrangements?

15. a. Why were insurers reluctant until recently to cover nursing home expenses?

b. Do you believe that dental care insurance will be popular? Why or why not?

c. To what extent are nervous disorders and mental conditions covered under medical expense contracts?

SUGGESTIONS FOR ADDITIONAL READING

Dickerson, O. D.: *Health Insurance* (3d ed., Homewood, Ill.: Richard D. Irwin, Inc., 1968), chaps. 5–16.

Eilers, R. D.: *Regulation of Blue Cross and Blue Shield Plans* (Homewood, Ill.: Richard D. Irwin, Inc., 1963), chaps. 1–5 and 8–11.

Follman, J. F.: *Medical Care and Health Insurance* (Homewood, Ill.: Richard D. Irwin, Inc., 1963).

Gregg, D. W. (ed.): *Life and Health Insurance Handbook* (2d ed., Homewood, Ill.: Richard D. Irwin, Inc., 1964), pp. 21–24, 27.

Somers, H. M., and Somers, A. R.: *Doctors, Patients, and Health Insurance* (Washington, D.C.: The Brookings Institution, 1961).

21

business uses of individual life and health insurance

The contracts discussed in the two preceding chapters have many uses. A business firm may use these policies (1) to protect itself or (2) to protect its employees on an individual instead of on a group basis. This chapter describes these business uses and the decisions they entail.

In connection with some of these applications, the firm will probably need the services of a four-man team—a lawyer, an accountant, a trust officer, and an insurance agent.

Insurance for the Firm

The firm uses individual personnel insurance to protect itself against credit losses, key-man losses, and business-liquidation losses. Since credit life and health insurance were described in Chapters 19 and 20, the discussion here will be limited to key-man insurance and business purchase insurance.

KEY-MAN INSURANCE

Key-man insurance is insurance purchased by a firm to protect itself against financial losses caused by the death or disability of a key man. These losses were described in Chapter 8. If the potential losses are serious, most firms will elect to purchase insurance because the uncertainty will be great and there will be no other way to transfer the risk. However, even after risk analysis has determined the amount of the potential loss and the duration of the exposure, and after the risk manager has decided that a private insurance contract will be used to protect the firm, he must still make several decisions. These involve the amount of insurance, the type of policy, and the disposition of the policy if the key man resigns or retires.

The amount of insurance will depend upon the estimated losses, the cost of providing various degrees of protection, and the alternative uses for the premium dollars. Because protection is the purpose of key-man life insurance, the insurance policy should emphasize protection as opposed to investment. Term insurance (in some cases, decreasing term insurance) is in order if the protection need is of short duration, but the longer the duration, the stronger is the case that can be made for straight life insurance (with perhaps a decreasing-term rider) because of its flexibility and, in some cases, its cost advantage. A contract with some investment element may also be proper if the firm wants to meet protection and investment objectives with one contract. For example, the firm may want to protect itself against a key-man replacement loss if the key man dies during his employment period, and if he survives to retire, it may want to provide him with an income out of the cash values during retirement. Another possibility is that the cash value would be used by the firm itself to cover the costs of replacing the retired key man. A final consideration in selecting the contract is the physical condition of the key man, for the age and health of the person to be insured may limit the number of available contracts. An application for term insurance is more likely to be refused for these reasons than is an application for any other type of insurance.

If the key man retires or resigns, the firm may continue the policy in force, surrender the policy for its cash value if any, sell the policy to the key man, or, as noted above, use the policy to provide an income for the key man during his retirement.

Because of the nature of the insurance, no question arises concerning the owner and beneficiary of the policy. The employer applies for the policy, pays the premiums, owns the policy, and is the beneficiary under the policy. The premiums are not a deductible expense for Federal income tax purposes, but the proceeds are not subject to income tax.

Key-man health insurance may include any of the loss of income contracts discussed in Chapter 20.[1] The duration of the potential loss is a key consideration. Noncancelable and guaranteed renewable contracts pose a decision similar to life insurance if the key man resigns or retires. The ownership, beneficiary, and tax considerations are identical with those mentioned in connection with life insurance.

---

[1] A sole proprietor may also be interested in an *overhead expense* insurance contract which will reimburse him for the expenses that continue during his temporary disability. Note the similarity to business interruption insurance discussed on pp. 293–296.

BUSINESS PURCHASE INSURANCE

Business purchase insurance is insurance purchased in connection with a business purchase agreement. Under this agreement, the firm, the co-owners, or some employees have agreed to purchase some or all of the decreased or permanently disabled owner's business interest. In a case of temporary disability, an agreement is usually made to continue part of the disabled owner's salary. The purpose of the agreement and the insurance is to avoid the business-liquidation losses described in Chapter 8. The advantages of the agreement are thus the converse of the potential losses. For the heirs, the agreement provides:

1. A fair valuation of their interest. (Protection against harsh bargaining or a "freeze-out" by the survivors is assured.)
2. A continuous market for their interest.
3. A speedier and more orderly settlement of the insured's estate.

For the surviving owners, the advantages are:

1. A fair purchase price for the interest of the deceased
2. A speedier and more orderly settlement of the deceased's or disabled person's interest
3. Protection against the inclusion of undesirable business partners
4. Protection against restrictions in credit following the death or disability of an owner
5. Protection against lowered employee morale following the death or disability

Finally, the firm benefits, even if the owners do not die or become disabled, for the following reasons:

1. The firm's credit standing is improved.
2. Employee morale is improved.

Although a business purchase agreement need not be funded with life insurance or health insurance, insurance is an ideal funding vehicle because it provides the funds at the exact moment and only if they are needed.

In preparing the agreement and purchasing the insurance, a risk manager must make decisions with respect to the purchase price, the type of insurance, the ownership of the insurance, the beneficiary under the insurance policy, and the disposition of any ownership interest of the deceased or disabled owner in policies covering the other owners. We shall discuss each of these decisions. Because business purchase agreements covering disability are still relatively rare, most of the discussion will relate to the agreements covering death and retirement.

As in Chapter 8, unless otherwise noted, the discussion of business purchase agreements applies to all three forms of business organization— sole proprietorship, partnership, and close corporation.

Valuation   The valuation of a business interest is always difficult, and in business purchase agreements this difficulty is compounded by the fact that the value to be estimated is the value at some uncertain date in the future. Consequently, it is common practice not to set a fixed amount as the purchase price but to establish a formula for determining the value at the date of death or permanent disability. Sometimes a fixed amount is established with the understanding that this amount will be corrected periodically, but these revaluations are usually few and far between.

Despite the inaccuracies inherent in any of these valuation procedures, the value arrived at is more likely to be just than one left to chance and possibly influenced greatly by the unequal bargaining positions of the heirs and the prospective purchasers. An additional advantage to the heirs of a definite business purchase agreement valuation is that this valuation will, with the proper precautions, be accepted by the tax authorities as the valuation for estate tax purposes. Otherwise the business interest may be valued at much more than it is worth for this purpose.

Type of insurance   Business purchase life insurance contracts, like key-man life insurance contracts, should emphasize protection rather than investment. The case for term insurance is weaker, however, because the need for the protection is likely to be long-term. Business purchase health insurance contracts should provide disability income until a relatively advanced age. A nonterm life insurance policy with waiver of premium and disability income riders will often be useful because it provides benefits in case of death or disability.

Ownership of the insurance   Ownership considerations vary, depending upon the type of business organization. The prospective purchaser of a sole proprietor's business interest is typically a key employee, and that employee usually owns the policy and pays the premium. In a partnership or a close corporation, there are two possibilities. The firm may own the policy and pay the premiums, or each owner may purchase insurance contracts covering his associates. Factors affecting this decision include the number of policies involved, tax considerations, and whether creditors would have access to the proceeds.

Disability insurance policies may be arranged in the same way, but another common practice is to have each owner carry his own disability income insurance. If the owner becomes disabled for more than a specified period, the survivors agree to buy out his interest in installments through a series of promissory notes payable over a specified period.

Beneficiary The beneficiary under the life insurance policies may be (1) the surviving purchasers, (2) the firm (not possible in a sole proprietorship), (3) the heirs of the deceased, (4) the estate of the deceased, or (5) a trustee. Although the surviving purchasers or the firm are legally bound under the purchase agreement to pay the purchase price to the heirs in exchange for the business interest, there may be some delay and unpleasantness if they are named as beneficiaries. The danger that all will not proceed according to plan is even greater when the heirs or the estate are named because the heirs and the executor or administrator will then control both the proceeds and the interest.[2] If the agreement contains any loopholes, it may never be executed. The advantage of a trustee is that an unbiased intermediary is charged with the proper use of the insurance proceeds.

The beneficiary under the disability income contracts is the disabled sole proprietor or partner. In the case of a corporation, the disabled stockholder is the beneficiary if the stockholders buy the policy; otherwise, for tax reasons, the corporation is the beneficiary.

Disposition of policies no longer needed If the prospective employee purchaser of a sole proprietorship should resign, be discharged, or die, the purchase agreement is terminated, and the sole proprietor should have the right to purchase the policy from the employee or his heirs, because the original purpose for the policy no longer exists. Although some tax problems may arise, the sole proprietor may in turn transfer this value to a prospective purchaser under a new agreement. The purchase price is usually the cash value or some similar price.

In a partnership or corporation, the same situation arises when the partners or stockholders are the owners of the policies, as opposed to the firm. The surviving associates should be able to purchase the policies on their own lives from the retiring or deceased owner or his legal representatives.

Excess payments The purchase price of the deceased's business interest may exceed the face amount of the life insurance on his life or the payments under the disability insurance contract. For example, if the purchase price is to be determined by a formula, no one knows what the price will be at the time the insurance is purchased, and the amount purchased may turn out to be too small. Provision must be made in such a case for making

---

[2] One reason for naming the heirs as beneficiaries is that they would then be in a position to select the most appropriate settlement options. Many insurers, however, now make it possible for them to select the options when a trustee is the direct beneficiary.

the excess payments immediately or in installments secured by promissory notes and other safeguards.

An extreme example of an excess payment occurs when one or more of the owners are uninsurable and there are no existing policies which could profitably be transferred for value to fund the agreement.

Insurance for Employees

Key-man insurance and business purchase insurance are designed to protect the firm against key-man or liquidation losses. The other major business uses of individual insurance are to protect the employee. They fall into the following categories: (1) tax-free death benefit insurance, (2) disability salary continuation insurance, (3) split-dollar insurance, (4) deferred compensation insurance, (5) individual policy pension trusts, (6) wholesale insurance, and (7) franchise insurance. Most insurance protecting employees is group insurance, but individual insurance is also used extensively because (1) many firms are too small to qualify for group insurance; (2) the individual insurance plan may actually be no more costly for small groups than a group insurance plan; (3) the employer may wish to choose the employees to be protected on some basis (say, key employees) that would not be practicable or even permitted under group insurance; or (4) the employer may not wish to formalize the benefit. Each of the seven uses specified above will now be discussed separately.

TAX-FREE DEATH BENEFIT INSURANCE

An employer may pay up to $5,000 directly to the dependents or estate of any deceased employee on either a contractual or voluntary selective basis without entailing any income tax liability for the dependents. Moreover, the payment is a tax-deductible item for the firm. Although the firm need not purchase insurance to fund these payments, such a practice is common because the uncertainty is great and the cost of transferring the risk to an insurer is relatively low. Although the premiums on the insurance are not tax-deductible, the proceeds are not taxable to the employer.

DISABILITY SALARY CONTINUATION INSURANCE

Individual disability insurance may be used to provide an income partially or entirely tax-free for a disabled employee.[3] If the insurer sends the periodic

---

[3] In determining his taxable income, an employee can deduct up to $100 a week from any sick pay provided by his employer, following a 30-day waiting period.

If the sick pay amounts to less than 75 per cent of his regular earnings, he may deduct as much as $75 weekly, beginning one week after he is disabled, unless he is hospitalized, in which case there is no waiting period. After 30 days the maximum weekly deductible is $100.

checks directly to the employee, the firm may deduct the premiums as a business expense. If the insurer pays the firm, the premiums are not deductible, but the insurance proceeds are not taxable income for the firm, and its payments to the disabled employee are a deductible expense.

If a plan provides for salary continuance in case of death or disability, a life insurance policy with a disability income rider can be very useful.

SPLIT-DOLLAR INSURANCE

As was pointed out in Chapter 8, the protection needs of an insured tend to decline with age. Split-dollar insurance is a way of providing decreasing insurance for employees at an attractive price. A specified amount of insurance is purchased on the life of the employee, and the annual premium is split into two parts. Each year the employer pays a portion which is equal to the increase in the cash value during the policy year. The employee pays the difference—a decreasing amount.

The employer owns the policy and is the irrevocable beneficiary with respect to the cash value, which always equals or exceeds his contribution toward the policy. Thus his only loss is the interest he might have earned on his contributions. The employee's beneficiary receives the difference between the face amount and the cash value.[4] The employee gains because he receives what is in effect an interest-free loan.

DEFERRED COMPENSATION PLANS

Deferred compensation plans provide for the payment of an annual income to a key employee after he retires, in exchange for a reduced salary during his earning career. The advantage to the employee of a deferred compensation agreement is that he does not have to pay any income tax on the funding payments, whereas he would have to pay a tax on an equivalent increase in salary. He will have to pay a tax on the retirement payments when they start, but presumably at that time his income tax bracket will be much lower. The firm cannot deduct the funding payment, but the retirement payments by the firm are deductible as a business expense.

Large firms may elect to fund deferred compensation plans by accumulations of cash or securities during the employee's earning career. Many of these plans, however, are funded by insurance. Insurance is particularly popular with small firms, regardless of the types of benefits, and with both large and small firms when death and disability benefits are also included in the agreement. As we have already noted earlier in this chapter, the same policy may serve as key-man insurance and as a funding vehicle for

---

[4] If dividends are applied under the fifth dividend option to purchase term insurance equal to the cash value, the employee's beneficiary will receive the face amount of insurance.

a deferred compensation plan. The type of life insurance to be used also depends upon the combination of benefits included in the agreement. The firm pays the insurance premiums and collects the proceeds. The proceeds do not constitute taxable income for the firm.

Certain precautions are usually taken for tax reasons. First, the plan requires that the employee remain with the firm until retirement and that after his retirement he make himself available as a consultant and not enter into any competing employment. In other words, the promise to pay retirement benefits is conditional, not absolute. Second, the plan is not technically secured by the fund or the insurance. The conditional features of the plan necessitate this proviso.[5]

INDIVIDUAL POLICY PENSION TRUSTS

Pension plans designed to provide benefits for large groups of employees are discussed in the next chapter. Individual insurance policies can be used as the funding instrument for these pension plans. In fact, although group pension plans cover far more employees than individual policy plans, the individual policy plans are much more numerous. Many insurers limit their group plans to employee groups including at least twenty-five lives. For groups including fifty lives or less, the individual plan may be no more costly than the group plan. Further discussion of individual policy pension trusts will be deferred until the next chapter, under "Insured Plans," in order to avoid repetition of certain concepts and to facilitate comparisons among various funding instruments.

WHOLESALE INSURANCE

Wholesale insurance is life insurance written on groups that are too small to qualify for group insurance. The employer arranges for the collection and payment of the premiums on a group basis, but individual contracts are issued and the insurability of each individual applicant is evaluated separately. Physical examinations, however, are usually waived. As in group insurance, the amount of the protection is determined automatically on the basis of salary, position, service, or some other factor.[6] In short, wholesale

---

[5] Another compensation method inspired by tax factors is the restricted stock option. Under this method, the firm gives certain employees the option to buy a stated number of shares of the firm's common stock at a specified price. The option must be exercised within an agreed time. If the price of the stock should rise within that time, the option becomes highly valuable. The employee may purchase life and health insurance in connection with this option for two reasons: First, if the employee exercises the option but must pay the purchase price in installments or with borrowed funds and then dies or becomes disabled, the insurance proceeds can be used to continue the installment payments or to pay back the loan. Second, if he dies or becomes disabled before he has elected to exercise this option, the insurance proceeds can be used to make the purchase.

[6] See p. 411.

insurance, like individual policy pension trusts, is a hybrid of group insurance and individual insurance. The contributions by the firm are tax-deductible as a business expense but do not constitute taxable income to the employee.

Wholesale insurance has been growing rapidly as more small firms seek to protect their employees.

FRANCHISE INSURANCE

Franchise insurance is the health insurance equivalent of wholesale insurance and is often referred to by that name.

Retirement Plans for the Self-employed

Until the enactment of the Self-Employed Individuals Retirement Act of 1962, self-employed persons did not receive any tax incentives in connection with their personal retirement programs. Consequently many self-employed persons incorporated their business in order that as employees they might share the employee benefit plan tax advantages cited at several places in this chapter and the next. Under the 1962 act, as liberalized in 1967, self-employed persons may deduct for Federal income tax purposes the annual amount they set aside for retirement but in no case more than 10 per cent of their earned income or, if less, $2,500. In addition, earnings on the retirement fund are not taxed prior to retirement. When the self-employed person retires and withdraws money from the retirement fund, he must pay a tax on the withdrawals, but presumably he will at that time be in a lower tax bracket and eligible for special exemptions.

In order to receive these tax benefits, the self-employed must qualify their retirement programs (called H.R. 10 or Keogh plans, after the act's sponsor) with the Internal Revenue Service. The three principal methods of funding these plans are (1) individual annuity contracts issued to individual self-employed persons or group annuity contracts issued to members of a professional association, (2) transfer to a trustee who can invest the funds in almost any form of investment—typically common stocks, mutual funds, or life insurance, or some combination of these investments, or (3) a special custodial account with a bank which would usually invest the moneys wholly in a mutual fund.

If the self-employed person has any full-time employees who have worked for him three years or more, he must contribute toward their retirement at least the same percentage of their compensation as he applies to his own earned income. If an employer prefers, he may use a formula that relates his contributions to his profits. In either case, his contributions are a tax-deductible item for him, and his employees enjoy the tax advantage associated with other employees' pension plans.

REVIEW QUESTIONS

1. The Ajax Manufacturing Corporation has a key engineer, aged 40, who has been largely responsible for the firm's outstanding success. He is considered replaceable within ten years if he should die or become disabled, but in the meantime the profits of the firm would be reduced about $25,000 per year. Key-man insurance seems advisable.
   a. How much insurance should the firm buy?
   b. What type insurance should be purchased?
   c. What beneficiary designations should be made?
   d. What are the tax implications of this insurance?
   e. What should be the disposition of the insurance policies if the key man retires or resigns?

2. Messrs. Adams and Brown are equal partners in a small wholesaling firm. What would be the advantage of a business purchase agreement (a) to the heirs if either Adams or Brown should die? (b) to Adams or Brown if either died or became disabled?

3. An abbreviated balance sheet for the Adams-Brown partnership is presented below:

Balance sheet for Adams-Brown partnership

Cash		$ 5,000
Accounts receivable	$42,000	
Less reserve	2,000	40,000
Merchandise		100,000
Equipment		55,000
Real estate		40,000
Goodwill		10,000
		$250,000
Accounts payable		$ 80,000
Mortgage on real estate		20,000
Adams, capital		75,000
Brown, capital		75,000
		$250,000

The annual earnings have been averaging around $25,000. The average price-earnings ratio in the stock market for a business of this quality is about ten times earnings. What should be the valuation in the business purchase agreement?

4. If Adams and Brown agree to fund the agreement through insurance.
   a. Who should purchase the insurance? Why?

b. What type of insurance should be purchased?

c. Who should be the beneficiary under the insurance policies?

5. Would your answer to question 4 be different if Adams and Brown were stockholders in a close corporation instead of partners?

6. Carter is a sole proprietor.

a. Does he need a business purchase agreement?

b. If so, what would be the nature of the agreement and the insurance arrangements?

7. Since group insurance is less expensive than individual insurance, why should any firm consider the purchase of individual insurance to protect employees against their personnel losses?

8. Explain the tax features of:

a. Tax-free death benefit insurance

b. Disability salary continuation insurance

c. Deferred compensation plans

9. a. What is split-dollar insurance?

b. How does the employee benefit from split-dollar insurance?

10. Compare wholesale insurance and franchise insurance with group insurance.

SUGGESTIONS FOR ADDITIONAL READING

Advanced Underwriting and Estate Planning Service, Vol. II (Indianapolis: Research and Review Service of America, Inc.).

Dickerson, O. D.: *Health Insurance* (3d ed., Homewood, Ill.: Richard D. Irwin, Inc., 1968), chap. 21.

Gregg, D. W. (ed.): *Life and Health Insurance Handbook* (2d ed., Homewood, Ill.: Richard D. Irwin, Inc., 1954), chaps. 45–51.

Mehr, R. I.: *Life Insurance: Theory and Practice* (4th ed., Austin: Business Publications, Inc., 1970), chap. 22.

The Diamond Life Bulletins Service, Business Insurance Volume (Cincinnati: National Underwriter Company).

White, E. H.: *Business Insurance* (3d ed., Englewood Cliffs, N.J.: Prentice-Hall, Inc., 1963).

22

employee benefit plans

Employee benefit plans have become an important condition of employment for most employees. A business should be vitally interested in these plans because of their impact on industrial relations and the sizable expenditures they require. Some components of employee benefit plans have already been discussed in Chapter 21, but the major discussion has been reserved for this chapter.

After outlining the nature and scope of employee benefit plans, we will examine the arrangements that are usually made to provide the most common types of benefits. In most instances these arrangements involve group insurance, but some leading uses of retention will also be described.

Nature and Scope of Employee Benefit Plans

In recent years the *Social Security Bulletin* has reported annually on the operations of privately organized "employee-benefit plans." An employee benefit plan is defined as

> . . . any type of plan sponsored or initiated unilaterally or jointly by em- ployers and employees and providing benefits that stem from the em- ployment relationship and that are not underwritten or paid directly by government (Federal, state, or local). In general, the intent is to include plans that provide in an orderly, predetermined fashion for (1) income maintenance during periods when regular earnings are cut off because of

Number of employees covered by benefits expressed as percentage of all wage and salary workers*

Benefits	1950	1960	1968
Life insurance and death	38.9%	58.2%	64.9%
Accidental death and dismemberment	16.2	35.5	46.8
Hospitalization	48.7	68.9	75.4
Surgical	35.5	65.5	73.2
Regular medical	16.4	50.2	63.3
Major medical expense	....	16.5	31.7
Temporary disability, including formal sick leave	46.2	49.0	49.3
Long-term disability	....	....	7.9
Retirement	22.5	42.4	47.2
Supplemental unemployment	....	3.4	3.8

* Proportion of wage and salary workers in private industry only for last three benefits.

death, accident, sickness, retirement, and unemployment and (2) benefits to meet certain specified expenses usually associated with illness or injury.[1]

This definition does not include all personnel insurance benefits for employees (for example, it excludes split-dollar and deferred compensation benefits, which are provided through individual insurance contracts as noted in Chapter 21), but it does include the protection against personnel risks provided most employees. It also does not include the newly developing group property and liability insurance programs described at the end of this chapter, but these plans are still in their infancy. Consequently, the data in the *Bulletin* articles enable a reader to obtain an excellent understanding of the nature, scope, and growth of the employee benefit field.

The number of employees covered by each type of benefit included in these reports expressed as a percentage of all wage and salary workers for 1950, 1960, and 1968 is shown in the table at the top of the page.

These data show the rapid growth over a relatively short period in the number of persons covered and the large numbers of employees protected against death, poor health, and old age. They also indicate that there is still considerable room for expansion with respect to some types of benefits.

Another measure of the importance of these plans is the estimated contributions toward the various types of benefits. If these contributions are expressed as a percentage of all wages and salaries, the results for

[1] Walter Kolodrubetz, "Employee-Benefit Plans in 1968," *Social Security Bulletin,* XXXIII, No. 4 (April, 1970). This entire section is based largely on this article and on earlier articles in the same series.

1950, 1960, and 1968 are as shown in the table at the foot of the page. The high cost of pensions relative to other benefits is particularly noteworthy.

The death, medical expense, and disability income (excluding paid sick-leave) benefits are usually provided under *insured* plans.[2] Paid sick-leave and supplemental unemployment benefits are always self-insured. About 30 per cent of the employees covered under pension plans belong to insured plans, the remainder to self-insured programs.

The following detailed analysis of employee benefit plans is restricted to plans covering employees of a single employer, partly to simplify the presentation and partly because most employees are covered under single-employer plans. The increasing importance of the multi-employer plans, however, must be acknowledged. These plans cover the employers of two or more employees in an industry, in an area, or in an industry within an area. The two most important types are (1) plans covering employers of members of a trade association such as the Minnesota Employers' Association and (2) plans covering members of a union who work for two or more employers. This second type of plan, which is exemplified by the United Mine Workers Welfare and Retirement Fund, involves a welfare fund managed by trustees.[3] Two major characteristics of these multi-employer welfare funds are (1) the continuation of coverage if an employee moves from one firm under the plan to another firm under the same plan, and (2) the nature of the financial support. The plans are usually financed completely by em-

[2] "Insured plans" are interpreted broadly in this text to include plans underwritten by any agency which pools the risks of many insureds.
[3] For some details of "independent" health plans which include many multi-employer plans such as this one, see Chap. 20.

Estimated contributions to benefits expressed as percentage of all wages and salaries*

Benefits	1950	1960	1968
Life insurance and death	0.34%	0.54%	0.65%
Accidental death and dismemberment	0.01	0.03	0.04
Hospitalization	0.40	0.96	1.23
Surgical } Regular medical }	0.21	0.49	0.64
Major medical expense	....	0.18	0.37
Temporary disability, including formal sick leave } Long-term disability }	0.40	0.53	0.61
Supplemental unemployment	....	0.05	0.03
Retirement	1.67	2.47	2.88

* Proportion of wages and salaries in private industry only for the last three benefits.

ployer contributions based on payroll or some production unit such as tons of coal mined. Although many of these plans handle their own losses, any single employer may choose to regard the plan as an insurer because of the pooling of the risks of many employers.

Other groups whose insurance protection plans will not be discussed in the following sections are union members under union-controlled plans, professional associations, credit unions, and borrowers from banks.

Before turning to those benefits usually provided by insured plans, we shall contrast the group method of underwriting insurance protection with individual underwriting.

Group Underwriting Contrasted with Individual Underwriting

Group underwriting differs from individual underwriting in several respects.

1. Group selection is substituted for individual selection. If the group is acceptable to the insurer, everyone in the group is eligible for the protection. As a result, the insurer covers some persons who could not obtain individual insurance at any price. In order to keep the proportion of such persons in each insured group at a minimum, certain underwriting safeguards have been adopted with respect to life and health insurance plans.[4]

First, only those types of groups are acceptable (a) for which insurance is incidental to the major purpose of the group, (b) in which there is a constant flow of younger persons into the group while older and impaired lives are leaving it, and (c) for joining for which some physical qualifications are required. By these standards, a group of employees working for a single employer is most satisfactory. As insurers gain more experience with group insurance and as competition increases, these standards have been relaxed, and today insurers write such groups as members of a professional association or a college alumni society.

Second, the number of insureds in the group must exceed a certain minimum. This requirement decreases the chance that impaired lives will form an important part of the group and reduces the administrative costs per insured life. In group life insurance, the most common size requirement is 25 or more, although "baby group" insurance is written on as few as 10 lives.[5] In group health insurance, groups of 10 or less are fairly common. Groups of 2 have been reported. In pensions, the minimum number of lives is usually 25, but smaller minimums are becoming more common.

Third, if participation is voluntary, a certain percentage, usually 75 per cent, of the employees is required to participate. Otherwise, the partici-

---

[4] In most states, all or some of these safeguards are required by law.
[5] This term is sometimes used to describe wholesale and franchise insurance. See Chap. 21.

pating group might include an abnormally high percentage of impaired lives since those in poor health will almost certainly elect to participate. This requirement, however, has also been relaxed in recent years.

Fourth, the employees must meet certain eligibility requirements. For example, an employee must accept the coverage within a certain period after he becomes eligible. Otherwise he must prove individual insurability to join the group. Another eligibility requirement states that insured members must be active employees, not inactive members of the board of directors. Transitory workers are commonly excluded by a one-to-six-month qualification period.

Fifth, the benefit amounts must be either the same for all participants or determined automatically on some basis such as salary, position, service, or some combination of these factors. Otherwise the impaired lives would probably select large amounts of life and health insurance while the healthy lives would select smaller amounts. It has become fairly common, however, to give the employee some choice, such as an amount equal to his annual salary or an amount equal to his salary for two years.

Sixth, some maximum must be placed on the amount of life insurance and disability income protection on any single life. This maximum is generally related to the total amount of insurance in force on the group because one objective is to avoid a disproportionate amount of protection on any one life.

2. A master contract is issued to the employer as the policyholder. The employees, who are not technically parties to the contract, receive individual certificates as evidence of their protection.

3. Salaried employees of insurers who are specially trained in group insurance almost always assist the commissioned agent or broker originating the sale and handle the details associated with installation of the plan.

4. The employer assists the insurer in administering the plan. In some instances, the employer performs all the administration, even to the point of paying the claims.

5. The group contract may be designed within limits to meet the specific needs of the particular employee group. In this respect, group insurance has considerably more flexibility than does individual insurance.

6. Statutory standard provisions are less important than in individual insurance. Not all states have laws providing for standard provisions, and those which do have such laws do not, except for group life insurance, include more than a few provisions.[6]

7. Because the wholesale method of distributing the coverage permits reduced administrative costs and commissions, and because the employer

[6] The group life standard provisions cover such matters as a grace period, incontestability, misstatement of age, and conversion rights.

performs some of the administrative tasks, the premium for group insurance is less than the premium for equivalent individual insurance. Furthermore, the experience of the particular group may be considered in determining the final cost of the group protection.

Group Life Insurance

Group life insurance plans, which are underwritten almost exclusively by commercial insurers, may provide either yearly renewable term insurance or permanent insurance for the participating employees. Because over 90 per cent of the group life insurance in force is yearly renewable term insurance, we discuss that type of protection in more detail than the other types.

YEARLY RENEWABLE TERM INSURANCE

Group yearly renewable term insurance provides for the payment of a specified amount, commonly one or two years' salary but not in excess of $40,000,[7] to the beneficiary of a deceased employee. The proceeds are payable in a lump sum or according to the installment-time or installment-amount options. The interest and life annuity options are rarely available.

If the employee withdraws from the group, he usually has the right, without proving his insurability, to purchase within 31 days an individual nonterm insurance contract bearing a premium based upon his attained age. During the 31-day decision period, the group insurance protection continues. This right to convert the group protection to individual protection is valuable if the insured is uninsurable or if he would have to pay substandard rates for an individual contract. If the employer or the insurer terminates the master contract, employees with several years of service may convert at least part of their group protection, commonly up to $2,000 of their group-protection amount.

Under this type of plan, the cost of insuring any single employee increases over time, but if the age composition of the group remains approximately the same,[8] the total premium for the group does not change greatly. If the plan is *contributory* (i.e., if the employee also contributes to the cost), the employee's contribution is typically $0.60 or less per month per $1,000 of insurance during his membership in the group. At the younger ages this contribution is usually more than enough to pay for his personal

---

[7] Most states limit the amount of group coverage on the life of one person, $40,000 being the typical maximum. Some states, however, place no limit on the coverage. Amounts in excess of $100,000 have been written under many group policies.

[8] The age composition, not the average age, must remain about the same. To illustrate, the cost of insuring two persons, aged 20 and 60, exceeds the cost of insuring two persons, aged 40.

protection. It may even be more than enough to pay the annual premiums on individual 5- or 10-year term insurance. In later years, however, his total cost will far exceed the employee's contribution. Some employees may, if the plan is voluntary, elect not to participate under the plan until the premium for individual protection exceeds the required contribution under the group plan, but they will have to prove insurability at that time. If they become uninsurable, they will have good reason to regret their earlier decision.

The initial group premium depends primarily upon the age composition and the size of the group. The size is important because the expense loading does not increase proportionately with the amount of insurance in force. An additional charge is also levied for certain substandard industrial classifications. The final cost, however, depends also upon the dividends paid by participating insurers and the retrospective premium adjustments of non-participating insurers. The dividends and premium adjustments for large groups are roughly a return of the premiums not needed for (1) the claims and expenses of the particular group and (2) some contribution to contingency reserves and deficiencies in the premiums collected from some groups. As the size of the group decreases, the claim experience fluctuates over a wider range, and the insurer's experience on all groups combined is weighted more heavily in the formula.

The employer's contribution toward the cost of a qualified group term insurance plan is a business expense for the firm. The employee can exclude from his taxable income that portion of the employer's contribution used to purchase the first $50,000 of protection. Beneficiaries do not have to pay any Federal income tax on the proceeds. This tax feature, plus the inclusion of noncontributory insurance benefits in union demands, has been largely responsible for the trend toward noncontributory plans. For example, for an employee in a 20 per cent Federal income tax bracket, an employee is as well off with an $80 annual contribution by the employer to a group life insurance plan as with a $100 salary increase, $20 of which must be paid to the tax collector and the remaining $80 contributed to the group plan.

In addition to this tax feature, other arguments in favor of a noncontributory plan are that (1) the employer has more freedom in designing, administering, and revising the plan and (2) all eligible employees are covered, thus reducing (a) the problems with would-be beneficiaries where there is no coverage and (b) the expenses of keeping records of contributions. On the other hand, a contributory plan (1) makes it possible to provide larger benefits and (2) may increase the employees' interest in the plan. They may appreciate more what the employer is doing for them, and they may sometimes make valuable suggestions. Employee interest, of course, may also be developed in other ways, such as improved communications between labor and management. Many group term insurance plans include dependents as well as employees, but for a lesser amount.

NONTERM INSURANCE

Group life insurance written on the nonterm basis assumes two forms: (1) group paid-up insurance (a two-part protection plan combining an increasing amount of single-premium whole life insurance with a decreasing amount of term insurance) and (2) level-premium group permanent insurance. Both forms differ from group term insurance in that they provide the withdrawing employee with certain nonforfeiture values. These values are especially attractive to employees retiring at advanced ages because of the sizable premiums they would have to pay for converted protection under group term insurance. Business firms are aware of this problem of the aged, and many continue the group term insurance in decreased amounts on retired employees. The cost to the firm is a sizable increase in the total premium without any contribution by the retiree. Group permanent insurance spreads the cost of the protection after withdrawal over the working career of the employee, and in addition, the employee frequently shares the cost.

Health Insurance

Group health insurance plans provide (1) disability income protection and (2) medical expense protection. Each type of protection will be discussed separately.

To save space, however, we shall first summarize briefly the tax situation with respect to both these coverages. With some exceptions, the employer contributions are tax-deductible by the employer and nontaxable income for the employee. The benefits provided by the employer contributions are tax-free, except that disability income provided through these funds is taxable on the basis described in "Disability salary continuation insurance," under "Insurance for Employees" in Chapter 21. Although these tax rules are not quite so favorable toward noncontributory plans as the life insurance tax rules, they offer a strong reason for favoring employer-pay-all plans. The other arguments with respect to contributory and noncontributory arrangements are the same as those presented under "Group Life Insurance" earlier in this chapter.

DISABILITY INCOME INSURANCE

Group disability income insurance is underwritten almost exclusively by commercial insurers. This protection is provided through (1) temporary disability income insurance, (2) permanent disability income insurance, (3) dismemberment insurance, (4) disability provisions in group life plans, and (5) disability provisions in group pension plans. Dismemberment insurance which is written in conjunction with accidental death insurance provides for the payment of a lump sum if the insured suffers a loss of life or a scheduled dismemberment or loss of sight sustained solely as a result of accidental means within 90 days after the accident. The other protection types are important enough to be discussed separately.

Temporary disability income insurance   Group temporary disability income insurance, often referred to as group accident and health insurance, provides a specified weekly benefit for a totally disabled person for a maximum duration of 13 or 26 weeks, or less commonly, 52 or 104 weeks. No distinction is made between disabilities caused by accident or sickness except that no benefits are usually payable for at least the 7 days of sickness-incurred disability, whereas a shorter waiting period or none at all may apply to disabilities caused by accidents. The weekly benefit is usually related to the weekly earnings, the maximum benefit being generally under $70.[9]

Occupational injuries and diseases are usually excluded under the contract, but because of the restrictions on maximum workmen's compensation benefits, the temporary disability income benefits sometimes exceed the statutory payments. Consequently, some employers prefer to cover occupational injuries as well, but workmen's compensation payments are deducted from the group insurance benefit. Pregnancy, childbirth, or miscarriage may be excluded or the benefits limited to 6 weeks' duration.

If an employee terminates his employment, his insurance automatically terminates except that an employee who is absent on account of injury or sickness continues to be covered until premium payments are discontinued or, if earlier, until maximum benefits have been paid for any one disability.

The initial premium rate for a specified set of temporary disability benefits depends primarily upon the proportion of female lives and the size of the group. Females are much more susceptible to short-term disability and therefore increase the costs. Expenses do not increase proportionately with the weekly indemnity in force. If other group health insurance coverages are to be included in the plan, the expense loading is usually less than the sum of the expense loadings applicable to each component. Loadings are also added for certain substandard industries and when an abnormally large proportion of the group is in the upper age brackets. As in group life insurance, dividends and retroactive premium adjustments must be con-

[9] *Source Book of Health Insurance Data, 1969* (New York: Health Insurance Institute, 1969), p. 33.

sidered in determining the final costs of all forms of group health insurance underwritten by commercial insurers.

Permanent disability income insurance   Separate group protection against long-term disability is a relatively new form of protection but it has grown rapidly in the past decade, particularly among higher-paid employees. The most highly developed contracts pay a specified monthly amount to a totally and permanently disabled person from the completion of a waiting period such as 6 months until some advanced age such as 65.

Disability provisions in group life insurance plans   Most group life insurance contracts being issued today waive future premiums for a totally and permanently disabled employee. Some new contracts (and some very old ones) provide for the payment of the face amount if the employee either dies or becomes totally and permanently disabled. A one-year waiver of premiums, called an "extended death benefit," is found in some old contracts.

Disability provisions in pension plans   Insured pension plans rarely contain an *insured* promise to pay disability income benefits. Early retirement and withdrawal benefits are available to totally and permanently disabled persons as well as to others, but the use of these options reduces or eliminates the retirement benefit. Sometimes early retirement is possible only if the employee is totally and permanently disabled. Another approach in such cases is to liberalize the vesting conditions. The most liberal benefits, found in very few insured plans, provide for the waiver of future contributions toward the pension plan, the payment of a total and permanent disability income, or both.

MEDICAL EXPENSE INSURANCE

Group medical expense insurance, like its individual counterpart, is underwritten by commercial insurers, by Blue Cross and Blue Shield associations, or by independent plans.

Plans underwritten by commercial insurers   The group insurance contracts underwritten by commercial insurers so closely resemble their individual contracts that only a few differences and special characteristics need be noted here.

First, group contracts are generally more liberal than individual contracts. For example, the exclusions in group contracts are usually less important, and under many group major medical expense contracts, the expenses associated with a given illness need not be incurred within a short specified period. The experiments in prepaid group practice described under "Contracts issued by independent plans" (under "Medical Expense Contracts") in Chapter 20 involve primarily group insureds.

Second, the deductibles in group major medical expense insurance are more varied. Of particular interest are two deductibles used where there is also a basic plan. Under a *corridor* deductible arrangement, the deductible is the basic-plan benefits, if any, plus a stated dollar amount such as $100. Under the *integrated* deductible arrangement, the deductible is the greater of (1) the base-plan benefits or (2) a specified dollar amount.

Third, most group contracts contain a "coordination of benefits" clause that prevents insureds from collecting more than 100 per cent of their expenses from private and public programs. The clause states the order in which various insurances shall apply to the loss before the next type of insurance applies. For example, if a working wife is covered by her employer and as a dependent under her husband's policy, her own policy applies before her husband's. Her husband's policy pays nothing if her policy covers all her expenses.

Fourth, although an increasing number of group insurance contracts make it possible for a withdrawing employee to convert his group protection to a specially designed individual contract, under many plans the employee does not have this right.

Fifth, the costs of the basic coverages depend upon essentially the same factors as those described in the section on temporary disability income insurance. Major medical expense insurance costs, on the other hand, depend only slightly upon the proportion of females in the group. The most important rating factor is the age composition of the group.[10] In either case, dependents are also eligible for these coverages, and the dependent rate may be a single rate, two rates (one dependent or two or more dependents), or three rates (spouse, children, or spouse and children).

Plans underwritten by Blue Cross or Blue Shield associations   Group plans underwritten by Blue Cross and Blue Shield associations are often more liberal than the individual contracts written by these associations, but the similarities between the individual and the group contracts far outweigh the differences. Consequently, instead of describing the contracts in detail here, we refer the reader to the discussion of Blue Cross and Blue Shield contracts in Chapter 20.

There are three notable differences between Blue Cross and Blue Shield group plans and those underwritten by commercial insurers. First, an individual policy, rather than a certificate, is issued to each employee; no master policy is issued to the employer. Second, Blue Cross and Blue Shield associations commonly underwrite group protection for groups that would be

---

[10] Income is also an important consideration, but income is highly correlated with age.

too small to qualify for commercial group insurance. Third, although the contracts do not always specifically grant this right, withdrawing employees are usually permitted to convert their group protection to some individual contract. Fourth, although Blue Cross and Blue Shield prefer community rating—i.e., to charge all groups the same employee rates—competition from private insurers has forced many associations in recent years to rate on the basis of the characteristics and experience of the particular group.

Independent plans   Independent plans cover groups of employees on essentially the same basis as they cover individual employees. Rates for dependents generally vary only according to whether a single-rate basis or a double-rate basis (spouse or spouse and children) is chosen.

Sick-leave Plans

Sick-leave plans are underwritten exclusively by the employer. These plans usually continue the wages or salary of the disabled worker in full for a specified period, which may be graduated by length of service. Under most plans, sick leave is not cumulative. Many sick-leave plans supplement in some way an insured program providing benefits in case of temporary disability, e.g., by payments during the first two weeks.

   The sick-leave risk is retained because the loss can be predicted with a fair degree of accuracy, the loss severity is small, and employees, it is claimed by many, are less likely to feign illness if they are accountable to their employer. In addition, insurers are reluctant to provide benefits equal to the full wage. Sick-leave payments are usually made out of current operating income.

Supplementary Workmen's Compensation

Because maximum workmen's compensation benefits have not kept pace with wage levels or nonoccupational disability benefits, supplementary workmen's compensation benefit plans have become more common in recent years. These plans supplement the workmen's compensation payment, generally bringing it up to the level of the nonoccupational disability benefit or even of the full wage. Most firms maintain a distinct, separate self-insured program for these supplemental payments, but sometimes a paid sick-leave plan or insured temporary disability income plan is used. The reasons for preferring retention over insurance are essentially the same as those advanced earlier in connection with paid sick-leave plans. As was indicated in Chapters 9 and 18, many large firms also retain the basic workmen's compensation risk.

Supplementary Unemployment Compensation

Unemployment compensation provided under social insurance has, in recent years, like workmen's compensation, lagged behind wage levels. (These social unemployment insurance benefits are described in Chapter 31.) Consequently during the fifties several major unions negotiated supplementary unemployment plans for their members. No major SUB plans have been adopted since 1956, but unions continue to express considerably interest in these benefits.

Supplementary unemployment compensation plans vary greatly in detail, but the purpose generally is to provide a combined weekly basic and supplementary unemployment compensation benefit equal to a specified percentage (e.g., 95 per cent under the United Automobile Workers plan reduced by $7.50 per week because of the elimination of work-related expenses) of the employee's take-home pay, excluding compensation for overtime. The duration of the benefits depends principally upon how long the employee has worked for the firm. The payments are generally made out of trust funds financed by fixed employer contributions per employee. The plans are administered jointly by the employer and the union.

A second approach to private unemployment compensation is made by *conventional guarantee* plans, under which eligible employees are usually guaranteed a specified number of weeks of work or income per year. Employers try to meet their obligations under these plans by keeping their employees at work. The plans are operated on a pay-as-you-go basis and are administered by the employer alone or, less commonly, in conjunction with a union. Despite the fact that these plans antedate supplementary unemployment compensation plans by many years, they cover far fewer employees.

A third method is embodied in the *dismissal compensation* plans. Payments are made under these plans for a permanent severing of the present employment relationship. The employee need not remain unemployed. The benefits usually depend upon the duration of employment and the wage or salary and are in most cases payable in a lump sum. Some plans, for example, provide one week's pay for each year of service. Employers meet these payments out of current income, but there is a trend toward creating an advance fund for these benefits. Usually the employer is solely responsible for the active administration of the plan, but a union often reserves the right to protest the administrative decisions of the employer. Although dismissal compensation plans do not cover as many employees as supplementary unemployment compensation plans, they are more numerous, especially among the medium- and small-sized firms.

Pensions and Deferred Profit-sharing Plans

As we have indicated earlier, employers contribute more money toward pension and deferred profit-sharing plans than to any other type of employee benefit plan. Pension plans provide a retirement income, usually for life, the size of the benefit being generally determined by such factors as service and compensation. Profit-sharing plans, on the other hand, are established by an employer for the purpose of permitting his employees to share in his profits. For example, the employer may contribute each year to the plan a certain percentage of gross profits, of net profits, or of net profits in excess of some specified amount. Many profit-sharing plans provide for the distribution of these contributions immediately or periodically. Deferred profit-sharing plans, however, generally provide for distribution of the funds credited to a particular employee only upon the occurrence of certain events such as retirement, disability, death, or termination of employment.

Because over 75 per cent of the employees covered under pension and deferred profit-sharing plans are covered under pension plans,[11] most of the discussion which follows will be devoted to these plans. As a pension vehicle, deferred profit-sharing plans are at a disadvantage because (1) the profits and consequently the retirement income to be provided by the employer's contributions cannot be predicted with a high degree of certainty; (2) unless the trustee of the fund purchases annuities with the employer's contributions,[12] the plan cannot guarantee a lifetime income; and (3) if the plan is to qualify for certain tax advantages under the Internal Revenue Code, it is impossible to give adequate recognition to service rendered by older employees prior to the establishment of the profit-sharing plan. On the other hand, a profit-sharing plan has many relative advantages. For example, because the employee shares the firm's profits with the employer, he has a direct interest in the success of the firm and will probably do his best to contribute to it. Deferred profit-sharing plans also have more appeal for many employers than do pension plans because they fear that their long-term obligation under a pension plan may prove to be quite a burden, particularly in years when the firm is not earning large profits. Under deferred profit-sharing plans, their contributions are related to actual profits. Many firms supplement a pension plan with a deferred profit-sharing plan. Some use a deferred profit-sharing plan to fund benefits for future service and a pension plan for past-service benefits.

In establishing or modifying a pension plan, the risk manager must make certain crucial decisions. He must consider the total impact of his decision upon the firm's industrial relations, the costs involved, and the tax implications (to be discussed in the section "Source of Funds"). The

---

[11] A recent comprehensive study of deferred profit-sharing plans estimates that at the end of 1967 about 6 million employees participated in these programs. See Bert L. Metzger, *Investment Practices, Performance, and Management of Profit-sharing Trust Funds* (Evanston, Ill.: Profit Sharing Research Foundation, 1969).
[12] The trustee could purchase an immediate annuity at the time the employee retires, or he could purchase deferred annuities during the employee's working career.

major decisions to be made involve (1) the eligibility requirements, (2) the retirement benefits, (3) other types of benefits, (4) the source of funds, (5) the actuarial cost method, and (6) the funding agencies.

ELIGIBILITY REQUIREMENTS

Although pension plans may be designed to cover all employees, normally some eligibility requirements are established. This observation could also have been made with respect to the other employee benefit plans, but the requirements are commonly higher for the pension plans. Four types of requirements are in common use either singly or in some combination: (1) Employees may be required to have worked for the employer some minimum period. The purpose here is to reduce the administrative costs associated with rapid turnover. (2) A minimum-age requirement may be established in order to reduce the turnover costs mentioned above. Persons above a maximum age may not be permitted to participate because of the high cost of providing them with an adequate pension. (3) Because the Old-Age, Survivors, Disability, and Health Insurance program of the Federal government provides benefits based only upon annual earnings up to some specified dollar value, the plan may exclude employees whose earnings are less than that amount. A more usual procedure today, however, is to adopt a pension formula which recognizes that OASDHI benefits will be paid on that portion of an employee's wages. (4) The type of employment may determine whether the employee is eligible. For example, the plan may be limited to full-time employees, salaried employees, union employees, or the employees of one particular plant.

In addition to meeting these coverage requirements, employees must satisfy certain other conditions in order to receive the different types of benefits. These conditions will be described in connection with their respective benefits.

RETIREMENT BENEFITS

The principal benefit under a pension plan is a lifetime income for the employee after his retirement.

Qualification requirements   In order to receive the full benefit produced by the benefit formula, an employee must usually have attained a normal retirement age. Age 65 is the normal retirement age in most plans, but many persons have suggested raising the age limit to 68 or 70 because of the increasing proportion of older persons in our population and their improved health and abilities. Many others have suggested reducing the retirement age as an offset to the loss of jobs threatened by increased automation.

Retirement at the normal retirement age may be compulsory or voluntary. If voluntary, there is commonly some more advanced age, such as 68, at which retirement is compulsory. If there is no compulsory retirement age, the business must decide which employees it will permit to continue beyond the normal retirement age. This can be a painful and difficult decision.

Sometimes the employee must also have satisfied a minimum service requirement (in excess of any service requirement for participation under the plan) in order to qualify for retirement benefits. Service requirements are most common among plans covering public employees.

Early retirement is possible under most plans under certain conditions. If the employer's consent is necessary, attainment of age 55 is a common requirement. If the employer's consent is not necessary, a combination age and service requirement is usually found. Sometimes the worker must be totally and permanently disabled, in addition to meeting the other requirement. Early retirement pensions are generally much smaller than normal retirement pensions because fewer contributions have been made, the contributions have been accumulated at interest for a shorter period, and the pay-out period is much longer. Occasionally, however, a supplement is provided because the worker is totally disabled or because the early retirement is in the interest of the employer.

Benefit formulas   A generally accepted goal of pension planners is to provide a pension, including OASDHI benefits, equal to 50 or 60 per cent of the employee's annual average earnings during the past five or ten years of employment. In practice, two types of formulas for determining benefits are in common use: (1) defined contribution or money purchase formulas and (2) defined benefit formulas.

Under a *defined contribution* formula, the benefit is the amount that can be provided by annual contributions expressed as a percentage of the employee's pay. The cost to the employer is known, but the benefits are not. The formula also provides very limited benefits for newly covered older workers and is more difficult to explain to the participants. This method is not in common use today except among educational institutions.[13]

Under a *defined benefit* formula, the benefits are specified and the contributions are the amount necessary to produce these benefits. Usually the benefit is (1) a specified percentage of the employee's earnings per year of service, (2) a flat dollar amount per year of service, (3) a flat

[13] Almost half of the educational institutions have pension plans written by one specialized insurer.

percentage of the employee's earnings, or (4) a flat amount per month. For example, the benefit may be (1) 2 per cent of average earnings per year of credited service, (2) $6 per month per year of service, (3) 50 per cent of his final earnings, or (4) $200 a month.

Under some plans using these last two formulas, the employee must have completed some minimum period of service to receive this benefit. For shorter service periods, the benefit is proportionately reduced.

Most plans use a formula based upon average earnings. The average earnings may be based on the total compensation during the employee's service under the plan, but there has been a marked trend in the past two decades toward the use of the average salary during the last five to ten years, called the "final-average salary." The reason for this trend is that most retirees, past and future, judge pension plans on the relation between the benefits and their final salaries, not their average-career salaries, and final salaries may be substantially higher than career salaries because of promotions or inflation.

Annuity forms Under most pension plans, the normal method of paying out the retirement benefits is to provide an income for the remainder of the employee's life. If the employee has contributed to the cost of the pension, provision is made for the return in cash or in installments of the excess of the employee's contributions, with or without interest, over the benefits received prior to his death. In more technical terms, the normal benefit is a straight life annuity if the employee does not contribute, a modified cash refund or installment refund annuity if he does.

Other types of annuities can usually be selected, but the monthly benefits are adjusted until they are actuarially equivalent. Common options are a joint and survivorship annuity (payments during the joint lifetime of the insured and his beneficiary plus payments, usually of a reduced amount, during the lifetime of the survivor), a life annuity with n years certain (a lifetime income with a guarantee that the payments will be continued for at least n years), and an annuity which provides larger monthly income before OASDHI benefits become available in order to produce a level income throughout the retirement period.

Cost of living adjustments Since the post-World War II period there has been considerable interest in the effects of inflation on pension benefits. Increases in the cost of living during the employee's working career and after his retirement can reduce drastically the purchasing power of a pension benefit. Basing the benefit upon the employee's final salary is one way of recognizing increases in the cost of living during his earning career, but this approach does not solve the problem after retirement. Another solution is to adjust the monthly benefit during and after retirement according to changes in the consumer price index. A third solution is to allow the monthly benefit to rise and fall with the value of the investments in the pension fund, the changes in which are presumed to correspond roughly with changes in the cost of living. Sometimes under this approach, a conventional annuity is provided in conjunction with a variable annuity backed entirely by equities, while in other plans there is only one annuity backed by a balanced investment portfolio. Starting in the late sixties, variable annuities have become a common feature of pension plans.[14]

Past-service benefits   Past service is usually credited under the plan but is often limited in its effect because of the costs involved. In addition, under defined benefit formulas expressing the benefit as a percentage of average earnings and under money purchase plans, it is usual, for the sake of administrative simplicity, to assume that during the employee's eligible past-service period his earnings were equal to his earnings the date the plan is installed.

OTHER TYPES OF BENEFITS

Three other types of benefits commonly found in pension plans are (1) death benefits, (2) disability benefits, and (3) withdrawal benefits.

Death benefits   If the employee dies before retirement, his beneficiaries are entitled to a return of his contributions, with or without interest. Sometimes a widow's benefit provides a lifetime income, expressed as a percentage of the employee's pension, for widows of long-service, older employees. Survivor income plans, a newer concept, provide the survivor of a deceased employee (not just long-term employees) with some percentage of the employee's monthly pay until the survivor dies or retires.

Disability benefits   Specific total and permanent disability benefits are found in most plans, but usually an employee must have completed several years of service to be eligible for this protection and must have been disabled for a minimum number of months. These benefits usually supplement early retirement or withdrawal benefits, but they may be completely independent of those benefits. Sometimes they waive any future contributions to the pension plan in behalf of the employee.

Withdrawal benefits   If the employee terminates his employment relationship with the firm, he is entitled to a return of his contributions, with or without interest. Often he may elect to receive these contributions as an annuity at

[14] See "Annuity Contracts," under "Types of Contracts," in Chap. 19.

retirement age. Whether he will receive any part of the employer's contributions will depend upon the vesting provisions. The two extreme provisions are immediate full unconditional vesting and no vesting. Most vesting conditions fall between these two extremes and relate the degree of vesting to the period of service, require the employee to receive his and the employer's contributions as a paid-up annuity beginning at retirement age, provide for partial vesting only, or assume some other form. Immediate full vesting encourages mobility of labor and may improve employer-employee relations, but this type of vesting is costly, and from the viewpoint of the firm, the increased mobility may mean increased turnover. Vesting provisions have been liberalized considerably in recent years.

SOURCE OF FUNDS

Pension plans, like group life and group health insurance plans, may be contributory or noncontributory. The arguments for each approach have been presented earlier in this chapter. A noncontributory pension plan, however, may not enable the employee to avoid completely the tax on the employer's contributions; it *may* only reduce or defer that tax, as we shall explain in the next paragraph. This can still be an important advantage.[15]

If the pension plan, contributory or noncontributory, is qualified with the Internal Revenue Service, the employer may deduct his contributions as a business expense; the employee need not report these contributions as income *at that time;* and the earnings on the pension funds are tax-exempt. When the employee retires, however, he must, under a noncontributory plan, report his pension benefits as taxable income. If the plan was contributory, he is permitted to deduct from the pension benefits each year his "cost basis," which, for a straight life annuity, would be the total of his own contributions divided by his life expectancy according to IRS tables. Similar rules apply in other situations. If the pension benefit, less allowable deductions for charity, property taxes, and the like, is less than the exemptions available at that age, the employee may escape the tax.[16] In the more usual case, some of the pension income will be taxed but at lower tax rates than those which would have been applied to the employer contributions during his working career.

To qualify a plan, a firm must demonstrate, among other things, that the plan is a legally binding arrangement and does not discriminate in favor of officers, stockholders, supervisors, or high-salaried employees. The risk

[15] Even if the tax is merely deferred, the plan provides the employee with the use of his money in the meantime without any interest charge. In other words, he has an interest-free loan.
[16] At age 65, the personal exemption is doubled. In 1970 a man and wife, both aged 65, were entitled to a $2,500 exemption.

manager must keep IRS requirements in mind as he makes each decision with respect to the pension plan.

ACTUARIAL COST METHOD

The manner in which the cost of the benefits is to be budgeted is called the "actuarial cost method." Some plans are operated on a pay-as-you-go basis with no advance preparation. Most plans, however, are funded, in the sense that contributions to the pension fund in the early years exceed current disbursements. The excess amounts are invested, and the accumulated amounts plus the income from investments are available to pay part of the costs in the future.

Several methods of advance preparation are possible. Under one method, the annual contributions are estimated to be sufficient to provide the full retirement benefit for employees retiring that year. No advance preparation is made for the future retirement of active employees. Another procedure is to contribute each year the "normal cost" of the plan according to some actuarial assumption plus the assumed interest on any "supplemental liability."[17] For example, the normal cost may be the sum of the level annual contributions that would have been required to provide the specified pension benefits for each employee if level contributions had been made since each employee entered the service of the employer. Because such contributions have not been made for the participants who were employed when the plan was installed, the fund starts off with a "debt." In more technical terms, there is an initial supplemental liability.[18] The interest payments on this liability prevent the debt from increasing. Under this method, the fund is usually greater than it is under the first method, but the advance preparation is not complete. Full funding could be accomplished by liquidating the supplemental liability over a period of time,[19] but failure to do this will not usually prevent the plan from meeting its promised payments if the plan continues to operate indefinitely.[20] Usually enough new contributions will be made to provide benefits for retired persons without exhausting the funds. But if the plan is terminated, the deficiency will become

---

[17] This is the minimum deductible contribution permitted by the Internal Revenue Service under this method.

[18] This liability is equal to the present value of the benefits which will be paid the current participants in the plan less the present value of the normal cost contributions in behalf of these participants. Alternatively, it may be viewed as the accumulated value of the past normal cost contributions that have not been made.

[19] A common procedure is to contribute the normal cost under the assumption made above plus 10 per cent of the initial supplemental liability until it is liquidated. This is the maximum deductible contribution permitted by the Internal Revenue Service under this method.

[20] Compare this statement with the one made under "Funding" in Chap. 31 with respect to OASDHI and with the one made in Chap. 24 with respect to private life insurers.

apparent.[21] Although many different actuarial cost methods could be described, this discussion should be sufficient to indicate the principles involved and the variations possible.[22]

FUNDING AGENCIES

The pension plan may be (1) self-insured or (2) insured. There are several types of insured plans, some of which arose as a direct response to competition from self-insured plans.

Self-insured plans   Under most self-insured plans, the employer transfers funds periodically to a trustee, commonly a bank or trust company. The trustee invests these funds and often performs certain administrative tasks such as sending out the pension checks. The trustee, however, assumes no risks, the mortality, investment, expense, turnover, and other risks being assumed by the employer. A consulting actuary, who advises the employer with respect to the funding arrangements, also assumes no risks.

Although self-insured plans can be and often are operated on a conservative basis, they permit considerable flexibility in (1) designing benefit formulas, (2) budgeting costs over time, and (3) investing the pension moneys. For example, the funds may all be invested in common stocks. As explained below, insured plans originally permitted much less flexibility, but in recent years they have improved their position substantially with respect to these matters. An employer may still prefer a self-insured plan because it affords even greater flexibility. He may also reason that he can avoid commissions and premium taxes (in states where annuities are taxed), but the self-insured firm must pay the trustee and the consulting actuary and perform certain services itself. The primary disadvantage is the risk involved.[23] The mortality risks alone are enough to restrict this approach to large employers, but, as noted above, there are also no guarantees from an outsider with respect to investment results or expenses of operation.

Insured plans   Insured pension plans can be characterized as (1) group deferred annuity plans, (2) deposit administration plans, (3) separate ac-

---

[21] Under the plan provisions, however, the employer's liability is generally limited to the contributions already made.

[22] Another method which is commonly used with insured plans is discussed in the section below, "Insured plans."

[23] However, the employer usually reserves the right to discontinue the pension plan, with his liability limited to the contributions he has already made. His contributions may not be sufficient to provide the benefits earned to that date. Some of the risk, therefore, is transferred to the employees. This is especially true when the employer's obligation has been established by collective bargaining at a fixed amount per man-hour, per ton, or relative to some other variable. The risk to the employer in this case is that future collective bargaining will raise his contribution.

count plans, and (4) individual policy pension trusts. Since each type presents different advantages and problems for the employer, we shall discuss each separately.

1. Until the middle sixties, most of the insured group pension plans were *group deferred annuity plans,* which provide for the annual purchase of a number of single premium deferred annuities. These plans still cover almost one-fourth of the persons covered under insured pension plans. Under these plans, the usual monthly retirement benefit for future service is a stated percentage of average earnings over the credited years of service times the number of years of service. This benefit is equal to the sum of the amounts obtained by multiplying the earnings each year by the specified per cent. For example, if the benefit is 2 per cent of average earnings over the credited years of service and an employee has 5 years of credited service, during which he earned $11,000, $12,000, $13,000, $14,000, and $15,000, respectively, his monthly retirement benefit is .02($13,000) 5 = $1,300 or $220 + $240 + $260 + $280 + $300 = $1,300. Consequently, if the employer (by himself or together with the employee) purchases each year a single premium deferred annuity providing at retirement age the specified percentage times the earnings during that year, he will have purchased by that retirement age the annuity contracts necessary to pay the specified retirement benefit. Furthermore, at the end of any year, he will have purchased the contracts necessary to pay the pension benefits earned to that date. The annual purchase of annuity contracts in these amounts is the usual procedure under a group deferred annuity plan.

Past-service liability is liquidated by purchasing over a specified period deferred annuities sufficient to provide past-service benefits. Many purchase patterns are possible, but under most plans annuity contracts are purchased first for those employees nearing retirement.

As compared with self-insured plans, group deferred annuity contracts offer both advantages and disadvantages. The primary advantage to the employer (and to the employee) is the actuarial soundness of the arrangement. A third party guarantees that the pension payments will be made for life, and if the plan were to be terminated at any time, the pension benefits earned to date (with the possible exception of some past-service benefits) would be completely funded. The employer can fulfill his promises to his employees without any sizable risk to himself. The employer need not be concerned about survival rates in excess of those assumed in the annuity premiums, about lower interest earnings, or higher expenses. Some risk remains, however: (1) The purchase prices of the annuities are subject to change after an initial guarantee period, and (2) the purchase prices are established at a conservative level to permit the types of dividend and retroactive premium adjustments already noticed in connection with group insurance. Another advantage of this approach is that the employer transfers to the insurer most of the administrative worries (actuarial, financial, legal, loss-adjustment) associated with operating a pension plan.

The principal disadvantage is the relative inflexibility of the group deferred annuity plan with respect to benefit formulas, premium payments, and supporting investments. Although other benefit formulas can be used, the career-average formula is the only formula other than a money purchase arrangement for which the group annuity has all the advantages cited above. The funding discipline imposed by the group annuity plan also limits the freedom of the employer and may prove a hardship in some years. Temporary cessations of premium payments, however, can be arranged under certain conditions. Finally, the group annuity premiums must be invested by the insurer in investments subject to certain legal restrictions. Only a small portion of a life insurer's general investments can usually be invested in equities. It is true that investment in equities has some dangerous aspects, but stocks have been a particularly attractive type of investment in the long run. In addition to these disadvantages, the operating expenses of an insured plan may exceed the corresponding cost of a self-insured plan, largely because of state premium taxes.

2. *Deposit administration plans* are more flexible than group deferred annuity plans, but they also include fewer guarantees by the insurer. These plans now outnumber group deferred annuity plans and cover over half of the persons under insured pension plans. Under deposit administration plans, which are usually noncontributory, the employer's contributions or deposits are paid into a fund which accumulates at interest. The accumulations constitute an undivided fund; i.e., there are no accounts for individual employees. No annuity contracts are purchased until the employee retires or, in some cases, until his pension is vested. Employee contributions, if any, are usually segregated, and individual records are established. Sometimes annuities are purchased immediately with these contributions.

Deposit administration contracts can be used with any type of benefit formula because the necessary contracts can be purchased at the time of retirement. The funding arrangement can also be flexible because, except for the purchase of contracts on retiring employees, the employer has great freedom with respect to his annual contributions, although probably not quite as much as he would have under a self-insured plan. The insurer or perhaps a consulting actuary usually recommends a range within which the contributions should fall, but the latitude within this range is great, and the employer may sometimes ignore the recommendation.[24] The invest-

[24] Insurers generally require some minimum contribution. The Internal Revenue Service also establishes some minimum amount if the plan is to remain qualified. See footnote 17.

ment of the pension funds is subject to the restrictions on insurance investments already noted.

The third-party guarantee under deposit administration plans is not
as complete as that under group deferred annuity plans. For this reason
and because of the greater minimum administrative costs involved, the deposit administration plan is usually reserved for larger firms. On the other
hand, the deposit administration plan does contain some important guarantees by the insurer. The most important guarantee is the promise of a
lifetime payment to the retired employees. The other guarantees are a minimum interest return and annuity rate schedule applicable to the moneys
deposited in the undivided fund. Although these guarantees may change
over time, they always apply with respect to the dollars received while they
were in effect. The principal of the fund, of course, is not subject to any
fluctuations.

3. *Separate account plans* are the most recent addition to and most
rapidly growing type of insured pension plan. Basically separate account
plans are deposit administration plans but the insurer places at least part
of the employer's contributions in a separate account which is not com-
mingled with the insurer's other assets and which is not subject to the
investment limitations placed on insurers. For example, the entire account
may be invested in equities. Although some employers are large enough
for the insurer to establish a separate account for their individual pension
plans, generally a separate account commingles the contributions of many
employers. Thus separate accounts permit considerable flexibility with respect to the investment of pension funds but the employer generally cannot
dictate the particular investments to be made.

Separate accounts were made possible during the 1960s when most
states adopted enabling legislation and the Securities and Exchange Commission approved such plans.

Separate account plans may be used to fund a plan that provides
a retirement benefit which is adjusted according to changes in the cost
of living or in the value of the separate account investment portfolio. Their
more common use, however, is to fund plans that provide a defined fixed-
dollar benefit. In this instance stock market fluctuations affect only the
cost to the employer or, alternatively, the fixed-dollar benefit the employer
is willing to pay the employee when he retires.

4. Under the individual policy plan, known as an *individual policy
pension trust* (often shortened to *pension trust*), the employer and perhaps
the employee transfer funds to a trustee who purchases individual level-
premium insurance policies on the lives of the participating employees. The
trustee owns the contracts subject to conditions outlined in the trust
agreement.

Group pension plans cover far more employees than individual policy plans, but individual policy plans are much more numerous. Many insurers limit their group plans to employee groups including a minimum of 25 lives. For groups including 50 lives or less, the individual plan may be no more costly than the group plan.

The policies under a pension trust are usually retirement annuities or retirement income annuities. The initial contract for each employee is generally sufficient to provide his retirement benefit if the formula is unchanged and if his present compensation is continued until retirement date. If his retirement benefit is increased or decreased because of changes in his compensation or the benefit formula, new contracts are purchased or old ones reduced. This procedure can become awkward, especially since evidence of insurability may be required in connection with all retirement *income* contracts because of the death benefits.

PUBLIC POLICY AND PRIVATE PENSIONS

In 1965 the President's Committee on Corporate Pension Funds and Other Private Retirement and Welfare Programs raised several questions concerning the treatment of employees under many private pension plans, the solvency of the plans, and their effect upon the mobility of labor. Legislation reflecting the Committee recommendations has been introduced periodically since that time that would accomplish one or more of the following: (1) establish minimum vesting standards, (2) raise funding requirements, and (3) provide Federal reinsurance protection for employees in plans that terminate before they are fully funded. Opponents of new vesting and funding requirements argue mainly (1) that pension planners should be free to determine the proper mix of eligibility requirements, vesting, benefit levels and structure, and financing and (2) that reducing the flexibility in person planning would retard the development of new plans. The reinsurance program has been opposed on the grounds that it is impractical and would discourage adequate funding of individual pension plans.

Group Property and Liability Insurance

Until recently employee benefit plans were limited almost exclusively to personnel risks. In the past few years many plans have been established to provide employees some protection against their property and liability risks—typically, automobile insurance and homeowner's insurance. Such plans will probably become much more popular in the next decade. The reasons why these programs were not introduced at a much earlier date fall into two major categories: First, until recently there was little demand for this protection among employers or employees. Because employers are the source of the income payments interrupted by poor health, unemployment, death, or retirement, it was natural for them to think about and for employees to demand some employer-arranged protection against those risks. The link between the employment relationship and an employee's property and liability risks is much less direct. Furthermore, whereas all employees are exposed to serious losses associated with personnel risks, property and liability exposures can vary widely among employees. For example, not all employees may own automobiles or dwellings. This disparity was much greater in the past than it is at present. Finally, the Federal government contributed greatly to the development of plans covering personnel risks through various tax incentives described earlier in this chapter. There are no tax incentives to encourage group property and liability insurance plans.

Second, until a few years ago property and liability insurers did little to develop group property and liability insurance. Individual insurance provided a sufficient volume of sales to keep these insurers occupied, and there were legal, technical, and marketing problems associated with group insurance that they were not prepared to handle. Almost all state insurance departments considered group plans, particularly the "true" group variety with group selection and uniform group rating, to be (1) unsafe and (2) unfair to persons outside the group and to the better-quality insureds within the group. Group property and liability insurance poses more technical problems than group life and health insurance because property and liability insurance exposures vary more in quality among employees, underwriting experience of the group depends upon the behavior of persons who are not members of the group (e.g., dependents and friends driving the employee's car), and much more attention must be paid to post-sales servicing. Because insureds are much concerned about the servicing of property and liability insurance, selecting an acceptable insurer is a difficult task and many employees may prefer to retain their individual insurers. If the plan is a voluntary, employee-paid arrangement, the participation ratio may be unsatisfactory for this and other reasons. Finally, many property and liability insurance agents have opposed the extension of group insurance because, unlike group life and health insurance, which often stimulates the sale of individual insurance,[25] group property and liability insurance could provide almost all of the property and liability protection required by the typical employee, thus lessening significantly the demand for individual insurance.

Despite these barriers some group property and liability insurance has been written for some time; most of this insurance, however, was written

[25] Many life and health insurance agents also opposed the development of group insurance in its early years. They still favor dollar limits on the amount of protection that can be written on an individual life and on the types of groups that can be insured. They argue, with some support from more objective observers, that unlimited extension of the group concept is unsafe and deprives the individual counseling and tailor-made protection.

for trade associations, professional associations, or franchise dealer groups. Employee groups were rare. This insurance was provided by "circuitous but legal" means[26] such as (1) buying the insurance from a non-admitted alien insurer not subject to state regulations, (2) declaring special dividend rates for members of a group, and (3) developing special policies for and soliciting only members of a group. In the middle sixties, however, it was generally agreed that group property and liability insurance amounted to much less than 10 per cent of the total premium volume.

In the late sixties several events improved the prospects for the future development of group property and liability insurance for employee groups. First, union leaders looking for new fringe benefits for their members became interested in group property and liability insurance as an employer-provided benefit. The United Automobile Workers was a leader in this movement. Employer interest in group protection also increased. Second, several large insurers began to market aggressively this form of insurance. They believed that in this way they could increase significantly their share of the family insurance market; the method they used avoided some of the technical, legal, and marketing problems that had hindered earlier attempts; and some state regulatory officials and legislatures adopted a more favorable outlook toward the group concept. At least two states have amended their property and liability insurance rating laws to state explicitly that rates are not unfairly discriminatory if they attempt to spread the risk broadly among persons insured under a group policy.

To date property and liability insurance protection for employee groups is still uncommon. "True" group insurance is rare. Most of the present programs are "mass merchandising" plans under which individual policies are sold to the employees of a business on a payroll deduction basis. Employees pay the entire premium; the employer makes the necessary arrangements and deducts the premium from wages. Some of these plans include life insurance, health insurance, and mutual funds as well as property and liability insurance. Because of expense savings (e.g., lower commissions and the premium collection service provided by the employer) and the opportunity to render more effective loss-prevention services, initial rates (or rates less dividends) are less than for comparable individual insurance from the same insurers. However, the rate structure is the same as for individual insurance; i.e., each employee pays the same rate relative to that paid by other employees that he would pay if they all purchased individual insurance from the same insurer. Furthermore, although the standards are more liberal than for individual insurance, the insurer reserves the right to reject individual applications. Personal counseling is provided through a representative who often has an office on the employer's premises. Some insurers write

[26] James J. Chastain, "Group Property and Liability Insurance," chap. 39 in R. D. Eilers and R. M. Crowe (eds.), *Group Insurance Handbook*.

this business through a single agency; others permit any of their agents to solicit the business. "Mass merchandising," therefore, is a hybrid of individual and group insurance.

"True" group property and liability insurance, like group life and health insurance, is characterized by group selection and a uniform average rate for all employees. Employers would normally be expected to pay part or all of the cost per employee. Because this concept represents a more revolutionary break with the past and introduces more technical and legal problems, it is still largely in the discussion stage, but a few plans have been established.

For the employee, group property and liability insurance offers possibly lower rates, installment payment of premiums through periodic payroll deductions, more liberal underwriting, loss-prevention services, and possibly more sympathetic treatment of claims (through group pressure). Nevertheless, participation rates in the voluntary "mass merchandising" plans in effect have been low (typically under 20 per cent of eligible employees). Partly this can be explained by the novelty of the idea, but for some employees there are no premium savings and for others the savings have not been substantial enough to disrupt their existing relationship. The future growth rate of group property and liability insurance will depend to a large extent upon (1) insurers' ability to increase the premium reductions and to publicize the savings and (2) employer willingness to assume part or all of the premium cost.

REVIEW QUESTIONS

1. Under group insurance, group selection is substituted for individual selection.
   a. What is group selection? How does it work?
   b. In what respects is group insurance more attractive than individual insurance? less attractive?
2. An employer is concerned about purchasing group yearly renewable term insurance because he fears that as each employee grows older, the premium will increase until finally it becomes prohibitive. How would you advise him?
3. Unions have pressed for noncontributory plans in recent years.
   a. What is a noncontributory plan?
   b. What are the advantages and disadvantages of a noncontributory plan?
4. An employee, aged 45, who has worked for a firm for 20 years, resigns to take a job with a new firm in another state. The employee has been covered during the past 15 years under a $10,000 group life insurance. What rights does the employee possess if the group life insurance plan provided:
   a. Term insurance
   b. Nonterm insurance

5. How would you answer question 4 if the employee was retiring at age 65 instead of resigning?

6. Comment briefly upon the following characteristics of group temporary disability income insurance:

   a. Duration of benefits

   b. Waiting period

   c. Weekly benefit amount

   d. Conversion rights

7. Each of two firms employs the same number of employees and provides the same group life insurance and temporary disability insurance. One firm, however, pays a higher group life insurance premium and a lower group temporary disability life insurance premium than the other. How would you explain these differences?

8. What insured disability benefits exist other than temporary disability insurance?

9. Distinguish between the group medical expense insurance underwritten by commercial insurers and by Blue Cross and Blue Shield associations.

10. Answer question 4 with respect to the firm's group health insurance programs covering disability income losses and medical expenses.

11. How does a deferred profit-sharing plan differ from a pension plan?

12. In designing a pension plan, the employer may elect to use one or more of four types of eligibility requirements. Describe each type briefly.

13. At what age should an employee be permitted to retire?

14. An employee worked for 30 years for the ABC Manufacturing Corporation. His starting salary of $3,000 was increased $1,000 every 5 years until it reached $8,000.

   a. What would be his monthly pension if the ABC pension plan provides for each year of service 1½ per cent of average salary? of "final salary"?

   b. What is the normal annuity form?

15. a. What is a money purchase plan?

   b. Why have unit benefit formulas proved more popular than the money purchase formula?

16. The variable annuity is one approach to cost-of-living adjustments in pension plans. Describe and evaluate some other approaches.

17. A firm is considering the establishment of a pension plan providing 0.5 per cent of average salary for each year of service for employees earning less than $10,000 a year and 5 per cent of salary for each year of service for employees earning $10,000 or more. How would you advise them?

18. Compare the tax advantages of a noncontributory pension plan with the tax advantages of a noncontributory group life insurance plan.

19. Answer question 4 with respect to the pension plan.

20. If a pension plan is terminated, discuss the implications under each of the actuarial cost methods described in the text.

21. Some observers are disturbed about the funding of some private pension plans. Why?

22. One of the major decisions in pension planning is whether to self-insure or to insure. What factors should be considered in making this decision?

23. Compare the four most popular types of insured pension plans with respect to flexibility in benefit formulas, flexibility in budgeting, responsibility of the insurer, and flexibility in investments.

24. a. Distinguish between "mass merchandishing" and "true" group property and liability insurance.

    b. What do you predict will be the future growth of group property and liability insurance?

SUGGESTIONS FOR ADDITIONAL READING

Dickerson, O. D.: *Health Insurance* (3d ed., Homewood, Ill.: Richard D. Irwin, Inc., 1968), chaps. 6–10, 15, and 16.

Eilers, R. D., and Crowe, R. M.: *Group Insurance Handbook* (Homewood, Ill.: Richard D. Irwin, Inc., 1965).

Field, Irving M.: *Employee Group Property and Liability Insurance* (Eugene: School of Business Administration, University of Oregon, 1967).

Follmann, J. F., Jr.: *Medical Care and Health Insurance* (Homewood, Ill.: Richard D. Irwin, Inc., 1963).

Gregg, D. W.: *Group Life Insurance* (3d ed., Homewood, Ill.: Richard D. Irwin, Inc., 1962).

——— (ed.): *Life and Health Insurance Handbook* (2d ed., Homewood, Ill.: Richard D. Irwin, Inc., 1964), chaps. 28–45.

Kimball, S., and Denenberg, H.: *Mass Marketing of Property and Liability Insurance,* Department of Transportation Automobile Insurance and Compensation Study (Washington, D.C.: U.S. Government Printing Office, 1970).

Kolodrubetz, W. W.: "Employee-Benefit Plans, 1950–68," *Social Security Bulletin,* XXXIII, No. 4 (April, 1970), 35–47, 49.

McGill, Dan M.: *Fundamentals of Private Pensions* (2d ed., Homewood, Ill.: Richard D. Irwin, Inc., 1964).

Melone, J. J., and Allen, E. T., Jr.: *Pension Planning* (Homewood, Ill.: Richard D. Irwin, Inc., 1966).

Pickrell, J. F.: *Group Health Insurance* (rev. ed., Homewood, Ill.: Richard D. Irwin, Inc., 1961).

Somers, H. M., and Somers, A. R.: *Doctors, Patients, and Health Insurance* (Washington, D.C.: The Brookings Institution, 1962).

Webb, Bernard L.: *Mass Merchandising of Automobile Insurance* (Indianapolis: Insurers Press, 1969).

E. Implementing an insurance decision

23

selecting the insurer: I

A risk manager must select an insurer or insurers to implement the insurance program. He will need to understand the different types of insurers and their principal characteristics, but he should realize that the variations among the insurers of each type are more important than the variations among the average insurers of different types. This chapter discusses the types of insurers according to several methods of classification. It also describes the role of groups, reinsurance associations, and business combinations marketing both insurance and noninsurance products and services. Chapter 24 deals with necessary considerations in choosing among particular insurers and the sources of information concerning them.

Types of Insurers

About five thousand insurers write insurance in the United States. They can be classified in various ways, of which the following are the more important: (1) by the type of insurance written, (2) by the legal form of business organization, (3) by domicile and admission status, (4) by pricing policy, (5) by marketing method, and (6) by the kinds of insureds serviced.

TYPES OF INSURANCE WRITTEN

Insurers can be classified first according to the types of insurance they write. Two methods of classifying insurers are of interest here. By the first, insurers can be classified according to whether they are primarily or solely (1) originating or direct insurers or (2) reinsurers. Direct insurers do most of their business with the public, while reinsurers are primarily engaged in insuring those portions of the direct business which the direct insurers for one reason or another do not wish to retain.[1]

By a second method of classification, insurers can be grouped according to whether they write personnel, property, or liability insurance or some combination of these major divisions of insurance. Some insurers write only one of the many kinds of insurance under one of these major divisions (e.g., life insurance, fire insurance, or automobile insurance); others write practically all kinds of insurance under all three divisions (e.g., most kinds of property and liability insurance plus health insurance). Many insurers fall between these two extremes.

Legally insurers can be divided into two groups: (1) life insurers who can write life insurance and health insurance and (2) nonlife insurers who can write any type of insurance other than life insurance.

LEGAL FORM OF BUSINESS ORGANIZATION

Probably the best-known classification of insurers is according to the legal form of business organization. Three major classes exist—private proprietary insurers, private cooperative insurers, and government insurers—but each of these classes includes a variety of subclasses.

Proprietary insurers   Proprietary insurers are characterized by profit-seeking owners[2] who are responsible for the management of the firm and who bear the risks of the insurer. There are two types of proprietary insurers: (1) capital stock insurers and (2) Lloyds Associations.

The *capital stock* insurer is a corporation whose owners are stockholders. The operations of a stock insurer closely resemble the operations of profit-seeking corporations in any line of endeavor. The stockholders elect the board of directors, which delegates the management responsibilities to the officers of the insurer. Stockholders receive dividends declared by the board of directors and may sell their shares of stock to others at the

---

[1] For some of these reasons and a more complete statement of the role of reinsurance, see Chap. 24.

[2] Because capital stock insurers, the leading proprietary insurers, are usually more easily organized under state laws than are mutual insurers, some persons interested in forming a mutual insurer organize instead a stock insurer and minimize the profit objective. Many are converted at a later date to a mutual.

To organize a stock insurer, one must satisfy certain capital and surplus requirements. To organize a mutual, one must meet initial surplus requirements and in addition have applications from more than a stated number of persons on more than a stated number of separate exposures with aggregate premiums in excess of a certain amount.

Some stock insurers are owned by a parent mutual as part of a group operation.

market price. The dividends and the market value will depend to a large extent upon the success of the operations of the insurer. The corporation possesses a cushion against unfavorable years consisting of the capital and paid-in surplus subscribed by the original stockholders and the additional surplus retained from gains during years of favorable operation. This cushion permits stock insurers to follow their customary practice of charging policy-holders a definite premium (subject, in some instances, to a retrospective rating plan, discussed in Chapter 25).[3] The importance of the capital stock method of operation is evident from Table 23.1, which shows the proportion of each kind of insurance written by each of the major forms of business organization. It is clear that capital stock insurers predominate in property and liability insurance but not in personnel insurance. The difference in size between stock life insurers and stock property and liability insurers is demonstrated by the fact that the relatively small share of the life insur-ance market was written by about 1,650 insurers, while less than half that number of stock property and liability insurers dominated that field. The increasing number of stock life insurers (there were only 708 in 1954) is having its impact, however, and the proportion of life insurance written by stock insurers was higher in 1969 than it was in 1954 (36 per cent).

Table 23.1 also indicates that stock insurers write practically all forms of property and liability insurance. Table 23.2 indicates the diversified inter-ests of stock insurers in a different way. This table shows the distribution of the premium income of each type of insurer by kind of insurance.

Lloyds Associations derive their name from the resemblance between their operations and those of Lloyd's of London. *Lloyd's of London* is an association of individuals who underwrite insurance as individuals.[4] The function of the association is merely to provide certain services, such as underwriting information, policy writing, loss adjustments, and office space; to screen carefully prospective members; and to prescribe certain regulations aimed at maintaining the financial solvency of members. The association was formed in 1769 by a group of underwriters who used to gather at Edward Lloyd's coffee house to transact their business.

About 6,000 members currently underwrite insurance as individuals through Lloyd's of London. Most of these underwriters are engaged in other

---

[3] In some lines, particularly in life insurance and workmen's compensation insurance, stockholders' dividends are often limited in some way, and policyholders share in the profits. Sometimes policyholders are also given a vote in the management of the firm. In no cases, however, do policyholders share the losses except through a reduced dividend.

Stock life insurers issuing participating insurance often issue nonparticipating insurance at lower guaranteed rates.

For an interesting study of stock participating life insurance, see J. M. Belth, "Participating Life Insurance: The Stock Company Version," *Journal of Insurance*, XXIX, No. 2 (June, 1962), 229–237.

[4] For a recent report on Lloyd's, see "The Risky Future at Lloyd's of London," *Business Week* (October 18, 1969), 102–113.

Table 23.1   Premium income of United States private insurers, 1969

Property and liability insurers

Type of insurance	Premium income,* $ millions	Proportion (per cent) written by			
		Stock insurers	Mutual insurers	Reciprocal exchanges	Lloyds Associations
Homeowners multiperil	$ 2,203.3	76.1	21.8	2.1	†
Commercial multiperil	1,023.4	84.2	15.2	0.5	†
Fire	1,986.4	81.8	16.7	1.5	†
Extended coverage	566.3	82.0	16.3	1.6	0.1
Allied fire	262.6	71.0	28.0	1.1	†
Ocean marine	399.6	87.4	12.3	0.4	†
Inland marine	699.0	86.4	10.8	2.7	0.1
Theft	124.5	86.4	12.8	0.8	†
Fidelity and surety	503.9	95.4	4.5	0.1	†
Glass	40.1	81.7	17.3	1.0	†
Boiler and machinery	106.4	88.2	11.8	†	†
Automobile physical damage	4,356.0	63.5	28.9	7.3	0.2
Automobile bodily injury liability	5,772.1	60.4	31.8	7.7	†
Automobile property damage liability	2,469.7	60.1	32.2	7.6	0.1
Miscellaneous bodily injury liability	1,265.9	78.4	19.8	1.7	†
Miscellaneous property damage liability	378.8	81.5	17.5	1.0	†
Workmen's compensation	3,167.9	68.6	30.1	1.2	†
All other‡	453.2	56.4	43.4	0.3	†
Total	$25,780.0	69.6	25.9	4.4	†

Life and health insurers

Type of insurance	Premium income, $ millions	Proportion (per cent) written by		
		Stock insurers	Mutual insurers	Blue Cross-Blue Shield and other health insurers
Life, including annuities§	$24,253	48	52	—
Disability income ¶	2,855	100.0		—
Medical expense	14,430	50.9		49.1
Total	$41,538	82.9		17.1

* Net premiums earned for property and liability insurers.
† Less than 0.1 per cent.
‡ Mutual premium volume includes $131.5 million written by the Factory Mutuals (see p. 458), which are not reported on a segregated basis.
§ The life insurance premium income of fraternals, assessment associations, and mutual savings banks is omitted. These insurers write about 5 per cent of the life insurance in force.
¶ A very small fraction of the premium income of the independent plans (included in the table as other health insurers) is for disability income insurance.

Sources: Property and liability insurance data from Best's Review, Property/Liability Insurance Edition, LXXV, No. 6 (October, 1970), 22–23. Data are based on reports of 739 stock insurers, 318 mutual insurers, 43 reciprocal exchanges, and 11 Lloyds Associations, which account for most of the premiums written in 1969.
Life insurance data from 1970 Life Insurance Fact Book (New York: Institute of Life Insurance, 1970), pp. 25, 57.
Health insurance data from Source Book of Health Insurance Data, 1970 (New York: Health Insurance Institute, 1970).

Table 23.2 Premium income of each major type of United States private insurer, 1969*

Property and liability insurers

Type of insurance	Stock insurers Premiums, $ millions	% of total	Mutual insurers Premiums, $ millions	% of total	Reciprocal exchanges Premiums, $ millions	% of total	Lloyds Associations Premiums, $ millions	% of total	All insurers Premiums, $ millions	% of total
Homeowners multiperil	$ 1,666.7	9.3	$ 489.6	7.3	$ 46.9	4.1	$0.1	1.0	$ 2,203.3	8.6
Commercial multiperil	863.0	4.8	155.5	2.3	4.9	0.4	†	†	1,023.4	3.9
Fire	1,625.0	9.0	331.7	5.0	29.0	2.6	0.7	7.8	1,986.4	7.7
Extended coverage	464.9	2.6	92.2	1.4	8.9	0.8	0.3	3.1	566.3	2.2
Allied fire	186.2	1.0	73.5	1.1	2.9	0.3	†	0.2	262.6	1.0
Ocean marine	348.9	2.0	49.2	0.7	1.5	0.1	†	0.3	399.6	1.5
Inland marine	604.6	3.4	75.4	1.1	18.6	1.6	0.4	4.3	699.0	2.7
Theft	107.5	0.6	16.0	0.2	1.0	0.1	†	†	124.5	0.5
Fidelity and surety	480.7	2.7	22.6	0.3	0.6	0.1	†	0.1	503.9	1.9
Glass	33.5	0.2	7.1	0.1	0.4	†	†	†	41.0	0.2
Boiler and machinery	93.8	0.5	12.6	0.2	†	†	†	†	106.4	0.4
Automobile physical damage	2,768.5	15.4	1,252.0	18.9	318.7	28.2	6.8	78.4	4,356.0	16.9
Automobile bodily injury liability	3,435.6	19.4	1,840.8	27.5	445.4	39.4	0.3	3.1	5,772.1	22.4
Automobile property damage liability	1,483.7	8.3	798.3	11.9	187.5	16.6	0.2	1.8	2,469.7	9.6
Miscellaneous bodily injury liability	993.6	5.5	250.6	3.8	21.7	1.9	†	†	1,265.9	4.9
Miscellaneous property damage liability	308.9	1.7	66.2	1.0	3.7	0.3	†	†	378.8	1.5
Workmen's compensation	2,174.4	12.1	954.4	14.3	39.1	3.5	†	†	3,167.9	12.3
All other	255.4	1.4	196.5	2.9	1.3	0.1	†	†	453.2	1.8
Total	$17,944.9	100.0	$6,694.2	100.0	$1,132.1	100.0	$8.8	100.0	$25,780.0	100.0

Life and health insurers

Type of insurance	Commercial insurers Premiums, $ millions	% of total	Blue Cross-Blue Shield and other health insurers Premiums, $ millions	% of total	All insurers Premiums, $ millions	% of total
Life, including annuities	$24,253	70.4			$24,253	58.4
Disability income	2,855	8.3			2,855	6.9
Medical expense	7,342	21.3	$7,088	100.0	14,430	34.7
Total	34,450	100.0	7,088	100.0	$41,538	100.0

* See Table 23.1 for other footnotes.
† Less than $50,000, or less than 0.1 per cent.

Sources: See Table 23.1.

businesses (e.g., bankers, industrialists, and members of Parliament) and limit their participation in this insurance operation to the furnishing of the necessary capital and the risk-bearing function. Usually the insurance decisions are made by a managing agent who has the authority to speak for a number of underwriters belonging to his "syndicate." Even if the insurance is placed in one or more syndicates, however, the liability of each member of the syndicates is several and not joint. A member is not responsible for the failure of other members to fulfill their promises. Syndicates or underwriters not participating in the particular contract are technically outsiders to the entire transaction.

At first glance, the financial guarantee behind a contract from Lloyd's of London may appear somewhat questionable because of the heavy reliance upon the financial conditions of the particular underwriters signing the contract. This fear should be erased, however, because the applicants are carefully screened with respect to their financial and moral integrity; their liability is unlimited; their accounts are supervised by the association; various deposits are required which serve as security behind the underwriter's promise; and a central guarantee fund is maintained by the association, which can be used to pay any unsatisfied obligations. In addition, the reputation of Lloyd's of London is jealously guarded by the membership. Not until 1969 were non-Commonwealth citizens admitted to membership.

Another possible defect is that technically the insured has purchased a separate contract from each underwriter and must proceed in case of a dispute against each underwriter. In practice, however, Lloyd's underwriters accept the outcome of a suit against one member.

Lloyd's of London members possess almost unlimited freedom with respect to the types of insurance they may write and the rates they may charge. Members, in fact, differ with respect to these matters, although there is a tendency to follow the established leaders in certain fields. This extreme flexibility has led to some of the unusual contracts attributed to Lloyd's of London, but most of the insurance written is less spectacular. Marine insurance is the major line. Because individuals are the insurers, only short-term life insurance contracts are written, and the volume of business is small. However, the underwriters have considered writing permanent insurance through a separate corporation. In order to place business with underwriting members, one must operate through a Lloyd's broker. This fact poses a problem for an insured in the United States because Lloyd's of London underwriters can be represented in the United States with respect to all lines of insurance only in the two states in which they are licensed—Illinois and Kentucky. In addition, in a number of states, Lloyd's and other nonadmitted insurers can be represented by a broker with respect to "surplus-line" insurance, i.e., insurance that is not available from duly licensed insurers in that state. In the other states, tech-nically the buyer must contact a Lloyd's representative in Illinois, Ken-tucky, Canada, or London, but it is customary for a licensed agent to conduct the negotiations in the insured's name. Most American insurance with Lloyd's of London is insurance that is not readily available in the local market or reinsurance purchased by American insurers. Nevertheless about one-half of the premium volume developed by Lloyd's underwriters is purchased by insureds or insurers in the United States.

Although Lloyd's is licensed only in two states, the underwriters agree in the insurance contract to submit to and abide by the decisions of United States courts. Moreover, they have established an American trust fund for the specific protection of United States policyholders.[5]

Lloyds Associations in the United States pattern their operations after those of Lloyd's of London but there are many significant differences. The number of underwriters is very small; their financial resources are meager compared with those of Lloyd's of London underwriters; their liability may be limited; an attorney-in-fact speaks for all the underwriters in the associa-tion; and the insurance operations are commonly restricted to one state (usually Texas) and to one line of insurance.[6] Although some Lloyds Associa-tions have enviable reputations, others have been conducted in such a way as to shed doubt on the value of this form of business organization in the United States. Only about fourteen associations are currently in operation. Tables 23.1 and 23.2 indicate the relatively small role played by these associations and the limited kinds of insurance they write.

Cooperative insurers   Cooperative insurers are organized not for profit but for the benefit of the policyholders, who elect the management and bear the risks of the insurer. Three types of cooperative insurers will be discussed in this chapter: (1) advance premium mutual corporations, (2) pure assess-ment mutual associations or corporations, and (3) reciprocal exchanges, sometimes referred to as "interinsurance exchanges." Three other types of cooperative insurers, which closely resemble the advance premium mutual corporation but which possess some unique characteristics[7] and which are usually regulated under a separate section of the state insurance laws, are fraternals, mutual savings bank insurers, and medical expense associations such as Blue Cross and Blue Shield. These organizations have already been

---

[5] The underwriters have also made deposits in Illinois and Kentucky for the specific bene-fit of policyholders in those states.
[6] Several states (New York, for example) forbid the formation of new Lloyds Associations, but in most states such an association is formed with comparative ease. All that may be required is a certain minimum number of underwriters, each of whom can demonstrate a certain minimum net worth. In some states, however, certain minimum deposits are also required.
[7] For example, doctors and hospitals usually control the medical expense associations.

described elsewhere in this text, and the reader should review those discussions in connection with this section.

The *advance premium mutual* is a corporation owned by its policyholders. The corporation sets premium rates at a level which is expected to be at least sufficient to pay the expected losses and expenses and to add to the contingency reserves.[8] Policyholders receive the dividends, if any, declared by the board of directors, the dividends representing the amount by which the premium and other income exceeds the needs of the insurer. The surplus built up out of past operations serves as a cushion against years of poor experience.

The contracts issued by the advance premium mutual may be assessable or nonassessable. If assessable, the assessment may be unlimited or limited. In either case, however, the mutual never expects to exercise this right, though it may be forced to do so. Nonassessable policies can be issued by mutuals whose surplus position is strong enough to satisfy the state requirements on this score.

Advance premium mutuals write most of the life insurance in force and one-quarter of the property and liability insurance. However, although only about 160 advance premium mutuals are active in the life insurance field, about 700 such mutuals write property and liability insurance. Mutual life insurers tend to be large, whereas most mutual property and liability insurers are small.

Although some mutuals write all types of property and liability insurance, most mutuals engage in a much more limited operation. Table 23.1 indicates that advance premium mutuals, which are responsible for most of the mutual premium volume, are most important in the more common property and liability lines, such as workmen's compensation and automobile insurance. Because these kinds of insurance have grown rapidly and because mutuals have gained more than the stock insurers from the public's increasing price consciousness, the mutuals' share of the property-liability insurance market has been increasing (it was less than one-quarter in 1952). Some authorities believe that because of the movement toward financial-services complexes this trend will soon be reversed.

Assessment mutuals are much more numerous than advance premium mutuals, but they write a very small proportion of the total premium volume, most of which was paid for fire insurance on farm properties.[9] Assessment

[8] The first mutual insurer in the United States, the Philadelphia Contributorship for the Insurance of Houses from Loss by Fire, founded in 1752, is still in operation. This insurer and a few others issue perpetual policies. The insured pays a very large initial premium the first year and nothing thereafter. The investment return on the premium is sufficient to pay the costs of the insurer and to return a dividend to the policyholder. The initial premium is returned when the insured drops his insurance.
[9] For more details, see the most recent edition of *Directory of Mutual Companies in the United States, Property and Casualty Insurance* (Chicago: American Mutual Insurance Alliance).

mutuals play an even less important role in personnel insurance, but there are a few large assessment health insurance associations.

Assessment mutuals differ from advance premium mutuals in that they always have the right to assess their policyholders and the chance of an assessment is high. A "pure" assessment mutual would charge an initial premium large enough to cover the expenses which will be incurred even if no losses are experienced and would assess the policyholders to pay any extra costs arising in connection with losses. At the other and much more common extreme, the assessment mutual would collect an initial premium sufficient to pay expenses and typical losses. Assessments are levied whenever unusual losses occur, the assessment in some instances being limited in advance to some specified amount. Some mutuals, legally termed "assessment mutuals," have never levied an assessment and could, in fact, be classified as advance premium mutuals.

Property and liability assessment mutuals usually confine their operations to a county or counties and at most operate in a few states. Because of the limited scale of their operations, their experience may show wide fluctuations from one year to the next; some, however, are large enough to maintain a fairly stable experience. Most personnel insurance assessment mutuals are also small, but some have a large number of policyholders in widely scattered geographical areas and maintain legal reserves similar to those established by advance premium mutuals.

Reciprocal exchanges resemble advance premium mutuals, but in their purest form they differ from these mutuals in many ways. First, they are not corporations but unincorporated associations.[10] Second, the association is not technically the insurer. Instead, the association makes it possible for the policyholders to insure one another individually and not jointly. Each member of the reciprocal insures and is insured by every other member of the reciprocal. There is a reciprocal exchange of contracts. In order to simplify the administration of the agreement, each subscriber receives only one contract, which states that he is in effect exchanging contracts with other members of the association. The administration of the agreement is in charge of an attorney-in-fact, who performs such duties as soliciting new members, rejecting undesirable applicants, paying losses, investing funds, and establishing premiums. Third, individual accounts are maintained for each member, the accounts of the association being the sum of the accounts of the members. The accounts are credited with the premiums and a share of the investment income and debited with a share of the expenses and losses. Deficiencies in the account are not expected, but if they occur, they

---

[10] A reciprocal is easier to form than a mutual. A minimum deposit may be required, but usually all that is needed is a minimum number of applications with aggregate premiums or exposure units in excess of a certain amount. If no minimum deposit is required, the only funds necessary are the advance premiums deposited by the subscribers.

can be repaired by an assessment, which may be limited. A surplus in the account may result in a dividend, and if any surplus remains in the account when the member terminates his membership, it is returned to him.

In practice, however, so many modifications have been introduced that it is often difficult to distinguish a reciprocal exchange from an advance premium mutual. First, undivided surplus funds are commonly kept in addition to the individual surplus accounts, and in some instances the undivided surplus funds replace completely the individual accounts. Second, because assessments are seldom necessary, the distinction between individual liability and joint liability is almost never effective. In fact, if sufficient undivided surplus funds exist, some states permit the issuance of nonassessable contracts.

Less than 50 reciprocals exist today. They write no life insurance and less than 5 per cent of the property and liability insurance.[11] Tables 23.1 and 23.2 show the limited number of lines in which they are active. Many reciprocals are associated with a trade association or an automobile association, but a few are multiple line insurers seeking with considerable success insureds of all types in most states.

A key factor in the success of a reciprocal exchange is the attorney-in-fact. The prospective subscriber should examine carefully the ability and reputation of the attorney-in-fact as well as the power of attorney which prescribes his authority and duties. In some cases, a policyholder's advisory committee may exist, and its effectiveness should be determined. This investigation is important because the attorney-in-fact, who has nothing to lose from the failure of the reciprocal other than his job,[12] may be tempted to increase the volume of business, regardless of its quality, because he is reimbursed on a commission basis. On the other hand, it should be emphasized that many excellent, progressive reciprocals can be found.

Government insurers   The last form of business organization to be discussed is the government insurer. The principal government insurers are operated by the Federal and state governments, but some are local government agencies. In most instances, the government plans are intended to be self-supporting, but in a few instances there is a direct subsidy, and in all cases the governmental unit would probably supply funds in times of financial distress.

---

[11] See Dennis Reinmuth, *The Regulation of Reciprocal Insurance Exchanges* (Homewood, Ill.: Richard D. Irwin, Inc., 1967), and Richard L. Norgaard, "Reciprocals: A Study of the Evolution of an Insurance Institution," unpublished doctoral dissertation, University of Minnesota, 1962, for more details.

[12] The retention of his job may of course be a sufficient incentive. His future employment may also be affected.

The *Federal government* insurers are fewer in number but extremely important. The largest insurance operation in the world is the Old-Age, Survivors, Disability, and Health Insurance program under the Social Security Act. Other important Federal government insurers include the Railroad Retirement Board (benefits under the Railroad Retirement System), the Veterans Administration (servicemen's life insurance and veterans' mortgage and property improvement loan insurance), the Federal Housing Administration (mortgage and property improvement loan insurance), the Federal Deposit Insurance Administration (insurance of bank deposits), the Federal Savings and Loan Insurance Corporation (insurance on savings and loan association shares), the Federal Crop Insurance Corporation (insurance of farmers' crops against natural hazards), the Atomic Energy Commission (nuclear energy liability protection in excess of that available from private sources), the Maritime Administration (war risk marine insurance binders, which become effective during time of war after private insurance is canceled, the Export-Import Bank of Washington (protection on exports against such political losses as inconvertibility of foreign currencies), the National Insurance Development Fund (reinsurance for private insurers against the risk of catastrophe losses from civil disorders, the National Flood Insurance Fund (flood reinsurance for private insurers), and the Securities Investor Protection Corporation (protection for investors in case of brokerage house insolvencies).

The two most important types of *state* funds are the unemployment insurance funds in all states and the workmen's compensation insurance funds, which compete with private insurers in twelve states[13] and possess a monopoly in six states.[14] The variation among these funds with respect to services rendered, acceptable classes of insureds, pricing policies, tax status, and other matters is too great to detail here. Another type of state fund associated with workmen's compensation laws is the second-injury fund.[15]

Other state funds include temporary disability insurance funds in California, Hawaii, New Jersey, New York, and Rhode Island, a life insurance fund in Wisconsin and Torrens title insurance funds in California, Massachusetts, North Carolina, and Ohio.[16]

Government underwriting of insurance on its own property and personnel insurance benefits for its employees is best classified as self-insurance or retention. Sometimes, however, a state fund underwrites insurance benefits for local government employees (say, teachers).

It is clear that some of these government insurers are providing protec-

---

[13] Arizona, California, Colorado, Idaho, Maryland, Michigan, Montana, New York, Oklahoma, Oregon, Pennsylvania, and Utah.
[14] Nevada, North Dakota, Ohio, Washington, West Virginia, and Wyoming.
[15] Second injury funds exist in all but four states: Georgia, Louisiana, Nevada, and Virginia. See Chap. 7 for more information on these funds.
[16] County Torrens title funds are active in several states.

tion in direct competition with private insurers; but many are underwriting risks that private insurers have generally considered to be uninsurable. Table 11.3 permits some comparisons between the scope of some leading government insurance operations and private insurance.

DOMICILE AND ADMISSION STATUS

Insurers are classified as domestic, foreign, or alien insurers, depending upon whether they are organized under the laws of the state to which the classification is applicable, of some other state, or outside the United States. All domestic insurers must be authorized by state insurance officials to conduct an insurance business. Foreign and alien insurers are considered to be admitted insurers if they have been licensed by the state insurance official. An unlicensed or nonadmitted insurer cannot be represented by agents (other than the surplus line agents described in the section below under "Marketing methods") within the state. Government insurers are not classified in this way.

PRICING POLICY

Differences in pricing policies of insurers have become more marked in recent years, though the differences are more notable in property and liability insurance than in personnel insurance. Insurers can be classified according to whether they issue participating or nonparticipating contracts and according to whether they use independent or bureau rates.

Participating or nonparticipating insurers   Policyholders of participating insurers share in the experience of the insurer through dividends, assessments, or both. Policyholders of nonparticipating insurers pay a definite premium (subject in some cases to retrospective rating). The same insurer may issue participating and nonparticipating insurance. Insurers issuing participating insurance include some capital stock insurers (mostly life insurers), most advance premium mutuals, all assessment associations, and most reciprocal exchanges. Nonparticipating insurers include most capital stock insurers (for at least part of their business), some advance premium mutuals, and some reciprocal exchanges. Most government insurers are nonparticipating insurers.

Some participating insurers set their rates at a high level to permit the payment of large dividends, while others establish lower rates and expect to declare lower dividends. Some advance premium mutuals and reciprocal exchanges are classified as nonparticipating insurers because they issue nonassessable contracts, fix rates at the lowest feasible predictable level, and pay no dividends.

Independent or bureau insurers   The second classification according to price policy is not important in personnel insurance, where each insurer uses its own independent rate structure. In property and liability insurance, however, an insurer may develop its own rates or, as a member or subscriber to a rating organization, called a "rating bureau," it may use the rates developed by the bureau from pooled experience.[17] Many bureau members or subscribers modify the bureau rates in some respect, thus occupying a position midway between the independents and those using the bureau rates.

MARKETING METHODS AND SUPERVISORY SYSTEMS

Insurers may market their product in four different ways: (1) through independent agents, (2) through employees or by mail or vending machines on a direct writing basis, (3) through exclusive agents, or (4) through brokers. Insurers may supervise their agents and sales representatives under (1) a general agency system, (2) a branch office system, or (3) a direct reporting system. A particular insurer may use two or more of these methods or supervisory systems.

Marketing methods   *Independent agency insurers* market their product through agents who may represent several insurers.[18] The agent is an independent businessman who receives a commission as compensation for his services and who retains the right to renew the insurance contracts of his customers with a different insurer. The agency expiration list, which records the names and addresses of present policyholders and the dates their policies expire, belongs to the agent, and if he and the insurer agree to sever their relationship, the insurer cannot give any information in this list to a new agent. Independent agents may write their own policies and handle all financial transactions (billing, collecting, and extending credit) with their insureds. Increasingly, however, independent agency insurers are taking over the policy writing, billing, and collecting functions. In this way independent agency insurers have been able to reduce selling and servicing costs, including commissions, and to strengthen their relationships with their insureds.

Despite their independent status independent agents have the authority to commit immediately the insurers they represent to insure most applicants. Moreover, all agents are considered legal agents of the insurer, who is bound by their actions and knowledge.

All forms of business organization in property and liability insurance

---

[17] Rating bureaus are described more fully in Chap. 25.
[18] Office agents are sometimes appointed by a few agency insurers. These agents are based in the home or branch office, receive more administrative assistance, and are paid lower commissions.

include some agency insurers. In fact, most stock and most mutual property and liability insurers are agency insurers.

Direct writers sell insurance through commissioned or salaried (plus bonuses) employees, called "sales representatives," or by mail. Relatively little insurance, most of it health insurance, is sold by mail because relatively few persons are willing to take the initiative to buy insurance. Sales representatives represent only the insurer employing them. Generally the insurer does more of the policy writing, billing, and collection work under this system than under the agency system. Sales representatives usually have the power to bind the insurer they represent and are legally that insurer's agents. Consequently their errors are attributed to the insurer.

All forms of business organization in property and liability insurance include some direct writers, but most direct writers are cooperative insurers, including most of the larger mutuals. All government insurers are direct writers.

Exclusive agency insurers occupy a position somewhere between independent agency insurers and direct writers. Like direct writers, these insurers require exclusive representation (at least for their regular business), regard the policyholders as their customers, and perform much of the administrative work in behalf of the agent. On the other hand, the agents are regarded as independent businessmen and are always reimbursed on a commission basis. Typically, however, the renewal commission is much less than the commission on new business. Many authorities prefer to classify exclusive agency insurers as a modified version of the direct writers.

The leading examples of exclusive agency insurers are some leading mutual insurers and almost all life insurers, regardless of the form of business organization. In life insurance, however, the renewal commissions usually belong to an agent who has completed a certain period of service, even if he leaves the insurer.[19]

Insurers accepting brokerage business are the fourth and final category of insurers classified according to marketing methods. Unlike the insurers' producers discussed above, *brokers* are independent businessmen who do not represent any insurer. Brokers offer to analyze risks for their clients and to shop among insurers to obtain the optimum protection at the optimum price. For their services, brokers receive part or all of the producer's commission from the insurer or producer with whom they place the business. Some insurers accept and even encourage the direct placement of insurance with brokers, while others require the placement through one of their producers.

---

[19] Unlike property and liability insurance contracts, life insurance contracts, except for term insurance, do not have to be resold periodically. Also, the insured would usually suffer if the contract were surrendered and rewritten in another insurer just to maintain the relationship with the agent.

Some insurers will not pay the broker any commission for business he places with them, and the broker may hesitate to suggest the use of their facilities.

Because brokers are not legal agents of the insurer, they cannot bind any insurer, and no insurer can be held responsible for their mistakes. However, in several states statutes make the broker the agent of the insurer with respect to the acceptance of premium payments from the insured. In other states this practice is customary and in many instances has been supported by the courts.[20]

In practice, brokers do develop relationships with particular insurers and place most of their business with them. These relationships speed up and cut the cost of placing the insurance for the broker and often enable him to place business that would otherwise be impossible to insure.

Brokers may be one-man operations concentrating upon risk analysis and the purchase of insurance for families and small firms or they may be sizable operations providing, in addition, engineering, appraisal, actuarial, and other services and specializing in the accounts of large business firms. The latter are more common because (1) these clients are more likely to demand the services of the broker,[21] and (2) since the broker often receives a lower commission rate than the insurer's producer, the broker usually prefers larger premium accounts. For the same reasons, brokers tend to concentrate their operations in large cities.

Brokers are most important in property and liability insurance; they rarely specialize in life insurance. On the other hand, property and liability insurance brokers also originate a considerable amount of personnel insurance, particularly group insurance and pensions. Independent agency property and liability insurers are much more likely to accept brokerage business than are direct writers and exclusive agency insurers.

In some states the law does not provide for brokers, and brokerage concerns must here represent the insurers with whom they do business. In these states the difference between the agency representing several insurers and the so-called "broker" is primarily a matter of philosophy. The broker is supposedly less hesitant to seek new insurer connections if the needs of his client require them. The term which has been used to describe brokers operating in this fashion is *broker-agents*.

Broker-agents are also common in states which do permit the licensing of brokers. Sometimes the broker is licensed as both an agent and a broker; sometimes he is licensed only as an agent and operates in accordance with the philosophy described in the preceding paragraph. Finally, it is a common

---

[20] Edwin W. Patterson, *Essentials of Insurance Law* (New York: McGraw-Hill Book Company, 1957), p. 492.
[21] In the highly technical field of ocean marine insurance, the broker occupies a commanding position.

practice for agents to place business which their regular channels reject with some insurer they do not normally represent.

In most states, *surplus or excess line brokers* may be licensed to obtain insurance from nonadmitted insurers. Under these statutes, the excess line broker must demonstrate that the insurance sought is not available in the admitted market, pay the state premium tax, and post a bond guaranteeing that he will comply with the statute. Excess line brokers are sometimes also agents or brokers engaging in regular business, but more often they are specialists serving ordinary agents and brokers and sharing their commissions with them.

Although they are often confused with brokers or broker-agents, *insurance consultants* are independent businessmen who offer advice about insurance to their clients. Like brokers, they do not represent any insurers, but unlike brokers, they are paid by their clients on a fee basis and do not share in the commissions paid by insurers. Because their remuneration is not tied to the amount of insurance purchased by the client or to the particular insurer providing the protection, it can be argued that the suggestions of the consultant are more likely to be objective than those of agents, sales representatives, or brokers. On the other hand, the extra fee involved limits their appeal, and their interest in the risk problems of the firm may not be a continuing one. Insurance consultants operate for the most part only in large cities, and their clients are usually firms or public bodies large enough to have complicated insurance problems but not large enough to have a full-time risk manager on their staff.

Supervisory systems   Under the *general-agency system* of supervising agents, the insurer appoints a general agent to represent it in a specified territory.[22] The general agent may sell insurance himself and in addition may appoint other agents to work under him. The general agent's compensation includes a commission on the business he personally produces, an overriding commission on the business produced by his agents, and, in an increasing number of cases, a contribution toward his expenses.

By definition, this system is not applicable to direct writers. The other two systems to be noticed are used by both agency insurers and direct writers.

In life insurance, a general agent usually represents only one insurer, and much of his activity centers around the recruiting, training, and supervision of agents. In property and liability insurance, where the system is much less common and is diminishing in importance, the general agent

---

[22] Agents may also be involved under more than one system. For example, the authors know one local agent who has contracts with (1) a managing general agent, (2) two insurers through their branch offices, and (3) a few insurers operating under the direct reporting system.

usually represents several insurers, and in addition to his production function, he is often authorized to underwrite some of the business written
through the agency, provide engineering services, and settle most claims.
In many cases, the general agent who provides extensive services of this
nature produces no business personally and is termed a "managing general
agent."[23]

The general-agency system is most attractive to small insurers and
large insurers entering new areas because (1) when the volume of business
is small, the overhead cost is reduced and (2) if an established general
agency is used, the insurer gains the prestige of the agency plus a network
of agents and their customers. Insurers, regardless of size, often prefer
this agency system; they argue that because of the method of remuneration,
the general agent has the maximum incentive to produce new business,
service his present insureds, and run an efficient operation.

Negative aspects from the insurer's point of view are (1) the relatively
high costs of operation when the volume of business is high, (2) the diverse,
and sometimes inefficient, practices employed by general agents, (3) the
pressures that a general agent can exert through a threat that he and his
appointed agents will cease representing the insurer, and (4) the failure
of most insureds to recognize the insurers with whom the general agency
has placed the insurance.

There is a definite trend, however, toward reducing the independence
of the general agent, particularly in life insurance. Insurers now pay more
of his expenses, exercise more supervision over his selection and training
procedures, and perform more of his clerical chores. Consequently, the differences between the general agency system and the branch-office system are
diminishing.

Under the *branch-office system*, the insurer establishes a branch of
the home office, sometimes called a "service office," in the territory and
places an employee, called a "branch manager," in charge of the office.
The branch manager may sell insurance himself, but he is less likely to
do so than a general agent. The branch manager appoints agents, but the
contracts are between the agents and the insurer, not between the agents
and the branch manager. The branch manager usually receives a salary
plus a commission or bonus depending upon the extent and quality of business produced by the branch.

By definition, the branch office represents only one insurer or group.
In property and liability insurance, the branch is usually authorized to perform most of the home office underwriting and claims functions.

The branch-office method of operation is becoming more popular in

---

[23] The distinction between a large local agency and a general agency which is not a
managing general agency is often vague.

all lines of insurance. Reasons for this preference include (1) the relatively low cost when the volume of business is great, (2) the degree of control that the home office has over the branch manager and his methods of operation, (3) the increasing importance of electronic data-processing equipment and its emphasis on uniformity, and (4) an increasing desire to acquaint insureds with the name of their insurers. On the other hand, the branch-office method is an expensive system for the small insurer or, to a lesser extent, a large insurer entering a new territory, which must struggle with a low volume of business to create a market for itself. Moreover, some insurance executives argue that, despite the incentive arrangements for branch managers, the independent status of the general agent is the most effective incentive plan that can be devised.

Under the *direct-reporting system,* the agents report directly to the home office of the insurer. The identifying characteristic of this system, then, is the absence of either a general agent or a branch office.

The principal appeal of this system is the absence of branch-office and general-agency costs. This appeal is greatest when the volume of business in the area is small and the problems simple, and when the insureds can be serviced by one or at most a few agents. The principal drawback is the absence of local supervision and assistance.

Life insurers seldom use this system, but property and liability insurers employ it extensively, particularly in rural areas and small towns.

Special agents or fieldmen are salaried (or salaried plus bonus) representatives of insurers marketing their product under the nonexclusive agency system. A special agent serves as the liaison between the insurer and the agent or broker. His work includes the following: locating new agents and brokers for his insurer; persuading existing agents and brokers to place more business with his insurer; educating the agent or broker with respect to coverages, agency management, and sales techniques; assisting the agent or broker in actual sales presentations, particularly with respect to the more technical aspects; and in general creating a favorable image for his insurer.

In exclusive agency and direct-writing insurers, representatives from the home or branch office provide similar services and in fact are also often referred to as "special agents."

INSUREDS SERVICED

Insurers may finally be classified according to the types of insureds serviced. Some insurers seek all types of insureds, subject to certain underwriting restrictions (and these vary widely), whereas others limit rather severely the types of insureds they will underwrite. For example, a manufacturing firm may establish a captive insurer as part of its risk management program for reasons cited in Chapter 9 (tax savings and access to reinsurance markets), and this insurer may underwrite only the risks of the parent company. Some insurers are organized by finance companies to write property insurance on automobiles financed through dealers using the finance company services. Other insurers, usually cooperative insurers, limit their customers to the members of a trade association, an automobile association, an industry, a church, an occupation, or some other group. Some government insurers also operate in a restricted area; e.g., the Railroad Retirement System and the Veterans Administration.

Groups and Cooperative Reinsurance and Underwriting Associations

In addition to individual insurers, the insurance market includes important (1) groups, (2) underwriters' associations, and (3) reinsurance associations.

GROUPS

A group or fleet of insurers includes two or more insurers operating as a team under common ownership or management.[24] Group operations are most important in property and liability insurance but are becoming more commonplace in life insurance. In early 1969 about 1,770 insurers organized into 549 groups, 30 more than in 1967.[25] Almost half of these groups wrote all lines of insurance. Among the 1,062 insurers in these all-lines groups, 86 per cent were stock insurers and 61 per cent were nonlife insurers.

Group operations were originally important for two reasons which do not exist today. First, the property and liability insurance industry at one time limited through a voluntary agreement the number of agencies per insurer, and second, prior to multiple line legislation, as noted earlier, fire and marine insurers could not write casualty insurance and vice versa. Though these two reasons no longer exist, organizations which have operated for many years are not easily scrapped. Personnel problems, goodwill values, and the costs of consolidation have prevented many groups from reducing the number of separate insurers in the group, but a few have made extensive changes.

Some factors favor more and larger group operations. First, an insurer can expand its scope more rapidly by obtaining the controlling interest in an existing firm than by extending its own operations. Second, property and liability insurers have been organizing new life insurers or acquiring

[24] The first group was formed in 1898.
[25] Richard deR. Kip, "Insurance Company Groups—1969," *CPCU Annals*, XXII, No. 3 (September, 1969), 197–202.

old ones at a much more rapid rate than in the past, and life insurers are beginning to reciprocate.[26] Third, many insurers within the past few years have formed new corporations to write substandard or preferred automobile business. The preferred automobile business is often billed directly from the home office, and the agent's commission is reduced. Forming a new insurer avoids the underwriting problems associated with transacting this special class of business within the same corporate structure as the conventional business. It also avoids problems under state rate regulatory laws.[27]

UNDERWRITERS' ASSOCIATIONS

Especially in fire insurance, insurers often cooperate in the underwriting of some or all of the policies they issue. These cooperative underwriting organizations are generally associated with one or more of the following conditions: (1) a unique or particularly hazardous exposure, (2) very high policy limits, or (3) a need for highly specialized talent.[28] Some examples will illustrate the nature of these associations.

The Factory Mutual Insurance Companies includes five mutual insurers specializing in sprinklered properties of superior construction.[29] These associated insurers are noted for their engineering advice and services, the unique contract they issue (for example, vandalism is always included, and there is no coinsurance clause), and their conservative pricing method, which requires the payment of a sizable premium deposit, most of which is returned at the end of the policy period. For example, the usual return on 3-year (the most common) term policies is about 65 per cent. Typically, one of the five insurers writes a direct policy, and the other four members act as reinsurers, the percentage of risk reinsured by each insurer being indicated in a rider to the contract. The association provides appraisal, inspection engineering, loss adjustment, and rate-making services for its members.

The stock insurers' equivalent (in many ways) of the Factory Mutuals is the Factory Insurance Association, an organization including about 100 of the leading stock insurers and devoted to the underwriting of highly protected properties. The FIA issues the policies directly, and its liability is uniformly apportioned among the member insurers. Unlike the Factory

---

[26] Life insurers have been slower to act because of legal restrictions and because several recent years have been marked by underwriting losses for nonlife insurers.

[27] For example, in order to charge a rate in excess of their usual rate for the insured's class, the insurer might have to get the written consent of the insured.

[28] G. F. Michelbacher, *Multiple-line Insurance* (New York: McGraw-Hill Book Company, 1957), p. 294.

[29] A stock insurer owned by the five Factory Mutual insurers accepts good insureds who do not meet the association standards. It is also licensed to write liability insurance.

Mutuals, the FIA operates through agents, and its member insurers write only a small portion of their business through FIA.

Property and liability insurance for the operators of atomic reactors are supplied by two stock associations—the Nuclear Energy Property Insurance Association and the Nuclear Energy Liability Insurance Association—and one mutual association—the Mutual Atomic Energy Pool. The liability of the member insurers is several and not joint.

The American Foreign Insurance Association is an underwriting association which extends the insurance operations of its stock members to foreign countries. United States Aircraft Insurance Group is a group handling the aviation insurance business of its stock members. The Cotton Insurance Association represents its stock members in the writing of reporting form policies on cotton. The Improved Risk Mutuals organization serves its twelve mutual members in about the same way as the FIA serves its stock members, except that the liability of each member is several and not joint. Assigned risk pools in automobile and workmen's compensation insurance assign insureds unable to procure insurance directly in proportion to the premium volumes of the members in the area covered by the pool.

Numerous other associations could be cited, but these examples are sufficient to indicate their number and importance and the fact that they compete against one another as well as against nonmember insurers.

REINSURANCE ASSOCIATIONS

Insurers are also organized into associations to provide reinsurance facilities. Some reinsurance associations, such as the Excess and Casualty Reinsurance Association, an association of stock insurers, reinsure primarily nonmembers. Most associations, however, such as the stock Workmen's Compensation Reinsurance Bureau and the American Mutual Reinsurance Company, which operates in all lines except life insurance, exist mainly to reinsure members. Reinsurance pools are much more common in property and liability insurance than in personnel insurance.

Financial Services Combinations

Beginning in the late sixties, many insurers became for the first time part of some business combination marketing noninsurance products and services. In some instances stock insurers have been acquired by some corporation, including conglomerates, whose primary business is not insurance. In more instances, a holding company has been formed by the persons who own a stock insurer, the stock of the holding company has been exchanged for the stock of the insurer, and the holding company has then acquired or established subsidiaries in fields that insurers have been forbidden to enter. Both of these routes to diversification are closed to mutual insurers unless they first convert their mode of operation to that of a stock insurer, a change that is permitted under the laws of some states. In order to correct this competitive disadvantage of the mutuals and to discourage the use of holding companies, which pose some important regulatory problems, many states have relaxed laws limiting the proportion of their assets insurers can invest (1) in the aggregate in common stock or (2) in the common stock of one corporation. Generally these new laws permit insurers to own a controlling interest in subsidiaries engaged in closely related or ancillary activities. Such activities include but are not limited to some other form of insurance, mutual fund investment management, mutual fund broker-dealerships, personal finance companies, banks, savings and loan associations, computer services, computer leasing, and real estate development. In short, insurers are permitted under this legislation to expand their operations to include a broad range of financial services and closely related services; they are not permitted to enter unrelated fields. The scope of holding companies is not limited in this way, but most holding companies formed by insurers have elected to concentrate on financial services. For this and other reasons, most stock insurers expanding into noninsurance areas have formed or become part of a parent holding company. Mutual insurers have become the parents of subsidiaries.[30]

Why have insurers sought product diversification through business combinations?

1. Life insurers have decided that in order to increase their share of the consumers' savings dollar they need to market equity products, which they cannot legally do directly, except for variable annuities.
2. Insurers for both selfish and unselfish reasons wish to improve their services to policyholders. They believe that "one-stop service" is more convenient for the customer and improves the likelihood that he will receive unbiased advice (e.g., in choosing between mutual funds and cash-value life insurance).
3. Insurers hope to improve their profit picture in the following ways:
    a. Synergism, or the concept that the whole may be greater than the sum of its parts. For example, the demand for one product may stimulate the demand for another, and certain overhead costs may not increase as rapidly as the business expands.
    b. Entering new fields that are profitable even without the influence of synergism.

---

[30] In some instances, mutuals have become the parents of holding companies which then acquire or form subsidiaries. Some mutuals have been converted into stock insurers in order to achieve more flexibility.

c. Reducing annual fluctuations in profits through diversification.

d. Investing the "surplus" surplus of insurers in more profitable ventures than insurance.

e. Securing more freedom in external financing. Although insurers may have the authority to borrow through bonds or debentures, they are reluctant to do so.

4. Insurers hope by increasing the range of their operations to improve their ability to attract and retain high-quality manpower.

Few leading insurers at the present time are not part of some business combination marketing noninsurance products and services. Much attention will probably be devoted in the next decade to developing integrated packages of insurance and other financial services sold by the same family of companies.

REVIEW QUESTIONS

1. The Beacon Casualty Insurance Company sells fire insurance.
   a. Was this possible in 1945?
   b. Is the Beacon Casualty Insurance Company a "casualty" company? If not, how would you classify It?

2. "Stock insurers, which are always nonparticipating, independent agency, proprietary insurers, write most of the premium volume in all branches of insurance."
   a. In what respects is this statement false?
   b. In what respects is this statement true?

3. Lloyd's of London is internationally renowned for its insurance activities, but technically Lloyd's is not an insurer. Explain this statement.

4. a. Are Lloyds Associations United States branches of Lloyd's of London?
   b. In what ways do Lloyds Associations differ from Lloyd's of London?

5. Some risk managers refuse to purchase insurance from mutual insurers because they believe that all mutual policies are assessable. Are they correct in their reasoning?

6. a. In which lines of insurance do mutuals account for at least 40 per cent of the premium volume?
   b. Is the mutuals' share of the insurance market increasing?

7. Compare the following types of insurers with respect to (1) the controlling group, (2) the liability of the "owners," i.e., whether it is joint and several or individual, and (3) ownership of the surplus.
   a. Reciprocal exchange
   b. Advance premium mutual

    c. Lloyds Association

    d. Capital stock insurer

8. The Buttonwood Mutual is legally a small township mutual operating in one state on the assessment basis.

    a. Should an insured be disturbed if the management collects an assessment each year?

    b. Do all assessable mutuals levy assessments?

9. The Gray Company is considering the formation of a captive insurer. Which of the following legal forms would be easiest to establish? Why?

    a. Capital stock insurer

    b. Advance premium mutual insurer

    c. Reciprocal exchange

10. a. Which government insurers compete with private insurers?

    b. Which government insurers provide insurance not available from private insurers?

11. An insurer domiciled in Nebraska wishes to sell insurance in Minnesota.

    a. If this insurer is not licensed by your state insurance department, what terms would you use to describe its status in your state?

    b. Why is this status important to insureds? to the insurer?

12. "All participating insurers are cooperative insurers, and all cooperative insurers are participating insurers." Comment on the truth or falsity of this statement.

13. a. What is the function of rating bureaus?

    b. Contrast the importance of rating bureaus in property and liability insurance with that of rating bureaus in personnel insurance.

14. a. Distinguish among agency insurers, direct writers, and exclusive agency insurers.

    b. Do parallel marketing systems exist in other businesses?

15. Does the fact that an insurance representative calls himself an agent, a broker, or consultant mean that he is functionally what the term implies?

16. Compare a property and liability insurance agent, a property and liability insurance sales representative, a property and liability insurance exclusive agent, and a life insurance agent with respect to:

    a. Binding authority

    b. Commissions

    c. Number of insurers represented

17. "One-stop selling" is an important trend in insurance as it is in other businesses.

    a. What does "one-stop selling" mean in insurance?

    b. What advantages and disadvantages does it offer?

18. Compare a broker, an agent, and a consultant with respect to:

    a. Binding authority

   b. Commissions
   c. Legal responsibility of insurers for their actions
   d. Number of insurers represented
19. In many states the law provides only for agents' licenses.
   a. Are there any brokers in those states?
   b. Do broker-agents exist in the other states? Why?
20. Special agents or fieldmen and group representatives play an important role in the marketing of insurance, regardless of the type of marketing structure. What is this role?
21. a. The general-agency system is most attractive to small insurers and to large insurers entering new areas. Why?
   b. What are the other marketing systems, and what are their advantages and disadvantages from the insured's point of view?
22. a. What is a group or fleet operation?
   b. Are groups or fleets increasing or decreasing in importance?
23. The Factory Mutuals and the Factory Insurance Association are two major underwriting associations.
   a. In what ways do these two associations resemble one another?
   b. In what ways do they differ?
24. Describe briefly the purpose of each of the following:
   a. Nuclear energy insurance pools
   b. Assigned risk pools
   c. Reinsurance pools
25. Why and how have insurers sought product diversification through business combinations?

SUGGESTIONS FOR ADDITIONAL READING

See suggestions for Chapter 24.

24

selecting the insurer: II

This chapter deals specifically with the considerations that must control the choice of a particular insurer and cites some useful sources of information.

Considerations That Affect the Choice of an Insurer

in selecting a particular insurer or underwriters' association, a risk manager must consider three factors—security, service, and cost. We discuss each of these matters in more detail below and evaluate each of the legal forms of business organization utilized by insurers with respect to the factor under discussion. We should reemphasize, however, that *because variations among the insurers of the same type are greater than the variations among the average insurers of different types, it is dangerous to select one insurer in preference to another simply because of its legal form of business organization.* Thinking in terms of stereotypes can be very misleading.

SECURITY

Security refers to the financial ability of the insurer to fulfill its promise when the occasion demands. If the promise covers a long term, as is true in life insurance, the security of the promise is especially difficult to determine because many changes can occur over a lengthy period.

Security depends upon many variables, including the ratio of the policyholders' surplus (capital plus surplus, including *voluntary* contingency reserves) to the liabilities, the volume of business written,[1] the nature and valuation of the assets, the nature and valuation of the liabilities, the profitability of past operations, the stability of the lines of insurance written, the pricing methods, the capability of the management, the underwriting policy, reinsurance facilities, and many others.

Some of these terms may be unfamiliar to the reader and the implications of others may not be clear. This ambiguity will most probably apply to the composition of the assets and liabilities of an insurer, the underwriting policy, reinsurance, past profitability, and pricing methods. Pricing methods have been mentioned in the preceding chapter and are developed in detail in Chapter 25, but a brief discussion of the other topics at this point will add to an understanding of insurer solvency.

Liabilities   The principal liabilities of an insurer are claim or loss reserves and premium reserves required by state law. They comprise over 90 per cent of the liabilities of both property and liability insurers and life insurers.

Loss or *claim reserves* must be established because on any given date the insurer has some claims which have been reported but not paid and others which have not even been reported. Reported claims may not have had time to clear the normal channels; they may be doubtful claims; they may have presented unusual problems whose solution is time-consuming; or they may have been settled under an agreement to make payments to the insured or other claimant over a long period of time. Claims may not have been reported because the insured is slow in notifying the insurer or because an agent is tardy in transmitting the insured's notice. Some losses are not even discovered by the insured until some time after they occur.

Insurers use a variety of methods to determine their claim reserves. A discussion of these methods is beyond the scope of this text,[2] but it should be noted that subjective estimates of reserves on individual claims and several averaging techniques are in common use. An analysis of the insurer's annual statement to the state insurance department will reveal

---

[1] Other things being equal, the policyholders' surplus ratio should be greater the smaller the volume of business written, because, on the basis of the law of large numbers, one would expect a smaller volume of business to fluctuate more widely.

[2] For a concise comprehensive discussion, see G. F. Micheibacher and Nestor Roos, *Multiple-line Insurers* (2d ed., New York: McGraw-Hill Book Company, 1970), pp. 182–190.

whether the insurer has been underestimating its claim reserves in the lines where they are most important.[3]

Property losses tend to be reported and settled promptly, but liability claims are often reported late, may take months and even years to settle, and may involve a promise to pay a claimant an income for life. Consequently, the claim reserves of an insurer specializing in property insurance will be relatively unimportant, whereas the claim reserves of a liability insurer will be a major portion of its liabilities. The small claim reserves of a personnel insurer are associated primarily with its health insurance business, its matured annuities,[4] and the life insurance proceeds placed under settlement options.

The second statutory reserve is the *premium reserve*. Property and liability insurers must maintain an unearned premium reserve on each unexpired contract which is equal to the premium on the contract times the fraction of the policy period which has not expired. For example, the unearned premium reserve on December 31 necessitated by a $300 premium one-year contract written on July 1 is $\frac{1}{2}$ ($300), or $150. If the contract had been for three years instead of one year, the unearned premium reserve would have been $\frac{5}{6}$ ($300), or $250. In practice, instead of computing the unearned premium reserve for each contract, it has been customary to assume either that all business written during the year was produced on July 1 or, under a more accurate procedure, that all business written during each month was produced in the middle of that month. The result of the approximation has been that the unearned premium reserve is understated when the insurer's premium volume increases steadily throughout the year and overstated when the premium volume declines. Computers now make it possible for many insurers to compute the unearned premium for each policy and add the results.

It is more important, however, to recognize the hidden equity in this reserve. The pro rata requirement assumes that the insurer should recognize as a liability the amount it would have to pay its insureds if it were to cancel its outstanding contracts on the statement date. The insurer could, however, probably reinsure its entire business with another insurer for considerably less than the unearned premium reserve, because the reinsurer would recognize that most of the expenses other than claims expenses (commissions, underwriting expenses, policy-writing costs) associated with the

---

[3] See Schedule P, parts 5, 5A, and 5B, in the annual-statement blank, which shows how the estimates of incurred losses in the compensation and liability lines have changed in the past as more experience became available. One would expect these periodic estimates to be more stable for the larger, more mature insurers because they have a larger volume of experience on which to base their results.

[4] Reserves on matured annuities and proceeds placed under settlement options are in fact often considered part of the policy reserve (see pp. 467–469 in this section) instead of claim reserves.

business have already been paid.[5] For the same reason, if the insurer continues in business, it could probably meet its future obligations under outstanding contracts with a portion of the unearned premium reserve. As a result, financial analysts generally consider most of the expense portion of the unearned premium reserve (less the Federal income tax liability on this amount) or, for many insurers, about 30 to 40 per cent to be hidden surplus which should be added to the policyholders' surplus in evaluating the solvency of an insurer.[6]

This same reasoning explains why an insurer that is increasing its premium volume at a rapid pace often appears to have a decreasing surplus account. The surplus is being absorbed by the increasing unearned premium reserve, and the insurer is considered to be approaching what is termed a "capacity" problem.[7] Thus the unearned premium reserve does not correctly measure the liability of the insurer for future losses, but it errs on the conservative side, and no generally acceptable alternative has been proposed. Moreover, the redundancy does not pose a major problem for the large insurers, whose relative growth tends to be less.

In the past, unearned premium reserves were very important liability items for insurers writing primarily fire and marine insurance because a large portion of the business was written for terms of three or five years. The introduction of installment-payment plans has reduced the importance of the premium reserve. Premium reserves are a less important item for liability insurers because the policy terms are generally short; much of the premium is payable on an audited basis, which means that it is earned when paid; and the claim reserve item is much larger.

The premium reserve for life insurers is called the "policy reserve." This reserve may be calculated according to the net level premium reserve method or by one of the "modified" reserve methods. The net level premium reserve, which is the most conservative measure, is the difference between the present value (based on certain interest and mortality assumptions) of the obligations assumed by the insurer under the outstanding contracts less the present value of the net premiums (premiums less the expense allowance included in the premium) to be paid under those contracts.

To illustrate the net level reserve method, assume that 10 years ago an insurer issued $1,000 straight life insurance contracts to each of a

---

[5] Even if the contract were canceled, the agent would be expected to return a pro rata portion of his commission to the insurer. Hence, even under these circumstances the pro rata portion of the premiums exceeds the needs.
[6] Other sources of redundancy are (1) the duplication of the reserve for premium taxes with the unearned premium reserve and (2) the disallowance of certain uncollected premiums as assets while including the unearned portion of these premiums in the reserve.
[7] For a measurement of the risk-bearing capacity of United States insurers and an analysis of many possible reasons why these insurers operate at much less than this capacity, see Ingolf Otto, "Capacity," *Journal of Insurance*, XXVIII, No. 1 (March, 1961), 53–70.

group of males, aged 35, assuming a 3 per cent interest return and the 1958 Commissioners Standard Ordinary Mortality Table.[8] The lump-sum value of the insurer's obligation to each surviving policyholder under the outstanding contracts is about $459. This is the net price that a person, aged 45, would have to pay for the same protection if he were to buy now into the group. The lump-sum value of the remaining premiums to be paid under these outstanding contracts is about $303 per contract. Thus the reserve per contract is about $156. At the issue date, the reserve was zero because the two present values were the same, namely, $359. Twenty years after the issue date, the reserve would be $573 — $239, or $334. Because no one was expected to live beyond age 100 under the 1958 CSO table, the reserve 65 years after the issue date would be $1,000 — 0, or $1,000.

If the insurer were to cease issuing new contracts, the net premium income from the contracts in force plus a lump sum equal to this policy reserve would, if the mortality and interest assumptions were correct, enable the insurer to meet exactly its obligations as they came due.

Note that this concept is far more complicated than the unearned premium reserve. The complication is introduced because mortality rates increase over time, while the usual life insurance contract is a long-term obligation purchased by a level premium.[9]

The explanation of the reserve presented above is in prospective terms. An alternative explanation in retrospective terms may be easier to understand. Under the retrospective method, the reserve is that portion of the net premiums plus assumed interest which remains after the insured's share of the assumed death claims has been paid. If the same mortality and interest assumptions are made, the reserve produced in this way is exactly the same as the one produced by the prospective method. Except for the treatment of expenses, this explanation of the reserve is the same as the explanation of the cash value presented in Chapter 19. It should be remembered, however, that the two concepts serve entirely different purposes. The reserve is a measure of how much the insurer should have on hand to meet its obligations in the future; if the mortality assumptions are over-optimistic, the correction that is needed is an increase or strengthening of the reserves. The cash value, on the other hand, results from the excess premiums paid by the insureds during the early years of their contracts; if the mortality assumptions underestimate the death rates, the insurer cannot reduce its contractual cash values, but it will wish that it could do so.

---

[8] States prescribe the basis upon which minimum reserves are to be computed. See below and in Chap. 25.

[9] Unearned premium reserves are established for one-year term life insurance contracts.

The net level premium reserve method is a conservative approach for essentially the same reason that the unearned premium reserve is redundant. The expense loading in the premiums is ignored in the computation, on the assumption that the expenses will be incurred as the expense loadings are received. Actually, the insurer will incur most of its expenses the first year, and if the full net level premium reserve is to be maintained, the insurer will have to reduce its surplus position. In future years, the expense allowances will exceed the expenses incurred, and the surplus withdrawn because of that contract will gradually be replaced. Unlike their treatment of property and liability insurance, however, state authorities have recognized this problem and permit insurers to use one of several modified reserve systems instead of the net level premium reserve method. A description of these systems is beyond the scope of this text,[10] but in effect they work on the assumption that the net premium is less than the actual net premium in the first year and greater in later years. The present value of the modified premiums must, however, equal the present value of the actual net premiums. As a result of the modification, the reserve at the end of the first year is less than the net level premium reserve, but it grows more rapidly after that date until at some point, which varies among the different methods, the modified reserve equals the net level premium reserve.[11] Insurers tend to be more conservative than the law requires in their application of these modifications.

Interest and mortality assumptions also affect the reserves. The lower the interest rate and in most cases the more rapid the increase in mortality rates with age, the higher the reserves. The usual assumptions are 3 per cent interest and the 1958 Commissioners Standard Ordinary Table.

Health insurance premium reserves are primarily unearned premium reserves, but the premium reserves on noncancelable and guaranteed renewable contracts are based upon the same principles as the policy reserves of life insurers.

Other liability reserves in addition to claim reserves and premium reserves include reserves for taxes, reserves for dividends voted to policyholders and stockholders, reserves for dividend accumulations (life insurance only), and reserves for other expenses incurred but not paid. Since 1951, life insurers have also been required by state law to maintain a specified security valuation reserve to provide for possible future losses in the values of stocks and bonds. Contingency reserves or earmarked surpluses include such items as voluntary reserves for fluctuations in securities or loss experience.

---

[10] See any standard life insurance text.
[11] The modified reserves are thus closer to the actual cash values than is the net level premium reserve, but the legal minimum reserves do exceed the legal minimum cash values during the early years.

Assets   Primarily because of the time lags which compel insurers to establish claim reserves and premium reserves, because of stockholder contributions to capital and surplus, and because of retained earnings, insurers
have sizable assets. At the close of 1969, the assets of life insurers totaled
over $197 billion, while property and liability insurers controlled assets of
about $51 billion.

Both types of insurers keep most of these assets invested in order
to cut the cost of the insurance to policyholders, increase dividends to
stockholders, or accomplish both of these objectives. The importance of
the investment return in property-liability insurance is emphasized by the
fact that during 1968, while approximately 820 leading stock property-liability insurers reported an (unadjusted for the hidden profit in the increase
in the unearned premium reserve[12]) underwriting loss of about $200,000
on premiums of $17 billion, they had an investment profit of over $2
billion. Net investment profit includes realized and unrealized capital
gains. Net investment income (not including realized or unrealized capital
gains and less investment expenses) was about $1.2 billion. During the same
period, net investment income was responsible for about 21 per cent of
the total income of United States life insurers. The portfolios of the property-
liability insurers and the life insurers differ, however, because of basic differences in the insurance products they market.

Property and liability insurers issue for the most part short-term contracts; their benefits tend to vary with the price-level indices; they are subject
to catastrophe losses; and they do not consider directly the return on their
investments in their pricing procedures. Consequently, in addition to the
obvious requirement that investments should be of high quality and secure,
the investment portfolio should provide liquidity and some opportunity for
appreciation during periods of inflation. Although investment return does
not enter into the rate-making formulas directly, a satisfactory yield is desirable for competitive purposes and for the benefit of the stockholders,
if any. Stockholder dividends are in fact usually limited to part of the investment earnings, these earnings being much more stable than the underwriting
profit.

An investigation of the actual portfolios will illustrate the application
of these principles. On the average, about one-half of the assets are invested
in bonds, United States government bonds accounting for about one-fifth
of this type of investment. Common stocks in well-known corporations with
a ready market account for another one-third of the assets. There are some
significant differences among individual insurers, however. Some insurers
consider the insurance business itself to be risky enough and place more
of their money in government bonds. Most mutual insurers fall into this

---

[12] See pp. 466–467. In 1969 these insurers suffered both an underwriting loss and an
investment loss.

group. Other insurers are more impressed by the threat of inflation and as a result invest more heavily in common stock. Some insurers are specialists in particular classes of securities such as municipal bonds.

Life insurers, on the other hand, issue long-term fixed-amount obligations, are seldom faced with a catastrophe, and use an assumed interest rate in their premium, reserve, and cash value computations. Hence in addition to security, their investment portfolios must emphasize stability and yield. Liquidity is of minor importance. A yield equal to at least the assumed rate of return is vital if the insurer is to continue its operations.

About one-half of the assets of life insurers is invested in bonds, but because of their relatively low rate of return, government bonds account for less than one-fifth of the bond total. The second most important type of investment is mortgages, which make up about 35 per cent of the total assets. Both the bonds and the mortgages are usually long-term commitments. Stocks, real estate, and policy loans each amount to only about 3 to 5 per cent of the assets, but interest in stocks and real estate is increasing. Because of more severe investment restrictions imposed by state laws and because of more general agreement on the best composition of the portfolio, the assets of one life insurer are more likely to resemble the assets of another than do the assets of property and liability insurers, but there are still some considerable variations, particularly with respect to the relative importance of bonds versus mortgages.

The valuation of the more important assets by all types of insurers is also important. Bonds that are amply secured and not in default as to interest or principal are carried at their amortized value. For bonds purchased at more than their par value, this means that their value decreases from the purchase price to the par value at the maturity date. The value increases when the bond is purchased at a discount. In either event the values are independent of market fluctuations, on the assumption that the bonds will be held to maturity. Mortgages, if properly secured, are set equal to the amount loaned. Stocks are valued according to "convention values" prepared by a committee of the National Association of Insurance Commissioners. For the most part, these are the market values on the preceding December 31. Certain assets, such as the home office building, are usually valued at nominal amounts.[13]

Underwriting   The underwriting policy of the insurer determines the kinds of insurance it will write, the provisions it will use in its contracts, the

---

[13] During the Great Depression (1931–1934) and on several occasions between 1907 and 1922, the NAIC established values in excess of the market value on the ground that the market values were temporarily depressed below their real worth.
Because a market value does not exist for some stocks, a special formula must be employed.

pricing system it will apply, the persons it will insure, and the amounts of insurance it will issue to individual insureds or in particular areas. Initiation of policy decisions with respect to the kinds of insurance to be written is likely to come from top management, but the other policy decisions are likely to originate in the underwriting department of the insurer or in two or more departments including the underwriting department. The implementation of the policy decisions is usually the function of the underwriters.

The variety in the kinds of insurance written has already been noted, the range extending from the insurer writing only one kind of insurance, say, automobile insurance, to the insurer that writes all kinds of insurance except a few highly specialized lines. Because some lines of insurance are more profitable and stable than others and because several accounting ratios such as the ratio of losses incurred to premiums earned depend to a large extent upon the mix of business written, the types of insurance issued must be considered in evaluating the solvency of the firm.[14]

The contract provisions describe the product which the insurer is selling, and care must be taken not to expose the insurer to losses not anticipated in the price through contract provisions which are ambiguous or over-generous or which enable the insured to wait until a loss is fairly certain before he purchases the contract. The contracts should encourage the insured to prevent losses and to minimize those which do occur. As we have noted elsewhere, many[15] property and liability insurance contracts are drafted by rating bureaus.

The pricing system to be used is extremely important and is related to the types of insureds to be covered.[16] Some insurers are very selective and operate with low average rates, while others are interested in all grades of insureds. Still others solicit only the less desirable kinds of insureds. The pricing systems of some insurers permit them to discriminate greatly among insureds, whereas others have only a few prices which they apply to broad classes of insureds. The prices in most instances are determined by the actuarial department of the insurer or by property and liability insurance rating bureaus, but the underwriters are usually consulted in connection with the actuarial decision, they apply the rating system to insureds or check the application of the rates by producers, and they actually make the rates in situations which are not covered by the rating system.[17]

Once the rating system has been established, the underwriting department must determine the policies that are to be followed in selecting those persons they are willing to insure and on what terms. Their objective is

---

[14] In fire insurance, for example, the losses incurred are usually over 50 per cent of the premiums earned, while the same ratio for fidelity and surety bonding is often under 40 per cent.
[15] See p. 250.
[16] Since pricing methods are described in Chap. 25, this discussion will be brief.
[17] For example, fire insurance on snow fences is usually priced in this way.

to select insureds consistent with their pricing system. Some selection is necessary because if the insurer were to accept every applicant, the persons who would be most likely to seek insurance would be those normally uninsurable at any price or else insurable but only at a higher price than is provided under the rating system. In addition, all insureds would seek the lowest price under the rating system. Selection against the insurer in this way is referred to as *adverse selection*. In practice, the insurer cannot avoid underpricing the insurance protection for some insureds, but in the interest of equity to its policyholders and its own continued solvency, it should seek to minimize this problem. On the other hand, it cannot be so selective that it insures only a small number of persons, because in that event its experience will be unstable.

The underwriting department accomplishes its objectives first through instructions to agents and through their cooperation. This approach is of particular importance to the insurer in property and liability insurance, where the producer normally has the authority to bind the insurer. These instructions will usually specify (1) those persons considered so undesirable that the producer should not even solicit their business, (2) questionable insureds concerning whom the producer should communicate with the underwriting department, and (3) those prospective insureds whom a producer is encouraged to solicit. The list differs among insurers. The cooperation of the producer is essential because there are always persons in the acceptable class who are clearly not acceptable on the basis of information available to the producer.

If the producer does not have binding authority with respect to the contract, the underwriting department has the opportunity to pass on the application before the insurance goes into effect. Where binding power exists, the underwriting department has this chance only with respect to renewals which are reviewed in advance of the binding date. As a result of its investigation, the underwriting department may accept the application, reject it, or make an alternative offer. The alternative offer may take the form of an entirely different contract (e.g., a twenty-year endowment contract for a twenty-year term insurance contract), some modification in the contract provisions (e.g., an exclusion of disability claims arising out of some preexisting condition), or an increased premium.

If the producer has already bound the insurer with respect to the contract, the underwriter can at most cancel the contract in accordance with the policy provisions. The cancellation may be accompanied by an alternative offer. Because cancellation, however, is unpleasant for the insurer and the insured and is a source of poor public relations, the underwriter is more likely, except in extreme cases, to give advance notice of its intention not to renew the contract.

Underwriters rely upon several sources in their investigation. First, information is provided by the prospective insured and the producer. Second, sources of information are available in the offices of the underwriting department. For example, most life insurers belong to the Medical Information Bureau. These insurers must report to the bureau all applicants for insurance with an impairment named on an official list. This information is considered highly confidential, and impairments are reported in code. The bureau disseminates the information it receives to member insurers. Insurers also cooperate for the exchange of information concerning suspicious fires. Financial ratings of insureds can be checked in various reporting services. Fire exposures can be checked by consulting the inspection report completed for schedule rating purposes and by detailed area maps which, through a coding system, give an experienced underwriter a mental picture of the construction, occupancy, protection, and exposure features of the property. On renewal business, the underwriter can analyze past experience. Supplementary information may also have been provided or may be available in the claim department, the department which audits the insured's books for pricing purposes, or in the engineering or inspection department which has been providing loss-prevention services. In addition to the information provided by these two sources, the underwriter can also gather additional information on his own initiative. In personnel insurance, for example, a medical examiner's report may be required. In all lines of insurance, the insurer's own inspection department or, as is more likely, an independent agency may be asked to prepare a confidential report on the applicant. Although the content of these reports varies among lines of insurance, all are designed to answer questions that the underwriter considers important. In fire insurance, for example, the report gives the applicant's net worth, age, racial descent, line of business, reputation, and other characteristics as well as a description of the premises and the neighborhood. The information is obtained from business acquaintances, neighbors, and other persons (in some cases including the applicant himself) and from files based on previous reports, newspaper clippings, and court and government records. Personnel insurers make more extensive use of these reports than do property and liability insurers.

Reinsurance   In addition to selecting insureds whose quality is consistent with the insurer's pricing system, the underwriter must avoid exposing the insurer to excessive losses caused by any one event. Otherwise the uncertainty for the insurer is great, and its financial solvency may be jeopardized. Excessive losses can result because the protection issued to one insured is too great or because many insureds are affected by the same event.

The maximum loss the insurer believes it can safely absorb is called the "line," "net line," "line limit," or "retention." This retention varies with the size of the insurer, its financial condition, its management philosophy, the characteristics of the exposure under consideration (death of a person, fire damage to a frame building, or workmen's compensation claims from a single accident), and other factors. Setting a high retention exposes the insurer to more risk; setting a low retention may deprive the insurer of some highly desirable business.

Underwriters can attack this problem in part by refusing to write insurance for amounts in excess of their retentions. They may, for example, refuse to write life insurance on an applicant in excess of $100,000, automobile bodily injury liability insurance policy limits in excess of $25,000 per person and $50,000 per accident, or fire insurance with respect to properties in a city block if the property is adjacent to one that is already insured or if the total insurance on properties in the block will exceed $500,000.

This approach will not, however, prevent catastrophe losses from occurring when a large number of small exposures covering a broad area are damaged by a single event such as a hurricane. It will also fail when the exposures are mobile and happen to be concentrated at the same spot when an accident occurs. For example, a ferry may sink, taking down with it 100 automobiles, most of which are insured by the same insurer. A third possibility is that the insurer may write several kinds of insurance and that the aggregate loss under the several different kinds of insurance in a single event may be substantial. Finally, although no single event may be troublesome, the losses for the year may be excessive.

To the enumeration of these unsolved problems we might add that it is not good business to refuse to write insurance in excess of the retention amount. Imagine the displeasure of the applicant and particularly of the producer when the application is rejected or accepted in part! For these reasons and others to be noted later, insurers commonly insure that portion of their liability under their contracts in excess of their retention with one or more insurers. This process is called *reinsurance*, the originating insurer the ceding insurer (and sometimes the direct writer—a term which has already been used in a different connotation), and the accepting insurer the reinsurer. An alternative approach which is less often used is to issue a joint policy with one or more other insurers. Some examples of this latter practice were presented in Chapter 23.

Reinsurance may be arranged in many ways. At one extreme there is facultative reinsurance, which is arranged on a particular exposure after the problem has arisen. The advantages of this approach are the opportunities for tailor-made protection and for underwriting advice from the reinsurer. The disadvantages are the delay, the possible failure to obtain coverage, and the administrative expenses involved. At the other extreme is the automatic treaty, under which the ceding insurer agrees to pass on to the reinsurer all business included within the scope of the treaty, the reinsurer agrees to accept this business, and the terms—e.g., the premium rates and the method of sharing the insurance and the losses—of the agreement are set. The advantages and disadvantages are the counterparts of those cited for facultative reinsurance. An example of an arrangement between these two extremes is the facultative treaty, under which the terms are set but neither the ceding insurer nor the reinsurer is obligated to participate in the arrangement with respect to any particular business.

The reinsurer may be another insurer whose major business interest also is dealing directly with the public. Some insurers of this type have very active reinsurance departments which aggressively seek business from other insurers, but most are reinsurers only because many reinsurance agreements obligate the ceding insurer to reinsure some of the liability assumed by the reinsurer under its direct business. The second type of reinsurer is a pool which may or may not include the ceding insurer. These associations were discussed in Chapter 23. Finally, the reinsurer may be engaged exclusively in the reinsurance business.

In 1968 United States insurers paid almost $408 million for reinsurance protection to foreign insurers, most of whom were located in the United Kingdom. Lloyd's of London was a principal reinsurer. On the other hand, United States reinsurers received only about $171 billion on reinsurance assumed from abroad. Since 1961, however, the premiums paid have increased only 43 per cent, while the premiums received have increased almost 176 per cent.[18] Moreover, United States insurers purchase the bulk of their reinsurance protection in the domestic market.

Reinsurance arrangements may distribute the insurance and the losses in many different ways. Four of these distribution methods will be described for illustrative purposes: (1) Under a *quota-share* split, the insurance and the loss are shared according to some preagreed percentage. For example, if a $100,000 policy is written and the agreed split is 50–50, the reinsurer assumes one-half of the liability; the insurer and the reinsurer each pay one-half of any loss. (2) Under a *surplus-share* agreement, the reinsurer accepts that amount of the insurance in excess of a stated amount, and the loss is prorated according to the amount of insurance assumed. For example, if $50,000 is the stated amount, the liability under a $100,000 policy would be split in the same way as under the previous arrangement, but under a $50,000 contract the reinsurer would accept no liability. (3) Under an *excess-loss* arrangement, the reinsurer agrees to pay that portion of the loss incurred under an individual contract in excess of some

---

[18] "Record '68 Payment on Reinsurance Activities Abroad," *The National Underwriter* (December 5, 1969), p. 4.

specified amount, such as $50,000. (4) *Catastrophe* reinsurance, like ex-cess-loss reinsurance, requires the reinsurer to pay excess losses, but in this instance the losses are those incurred by the insurer as a result of single event under all contracts covered under the agreement. For example, the reinsurer might be obligated to pay that portion in excess of $250,000 of the losses incurred (less losses reinsured in other ways) as a result of a hurricane.

Variations are possible under all these methods. For example, the re-insurer may accept only part of the excess insurance under the surplus-share arrangement or pay only part of the excess loss under the excess-loss method. In life insurance, the reinsurance agreement may apply only to the decreasing pure protection portion of nonterm insurance policies and not to the savings or investment element. In all lines and under all arrange-ments, the insurer may limit the maximum amount it wishes to reinsure.

It is clear that not all these methods of distributing insurance and losses provide the same protection or have the same effect on the balance sheet. Under the first two methods, for example, a pro rata proportion of the premium less a commission for originating the business is transferred to the reinsurer. The unearned premium reserve on that premium is also transferred,[19] and through the commission the equity in the unearned pre-mium reserve is released. Some insurers, especially new and rapidly growing insurers, use these two methods for this very reason.

Other uses of reinsurance are to retire completely or in part (in an area or a line of business, for example) from the insurance business, to transfer insurance from one member of a fleet to another, and to obtain advice from an outsider (the reinsurer) with respect to a particular insured or a new line of business. The major contribution of reinsurance to insurer solvency, however, is the more widespread distribution of risk it makes possible.

Past profitability   For property and liability insurers annual increases in retained earnings depend upon (1) underwriting profit, (2) net investment income (dividends, interest, and rents), (3) realized capital gains, (4) un-realized capital gains, (5) dividends to policyholders, (6) income taxes, and (7) dividends to stockholders. Statutory underwriting profit, which is the official measure required under state regulation, is determined by subtracting from the premiums earned the losses and expenses incurred. Many analysts believe that when an insurer's premium volume is increasing (decreasing), statutory underwriting profit understates (overstates) the "true" profit be-cause it ignores the hidden profit in the increase in the unearned premium

[19] Unless the reinsurer is not an authorized reinsurer under state law.

reserve.[20] Consequently they would add to (subtract from) the statutory profit some (commonly 30 to 40) per cent of the increase (decrease) in the unearned premium reserve less the additional (reduced) income taxes that this would create.

Another adjusted measure of underwriting profit would add (1) the loss ratio (losses incurred divided by premiums earned) to (2) the expense ratio (expenses incurred divided by premiums written). Premiums written exceed premiums earned when the premium volume is increasing because the insurer receives many premiums in a year that will be only partially earned that year. Because insurers incur most of their expenses in the first month a contract is in force, their expenses tend to be more closely related to premiums written than to premiums earned. Hence it is considered more appropriate to use premiums written in calculating expense ratios. If the combined loss and expense ratio is less than 100 per cent, the insurer's underwriting has been profitable. Otherwise, it has not.

Profit, of course, should be related to some base such as net worth, and the variation in annual profit rates as well as the average level should be considered in analyzing profitability.[21]

Unlike property and liability insurers, life insurers do not distinguish between their underwriting profit and their net investment profit. Their increases in retained earnings depend upon (1) their net gain from operations, (2) dividends to policyholders, (3) income taxes, (4) net realized and unrealized capital gains, and (5) dividends to stockholders. Net gain from operations is determined by subtracting from income (principally premiums and net investment income consisting of interest, dividends, and rents) benefit payments, increases in policy reserves, and operating expenses and taxes. The use of modified reserves, mentioned earlier on page 469, partially corrects for the disparity between the timing of expenses and the uniform expense loading in each annual premium.

Security comparisons among types of insurers   Now that we have explained the principal factors affecting solvency, we turn to a comparison of the different types of insurers with respect to the many variables affecting solvency. In this exceedingly difficult task a few statements are possible.

[20] See earlier, on pp. 466–467.

[21] The profit levels of property and liability insurers have been a major topic of research in recent years. According to a report prepared by Arthur D. Little, Inc., for the National Association of Independent Insurers the total industry average rate of return (measured by the net income including unrealized capital gains divided by total investable funds) for 1955–1967 was 3.6 per cent. Related to policyholders' surplus, the average rate of return was 8.4 per cent. The report argues that, considering the risk associated with these returns, they were not excessive. For one of several critical reviews, see J. D. Hammond and N. Shilling, "The Little Report on Prices and Profits in the Property and Liability Insurance Industry," *Journal of Risk and Insurance*, XXXVI, No. 1 (March, 1969), 129–145.

First, stock and advance premium mutual life insurers are so similar in their methods of operation that one type is probably no more financially sound than the other.[22]

Second, according to Table 24.1, at the close of 1969, 829 stock property and liability insurers reported a policyholders' surplus ratio (policyholders' surplus divided by total liabilities) of 0.50 while 324 advance premium mutuals indicated a ratio of 0.37. The variation among individual insurers was great.[23]

[22] Mutual insurers which set their initial premiums very high in order to return a sizable dividend have a safety factor built into their premiums which is not available to stock nonparticipating insurers, but the chance that this cushion will be needed is extremely small. On the other hand, stock insurers have an additional cushion in their capital stock, but this too in most instances is relatively unimportant.

[23] Because of the variety of ways in which insurers establish their estimates of total liabilities, Roger Kenney has suggested that if the objectively computed unearned premium reserve is the major liability item (this would be true in property insurance), a more satisfactory measure of solvency is the ratio of the policyholders' surplus to the unearned premium reserve. He believes that this ratio should be at least 1:1 (i.e., policyholders' surplus = unearned premium reserve) unless certain other factors (conservative investments, stable underwriting experience, etc.) suggest a lower standard. If loss reserves, which are less reliable estimates, dominate the liability items, he favors computing the ratio of the premiums written to the policyholders' surplus. Subject to certain exceptions, he suggests a ratio of no more than 2:1. See Roger Kenney, *Fundamentals of Fire and Casualty Insurance Strength* (4th ed., Dedham, Mass.: The Kenney Insurance Studies, 1967). For a critical analysis of the Kenney Ratios, see the book review by A. E. Hofflander in the *Journal of Risk and Insurance*, XXXV, No. 3 (September, 1968), 437–439.

Table 24.1 Stock and mutual property and liability insurer policyholders' surplus ratios, loss ratios, expense ratios, and adjusted underwriting profits, 1960–1969

Year	Policyholders' surplus ratio		Loss ratio*		Expense ratio†		Adjusted underwriting profit‡	
	Stocks	Mutuals	Stocks	Mutuals	Stocks	Mutuals	Stocks	Mutuals
1960	71%	48%	63.6%	64.2%	34.8%	25.6%	1.6%	10.2%
1961	85	53	64.4	63.6	35.0	25.6	0.6	10.8
1962	76	54	64.5	66.7	34.5	25.7	1.0	7.6
1963	82	50	66.3	71.4	34.7	26.5	−1.0	2.1
1964	84	49	68.0	73.4	33.9	25.9	−1.9	0.7
1965	77	47	69.2	73.1	32.7	25.0	−1.9	1.9
1966	63	44	66.1	70.9	31.9	24.2	2.0	4.9
1967	66	44	67.2	72.7	31.7	24.5	1.1	2.7
1968	65	43	68.8	74.4	31.2	24.6	0.0	1.0
1969	50	37	70.3	76.5	30.3	24.1	−0.6	−0.6

* Loss ratio = Losses incurred/Premiums earned
† Expense ratio = Expenses incurred/Premiums written
‡ Adjusted underwriting profit = 1 − Loss ratio − Expense ratio

Source: Best's Aggregates and Averages, 1970, pp. 1, 142, 213.

Moreover, the ratios vary over time, the average stock and mutual ratios moving closer together when the stock market declines because stock insurers invest more heavily in equities.

Mutual insurers report higher adjusted underwriting profits than stock insurers because many mutuals charge premiums close to or equal to those charged by many stock insurers and are able to return a dividend because of more selective underwriting or lower expense ratios. The effect of investment income on profits has already been noted earlier in this chapter under "Assets."[24]

Third, in analyzing other types of insurers we must consider special characteristics. The policies of assessment mutuals and many reciprocals are assessable, and this assessment right constitutes at the same time a source of strength and of concern. Assessments are less likely, however, when the policyholders' surplus ratio is at a satisfactory level. The evaluation of a Lloyds Association would require an investigation into the financial liability and the financial strength of each underwriter. The financial strength of Lloyd's of London, according to this criterion, is beyond question. Finally, many government insurers, such as the Social Security Administration with respect to Old Age, Survivors, Disability, and Health Insurance, are the only suppliers of a certain type of insurance that is compulsory for some persons. Consequently, they may conduct their business affairs on the assumption that larger revenues in the future will correct any current deficiencies. In some instances, however, the government insurer is supposed to be self-supporting and competitive. Nevertheless it is doubtful that the sponsoring government would ever fail to appropriate funds in case of a financial catastrophe. Most government insurers also have the advantage of a large number of exposures widely distributed.

No type of insurer can claim to be clearly superior to the others in terms of its financial strength. If any superiority exists, it must probably be conceded to government insurers because of their special characteristics. On the other hand, there are many differences among individual insurers with respect to financial strength, and these must be carefully investigated. Even experts make mistakes on these analyses, but often investigation shows that one insurer is financially sounder than another.

SERVICE

Service is an intangible factor and one which it is difficult to define. Service is generally considered to include (1) assistance in the recognition and evaluation of risks, (2) the provision of insurance contracts which meet the specific needs of the insured, (3) aid in loss prevention and reduction,

[24] For current data, see the most recent issue of *Best's Aggregates and Averages*.

(4) a "fair" attitude toward cancellations, and (5) promptness and fairness in the settlement of claims. It may also include the extension of short-term credit with respect to the premiums. The need and desire for these services differs among insureds, and the ability and willingness (as expressed through its underwriting policies) of insurers to service a particular insured also varies. In property and liability insurance, the insurer's ability and desire to service the insured depends upon such factors as the insured's industry, location, quality of exposure, complexity of operations, and desire for unusual coverages or limits. In personnel insurance, illustrative factors are occupation, location, state of health, economic status, family status, investment opportunities, and the amount and type of coverage sought.

Evaluation of the types of insurers in terms of the service they render is even more difficult than their evaluation according to financial strength because all the judgments must be qualitative. Again, however, certain statements are possible.

First, stock and mutual life insurers must be rated on a par with respect to service because of the similarity of their contracts, claims procedures, support of medical research and distribution of medical information, and loss-adjustment procedures.

Second, stock and mutual property and liability insurers both claim superiority with respect to loss prevention. Both have a record of substantial activity at the association and individual-insurer level, and quantitative evaluation of their relative merits is impossible. Only in workmen's compensation is there any objective information with respect to promptness of claims handling, and this evidence indicates that neither type of insurer is superior to the other. With respect to assistance from the producer regarding risk analysis, design of the insurance program, and aid in presenting claims, it is generally agreed that the distinction between direct writing and agency insurers is more important than the difference between stock and mutual insurers. Both stock and advance premium mutual insurers usually operate through agents, but among the largest mutuals the direct writing system is more important. Other things being equal, the agency system is considered by many to result in superior service because of the independence of action, the smaller number of customers served, the greater emphasis upon continued service, and the attraction of higher-quality personnel. Other things are seldom equal, however, and this generalization is subject to numerous exceptions. Even the generalization is by no means universally accepted. On one point, the stocks do have a clear superiority. Their insurance offerings are more varied, and they write practically all coverages. For confirmation of this point, see Table 23.2. There is also some evidence to indicate that they may be more liberal in their underwriting standards. This greater liberality may result in less stringent initial underwriting, fewer cancellations, or both.

Third, with respect to the other insurers, several brief observations should be made. Assessment mutuals are generally close to their insureds and render personal service, but their contract offerings are limited, often by statute.[25] With some notable exceptions, reciprocals and Lloyds Associations apparently stress service less than stock and mutual insurers and operate in narrower fields. Lloyd's of London is noted particularly for its willingness to write unusual contracts that cannot be obtained elsewhere. Risk managers for large firms often turn to Lloyd's and other nonadmitted insurers for protection not available through usual channels. Government insurers are often accused of excessive red tape and delay in claims handling, but this is a debatable point. Some state workmen's compensation funds provide little or no loss-prevention services; others are slow-paying claims. On the other hand the service record of some state funds is excellent. Their only major limitation is that they cannot provide multiple line or interstate coverages.

COST

The cost of the insurance protection is an obvious basic consideration. In our discussion *cost* refers to the initial premiums paid to the insurer less any returns because of dividends or rate adjustments. In this sense, cost is measurable, and its apparent objectivity is one reason why undue emphasis is often placed upon this factor. Cost is not always measurable *in advance,* however, and the inability to foresee complicates the decision. Furthermore, relative costs should always be balanced against relative services. Financial strength, of course, should never be compromised.

In personnel insurance, the distinction between stock and mutual insurers is not nearly so important as the distinction between participating and nonparticipating insurers. The dividends paid to stockholders are a relatively insignificant cost element, the major factors being the mortality, investment, and expense experience.[26] Participating insurers charge more than nonparticipating insurers for the same coverage but return a dividend on the basis of their actual experience.[27] The dividends may or may not be sufficient to offset the additional premium. There is no inherent reason why the dividends should be more or less sufficient, but historically the nonparticipating insurers have on the average and at most times proved to be

[25] For example, in Minnesota, township mutuals until recently could write only fire, theft, and additional lines (extended coverage less windstorm) in a package.

[26] In 1969, stockholder dividends amounted to 1.5 per cent of the premium income of life insurers. Since 3.9 per cent of the life insurance in force was nonparticipating, stockholder dividends amounted to roughly 4 per cent of the premiums paid for nonparticipating insurance. This analysis ignores profits which are not distributed to policyholders. It also ignores investment income, which accounts for about 22 per cent of the total income of life insurers.

[27] Additional expenses introduced by this procedure include extra commissions (if the commission rate is unchanged) and the costs of determining and distributing the dividends.

too conservative in their estimates. Whether this ultraconservatism will be true in the future is an open question. In short, the difference in costs under the two procedures cannot be determined in advance.[28] The choice is largely a matter of the insured's estimates regarding the future in relation to the nonparticipating insurer's estimates and any value he assigns to the possible uses of dividends.

In practice, the projected annual "net cost" of a life insurance policy is often computed in the following way: First, add up the premiums for the period over which the net cost is to be determined. This period is usually 20 years. Second, subtract the projected dividends, if any, from the premiums. Third, subtract the cash value at the end of the period. Fourth, divide the result of the first three steps by the number of years in the period. To illustrate, if a nonparticipating straight life insurance policy requires an annual premium payment of $22 and provides a cash value of $335 at the end of 20 years, the 20-year annual net cost, according to this method, is [20 ($22) − $335]/20, or $5.25. This method has been severely criticized. Two major defects are (1) the emphasis upon 20-year annual net costs, there being no reason why the cost over a 20-year period should be more important than the cost over some other period, and (2) the failure to recognize the loss of possible interest returns on the premiums paid. The importance of this second factor is obvious when this method yields a negative cost.

Net cost calculations of this sort have also been used to compare insurers with respect to cost. The comparisons are of limited value because (1) the contracts may differ in their degree of liberality (for example, the settlement options may be more liberal in the contract with the higher net cost), (2) the ranking of two insurers may change depending upon the type of policy, age, and the period for which the net cost is guaranteed, and (3) ignoring interest rates may favor one insurer over another.

A more satisfactory way to compare the costs of two or more life insurance contracts is to calculate the respective rates of return as described earlier in Chapter 19 on pages 352 to 354.

In property and liability insurance it is possible to make some definite statements regarding relative average costs. The average advance premium mutual insurer charges lower initial premium rates than the average stock insurer or charges the same premiums and pays a dividend. The mutual

[28] Insureds who die during the early years of their contracts will almost always pay less under nonpar contracts because dividends under par contracts during these years are generally small.
[29] For more information on costs, see J. M. Belth, *The Retail Price Structure in American Life Insurance* (Bloomington, Ind.: Bureau of Business Research, Graduate School of Business, Indiana University, 1966).
   See also Price Gains, Jr., *Cost Facts on Life Insurance* (Cincinnati: The National Underwriter Co., 1969), which compares the costs of contracts issued by leading life insurers on several bases.

contract may be assessable, in which case the cost may exceed the stock premium, but an assessment by an advance premium mutual is a rare event. Consequently, the average stock insurer charges more for a specific contract than does the average advance premium mutual. Some of the difference in cost may be attributable to more selective underwriting by the mutuals, but the major reason is the difference in acquisition costs. Table 24.1 provides some insight into the relative importance of these two factors, but the stock and mutual ratios are not strictly comparable because these two types of insurers charge different average premiums. Differences in service and financial strength, it has been shown, are difficult to evaluate. The difference in acquisition costs is decreasing, however; a marked reduction occurred in the late 1950s and the 1960s, when several leading stock insurers cut their commission rates. Moreover, the variation in costs among the insurers of each type is sizable.

Assessment mutuals are low-cost operations; the expenses are generally held to a minimum, and the insureds are of high quality and have a more personal relationship to the insurer. The cost, however, is indefinite. Reciprocals also tend to be low-cost insurers because they often deal directly with the subscribers and are selective in their underwriting. Their contracts may be assessable, but this option is seldom exercised and may not even appear in the contract. Lloyds Associations charge a definite premium, and their expenses of operation also tend to be low. Lloyd's of London, however, is relatively expensive. Finally, government insurers are characterized by low administrative expenses and the absence, in most instances, of acquisition costs. These observations apply with special force to monopoly insurers. The maximum cost for a given period is also definite, but some government insurers return dividends to policyholders. In comparing the costs of private and public insurers, however, one must recognize that the government may be assuming some of the costs, providing some of the services, or exempting the insurer from certain taxes. Moreover, the state insurers tend to restrict their activities to lines of insurance which are relatively inexpensive to administer.

SOURCES OF INFORMATION

Several sources are available to the insured who wishes information concerning an insurer's financial strength, service, and cost.

Published sources provide the most detailed information. The sources to be noted are illustrative only and are not meant to be exhaustive.[30]

---

[30] For a detailed list of published sources of information, see A. H. Mowbray, R. H. Blanchard, and C. A. Williams, Jr., *Insurance* (6th ed., New York: McGraw-Hill Book Company, 1969), pp. 642–646.

The annual reports which insurers must submit to the state insurance department provide extensive information on the financial affairs of the insurer and may be consulted by the public. Sometimes the insurance commissioner issues an annual report which condenses much of this information, and many insurers will send interested parties copies of their reports to stockholders. Reporting services, however, are the most frequently consulted sources.

In life insurance, illustrative reports are *Best's Life Reports* and *The Spectator Insurance Year Book*, which present the background history of most insurers, the lines they write, the states in which they operate, and detailed financial data;[31] *Flitcraft* and *Little Gem Life Chart*, which indicate the principal policy provisions, the premium and dividend rates, and the settlement option values used by most life insurers;[32] *The Handy Guide*, which reproduces one insurance contract issued by each of the leading insurers and in addition presents important premium information;[33] *Settlement Options*, which also contains tables of settlement option values but which in addition describes in detail the practices of most insurers with respect to settlement options;[34] *Who Writes What in Life, Accident and Sickness?*, which lists the contracts and underwriting practices of the leading life and health insurers;[35] and *Time Saver*, which analyzes the policies and rates of most health insurers.[36]

In property and liability insurance, *Best's Insurance Reports, Fire and Casualty* occupies a position analogous to *Best's Life Reports* in life insurance.[37] For each insurer this report describes the history, the management, and the general underwriting policy of the insurer and presents detailed financial data. An additional feature is the rating of each insurer according to the quality of its underwriting results, the economy of its management, the adequacy of its reserves, the ability of its capital and surplus (including the hidden equity in the unearned premium reserve) to absorb unfavorable operating results, and the soundness of its investments. Grades run from A+ and A (excellent) to C (fair). Because of the large proportion of insurers receiving high grades, the major value of the grades is the assistance they afford in detecting questionable insurers. They can also

---

[31] *Best's Life Reports* (Morristown, N.J.: Alfred M. Best Company, Inc., annual); *The Spectator Life Insurance Year Book* (Philadelphia: Chilton Company, annual).
[32] *Flitcraft Compend* (Morristown, N.J.: Flitcraft, Inc., annual); *Little Gem Life Chart* (Cincinnati: The National Underwriter Company, annual).
[33] *The Spectator Handy Guide* (Philadelphia: Chilton Company, annual).
[34] *Settlement Options* (Morristown, N.J.: Flitcraft, Inc., annual).
[35] *Who Writes What in Life, Accident and Sickness?* (Cincinnati: The National Underwriter Company, annual).
[36] *Time Saver* (Cincinnati: The National Underwriter Company, annual).
[37] *Best's Insurance Reports, Fire and Casualty* (Morristown, N.J.: Alfred M. Best Company, Inc., annual).

prove useful when a risk manager is approached by an insurer about which he knows little or nothing. Often these less-known insurers would be desirable.[38] *Who Writes What?* is analogous to *Who Writes What in Life, Accident and Sickness?*[39] *Best's Aggregates and Averages* reports important financial data for leading insurers and the industry.[40] The *Fire, Casualty, and Surety Bulletins* provide up-to-date information on leading property and liability insurance coverages.[41] One state (Georgia) insurance department has distributed tables of rates charged by different insurers.

Other sources of information are contacts with individual insurers and agents who can supply specimen contracts and premium information; other insureds, especially those facing the same problems; meetings such as those sponsored by the American Management Association's Insurance Division and the American Society of Insurance Management; and the insured's personal experience.

Of the three factors to be considered in selecting an insurer, service is not only the most difficult factor to evaluate but also the one about which objective information is most scarce. Other risk managers can be consulted, but the value of their opinions depends upon their objectivity, their experience, and the similarity of their risk problems to those of the manager making the investigation.

Considerations That Influence Selection of a Producer

In selecting an insurer, a risk manager must pay attention to financial strength, service, and cost. In selecting a producer, he must realize that service and cost are the primary factors to be considered. The producer's ability to service the insured depends upon his knowledge of the insurance business, his understanding of the risk manager's special problems, and his ability (in terms of time, interest, analytical skill, markets, and facilities) to help the risk manager to design and implement with minimum delay and cost an optimum protection program. The producer's task does not terminate, however, with the design and implementation of the original program. Insurance needs are constantly changing, and the program must be kept up to date. In addition, when losses occur, the producer can render

---

[38] *Best's Life Reports* does not grade the insurers in this way, but for each insurer there are comments on whether (1) the results achieved by the insurer have been "favorable," "very favorable," or "most favorable" and (2) whether the overall margins for contingencies are "considerable," "substantial," "very substantial," or "most substantial." Comparative comments are also made on investment yields, expenses, mortality costs, and lapses and surrenders.

[39] *Who Writes What?* (Cincinnati: The National Underwriter Company, annual).

[40] *Best's Aggregates and Averages* (Morristown, N.J.: Alfred M. Best Company, Inc., annual).

[41] *Fire, Casualty, and Surety Bulletins* (Cincinnati: The National Underwriter Company, monthly reporting service).

valuable assistance. He may also provide or request additional services such as appraisals or loss-prevention advice.

As was true of insurers, *the variation among producers of a single type is more marked than the variation among types of producers.* From what was said earlier, however, property and liability insurance agents, brokers, and insurance consultants probably rate somewhat higher than exclusive agents and sales representatives with respect to service because of their independence of action and their ability to concentrate on fewer customers.

With respect to cost, exclusive agents and sales representatives generally receive less compensation than independent agents and brokers, while an insurance consultant charges an additional fee. The risk manager is likely to turn to agents, brokers, and consultants when he places a high value on their possible "extra" service. This is evident from the fact that the exclusive agents and sales representatives have been most successful in the mass market, where the service demands are at a minimum. In other words, business risk managers have been more prone to turn to agents, brokers, and consultants than have family risk managers. As noted previously, however, independent agency insurers have been adopting certain practices of the direct writers and vice versa. Authorities differ on the relative roles each type of insurer will play in the business and family markets of the future.

SOURCES OF INFORMATION

Obtaining information about prospective producers is much more difficult than investigating insurers. The service to be provided by the producer is the principal issue, and, as noted above, published sources cannot provide this information. Other risk managers may be able to provide useful evaluations of producers as well as of insurers, but the most satisfactory source of information is personal contact with the producer. The more informed the risk manager, the more fruitful this contact is likely to be.

One positive indication of a producer's ability is a Chartered Life Underwriter (CLU) or Chartered Property and Casualty Underwriter (CPCU) designation. To obtain one of these designations, a candidate must have passed a series of examinations covering such diverse fields as insurance, law, economics, social legislation, finance, accounting, and management. The examinations are prepared and graded and the designations awarded by the American College of Life Underwriters and the American Institute of Property and Liability Underwriters, respectively. Although it is true that many highly competent producers do not have either designation and that the designations do not necessarily indicate competence, the risk manager should be aware of the existence and meaning of CLU and CPCU.

Selection Procedures

Up to this point the text has dealt with types of insurers and the factors to be considered in selecting particular insurers and producers. The discussion now turns to several different *procedures* which the risk manager may use in the selection process. The discussion is meant to be indicative rather than exhaustive. First, the risk manager may select a single agency or group of cooperating agencies to control the entire program, or he may select different agencies or sales representatives for the various parts of the total program. Second, in selecting insurers or producers he may use open competitive bidding, modified competitive bidding, or individual negotiations.

CONTROLLING-AGENCY OR PIECEMEAL APPROACH

Under the controlling-agency arrangement, one agency or two or more cooperating agencies are charged with responsibility for the total program and with obtaining the necessary protection from the insurers they represent. The controlling agency may be a broker or an insurance consultant but is seldom a sales representative representing one insurer. Relationships with the controlling agency are expected to be close and to continue indefinitely. The major advantage of this system is centralized authority and responsibility, which should minimize the possibility of gaps and overlaps in the program, reduce the time and effort the risk manager must spend on insurance, and simplify loss adjustments. The principal disadvantage is a potentially higher premium.

Under the piecemeal approach, responsibility for the insurance portion of the risk management program is divided among several agencies, brokers, or sales representatives. The major advantage of this approach is that in each area the risk manager can seek out the agency offering the best combination of service and cost. The result may be better overall service, lower cost, or both. Two possible disadvantages are an uncoordinated program with gaps and overlaps and increased demands upon the risk manager.

COMPETITIVE BIDDING OR NEGOTIATIONS

Under open competitive bidding the risk manager or insurance consultant draws up a set of rigid specifications and invites competitive bids for all or separate parts of the program. The principal appeal of competitive bidding lies in the lower premium cost it produces[42] and, if price is the only consideration, the relative simplicity and objectivity of the decisions involved.[43]

Objections to open competitive bidding are that price may be overem-

[42] For example, one municipal body found that the bids on its automobile liability insurance ranged from $1,500 to $5,500.
[43] The decision may not be simple, however. For example, should mutual dividends, which cannot be guaranteed, be ignored?

phasized; framing the specifications is a sizable complex task; the specifications may be incomplete or incorrect; and bidders are not free to suggest alternative ideas which, in the long run, may produce less costly protection. If the process is repeated too frequently, the insurer or producer may not have the time or the inclination to develop a close working relationship with the business. An opposite viewpoint is that the service provided by the insurer and the agent is sharpened by this competitive threat.

These problems affect part-time risk managers more adversely than full-time risk managers. Employing an insurance consultant would eliminate some of these disadvantages for the part-time risk manager but the consultant's fee would have to be added to the cost.

Under modified competitive bidding, the risk manager invites the bidders to suggest substantially different insurance coverages as long as they satisfy certain broad directives. Such a procedure would complicate the decision process and make it more subjective, but it is more flexible than open competitive bidding and stimulates qualified insurance personnel to do more thinking about the program.

Individual negotiations with insurers and agents is the most common procedure, particularly among small businesses that do not have the desire or the ability to frame specifications or broad directives. Sometimes the business contacts only one agent or insurer with respect to the total program or part of that program. The result may or may not be the optimum, considering the premium paid, the services rendered, and the implicit and explicit cost of a more thorough selection procedure.

REVIEW QUESTIONS

1. Security is generally considered to be the most important consideration in selecting an insurer.
   a. What is meant by security?
   b. What variables determine the security of an insurer?
2. The balance sheet for Insurer A indicates unearned premium reserves equal to 10 per cent of liabilities and loss reserves equal to 79 per cent of liabilities.
   a. What is the unearned premium reserve?
   b. What is the loss reserve?
   c. What types of insurance does this insurer probably write?
3. Financial analysts often subtract a fraction of the unearned premium reserve from the total liabilities and add it to the surplus to determine the policyholders' surplus ratio.
   a. What is the policyholders' surplus ratio?

b. Why do financial analysts make this correction?

4. The redundancy in the unearned premium reserve has sometimes been blamed for "capacity" problems.

   a. What is a capacity problem?

   b. What is the relationship of this problem to the unearned premium reserve?

5. How do life insurers determine net level premium reserves?

6. To what extent is there a redundancy in the policy reserves of life insurers?

7. If a life insurer's interest return drops permanently to a lower level,

   a. What action should it take with respect to its reserves?

   b. What action can it take with respect to its cash values?

8. Life insurers control about four times as many assets as property and liability insurers even though the annual premium volume of both types of insurers is about the same. Why?

9. a. Compare the investment portfolio of the typical life insurer with the portfolio of the typical property and liability insurer.

   b. Explain the major differences.

10. The balance sheet of an insurer indicates that its assets consist primarily of bonds, mortgages, and common stocks. How are each of these types of investments valued?

11. a. What is meant by "underwriting policy"?

    b. What are some of the more common variations in underwriting policy? How does each of these variations affect insurer solvency?

12. Insurer A reports an expense ratio of 0.30 while insurer B reports an expense ratio of 0.45. Does this mean that insurer A is the more efficient insurer?

13. Insurance underwriters can turn to several sources for information concerning the desirability of an applicant for insurance.

    a. What are these sources?

    b. How does the binding authority of the agent affect the underwriter's possible courses of action?

14. Reinsurance facilities affect the insurer's solvency and its ability to service its policyholders. How?

15. Distinguish between facultative reinsurance, facultative treaty reinsurance, and automatic treaty reinsurance.

16. An insurer wishes to enter into one of the following reinsurance arrangements:

    a. A quota-share arrangement with the ceding insurer retaining 60 per cent of any loss

    b. A surplus-share arrangement, under which the ceding insurer will retain policy amounts up to $50,000

    c. An excess-loss arrangement, under which the ceding insurer will retain all losses under $50,000

How much will the reinsurer pay under each of these arrangements if the loss is

(1) $ 20,000 under a $ 40,000 policy

(2) $ 20,000 under a $100,000 policy

(3) $100,000 under a $100,000 policy

17. a. How does catastrophe reinsurance differ from the arrangements cited in question 16?

b. What other functions are performed by the underwriting department in addition to selecting among applicants and avoiding undue concentrations of exposure?

18. a. Which are safer operations on the average, stock insurers or mutuals?

b. Even if one could determine that one type of operation was safer on the average, how significant would this finding be in selecting a particular insurer?

19. What special characteristics of government insurers affect their financial strength?

20. Many insurers claim that they render superior service; but a survey of agents a few years ago determined that few of them were able to define what *service* means. What are some of the ingredients of superior service?

21. A supporter of mutual insurers argues that mutuals render better service because the policyholders own the insurer. Comment on this claim.

22. a. "The average mutual property and liability insurer charges lower rates than the average stock property and liability insurer." Is this statement correct?

b. "The average mutual life insurer charges lower rates than the average stock life insurer." Is this statement correct?

23. "The cost of administering OASDI is about 2 per cent of benefits paid. The cost of administering workmen's compensation insurance through private insurers is about one-third of the premiums written. Therefore, public insurers are much more efficient than private insurers." Comment on this statement.

24. What sources can the risk manager consult to obtain information concerning an insurer's financial strength, service, and cost?

25. Would you favor the use of competitive bidding in the selection of an insurer?

A REVIEW CASE ON CHAPTERS 23 AND 24

A Memorandum on Selection Factors

As risk manager you have been asked to prepare a general memorandum to management concerning the various factors which you have considered in placing the insurance coverage of the firm. Identify the importance of each of the following concepts in this memorandum.

1. Selecting the company
   a. Importance of financial strength
   b. Measurement of financial strength
   c. Operating ratios such as: expense ratio, loss ratio, investment return, etc.
   d. Age of company
   e. Geographical licensed areas
   f. Policyholder services
   g. Independent company ratings
   h. Philosophy of management
   i. Other factors, such as type of company, etc.
   j. Cost of insurance
2. Selecting the agent or broker
   a. Type of agency system used
   b. Age, experience
   c. Volume of business of agent or broker
   d. Reputation in community
   e. Extension of credit
   f. Other services or factors
   g. Commission structure

SUGGESTIONS FOR ADDITIONAL READING

Best's Aggregates and Averages (Morristown, N.J.: Alfred M. Best Company, Inc., annual).

Best's Insurance Reports, Fire and Casualty (Morristown, N.J.: Alfred M. Best Company, Inc., annual).

Best's Life Reports (Morristown, N.J.: Alfred M. Best Company, Inc., annual).

Bickelhaupt, D., and Magee, J.: *General Insurance* (8th ed., Homewood, Ill.: Richard D. Irwin, Inc., 1970), chap. 5.

Denenberg, H. S., et al.: *Risk and Insurance* (Englewood Cliffs, N.J.: Prentice-Hall Inc., 1964), chaps. 14 and 28–30.

Greene, M.: *Risk and Insurance* (2d ed., Cincinnati: South-Western Publishing Company, 1968), chaps. 5–7.

Gregg, D. W. (ed.): *Life and Health Insurance Handbook* (2d ed., Homewood, Ill., Richard D. Irwin, Inc., 1964), chaps. 70–74.

Kenney, Roger: *Fundamentals of Fire and Casualty Insurance Strength* (4th ed., Dedham, Mass.: The Kenney Insurance Studies, 1967).

Kulp, C. A., and Hall, J. W.: *Casualty Insurance* (4th ed., New York: The Ronald Press Company, 1968), chaps. 17, 18, and 23.

Life Insurance Fact Book (New York: Institute of Life Insurance, annual).

Long, J. D., and Gregg, D. W. (eds.): *Property and Liability Insurance Handbook* (Homewood, Ill.: Richard D. Irwin, Inc., 1965), chaps. 58–71 and 74.

Mehr, R., and Cammack, E.: *Principles of Insurance* (4th ed., Homewood, Ill.: Richard D. Irwin, Inc., 1966), chaps. 24–27 and 29.

———— and Hedges, B. A.: *Risk Management in the Business Enterprise* (Homewood, Ill.: Richard D. Irwin, Inc., 1963), chaps. 16 and 19.

Michelbacher, G. F., and Roos, N.: *Multiple-line Insurers: Their Nature and Operation* (2d ed., New York: McGraw-Hill Book Company, 1970), chaps. 4, 5, and 8–12.

Mowbray, A., Blanchard, R. H., and Williams, C. A., Jr.: *Insurance* (6th ed., New York: McGraw-Hill Book Company, 1969), chaps. 24–26, 28–30, 32, and 33.

Riegel, R., and Miller, J.: *Insurance Principles and Practices* (5th ed., Englewood Cliffs, N.J.: Prentice-Hall, Inc., 1966), chaps. 3–5, 13, and 15.

Thompson, K.: *Reinsurance* (4th ed., Philadelphia: The Spectator Company, 1966).

25

insurance pricing methods

We have already emphasized the importance of considering cost in the selection of an insurer. In order to evaluate properly the cost of the protection provided by a particular insurer, the risk manager must understand the principles and procedures of insurance pricing. Moreover, once the insurer has been selected, the risk manager can use this knowledge to obtain the lowest possible price for his firm. Finally, because insurance is a public-interest business,[1] the risk manager, as a citizen, has a strong interest in insurance pricing.

This chapter is designed to provide an understanding of the objectives of insurance pricing, the principal pricing methods, rating bureaus, and dividend-distribution formulas.[2] In addition, the price structures in some specific kinds of insurance are discussed in order to illustrate (1) the application of these general concepts and (2) the important differences which exist among lines of insurance because of variations in the problems presented and in pricing philosophies.

Pricing Objectives

An insurer's pricing objectives are determined by law and by business considerations. State law usually requires that most property and liability insur-

[1] *German Alliance Ins. Co. v. Lewis,* 233 U.S. 389 (1914).
[2] Insurance pricing has already been mentioned briefly in Chaps. 23 and 24. Illustrative premiums have also been presented in connection with some of the coverages.

ance rates be reasonable, adequate, and not unfairly discriminatory. (An insurance rate is the price per unit of insurance or exposure. An insurance premium is the total price, which is usually calculated by multiplying the rate times the number of units of insurance or exposure. For example, the premium for a $10 million property insurance policy may be $20,000, or 100,000 times a rate of $0.20 per $100 of insurance.) Life insurance rates must be adequate and not unfairly discriminatory; it is assumed that because there are no rating bureaus in life insurance, competition will prevent these rates from becoming unreasonable. Health insurance rates are generally subject to the same standards as those of life insurance. In addition, about one-third of the states have laws that prohibit approval of a health insurance policy if the benefits provided therein are unreasonable in relation to the premium charged.

Insurance rates for a given policy are reasonable if they are not, on the average, too high. The profits of the insurer should not be excessive. Insurance rates for a given policy are adequate if they are, on the average, high enough. They must be sufficient to cover the expected losses and expenses of the insurer; otherwise the insurer may become insolvent and the policyholders will suffer. Insurance rates are not unfairly discriminatory if each insured pays his "fair" share of the cost. This is a vague requirement, but it is generally (though not universally) considered to mean that rate differences among insureds should, subject to practical limitations, reflect differences in expected losses and expenses. If the expected losses and the expected expenses for one individual are twice the sum of these items for a second person, the insurance premium for the first insured should be twice that for the second.[3]

It can be argued that these three objectives are also dictated by business considerations.[4] An insurer whose rates are excessive for all of its customers will, if it is subject to competition, not be attractive to knowledgeable clients. If the *general* rate level is excessive but some of the prices are unduly low, the result may be a large volume of business at inadequate prices. This same result may obtain even if the general rate level is proper

[3] This definition is still vague, however, because it is extremely difficult to make expected loss estimates, and there is room for much honest disagreement. Some expenses vary with the expected losses and consequently are subject to the same uncertainties. Finally, some of the expenses must be shared with other insureds and other kinds of insurance, and the allocation of these costs is necessarily arbitrary. A question also arises as to whether the relevant cost concept is average cost or marginal cost—the additional cost of writing another policy. For further discussion of these and other problems, see C. A. Williams, Jr., *Price Discrimination in Property and Liability Insurance*, University of Minnesota Studies in Economics and Business No. 19 (Minneapolis: The University of Minnesota Press, 1959). These difficulties suggest that the test of unfair discrimination should not be rigidly applied.

[4] The market is not so perfect as this discussion would lead one to believe, particularly with respect to the *relative* prices charged by one insurer, but the general tendencies are present.

but some individual rates are too low. The dangers of inadequate rates for all insureds are obvious.

Business considerations also suggest some other criteria. The pricing structure must be workable, understandable, impossible (or at least difficult) to manipulate to the insured's advantage, and relatively inexpensive to apply. If necessary, some accuracy must be sacrificed to attain these goals. The rates should be responsive to changes in the long run, but because of the adverse public relations and the administrative costs associated with frequent rate changes, the rates should be stable in the short run unless a significant, presumably long-term, change in the risk environment becomes evident. Finally, the rates should encourage loss-prevention activities. The insured should be able to recognize the effect that his own efforts will have on the general rate level, and on his own premium relative to that paid by other persons. Some authorities argue that there is a social gain even if the incentive exceeds the reduction in the expected cost that is likely to result from the loss-prevention activities.

Public policy considerations may suggest the socialization of some risks on some basis other than private equity.[5] For example, in order to keep the price of automobile insurance within the reach of younger drivers, older drivers may be asked to pay more than their fair share of the total costs. This objective conflicts with the unfair discrimination standard noted earlier and requires special pricing arrangements.[6]

Principal Pricing Methods

Insurance-pricing methods can be divided into three major categories: (1) individual rating, (2) class or manual rating, and (3) modification rating, usually referred to as "merit rating."

INDIVIDUAL RATING

Under individual rating, each insured is charged a unique premium based largely upon the judgment of the person setting the rate, supplemented perhaps by whatever statistical data are available and by a knowledge of the premiums charged similar insureds. It takes into account all known factors affecting the exposure, including competition from other insurers. Under this method the person *applying* the rating method to the individual insured is also the rate *maker*.

This method is not in common use in insurance today. Ocean marine insurance rates and, to a much lesser extent, inland marine insurance rates

[5] Spencer L. Kimball, "The Purpose of Insurance Regulation," *Minnesota Law Review,* XLV (1961), 512–514.
[6] See the three objectives given at the beginning of this section.

are set in this fashion. Individual rating is used in other lines of insurance only for unusual exposures which cannot be handled under the other two rating methods, and it is used in pricing reinsurance. Consequently, risk managers of large business firms are much more likely to encounter this method than are other risk managers. Some risk managers of giant firms which self-insure the more common exposures and seek outside protection only for the unusual may be concerned solely with individual rating.

CLASS RATING

Under class rating, insureds are classified according to a few important and easily identified characteristics, and the insureds in each class are charged the same rate. This method of rating is often referred to as "manual rating" because the class rates are printed in a manual which the producer can consult to determine the appropriate rate for the insured. Under this method, the person applying the rates to determine the premium is not the rate maker. Except for determining the correct class for the insured, the person applying the rates has no decisions to make and, at least in theory, the rate should be the same, no matter who applies the rates. Determining the correct class, however, often involves considerable judgment, and the risk manager should check to see that his firm has been placed in the most favorable class possible.

The typical insured is more likely to encounter this method than any other, since the procedure is used to set most individual life insurance and health insurance rates, family automobile insurance rates, homeowner's insurance rates on dwellings, general liability and workmen's compensation rates for small businesses, and many others.

Besides simplifying and speeding up the application of the rates, class rating makes it possible to use statistical methods more extensively in making the rates. Class rating groups together similar insureds, and the exposure units in the class may be numerous enough to provide a useful indication of the loss experience to be expected in the future. The attention paid to the statistical indications varies greatly among lines and even among states within the same line. This diversity can be attributed to variations in the rating problems presented, the data available, the prevailing rating philosophies, and the statistical support required to satisfy the state rate regulators.

At one extreme (represented by fire insurance and marine insurance), past experience is classified only by line, policy, or groupings of rate classes. For each of these statistical classes, a *loss ratio* is computed, the loss ratio being the ratio of the losses incurred (sometimes paid) to premiums earned (sometimes written). This loss ratio is then compared with the permissible or expected loss ratio.[7] If the statistical indications are accepted at face value, the rate change for that class is determined by the formula $(r - R)/R$ where r is the actual loss ratio and R is the permissible loss ratio. For example, if r is 0.27 and R is 0.54, the indicated rate change is a 50 per cent decrease. If r is 0.65, the indication is a 20 per cent increase. It is assumed that expenses increase proportionately with premiums[8] and that if the premiums over the period covered by the experience had been at the level suggested, the loss ratio would have equaled the permissible loss ratio. For example, if the premiums over the experience period *at the level currently in effect* had been $1 million and the actual losses were $270,000, the indicated rate change as noted above is a 50 per cent decrease. With this reduction in rate level, the premiums would have been $500,000 and the actual loss ratio 0.54 or the same as the permissible loss ratio.

Statistical indications may not, however, be accepted at their face value. The number of exposure units in the statistical class may not be large enough for the results to give a true picture of the expected losses. In some instances this fact will be taken into account by consulting a table of credibility factors which increase as the number of exposure units increases. These credibility factors measure the reliability of the statistical evidence or the degree of belief that the rate maker should place in the actual experience. Some statistical methods, a discussion of which is beyond the scope of this treatment,[9] *may* be used in constructing this table, but the tabled values always depend to some extent and sometimes completely upon the judgment of the persons constructing the table. When the credibility factor is 100 per cent, the actual experience is considered completely reliable *relative to any other available information.* When the factor is 0 per cent, it is ignored. When it is between these values, both the actual experience and the current rate level (or some other information such as the actual experience for all statistical classes combined) affect the rates to be charged in the future, the weight assigned to the actual experience increasing as the credibility factor increases. The rating formula including the credibility factor C is $(r - R)/R \times C$. In the examples presented

---

[7] The permissible loss ratio is unity minus the expected ratio of the expenses to the premiums and the profit and contingency allowance. For example, if the expected expense ratio is 0.41 and the profit and contingencies factor 0.05, the permissible loss ratio is $1 - 0.41 - 0.05 = 0.54$.

[8] Commissions, taxes, loss-adjustment expenses, and others comprising about three-fourths of the expenses do tend to behave in this manner in most lines. Whether they should so behave is an interesting point for debate.

[9] For example, the 100 per cent point may be established by the method we suggested a risk manager might employ to determine the number of exposure units required for a given degree of stability in his loss experience. See Chap. 5.

For those interested in pursuing this point further, see L. H. Longley-Cook, *An Introduction to Credibility Theory* (New York: Casualty Actuarial Society, 1962).

earlier, if the credibility factor had been 50 per cent, the indicated rate changes would have been −25 per cent and +10 per cent, respectively.

Under the loss-ratio approach, however, such an objective approach is unusual. The actual loss-ratio indications are usually modified according to the underwriting judgment of the rate maker. Where this is done, the argument is that the statistical approach is too inflexible and that many factors must be considered in addition to the statistical experience.

So far, we have assumed that the environment is not changing and that the objective is to obtain a true picture of the expected losses in the past which will serve as a guide to the future. If the environment is changing, the loss-ratio indications cannot be accepted at their face value, and the role of judgment is increased. Sometimes statistical trends can be used to modify the data and reduce the element of judgment.

Once the rate changes, if any, for the *statistical* classes are obtained, the task remains of determining the changes for the *rating* classes. One statistical class, for example, may include five rating classes. These five rating classes will probably receive the same rate increase or decrease. If the relation among the five class rates is to be changed, the change will be based almost entirely on the judgment of the rate maker because the statistical experience, even if available, is not considered credible.

At the other extreme, represented by automobile insurance, workmen's compensation insurance, and life insurance, past experience is segregated into approximately the same or even more classes than the insureds. Although changes in the general rate level are sometimes based on a loss-ratio formula of the type described above, changes in the rate relativities or class-rate relations are determined by the *pure-premium* method.[10] Basically, the approach is to compute first an indicated pure premium or the actual losses per unit of exposure, such as one car-year or $100 of payroll.[11] If this pure premium is fully credible, as determined by a table of credibility factors of the type described above, the indicated pure premium is loaded for expenses and profit to arrive at the manual rate.[12] For example, if the pure premium is $20 per automobile and the permissible loss ratio is 0.60, the indicated class premium rate is $20/0.60 = $33. If the indicated pure premium is not fully credible, the estimated pure premium is

[10] Mathematically, the two methods are equivalent so long as the expenses are assumed to increase proportionally with the premiums. The pure-premium approach, however, presents the information in a different fashion and appears to stimulate a more careful analysis. See C. A. Kulp and J. W. Hall, *Casualty Insurance* (4th ed., New York: The Ronald Press Co., 1968), 796–804.

[11] The pure premium is, therefore, a rate. This terminology is confusing but generally accepted.

[12] If the change in the general rate level is computed separately, an adjustment in the class rates is usually necessary after all the class rates are determined, because the class rate changes should produce the desired change in the overall rate level. This will clearly not be true if the class experience credibility varies by classes.

the weighted average of the indicated pure premium and some other indication such as the pure premium underlying the present rates. The credibility factor is the weight assigned to the indicated pure premium. For example, if the credibility factor in the preceding example had been 40 per cent and the pure premium underlying the present rates $15, the estimated pure premium would be 0.40($20) + 0.60($15) = $8 + $9 = $17. The class premium rate would be $17/0.60 = $28.[13]

As under the loss-ratio method, changes in the environment may make past experience a misleading guide for the future. Under the pure-premium method, however, there is a much greater reluctance to depart from the statistical indications, and statistical trend factors are used whenever possible to make the necessary adjustments. For example, if the average cost of settling automobile claims is increasing, the actual losses may be adjusted to reflect the current or even expected future costs.

Life insurance rating is a special case because of the long-term contracts, the increase in mortality rates with age over the contract term, the direct recognition of the investment return, and the quality of the statistical information available. Further dissussion will be deferred to the sections on specific premium structures.

MODIFICATION RATING

Under modification or merit rating, the rate maker distinguishes among insureds in the same rating class[14] on the basis of differences in expected losses or expenses per exposure unit. The variations may be expected because of differences in past experience, size of the exposure, or a detailed analysis of the quality of the exposure. Four principal modification rating methods will be discussed: (1) schedule rating, (2) experience rating, (3) retrospective rating, and (4) premium discount plans.

With some exceptions (particularly among some of the newer multiple line developments), these plans are reserved for the larger firms. A small relative difference between the modified rate and the class rate becomes important only when the premium is large; the loss experience of a particular insured becomes credible only when the number of exposure units is large; the expenses associated with modification rating become reasonable only when they result in substantial dollar premium changes; and expense savings for the insurer become more noticeable as the premium increases.

---

[13] This example is designed to illustrate the principles involved. The reader should recognize that it is possible to apply these steps in a different order to arrive at the same result. In addition, several refinements are usually introduced which need not be considered in this survey.
[14] Sometimes the insureds are not technically in the same rating class. See the later discussion of fire insurance schedule rating.

Schedule rating   Under schedule rating, the modification is based upon a comparison between some specified characteristics of a standard insured and the corresponding characteristics of the insured who is being rated. The person applying the schedule adds a charge to the standard rate for each way in which the rated insured is worse than the standard and subtracts a credit for each way in which the rated insured is better. The characteristics considered in the schedules and the charges and the credits are sometimes very precisely stated, and two persons applying the same schedule will arrive at approximately the same result. Other schedules are so highly flexible—the characteristics are so vaguely defined and the credits and charges can fall anywhere within a broad range (e.g., up to 55 per cent)—that schedule rating approaches individual rating. Regardless of whether the schedule is flexible or inflexible, the persons constructing (not applying) the schedule are forced to rely almost entirely on their judgment in choosing the characteristics to be compared and in evaluating their importance.

One great advantage of schedule rating is that an analysis of the schedule will reveal those areas where the quality of the insured's exposure could be improved. As such, schedule rating is a boon to loss-prevention efforts because it enables the insured to estimate the insurance savings associated with a preventive undertaking.

Detailed, inflexible schedule rating is less important today than it was previously because a detailed schedule is expensive to apply and because the less flexible schedules have placed too much emphasis upon tangible or physical factors. In some lines such as workmen's compensation insurance, this emphasis has proved to be very misleading. The most important application of detailed schedule rating is the pricing of fire insurance and some inland marine insurance for most business exposures. High flexible schedules are in common use in such lines as automobile liability and general liability insurance.

Experience rating   Under experience rating (sometimes called "prospective experience rating"), the modification is based upon the relative loss experience of the individual insured during some representative period in the past. Although the formulas used in practice assume a variety of forms, the following formula illustrates the basic principles:

$$\text{Experience modification} = \frac{A - E}{E} \times C$$

where A represents the actual losses of the individual insured during the experience period, E represents the expected losses if the insured had been the average insured in his class (expected losses = permissible loss ratio times the premium over the experience period at class rates), and C is the credibility factor, which in this case depends upon the relative credibility of the individual experience and the class experience.[15] A table of credibility factors contains credibility factors which increase with the quantity of the exposure of the insured during the experience period. The credibility factor exceeds zero only for the 10 to 20 per cent of the insureds eligible for experience rating. Judgment always plays an important role in the construction of this table, but in some lines statistical theory also enters the picture.

To illustrate the application of experience rating, if the expected losses for the insured over a three-year experience period were $10,000, the actual losses $7,000, and the credibility factor 60 per cent, the experience modification is an 18 per cent decrease. If the manual premium to be paid during the next year had been $8,000, the premium after experience rating would be 0.82($8,000) = $6,560.

An important feature of experience rating which has not been recognized in the preceding discussion is the emphasis it places upon loss frequency as opposed to loss severity. Loss severity is considered to be largely a matter of chance, and various devices are used to limit the effect of a single loss upon the experience rate. Consequently, an experience-rated insured who suffers one $50,000 loss over the experience period will probably pay a much lower premium than another insured whose class premium would have been the same as that of the first insured but who suffered twenty losses of $2,500 each.

Experience rating, therefore, varies the premium according to the loss experience of the insured, but the effect of single losses is limited, and the credibility factor dampens the effect of both good and bad experience unless the insured's exposure during the experience period was very large and the plan provides for full credibility.

Experience rating affects relatively few insureds because of its eligibility requirements, but in the liability lines, including workmen's compensation where it is most important, these insureds pay much and sometimes most of the premiums.[16]

Retrospective rating   Under retrospective rating (sometimes called "retrospective experience rating"), the modification depends upon the insured's experience during the *policy* period and a premium discount for expense savings attributable to the size of the insured. Theoretically the retrospective premium equals the actual losses and expenses of the insured during the policy period plus a net insurance charge, but the premium is not permitted

---

[15] Note the similarity to the loss-ratio formula used to establish class rates.
[16] In workmen's compensation, less than 15 per cent of the insureds are experience rated, but they pay about 75 per cent of the premiums.

to exceed a specified maximum or fall below a specified minimum. The purpose of the net insurance charge is to make up the premium deficiency for the insurer which results because the excess premiums paid by those insureds charged the minimum premium are less than the premium deficiencies of those insureds paying the maximum premium. In effect, then, the insured is paying the insurer to service a self-insurance operation except for the maximum and minimum premium features.

The following formula or some slight variation is used in practice:

Retrospective premium = [basic premium

+ (losses)(loss-conversion factor)] × tax multiplier

subject to stated maximum and minimum premiums.

The basic premium includes the net insurance charge, which is based upon a statistical analysis of a frequency distribution of losses, and the expenses less taxes that do not vary directly with the losses. The basic premium does not increase proportionately with the size of the insured in recognition of the fact that the expenses of serving an insured do not increase this rapidly.[17] The loss-conversion factor adds to the losses the expenses which do vary with the losses. The tax multiplier loads the premium for taxes.

The effect of retrospective rating can be demonstrated graphically in Figure 25.1. The insured's premium cannot be specified at the beginning of the policy period, but assuming that the extent of his exposure can be estimated fairly closely, the premium will fall somewhere on the line in the diagram.

Because the insurer cannot make a good estimate of the losses incurred until some time after the policy period has ended, the plan provides for

[17] In addition, because these insureds are much less likely to pay maximum premiums, the net insurance charge can be reduced.

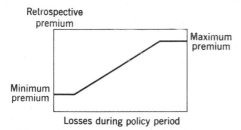

Figure 25.1   Retrospective premium as a function of the losses.

provisional premiums with subsequent adjustments upward or downward depending upon the experience.

Retrospective rating is very responsive to fluctuations in the insured's experience. Insurers limit its use to very large firms whose fluctuations are likely to be small and who are financially able to absorb those fluctuations which occur. For the large firm with a superior experience record, retrospective rating is very attractive. It is even more attractive for the insured whose past experience is such that experience rating results in a debit or increase over the manual rate but who believes that his future experience will be excellent. Insurers will sometimes insist upon retrospective rating when they have reason to expect poorer experience than anticipated under experience rating.

The risk manager may be called upon to make some important decisions with respect to restrospective rating. These decisions will all be subject to the consent of his insurer. First, the plan is usually elective, and the insured must decide whether to stick with the experience-rated premium to which the firm is usually otherwise entitled or to assume some risk. Second, if the plan is elected, the risk manager has to choose the applicable minimum premium and maximum premium factors and in some cases the loss-conversion factor. The considerations affecting these choices are too advanced for this text, but one example can be presented. The insured may reason that decreasing the maximum premium would reduce the chance of a sizable premium loss. There is a cost associated with this decision, however. The net insurance charge and the basic premium will have to be increased, and the premiums over the most likely range of losses will be increased.

Very few risk managers will be called upon to make these decisions, but those who do pay a good share of the premiums in some lines of insurance. Retrospective rating is found in most lines of insurance where experience rating is used.[18]

Size-discount plans   Size-discount plans produce relatively lower class premiums, schedule premiums, or experience premiums for large-premium insureds on the ground that they will probably experience more favorable expense ratios, loss ratios, or both merely because they are large. The most important size-discount plans are those which recognize that not all the expenses of servicing an insured increase proportionately with the size of his premium. Size-discount plans usually provide a table of discounts which are applied to the premiums otherwise developed. For example, if the experi-

---

[18] In workmen's compensation, where this method is more important than in other lines, only about 1 per cent of the insured firms are retrospectively rated, but they pay about 10 to 15 per cent of the premiums.

ence premium is $1,500, the amount in excess of $1,000 may be discounted 10 per cent to produce a premium of $1,450.

Rating Bureaus

In personnel insurance, the actuarial staff of each insurer establishes its price structure. In property and liability insurance, as was noted earlier, many or all insurers price some insurance policies in concert. The cooperating insurers are members of, or subscribers to, a rating bureau which pools the experience of these insurers to arrive at a common premium structure. Adherence to this premium structure may or may not be required.

Bureau operations have been defended on the ground that they produce more credible statistical data for rate making, they make available a group of highly qualified experts at minimum cost, and, to the extent that they require adherence to their rates, they reduce the possibility of cutthroat competition, unfair discrimination, and insolvency. They also reduce the number of rate structures to be reviewed by state regulators. The disadvantages of unbridled competition are considered especially important in insurance because, if insurers become insolvent, they will be unable to fulfill their promises to their insureds. Such competition is possible in insurance because the price is based on an estimate, and the insurer may be unduly optimistic in its attempts to meet competition. On the other hand, it has been argued that when rating bureaus seek adherence to their rates, they impede progress because all bureau decisions must be agreed upon by many insurers. In addition, a rigid rating bureau makes impossible or at least difficult price and coverage competition that would encourage new products and pricing methods and more efficient operations. It has also been argued that the threat of insolvency and unfair discrimination as a result of open competition has been greatly overemphasized.

At least five bureau systems are in operation in the United States. The arrangements may differ by line in the same state or by state in the same line. Under the first or most inflexible arrangement, all insurers must belong to one rating bureau, and no insurer can deviate from the bureau rates. Under a second system, all insurers must belong to one bureau, but individual insurers can deviate with respect to the general rate level if they can demonstrate to the satisfaction of the state regulators that their loss or expense experience differs from that of the average bureau insurer. Under a third system, all insurers must belong to one bureau, but individual insurers can deviate on the basis of demonstrated differences from either the general rate level or the relative rates paid by insurers. Under the fourth and, until recently, easily the most common arrangement, membership in a bureau is optional, and members or subscribers are free to deviate from the bureau rates, but the burden of the proof is again on the deviators. There may be only one rating bureau in the line, or there may be several. A common practice is separate bureaus for stock insurers and for mutual insurers. Finally, rating bureaus may be permitted to exist on an optional basis, and members and subscribers may elect to adhere to the bureau rates; but there can be no agreement to this effect. Starting in the late sixties an increasing number of states adopted legislation prohibiting agreements to adhere to bureau rates except those developed for workmen's compensation insurance. Other than tradition the two principal reasons for excepting workmen's compensation insurance appear to be (1) the social insurance nature of this coverage, which suggests close public supervision, and (2) the importance assigned to insurer solvency, coupled with the belief that rate agreements contribute to insurer solvency. In addition to these statutory changes, under the fourth system many insurers who were formerly bureau insurers now set their own rates. The bureaus themselves have become more permissive. Some approve deviations automatically and will, under an "agency filing" procedure, file with state insurance departments rates developed independently by a member or subscriber.

Dividends

About one-fourth of the property and liability insurance in force and over one-half of the personnel insurance in force is advance premium participating insurance, which provides for the payment of dividends to policyholders if the premiums exceed the actual losses and expenses, including contributions to contingency reserves. The cost of the insurance to the insured depends upon these dividends as well as the initial premiums, and dividend practices, therefore, can be considered part of the pricing procedures.

Property and liability insurers usually pay dividends out of their *underwriting* "profit," which may arise out of savings on losses or expenses. Investment earnings are used to build up contingency reserves and unassigned surplus. The dividend level is usually less than the underwriting profit in the most profitable years in order that the level need not be decreased in the poorer years.

The risk manager is interested not only in the general level of dividends but also in their distribution among insureds. Most property and liability insurers return the same percentage dividend, say 10 per cent, to all insureds purchasing a particular policy. Sometimes the dividends vary by classes or broad groups of classes, and in some instances, particularly in workmen's compensation insurance, the dividend varies with the loss experience of the particular insured and the size of his premium. Under this last practice, the large insured with good experience obtains the most substantial return. Less common practices vary the dividend according to either the loss experience or the premium size but not both.

Life insurance dividends come from more sources than property and liability insurance dividends and are apportioned according to a much more detailed formula. This discussion will be limited to individual life insurance because the relationship of group insurance dividends to the experience of the particular group has already been discussed in Chapter 22.

The three most important sources of dividends for a life insurer are (1) savings in mortality costs because the estimated death rates exceed the actual death rates, (2) savings in the allowances for expenses, and (3) an investment return in excess of that assumed in computing the premiums. Life insurers must also set aside some surplus in order to maintain a steady dividend policy and to establish contingency reserves. The divisible surplus, however, is a larger proportion of the total surplus than is the case for property and liability insurers and, as noted above, includes some excess investment return. These differences arise because investment return is relatively more important for life insurers, because an assumed investment return is part of the life insurance rate-making formula, and because a life insurer whose loss experience is relatively stable can operate more safely than can property and liability insurers with a low ratio of surplus to liabilities.[19]

In life insurance, the most common plan for distributing the divisible surplus among the insureds is the three-factor method. The essence of this method is that each insured receives a dividend from each of the three sources of dividends according to the contribution to that source of policies of the same type, issue age, and issue year. Younger persons, for whom the death rates are most likely to be overstated, receive the largest return on mortality savings. The same is true of insureds with policies having low cash values. Expense savings go mainly to those insureds paying large expense loadings and, if no size discount is applied to the initial premiums, may be much greater relatively for the larger contracts. Policyholders whose contracts have large cash values receive the largest dollar return from the excess investment return. There is a tendency for dividends to increase with the age of the contract because the cash value and the share in the excess investment return increase over time.[20]

---

[19] In fact, some states, such as New York, limit this ratio for mutual insurers to a certain per cent in order to avoid an unnecessary accumulation of surplus and to force payment of policyholder dividends.

[20] During periods of low investment earnings, however, the investment return may not be important enough to produce this effect and may even be negative.

Some Specific Premium Structures

The concepts discussed to this point will now be illustrated by a discussion of the pricing structures in some specific lines of insurance. The lines selected for illustrative purposes are fire insurance, automobile liability insurance, workmen's compensation insurance, and life insurance. These lines have been chosen either because of their importance or because they provide good examples of the major approaches to insurance pricing. Only the more important aspects of insurance pricing in each of these lines and only the typical rating patterns can be considered. In some states and for some insurers, the pricing procedures may differ greatly from those discussed.

FIRE INSURANCE

In most states, almost all fire insurers belong to a statewide or regional rating bureau or subscribe to its rating services. Usually only stock insurers can be members and vote at meetings of the bureau. Subscribers are more likely to deviate from the bureau rates than are members. Some subscribers use the bureau rates for some classes of business—usually those which are schedule-rated or less desirable—and file their own rates or belong to a different rating bureau (such as the Improved Risk Mutuals) for the other classes. The Factory Mutual Companies operate through the Factory Mutual Rating Bureau on a national basis.

Class rates Almost all fire insurance rates can be divided into two basic types: (1) class or manual rates and (2) schedule rates. Class rates are generally used to price such exposures as dwellings, private garages, and small apartment houses. The factors considered in classifying the insureds are the occupancy, whether the property is a building or contents, the grade of the community fire protection, the construction—generally brick, frame, or fire-resistant—and the amount of insurance purchased. The last factor was not included until the middle sixties, when it was recognized that low-valued dwellings had higher losses per $100 of insurance. Coinsurance clauses and discounts are not applicable to most class-rate exposures.

Class rates are based in part upon statistical data. A uniform statistical plan has been established for classifying all fire insurance premiums and losses in a state according to 115 occupancy classes, with further breakdowns for three classes of construction (brick, frame, and fire-resistant) and two grades of community fire protection (protected and unprotected). For some occupancy classes, the experience on buildings is separated from that on contents. In some areas, the 115 occupancy classes are compressed into about 45 classes for rate-making purposes.

The usual practice is to compute the actual loss ratio over the past five years on the assumption that the current rates have been in effect and to adjust the rates on the basis of underwriting judgment when the ratios appear unduly low or high. In some states, however, the procedure is more objective. A statistical indication is computed, using the loss-ratio method and a table of credibility factors.

In either event, the statistical class may include several rating classes. The rate relativities among these rating classes must be based upon underwriting judgment. For example, one rating factor, community fire protection, may recognize as many as ten grades of protection, but the statistical plan calls for only two classes—protected and unprotected. Consequently, the variation in class rates by grade of community protection is based largely upon underwriting judgment.

The protection grade for a particular community is based upon an inspection of that city by the American Insurance Association or, in smaller communities, by the local rating bureau. The schedule used by the inspectors assigns up to 5,000 points to the community for deficiencies in the following factors, listed in order of importance: water supply and distribution; fire department equipment, personnel, and efficiency; structural conditions and conflagration potential; fire alarm regulations; general hazards and enforcement of laws relating to hazardous materials; and building laws. Class 1 communities score 0–500 points, class 2 communities, 501–1,000 points, etc. Most cities with paid fire departments fall in classes 3 to 6. The risk manager may be able to reduce his fire rates and those of his neighbors by convincing his community to take steps to improve its grade.

Schedule rates   Schedule rates apply to most insureds who are not class-rated and are thus more likely to be of concern to risk managers of business firms.[21] Although there are hundreds of schedules in use, the basic approach is to add to the rate for the standard building in the risk manager's city a series of credits and debits based upon a detailed analysis of the rated building's construction (e.g., thickness of walls, concealed spaces), occupany (manufacturing, wholesale grocery), exposure (adjacent buildings such as churches or factories, distance from them), and protection (automatic sprinklers, watchman service). The schedule rates are prepared after a detailed inspection by the rating bureau, and the risk manager may obtain a copy of the schedule.

The schedules used to rate large insureds and superior properties with approved automatic sprinklers give the person applying the schedule much

---

[21] For a discussion of the schedule rating plans applicable to substandard properties under FAIR plans, see pp. 620–622.

more leeway in determining the features to be considered and the charges or credits to be added or subtracted from the rate.

Under an expense modification plan insureds developing a three-year premium of at least $10,000 may, if the insurer agrees, have their rate reduced to reflect savings in acquisition costs or other expenses. This discount is most likely to be granted when there is competition for the insured's account.

The features to be included in the schedules and the size of the credits and the debits are based upon the combined judgment of the schedule makers. The statistical experience noted earlier does indicate the loss ratios of *classes* of schedule-rated risks, such as wholesale groceries in brick buildings in unprotected territories. The attention paid to these statistical indications varies as in the case of class rates.

AUTOMOBILE LIABILITY INSURANCE

Automobile liability insurance rating has many facets. First, independents write more automobile insurance than do bureau members and subscribers. Because of space considerations, however, and because the bureau-rating procedures are fairly typical, we shall limit this discussion to those procedures. Second, private passenger automobile rates depend upon different factors than do the rates for commercial cars (for example, trucks and delivery sedans) and public automobiles (for example, taxis and buses). Commercial and public automobile rates will be discussed only very briefly because the same basic principles underlie these rates and rates for private passenger automobiles.

Two countrywide bureaus are active in this field—the stock-controlled Insurance Services Office and the mutual-controlled Mutual Insurance Rating Bureau. The Insurance Services Office procedures are discussed in the following paragraphs; the Mutual Bureau structure is essentially the same. In some states the two bureaus file the same rates based on their combined experience.

Class rates   Most automobile liability insureds are class-rated. Private passenger car rates are determined as follows: First, for each car to be insured under the contract, a base premium is determined from the rating manual. The base premium depends only upon the policy limits desired and the territory in which the car will be principally garaged. Because claims in excess of $25,000 are relatively few, limits covering claims in excess of this amount can be purchased for only a modest increase in base premiums. For example, the base premium for 50/100 limits under a Family Automobile Policy is only about 30 per cent higher than the base premium for a 10/20 policy.

Second, a rating factor stated as a percentage of the base premium is calculated by adding together a primary classification rating factor and a secondary rating factor. The primary rating factor varies among insureds depending upon the use of the automobile (pleasure but not driving to work, driving to work less than 10 miles, driving to work 10 miles or more, business use, or farm use); the age, sex, and marital status of operators; whether any youthful operators have completed an approved driver-training course; and whether any youthful operators are good students. There are 480 possible factors, only a few of which can be described here. For example, if the car is used only for pleasure driving and the only operator in the household is a female driver, aged 30 to 64, the primary classification rating factor is 0.90. If the car is used by this female operator to drive to work a one-way distance less than 10 miles, the factor is 1.00. If a car used only for pleasure driving is owned by an uninsured male 17 years of age without driver training and with low grades, the factor is 3.30. A driver-training course and good grades would reduce this factor to 2.05. Other things being equal, the rates for youthful male owners decrease each year until they are aged 30, at which time they are no longer considered to be youthful owners who are charged extra for the additional expected losses associated with this group.

The secondary rating factor, of which there are ten possibilities, depends upon whether more than one car is being insured and the number of driving record points assessed against the insured under a safe-driver insurance rating plan. Under this plan the insured is assessed one point for each accident during the past three years causing bodily injuries or property damage exceeding $50 involving a car operated by the named insured or a resident relative. However, no point is assigned if the named insured can demonstrate that the accident occurred under certain circumstances—e.g., if he has secured a judgment against the other person. One point is assigned for two or more accidents during the past three years involving only minor property damage. Up to three points may be assigned for various traffic convictions such as drunken driving. Finally, one point is assigned if the principal operator has been driving for less than three years. The factor is zero for a person insuring only one car with no points. If he were insuring two or more cars, the factor would be −0.15. The highest secondary factor is 1.80 for a person with five points insuring a single car.

The final step is to multiply the base premium by the sum of the primary and secondary classification rating factors.[22] For example, assume

[22] If the number of youthful operators is less than the number of cars, the youthful-operator classification is applied only to cars equal in number to the number of youthful operators. The cars with the highest base premiums are assigned to the youthful-driver classification.

a base premium of $50 for a given territory and policy limits. A youthful male owner, aged 17, without driver training, with low grades, and with five points under the safe-driver plan would pay $50(3.30 + 1.80) = $255 to insure one car.

Rates for most commercial automobiles, other than trucks used to transport commodities for persons other than the insured, depend upon the territory of principal garaging, the use of the automobile, its size, and its radius of operations. Rates for truckmen depend upon whether they are local truckmen or long-haul truckmen, their radius of operation, and the territories in which they operate.

Public automobile rates vary according to the territory of principal garaging and the business classification—private livery, public livery, taxi-cabs, and buses classified by number of passengers.

The bureaus make extensive use of statistics in establishing both the general rate level and the rate relativities. The statistical classes correspond fairly closely with the rating classes. In the private passenger rate-making procedure, the first step is to determine the statewide rate-level change by applying the loss-ratio method with a credibility factor taken from a table. In computing the actual loss ratio, the losses are adjusted to reflect trends in average claim costs, and the premiums are developed at the current rate level. The second step is to develop the proposed rate-level changes by territory. Finally, countrywide data are analyzed to determine whether any changes should be made in the rate relativities among classes in the same territory.

Modified rates   Modification rates assume many forms in automobile liability insurance. Important modification rating plans include a fleet-rating plan, an experience-rating plan with or without a schedule-rating supplement, and retrospective rating.

The automobile fleet plan provides discounts if five or more automobiles under one ownership are insured. It is assumed that some of the automobiles in a large fleet are always out of operation because of repairs, spares, or some other reason.

The experience-rating plan, which is fairly typical, is also available for fleets of automobiles. In most states the experience rate may be further modified according to a highly flexible schedule. The schedule provides for a maximum credit of 25 per cent and a maximum debit of 20 per cent based on very broad directives with respect to management, employee charac-teristics, condition of equipment, and safety organization. The experience and schedule rate may in turn be reduced if the expenses—usually commis-sions—incurred in producing the business are less than normal. This schedule and expense modification plan was the forerunner of the comparable plan for fire insurance described on page 510.

The retrospective-rating plan is Plan D described below in connection with workmen's compensation insurance rates.

WORKMEN'S COMPENSATION

Workmen's compensation insurance may be underwritten by private insurers or by state funds. Only the rate structures of private insurers will be considered here. Although state-domiciled private bureaus (called "independent bureaus") or state-controlled bureaus make the rates in many states, the principal rating bureau is the National Council on Compensation Insurance, which makes the rates in about half of the states and serves in an advisory capacity in most of the others. The council includes both stock and nonstock members and subscribers. Except in a few states, independent insurers do not exist. Because all insurers in most states use the same initial rates, more workmen's compensation insurance is written by both stock and mutuals on a dividend basis than any other line of property and liability insurance.

About 85 per cent of the workmen's compensation insureds are class-rated. Their payroll is divided into classes on the basis of the type of industry (piano manufacturing), the occupation of the employee (clerical office employee), or the industrial operation performed (manufacturing concrete at the job location by a contractor constructing bridges). Generally the entire payroll falls into one class determined by the industry except for clerical office employees, drivers, and certain other "standard exceptions." Because the payroll (to which the rate per $100 of payroll must be applied to determine the premium) can be estimated only at the beginning of the year, the insured pays a deposit premium which is adjusted at the end of the policy period or on an interim basis.

In no property and liability insurance field do the rate makers pay more attention to statistical indications than in workmen's compensation insurance. For each of the payroll classes, there is statistical information concerning the exposures in terms of $100 of payroll, and the losses are subdivided into three classes—serious disability losses, nonserious disability losses, and medical expenses.

The first step in revising workmen's compensation class rates is to determine the statewide rate change by what is essentially a loss-ratio approach. Losses are adjusted for amendments to the workmen's compensation law, and the premiums are converted to the current rate level. The second step is to determine the pure premiums for each of the payroll classes. Finally, the class pure premiums are loaded for expenses in the usual fashion.

Modified rates   Modification rating plans are extremely important in workmen's compensation insurance. These include an experience-rating plan, a premium-discount plan, and several retrospective-rating plans. Experience rating and retrospective rating were first developed as workmen's compensation insurance rating tools.

An insured whose annual premium at manual rates would average about $750 must be experience-rated. The detailed plan cannot be discussed here, but we should note that it is the most carefully and objectively designed experience-rating plan in insurance.

If the insured's annual premium exceeds $1,000, his premium is subject to a discount because of expense savings. The discounts are tabled and increase as the premium increases. Two sets of discounts are provided—stock discounts and nonstock discounts. Nonstock discounts are smaller because the insurers using these discounts prefer to pay dividends.

As an alternative to the premium-discount plan, an insured whose annual premium exceeds $1,000 may elect to be retrospectively rated under plan A, B, C, or J. Each of these plans specifies the set of maximum and minimum premiums corresponding to the standard premium—the premium that would be paid without the benefit of retrospective rating or premium discounts. Because of their importance, each of these plans will be described briefly.

Under plan A, the maximum premium is the standard premium, and the minimum premium exceeds the basic premium. At most, the insured loses his premium discount. Under plan B the maximum premium is greater than the standard premium, and the minimum premium is less than the plan A minimum. In other words, the possible fluctuation in the premium is much greater. The basic premium is considerably less. Plan C has the same maximum premium as plan B, but the minimum premium is much less since it is the basic premium times the tax multiplier. This plan produces a lower premium than plan B only when the experience is superior, because dropping the minimum premium increases the basic premium. Plan J is characterized by a lower maximum premium than either plan B or plan C, but the minimum premium is lower than under plan A. It is suitable for insureds who find A too conservative and B or C too risky.

Plan	Basic premium, per cent	Minimum premium, per cent	Maximum premium, per cent
A	31.9	83.5	100
B	24.6	62.0	165
C	36.9	36.9 × tax multiplier	165
J	31.8	69.4	130

To illustrate these differences, assume that an insured has a $10,000 standard premium. In one state, the ratios of his basic, minimum, and maximum premiums to this standard premium would be as shown in the table at the bottom of page 514.

An insured whose annual premium exceeds $5,000 may also elect plan D, which has two distinctive characteristics. First, the insured may, subject to the consent of the insurer, select any reasonable set of minimum and maximum premiums. In other words, plans A, B, C, and J are special cases of plan D. Second, plan D can be applied, separately or in some combination, to workmen's compensation insurance, automobile liability insurance, general liability insurance, automobile physical damage insurance, burglary insurance, and glass insurance.

LIFE INSURANCE

In the property and liability insurance lines discussed, rating bureaus either establish the rates for much of the insurance written or have played an important role in developing the rating methods used in those lines. Consequently, particular attention has been focused upon bureau rating methods. In life insurance there are no rating bureaus; each insurer has a staff of actuaries to set its own prices or relies upon the services of consulting actuaries. Despite this independence of action, however, the same basic principles underlie the approach of all life insurers. Because the special characteristics of pricing group insurance and pension plans have already been noted briefly, this discussion will be limited to individual life insurance.

Class rates predominate in individual life insurance. For standard lives, the rates for a particular contract depend upon the age at issue and in most cases upon the face value of the contract. The class rates for substandard lines also depend upon the severity of their impairment or the dangers associated with their occupation.

Life insurance class rates can be and are established on a much more mathematically precise basis than is possible in the other lines of insurance. This statement is not meant to imply that life insurance rating is a completely objective, accurate process; as will be shown below, considerable judgment enters into the making of life insurance rates.[23]

The primary reasons why life insurance rating can be more precise than rating in other lines are that (1) because all losses are total and a fixed amount is paid in case of death (or survival under an annuity contract), the only loss information required is the probability of death at each age and (2) the mortality rates at each age, although subject to long-term trends, are fairly stable in the short run. Furthermore, because all insurers

---

[23] For a critical comment on the scientific accuracy of insurance rates, including life insurance rates, see A. H. Mowbray, R. H. Blanchard, and C. A. Williams, Jr., *Insurance* (6th ed., New York: McGraw-Hill Book Company, 1969), pp. 414–416.

use the same simple classification for standard lives, the experience of the principal insurers can be combined to provide highly credible experience, which may or may not be adopted by a particular insurer as a basis for its rates.

This combined experience or an insurer's individual experience forms the foundation for a mortality table which shows the mortality rates at each age. These mortality rates differ from the pure experience in that they have been (1) graded to eliminate irregular chance fluctuations and (2) loaded to provide a margin of safety. On the assumption that some arbitrary number of persons, such as 10 million, is alive at the initial age in the table, the table shows, in addition to the mortality rates at each age, the number of deaths which will occur at that age out of the initial 10 million and the number who will survive to the next age.

The most recent mortality table based upon combined experience is the 1958 Commissioners Standard Ordinary Table, so-called (1) because in 1958 the National Association of Insurance Commissioners approved its use for minimum reserve valuations and (2) because the table applies to ordinary insurance on standard lives. This table is reproduced as Table 25.1. Several other combined mortality tables are in current use, such as the Group Annuity Table for 1951 and the 1941 Standard Industrial Table. The safety margins in the annuity tables must of course work in the opposite direction. Most participating insurers use one of these combined experience tables to establish their premiums, but nonparticipating insurers, in order to compete, modify these mortality rates according to their own experience or other combined experience with no safety margins.

Life insurance rates, unlike property and liability insurance rates, also depend upon an assumed interest return on the insurer's investments. The importance of this assumed interest return will be evident in the example presented in the next paragraph. Participating insurers, because of their dividend policy, can be conservative in their interest assumptions, while nonparticipating insurers must be as realistic as possible.

To illustrate the uses of the mortality data and the assumed interest rate and the basic principles of life insurance rate making, the following simplified example is presented. Assume that a man, aged 35, wants to pay one lump sum for a $1,000 five-year term insurance contract. What is the appropriate lump sum on the assumption that the 1958 CSO mortality rates and a 3 per cent interest return will be maintained and that expenses can be ignored? This lump sum is called the "net single premium." For explanation purposes,[24] assume that this man is one of the 9,373,807

---

[24] Most actuaries prefer an explanation in terms of probabilities, but the approach used here is easier for the nontechnical reader to understand.
Fortunately actuaries have developed tools called "commutation tables," which reduce greatly the work in premium computations.

Table 25.1 1958 CSO mortality table

Age	Number living	Number dying	Mortality rates per thousand
0	10,000,000	70,800	7.08
1	9,929,200	17,475	1.76
2	9,911,726	15,066	1.52
3	9,896,659	14,449	1.46
4	9,882,210	13,835	1.40
5	9,868,375	13,322	1.35
6	9,855,053	12,812	1.30
7	9,842,241	12,401	1.26
8	9,829,840	12,091	1.23
9	9,817,749	11,879	1.21
10	9,805,870	11,865	1.21
11	9,794,005	12,047	1.23
12	9,781,958	12,325	1.26
13	9,769,633	12,896	1.32
14	9,756,737	13,562	1.39
15	9,743,175	14,225	1.46
16	9,728,950	14,983	1.54
17	9,713,956	15,737	1.62
18	9,698,230	16,390	1.69
19	9,681,840	16,846	1.74
20	9,664,994	17,300	1.79
21	9,647,694	17,655	1.83
22	9,630,039	17,912	1.86
23	9,612,127	18,167	1.89
24	9,593,960	18,324	1.91
25	9,575,636	18,481	1.93
26	9,557,155	18,732	1.96
27	9,538,423	18,981	1.99
28	9,519,442	19,324	2.03
29	9,500,118	19,760	2.08
30	9,480,358	20,193	2.13
31	9,460,165	20,718	2.19
32	9,439,447	21,239	2.25
33	9,418,208	21,850	2.32
34	9,396,358	22,551	2.40
35	9,373,807	23,528	2.51
36	9,350,279	24,685	2.64
37	9,325,594	26,112	2.80
38	9,299,482	27,991	3.01
39	9,271,491	30,132	3.25

Table 25.1 (continued)

Age	Number living	Number dying	Mortality rates per thousand
40	9,241,359	32,622	3.53
41	9,208,737	35,362	3.84
42	9,173,375	38,253	4.17
43	9,135,122	41,382	4.53
44	9,093,740	44,741	4.92
45	9,048,999	48,412	5.35
46	9,000,587	52,473	5.83
47	8,948,114	56,910	6.36
48	8,891,204	61,794	6.95
49	8,829,410	67,104	7.60
50	8,762,306	72,902	8.32
51	8,689,404	79,160	9.11
52	8,610,244	85,758	9.96
53	8,524,486	92,832	10.89
54	8,431,654	100,337	11.90
55	8,331,317	108,307	13.00
56	8,223,010	116,849	14.21
57	8,106,161	125,970	15.54
58	7,980,191	135,663	17.00
59	7,884,528	145,830	18.59
60	7,698,698	156,592	20.34
61	7,542,106	167,736	22.24
62	7,374,370	179,271	24.31
63	7,195,099	191,174	26.57
64	7,003,925	203,394	29.04
65	6,800,531	215,917	31.75
66	6,584,614	228,749	34.74
67	6,355,865	241,777	38.04
68	6,114,088	254,835	41.68
69	5,859,253	267,241	45.61
70	5,592,012	278,426	49.79
71	5,313,586	287,731	54.15
72	5,025,855	294,766	58.65
73	4,731,089	299,289	63.26
74	4,431,800	301,894	68.12
75	4,129,906	303,011	73.37
76	3,826,895	303,014	79.18
77	3,523,881	301,997	85.70
78	3,221,884	299,829	93.06
79	2,922,055	295,683	101.19

Table 25.1   (continued)

Age	Number living	Number dying	Mortality rates per thousand
80	2,626,372	288,848	109.98
81	2,337,524	278,983	119.35
82	2,058,541	265,902	129.17
83	1,792,639	249,858	139.38
84	1,542,781	231,433	150.01
85	1,311,348	211,311	161.14
86	1,100,037	190,108	172.82
87	909,929	168,455	185.13
88	741,474	146,997	198.25
89	594,477	126,303	212.46
90	468,174	106,809	228.14
91	361,365	88,813	245.77
92	272,552	72,480	265.93
93	200,072	57,881	289.30
94	142,191	45,026	316.66
95	97,165	34,128	351.24
96	63,037	25,250	400.56
97	37,787	18,456	488.42
98	19,331	12,916	668.15
99	6,415	6,415	1,000.00

who have survived to age 35 according to Table 25.1 and that all these persons are interested in the same insurance.[25] According to Table 25.1, out of these 9,373,807 persons, 23,528 will die the first year, 24,685 the second, 26,112 the third, 27,991 the fourth, and 30,132 the fifth. The actuary assumes that these death claims will not be paid until the end of the year in which the death occurs. Because of this time lag and because of the assumed interest return, he need not collect $23,528,000 now to pay the death claims occurring the first year. The necessary fund is only $23,528,000/1.03, or $23,043,335, because this amount invested for one year at 3 per cent will yield $23,528,000. The amount which must be collected now to meet the claims payable at the end of the second year is $24,685,000/(1.03)^2, or $23,268,081, because this amount invested for two years at 3 per cent will yield $24,685,000. A similar procedure is followed for the other three years. The increasing importance of the interest assumption in the later contract years is obvious.

[25] The fact that the number of persons purchasing the insurance almost certainly will be different from 9,373,807 will not affect the answer so long as the mortality *rates* still apply.

(1)	(2)	(3)	(4)
		Present value of	Present value of
Contract	Death	$1 payable at	death claims
year	claims	end of year, 3%	(2) × (3)
1	$23,528,000	$0.9709	$ 23,043,335
2	24,685,000	0.9426	23,268,081
3	26,112,000	0.9151	23,895,091
4	27,991,000	0.8885	24,870,004
5	30,132,000	0.8626	25,991,863
			Total $121,068,374

The computation is shown in tabular form at the top of the page.

The net single premium is equal to this fund divided by the number of insureds. In this case, the net single premium is $121,068,374/9,373,807, or $12.92.

If the insureds pay for this contract with five annual premiums, the five annual premiums will have to be greater than a single premium payment at the beginning of the five years, because (1) not all insureds will live to pay the five annual premiums and (2) the insurer will not have the use of all the premiums for five years. The actuary first determines the lump-sum equivalent of a $1 annual premium over the next five years on the assumption that the premiums are paid at the beginning of the year. All 9,373,807 insureds will pay $1 on the issue date, but only 9,350,279 insureds will pay $1 one year later, and because of the loss of interest on this money, its present value is only $9,350,279/1.03, or $9,078,186. Similar computations are made for the other years and are summarized in the table following.

(1)	(2)	(3)	(4)
		Present value of	
		$1 payable at	Present value of $1
Contract	Premium	beginning of year,	premium payments,
year	payors	3%	(2) × (3)
1	9,373,807	$1.0000	$ 9,373,807
2	9,350,279	0.9709	9,078,186
3	9,325,594	0.9426	8,790,305
4	9,299,482	0.9151	8,509,956
5	9,271,491	0.8885	8,237,720
			Total $43,989,974

This present value of the $1 premium payments per policyholder is $43,989,974/9,373,807, or $4.69. The present value of $2 premium payments would be twice this value, $3 premium payments three times this value, etc. Consequently,

$$\begin{array}{l} \text{Desired} \\ \text{annual} \\ \text{premium} \end{array} \times \begin{array}{l} \\ \text{present value of \$1} \\ \text{premium payments} \end{array} = \begin{array}{l} \text{net} \\ \text{single} \\ \text{premium} \end{array}$$

or

$$\begin{array}{l} \text{Desired annual} \\ \text{premium} \end{array} = \frac{\text{net single premium}}{\begin{array}{l}\text{present value of \$1} \\ \text{premium payments}\end{array}}$$

$$= \frac{\$12.92}{\$4.69} = \$2.75$$

Although these principles have been stated in terms of a specific example, they are general in their application. For example, in order to determine the net annual premium for a straight life policy, the only difference would be that each table would be extended to include 65 contract years, i.e., to age 100, at which time it is assumed that all of the 9,373,807 insureds will have died.

The gross premium is the net premium loaded for expenses. Participating insurers usually add to the net premium a percentage of the premium plus (1) a constant per $1,000 of insurance or (2) a constant per $1,000 of insurance and a constant per policy. As might be expected, nonparticipating insurers must be more precise in their initial premium computations.

REVIEW QUESTIONS

1. a. Most state laws require that property and liability insurance rates be *reasonable, adequate,* and *not unfairly discriminatory.* What do these terms mean?
   b. What are the legal requirements with respect to life insurance rates? Why do they differ from the requirements with respect to property and liability insurance rates?
2. a. Distinguish between individual and class rates.
   b. Cite some examples of each of these two types of rates.
   c. What risk managers are most likely to be concerned about individual rates?
3. The loss-ratio and pure-premium approaches to class rate making are equivalent mathematically but differ in some other ways. Explain this statement.

4. a. Suggest ways in which an insurer might establish the volume of experience required to merit 100 per cent credibility.
   b. What is meant by "60 per cent credibility"?
5. a. How can a risk manager make use of the results of schedule rating?
   b. When does schedule rating approach individual rating?
6. a. The class premium for a firm would have been $4,000, but the firm is eligible for experience rating. During the experience period, the firm had actual losses totaling $6,000. An average firm in its rating class would have suffered losses totaling $8,000. The credibility percentage for this firm is 40 per cent. How much will the class premium be reduced as a result of experience rating?
   b. How would you answer a if the actual losses were $10,000?
   c. Does it make any difference under experience rating whether a firm has 5 losses of $10,000 each or 50 losses of $1,000 each? Explain.
7. a. Compare retrospective rating with self-insurance.
   b. Under what conditions might an insurer require retrospective rating?
8. How is the retrospective premium affected by:
   a. Lowering the maximum premium and raising the minimum premium
   b. Raising both the maximum premium and the minimum premium
9. Rating bureaus are less important in property and liability insurance than they were formerly.
   a. Which of the five bureau systems do you prefer? Why?
   b. What are the advantages of rating bureaus?
   c. Why have rating bureaus declined in importance?
   d. How important are rating bureaus in life and health insurance?
10. a. Do property and liability insurers always pay all policyholders in the same rating class the same percentage dividend? If not, what do they do?
    b. If a life insurer earns 1 per cent more on its investments than it assumed in establishing its rates, which policyholders will receive the greater dividend return as a result—term insurance policyholders or straight life insurance policyholders? Which group would gain more from mortality savings? Why?
11. a. What types of business firms are class-rated by fire insurers?
    b. Are fire insurance class rates based on statistical analysis?
    c. How can a class-rated business firm cut its rates?
12. Describe briefly the basic approach to schedule rating in fire insurance.
13. a. What factors affect the automobile liability class rate which a sole proprietor will have to pay?
    b. How do the policy limits affect the class rate?
    c. Is automobile insurance merit rating experience rating? Explain your answer.

14. Are the automobile liability insurance class rates paid by persons in a medium-sized city in your state based solely upon the automobile liability experience in that city? Explain your answer.

15. A large firm has a fleet of automobiles consisting of 40 private passenger automobiles and 15 trucks. What automobile liability insurance modification rating plans are applicable to this firm?

16. a. What factors affect workmen's compensation class premiums?
    b. To what extent do the class rates paid by a firm in a particular industry depend upon the loss experience in that industry?

17. On what basis should a firm decide among workmen's compensation retrospective-rating plans A, B, C, D, and J?

18. Compute the net level annual premium for each of the following policies:
    a. A three-year $1,000 term life insurance policy issued at age 25
    b. A three-year $1,000 endowment policy issued at age 25

19. Compare life insurance, workmen's compensation, and fire insurance rating with respect to:
    a. Reliance upon statistical data
    b. Recognition of investment return

20. Participating and nonparticipating life insurers differ somewhat in their approach to pricing. How and why?

SUGGESTIONS FOR ADDITIONAL READING

Automobile Insurance Ratemaking (New York: Casualty Actuarial Society, 1960).

Crane, F.: *Automobile Insurance Rate Regulation,* Bureau of Business Research Monograph No. 105 (Columbus, Ohio: Bureau of Business Research, The Ohio State University, 1962).

Fire Insurance Rate Making and Kindred Problems (New York: Casualty Actuarial Society, 1960).

Hartman, G. R.: *Ratemaking for Homeowners Insurance* (Homewood, Ill.: Richard D. Irwin, Inc., 1967).

Jordan, C. W., Jr.: *Life Contingencies* (2d ed., Chicago: Society of Actuaries, 1967).

Kulp, C. A., and Hall, J. W.: *Casualty Insurance* (4th ed., New York: The Ronald Press Co., 1968), chaps. 11 and 19–22.

Marshall, R. M.: *Workmen's Compensation Insurance Ratemaking* (rev. ed., New York: Casualty Actuarial Society, 1961).

McGill, D. M.: *Life Insurance* (rev. ed., Homewood, Ill.: Richard D. Irwin, Inc., 1966), chaps. 8–12.

Menge, W. O., and Fischer, C. H.: *The Mathematics of Life Insurance* (2d ed., New York: The Macmillan Company, 1965).

Proceedings of the Casualty Actuarial Society (annual).

Riegel, R., and Miller, J.: *Insurance Principles and Practices* (5th ed., Englewood Cliffs, N.J.: Prentice-Hall, Inc., 1966), chaps. 11, 12, 19, 28, and 34.

Transactions of the Society of Actuaries (periodic).

Williams, C. A., Jr.: *Price Discrimination in Property and Liability Insurance,* University of Minnesota, Studies in Economics and Business No. 19 (Minneapolis: The University of Minnesota Press, 1959).

26

preparation for loss adjustments

In addition to analyzing risks faced by his firm and designing and implementing the best insurance program for it, the risk manager must know how to deal with insurers following a loss in order to assure a prompt and equitable adjustment of his claim. This chapter discusses, first, the different types of adjusters who may be involved in the negotiations, and second, several important loss-adjustment principles and procedures. The second topic is discussed separately for property insurance, liability insurance, and personnel insurance.

Types of Adjusters

Not all insurers employ the same types of adjusters to handle claims, and the same insurer may use different types of adjusters, depending upon the size or type of loss or the geographical location. The risk manager should be aware of the various types of adjusters and their role in the insurance mechanism. The types to be discussed here are (1) agents or sales representatives, (2) salaried adjusters on the insurer's staff, (3) employees of insurer-owned adjustment bureaus, (4) independent adjusters, and (5) public adjusters.

AGENTS AND SALES REPRESENTATIVES

Small property insurance claims (e.g., losses of $100 or less) are often adjusted by the agent or, much less frequently, by the sales representative.

Producers may also render valuable services for insureds in connection with other losses.

STAFF ADJUSTERS

Most insurers writing a large volume of property and liability business in a particular area have a staff of salaried adjusters to service that area. These specialists are used except when the insurer has written only part of the insurance involved in a loss (a common situation in fire insurance), in which case it is generally considered more efficient and economical to turn the claim over to an adjustment bureau or an independent adjuster. The authority of these adjusters varies according to the insurer. Staff adjusters of some insurers are authorized to use their own judgment in settling almost every claim, while others must refer practically every case to the home or branch office. Still others possess final authority on claims up to some specified amount. The adjuster is more likely to possess final authority with respect to property claims than to liability claims.

Most life insurance claims are handled very promptly by the claims departments in the branch or home offices. Field adjusters, however, are employed extensively with respect to health insurance claims.

ADJUSTMENT BUREAUS

Adjustment bureaus are separate organizations owned by insurers. At present there are only two adjustment bureaus, the General Adjustment Bureau, Inc., which operates on a nationwide basis, and the Underwriters Adjusting Company, which operates only in the Midwest. Both provide services primarily for their stock insurer owners but also service other insurers. Insurers are most likely to seek the services of the bureau if the insurance is shared with other insurers and in those areas where their volume of business does not justify the employment of a staff adjuster. In January, 1971, following an antitrust investigation by the Department of Justice, the insurer-owners of the General Adjustment Bureau agreed to divest themselves of their stocks in this organization. The bureau will continue under public ownership.

INDEPENDENT ADJUSTERS

Independent adjusters are persons or firms engaged in loss-adjustment work as independent businessmen. They service insurers on a fee basis. Sometimes they specialize in a particular line of insurance such as automobile insurance. Insurers often hire independent adjusters to handle claims in areas where they write little business, to supplement staff adjusters during peak claim periods, and to adjust claims requiring highly specialized skills. Independent adjusters, like adjustment bureaus, have extensive authority. Many self-insurers hire independent adjusters to service their plans.

PUBLIC ADJUSTERS

Although an insured can represent himself in a loss adjustment, it is common practice in property insurance for an insured with a large loss to be represented by a public adjuster.[1] The public adjusters assist the insured in the preparation of the necessary records (to be discussed later) and in negotiations with the insurer's representative. Because of the public adjuster's familiarity with loss-adjustment principles and procedures, it is argued that in many cases he increases the insured's recovery. As his fee, the public adjuster commonly receives a stated percentage, say 10 per cent, of the amount paid by the insurer.[2]

Principles and Procedures

Although loss-adjustment principles and procedures in property, liability, and personnel insurance have much in common, considerable variation exists among the most important problems in each branch. For this reason, the three branches will be discussed separately.

PROPERTY INSURANCE

Insurance contracts impose certain obligations upon the insured following a loss. Failure to meet these obligations may prevent the insured from recovering on what is otherwise a valid claim. In property insurance contracts, the insured is usually instructed to (1) notify the insurer, (2) protect the property from further damage, and (3) assist the insurer in its investigation of the loss.

Notice of loss   The insured must usually notify the insurer or, in most instances, a duly authorized agent "immediately" or "as soon as practicable." The courts interpret both terms to mean as soon as is reasonably possible. Furthermore, notice to the agent is always sufficient. A few contracts require that the notice be given within a specified period following the loss.

The policy usually requires that the notice be given in writing. Actually, however, oral notice to the insurer is usually sufficient unless the insurer or its agent objects. Even if it makes an objection, the policy requirement is ineffective if the insurer then proceeds to adjust the claim. In spite of these liberal interpretations, however, the insured will be wise to give the notice in writing because he may need a copy as evidence in case the notice is questioned. Some policies, such as those covering theft losses,

---

[1] Compensation claimants' attorneys play a similar role in liability insurance.
[2] Some public adjusters must unfortunately be classified as "ambulance chasers," but the merits of others are widely recognized—even by adjusters for the insurers.

where prompt action may reduce substantially the amount of the loss, require telegraphic notice or some other special form of communication.

The insured may also be expected to notify someone other than the insurer. Under a theft insurance policy, for example, the insured must tell the police, as well as the insurer, about the loss.

Protection of property from further damage All property insurance contracts require the insured to protect the property from further damage. Failure to meet this requirement will release the insurer from any responsibility for further damage. Although not all policies specifically state that the insurer will reimburse the insured for any reasonable expenses incurred in protecting the property, such reimbursement is usually made. Only in marine insurance contracts, however, is this reimbursement in addition to the face value of the contract. In some contracts, such as business interruption insurance, the reimbursement is specifically limited to the reduction in the loss.

Ideally, the adjuster will arrive promptly on the scene and suggest the types of protective measures that should be adopted. The degree of supervision exercised by the loss adjuster over the insured's protective work depends upon the loss situation and the adjuster's evaluation of the insured. Sometimes the adjuster assumes the insured's responsibility completely. The insured should not hesitate, however, to take any action that appears reasonable and necessary before the arrival of the adjuster.

Examples of protective measures which have proved beneficial in some instances are the following: nailing of tar paper over holes in a roof, draining of plumbing in cold weather, separation of wet debris from woodwork, removal of contents from a building threatened by further damage, drying and greasing of wet machinery, prompt distribution of perishables to retailers or consumers or to cold-storage plants, separation and drying of wet merchandise, and coverage of exposed equipment with tarpaulins.

Assistance in the investigation The third duty of the insured following the loss is to assist the loss adjuster in his investigation. The adjuster must determine (1) whether the loss actually occurred, (2) whether it is covered under the contract, and (3) the extent of the loss. The burden of proof is upon the insured, and the better prepared he is to aid in these determinations, the more satisfactory and prompt the final loss adjustment is likely to be. If the adjuster has some doubt concerning whether the loss is covered, he may ask the insured to sign a nonwaiver agreement which states that the insurer is not admitting its liability by its investigation. Despite the nonwaiver agreement, however, the insurer may be held liable if it causes the insured undue expense or inconvenience. Sometimes in a doubtful situation the insurer does not request a nonwaiver agreement but sends the insured a reservation-of-rights letter in which it reserves the right to deny the claim later.

Usually it is a simple matter to determine whether the loss occurred, and the insured will have no difficulty in proving his case. In some instances, however, particularly with respect to theft and mysterious disappearance losses, the adjuster may have to rely heavily upon the reputation of the insured.

To determine whether the loss is covered, the adjuster must be thoroughly acquainted with the property insured, the circumstances surrounding the loss, and the insurance contract. He must know whether the contract was in force at the time of the loss and whether the contract covers the peril, the person(s), the property, the location, and the type of loss (direct or consequential) involved in the claim. The contract may also specify some conditions not falling into any of these categories which, if they exist, suspend or terminate the coverage. The insurer can supply contract information, but the adjuster must rely upon the insured to provide information concerning the property and the circumstances of the loss. This the insured can do by exhibiting the remains of the property and the space it occupied and by offering testimony, fire-department or police-department records, plans and specifications, deeds, bills of sale, or other evidence.

The most difficult task in adjusting property losses in the valuation of the loss. For direct property losses, the usual basis of recovery is the actual cash value of the loss. As pointed out in Chapter 16, this measure is usually the cost of repair or replacement new less depreciation (including obsolescence) or the decrease in market value, but other measures are possible. Even after a measure has been agreed upon, disagreement may arise concerning such concepts as depreciation and market value.

The insured and the adjuster may use one or more of several methods to establish the value of the property and the loss. For example, they may look at the property together and agree on the loss;[3] they may make or have made separate estimates and reconcile their differences; they may prepare specifications for repair or replacement and submit these to be bid upon; they may accept the valuation of a single expert; or they may accept the amounts shown in accounting records.[4]

Property insurance contracts generally require the insured to produce upon request at reasonable times and places all records pertinent to the valuation procedure. If the records have been destroyed or if they are otherwise unavailable, the insured does not usually lose his right to press the

---

[3] Most small- and moderate-sized losses are adjusted in this way. P. B. Reed and P. I. Thomas, *Adjustment of Property Losses* (3d ed., New York: McGraw-Hill Book Company, 1969), p. 9.
[4] *Ibid.*, pp. 8–13. Reed and Thomas list eleven different methods.

claim, but his own best interests are served if he can provide records substantiating his claim because the adjustment process will then be speeded up and is more likely to be equitable. Under some contracts, the insured is required to keep records of the insured property which will enable the insurer to determine accurately the amount of the loss.

Consequential property losses are even more difficult to evaluate than direct property losses. The length of time required to restore premises to a tenantable condition, the net profit and continuing expenses that would have been covered by sales during the period a store must be out of operation, and the profits that a manufacturer would have made on the sale of some finished goods are examples of losses falling in this category. Often the losses must be estimated from sketchy accounting data.

The difficulties in measuring losses are compounded when the contract contains a coinsurance clause because this clause makes necessary a valuation of the undamaged as well as of the damaged property. Except when the loss is small, the insurer is likely to require a detailed inventory of the damaged and undamaged property, and the insured is well-advised to keep adequate up-to-date records for this purpose. The fire insurance contract specifically charges the insured with the preparation of such inventory records after any loss, but this provision is seldom enforced with respect to the undamaged property unless there is a coinsurance clause.

Within some specified period following the loss, such as 30 or 90 days, the insured must file a sworn detailed proof of loss with the insurer. The insurer usually furnishes a blank proof-of-loss form, which the insured completes and signs. Most claims are adjusted swiftly and without difficulty, and in such cases it is common practice for the adjuster to complete the proof-of-loss form for the insured's signature after the adjustment has been completed. In situations where the insured's story may change over time or where a dispute has arisen, the adjuster may refuse to proceed with the adjustment until the insured has executed a proof of loss.

Several legal interpretations and statutes soften the impact of the proof-of-loss requirement upon the insured. Although contracts specify the number of days within which the proof of loss must be filed, several states by statute or by court interpretation have either made it unnecessary for insureds to comply with this time period or require the insurer to give additional notice of its intention to enforce this provision. The courts have also held that a material misstatement by the insured in the proof of loss shall not affect the insured's right of recovery unless the misstatement was intentional. The insurer or its representatives may be held to have waived the proof-of-loss requirement if they deny liability, if they promise to prepare the proof-of-loss statement for the insured, or if they begin to adjust the loss without notifying the insured that proof of loss will be required. The insured cannot be accused of failure to comply with the proof-of-loss provisions because of some defect which the insurer does not promptly point out. The insured can change the filed proof-of-loss form if he believes that his initial loss estimates were in error. Despite these favorable interpretations, the insured should make every attempt to comply with the policy provisions. His case may be the exception which proves the rule.

Usually the insurer will pay the claim shortly after the insured files the proof of loss. Some contracts specify a time period within which the claim must be paid.

Special problems   In some property-loss adjustments, problems arise which necessitate additional steps in the loss-adjustment procedure. For example, the procedure may be more lengthy and complex when there is (1) other insurance, (2) a third party who is responsible for the loss, (3) some dispute over the valuation of the loss, or (4) any disagreement which might eventually result in a court case.

If two or more contracts cover the loss, it is usually clear from contract provisions how the loss is to be apportioned among the various insurers, but sometimes the situation is ambiguous. For example, there may be two contracts, each of which claims to provide excess insurance over any other insurance covering the loss. The courts usually resolve such situations in a way that is beneficial to the insured. In the case cited, they would probably require the insurers to share the loss on a pro rata basis. Most cases of this sort, however, are handled without going to court.

Most insurers abide by Guiding Principles (1963), which prescribe certain rules to be followed in settling disputes because of overlapping coverages. A few examples will illustrate these principles. If two or more policies cover the same property and the same interest, the insurance which is specific as to property and location is primary to any other insurance such as blanket or floating insurance. Bailee's customers' insurance is primary insurance to other insurance purchased by the same named bailee-insured. If the owner of a building and its contents has one policy covering the building and another policy covering the contents, the policy on the building is primary with respect to wall-to-wall carpeting if the carpeting is included in the realty mortgage.

Many controversies among insurers which are covered by the rules are submitted to arbitration instead of to the courts. The arbitrators are sometimes trade-association committees.

The insured and his insurance advisor can reduce the number of these controversies by avoiding needless nonconcurrencies and overlaps in his program.

The second special problem to be discussed arises when the insured has a legal right to recover his loss from some third party. The third party may be responsible as a result of negligence, a contract, or a statute. Common law and the subrogation clause in the insurance contract provide that the insurer, upon payment of the loss, may take over the right of the insured to collect from the responsible third party to the extent of the insurance payment. The insured, therefore, must be careful after (and before) a loss not to prejudice this right of the insurer. The right is particularly important in transportation insurance because of common carrier liability and in automobile collision insurance because another party is often at fault.[5] In no event should the insured release the party responsible without the consent of the insurer simply because he is willing to pay the part of the loss that is not insured.

The insurer may seek to recover from the third party in the name of the insured or in its own name. If the loss exceeds the insurance payment, the insured may join in the suit, sue in his own name for the entire amount or his interest only, or rely on the insurer to sue for the entire loss. In any event, the insurer is usually entitled only to the amount by which the net recovery (excluding recovery costs) exceeds the net loss (excluding any insurance payments) to the insured. For example, an insured may have a $15,000 loss for which he recovers $10,000 from an insurer. If the net recovery from some third party who caused the loss is $14,000, the insured recovers $5,000 and the insurer $9,000. Some contracts, e.g., some fidelity bonds, stipulate that the net recovery is to be shared by the insurer and the insured in proportion to their losses. Under a few contracts, the insurer has primary rights to the recovery.

The third special problem occurs when the insured and the adjuster cannot reach an agreement concerning the valuation of the property or the loss. In such an event, two contract provisions are pertinent. Under the first, either the insurer or the insured has the right to demand in writing that the differences be resolved by an appraisal. Each party names an appraiser to represent him, and the appraisers then select a competent and disinterested umpire. If the appraisers cannot agree on an umpire, provision is made for his selection by the courts. The appraisers then value each property item and the loss to that item. Only their differences are submitted to the umpire. In the absence of fraud, collusion, or mutual mistake, an award signed by any two of the three persons is binding. The insured must pay his representative's fee plus one-half of the bill of the umpire and other appraisal charges.

The insured must submit to the demand of the insurer for an appraisal,

---

[5] Automobile collision subrogation claims often involve two insurers. Under a Nationwide Inter-company Arbitration Agreement, most insurers have agreed to submit to local arbitration committees all automobile physical damage subrogation claims below a stated amount. Almost all claims are settled merely on the basis of claim files.

but in most instances,[6] if the insurer refuses to submit to a similar demand of the insured, the insured's only remedy is to sue.

The second provision which becomes pertinent in a valuation dispute gives the insurer the right instead of paying the loss in cash to buy all or any part of the property at the agreed or appraised value or to repair, rebuild, or replace the property. Although this provision gives the insurer an out if it disagrees with either the insured's or the appraisers' estimate of the loss, in most property lines the insurer seldom exercises this option because of the difficulties involved in disposing of property or in repairing, rebuilding, or replacing to the insured's satisfaction.

These options are used, however, in settling personal property claims when the insurer is in a better position to dispose of the property than is the insured. For example, some merchandise damaged by smoke can often be reclaimed and sold by salvors employed by the insurer more advan- tageously than they could be sold by the insured. In other instances, the insured himself conducts the sale under the supervision of the insurer.

Replacement in kind instead of a cash payment is the usual rule when the insurer can replace the property more promptly or more economically than can the insured. Two illustrations of losses of this type are glass losses and jewelry losses.

The final special problem to be considered is fortunately relatively rare. In some instances, the insured is unable to resolve his differences with the insurer and must resort to a suit. The insured must have complied with all the requirements of the contract before he can successfully sustain a suit against the insurer. These include, among other things, the commence- ment of the suit within a certain time period which may be stated either in terms of a date after or before which suit cannot be brought or of a time interval during which the suit must be started. The minimum time limit gives the insured time to consider its action on the claim, while the maximum time limit permits the insurer to close its books on old claims after a reasonable time. Sometimes the insured may be excused from the maximum time limit. For example, the time limit would not be enforced if the insured and the insurer were still involved in the investigation of the loss at the terminal date.

LIABILITY INSURANCE

Liability insurance claims present some responsibilities and problems for the insured which differ from those associated with property insurance

---

[6] There are exceptions. For example, under the Minnesota statutory fire policy, if either party fails to select an appraiser within twenty days after the demand is made, a presiding judge of the district court of the county where the loss occurs may appoint an appraiser for the party which fails to appoint one itself.

claims. Whereas property insurance claims are termed first-party claims because the insured has suffered the loss, liability losses are called third-party claims because the insured is legally obligated to pay some injured third party. The discussion in this section will emphasize the special characteristics of liability insurance claims. Workmen's compensation and medical payments claims, which are more closely akin to health insurance claims, are covered in the next section.

Special interest of business risk managers　Business risk managers are much more interested in the outcome of a liability claim than are family risk managers. Family risk managers, to be sure, are extremely concerned about escaping any possible loss to themselves, but they commonly have little direct interest in the manner in which the claim is handled unless they know the injured party. Business risk managers, on the other hand, do have a direct interest because every claimant is a potential customer or because the integrity of their business is at stake. A lengthy publicized trial alleging some defect in the firm's product, for example, can do the firm immeasurable harm. Furthermore, because of experience and retrospective rating, the firm is interested in minimizing losses which have occurred and in gathering important loss-prevention data for the future. The same observation with respect to experience and retrospective rating could have been made with respect to property losses.[7]

Common principles and procedures　Whenever an accident occurs, the insured should notify the insurer as soon as possible. The observations made earlier with respect to notices of property losses also apply here, but three differences should be noted. First, the insured should notify the insurer concerning any accident which might result in a claim from a third party. The notice must contain any reasonably obtainable information concerning the time, place, and circumstances of the accident and the names and addresses of injured persons and witnesses. The insured should not withhold the notice until the injured party presents a claim. Even if the injured party maintains that he was not injured, the insured should notify the insurer. Second, the courts will interpret the notice requirement in liability insurance contracts more strictly, because a prompt investigation of the circumstances surrounding the accident is essential to protect the insurer's interest. The major problem in investigating liability claims is that of gathering the facts and interpreting them in the light of the law, the judge, the jury, and the

---

[7] For a more detailed explanation of the reasons for this interest and the claim follow-up practices which have been adopted, see the three articles by William L. Hollingsworth, Joseph A. Edwards, and Jack C. Else on "Improving Claim Follow-up Practices," *Facing New Problems in Risk Management,* AMA Management Report No. 64 (New York: American Management Association, 1961).

plaintiff's attorney. Witnesses and evidence can quickly disappear, or witnesses can change their stories, and with the passage of time, minor injuries can assume major proportions in the mind of the claimant. Third, in addition to the notice of accident requirement, the contract demands that the insured forward *immediately* to the insurer every notice of a claim or suit, summons, or other process delivered to him or his representative.

During the adjustment process, the insured must cooperate with the insurer. The insurer provides the lawyers and is responsible for, and in charge of, the defense of the claim, but if the insurer requests the insured to do so, the insured must attend hearings and trials and assist in the general conduct of the suit by such means as securing and giving evidence, obtaining witnesses, and effecting settlements if the insurer believes that this process offers the best solution.[8] For this assistance the insurer reimburses the insured for all reasonable expenses incurred at the insurer's request. Except in some automobile policies issued to families, the insurer does not reimburse the insured for his loss of earnings.

The insured must be careful both at the time of the accident and after it not to make voluntarily any payment, assume any obligation, or incur any expense other than the cost of essential immediate medical treatment of others. Paying these medical expenses is not regarded as an admission of liability but the mark of a decent person and a wise precautionary measure because it may substantially reduce the ultimate loss. The other acts, however, can prejudice the insurer's ability to defend the claim.

The insured need not submit a proof of loss in connection with liability losses. Such proof is unnecessary because the amount of the loss is fixed either by the judgment awarded by the courts or in an out-of-court settlement between the insurer and the claimant.

Special problems   Special problems sometimes arise in connection with liability insurance claims. They may occur when (1) some third party is primarily responsible for the loss, (2) the suit or the judgment is in excess of the policy limits, or (3) the insured and the insurer cannot resolve their differences without resorting to a suit.

If some third party is primarily responsible for the accident for which the insurer pays a judgment in behalf of the insured, the insurer takes over any right the insured may have to sue the third party. This right may arise, for example, under a hold-harmless agreement or because some other

[8] Under a few professional liability contracts, the insurer cannot settle the claim out of court, without the consent of the insured. Under most liability contracts, however, the insurer has the right to effect a settlement if that appears to be the most economical solution. Most claims are in fact settled in this fashion. Business risk managers, however, often attempt to influence the settlement of product liability claims. See above.

party, such as an agent, is primarily responsible. Although insurers seldom exercise this right with respect to liability losses, the insured must be careful to preserve whatever right exists.

Often the injured party will sue for an amount far in excess of the policy limits. In such a case, the insurer is expected to notify the insured immediately in order that he may participate in the defense if he so desires because he also faces a potential loss.

A related problem arises when the claimant agrees to settle for an amount within the policy limits but threatens to sue for a much larger amount. If the insurer refuses and the claimant sues for and is awarded an amount in excess of the policy limits, the insurer is responsible for this excess only if a court decides that the adjuster was negligent or that he did not act in good faith in behalf of the insured.

Liability insurance contracts do not specify any interval during which the insured must commence suit against the insurer in case of a disagreement, but they do assert that no one has a right of action against the insurer (1) unless the insured has complied with all the policy provisions and (2) until the insured's liability has been established either by a judgment awarded by a court or by a written agreement among the insured, the insurer, and the claimant. These conditions affect both insureds and claimants. If the insurer claims that the insured has violated the contract, the insured must defend himself in court against the claimant before he can sue the insurer. The claimant has no rights under the contract if the contract is void with respect to the insured. Except in a few states with direct-action statutes which supersede these policy provisions, the claimant can never proceed directly against the insurer until the insured's liability has been established by the courts.

PERSONNEL INSURANCE

Personnel insurance losses may be caused by death or the attainment of a specified age or by an accidental injury or sickness. Losses of the first type are much easier to adjust than are those of the second type.

Death   When an insured dies, a life insurance contract instructs his beneficiary to submit written proof of loss to the insurer. Because it is easy to verify whether death has occurred, because there are few, if any, exclusions in the contract, because the incontestable clause eliminates after a few years the possibility of a defense of misrepresentation, and because the amount to be paid is stipulated in the policy, almost all claims will be paid within twenty-four hours after the insurer receives the proof of loss.

The three most troublesome areas in the adjustment of life claims are vague beneficiary designations, disappearance cases, and double indemnity claims. Beneficiaries are sometimes designated in terms which are broad enough to include several persons, e.g., "my wife," or are changed immediately preceding death in a manner which is not strictly correct. Insurers handle these problems by paying the proceeds into court under what is called an "interpleader action" and letting the court make the decision. Disappearance cases are relatively rare but happen often enough to pose a problem. At common law a person is presumed to be dead seven years after he mysteriously disappears, and if the contract is still in effect at the expiration of that period, the insurer must pay the claim. Double indemnity causes problems because of its restrictive insuring clause and the suicide exclusion.

Group life insurance claims are handled in essentially the same way as individual life insurance claims, but the proof of loss is usually transmitted to the insurer through the employer. Some large firms are even authorized to pay their own claims.

Attainment of a specified age   Annuity contracts involving life contingencies require that the insured post proof that he has attained that age. He may also be asked to present evidence that he is living on the due date of each annuity payment which is contingent upon his continued survival.

Group pension plans may require in addition certification that the employee has retired. If the pension plan is self-insured by the employer and if the trustee is to mail the checks, the employer must provide the trustee with the necessary information.

Poor health   The procedure to be followed in adjusting health insurance claims is discussed at length in the mandatory standard provisions in the health insurance contract. The insured (or his beneficiary, if a death benefit is involved) is to notify the insurer or its authorized agent in writing within 20 days after the occurrence or commencement of any loss or as soon thereafter as is reasonably possible. The insurer must furnish the insured proof-of-loss forms within 15 days after the insured notifies the insurer. If the insurer fails to meet this dead-line, the insured can satisfy the proof-of-loss requirement by submitting written proof describing the occurrence and the character and extent of the loss. If the claim is for an income benefit, the insured must return the proof-of-loss form or the substitute written proof within 90 days after the termination of the period for which the insured is liable. If the claim is for other benefits, such as medical expense reimbursements, the proof must be submitted within 90 days after the loss, e.g., when the hospital bill is paid. These 90-day limits are waived if it is not reasonably possible to give proof within such time. In that event, proof must be submitted as soon as possible, but unless the insured lacks the legal capacity to submit proof of loss, the deadline is one year from the time proof is otherwise required.

The insurer promises to pay losses other than income losses immediately after it receives due written proof of the loss. There is a trend toward the use of forms under which the insurer pays directly the hospitals, doctors, and others, but the insured can always request that he receive the payment. Claims for income losses will, subject to due written proof of loss, be paid at the expiration of each 4 weeks during the benefit period. If the disability lasts many months, this 4-week payment schedule can be very advantageous for the insured.

The standard provisions also give the insurer the right, at its own expense, to examine the insured at reasonable times and places and to perform an autopsy in case of death. The right of examination is exercised only in troublesome cases. The autopsy right is seldom used.

Finally, the standard provisions state that suits against the insurer must be commenced no earlier than 60 days after the insured has furnished the insurer written proof of loss and no later than 3 years after the date the proof was supposed to be furnished.

The discussion to this point has been concerned with individual health insurance issued by commercial insurers. Under group insurance contracts, the procedures are simplified. The employee usually obtains his proof-of-loss form from the employer. After the forms are completed, the employer forwards them to the insurer. If the claim is approved, the insurer sends the payment to the employee through the employer or directly to the vendors of the medical care. Sometimes a business firm has the authority to approve all claims up to a certain size and to draw drafts on the insurer with respect to the approved claims.

The Blue Cross or Blue Shield procedure is even simpler. The insured presents a subscriber's identification card or his contract to the doctor or hospital, which in turn completes the necessary claim forms and sends them to the appropriate medical expense association. The hospital or doctor bills the insured for the excess of the total bill over the medical-association payment.

Medical payments losses under liability insurance contracts are not subject to the standard provisions under individual health insurance, but the liability contracts do provide for prompt notice to the insurer, written proof of loss, examinations by physicians selected by the insurer and authorization for the insurer to obtain pertinent medical reports, permission for the insurer to pay directly the person or organization providing the medical services, and suits against the insurer.

Workmen's compensation claims resemble health insurance claims in some respects and liability claims in others. They are like health insurance claims in that (1) if the circumstances surrounding the injury or disease satisfy certain criteria (established in this instance by the workmen's compensation law of the state), the claim is to be paid; (2) the insurer is directly and primarily responsible to the injured party; (3) the insurer may be sued directly by the injured party; and (4) the principal adjustment problems are the same as those to be discussed shortly for health insurance. On the other hand, they resemble liability insurance claims in that (1) the contract contains both a notice-of-injury provision and a notice-of-claim or suit provision; (2) the insured must assist and cooperate with the insurer in the handling of the claim; (3) failure of the insured to meet his obligations under the contract may give the insurer the right to recover from the insured the amounts paid to the injured party; and (4) the insurer possesses subrogation rights. All claims must be filed with the state workmen's compensation board, and disagreements between the injured employee and the employer are handled first by a hearing before the board.

The key problem in adjusting claims involving accidental injuries and sickness is the subjectivity of many elements included in the claim. The insured may or may not be ill, his illness may or may not be disabling, the medical treatment may or may not be necessary, and the hospital and doctor bills may or may not be reasonable. An insured who was legitimately disabled for a time may be guilty of malingering, perhaps because of the insurance payments, or he may truly not have recovered. The above statements are not meant to imply that the situation is hopeless for the insurer; relatively standard patterns can be expected with most illnesses. The insured, however, should appreciate the importance of an untarnished reputation and a cooperative attitude in securing a favorable hearing on his claim.

A Fair Settlement

The objective of the loss adjustment is a fair and prompt settlement of the claim. Insureds should realize that it is as wrong for an insurer to overpay its claims as to underpay them. Overpayments will usually be reflected in increased insurance costs or in a weakened financial condition of the insurer.

Small losses which, strictly speaking, are not covered under the contract are paid by some insurers as nuisance claims. The loss in goodwill and the expenses of an extensive investigation are considered more costly than the claim itself. Other equally reputable insurers argue that this practice leads to a misunderstanding of the insurance coverage and can prove very costly if all insureds submit such claims.

Many insureds are disappointed by loss adjustments because they have not read their contract. A loss they thought was covered under the contract is either excluded or not specifically included, or the contract limits the amount of the recovery to less than they had expected. These disappointments are best averted at the time the risk management program is designed and not at the time of the loss adjustment.

Other insureds will be disappointed because of honest disagreements concerning the circumstances of the loss and the interpretation of the contract. If they are convinced that they are correct after continued discussions with the insurer and if their conviction is confirmed by some informed, objective third party, they should contact their state insurance department, which, if it agrees with the insured, may be able to force the insurer to act more favorably by moral suasion or by a threat to cancel its license to operate in the state. The insured may also resort to the legal remedies provided under the contract.

Still other insureds, whose ethics are normally unquestionable, tend to exaggerate their claims either (1) because they consider it smart and socially acceptable to collect an excess amount from the impersonal insurer (which, they point out, has been collecting much more in premiums from the insured than it has paid in losses) or (2) because they consider it necessary to ask for too much initially in order to receive a fair settlement. The first attitude would be disastrous if it were adopted by everyone, and yet it is true that society does to a certain degree condone such procedures. The second attitude is unnecessary so far as most (but unfortunately not all) adjusters are concerned.

Some risk managers whose firms are experience- or retrospectively rated have accused insurance adjusters of loose and indifferent handling of claims because they have no incentive to keep costs down. Some insurers, on the other hand, point out that they are sometimes pressured to pay product liability and workmen's compensation claims which they would have preferred to fight. Neither practice is in the long run in the best interest of the insurer or of the risk manager.[9]

Often the insured is dissatisfied, not with the final settlement, but with the treatment he received at the hands of the adjuster and the work he was asked to do. Some adjusters—but not most—are discourteous and overdemanding. In defense of some of the actions of adjusters, it should be noted that they are continually dealing with some insureds who are misinformed, uncooperative, or dishonest, even to the point of purposely causing the loss to make a profit on the insurance. If the insured can erase at

---

[9] J. T. Parrett, "Loss Control after the Fact," *The Growing Job of Risk Management,* AMA Management Report No. 72 (New York: American Management Association, 1962), pp. 215–223.

an early date any doubt the adjuster may have concerning the insured's motivations, the stage should be set for a more amicable and fair adjustment. If the insured and the insurer cannot reach an agreement, the courts will also look with more favor on the insured who has played the game openly, fairly, and intelligently.

REVIEW QUESTIONS

1. With what types of loss adjusters may a risk manager have to deal? How do they differ?
2. When should a risk manager turn to a public adjuster for assistance in preparing a claim?
3. What is the insured obligated to do under a property insurance contract following a loss?
4. What is the most difficult problem encountered in adjusting property losses? How is the problem handled?
5. What are the Guiding Principles?
6. Why are Guiding Principles important to risk managers?
7. A firm has a $40,000 fire insurance contract covering a $100,000 building. Because of the negligence of an employee of a neighboring firm, a fire starts which spreads to the insured's property causing a $60,000 loss.
   a. How will the insured and the insurer handle this loss?
   b. If there is a net recovery of $50,000 from the neighboring firm as a result of a suit, how will this amount be shared?
8. If the insured and an insurer cannot agree upon the amount of a property loss, what can they do?
9. Why are business risk managers especially interested in the settlement of liability claims?
10. Under the liability insurance contract, what is the insured obligated to do after an accident?
11. A firm has a bodily injury liability insurance contract with limits of $50,000 per person and $100,000 per accident. An injured person offers to settle his claim for $30,000 but threatens to sue for $80,000 if his offer is refused. The insurer prefers to refuse his offer. What is the situation if the injured party sues and wins?
12. One firm has a liability claim against another firm which the risk manager of the first firm knows is insured by a particular insurer. The vice-president of the risk manager's firm suggests that his firm sue that insurer in court. What will probably be the risk manager's reply?

13. "Life insurance claims adjusting is trouble-free." Comment upon this statement.

14. Many of the mandatory standard provisions in a health insurance contract deal with the obligations of the insured and the insurer following a loss. What are these obligations?

15. a. In what respects do workmen's compensation loss adjustments resemble health insurance loss adjustments?

    b. In what respects do workmen's compensation loss adjustments resemble liability insurance loss adjustments?

16. What is the employer's role in adjusting employee claims under group personnel insurance contracts?

17. What in your opinion is a "fair" settlement of a claim?

18. Why is a firm which is experience- or retrospectively rated directly concerned about its insurer's claims practices?

SUGGESTIONS FOR ADDITIONAL READING

Dickerson, O. D.: *Health Insurance* (3d ed., Homewood, Ill.: Richard D. Irwin, Inc., 1968), chap. 20.

Donaldson, J. H.: *Casualty Claims Adjustment* (rev. ed., Homewood, Ill.: Richard D. Irwin, Inc., 1969).

Johns, Corydon T.: *An Introduction to Liability Claims Adjusting* (Cincinnati: National Underwriter Company, 1965).

Michelbacher, G. F., and Roos, N.: *Multiple-line Insurers: Their Nature and Operation* (2d ed., New York: McGraw-Hill Book Company, 1970), chap. 7.

Reed, P. B., and Thomas, P. I.: *Adjustment of Property Losses* (3d ed., New York: McGraw-Hill Book Company, 1969).

Thomas, P. I.: *How to Estimate Building Losses and Construction Costs* (Englewood Cliffs, N.J.: Prentice-Hall, Inc., 1960).

F. Review case

27

business risk management—an illustrative case: the ABC corporation

This final chapter on business risk management applies many of the concepts presented in Chapters 3 to 26 to the risk management problems of a hypothetical firm. There are dangers in such an undertaking because (1) a complete analysis would require much more space than is available in this chapter; (2) although pricing considerations are an important part of the analysis, it has been impossible in an Introductory text to discuss insurance pricing in much detail; and (3) the reader may be looking for one solution when actually many good solutions can be suggested. In addition, in order to focus attention on the major concepts, the circumstances have been deliberately oversimplified. On the other hand, an illustrative case is the best way to review and integrate risk management concepts, and the authors believe that this case, despite its limitations, will serve the purpose.[1]

The ABC Corporation

The business whose risk management problems are to be analyzed is the ABC Corporation, a small concern manufacturing automobile parts. Mr. Adams, the president, owns 60 per cent of the stock; Mr. Brown, the vice-president, owns 20 per cent; and Mr. Carlson, the secretary-treasurer, owns the remaining 20 per cent.

---

[1] For other cases that illustrate the concepts presented in this text, see W. M. Howard, *Cases on Risk Management* (New York: McGraw-Hill Book Company, 1967).

The firm owns one brick building, which houses all the manufacturing operations and the executive offices. This building, which was built ten years ago at a cost of $150,000 plus the land, has three stories and a basement and provides 50,000 square feet of working space. The building has no automatic sprinklers. An appraisal firm has estimated that it would cost $250,000 to rebuild the building new today, but that because of depreciation the actual cash value of the building is $200,000. A railroad siding is adjacent to the east side of the building, for which the firm has assumed liability under a fairly typical sidetrack agreement. A parking lot for 100 cars is on the west side of the building. The remainder of the two acres owned by the firm is landscaped with trees, shrubs, and a lawn. The building is 200 feet from the street.

The firm also rents a brick building across the street as a warehouse for finished goods and as a garage for a fleet of 10 private passenger cars and 15 delivery trucks. The actual cash value of the building is $100,000. Each private passenger car and truck could be replaced in the used-car market for $2,500 and $6,000, respectively. The rent under a lease which has ten years to run is $500 a month, but the firm estimates that the value of equivalent premises would be $1,000 at today's rentals.

The firm sells its products only to wholesalers and manufacturers. There is little seasonable fluctuation, and business has remained fairly stable over the years. About 80 per cent of the sales are made to customers within a radius of 50 miles; deliveries are usually made by employees driving the firm's own automobiles. The deliveries to other areas are effected by motor truck or rail common carriers. No shipments are made outside the United States.

The machinery in the factory would cost $100,000 to replace with new machinery, but physical depreciation is estimated at $20,000. Raw materials, goods in process, and finished goods are valued as shown in the balance sheet with no allowance for depreciation.

The firm has 60 employees, about 30 of whom are involved in the manufacturing process. The others are the officers, the office force, warehouse employees, and salesmen. One of the employees is a key engineer, aged 40, whose ingenuity has been largely responsible for the success of the firm. Salesmen drive company cars in their work. The annual payroll is $400,000; payments by check are made bi-monthly. Because of a labor shortage in its locality, the firm would prefer to continue its employees on the payroll during a shutdown of two months or less. Otherwise, it would consider dropping about one-half of the employees, for whom the annual payroll is $150,000.

The most recent balance sheet and income statements are presented as Tables 27.1 and 27.2.

Table 27.1   ABC Corporation balance sheet, December 31, 1970

Assets			
Current assets:			
Cash		$ 5,000	
Accounts receivable	$110,000		
Reserve for doubtful accounts	10,000	100,000	
Inventories			
Finished goods	$ 60,000		
Goods in process	50,000		
Raw materials	20,000	130,000	
Supplies on hand			
Factor and shipping supplies	$ 3,000		
Stationery and supplies	2,000	5,000	$240,000
Fixed assets:			
Building	$150,000		
Reserve for depreciation	50,000	$100,000	
Machinery and equipment	$ 50,000		
Reserve for depreciation	10,000	40,000	
Furniture and fixtures	$ 20,000		
Reserve for depreciation	10,000	10,000	
Goodwill		10,000	160,000
Total assets			$400,000
Liabilities			
Current liabilities:			
Accounts payable			$100,000
Total liabilities			$100,000
Stockholders' equity			
Capital stock		$100,000	
Retained earnings		200,000	$300,000
Total liabilities and equity			$400,000

Risk Analysis

On the basis of the financial statements and other information regarding the firm's operations, the risk manager should first list in some orderly fashion the risks to which the firm is subject and provide some measures by which they may be evaluated. No attempt will be made here to perform a complete risk analysis, but the approach will be indicated by recognizing most of the potential losses faced by the firm and by listing for each kind of loss the maximum possible loss in dollars. The maximum loss is assumed to be a total loss unless otherwise indicated. The possible causes of loss or perils and the probabilities of the various losses are not stated. The analysis, which relates to this particular firm the risks discussed earlier,

Table 27.2 ABC Corporation: income statement for the twelve months ended December 31, 1970*

Sales	$760,000
Less returns and allowances	10,000
Net sales	$750,000
Less cost of raw stock used in production	200,000
Gross earnings	$550,000
Less payroll	250,000
Less other expenses	255,000
Net operating profit	$ 45,000
Less provision for income taxes	15,000
Net profit	$ 30,000

*The information in the usual profit and loss statement has been rearranged in order to simplify the presentation.

is presented in outline form in Table 27.3. The table is sufficiently self-con-tained not to require any further discussion, but the reader is reminded that the balance sheet values are used only when they are not in conflict with the values in the text and that the insured can incur several types of loss at the same time or during the same year.

Selection of Tools

Once the risk manager has defined his problem, he must decide which tool or combination of the five basic tools—avoidance, retention, loss preven-tion or reduction, transfer, and combination—he will use to handle the risks involved. Although it would be possible to use statistical decision theory to make this selection in the manner described in Chapter 13, enough has probably already been said about this approach, given the present state of the art. Instead, the more conventional analysis described in Chapter 12 will be used. First, the insurance contracts which seem to meet best the problems of this firm will be divided into three groups in order of decreas-ing priority—essential, desirable, and available—according to the criteria outlined in Chapter 12. Each contract will then be considered separately in order to determine whether some other tool would offer a more satisfactory approach to the problem.

INITIAL LISTING OF INSURANCE COVERAGES

The initial listing of *essential* insurance contracts includes the coverages that are either required by some outside party or that protect the insured against losses which would threaten the continued existence of the firm.

Table 27.3 ABC Corporation: risk analysis

Type of loss	Maximum possible loss
Property losses:	
Direct losses	
Main building	$200,000
Raw materials $20,000	
Goods in process 50,000	100,000
Finished goods	
In main plant or warehouse 30,000	
In transit 30,000	30,000
Machinery	80,000
Furniture	10,000
Motor vehicles	
Private passenger cars	25,000
Trucks	90,000
Cash	5,000
Consequential losses:	
Loss of net profits and continuing expenses during shutdown of manufacturing operations	Assuming 6 months as a maximum possible shutdown period, 1/2 ($550,000 gross earnings) less noncontinuing expenses, estimated at $50,000.
Loss of customers after resumption following shutdown	Difficult to estimate, but assumed to be small.
Depreciation (replacement cost new less actual cash value)	
Main building	$50,000
Machinery	20,000
Leasehold interest	$500 a month for remainder of 10 years starting as of date of loss.
Inability to collect on accounts receivable	$100,000 (but this is very unlikely).
Liability losses:	
Bailee liability for damage to warehouse and garage	$100,000 plus $500 a month rent for 8 months maximum replacement time.
Premises—operations	
Main building	
Warehouse and garage	
Operations on and off premises	Unlimited.
Elevators	
Main building	
Warehouse and garage	
Product	
Independent contractors	(None at present.)
Contract	
Sidetrack agreement	
Automobiles	
Owned vehicles	Unlimited.
Borrowed or hired vehicles	
Employee autos used on company business	

Table 27.3 (Continued)

Type of loss	Maximum possible loss
Personnel losses:	
To employees	
Losses of earning power and unexpected expenses caused by Death Poor health Old age Unemployment	Difficult to compute, but firm is only partly responsible, and needs are usually dictated by agreement with the union.
To the firm	
Loss of profits or replacement costs resulting from death or long-term disability of the key engineer.	Half of annual profits, or $15,000 for 3 years until replacement can be obtained and trained.
Liquidation losses if a stockholder dies or becomes disabled for a long period.	Difficult to estimate, but could be forced to sell assets at one-half of their book value.

Although a special multi-peril policy may be the best way for the business to obtain several of these coverages, separate contracts will be used in this initial listing to permit a more detailed analysis of the relative importance of various types of insurance. The essential coverages include the following:

1. *Workmen's compensation* insurance. This insurance is required by law.

2. *Group life, group health, and pension benefits.* These benefits are required under a contract with a union representing the factory employees. It will be assumed that the firm recognizes that it must protect the other emp'oyees in a similar fashion or it will lose them.

3. *Fire and extended coverage* insurance equal to the actual cash value of the building owned by the firm and the contents of that building and the rented building. The potential losses on these items are sizable enough to threaten the continued existence of the firm. In order to reduce the rate but allow some margin for an increase in value, the insurance on the building would be written on an 80 or 90 per cent coinsurance basis. Because the total contents value is fairly stable, there may be no reason to purchase a reporting form, but a blanket policy covering the contents at both the owned and rented locations would be highly desirable because the proportion of the finished goods at each location fluctuates markedly. It may be possible, however, to reduce the premium by placing separate amounts of insurance on the machinery, the inventory, and the furniture and fixtures.

4. *Business interruption* insurance, which will pay losses arising out of damage to the owned property arising out of fire or extended coverage perils. The gross earnings form with a 50 per cent coinsurance clause and no payroll endorsements would be desirable because of the estimated maximum shutdown and the nature of the payroll. The amount of insurance should be 0.50 (gross earnings according to Table 27.2), or 0.50($550,000) = $275,000 plus some safety margin in case the gross earnings increase.

5. *Boiler and machinery* insurance. On the assumption that a boiler explosion is very unlikely to affect more than one-quarter of the values at the main location and no other premises, a policy limit of $100,000 should be sufficient to take care of the most important direct property losses. The policy should be endorsed to cover business interruption losses of the same amount as the other business interruption insurance.

6. *Comprehensive general bodily injury liability* insurance. Liability losses have an unlimited potential. The comprehensive form was selected because the firm has several of the common sources of liability and may develop the others. Recent court awards in the state in which the firm is located indicate that the liability limits should be at least $250,000 per person, $1 million per accident.

7. *Comprehensive automobile bodily injury liability* insurance. Liability losses again have an unlimited potential, and the comprehensive automobile liability insurance policy has the advantages described in Chapter 18. Hired car and nonownership liability exposures already exist. The policy limit should be the same as the CGL policy—$250,000 per person, $1 million per accident.

8. *Insurance to fund a buy-and-sell agreement* which is to operate if one of the owners dies. The corporation is to own the policies. The insurance on Mr. Adams is to be 60 per cent of the present agreed valuation, the insurance on Mr. Brown, 20 per cent, and the insurance on Mr. Carlson, 20 per cent. The valuation at the date of death is to be determined by a trustee, the difference between the final valuation and the present agreed valuation to be paid directly by the survivors in installments over a period of 10 years. The present agreed valuation is $400,000, which exceeds the book value because the owners agree that the book value understates the asset values, including goodwill.

The *desirable* coverages are designed to handle those losses which would cause the firm serious economic distress but which would probably not force the owners to cease operations. The following contracts fall in this category:

1. *Vandalism* insurance, added by endorsement to the fire insurance policy on the owned building, its contents, and the contents of the rented building. Vandalism is unfortunately a frequent peril. Its consequences can be very great, but it has a smaller potential than, for example, windstorm or explosion.

2. *Automobile comprehensive and collision* insurance equal to the actual cash value of the owned motor vehicles.

3. *Transportation* insurance, covering shipments in the insured's own trucks or while in the hands of a common carrier. The limits depend upon the maximum value shipped in each vehicle.

4. *Comprehensive destruction, disappearance, and dishonesty policy,* including a primary commercial blanket fidelity bond, money and securities coverage on and off premises, and depositor's forgery coverage in the basic form and endorsed to cover payroll robbery and mercantile open-stock burglary. The fidelity bond penalty is difficult to determine, but a formula suggested by the Surety Association of America is often used as a guide.[2] Under this formula the first step is to compute a dishonesty exposure index as follows: (1) 5 per cent of the inventories plus (2) 20 per cent of the other current assets plus (3) 10 per cent of net sales. In this instance, this index is $0.05(130,000) + 0.20(110,000) + 0.10(750,000)$, or $162,000. The second step is to obtain the recommended penalty from a table prepared by the association. For an exposure index of $162,000, the table recommends a bond penalty between $50,000 and $75,000. The money and securities limit should be set at the level at which these assets are commonly kept on the premises, the payroll coverage being designed to handle the periodic payroll exposure. The depositor's forgery coverage is also difficult to determine; it would depend upon such factors as the nature of the check-signing authority, the maximum check amount written, and the frequency with which bank statements are checked. The mercantile open-stock coverage should equal the coinsurance limit to avoid a coinsurance penalty, but excess losses are very unlikely.

5. *Depreciation* insurance on the owned building, written as an endorsement to the fire insurance contract and converting that contract from an actual cash value basis to a replacement cost basis.

6. *Leasehold interest* insurance to protect against the loss of $500 per month for the remainder of the 10-year lease.

7. *Accounts receivable* insurance in an amount sufficient to satisfy the minimum coinsurance requirements.

8. *Comprehensive general property damage liability* insurance, with a $100,000 per accident limit.

[2] Peter A. Zimmerman, "Proper Limits for Fidelity Bonds," AMA Insurance Series No. 114 (New York: American Management Association, 1957), pp. 49–55.

9. *Comprehensive automobile property damage liability* insurance, with a $100,000 per accident limit.

10. *Fire legal liability* insurance, with a limit of $100,000 per accident because this approximates the value of the rented building plus the consequential losses if the building is damaged.

11. *Insurance to fund a buy-and-sell agreement,* which is to operate if one of the owners is totally and permanently disabled. The need for this agreement is deemed to be a little less critical than if one of the owners dies, but this division, like many other features of this analysis, is debatable.

12. *Life* insurance on the key engineer, with a total and permanent disability rider attached. The policy amount should be at least $30,000.

The *available* coverages include all those coverages which might be of some value to the business but which do not fall in the first two categories. Usually they deal with losses which are likely to be small or which happen very infrequently. This list could be very extensive; the more common items are the following:

1. Earthquake insurance
2. Plate glass Insurance
3. Water damage insurance
4. Extra expense insurance
5. Rental value insurance
6. Valuable papers insurance
7. Credit insurance
8. Depositor's forgery coverage on incoming instruments
9. Water damage liability insurance
10. Personal injury liability insurance in excess of bodily injury liability insurance

REVISED LIST

The second step in the analysis is to determine which of these losses could be better handled through some noninsurance method. Avoidance will not be considered in this analysis because avoidance is applicable only with respect to risks that have not yet been assumed, not those that already exist.[3] Combination can also be ignored because it is assumed that no

[3] Disposing of property exposed to loss is a definite possibility, but according to the definitions in this text, this disposal is an example of transfer, not of avoidance.

mergers are contemplated and that the size of the firm is fairly stable. This leaves, then, for consideration loss prevention and reduction, noninsurance transfers, and retention.

With respect to the *essential* coverages, there may be some opportunities for loss prevention and reduction. It is extremely doubtful that these efforts can reduce the frequency or the severity of the insured losses to such an extent that the classification of the insurance as essential will be changed, but safety measures may reduce significantly the insurance premium or the cost of retaining the losses. Opportunities to transfer any of the insured losses through some noninsurance device appear to be lacking. The classification of these coverages are essential implies that it would not be wise for the insurer to retain the *types* of losses included under these contracts except under two circumstances. First, the policy limits were established at a level which the losses are not likely to exceed or which represents the maximum coverage available. The firm retains losses in excess of these limits. Second, some of the essential coverages fall in this category solely because they are required by some other party even though the potential losses are small or predictable. In this case, the losses covered under the two required contracts are not small, but with 60 employees the firm may wish to consider a self-insurance program, particularly with respect to workmen's compensation. It would appear wiser for this firm to compromise by electing workmen's compensation insurance under a retrospective-rating plan if its experience has been consistently good. Finally, although the opportunities for retaining completely losses of these types are not great, the firm should consider seriously the possibility of using deductibles to retain small losses. More specifically, deductibles might be used advantageously with respect to the general liability insurance, the automobile liability insurance, the fire and extended coverage insurance, and the boiler and machinery insurance. Because the firm does not have enough exposure units to predict its losses within a narrow range, the deductible amount should be small, say, under $500 or $1,000. The exact amount will depend upon an analysis of the premiums, the willingness of the management to bear some risk, and the question of whether the deductible applies to each loss or to total losses during the year.

The noninsurance methods have somewhat more widespread application with respect to the *desirable* coverages. The observations made in the preceding paragraph with respect to loss-prevention and reduction activities are also applicable here. At least one noninsurance transfer device might be applicable. As was noted earlier, the firm could ask the owner of the warehouse and garage to excuse the firm under the lease from any responsibility for damage to the building as a result of fire or other specified perils.

It may be reluctant to do so, however, because the landlord may take this opportunity to change the terms of what is now a favorable lease. Another possibility is to ask the landlord to have the firm named in the landlord's insurance contract on the building, but it will be assumed that the landlord's insurer is unwilling to do this. Retention is a possibility with respect to all the losses included under these contracts, but the losses are serious enough to suggest insurance unless the premiums are unreasonably high. The firm is, of course, retaining losses in excess of the suggested policy limits. There are no opportunities for self-insurance because the number of units is small, but the risk manager should consider small deductibles under the vandalism insurance, the dishonesty insurance, and the general liability and automobile liability property damage insurance. The automobile physical damage insurance should definitely be subject to some deductible, such as $500 or $1,000 per vehicle, because of the substantial premium savings. Deductibles are not readily available under the other forms of property and liability insurance, but they may also be worthy of some investigation. The disability income insurance on the owners should contain a waiting period of at least one month.

The case for insurance is least strong with respect to the *available* coverages. It will be assumed that this firm's loss-prevention activities can be effective enough in some of these areas to make retention attractive because the resulting maximum loss or the loss frequency is very small. This assumption will be made with respect to water damage insurance, water damage liability insurance, credit insurance, personal injury liability insurance in excess of bodily injury liability insurance, valuable papers insurance, and depositor's forgery insurance. Earthquakes are considered so unlikely that this type of loss can be retained without any special loss prevention efforts. Since the chance that the firm will incur any extra expenses in order to continue operating is small, this loss can be retained, but it should be recognized that the firm by this decision is retaining any loss of customers following a business interruption.[1] Rental value insurance, it will be assumed, is more economically provided under business interruption insurance. Glass insurance, on the other hand, is to be purchased because the price is reasonable and the firm is very much interested in the replacement service.

Any losses for which insurance is not usually available, such as flood losses to real estate, strike losses, or war losses must of course be retained, although it may be possible to reduce the expected losses through loss-prevention measures or some noninsurance transfers.

---

[1] This protection can now be included under business interruption insurance, but it will be assumed here that this potential loss is retained.

THE RISK MANAGEMENT PROGRAM

The result of this analysis is the following combination of tools:

A. Loss-prevention and reduction measures—probably the installation of automatic sprinklers, safety inspections of vehicles, annual physical examinations for the owners and key employees, and many other activities whose benefits at least offset their costs
B. Retention
    1. Losses in excess of the limits of the insurance purchased
    2. Losses excluded under the insurance purchased
    3. Losses up to the deductible amount under the automobile physical damage insurance plus any other deductibles selected by the risk manager
    4. Earthquake losses
    5. Water damage losses
    6. Sprinkler leakage losses (unless the insurance is purchased following a decision to install sprinklers)
    7. Cost of replacing valuable papers other than merely copying them from a preserved source
    8. Forgery losses on incoming instruments
    9. Theft of property other than money and securities which is not classified as either robbery or burglary
    10. Flood losses
    11. War losses
    12. Loss of profits and continuing expenses during a shutdown of manufacturing operations as a result of a strike or any peril other than fire, the extended coverage perils, or accidents involving boilers and machinery
    13. Loss of customers following resumption of business after a shutdown
    14. Credit losses other than those arising out of the destruction or disappearance of accounts receivable records
C. Noninsurance transfers
    1. None
D. Insurance
    1. First priority
        a. Workmen's compensation
        b. Group life insurance, group health insurance, and a pension plan
        c. Fire and extended coverage insurance on owned building and contents in both buildings
        d. Business interruption insurance against fire and extended coverage perils

  e. Boiler and machinery insurance, including business interruption insurance
  f. Comprehensive general bodily injury liability insurance
  g. Comprehensive automobile bodily injury liability insurance
  h. Life and disability insurance on key engineer
  i. Life insurance on owners in connection with a buy-and-sell agreement
2. Second priority
  a. Vandalism insurance
  b. Automobile comprehensive and collision insurance
  c. Transportation insurance
  d. Comprehensive destruction, disappearance, and dishonesty policy
  e. Depreciation insurance
  f. Leasehold insurance
  g. Accounts receivable insurance
  h. Comprehensive general property damage liability insurance
  i. Comprehensive automobile property damage liability insurance
  j. Fire legal liability insurance
  k. Disability insurance to fund a buy-and-sell agreement
3. Third priority
  a. Glass insurance

Much of the property and liability insurance in this list can be obtained under the SMP policy. Without endorsements that contract will provide the fire and extended coverage insurance, $1,000 of extra expense insurance, depreciation insurance if repair costs do not exceed $1,000, and broad general liability insurance. Through Sections III and IV the insured can obtain the equivalent of a comprehensive destruction, disappearance, and dishonesty policy and boiler and machinery insurance. Through endorsements he can add vandalism insurance, business interruption insurance, mercantile open-stock burglary insurance, depreciation insurance, accounts receivable insurance, glass insurance, and comprehensive general liability insurance.

The risk manager must also decide which insurer or insurers should underwrite the insurance sections of the program and how it should be placed. The considerations involved have already been outlined earlier. If it is assumed that this firm has had very good loss experience, the risk manager would be well advised to make extensive use of experience- and retrospective-rating plans. He should also check on schedule rates to determine whether the evaluation of the firm's exposure is correct. The advance preparation which will help him if a loss does occur has been suggested earlier.

A Reminder

It is important at the conclusion of this analysis to remind the reader concerning what was said at the beginning of this discussion concerning the nature, purpose, and limitations of the analysis. The analysis is not perfect or complete, and alternate solutions may be better than the one suggested.[5] On the other hand, the case does review and integrate many of the concepts described earlier and illustrates how these concepts can be applied to actual situations.

REVIEW QUESTIONS

1. Criticize the risk management program for the ABC Corporation in this chapter.
2. Prepare an alternate risk management program for the ABC Corporation, and compare it with the program suggested in this chapter.
3. One aspect of the suggested risk management program for the ABC Corportation which was left somewhat indefinite was the use of deductibles. How would you advise the ABC Corporation on this point?
4. Prepare a risk management program for some firm in which you are interested.

SUGGESTIONS FOR ADDITIONAL READING

Howard, W. M.: *Cases on Risk Management* (New York: McGraw-Hill Book Company, Inc., 1967).

Mehr, R., and Hedges, R. A.: *Risk Management in the Business Enterprise* (Homewood, Ill.: Richard D. Irwin, Inc., 1963), Part VI.

Mielke, R. G.: *Insurance Surveys: Business-Personal* (5th ed., Indianapolis: The Rough Notes Company, 1962).

Selected Insurance Survey Cases (Philadelphia: American Institute for Property and Liability Underwriters, Inc., annual).

A REVIEW CASE

This case is designed to review the material presented in Chapters 3 to 26. Unlike the ABC Corporation case, which emphasized the management of property and liability risks, this case stresses personnel risks.

[5] For example, one alternate solution might include the manufacturers' output policy described on p. 305.

Apex Labs, Incorporated

Pending the outcome of a jurisdictional strike, a newly appointed risk manager is assigned responsibility for revising the firm's employee benefit plan for its employees and its personnel risk management program for the firm itself. The union, if successful, will probably be aggressive; it has a proved record of vigorously pressing for comprehensive fringe benefit packages in addition to liberal work rules. The risk manager and the Executive Safety Committee have been instructed to prepare for new union agreements, both temporary and permanent, which would add new coverages to be offered to the employees or increase benefits of the programs now in force.

Situated in the North Central part of the United States, this highly successful drug and chemical company specializes in producing patent medicines. The firm has made recent inroads into the ethical-drugs markets. The future of this expansion looks even brighter, but it is heavily dependent on the services of the very talented president and two expert scientists heading up the experimental laboratory.

Apex Labs has about 250 employees. Twenty-five per cent are women, most of them married, and their average age is 30. There are 40 office personnel, and the remainder are mostly highly skilled technicians, not easily replaced. There are 4 company-owned trucks (which are used for intermediate-haul deliveries) and 10 company-owned passenger cars, which are intended primarily for salesmen. Five officers of the company as well as members of their families also use the cars.

In analyzing the current income and expense statements, the risk manager notes that out of annual sales of nearly $10 million, gross earnings were $1.9 million and ordinary payroll for the year was $1.6 million. Plant operations are uniform throughout the year. Salaries totaled $280,000 and ranged from $32,000 for the president on down. In the past, stock options were offered to top executives, but the practice was voted out at a recent stockholders' meeting. The capital stock is not held widely nor is it listed; the largest block, held by an investment syndicate, is not controlling.

The risk manager considers the following as a fair statement of the existing security programs for the personnel. The firm insures its workmen's compensation exposure. This policy reimburses employees who are injured on the job for their medical expenses as well as for their loss of time. The policy is extended to cover sickness if it is caused by their employment. Apex pays its share of OASDHI and unemployment compensation taxes. The firm provides a full-time registered nurse during working hours and a visiting physician for an hour each morning. The employees are permitted to sign for any of the firm's products for their personal use without charge. A safety program includes classes, drills, and other loss-prevention activities.

The risk manager is now required to prepare cost estimates and specifications of various new plans of personal protection for the employees, for the edification and approval of the committee, to be used to satisfy any of the fringe-benefit demands of the successful union. In addition to this, and in lieu of agreements with the union, he has been asked to provide proposals that would include nonunion personnel, salesmen, executive officers, and staff.

1. a. List the kinds of personnel risks that can be retained by this firm. Label the kinds of programs that might effectively deal with these risks.
   b. Should this list include an investment club? a credit union? education for the employees' children? a guaranteed annual wage? profit sharing?
   c. Which items in the list are properly within the domain of the risk manager? Why?
2. In each of the items listed determine whether insurance could be a usable tool in handling the risk. Should a guaranteed annual wage be considered insurance?
3. a. Which of the insurable items are amenable to self-insurance schemes?
   b. What are the ingredients of self-insurance?
4. If the budget does not permit an adequate fund, is self-insurance ruled out?
5. Should a risk manager actively participate in bargaining with a union?
6. To what extent do conditions of the local labor market influence the decisions the risk manager must make? Does the effect of business cycles on the firm's operations influence risk management?
7. Can an employee of Apex be personally liable for an injury to a third party when he is using a company car? Should Apex provide personal protection for employees who use their own cars on company business? Should Apex provide car insurance for all employees? fire insurance for their houses?
8. a. If Apex provides a group nonoccupational accident and health insurance plan, what steps can be taken to keep the cost of the plan down for the firm?
   b. Would the risk manager be wise in pressing for major medical insurance as a substitute for a basic plan?
9. a. If the proportion of women to men were doubled, would the change have any effect on the costs of the various kinds of personal security that Apex could offer?
   b. What is the effect on a pension plan if the average employee age is increased? Is this true for a profit-sharing plan?

part 3
family risk management

Each family must manage its own risks. Consequently, every person has some interest in family risk management. Because risk management is of necessity a part-time concern for family managers, it is fortunate that the risks a family must face are much less complex and extensive than those encountered by a business firm.

Family risk management is important enough in its own right to merit intensive study, but an understanding of family risk management also sheds some light on business risk management, especially with respect to insurance coverages. Insurers customarily experiment in the safer and more simple family market. Consequently, an analysis of the newer family coverages should emphasize the present gaps in business insurance and provide clues to future developments.

The first chapter in Part 3 deals with property and liability risk management; the second, with personnel risk management. Much relevant material from preceding chapters is incorporated by reference.

28

family property and liability risk management

This first chapter on family risk management deals with the nature and importance of property and liability risks and how they might be handled by noninsurance and insurance tools.

Risk Analysis

A family, like a firm, must first recognize and measure its risks. The techniques and principles which can be employed have already been discussed in Chapters 4 and 5 and need not be repeated here. It is true, of course, that families do not maintain financial statements, but records are usually available or can be constructed that give a fairly accurate picture of the family's property and activities. When matched against a logically classified comprehensive list of all the property and liability risks that may be faced by any family, this picture can be converted into a portrayal of the circumstances of a particular family. The remainder of this section is devoted to the development of that logical classification of risks.

The basic risk classification is the same as that developed in Chapters 6 and 7. Potential property losses include (1) direct losses and (2) consequential losses, but the potential liability losses are only those associated with torts. An examination of detailed examples under each of these categories and a perception of their relative importance show how family exposures differ primarily from those of a firm.

A family's real and personal property is exposed to direct loss. The real property, if any, is typically a dwelling; the personal property includes such items as household goods, clothing, and the family automobile. A complete inventory of this property would indicate its present and probable location (commonly the permanent residence, a summer cottage, or property in the hands of some bailee) and the nature of the family's interest (usually sole owner, part owner, or mortgagee). The maximum possible loss is generally the cost of replacing the property new less physical depreciation and economic obsolescence.

Most consequential losses are associated with the loss of use of property. Although the family may suffer from the loss of use of personal property as well as of real property, the most important consequential losses occur with respect to real property because most items of personal property can be replaced much more quickly. The possible losses with respect to an owner-occupied family dwelling include *additional* living expenses of *all* types (for example, housing, food, transportation, laundry) incurred by the family during the period when they cannot live in the house.

Other types of consequential losses include (1) depreciation losses, (2) debris removal costs, (3) leasehold value losses, and (4) demolition losses, all of which have been described in Chapter 6. Very few families need concern themselves about leasehold losses and demolition losses, but debris removal costs are important for all families, and depreciation losses become important when an older piece of property is providing satisfactory service.

Families seldom have to worry about losses arising under workmen's compensation statutes because these laws apply to domestic service in only a few states.[1] Other tort actions, however, are very important and are frequently underestimated as a source of losses. The magnitude of the possible losses in the form of judgments, defense and court costs, and indirect expenditures of time, energy, and money has already been emphasized in Chapter 7. The fundamental legal principles associated with tort actions have also been discussed in that chapter. Only the sources of these tort actions for a family are discussed here.

The ownership, maintenance, or use of an automobile is the best-known source of liability, the awareness of this danger being stimulated by the various state statutes dealing with uncompensated automobile accident victims and the extensive publicity accorded to automobile accidents and suits. Less often appreciated are potential losses arising out of the ownership, maintenance, or use of other types of property, such as dwellings; the responsibility assumed under leases and other contracts; possible contingent

---

[1] In most states, however, families may voluntarily choose to bring their domestic servants under the workmen's compensation law.

liability arising out of the operations of independent contractors such as plumbers and painters, and the exposure through personal activities of various sorts, such as entertaining guests, engaging in sports, or merely walking down the street.

Use of Noninsurance Tools

Noninsurance tools can prove very useful in dealing with these risks. Families should consider particularly (1) avoidance, (2) retention, (3) loss prevention and reduction, and (4) transfer.

AVOIDANCE

A family may be wise to forego certain activities or the ownership of certain property if the risks involved are great relative to the advantages. For example, the ownership of a car by a college student may not be worth the risks involved. A young family may postpone a move to more luxurious quarters for the same and other reasons. Avoidance, however, is much less useful than the other tools.

RETENTION

Active retention is an extremely useful way to handle many potential *property* losses. Some of these losses cannot be avoided, prevented, or transferred at any price and therefore must be retained. War damage is an example of this sort. Another illustration is the loss of use of most types of personal property even though direct losses to this property may be insurable.

As we have explained in Chapter 9, retention is a particularly useful tool when potential losses which are transferable are so small that the family can handle them with relative ease out of current income or by withdrawals from savings accounts. Small automobile physical damage losses, small dwelling losses, and other small property losses fall in this category. The point at which these losses cease to be small depends upon the economic status and personality of the family, but most families should consider seriously the assumption of some small losses. Transfer fees are seldom likely to be so attractive that it is worthwhile to commit funds to this use; the cost to the transferee of adjusting small losses is relatively high.

As the potential losses become more predictable, retention also becomes more attractive, because the family can safely practice self-insurance with resultant expense savings and direct benefits from any improvements in loss experience. Most, if not all, of the family losses falling in this group—mysterious disappearance of fountain pens and pencils, tears in clothing, and misplaced tools—are also small losses, and the argument for retention of these losses is thus strengthened.

Retention is much less applicable to liability losses because they tend to be large and infrequent. Every family must be prepared, however, to bear some liability risk itself, since insurers, who usually offer the only transfer device, place limits on their maximum responsibility.

LOSS PREVENTION AND REDUCTION

Efforts to reduce the chance that the loss will occur or the severity of losses that do occur should always be tried when economically feasible. The development of safe driving habits, good housekeeping, participation in public efforts for improved fire protection and highways, and the selection of a well-built home are just a few examples of the efforts that can pay handsome dividends. It is true, except in automobile insurance, where owners are now commonly rated in part on the basis of their own experience, that insurance premiums do not vary with the experience of the individual family as they do in the case of large firms, but the family does benefit substantially with respect to the retained losses. In addition, if every family in the same rate class were to become more safety-conscious, the class rate could eventually be reduced.

TRANSFER

A family may transfer a property or activity to someone else. Although the motive for the transfer is generally something other than transfer of the associated risks, the transfer of the risks is an important by-product. Examples would be the sale of a car or the transfer of driving responsibilities to someone outside the family.[2]

Risks may be transferred without transferring the property or the activity. Tenants are likely to find this device very useful in their dealing with landlords. For example, the landlord may be made responsible for any damage to the property by certain specified perils, and it may be agreed that the rent is to cease if the property becomes untenantable. Generally speaking, however, transfer devices of this sort, other than insurance, are seldom available for families.[3]

---

[2] In the latter situation, the family may not escape completely the risks involved. For example, the car driven may be owned by the family in a state with a statute making the owner liable. See pp. 122–123.

[3] Families may move in with friends and relatives after a property loss, but unless the move had been anticipated prior to the loss, the change of domicile is a transfer of an actual loss, not risk.

Use of Insurance

Although noninsurance tools, particularly loss prevention and retention, are extremely important, all families are likely to turn to insurance for at least some protection, and most families will make extensive use of this tool. The contracts most likely to be used are (1) some homeowner's contract and (2) the Family Automobile Policy, the Special Package Automobile Policy, or some independent version of these two contracts. Families may also be interested in personal catastrophe liability insurance and fidelity and surety bonds.

HOMEOWNER'S INSURANCE PROGRAM

The homeowner's insurance program consists of package policies combining most of the property and liability insurance that a family needs into one contract. Prior to the development of the homeowner's program in 1950, families interested in broad protection had to purchase several different contracts to approximate their coverage under a homeowner's contract. For example, one set of contracts might be (1) a fire insurance contract with a dwelling and contents broad form attached that covers the insured's dwelling and personal property (other than his automobile and some other specified property) against many specified perils such as fire, windstorm, riot, vandalism, water damage, and glass breakage, (2) a theft insurance policy, and (3) a comprehensive personal liability insurance contract that covers most sources of liability other than automobile liability. Another set of separate contracts providing broader protection would include (1) a fire insurance contract with a dwelling building special form attached that covers the insured's dwelling against all risks not specifically excluded, (2) a personal property floater that provides similar all risks protection on personal property anywhere in the world not specifically excluded, and (3) a comprehensive personal liability insurance policy. Although these separate contracts and others are still available, most homeowners and tenants are eligible for and purchase homeowner's contracts.[4]

The reasons why homeowner's contracts have become so popular are that (1) they provide at least as broad coverage as the separate contracts, (2) they avoid gaps between and overlaps among separate coverages, (3) purchasing and renewing one contract is more convenient and more efficient than arranging several contracts, and (4) the premium is considerably less than the sum of the premiums for equivalent separate coverages. The cost is less because (1) it is less expensive to sell and service a package contract,

---

[4] The market for the older contracts is limited primarily to persons with low-valued dwellings, persons with undesirable exposures, and persons who do not occupy the dwellings but rent them to others.

(2) the "quality" of insureds purchasing homeowner's contracts tends to be better, particularly with respect to certain perils, such as theft, against which only the loss-prone seem to insure under separate contracts, and (3) some features of the homeowner's contracts cause insureds to purchase higher amounts of insurance relative to the values exposed to loss. Higher insurance-to-value ratios mean lower rates per $100 of insurance for the reasons specified on page 277.

A homeowner's contract consists of (1) a basic homeowner's policy, (2) a descriptive form, and (3) whatever endorsements, if any, are necessary. The heart of the contract is the descriptive form, of which there are five varieties: Form 1 (titled the "Basic Form"), From 2 (the Broad Form), Form 3 (the Special Form), Form 4 (the Contents Broad Form), and Form 5 (the Comprehensive Form). Owner-occupants of a dwelling used exclusively for private residential purposes (including incidental office occupancy) and containing no more than two boarders per family are eligible for all five forms. Owner-occupants of three- or four-family dwellings and tenants are eligible for Form 4 only. Form 2, the most popular form, is analyzed in detail below. The discussion of the other forms will be limited to the major ways in which they differ from Form 2. Table 28.1 permits a comparison of the premiums for each of the five forms.

Form 2   Form 2, like the other four, is divided into Section I dealing with property insurance and Section II dealing with liability insurance. The insured must buy both sections.

Section I protects the insured's property against the flowing specified *perils:* fire; lightning; windstorm; hail; riot; civil commotion; aircraft damage; vehicle damage; smoke; explosion; vandalism; theft; sonic boom; falling objects (including trees); weight of ice, snow, or sleet; collapse of all or part of a building; glass breakage to residence; sudden and accidental tearing asunder, cracking, burning, or bulging of a steam or hot water heating system or of a water heater; accidental discharge, leakage, or overflow of water or steam from within a plumbing, heating, or air conditioning system, or from domestic appliances; freezing of these systems or appliances; and sudden and accidental injury from artificially generated electric current to electrical appliances, devices, fixtures, and wiring. The insurer, however, is not liable when these perils are "caused, directly or indirectly, by (*a*) enemy attack by armed forces, including action taken by military, naval, or air forces in resisting an actual or an immediately impending enemy attack; (*b*) invasion; (*c*) insurrection; (*d*) rebellion; (*e*) revolution; (*f*) civil war; (*g*) usurped power." A fire set intentionally by public authorities is not covered unless their purpose is to prevent the spread of a fire not otherwise excluded under the contracts. Windstorm damage does not include damage by tidal wave, high water, ice, or snow, whether driven by wind

Table 28.1 Three-year prepaid premiums in one jurisdiction ofr the homeowner's policies for selected combinations of community protection and policy amounts ($50 disappearing deductible under Forms 1 through 4; $100 under Form 5.)*

Community protection class†	Form 1	Form 2	Form 3	Form 4‡	Form 5
	$15,000 insurance on dwelling				
1–6	$163	$207	$222	$ 92	$463
7 & 8	180	219	237	99	486
9	213	240	261	105	522
10	228	267	282	119	552
	$30,000 insurance on dwelling				
1–6	$311	$391	$419	$151	$754
7 & 8	339	413	448	163	802
9	402	453	493	176	873
10	430	505	533	201	934
	$45,000 insurance on dwelling				
1–6	$505	$635	$682	$211	$1,019
7 & 8	522	673	728	223	1,088
9	654	738	803	236	1,192
10	700	821	868	261	1,286

* Annual premium = 1.05 three-year premium ÷ 3 .
† For more details on this ten-class rating scale, see p. 509.
‡ Insurance on the contents is assumed to be 50 per cent of the insurance on the dwelling under the other forms.

or not. Damage by windstorm or falling objects to the interior of the dwelling is not covered unless the exterior of the roof or walls has been damaged first. Smoke from agricultural or smudging operations is excluded. Theft is defined as "any act of stealing or attempt thereat, including loss of property from a known place under circumstances when a probability of theft exists" even if an actual theft cannot be proved. The vandalism, residence glass breakage, and water damage perils are not covered if the residence is vacant for more than 30 days preceding the loss. During any period of vacancy or unoccupancy, losses caused by freezing of plumbing and heating systems and domestic appliances are not covered unless these items have been drained and the water supply shut off during the vacancy or unoccupancy. Falling objects, collapse of buildings, water damage, bursting of steam or hot water heating systems or heaters, and freezing are not covered if earthquake or landslide contributes to those perils.

The *property* covered is (1) the dwelling, (2) appurtenant private structures such as a detached garage but not including property used for commercial, manufacturing, or farming purposes or property other than a private garage rented to someone other than a resident-tenant, (3) trees, shrubs, plants, and lawns, but this property is not protected against damage caused by certain of the specified perils such as windstorm, hail, or vehicles owned or operated by an occupant of the premises, and (4) personal property. The dwelling item includes building equipment, fixtures, and outdoor equipment, if the property of the insured, and materials and supplies located on the premises intended for use in construction, alteration, or repair of the dwelling. All personal property that one would normally associate with a dwelling is covered except a few items that are specifically excluded. For example, all motorized vehicles (other than those used for the service of the premises and not licensed for road use), such as automobiles, golfmobiles, and snowmobiles, are excluded. There is also no coverage for business property or for animals, including birds and fish. Credit cards are not insured against theft. Forgery or alteration of checks or similar orders to pay a sum of money are excluded, but theft of these instruments is covered. Loss of a precious or semiprecious stone from its setting is excluded from theft coverage.

The *persons* whose property is insured include the named insured and, if they are residents of his household, his spouse, the relatives of either, and any other person under 21 in the care of an insured. In addition the policy covers legal representatives of the named insured, such as his guardian, if any; the executor of his estate, if he dies; a trustee in bankruptcy; or an agent. Personal property used or worn by an insured is protected even if he does not own it. If property owned by others is not being used or worn by an insured, it may still be covered under certain conditions, at the option of the named insured. If the loss occurs on the premises, it must happen on the portion of the premises occupied exclusively by the insured. A guest's property is also protected if the loss occurs in a temporary residence occupied by an insured. A servant's property is covered off premises if the property is in his custody or in a temporary residence of an insured.

The policy covers both direct and consequential *losses*. In addition to paying the cost of replacing damaged property, the policy covers the "necessary" increase in living expenses of all sorts incurred by the named insured while his property is rendered untenantable by an insured peril. Also covered are debris removal costs and the named insured's liability for fire department charges levied because of a fire on the insured's premises or exposing property.

Except for the limitations already noted in connection with the property of guests or servants away from the insured's premises, the protection extends to *locations* anywhere in the world. However, theft from an unattended unlocked automobile away from the premises is not covered unless it is a public conveyance or unless the insured parks his car in a public garage or parking lot and leaves his keys with an attendant. Also not covered away from the premises is theft from an unattended private watercraft unless it is from a securely locked compartment. Theft away from the premises of watercraft or trailers is also excluded.

The *term* of the contract is three years, but the premium is usually paid in annual or more frequent installments. The contract contains a typical cancellation provision.

If the policy covers a particular loss, several provisions affect the *amount* an insured can collect. The policy limits prescribe the maximum amount the insured can recover. Once the insured selects the amount of property insurance to be placed on the dwelling (the insurance on the dwelling must be at least $8,000), the minimum amount of insurance to be placed on each of the other property insurance items is fixed as a percentage of the dwelling insurance, as follows:

Appurtenant private structures	10% but may be increased
Personal property:	
On premises	50% but may be increased or reduced to 40%
Away from premises	10% of the on-premises limit but not less than $10,00
Additional living expense	20%

For example, if the insured selects $30,000 insurance on the dwelling, the four other insurance amounts are $3,000, $15,000, $1,500, and $3,000.

When the named insured moves from one principal residence to another within the United States, the unscheduled personal property on-premises limit applies at both locations.

Smaller internal limits per loss apply to certain types of property: money ($100); accounts, bills, deeds, and the like ($500); theft of watches, jewelry, and fur items ($500); manuscripts ($1,000); watercraft ($500); and trees, shrubs, plants, and lawns (5 per cent of the dwelling limit but no more than $250 per tree, shrub, or plant). Fire department charges are covered up to $250.

A replacement cost provision states that under certain conditions the insured can recover more than the actual cash value of any loss to building items (not personal property). The insurer promises to pay (1) the actual cash value of the loss or, (2) if higher, the amount obtained from the following calculation:

$$\frac{\text{Amount of insurance on building}}{80\% \text{ of replacement cost new of building}} \times \frac{\text{Replacement cost new}}{\text{of damaged portion}}$$

Consequently, if the insured maintains insurance equal to at least 80 per cent of the replacement cost new of the total structure (less the cost of excavations, underground flues and pipes, underground wiring and drains, and foundations), all his building losses will be paid on a replacement cost new basis up to the face value of the contract. For example, assume that a dwelling with a cash value of $30,000 would cost $40,000 to replace new today. To repair some fire damage to the dwelling would cost $10,000, but because of depreciation the actual cash value of the damage is $8,000. If the policy limit on the dwelling is at least 0.80($40,000), the insurer would pay $10,000. If the policy limit were some smaller amount, say, $28,000, the insurer would pay the higher of two amounts: (1) $8,000, the actual cash value, or (2) the value derived below:

$$\frac{\$28,000}{0.80(\$40,000)} \times \$10,000 = \$8,750$$

If the cost to repair the damage without any deduction for depreciation is more than $1,000, or 5 per cent of the insurance on the building item, the insurer will pay only the actual cash value until the damage is actually repaired or completed.

The contract contains a $50 disappearing deductible applicable to all perils. Under this clause, for losses up to $500 the insurer promises to pay 111 per cent of that portion of any losses in excess of $50. For example, if the loss is $450, the insurer pays 1.11($400), or $444.[5] The deductible is $6. For losses of $500 or more, there is no deductible. The deductible does not apply to additional living expense claims.

Section II include three separate and independent coverages: (1) liability insurance, (2) medical payments insurance, and (3) insurance against physical damage to the property of others. The *peril* under the *liability insurance* is an occurrence for which the insured is legally liable.

The liability may arise out of any *source* not specifically excluded. All premises on which the named insured or his spouse maintains a residence, including the private approaches thereto, are covered under this contract. So are other premises and private approaches thereto used in connection with the residence. Business or rental property (not including occasional rental of the insured's residence and some other specified rentals of the residence or garage) and farms are not covered. Other premises that are included are individual or family cemetery plots or burial vaults, non-owned premises such as a summer cottage in which an insured is temporarily

---

[5] In some states the insured can still select a disappearing deductible clause that applies only to windstorm and hail losses.

residing, and vacant land, other than farm land, owned or rented to an insured. The land is considered vacant even if independent contractors are constructing a one- or two-family dwelling for the insured.

Because business or professional pursuits are specifically excluded, the policy covers only personal activities. An important personal activity that is excluded is the ownership or operation of motor vehicles. However, recreational motor vehicles (such as snowmobiles) and motor vehicles not subject to registration because they are used exclusively on the premises (such as power lawn mowers and snowplows) or are kept in dead storage on the premises are covered with respect to on-premises losses. In addition, golf carts are covered while they are being used off-premises for golfing purposes. Coverage also applies to operations by independent contractors who are using vehicles not owned or hired by the insured to serve a nonbusiness function for the insured.[6] Another important exclusion applies to watercraft owned by or rented to an insured away from the premises if it has an inboard or inboard-outboard motor with over 50 horsepower or is a sailboat 26 feet or more in length. In addition, watercraft away from the premises powered at least in part by owned outboard motors with a combined horsepower of 25 or more are also excluded unless the motors were acquired after the policy was issued. All aircraft are excluded on or away from the premises.

Other important exclusions eliminate intentionally inflicted injury or damage, liability assumed by the insured under any agreement which is not in writing, and damage to property owned by, used by, rented to, or in the care, custody, or control of the insured, or over which the insured is for any purpose exercising physical control. However, the insurer does agree to pay any sums which the insured shall become legally obligated to pay as damages because of injury to or destruction of premises or house furnishings used by, rented to, or in the care, custody, or control of the insured, if the damage is caused by fire, explosion, or smoke caused by a sudden, unusual, and faulty operation of a heating or cooking unit. Employer's liability claims are not excluded, but the insured must declare the number of his residence employees if there are more than two, and there is no coverage against workmen's compensation claims.

The *persons* insured under the contract are the named insured and, if they are residents of his household, his spouse, the relatives of either him or his spouse, and any other person under 21 in the care of an insured. With respect to animals and watercraft owned by an insured, the contract also covers any person or organization having custody thereof with the per-

---

[6] For example, an electrician arriving to repair a defect in the house wiring may have an accident at the street corner. If the insured is brought into the case, he is protected, but this coverage is excess over any other insurance available to the insured.

mission of the owner. Any employee is also covered while operating a farm tractor or other farm implement.

The *losses* covered under the contract fall into the following categories: First, the insurer promises to pay all sums which the insured becomes legally obligated to pay as a result of bodily injury or property damage. Protection against both bodily injury and property damage claims is included under one insuring agreement. Second, the insurer will pay expenses incurred by the insured in order to provide immediate medical and surgical relief at the scene of the accident. Third, the insurer promises to defend the insured and pay the types of costs described on page 263, including the insured's loss of earnings up to $25 per day while attending hearings and trials.

There are no *location* limitations, and the *time* provisions are those common to liability contracts.

Medical payments insurance bears the same relation to the personal liability coverage that the medical payments coverages under the business general liability and automobile liability insurance contracts bear to the liability coverages under those contracts. This coverage is actually health insurance, not liability insurance, and receipt of these benefits does not prejudice the right of the beneficiary to sue the insured for the same loss. On the other hand, these payments may be made even if the insured is not liable. It is sufficient for the injury to be caused by accident (1) while the injured party is on the premises, as previously defined, with the permission of the insured, or (2) while he is elsewhere if the injury arises out of the premises, is caused by the activities of an insured, or is caused by or sustained by a residence employee while engaged in his employment by an insured. The insurer does not cover injuries to three groups of persons: any insured; any person, other than a residence employee, regularly residing on the premises or on the premises because of a business conducted thereon; and any person for whom benefits are required to be provided by his employer under a workmen's compensation law.

Physical damage to property insurance is in one sense the property-damage equivalent of the medical payments coverage. The insurer agrees to pay for damage to or destruction of the property of others caused by an insured. The liability of the insured is not an issue. The only exclusions applicable to this coverage are losses arising out of the ownership or use of motor vehicles, trailers, farm machinery, aircraft, or watercraft; loss to property owned by or rented to any insured, any resident of the named insured's household, or any tenant of the insured; or losses caused intentionally by an insured aged 13 or over. Note that these exclusions do not eliminate non-owned or nonrented property in the care, custody, or control of an insured. However, if coverage is provided under Section I, as it may be, that section is responsible for the loss.

The insurer promises to pay all liability claims up to a single limit per occurrence, the minimum possible limit being $25,000. There are no separate limits for bodily injury claims or for property damage claims, nor is there a separate limit per person injured. The supplementary payments —defense and settlement costs and the like—are paid in addition to the single liability limit. The medical payments insurance has a minimum limit of $500 per person and $25,000 per occurrence. The limit under the section covering physical damage to property is always $250 per occurrence.

Form 1   Form 1 differs from Form 2 primarily in two respects. First, the property insurance section covers fewer perils, and some of these perils are more narrowly defined. Form 1 covers only fire, lightning, windstorm, hail, riot, civil commotion, explosion, aircraft damage, vehicle damage, smoke, vandalism, residence glass breakage (up to $50 per occurrence), and theft. Explosions of steam boilers, however, are excluded. Vehicle damage is not covered if the vehicle is driven by an occupant of the premises. Smoke damage is limited to that resulting from the faulty operation of a heating or cooking unit in the described premises. Theft is defined as any act or attempt of stealing, but there is no reference to loss of property from a known place under circumstances when a probability of theft exists. Second, the additional living expense insurance limit is 10 per cent, not 20 per cent, of the dwelling limit.

Form 3   The principal difference between Form 3 and Form 2 is that the specified-perils insurance on the dwelling, but not the contents, is converted to all risks insurance. Excluded perils include earthquake, flood, war, wear and tear, rust, mold, contamination, inherent vice, latent defect, marring or scratching, termites, and rodents.

Form 4   Form 4 is used to provide protection for a tenant or a homeowner who is not eligible for the other forms. This form is the same as Form 2 except that there is no coverage on the dwelling or related private structures. The insured selects the amount of on-premises property insurance to be placed on his personal property, subject to a minimum requirement of $4,000. The off-premises limit is 10 per cent of this on-premises limit, subject to a minimum of $1,000. Additional living expenses are covered up to 20 per cent of the on-premises limit. In addition, if the named insured has any interest in improvements, alterations, or additions made to that portion of the premises used exclusively by the named insured, the limit on this improvements and betterments coverage is 10 per cent of the on-premises limit.

Form 5   Form 5, which is the most liberal of the homeowner's forms, differs from Form 2 in that (1) the property insurance is all risks with respect to both real and personal property and (2) the policy limits differ. The minimum policy limit on the dwelling is $15,000; the minimum personal property limit is 50 per cent of the dwelling limit for both on-premises and off-premises losses. Under the disappearing deductible clause, for losses up to $500 the insurer pays 125 per cent of that portion of the loss in excess of $100.

Endorsements   Endorsements may be attached to the contract to limit, modify, or expand the coverage. For example, one endorsement substitutes a flat $100, $250, or $500 deductible for the disappearing deductible in the forms. The premium credits for these deductibles are 10 per cent ($75 maximum), 20 per cent ($150 maximum), and 25 per cent ($225 maximum), respectively. Another permits the insured to schedule certain items of personal property, such as a fur coat, a diamond ring, or a musical instrument. Each scheduled item is protected on an all risks basis up to the amount specified in the schedule. If an insured has a business office on his principal residence that is incidental to the occupany of the premises as a dwelling, he can through an endorsement extend the definition of "personal property" to include the office furnishings and equipment and to include the liability exposure (other than professional liability) associated with this occupancy. A fourth example extends theft protection under Forms 2, 3, and 4 to property in unattended watercraft, motor vehicles, or trailers. Form 5 already provides this coverage. A fifth example covers another dwelling in the same state owned by the insured and used as a secondary residence. A most interesting final example is termed an "inflation guard endorsement." This endorsement increases the Section I coverage limits at a rate of 1 per cent per quarter for the first ten quarters of a three-year term and 2 per cent at the end of the eleventh quarter—a total of 12 per cent.

AUTOMOBILE INSURANCE

The other property and liability insurance contract that will be purchased by most families is an automobile insurance contract. Of the three standard-provisions contracts discussed in Chapter 18, most families will be interested in a family automobile policy or a special package automobile policy. Because these two contracts have already been discussed in detail in Chapter 18, no additional remarks will be made here.

PERSONAL CATASTROPHE LIABILITY INSURANCE

Many insurers issue a personal catastrophe liability insurance policy. One such policy provides $1 million or more excess liability insurance over a $50,000 comprehensive personal liability insurance policy (or Section II of a homeowner's contract) and a $300,000 automobile liability insurance policy. Where applicable, the policy also provides excess insurance over primary aircraft liability insurance, watercraft liability insurance, employer's liability insurance, and professional liability insurance. In addition, this policy covers losses not covered by these primary policies, but the insurer is responsible only for that portion of any such loss in excess of $10,000.

Examples of losses covered under this policy that are not covered under the primary insurance are personal injury claims based on false arrest, wrongful eviction or malicious prosecution, liability for automobile accidents occurring outside the United States and Canada, liability for losses to property (other than aircraft or watercraft) rented, leased, or in the care, custody, or control of the insured, and liability of others assumed under any contract, whether it be oral or written.

FIDELITY AND SURETY BONDS

The basic characteristics of fidelity and surety bonds and the major differences between bonding and insurance have already been described in Chapters 10 and 11. All that is necessary here is a brief discussion of the bonds that are important in family risk management.

A family will not ordinarily have any occasion to be an obligee under a fidelity bond. Some families will protect themselves in this manner against losses caused by dishonest domestic servants. Surety bonds are also not likely to play an important role in the risk management plans of most families, but in particular cases they can prove extremely important. Among the more commonly used surety bonds, all of which have been described on pages 333 to 334, are the following: probate bonds, such as the executor's bond, administrator's bond, or guardian's bond; court bonds, such as bail bonds, appeal bonds, or attachment bonds; and bonds for lost instruments. Under some of these bonds and under some circumstances, the family member will be the principal. For example, he may be the executor of a relative's estate. In other cases, the family member will be the obligee. For example, a moving and storage concern may furnish a bond to guarantee its safe handling of the family's property.

An Illustrative Case

The principles and practices which have been discussed will now be applied to a particular case. The reader is warned not to expect a single solution to the problems presented. He should also realize that as the family situation changes over time, the risk management program may have to be revised. Finally, he must recognize that so many considerations are involved in designing a risk management program that it is impossible to deal with more than the major dimensions in this short case.

RISK ANALYSIS

The first step in developing a risk management program is, as has already been stated, the recognition and evaluation of the risks facing the family. Assume circumstances as follows: John Smith, aged 35, has a wife, aged 35, and two sons, aged 8 and 3, respectively. John, who is the assistant plant manager for a small local manufacturing firm, earns $18,000 annually and his prospects for the future are excellent.

The Smiths have a home, valued at $28,000, including the land, which they built eight years ago. The unpaid balance on the mortgage, which has fifteen more years to run, is $20,000. The home, when furnished, would probably rent for about $300 per month and, if built new today, would cost about $35,000. The land, the cost of excavations, foundations, and the like, are valued at $5,000.

The Smiths also have a car valued at $2,500 with a replacement cost new of $3,500; typical furniture, clothing, and the like,[7] valued at $15,000 with a replacement cost new of $18,000; savings and checking accounts totaling $3,000; and in a safe deposit box, some common stocks and mutual fund certificates with a current market value of $9,000.[8]

The Smiths are an active family with a strong interest in sports. They participate in many social and civic activities. They often lend their car to friends or organizations, and they often drive cars belonging to others. John, in addition, frequently drives a company car on business trips.

Each summer the Smiths rent a cabin in the northern part of the state for two weeks. They drive to the cabin in their car, to which they attach a rented utility trailer containing about $1,500 in furniture, clothing, and the like.

The family circumstances have been deliberately oversimplified, but it is still necessary to sort out and arrange the risks in some systematic fashion. Using the basic risk classification developed earlier in the text,

[7] A detailed listing of this property is omitted here to save space and to simplify the discussion.
[8] The reader will probably notice the absence of any reference to life insurance cash values. This omission is intentional because the same illustration is to be used in the next chapter to develop a life and health risk management program, and the omission of any existing insurance simplifies that discussion immeasurably.

we have the following picture:

Types of risks	Maximum possible loss
Property risks	
Direct losses	
Dwelling	$28,000 including the land, cost of excavations, etc.
Furniture, clothing, etc.	
On premises	15,000
Off premises	1,500
Savings and checking accounts	3,000
Securities	9,000
Cash	500
Automobile	2,500
Consequential losses	
Additional living expenses	800 per month for 9 months
Depreciation	
Dwelling	7,000
Furniture, clothing, etc.	3,000
Automoblle	1,000
Debris removal	1,500
Liability risks	Almost unlimited in potential except for
Owned premises	bailee liability with respect to cabin
Owned automobile	
Business activities	
Personal activities	
Contractual liability under lease	
Contingent liability for operations of independent contractors	

All these losses are possible, but the chance of loss with respect to the savings and checking accounts and securities is slight. The other property losses can be caused by a very large number of perils, some of which are fairly common (for example, fire or an automobile collision), while the chance of others (for example, flood and earthquake in most areas) is very slight. The perils also differ according to whether they usually cause large or small losses.

Families seldom suffer contingent liability losses because of the operations of independent contractors, but many families experience the other liability losses, and their consequences may be very severe.

USE OF NONINSURANCE TOOLS

In designing their risk management program, the Smiths can use several noninsurance tools. Avoidance of risk may be a consideration if they have an opportunity to acquire new property or to engage in some new activity, but this technique will probably seldom be employed.

Retention, on the other hand, will play a very important role. Some of the causes of loss to real property such as flood, insect damage, and war cannot be handled in any other way. The same is true of some causes of loss to personal property, depreciation losses on personal property, and liability losses in excess of the limited amounts which can be transferred to an insurer or some other transferee. The Smiths should, in addition, retain as many small losses as possible. The exact amount depends upon the personality of the Smiths and the transfer costs in each instance,[9] but the Smiths should be able to bear losses up to at least $100 without too much inconvenience. The Smiths could also retain losses for which the probability of loss is very low, but their decision will depend upon the transfer costs.

The Smiths should, of course, take all economically feasible steps to reduce the frequency and the severity of the losses. Some specific examples of possible methods were cited on page 566.

The principal opportunity for the Smiths to employ the transfer device is with respect to the rented cabin, but it will be assumed here that the landlord will rent to the Smiths only if they assume responsibility for losses resulting from their own negligence.

USE OF INSURANCE TOOLS

The Smiths should make extensive use of the insurance device in their planning. Several alternative insurance programs are possible. One program, which in one company and one area would cost the Smiths annually about $270, would be the following:

---

1. Homeowner's Form 2 ($50 disappearing deductible)
    $25,000 Dwelling
      2,500 Appurtenant private structures
          Personal property
    12,500 On premises
      1,250 Off premises
      5,000 Additional living expense
    25,000 Liability
       500 Medical payments
       250 Physical damage to property of
          others

2. Special package automobile policy
    Actual   Comprehensive
      cash   Collision
     value   ($100 deductible)
    50,000 Liability
      2,000 Medical payments
      1,000 Accidental death
    20,000 Uninsured motorists

---

[9] A "bargain," for example, cannot be ignored, but bargains are rare with respect to small-loss coverage.

This program would provide fairly complete property and liability insurance protection for the Smiths at a reasonable cost. It covers most of the types of losses and perils to which the Smiths are exposed and includes deductibles which reduce the cost with no significant loss in protection. Because the dwelling limit exceeds 80 per cent of the replacement cost new of the dwelling less the land value and less exclusions such as the cost of excavations (80 per cent of $30,000) the policy covers building losses on a cost of replacement new basis. However, the program does not cover all property perils, liability as a result of business pursuits is retained, and covered liability losses may exceed the specified limits. Furthermore, the program still covers many small losses that the Smiths might be well advised to retain.

It is, of course, possible to tinker with this program in countless ways. For example, the dwelling limit could be cut to $24,000 without losing the replacement-cost feature if the dwelling value is stable. It is doubtful that the loss will exceed this amount, but it could, and the dwelling will likely increase in value. The limits applicable to the other property items would also be decreased. Finally, although this point is not effective here, the dwelling coverage cannot be cut below the protection required by the mortgagee. The inflation guard endorsement noted under "Endorsements" at the end of discussion of the homeowner's insurance forms would become especially important if the dwelling limit were reduced to $24,000.

Another possible change is an increase in the liability limits under both the personal liability and automobile liability components. Considering the loss potential and the small increase in premium for higher limits, this change would be a wise move. In fact, even if it is necessary to decrease some of the property limits to obtain the extra liability protection, this premium conversion deserves serious consideration. Substituting a flat $100 deductible for the $50 disappearing deductible would reduce the total premium by about $10. The automobile collision deductible is already $100, the maximum permitted under the special package policy, and the premium reduction for an automobile comprehensive deductible is small in absolute amount (in this instance, about $8 for a $50 deductible).[10]

Professional pursuits may result in extensive liability claims, and John should have these pursuits covered under his insurance program.

The other program to be considered in this analysis offers more complete protection. This program would include Homeowner's Form 5 and the Family Automobile Policy. Form 5 would cost the Smiths about $230 annually for limits roughly equivalent to those cited for Form 2; a flat $100 deductible would reduce the premium by 10 per cent. The Family Automobile Policy,

---

[10] Some authorities would argue against any automobile physical damage protection, particularly collision insurance, after the car is a few years old.

with roughly the same limits as the special package policy, would cost about $200.[11] The reader is referred to the earlier discussions of the differences between Form 5 and Form 2 and between the FAP and SPAP. It is sufficient to state here that this program would cover more perils but it would include some unnecessary benefits, such as the possible duplication of benefits under the FAP and health insurance.

REVIEW QUESTIONS

1. a. Outline the potential direct losses facing a typical family.
   b. Outline the potential consequential losses facing a typical family.
2. Outline the potential liability losses facing a typical family.
3. One man has observed that a family should never retain any losses which it can transfer at a reasonable price because a family cannot predict its losses with much confidence.
   a. Evaluate this observation with respect to property losses.
   b. Evaluate this observation with respect to liability losses.
4. a. Which of the homeowner's contracts is the most popular?
   b. Analyze this contract with respect to coverage and the amount of recovery.
5. a. Which of the homeowner's contracts provides the broadest coverage? How does it compare with Form 2?
   b. Which of the homeowner's contracts provides the most restricted coverage? How does it compare with Form 2?
6. Can tenants purchase a homeowner's contract? Explain your answer.
7. a. Explain the deductible clause in Form 2.
   b. How can this deductible provision be changed through an endorsement?
8. Explain why the premium for a homeowner's contract may be less than the sum of the premiums for separate contracts covering fire, the extended coverage perils, theft, and liability for activities other than automobile liability.
9. A family has a dwelling valued at $25,000 (replacement cost new $30,000) and contents valued at $10,000. This property is insured under a Homeowner's Form 2 with $24,000 insurance on the dwelling, a $50,000 liability limit, and a $1,000 per person medical payments limit. How much will the insurer contribute toward each of the following losses? Why?
   Assume that each of the property losses is stated in actual cash value terms. Replacement costs would be 20 per cent higher. For liability losses, assume the insured was negligent unless otherwise stated.

---

[11] In determining this price, we have assumed that the insured would not purchase the accidental death benefit. He would handle this problem under his life insurance program.

a. A windstorm destroys a detached garage valued at $3,000.
b. Fire causes $15,000 damage to the dwelling and $4,000 damage to the contents. The family must live elsewhere for four months while repairs are being made. Their monthly living expenses during these four months are $1,500 a month. The normal monthly living expenses for the family are $700 a month.
c. Vandals cause $500 damage to the interior of the premises.
d. Some furniture, valued at $1,000, stored in a warehouse, is completely destroyed in a warehouse fire.
e. Smoke from a fireplace in the living room causes $800 damage to wallpaper.
f. An automobile, valued at $2,500, is completely destroyed in a fire at a garage where it had been left for servicing.
g. A fire in the dwelling causes $100 damage to a camera which the husband borrowed from a friend.
h. A fire in the dwelling causes $200 damage to clothing belonging to an overnight guest.
i. A leak in a hot-water tank causes $500 damage to contents stored in the basement. Repairs to the hot-water tank itself cost $100.
j. Paint being sprayed on a neighbor's home is accidentally sprayed on the insured's home, causing $200 damage.
k. A thief steals $300 in cash from the premises.
l. A thief steals $400 worth of clothing from an unlocked car parked in front of a hotel.
m. A thief steals a $1,500 fur coat from a hotel room in West Germany.
n. A ring, valued at $500, mysteriously disappears.
o. A burglar breaks into a laundry and takes $100 in clothing belonging to the insured.
p. A thief breaks into the insured's home and takes a $200 fur coat belonging to an overnight guest.
q. The husband injures a companion while hunting. The companion suffers a loss of $8,000, including $1,000 in medical expenses. The husband is not legally liable.
r. The situation is the same as that described in q except that the husband is legally liable.
s. The wife injures a pedestrian with the family automobile. The pedestrian's loss is $6,000, including $1,500 in medical expenses.
t. A domestic employee falls off a defective chair, suffering a loss of $2,000, including $500 in medical expenses.
u. A son, aged 4, deliberately throws a rock through a neighbor's window, valued at $20. The parents are not legally responsible for their son's action.

v. The insured's son pilots a friend's 30-foot sailboat into a rowboat, causing $200 damage to the sailboat, $100 damage to the rowboat, and a $500 loss, including $250 in medical expenses, to the occupant of the rowboat.

w. The insured's young daughter falls down a stairway in the home. Her loss is $400, including $200 in medical expenses.

x. The family dog bites a guest, causing a loss of $80, including $50 in medical expenses.

y. While driving into his garage, the husband strikes a neighbor's child, cauing a loss of $30 in medical expenses.

z. Four dinner guests become violently ill as a result of certain impurities in the food. Each guest suffers a loss of $15,000 including $5,000 in medical expenses.

10. What additional protection would the family described in question 9 have if they purchased a personal catastrophe liability policy?

11. In what ways would you change the program suggested for the Smith family? Why?

12. Prepare a property and liability insurance program for your own family.

SUGGESTIONS FOR ADDITIONAL READING

Fire, Casualty, and Surety Bulletins (Cincinnati: The National Underwriter Co., monthly reporting service).

Guiane, G. E.: *1970 Homeowners Guide* (Indianapolis: The Rough Notes Co., Inc., 1970).

Pierce, J. E.: *The Development of Comprehensive Insurance for the Household* (Homewood, Ill.: Richard D. Irwin, Inc., 1958).

See suggestions for Chapters 17 and 18.

29

family personnel risk management

In addition to managing its property and liability risks, a family must make important decisions with respect to personnel risks associated with death, accidental injury, sickness, unemployment, and old age. This chapter deals with the recognition and measurement of these risks, the selection of the optimum tools of risk management, and the implementation of those tools.[1] The chapter concludes with an illustrative case.

Nature and Importance of Risks

The nature, severity, and frequency of losses faced by families as a result of the five personnel perils mentioned above have already been analyzed in detail in Chapter 8, and the reader is urged to review that analysis before continuing with the rest of this chapter.

The analysis of these personnel risks and the selection and implementation of the tools best suited to meet the needs and desires of a particular family are usually called *programming*, if the principal potential loss is a loss of earning power. If unexpected expenses (primarily taxes) following death are also very important, the process is usually called *estate planning*.

In illustrations of programming, a graphic portrayal of the income that the family needs and desires in case of the death, disability, or superannua-

---

[1] Since much of the material required for this presentation has already been discussed in previous chapters dealing with business personal risk management, it will be incorporated in this chapter by cross reference.

tion of one of its members (generally, but not exclusively the breadwinner) is extremely useful.[2] In addition to stating the needs clearly and precisely, the chart enables the family to view its total problems at a glance. If the family is concerned only with the loss of the breadwinner, one suggested chart would show the monthly income to be replaced if the breadwinner were to die immediately. The horizontal axis or the time axis would show the ages of the spouse and the children at frequent critical periods (for example, when the youngest child reaches age 18). An accompanying chart would show the amount that would be needed (1) if the breadwinner were to be disabled immediately and (2) because disability needs terminate at retirement, after the expected retirement age. In this instance, the horizontal

---

[2] Except for an occasional reference, unemployment is omitted from consideration in this chapter because the major tools used to handle this risk (loss-prevention measures by employers, social insurance, and supplementary unemployment benefits) involve no decision making by the family.

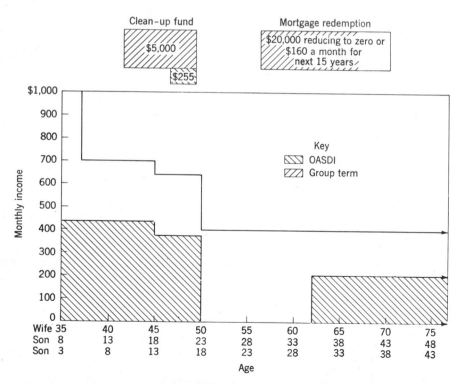

Figure 29.1   Smith family death needs and present protection. Death is assumed to occur immediately.

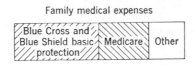

Family medical expenses

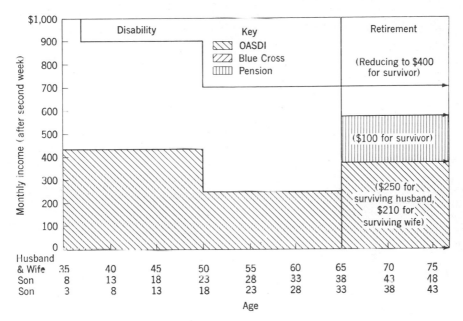

Figure 29.2 Smith family disability income, medical expense, and retirement needs and present protection. Disability is assumed to commence immediately.

axis should show in addition the age of the breadwinner. For examples of these two charts and their uses, see Figures 29.1 and 29.2.

If death or disability strikes at some later date, the desired monthly income pattern will probably change. These changes over time are most commonly either ignored, noted on the static chart, or otherwise recognized by nongraphic means, but to give a dynamic picture, a series of charts can be prepared with different starting dates.

Similar charts can also be prepared for other members of the family, particularly the spouse, but the need for such a representation is seldom felt because the losses associated with their death or disability are more easily described in words and because less attention is focused on these losses.

Boxed areas above or below the chart can be used to describe the need for emergency funds, clean-up funds, mortgage funds (although this item may be built into the monthly income needs), and a medical-expense fund. Clean-up costs include funeral expenses, probate costs, and estate taxes.

Use of Noninsurance Tools

All families utilize some noninsurance tools in dealing with personnel risks. As in the case of business firms, however, these noninsurance tools are almost always (1) loss prevention and reduction or (2) retention.

LOSS PREVENTION AND REDUCTION

Loss-prevention and reduction methods can be illustrated first by various health and safety practices and by education and training designed to keep each member of the family in good health and productive in an economic sense. Families differ markedly in the extent to which they practice these methods and in their effectiveness, but it is safe to say that more efforts along these lines would yield sizable dividends for most families. On the other hand, it is clearly impossible to rely completely upon loss prevention and reduction.

A second and entirely different type of loss prevention is the use of a will, gifts, and trusts to reduce the impact of estate taxes upon death. In estate planning, the proper application of these tools is an essential part of the procedure. Their proper use demands an extensive knowledge of legal instruments and taxes; but a few major principles can be enunciated here.[3] Only the Federal estate tax will be discussed, but state inheritance and estate taxes can also cause substantial estate shrinkages. Perhaps the most important estate tax consideration is the marital deduction. The amount of the net estate (gross estate less all expenses including probate costs) left to a surviving spouse (either outright or with the power to appoint the beneficiaries upon her death), but not in excess of 50 per cent of the net estate, is not subject to Federal estate taxes. Since there is a standard exemption of $60,000, a husband leaving all his $400,000 estate to his wife would subject only $400,000 − $200,000 − $60,000, or $140,000 of the estate, to estate taxes. Because the estate tax is a highly progressive tax, the difference in taxes would be even more marked. The estate tax on $340,000 (the taxable estate if he had left his estate to someone else) would have been $94,500, while the tax on $140,000 is only $32,700. In this example, note that the tax situation would not be changed if the

---

[3] The principles described in this discussion are also important in arranging the insurance part of the plan. For example, the proper designation of beneficiaries is extremely important. Life insurance policies are also useful as gifts in trust or as direct gifts.

husband had left only one-half of his estate to his wife and one-half to his children.

In addition to making certain that a person's estate will be distributed according to his wishes, a will can direct his estate into the most favorable tax channels.[4] If there is no will, the estate is distributed according to state law. Serious tax consequences may result.

The preceding discussion should not be interpreted to mean that a spouse should always leave one-half or more of his or her estate to the surviving spouse. Remember that when the survivor dies, there will be no surviving spouse (unless there has been a remarriage) and consequently no marital deduction. If the surviving spouse has sizable assets of his or her own, the part of the estate passed to the survivor may be taxed at higher brackets later. For example, in the preceding case, assume that the deceased's wife already had independent net assets of $400,000 when her husband died which, when added to her share in her husband's estate, gave her a net estate at her death of approximately $800,000.[5] The taxable estate is $800,000 − $60,000, or $740,000, and the tax is $229,700. If the husband had left one-half of his estate directly to his children, the tax upon his death would have been the same, but at the wife's death the taxable estate would have been only $600,000 − $60,000, or $540,000, and the tax $159,700. If the husband had left all his estate to the children, the taxable estate at the deaths of the husband and the wife would have been $400,000 − $60,000, or $340,000, and the tax $94,500. In this case, this last procedure would yield the smallest combined tax. This example illustrates the necessity for considering carefully all the circumstances involved.

Gifts can also be used to cut the estate tax. There is a tax on gifts, but each person has a $30,000 lifetime gift tax exemption plus an annual exclusion of $3,000 per donee. As both spouses are entitled to these exemptions, one spouse can, with the consent of the other, receive the benefit of the combined exemption. Furthermore, one-half of any gift from one spouse to the other is exempt. To illustrate these points, a husband could in one year, with the consent of his wife, give his wife and each of his two children $26,000 without incurring a gift tax. His annual exemptions would total $18,000, and his lifetime exemption would provide the difference. Much more could be said about gift taxes, but the preceding remarks are

---

[4] Tax laws and consequently the most favorable tax channels often change over time. For this reason and because it is much more important that the deceased's objectives should be satisfied, tax considerations should not be overemphasized.
[5] The sum of $800,000 ignores the reduction in the husband's estate because of the Federal estate tax at his death, changes in the values of the assets comprising the estate, the wife's withdrawals for living expenses, and the probable costs at the time of her death.

sufficient to indicate their significance in programming and especially in estate planning.

Trusts are useful in connection with both estate taxes and income taxes as well as in many other ways. Under a trust a donor transfers property to a trustee who manages and distributes the property in accordance with the terms of the trust agreement for the benefit of a third person, the trust beneficiary. Trusts can be divided into two major classes: (1) living trusts (*inter vivos* trusts), which operate during the donor's lifetime, and (2) testamentary trusts, which become effective at the donor's death. The latter could involve the proceeds of life insurance policies. The study of trusts is too highly specialized to be attempted in any detail in this text,[6] but the following example will illustrate their use: Through a trust arrangement, a father could transfer property to his child but have a trustee administer and distribute the property on the child's behalf. The property could include a life insurance policy on the father's life. Such a transfer would constitute a gift and might be subject to gift taxes, but the property is removed from the father's estate for Federal income and estate tax purposes. Probate costs would also be reduced for the same reason.

RETENTION

Retention is the second frequently used noninsurance tool. In three situations the use of this tool appears rational. First, insurance is about the only satisfactory method by which a family can transfer personnel losses to an outsider,[7] and complete insurance protection is almost always impossible to obtain because of underwriting restrictions, the cost involved, or both. In other words, in this situation a family has no choice. Recognition of this fact, however, together with some advance financial and psychological preparation, should make it easier to bear the losses when they do occur.

To illustrate this use of retention, contrast the amount of protection that a family should have against the death or disability of a breadwinner according to the needs approach described in Chapter 8 with the human life value loss. The family retains the difference between the values derived under these approaches. If the dependents know about the lower "minimum needs" value before the death or disability of the breadwinner, they should

---

[6] For a text describing trusts in a nontechnical manner, see Gilbert T. Stephenson, *Estates and Trusts* (4th ed., New York: Appleton-Century-Crofts, 1965).
For a one-chapter discussion of the subject, see F. C. Rozelle, Jr., "Trusts and Their Uses," in Davis W. Gregg (ed.), *Life and Health Insurance Handbook* (2d ed., Homewood, Ill.: Richard D. Irwin, Inc., 1964), pp. 781–791.
[7] Families sometimes transfer these risks to relatives or the public (through public-assistance plans), but this is seldom a satisfactory way of handling the loss.

be better able to adjust to the lower standard of living that almost inevitably follows.[8]

Second, although this decision must depend in part upon the income status and personality of the individual family unit, most families would be well advised to consider retaining such potential losses as (1) small medical expenses and (2) short-term income losses.

A third situation in which retention may be rational applies only to preparation for retirement. The advantages and disadvantages of insurance as an investment have already been discussed in Chapter 19. Risk managers were advised at that time to consider seriously the use of nonterm life insurance and annuities as one of their fixed-dollar investments. Families, however, should also use other types of investments, such as savings accounts, credit-union shares or deposits, and common stocks to prepare for their retirement. Some may have such attractive alternative investment opportunities and the self-discipline necessary to carry out their investment plans that they may not care to use any insurance in their preparation for retirement. Some may prefer to rely heavily upon other investments prior to retirement, at which date they will transfer some of the risk by using part of the accumulated funds to purchase an annuity. The proper balance is an individual family decision, but it must be made with knowledge and appreciation of the advantages of *all* forms of investments.

Uses of Insurance

Families make more extensive use of insurance to handle their personnel risk problems than do business firms for several reasons. First, many plans that create retained risks for the employer constitute insurance protection for the employee. For example, a pension plan which is self-insured by the employer provides insurance protection for the employee, the employer being the insurer. Likewise, supplemental unemployment benefits are insurance benefits for the employee even though they are self-insured by the employer. Second, a family is less able to retain risks because of its more limited exposure and less flexible financial position.

The average family has three layers of insurance protection: (1) social

[8] Sometimes, in constructing the statement of minimum needs, it is assumed that the standard of living will not have to be adjusted as radically as the statement of needs would indicate because (1) the wife can seek employment or (2) she can remarry within relatively few years. Earning a living, however, may not be easy for the wife, particularly if there are children, and in addition, she may lose some valuable OASDHI benefits. The probability that the widow will be remarried is not great enough to be depended upon. According to a recent remarriage table based on OASDHI experience, out of 100 females widowed at age 35, about 70 will still be living and unmarried 5 years later. See J. P. Jones, *Remarriage Tables Based on Experience under OASDI and U.S. Employees' Compensation Systems*, Actuarial Study No. 55 (Washington, D.C.: U.S. Government Printing Office, December, 1962).

insurance (usually OASDHI), (2) an employee benefit plan, and (3) individual insurance. The protection afforded by OASDHI will be explained in Chapter 31; the other two layers were discussed in Chapters 19 through 22.

To determine how much individual insurance and which combination of policies are best in the particular instance, the risk manager should follow these steps:

1. From the needs determined in the risk analysis, subtract the amounts already provided by programs that involve little or no decision making by the insured; e.g., OASDHI benefits and lump-sum payments under group life insurance programs.

2. From the needs that remain, subtract the benefits already provided by other programs (generally individual life insurance contracts) that do involve some decision—usually the choice of the proper settlement option.[9] In choosing these options, two important principles should be kept in mind. Life annuities are suggested if the mortality table used to compute the periodic payments contains relatively high death rates. This is most likely to be true in older policies. Contracts with high guaranteed interest rates should also be used to provide periodic payments over many years through life annuities or installment options of long duration. Conversely, contracts with options based upon relatively low interest rates should be used to fill the short-term needs.

3. From the needs that are not met by existing insurance protection, determine what amount the insured wishes to retain. These losses will supposedly be met out of assets already accumulated (stocks, bonds, savings accounts, and the like) or to be accumulated in the future.

4. The needs that remain after the completion of the first three steps must be met through insurance, and the problem is to select some combination of insurance policies that will meet those needs.

The death proceeds needed at any age and the cash value accumulations required at retirement age can be determined with the aid of settlement options. For example, assume that the need is (1) $200 a month for 20 years if the insured dies prior to age 65, there being no lump-sum needs, and (2) a life income of $245 a month for the insured (a male) after he reaches age 65, with payments certain for 5 years. Using the table of settlement options reproduced in part as Table 19.6, one can calculate the required death proceeds as 200/5.39 × $1,000, or $37,000, and the cash value accumulations as 245/6.62 × $1,000, or $37,000.

---

[9] Sometimes a change in existing contracts is in order, but generally speaking, a prima facie case exists for maintaining existing contracts. The primary argument against surrendering old contracts in order to purchase new ones or to use the funds in some other manner is the high initial expense in personnel insurance policies and the use of a large part of the premium dollar in the early years to pay for this expense.

These two amounts, plus the family's views on budgeting the premiums, suggest the types of life insurance and annuities to be provided. To illustrate, suppose the desired death proceeds are to be $37,000 in case of death at any time prior to age 65 but the amount of retirement income to be provided through insurance is zero. If the insured wishes to budget his premiums uniformly over his earning career, the appropriate contract is a term-to-65 contract. If the same circumstances prevailed but $37,000 is also accumulated at retirement age, as is true in the case illustrated, an endowment-at-65 would be the most suitable contract. The selection is not usually this simple, a combination of insurance policies usually being required to meet the stated needs. For example, if the desired death proceeds are $30,000 and the retirement accumulations at age 65 $24,000, one possible combination (but probably not the best) would be a $24,000 endowment-at-65 and a $6,000 term-to-65 contract. If a straight life contract produced a cash value at age 65 of $500 per $1,000, another possible combination is a $12,000 straight life insurance contract and an $18,000 endowment at age 65.[10] Because of quantity discounts it may be almost as cheap (or even cheaper) to purchase one contract which does more than the insured requires rather than purchase an exact fit.

After the cost of the combination selected has been computed, it is highly possible that the members of the family will wish to reconsider the losses they have agreed to retain, in which case a new combination of insurance policies must be selected.[11]

The need for disability income and medical expense contracts is met by selecting those contracts that (1) provide disability income payments at the desired times and in the desired amounts and (2) pay the prescribed medical expenses. Because health insurance contracts are less flexible than life insurance contracts, one will rarely be able to find a contract that meets the needs exactly. For example, it is not always possible to find a disability income contract that will provide an income to *any* specified age. Consequently, some revision of the potential losses to be retained is almost always a necessary part of this insurance decision. This decision will be described more fully in the illustrative case which follows, but two general remarks are in order here. First, the risk manager should remember that life insurance contracts can be endorsed to provide attractive disability income benefits. Second, noncancelable and guaranteed renewable contracts should be given very serious consideration because of the certain protection they provide to advanced ages.

[10] For a detailed discussion of more complicated examples, see the monograph on programming by Henry T. Owen, *Life Insurance Case Analysis* (Englewood Cliffs, N.J.: Prentice-Hall, Inc., 1952).
[11] Owen, *op. cit.*, pp. 40–45, suggests a technique for approximating the cost before selecting the actual combination of policies.

The graphic presentation suggested in the risk analysis section can also be used to advantage in selecting the tools of risk management. Different shadings or colors are used to represent OASDHI, group insurance, existing individual insurance, and retention, and these shadings or colors are used to fill in those portions of the needs that are met by these respective tools. The unshaded or uncolored area would represent the remaining needs, if any, to be met by new individual insurance. This graphic presentation simplifies and emphasizes the required changes in the total personnel insurance program. The graphic approach is illustrated in the case that follows.

Beginning in the late sixties insurers have made increasing use of computers to perform the necessary calculations and to prepare tabular and graphic presentations for insureds.

An Illustrative Case

The case to be presented is oversimplified in order to emphasize the principles involved instead of the details. The reader should also remember that (1) there are several possible solutions to the personnel risk problems posed by this family and that (2) a change in the circumstances of the family might make the suggested solution inappropriate. For the latter reason, any program should be subjected to some periodic review.

RISK ANALYSIS

John Smith, aged 35, has a wife, aged 35, and two sons, aged 8 and 3, respectively. John, who is the assistant plant manager of a local small manufacturing firm, earns $18,000 annually. His state and Federal income taxes total $3,600. John's prospects are excellent, it being generally assumed that he will eventually become plant manager. The compulsory retirement age at the plant is 65.

The Smith family has a $28,000 home, subject to a $20,000 mortgage with 15 more years to run. They have a car valued at $2,500, furniture, clothing, and the like valued at $15,000, savings and checking accounts and credit union deposits totaling $3,000, and some common stocks and mutual fund certificates with a current market value of $9,000. The savings accounts and the stocks produce an annual income of about $500.

If John should die, his family will lose the present value of his future earnings less his maintenance cost. Even if his salary is unchanged (an unlikely event in this case), this present value at age 35, assuming a maintenance cost of $2,400 and an interest return of 5 per cent, is about $185,000. The unexpected expenses would include such items as funeral expenses, estate taxes, and probate costs, which might be conservatively estimated at $5,000 at present but which would increase as his already acquired estate grows and would not terminate at retirement.

If John should become totally and permanently disabled, the economic loss would be even greater because the maintenance cost could not be deducted. At age 35, under the assumptions noted above, the economic loss would be over $220,000. Temporary disability would shorten the period of lost earnings. Medical expenses, of course, can be substantial even for a short-term illness.

When John retires, he will need sufficient income to provide for himself and his dependents at that time, probably his wife, for the rest of their lives.

If the wife dies or becomes disabled, the income lost is the amount required to replace the services she renders to the family. Income taxes and estate taxes will also increase as a result of her death. If the children die or become disabled, the family loses no income, but they do lose the money "invested" in the children. They may also assume an added burden after the age at which the disabled children would normally have become independent. Medical expenses are an important consideration in either case.

The "needs" approach is more realistic. The family members agree that they need to replace lost income only if the husband dies, becomes disabled, or retires. The same is true of unexpected expenses associated with death. With respect to medical expenses, however, the potential losses caused by the entire family are to be recognized. Implicitly then, the family has elected to retain the risks associated with the death or disability of the mother or the boys, with the exception of the medical expense risk. This decision may be based on the magnitude of the potential loss and is most questionable in the case of the wife.

The family also agrees to retain some of the losses associated with the husband's possible death, disability, or retirement, because no attempt is to be made to replace all the income lost or to provide a retirement income that will enable him to continue unchanged his standard of living.

The needs (and desires) of the Smith family are presented in the first column in Table 29.1. These needs are perhaps more clearly and dramatically stated in Figures 29.1 and 29.2. In these figures, the death and disability needs are expressed on the assumption that the father dies or becomes disabled immediately. If death or disability occurs later, certain needs, such as those for mortgage redemption and dependency-period income, change. These changes can be illustrated graphically by charts based on other assumed death or disability dates or by notations on the static charts. In order to conserve space, Figure 29.2 includes the medical expenses of the entire family.

Table 29.1 Smith family needs, present protection, and needs not covered

Need	Present protection*	Remainder
Death of father		
1. Cash needs:		
a. Clean-up fund—$5,000	a. $5,000 group insurance, $255 OASDHI	
b. Mortgage redemption—$20,000 decreasing to zero over next 15 years or $160 a month for the remainder of that period	b. $15,000 group insurance	b. $5,000 decreasing to zero over the next 15 years, or $40 a month for the remainder of that period
2. Income needs:		
a. Dependency period—$700 a month until oldest child reaches age 18, $640 for next 5 years	a. $435 a month (approximate OASDHI family maximum) until oldest child is aged 18, $375 a month until youngest child is 18	a. $265 a month until youngest child is 18 (wife aged 50)
b. Life income for wife—at least $400 a month when wife reaches age 50†	b. $205 a month after wife is 62—OASDHI	b. $400 a month from wife's age 50 to 62. $195 a month thereafter
c. Readjustment income—$300 a month for 2 years		c. $300 a month for 2 years
Disability of father		
1. Medical expenses:	Blue Cross and Blue Shield protection. Medicare after age 65 under OASDHI	Major medical expenses
2. Income needs after second week:		
a. Dependency period—$900 a month until youngest child reaches 18	a. $435 a month (approximate OASDHI family maximum) until youngest child is 18‡	a. $465 a month until youngest child reaches age 18 (husband aged 50)‡
b. Life income—$700 a month from age 50 to age 65	b. $250 a month from age 50 to age 65—OASDHI	b. $450 a month from husband's age 50 to 65
c. Readjustment income—$100 a month for 2 years		c. $100 a month for 2 years
Medical expenses of other family members	Blue Cross and Blue Shield basic protection. Medicare after age 65 under OASDHI	Major medical expenses

Table 29.1 (continued)

Need	Present protection*	Remainder
Superannuation of husband at age 65—$700 a month for husband and wife, $400 to survivor	$200 a month for both, $100 for the survivor— group pension $375 a month for both, $250 for surviving husband, and $210 for a surviving wife—OASDHI	$125 a month for both, $50 for a surviving husband, $90 for a surviving wife

*OASDHI benefits are those provided by the Social Security Act as amended in late 1969. See text for further explanation.
† If death occurs prior to the end of the dependency period, the life income for the wife after she reaches age 50 is to be $400 a month. If death occurs at a later date, the monthly income may be greater.
‡ In order to qualify for OASDHI disability income payments, Mr. Smith's disability must be expected either to result in death or to last at least 12 months. Furthermore, there is a 6-month waiting period.

RECOMMENDED TOOLS AND THEIR IMPLEMENTATION

Now that the problem has been defined, the next step is to determine the extent to which it has already been solved. The following facts are pertinent. Smith is entitled to the OASDHI benefits shown in Table 29.1. Because of publication deadlines, these benefits are those provided by the Social Security Act as amended in late 1969. Higher benefits are expected as a result of 1971 amendments. Smith is also covered, as a result of his employment, under a $20,000 group term life insurance plan, typical Blue Cross and Blue Shield basic medical expense contracts, and a company pension plan which, according to present indications, will pay him and his wife $200 a month after retirement, one-half being continued for the surviving spouse. The employer pays the entire cost of the life insurance and pension benefits; Smith pays one-half of the premiums for the Blue Cross and Blue Shield benefits. Smith has no individual insurance at the present time. Smith's other assets include the home, car, furniture and household effects, bank accounts, credit union deposits, and stocks noted under "Risk analysis."

The first step is to subtract from the needs the amounts provided under Smith's present insurance program. The life insurance proceeds under the group term insurance are applied to short-term needs and to pay off the mortgage because of the relatively low interest rates guaranteed under the settlement options. This determination of the needs not covered by the present protection is demonstrated in Table 29.1.

John Smith decides that his noninsurance assets are to be used (1) to meet those losses that the family has already agreed to retain because in its planning it elected to ignore some types of losses (e.g., disability incurred by the wife) and (2) to provide some supplementary benefits in connection with those needs that have been recognized (e.g., retirement income in excess of the amounts indicated in the table). In other words, the remaining needs shown in Table 29.1 are to be met through insurance.

Several insurance programs are possible, but a specific program will be developed for illustrative purposes. The desired death protection and retirement needs will be considered first. The protection needs may be reorganized and summarized as follows:

1. $195 a month for the widow beginning at age 50
2. $205 a month for 12 years beginning 15 years from now[12]
3. $265 a month until the youngest child reaches age 18
4. $40 a month until the end of the mortgage period
5. $300 a month for 2 years

Needs 1 and 2 should be filled first because the proceeds used to meet these needs can be placed under the interest option until they are required, thus reducing the earlier needs. If the appropriate settlement option values are those in Table 19.6,[13] the insurance proceeds which must be applied under the life income[14] and installment time[15] options, respectively, are approximately $46,900 (computed as 195/4.16 × $1,000) and $25,200 (computed as 205/8.13 × $1,000), a total of approximately $72,000.

Because needs 3 and 4 decrease over time and expire at the time the $72,000 proceeds are needed, a family income rider is appropriate. At first glance, a 1 per cent 15-year family income rider attached to a $30,000 base policy would seem to be in order. Actually, however, this amount can be reduced because the other $42,000 of proceeds purchased to meet needs 1 and 2, when placed on a 2¾ per cent interest option, will yield more than $42 × 2, or $84 a month. A trial-and-error procedure will reveal that in order to obtain about $300 a month during the remainder of the dependency period plus $72,000 at the expiration of that period, the insurance program

---

[12] $400 — $195 = $205. In order to simplify the problem, it is assumed that this protection is needed even if the wife does not survive the 12 years after age 50.

[13] Using the values in Table 19.6 is a conservative approach, because these values are guaranteed amounts. The actual payments may be higher. See Chap. 19.

[14] The value for the life income option with 5 years certain is used in this example because this is the smallest period certain for which a value is provided in Table 19.6. Using the 15 years certain value would have increased the amount only slightly and should be considered. If the wife should die before reaching age 50, these proceeds would be available to meet some other need. These "excess" proceeds can be avoided, but a discussion of the problem is beyond the scope of this book. See Dan McGill, *Life Insurance* (rev. ed., Homewood, Ill.: Richard D. Irwin, Inc., 1967), pp. 671–672.

[15] Table 19.6 does not give the installment time option applicable to a 12-year period, but the value is $8.13 per $1,000 proceeds.

should include $72,000 in basic insurance,[16] with a 1 per cent family income rider attached to $20,000 of this insurance.

Need 5 can be met by $7,000 (computed as $300/42.77 \times \$1,000$) placed under the installment time option for two years.

The death protection needed, therefore, is approximately $72,000 + \$7,000 = \$79,000$, plus a 1 per cent family income rider attached to $20,000 of this insurance.

The cash value required to meet the retirement need can be computed from a table of joint and two-thirds survivorship option values. Although a joint and two-thirds survivorship annuity does not meet the need exactly, it comes close to doing so. Assuming that this value for a husband and wife, both aged 65, is $6.23, the cash value required to meet the retirement need is about $20,000 (computed as $125/6.23 \times \$1,000$).

What is desired, then, ideally, is a $79,000 contract with a cash value of $20,000 with a 1 per cent 15-year family income rider attached to $20,000 of the face amount.[17] In other words, for each $1,000 of proceeds, the cash value should be $253. If the choice is limited to the contracts whose cash values are presented in Table 19.3, it is apparent that the cash values under the three contracts shown are too high. Some combination of term insurance and one of these contracts, however, would work. One combination that produces the correct cash value and $79,000 of basic insurance is $38,000 of straight life insurance and $41,000 of five-year renewable term insurance.[18]

---

[16] A trial-and-error procedure is not necessary. The following formula can be used:

$$2 \left(\$72 - \frac{\text{amount with rider}}{\$1,000} \right) + 10 \left(\frac{\text{amount with rider}}{\$1,000} \right) = 300$$

$$\$144 + 8 \left(\frac{\text{amount with rider}}{\$1,000} \right) = 300$$

$$\text{amount with rider} = 19\tfrac{1}{2} \times 1,000$$
$$= \$19,500$$

For our purposes, $20,000 is accurate enough.

[17] This contract would be ideal in the sense that it would provide exactly the protection and retirement needs specified in the analysis. Because these needs may change, guaranteed insurability options, variable life insurance, and other features might be included to provide some flexibility.

[18] This combination can be computed as follows:
Let x be the number of $1,000 units of straight life insurance and y the number of $1,000 units of term insurance. Then

$$x + y = 79$$

$$0.522x + 0.0y = 20$$

The rounded solutions to this set of simultaneous equations are $x = 38$ and $y = 41$. In this instance the simultaneous-equation approach does not save time because the cash value is provided entirely by one of the two contracts. If the two contracts had cash values bracketing the desired cash value, this would be a useful approach.

According to the premiums quoted in Table 19.3, for the first five years the basic insurance part of the program would cost annually [($38 × 17.61) + $10] + [($41 × 5.04) + $10], or about $900. Later the term insurance premium will increase. The family income rider from a typical insurer would cost about $80. Other possible combinations should be tried to see whether they achieve the same result at lower cost. Because the insurance premium does not increase proportionately with the face amount of the policy, one may prefer to purchase only that type of insurance which comes closest to meeting his needs, but in this instance that does not seem appropriate.

When the optimum combination has been selected, the premium may be more than the Smiths are willing and able to pay. If this is true, the objectives must be revised downward. The least important needs must be identified and treated. For many families, the two needs likely to be reduced first are those for a life income for the widow (because there may be time to adjust to the changed situation by then) and for retirement income. In this example, it will be assumed no downward revision is necessary despite the size of the premium. In any event the disability portion of the program should also be analyzed before any final decision is made.

When placed under the appropriate settlement options,[19] this new life insurance plus the existing protection will produce the income pattern stated in the objectives. The options may be selected by the insured or left to the discretion of the beneficiary, depending upon the wishes of the insured. Finally, the contracts should be checked carefully with respect to such details as the method of naming beneficiaries.

The discussion now turns to disability income and medical-expense needs. The disability needs must be rewritten in a slightly different fashion than they appear in Table 29.1 because, unlike life insurance proceeds, disability income benefits cannot be deferred under an interest option. The suggested revision is as follows:

1. $465 a month beginning 2 weeks after the disability commences and terminating when the husband is aged 65. (This $465 provides $15 more than is required after the disabled husband reaches age 50, but the additional cost is negligible and securing the necessary contracts is simplified.)

2. $100 a month beginning 2 weeks after the disability commences and terminating 2 years later.

[19] Insurers vary with respect to the flexibility of their settlement options. For example, some permit options to be changed at any time while others do not. Some permit commutation of payments under a family income rider while others do not. If the mortgage is to be paid in cash, this right is necessary under the suggested program. If this solution is not available, a separate mortgage redemption contract would be a better way to meet this need.

3. $435 a month beginning 2 weeks after the disability commences and terminating 6 months later. This need arises because of the waiting period under OASDHI.

As was demonstrated in Chapter 20, disability income contracts are not too flexible with respect to the maximum duration of benefits payable. Noncancelable contracts, however, are available which would take care of all the needs shown here because the required durations are (1) to age 65, (2) 2 years, and (3) 26 weeks. Three representative noncancelable contracts that would meet these objectives would cost roughly $260, $35, and $20, respectively. One way to reduce these costs would be to increase the waiting period. Although noncancelable or guaranteed renewable contracts are recommended, commercial contracts providing the same income benefits can also be used to lower the total cost.

Another approach to the first need would be to attach a disability income rider to part of the life insurance to be purchased. This approach is worthy of consideration because of the expense savings associated with the use of riders.

The life insurance and the disability income contracts, as well as the medical expense contracts to be noted next, should be endorsed, wherever possible, to provide for waiver of future premiums in case of total and permanent disability.

The medical-expense needs can be met by a guaranteed renewable major medical expense insurance contract with a $1,000 deductible, a 20 per cent participation provision, and a $20,000 or higher maximum benefit. A contract of this type would cost the Smith family about $210 annually.

In closing, we should note once again that the solution to a programming problem is not unique.[20] The suggested solution, however, indicates the type of reasoning that should be employed in order to select the proper tools to meet the stated needs.

REVIEW QUESTIONS

1. Illustrate how you would portray graphically the financial needs of a family in case the breadwinner dies, becomes disabled, or retires.
2. a. A family consists of a husband, aged 45, a wife, aged 40, and two sons, aged 21 and 18. The husband is the sole owner of assets totaling $500,000, including a $60,000 cash value under a $100,000 life insur-

[20] If John has a strong voice in company affairs, he would be well advised to suggest a strengthening of his firm's insurance and retirement program in lieu of salary increases. His individual needs and costs could be reduced in this way, and he would gain through the effort on his taxes.

ance contract. The other members of the family control very few assets. The husband and wife have agreed that all the assets except the life insurance are to pass directly to the children upon his death. Comment on this arrangement.

    b. Would your comments under a be different if the wife also controlled assets valued at $600,000?

    c. How could this family make use of gifts to reduce their estate tax?

3. a. Distinguish between an *inter vivos* and a testamentary trust.

    b. What advantages are afforded by trust arrangements?

4. Under what conditions is retention a rational approach to family personnel risk management?

5. Outline the steps you would follow to determine the additional personnel insurance required by a family.

6. Would you recommend that a contract issued when the assumed mortality rates were high be applied under a 5-year fixed-period option?

7. a. Prepare an alternate risk management program for the John Smith family.

    b. In what ways is your program superior to the one in the text? inferior?

8. In what sense does the use of the family income rider in the Smith program make that program dynamic?

9. Prepare a life and health insurance program:

    a. For the Smith family, assuming that John Smith is not covered under OASDHI.

    b. For a man, aged 50, and a wife, aged 45. Make any other assumptions you wish in this case.

10. Prepare a life and health insurance program for your family.

SUGGESTIONS FOR ADDITIONAL READING

Cohen, J. B., and Hanson, A. W.: *Personal Finance* (3d ed., Homewood, Ill.: Richard D. Irwin, Inc., 1964).

Dickerson, O. D.: *Health Insurance* (3d ed., Homewood, Ill.: Richard D. Irwin, Inc., 1968), chap. 21.

Fundamentals of Federal Income, Estate and Gift Taxes (15th ed., Indianapolis: The Research and Review Service of America, 1969).

Gregg, D. W. (ed.): *Life and Health Insurance Handbook* (2d ed., Homewood, Ill.: Richard D. Irwin, Inc., 1964), chaps. 55–64.

Mehr, R. I.: *Life Insurance: Theory and Practice* (4th ed., Austin: Business Publications, Inc., 1970), chaps. 20 and 21.

Stephenson, G. T.: *Estates and Trusts* (4th ed., New York: Appleton-Century-Crofts, 1965).

part 4
risk management, insurance, and public policy

Risk managers should be intensely concerned with public policy in the performance of their risk management function and as responsible citizens. The most important public policy issues that are directly related to risk management are discussed in the four concluding chapters of this text.

The first of these four chapters deals with the development and scope of regulation of the insurance business, which the Supreme Court, in *German Alliance Insurance Co. v. Lewis,* 233 U.S. 389 (1914), declared to be a "business in the public interest." Special attention is paid to the impact of the "age of consumerism" and programs in which the government and private insurers have joined forces to increase the availability of certain types of insurance.

The second chapter describes the leading social insurance programs in the United States and their place in the social security system. Old-Age, Survivors, Disability, and Health Insurance, workmen's compensation, temporary disability insurance legislation, and unemployment compensation are analyzed in some detail.

Poverty and ways to reduce it are the subject of the third chapter. Poverty is one of the most discussed topics of the day and the solutions adopted to control it have implications for risk managers.

Automobile insurance and other systems for compensating the victims of automobile accidents have been subject to numerous searching investigations during the past decade. The final chapter of this text describes the sources of dissatisfaction with the present system, the changes that have already been made, and those changes that have been proposed.

30

government regulation
of insurance

The business of insurance has been described by the courts as being "affected with the public interest." This chapter emphasizes the ways by which insurance consumer protection has been carried out in the past and the special problems that presently confront the regulators and the industry. Risk managers, as users of insurance, must be aware of the legal and economic environment in which insurers must operate in order to best avail themselves of their services.

The Purposes of Regulation

Regulation of insurance to protect the insurance consumer has always been a part of public policy in this country. In the past such policy objectives were broadly announced as (1) preserving financial solvency of the companies, (2) regulating rates to avoid excessiveness, inadequacy, or unfair discrimination in pricing, and (3) controlling trade practices to encourage fair competition and marketing. Today the emphasis is more directly on consumer needs and services which are or should be rendered by the private insurance institution. This consumer orientation undoubtedly is a result of increased emphasis developing on a national basis for giving the consumer better protection and remedies against unfair pricing and trade practices, as well as inferior product quality, that he allegedly suffers at the hands of other businesses. Truth in lending, truth in packaging, and other recent consumer protection legislation are evidence of growing Federal and state action in this area.

As further evidence of how the "age of consumerism" has affected the purposes and objectives of insurance regulation, if not its substance, one needs merely to examine the recent statements of government leaders in this area. In a recent speech, Richard E. Stewart, former Superintendent of Insurance of New York, remarked that government is trying to assist insurance consumers to "get the most insurance for their money." Within this broad purpose, Mr. Stewart suggests the following specific objectives of regulation:

1. *Insurance must be made available to those who want and need it.* Government must be expected to assist, strengthen, or replace (if need be) the private insurance mechanism when the shortage of insurance is serious enough to the consumer and the social cost of not acting is too high. Some consumers have had difficulty in purchasing private passenger automobile coverage, disability protection, and property insurance in ghetto areas, indicating availability problems.

2. *Regulators must make certain that the insurance product is of high quality and reliability.* Problems of removing restrictive contract language, limiting company freedom of cancellation and nonrenewability, and providing at least minimum guarantees against loss due to insolvency of an insurer would be a part of this quality and reliability objective.

3. *The price of insurance must bear some relationship to the quality of protection purchased and the ability to pay.* To the buyer, the best pricing system would seem to be one that yields prices as low as possible for even the poorer-quality risks. On the other hand prices must be reasonably fair and equitable among policyholders and still maintain the solvency of the companies upon which the insurance guarantee rests. Relevant government activity must see to it that rates are neither so low as to produce insolvency and thereby jeopardize quality nor so high as to preclude the purchaser's obtaining the necessary coverage.

Within this modern context, the sole purpose of insurance enterprise seems to be to provide quality protection at a reasonable cost to those who want and need it and to perform its business functions in a fair, efficient, and reliable manner. As will be shown in this chapter, there has been a change in emphasis in insurance regulation toward obtaining better distribution of services to poorer-quality risks, broder coverage at lower costs, and maintaining the supply and quality of insurance even in the more unprofitable markets. The basic questions to be answered are: (1) How has regulation been conducted to protect the consumer?, (2) What is the structure of regulation?, and (3) What are the problems confronting insurance regulators and consumers in today's economic and social environment?

The Background and Theory of Insurance Regulation

From the time of the special incorporation acts of the colonial legislatures to the present, the structure and destinies of the insurance business to a large degree have been guided by government. This phenomenon may appear to be unusual when the high degree of insurance regulation is contrasted with the extent of regulation of other business enterprises. On closer analysis, however, certain factors are found to be important in distinguishing insurance from other commodities and services marketed in a private enterprise economy:

1. Elimination of the marginal firm under a competitive environment is contrary to the basic purpose of the insurance institution, namely, to guarantee performance of future contingent financial obligations. Financial solvency is the foundation of public confidence in the private insurance mechanism and historically has been the primary objective of regulation.

2. The consumer is unable to evaluate the insurer's promises of future performance as distinguished from the similar evaluations that may be made with respect to tangible goods and services.

3. Complete freedom of entry of new insurance firms is not desirable because of the fiduciary nature of the policyholder-insurer relationship and the resulting opportunities for fraud and financial speculation by unregulated promoters.

4. Intensive unregulated competition in marketing insurance often produces inadequate rate levels and insolvency, sharp loss-adjusting practices, abortive policy language, and possible tendencies toward monopolization, all of which are recognized to be against the public interest.

Because of the unique position insurance holds in the marketplace and the desired social objectives the insurance mechanism must serve, regulation has been not only accepted but encouraged by the insurance business as well as by the consumer.[1]

COMPETITION AS A REGULATOR

Classical economic theory suggests that where the conditions of reasonably perfect competition are satisfied, the consumer is adequately safe-guarded

[1] Arthur C. Mertz, *The First Twenty Years: A Case Law Commentary on Insurance Regulation under the Commerce Clause* (Chicago: National Association of Independent Insurers, June, 1965), pp. 68–69.

against excessive profits, unfair price discrmination, and the lack of innovation and improvement in goods and services. As has been already stated, however, this theory of consumer protection breaks down when applied to insurance. The results of two important investigations by state legislatures illustrate this argument.

Fire insurance rates   Prior to the turn of the twentieth century, the underlying philosophy of fire insurance regulation was to prevent mergers and cooperative rating practices in order to preserve "atomistic competition" to protect the consumer. Anticompact laws, antirebating laws, and restrictions on cooperative rate making formed the heart of the regulatory framework. The many insolvencies which resulted from the enforcement of this legislation and the unrestrained competitive environment shook the foundation of state regulation.

The conclusions of the Joint Committee of the Assembly and Senate of the State of New York appointed to investigate corrupt practices in connection with legislation and affairs of insurance companies, published in 1911, vividly illustrate the difficulties of unregulated competition:

> We now consider the effect of open competition in fire insurance. It is not necessary to theorize about this for there is plenty of evidence in the rate wars which were formerly carried on and which to some degree prevail today. The universal effect of such periods of open competition wherever and whenever they have occurred has been a cutting of rates to a point that was below the actual cost of the indemnity. If the rate war had been general this would have meant the ultimate death of the company and rate wars of even a local character, if long continued, lead to the dissolution of the smaller and weaker companies. The effect on all companies is weakening. The policyholder gets his insurance very cheaply; too cheaply, for the weakening of the companies is not in the long run and on the whole an economic good for there is just so much less protection behind the insured in case of conflagration. The mutual character of insurance is so strong that nothing which tends to produce inferior protection can be for the public good. It has not done the policyholder any good to get cheap insurance if, when the test comes, the protection is found worthless.

But this is not all. In a state of open competition, insurance rates are often adjusted not to hazards but largely to the bargaining strength of the insured. Large buyers therefore may obtain their insurance too cheaply, as opposed to others who are not in a position to drive a sharp bargain.

As a result of this investigation, fire insurers were permitted to belong to rating bureaus and to agree to adhere to bureau rates, as long as the activities of these rating bureaus were subject to state regulation and as long as individual insurers could, if they wished, make their own rates.

Life insurance practices   After a long period of virtually unregulated activity and abuses in life insurance, the New York Legislature in 1905 conducted the famous Armstrong investigation, headed by Senator Armstrong assisted by Charles Evans Hughes, later Chief Justice of the United States Supreme Court. Testimony of this important study is contained in nine volumes; it disclosed many of the abuses and malpractices which had developed in the life insurance business up to that time, such as

1. Excessive commissions paid to agents
2. Illegal lobbying activities
3. Officers of insurers personally profiting from investment activities by their insurers
4. Officers of insurers controlling other business activities through common stock ownership

Much of the legislation which relates to the regulation of the life insurance industry today was enacted as a result of this investigation. Controls over life insurers' investment activities, reserves, commissions, and officers' activities stem from this study.

PRESENT THEORY OF REGULATION

The basic theory of regulation which has evolved over the 175-year history of insurance activities in this country has been to protect and preserve competition as the prime regulator of insurance activities and at the same time to superimpose boundary lines on trade, investment, and pricing activities in order to avoid the evils of monopolization or excessive profits on the one hand and insolvency and liquidation on the other.

Recent studies indicate that competition does exist in most areas of insurance. In the life insurance business there has been a considerable expansion in the number of insurers organized within the past decade, and the concentration of business in the top 50 insurers has been reduced. The Institute of Life Insurance reports that the net number of insurers has increased from 649 in 1950 to over 1,800 in 1969, even after accounting from some 989 companies that discontinued operations for various reasons during this same period. In the property and liability insurance business similar evidence is available to support the contention that competition is active. The rapid growth of the premium volume of insurers making rates independent of rating bureaus and the general expansion of the market controlled by mutual insurers are evidence that competition is operating. Many new insurers have recently been organized, a fact that suggests comparative freedom of entry into the business.

In addition to describing the present theory of regulation as one of *supervised and controlled competition* with government acting as a referee over the activities of companies to minimize conflicts with the consumer interest, there is also a positive role which some would ascribe to this function of government; namely, *to innovate, guide, and in some cases direct the explicit and detailed affairs of the companies for the purpose of accomplishing objectives which may not directly enhance the short-run profit prospects of insurers.*

The frustration and concern expressed by various industry and government regulators in this regard were best summarized recently by John F. Bolton, former Director of Insurance for the State of Illinois: "The insurance mechanism is made the dumping ground for difficult, perplexing and unresolved social problems . . . without sufficient forethought or research into the question of whether insurance was meant to be capable of solving structural problems of a complex and troubled society."

The National Advisory Panel on Insurance in Riot Affected Areas has suggested an approach which has and probably will become more and more common:

> When the public interest has required insurance to further basic social objectives, pragmatic programs have been developed by which government has joined with industry to obtain those goals. The approach has generally been to utilize the resources of the private insurance industry to the maximum extent. This private effort is then backed by government resources to fulfill purposes that can be achieved only by the partnership of government and private enterprise.

The discussion concerning the current problems of regulation which appears later in this chapter will illustrate this broader and more creative role which government is currently being asked to play for solving specific social problems through private-governmental insurance programs.

The Structure of State Regulation

In the early history of insurance in America insurers received their charters from state governments or were incorporated under state statutes, as were other business institutions. Early state legislation pertaining to insurance dealt with the licensing of agents and insurers, with contract provisions, and with investments. The two primary objectives of regulation in the early period were raising tax revenues and assuring financial solvency. Later, the basic aims of state regulation were enlarged to include assuring more liberal and ethical treatment of the policyholders and maintaining and expanding services and benefits to the insurance consumer.

THE STATE INSURANCE COMMISSIONS:
THEIR REGULATORY POWERS AND DUTIES

While insurance laws are important, providing the legal framework upon which all regulation rests, they have significance only when and if they are enforced and administered. The administrative agency, therefore, plays the most important role in the modern pattern of supervision, giving definition and meaning to what would otherwise be mere words.

The concept that regulatory law should be defined, administered, and interpreted by agencies possessing so-called "law-giving" and "judicial" powers is a relatively new tendency in Anglo-American law. The attempt to strike a balance between speed and fairness in the application of law has led to the delegation of power to specialists responsible to the executive as well as to the legislative branches of government. Likewise, the growth of administrative discretion is, at least in part, a result of the revolt against the rigidity and ritualism of the judicial process.

The powers of the insurance commissioner are based upon the police power reserved to the states under the Federal Constitution. In administering the affairs of this office, a wide range of discretion is allowed in enforcing decisions based upon the general welfare and safety of the community. The insurance commissioner has been best described by Professor Patterson:[2]

> Sometimes the insurance commissioner is an official clerk, sometimes he is a judge, sometimes he is a law-giver, and sometimes he is both prosecuting attorney and hangman. He is partly executive, partly judicial and partly legislative; and yet he is not confined within any of these categories.

DEVELOPMENT OF COMMISSION REGULATION

In 1851, New Hampshire appointed a three-man commission to examine insurers annually. In 1852, Massachusetts established a Board of Insurance Commissioners, composed of a secretary, treasurer, and auditor and charged with general enforcement of the insurance laws. Several other states created similar boards around the same time. By these acts, the modern system of state supervision came into existence. It was not until 1865, however, that Connecticut became the first state to appoint a single insurance commissioner.

The most famous of the early insurance commissioners was Elizur Wright, who served as a member of a two-man board in Massachusetts from 1858 to 1867. As a professor of mathematics, Wright had become interested in the mathematics of level premium insurance, the development

---

[2] Edwin W. Patterson, *The Insurance Commissioner in the United States* (Cambridge, Mass.: Harvard University Press, 1927), p. 6.

of reserves, and nonforfeiture laws, which are the foundations of modern life insurance activities. In 1850, Wright secured passage by the Massachusetts Legislature of a bill which required life insurance companies to maintain reserves that made it mathematically certain money would be available to pay the benefits promised in the policies. As commissioner of insurance, he secured passage of a nonforfeiture law and developed methods of reporting and accounting which became the blueprint for the future sound development of the entire private life insurance institution.

In 1866 a bill looking to Federal regulation and control of insurance under the commerce clause of the Constitution was presented to Congress, but there was a decided hesitation, and two years later came the first of several decisions of the United States Supreme Court holding that issuing a policy of insurance was not a "transaction in Commerce" and that "these contracts are not articles of Commerce."[3] These decisions were a great stimulus to state legislatures to establish permanent administrative agencies to supervise insurance company activities. By 1871 practically all the states had some supervision and control of insurers through established commissions.

With the evolvement of many separate state insurance commissions and their crazy quilt of insurance regulations, it became apparent that some form of national association was needed to eliminate many of the inconsistencies in state regulations. The New York superintendent of insurance requested a meeting of regulatory officers of all the states, and at this first meeting in 1871 the National Association of Insurance Commissioners was formed. Since that time the NAIC has continued to meet, at first annually and later semiannually, to discuss technical and legal problems relating to the development of uniform legislation and administrative solutions to the major problems confronting insurance regulators. All states now contribute to the work and the budget of the NAIC and have participated actively in its long list of legislative and administrative solutions. Several of the important accomplishments of this rather loosely knit organization are:

1. Creation of the valuation committee to establish uniformity in market values of stocks and bonds held by insurance companies
2. Development of the convention blank or annual statement forms which serve as a basis for insurance company reports to state insurance departments
3. Development of administrative procedures for integrating supervisory activities
4. Drafting of uniform legislation

[3] *Paul v. Virginia*, 8 Wall. 168 (1869).

FUNCTIONAL ORGANIZATION OF STATE COMMISSIONS

In every state, and in the District of Columbia as well, one or more officials are currently charged with the duty of administering the laws relating to private insurance. While the title given to these officials varies from state to state, there is nevertheless much in common as to their powers and duties. By far the most common designation is *insurance commissioner* and this title will be used in the following discussion. The prevailing type of administrative organization of the insurance departments of the various states is that of a single head with one or more subordinates. The most common method of selection of the insurance commissioner is by executive appointment, but other personnel in the departments are usually selected under civil service.

GENERAL STATUTORY POWERS AND DUTIES

In order to place the regulatory activities of the insurance commissioner in proper perspective, it becomes necessary to examine the departmental activities *in toto*. The state insurance commissioner's duties typically consist of the following:

A. Fiscal administration
   1. Supervising and collecting insurance taxes
   2. Supervising and collecting filing fees, license fees, and fees for certification of reserves
   3. Enforcing and supervising deposit requirements
   4. Managing funds of insurers in process of liquidation
B. Formation of insurers
   1. Ensuring compliance with laws pertaining to organization, such as those establishing minimum capital and surplus requirements
   2. Requiring the filing of all articles or certificates of incorporation
C. License and permit issuance
   1. Issuing insurers' licenses after verification of applicant's right to do business, financial status, and satisfaction of deposit requirements
   2. Issuing agents' licenses upon application or, in some cases, upon the passing of a qualification exam
   3. Issuing other miscellaneous licenses to brokers, adjusters, etc.
D. Examinations
   1. Power to examine and request information includes:
      a. Examining under oath officers and agents of the corporation
      b. Requiring the corporation, its officers, and its agents to produce its books and all papers relating to its business or affairs for inspection by officials making the examination

2. Power to request information, generally annexed to laws to permit more effective enforcement
E. Supervision of assets and liabilities
1. Requiring the filing of annual statements
2. Supervising the methods of determining the valuation of assets
3. Supervising the liability reserves which must be established
   a. Unearned premium reserves
   b. Reserves against losses
   c. Other contingent reserves
4. Jurisdiction over real estate
5. Jurisdiction over investments
6. Jurisdiction over financial character of business
F. Supervision of conduct of the business
1. Checking methods of advertising
2. Checking loss adjustments
3. Forbidding rebating or acceptance of less than full premiums and twisting or inducing a policyholder through misrepresentations to exchange one policy for another
G. Rate regulation

PRESERVATION OF INSURER SOLVENCY

One keystone in the structure of state regulation historically has been the preservation of the financial integrity of insurers, since the concept of insurance itself is based upon performance of a future financial obligation. In accomplishing this objective, insurance departments have directed much of their activity and legislation toward the periodic examination of insurers' financial affairs. Most insurance departments examine insurers at least once every three years for solvency and compliance with the respective state laws. In the interim between examination dates, insurers are required to file detailed annual reports concerning all their financial activities. In addition, the insurance commissioner may at any time choose to conduct special investigations or examinations or to request special information.

As a practical matter, most insurance departments are not adequately staffed to examine the affairs of insurers, both domestic and foreign, that are doing business within their borders. Therefore, insurance departments feel the greatest responsibility toward careful examination of domestic insurers. In addition, they participate with other insurance departments in what is referred to as a convention or zone examination, which enlists examiners from several states for checking the affairs of insurers doing[4] busi-

[4] For detailed presentation of examination procedures, see A. G. Straub, Jr., *Examination of Insurance Companies,* seven vols. (New York: New York State Insurance Department, 1953–1955).

ness beyond the borders of the state in which the insurer's office is located. Examination ranges far into the field of insurer services, activities of officers, management of investment portfolios, settlement of claims, and even the careful scrutinization of the minutes of all board of directors' meetings held by the company.

Beyond the examination reporting procedures, the insurance departments have promulgated important regulations concerning investment activities of insurers. State statutes, for example, describe certain types of securities which may be purchased and place restrictions on the distribution within the portfolio.[5] Difficulties may arise in this connection when insurers do business in states with differing investment statutes. Fortunately, the states have followed the principle of recognition of the existence of powers over corporations of another state to the extent that it does not offend public policy of the recognizing state. Following this rule, an insurer seeking to become licensed in a state other than its home state may be admitted, even though its investments do not any more than substantially comply with the general state statutes governing those investments. On the other hand, the applying insurer must be in absolute compliance with its own state's investment statutes. This reasonable approach to a seemingly impossible regulatory environment has proved workable.

With respect to other matters, such as the kind of business which can be written and commission or expense limitations, the insurance commissioner may demand that the insurer conduct its operations within and outside the state in accordance with the standards established for domestic insurers, on the grounds that the ability of the insurer to fulfill its obligations to policyholders within the state depends upon its total operations.

RATE REGULATION

Insurance commissioners also have authority over the pricing of insurance. The legal basis and method of regulation have been changing over the past few years, however. Most states still have a model rating law, developed by the NAIC in the late forties, which has five important features:

1. All rates must be reasonable, adequate, and not unfairly discriminatory, but these standards are not defined.

2. Rates and rating plans must be filed. The commissioner can request supporting information.

[5] For example, Section 81 (7) of the *New York Insurance Code* limits the ownership of real estate to 10 per cent of the total assets. Wisconsin Statutes Section 201.27 (4) limits the investment in stock and securities of any one corporation to 10 per cent of the insurance company's assets. See also Satterthwaite, "Regulation of Life Company Investment and the Rule of Comity," *Association of Life Insurance Counsel Proceedings*, XIII (1956), 401–407.

3. The filed rates cannot be used until a specified waiting period, which may be extended by the commissioner, has expired or until the rates have been specifically approved. In practice the waiting period has sometimes been extended for many months.

4. Rates that are permitted to go into effect may be subsequently disapproved.

5. Insurers may belong to or subscribe to the services of a rating bureau. Members may agree to adhere to the rates filed by the bureau.

The major alleged advantage of this approach is that it permits a reasonable blend of direct regulation and competition. The insurance commissioner is informed and can prevent a rate from becoming effective that in his opinion does not satisfy the standards. On the other hand, permitting the insurer to use the rate after a specified period even if the commissioner has not acted is supposed to protect the filer from unreasonable delays by the commissioner. Rating bureaus can exist as a stabilizing force but deviations and independent filings are possible.

Opponents argue that this approach does not permit insurers to respond rapidly enough to market pressures and changing loss experience. Even when the administration of the law is highly satisfactory, the waiting period causes some delays when approval of rate changes or new contracts is being sought. What is worse, however, is the fact that because the commissioner must act positively on each filing, he is subjected to political pressures, particularly with respect to rate increases. Consequently requests for rate increases are often denied, delayed, or reduced. Insurance department personnel, it is alleged, are sometimes unduly arbitrary and demanding. Rate making necessarily involves some judgmental decisions, and some regulators impose their own unfounded judgments on insurers. The results in many states are inadequate rates, an inadequate supply of insurance, and few innovations. Opponents also argue that insurance department resources required to administer a law of this sort would be more profitably devoted to the regulation of other matters such as insurer solvency.

Alternative approaches to rate regulation include both more restrictive and less restrictive regulation. The most common type of more restrictive regulation requires all insurers to belong to a single rating bureau whose rates must be approved by the insurance commissioner before they can be used. Under some of these laws, however, individual insurers may be permitted to make a case for using rates other than those developed by the bureau. The most restrictive regulation requires all insurers to use rates promulgated by state authorities. Supporters of these laws believe that they produce more accurate rates, promote rate stability, and best protect the public interest. Opponents deplore the interference with what they consider the prerogatives of private management and reiterate their objections to the model law.

Under file-and-use laws, one of the most common forms of less restrictive regulation, the major difference from the model law is that insurers may file and use their rates immediately, these rates being subject only to subsequent disapprovals. The least restrictive type of regulation, best exemplified by the California statute, is a no-filing statute under which rates need not be filed, except possibly for informational purposes within some time after they go into effect. The rates, however, are still subject to subsequent disapproval. All of the no-filing laws to date and some of the file-and-use laws permit rating bureaus to exist but prohibit insurers from agreeing to adhere to the rates developed by the bureaus. In other words, in those states the bureau rates are advisory only. Supporters argue that in states with these laws delays are eliminated, political pressures are reduced, more responsive rates result in a more adequate supply of insurance and encourage product innovations, and insurance departments can concentrate their attention on important matters. Opponents fear that this type of regulation may be too lax and that if price competition is "either insufficient or irresponsible," the public interest is better served by closer supervision.

In December, 1968, following an extensive investigation, the National Association of Insurance Commissioners concluded that price competition in property and liability insurance had become more intense than when it adopted the model law, although its effectiveness varies among lines and among states.[6] It recommended, therefore, that "where appropriate, reliance be placed upon fair and open competition to produce and maintain reasonable and competitive prices for insurance coverages wherever such competition exists, thus conserving the resources of insurance departments for other important areas of public interest where there is no substitute for enlightened government action, including increased attention to the growing lack of availability in personal lines markets sufficient to the demand for such insurance." Specifically, in states where greater reliance on competition seems appropriate, the Subcommittee recommended that new legislation either (1) "authorize the commissioner to suspend the prior approval requirement for any lines, subdivision or class of insurance where conditions warrant such action" or (2) repeal the prior approval requirement (except for certain lines deserving special consideration). In this latter instance, however, the commissioner should be authorized "to reimpose prior approval for any line, subdivision, or class of insurance in which he finds that competition is insufficient or irresponsible."

[6] "Report of Rates and Rating Organizations Subcommittee (F1)," *Proceedings of the National Association of Insurance Commissions, 1969,* Vol. I.

In the late sixties, either before or after the shift in the NAIC position, several states enacted file-and-use or no-filing laws, at least three of which contained the possibility of a return to the model law if competition proved insufficient or irresponsible. The most notable of these cases was New York, which had previously been a strong supporter of the model law.

Rate regulation in life insurance takes a form substantially different from that described for the property and liability business. Some states have set maximum rates which may be charged for credit life insurance, such as $2 per thousand dollars of coverage per month for level amounts of insurance, and $1 per thousand dollars for decreasing coverage. New York has established a maximum rate of 60 cents per thousand dollars per month for group life insurance sold in that state. Outside of these and other minor exceptions, life insurers are legally allowed to charge any rate that they feel would be proper and adequate as long as they do not discriminate unfairly among insureds, but they must establish sufficient reserves in their balance sheet, based upon the underlying assumptions of mortality, interest, and expense. State nonforfeiture laws prescribe the mortality tables and maximum-interest-rate assumptions for policy reserve computations. Therefore, any rating plan in life insurance that does not develop a sufficient quantity of assets to enable the insurer to satisfy these minimum reserves would be inadequate. Competition is expected to prevent excessive rates.

Some Current Problems in Regulation

A careful, detailed look at certain regulatory problems emphasizes the difficulties of implementing the concept of "giving the insurance consumer the most insurance for his money," as suggested by Superintendent Stewart. This subject may be divided into three general problem areas: (1) problems in providing a continuous supply of insurance; (2) company financial and structural problems, and (3) Federal versus state regulation.

PROBLEMS IN THE SUPPLY OF INSURANCE

There is considerable evidence that the private insurance mechanism is either unable or poorly equipped to serve the broad spectrum of consumer insurance needs. Poorer-quality risks, which have been isolated by credible company underwriting and profit studies, usually are eliminated in the selection process by restrictive underwriting rules or, if accepted, are priced at levels that few insureds would reasonably pay. This process has been described by its critics as "skimming the cream of the business" and as adverse to the public interest but is defended as rational economic conduct for sound company profit management. Although the less restrictive rate regulation described above is expected to increase the supply of property insurance (because insurers will have more freedom to set adequate rates), the premiums developed for some insureds, though justified, will be higher than those persons are able or willing to pay.

The central issue is: To what extent should the better, preferred classes of business be assessed higher premiums to help pay the claims or subsidize the rate structure for the marginal or residual risks within an overall competitive environment? Sound economic decisions by insurance company managers would dictate the elimination of unprofitable classes of business by either an unwillingness to write them in the first place, cancellation during the policy term, nonrenewal upon expiration, or setting very high rates—a procedure which makes the business profitable for the company but prices it out of reach of the consumer.

The loss-sharing concept of the insurance mechanism functions only so long as the concept of equitable or fair discrimination in rate making between and among classes of insureds is acceptable in the marketplace. If a particular company fails to define sharply the differences in risk quality in its rating plans, the preferred or higher-quality business will shift to other companies which do, with the result that the general quality of business written by the nondiscriminating company will deteriorate even more. The rendering of a value judgment as to what is desirable discrimination in insurance rates is, of course, subjective, and, hence, regulators, companies, and the general public are often in disagreement on this matter. More explicitly stated, should a farmer located hundreds of miles from an urban area be required to pay higher extended coverage premiums on his agricultural property because of riot losses to property located in the urban central core? Should the general level of automobile rates be raised to help pay the higher losses of particular classes of drivers (e.g., male, under age 25, single) that have generally experienced a much higher accident frequency and severity?

The failure experienced by certain insurance consumers to obtain adequate amounts and types of coverage at prices within their ability to pay creates a vacuum in the marketplace as well as problems for the society as a whole. For example, uninsured motorists, under our liability system of reparations, pose a serious threat to all persons involved in accidents with them. Financial-responsibility laws, unsatisfied-judgment funds, and compulsory insurance laws (described in Chapter 33), as well as uninsured-motorists coverage, are examples of attempts to relieve the adverse social and economic consequences of the uninsured vehicle or operator. The lack of available coverage in the voluntary market at prices that consumers can reasonably pay has also been attacked by creation of government-regulated or -controlled placement facilities. In automobile and workmen's compensation insurance, assigned risk plans operate to provide minimum coverage for the residual risks. These plans provide that each insurer doing business in the state be assigned its proportionate share of the risks not otherwise insurable in the voluntary market according to the ratio of its premium volume to the total state premium volume. The automobile plans are described in more detail in Chapter 33, which is devoted entirely to the social problems associated with automobile insurance.

Consumers have also argued that coverage availability has been lacking in the marketplace because of the lack of properly located agent facilities. Companies can avoid substandard markets by their selection and placement of agents. Mass merchandising of nonlife coverages through employee groups and associations (see Chapter 22) has been offered as one solution to this problem. Under these plans, coverage is provided to groups of insureds in order to reduce selling and administrative costs. Individual underwriting requirements have been somewhat relaxed in certain company plans because the insurers are getting a better overall distribution of business submissions. Still, the nonlife business has far to go in matching the group marketing operations of the life and disability companies where true group underwriting and rating is employed.

Special problems in supplying insurance have arisen for individual property owners and businessmen located in the urban core areas and in providing flood insurance on real property. In both instances Congress has enacted legislation designed to improve the supply of insurance.

Urban property insurance programs   In the light of the large number of urban riots which occurred in the summer of 1967, President Johnson appointed a committee referred to as the President's National Advisory Panel on Insurance in Riot Affected Areas (also known as the Hughes Committee). This committee conducted hearings and prepared a report which concluded that the property owners in urban core areas were having difficulty obtaining insurance in the private market.[7] The committee recommended the development of a state and national civil disorder insurance program requiring the meshing of both Federal and state governments and the insurance industry. Some of the states already had voluntary urban area programs in effect, most of which provided that no property owner in an urban area would be denied insurance until his property had been inspected, that no property would be rejected without telling the owner what improvements would make it acceptable, and that surcharged rates could be applied to acceptable

[7] *Meeting the Insurance Crisis of Our Cities, a Report by the President's National Advisory Panel on Insurance in Riot-affected Areas* (Washington, D.C.: U.S. Government Printing Office, 1968).

substandard property. The Hughes committee recommended extension and improvement of these plans, which they termed FAIR (Fair Access to Insurance Requirements) plans, and the formation of a Federal reinsurance corporation to protect insurers against catastrophe losses.

Following up on the Hughes Committee Report, Congress enacted on August 1, 1968, the Urban Property Protection and Reinsurance Act (titled XI of Public Law 90-448). Under this law the Secretary of the United States Department of Housing and Urban Development (HUD) administers a National Insurance Development Fund, which reinsures private insurers against catastrophic losses from civil disorders. Insurers, however, cannot purchase reinsurance on properties located in a given state unless the state (1) requires all property insurers in the state to belong to an approved FAIR plan and (2) agrees to reimburse the Fund for certain payments as described below. In 1970 almost thirty states had FAIR plans but fewer states had in addition provided the state "financial backup" for the Federal fund.

All FAIR plans cover both residential and commercial property, but most include only fire and the extended-coverage perils. Under the Federal legislation FAIR plans are not permitted to deny any applicant insurance merely because of environmental hazards such as a high crime rate, riot potential, or physical hazards other than those in immediately adjacent properties. State insurance commissioners have usually also required insurers to ignore these environmental hazards in their pricing but in turn have permitted in many states a special riot and civil disorder charge, averaging about 3 per cent, on all properties insured in the state, to enable insurers to recoup some of their expected losses on urban core property. The result is the socialization or broad pooling of certain risks associated with urban core property.

FAIR plan business is distributed among insurers in two ways. One approach is basically an assigned risk plan with a joint reinsurance association composed of all insurers assuming responsibility for (1) all or part of the insurance on property that has a significant exposure beyond the control of the insured and (2) that portion of the insurance on other property written under the FAIR plan in excess of the normal limit of liability that the insurer writing the policy has agreed to accept. The other approach is a direct underwriting pool.

Under the Federal reinsurance program, insurers interested in reinsurance must include all fire and extended coverage insurance, vandalism insurance, allied fire insurance lines, theft insurance, and those portions of multiple-peril policies covering similar perils. Other lines are optional. If individual insurers suffer property losses resulting from riots or civil disorders against which they have obtained reinsurance, such an insurer retains a portion of the total reinsured losses it sustains during the contract year up to

2.5 per cent of its reinsured premiums in the state plus 10 per cent of the losses in excess of this amount. The first layer of the remaining reinsured losses is paid by the Fund through assessments on those insurers whose losses in the state were less than the 2.5 per cent retention until all have sustained losses or assessments to the 2.5 per cent level. The Fund pays the second layer with the reinsurance premiums (originally 1.25 per cent of reinsured premiums but only 0.3 per cent in 1970) collected from insurers on properties insured in the state during the contract year. The state government must reimburse the Fund for the third layer up to 5 per cent of the aggregate property insurance premiums earned in the state during the preceding year on those lines of insurance reinsured by HUD. Most states that have enacted legislation to implement this "financial backup" will obtain this money from insurers, who in turn will be permitted to increase their insurance premiums to recover their loss from insureds. New Jersey, however, has enacted a program whereby policyholders are assessed $1\frac{1}{2}$ per cent of their fire insurance premium, to be accumulated in a contingency fund to be used when needed. Indiana has agreed to use general revenues for this purpose. The Fund pays the fourth layer with assets it has accumulated through excess reinsurance premiums paid in earlier years and current reinsurance premiums on properties located in other states. In other words not until this point does the national character of the plan become important. Finally, after its assets are exhausted, the Fund will borrow moneys from the United States Treasury, to be repaid out of future reinsurance premiums.

The program poses many problems. Not only must the insured be given access to the market, but the solvency of the participating companies must be properly safeguarded. Moreover, the cost of environment hazards must be reallocated while preserving the principle of price competition. Finally, there is an apparent conflict between Federal and state spheres of authority and activity. Because many property owners cannot secure adequate theft and vandalism insurance, there is pressure to add theft and vandalism insurance to FAIR plans. Because these perils are greatly influenced by environmental hazards, insurers are reluctant to add them without some provision for recouping their additional expected losses. Vandalism, however, has been added in many states. In late 1970 Congress enacted legislation that requires the Federal Insurance Administration to begin writing theft insurance August 1, 1971, in those states where no action has been taken to ease critical availability problems.

Flood insurance   The risk associated with flood losses to real property lacks many of the characteristics of an ideally insurable risk outlined on pages 202 to 203. Many persons are exposed to this loss, but a large proportion of these persons may suffer loss from a single event. Because most people with a serious interest in flood insurance have a high loss potential, the premium that would have to be quoted by a private insurer would be so large relative to the property value insured that the insurance would not be economically feasible. Consequently, private insurers have been reluctant to write flood insurance on real property except in rare cases. Flood insurance on personal property is readily available because this property is usually mobile.

Flood disasters, however, have created many hardships for the persons directly affected and for society. Loss-prevention and reduction measures need to be explored more fully, but a complementary alleviative program has been needed for some time. In 1956, following some serious flood losses in the northeastern United States in 1954, the Congress enacted a flood insurance program to be financed and administered by the Federal government with some participation by private insurers. Because Congress later became unhappy about certain portions of the law, it never appropriated any funds for the program.

Congress, however, continued its interest in some type of national flood insurance program and, following extensive research and debate, passed the National Flood Insurance Act of 1968. Under this act the Secretary of Housing and Urban Development administers a program that enables interested persons to purchase flood insurance on real or personal property located in states that have adopted satisfactory land-control and -use measures. Without this land-use restriction it was feared that the program would provide too much incentive for some people to build or to continue living or operating in areas that are highly susceptible to flood damage. Properties eligible for coverage include residential properties designed for one- to four-family occupancy and small commercial properties. Protection up to $17,500 per dwelling unit and $30,000 per multiple-dwelling unit, $5,000 for contents per dwelling unit, $30,000 for other single structures, and $5,000 for contents per business unit in a single structure is made available at "chargeable" premium rates (e.g., 40 cents per $100 insurance on dwellings and 50 cents per $100 insurance on their contents) that are less than the estimated losses and expenses in order to encourage the purchase of this insurance. The Secretary determines both the chargeable premiums and the "true" expected costs. The face amount of flood insurance in force at any one time is not to exceed $2.5 billion.

An advisory committee, including representatives of private insurers, state and local governments, lending institutions, home builders, and the general public, advises the Secretary in the preparation of regulations, on policy matters, and in any other way he may deem advisable.

Private insurers market and service the insurance, which is underwritten by the National Flood Insurers Association, created by those private insurers who wish to participate in the program as risk bearers as well as fiscal agents. The Federal government contributes the difference between the chargeable premiums and the premiums that would be required on a nonsubsidized basis. In addition, the National Flood Insurance Fund, in return for a premium paid by the pool, promises to reimburse the private pool for losses in excess of a specific amount. Thus the government's role in this program includes establishing the chargeable premiums and the true expected costs, paying the subsidy necessary to meet expected costs, and reinsuring the private pool.[8] The possibility of extending this concept of a joint private-public venture to other unusual perils such as earthquake is already under consideration.[9]

Other private-public plans   Two other examples illustrate the growing trend toward cooperative private-public arrangements designed to make insurance available in areas where private insurance alone has proved inadequate.

Exporters are concerned not only with physical damage to the goods they export but also with the possible insolvency of the buyer or with political risks such as inconvertibility of foreign currencies or expropriation of exported goods by a foreign authority. Insurance against physical damage and insolvency of the buyer is available through private sources, but private insurers have been reluctant to insure against political risks. Such insurance is now available through the joint efforts of the Foreign Credit Insurance Association, an underwriting pool of about 70 private insurers, and the Export-Import Bank, a Federal government agency. The Association sells a contract that protects exporters against both the insolvency of debtors and political risks, but the Export-Import Bank assumes responsibility for the political risks.

Liability for nuclear incidents poses catastrophic risks for the operators of nuclear reactors and potential claimants. Under a 1957 amendment to the Atomic Energy Act of 1954, Congress required operators of reactors to purchase certain amounts of nuclear energy liability insurance or to demonstrate their financial responsibility in some other way. It also limited the maximum responsibility for a nuclear incident to $500 million plus the required private protection. The private insurance is written by two underwriting pools—the stock Nuclear Liability Insurance Association and the Mutual Atomic Energy Reinsurance Pool. Congress also authorized the Atomic Energy

[8] An emergency program enacted in 1969 and to remain in effect until the end of 1971 permits the Secretary to make the flood insurance available without waiting for the completion of flood zoning studies for rate-making studies. Prior to this amendment insurance had become available in only three communities. The 1969 amendment also extended the flood insurance program to cover losses from water-caused mud slides.

[9] Medicare, consisting of the hospital and supplementary medical expense insurance programs for the aged, is based on a somewhat different concept of government and private insurer cooperation. The private insurers are not risk bearers under that program.

Commission itself to sell supplementary insurance to cover the excess $500 million liability. This joint private-public effort removed a significant impediment to the peaceful development of atomic energy.

FINANCIAL AND STRUCTURAL PROBLEMS OF COMPANIES

Insurance companies are faced with the same problems that confront many business firms, namely, maintaining a profitable and solvent operation in a highly inflationary and relatively unstable economy. Inflation exacts its toll from most financial institutions, including insurers, by raising the costs of operations perhaps more rapidly than price adjustments can be made to cover these rising costs. The property and liability insurance institution has the added problem of paying claims at inflated values which were not contemplated in the original rate-making and underwriting process. Life insurers have felt the impact of inflation in a slightly different way. Not only have their costs of operations increased, threatening the continued future of face-to-face selling, but life insurance buyers have become more interested in inflation-hedging–type investments such as mutual funds and variable annuities. As noted on pages 355 to 358, life insurers, in turn, have met this competition for the investment dollar by being licensed to sell variable annuities and, in some cases, by marketing mutual funds. Naturally, inflation has reduced the interest of consumers in cash value life insurance.

On the question of profitability, several studies have been made recently of the profits earned by property and liability insurers. These studies, conducted on behalf of the industry by the Arthur D. Little Company, Inc., in response to increasing interest in the role of investment income in rate regulations,[10] suggest that the rate of return on invested capital in the non-life insurance industry has lagged far behind that earned by other industries with comparable risks.

If accepted, the results, of course, have important implications for rate regulation. In addition they raise the question whether the private insurance industry can hold existing capital or attract new capital with these inadequate rates of return to meet the rising demand for insurance services. It has been suggested that failure by the insurance institution to be competitive in the capital markets will result in a contraction of insurance services and make it that much more difficult for consumers to obtain needed coverages.

According to the Little Reports, the entire industry earned approximately

[10] Arthur D. Little Company, Inc., Report to American Insurance Association, *Prices and Profits in the Property and Liability Insurance Industry* (November, 1967), and Report to the National Association of Independent Insurers, *Rates of Return in the Property and Liability Insurance Industry; 1955–1967* (June, 1969). For a sample critical review, see J. D. Hammond and N. Shilling, "The Little Report on Prices and Profits in the Property and Liability Insurance Industry," *Journal of Risk and Insurance*, XXXVI, No. 1 (March, 1969), 129–145.

3.6 per cent *on invested assets* for the period 1955 to 1967, including realized and unrealized investment gains, and after taxes. This compares unfavorably with an average rate of return for fifty-five industry groups for the same period which experienced a 10.7 per cent return after taxes. Moreover, annual rates of return for insurers fluctuated greatly during this period among insurers and over time. The rate of return *on net worth* for stock insurers was 7.0 per cent, compared with 11.8 per cent for companies included in Standard and Poor's COMPUSTAT annual industrial tape. Critics have contested the Little Report profit calculations, the use of invested assets as the major base of comparison, the way in which risk was measured, and the interpretation of the results. Some observers argue that *if* the profit rates of insurers are relatively low, the two most important reasons are (1) inefficiency in the conduct of the business and (2) the tendency of many insurers to write less premium volume than is optimal from a profit standpoint.

Those supporting the Little conclusions offer as further evidence of the comparative unprofitability of their industry what has occurred in the capital structure of some of the large insurers. Many companies have formed holding companies and have shifted a large part of their capital to these companies for investment outside the insurance industry. This drain of existing capital capacity has the effect of indirectly reducing future insuring capacity, a matter which has greatly disturbed insurance regulators. Also, unprofitable companies have been purchased by large conglomerate companies for the purpose of acquiring the assets of the insurer to be employed in their noninsurance activities. These inroads on the capital of the industry will continue, it is argued, unless and until insurance companies can show rates of return competitive with the rest of the economy. In a 1968 *Report of the Special Committee on Insurance Holding Companies* the New York State Insurance Department expressed grave concern about insurers being controlled by noninsurance industry groups, pointing to the need for new legislation to regulate such events.

In the long run, many observers have predicted, the insurance industry will inevitably integrate with other financial institutions and be a part of what is referred to as "one-stop financial service institutions." The merging of banks, investment companies, and insurers would offer the consumer complete financial services under one roof. Credit services, coupled with investment and insurance services, would give the consumer a total integrated financial counseling service meeting his credit, savings and investment, and protection needs in a more efficient manner. The advent of the computer and centralized data-processing facilities would make such plans possible. The public policy issue is whether such a system is desirable.

Another problem facing regulators has been that of the insolvent insurer and the disastrous effects that insolvent insurers produce for consumers and the general public. When an insurer becomes insolvent, not only do its investors lose their capital, but claims are not paid and unused premiums are not returned to policyholders. Public confidence in the particular insurer is thereby destroyed and, in turn, the confidence placed in the whole private insurance institution is threatened. Although insurers have an excellent solvency record, a rash of insolvencies among insurers specializing in substandard automobile insurance in the sixties focused national attention on this problem. Furthermore, although the frequency rate is low, the consequences for insurers and persons with liability claims can be disastrous.

Various plans have been proposed or enacted to meet this problem. Over 20 states, including such jurisdictions as California, Michigan, New York, and Wisconsin, have created guarantee funds that can be used to meet the losses of claimants and creditors of the insolvent company. The Federal government has also proposed a national guarantee program patterned somewhat after the Federal Deposit Insurance Corporation for banks. This plan, it is argued, would be more effective than the state plans because of the interstate character of the insurance business. Thus far, it has not been widely supported by most industry groups, as it would undoubtedly result in extensive Federal regulation of their business. Some insurers oppose any insolvency fund, mainly on the grounds that (1) well-managed insurers may be forced to pay costs generated by careless insurers and (2) regulators might relax their supervision of marginal insurers because the consequences to insureds of an insolvency will be reduced. Such opposition, however, seems to be declining in importance. These insolvency funds are discussed in more detail, particularly with reference to insolvency of automobile insurers, in Chapter 33.

State Versus Federal Regulation

Not only at issue is the problem of how the private insurance business should be regulated, but also the question: By which level of government, Federal or state? This jurisdictional problem is not new, but neither has it been settled after 175 years of litigation and dispute. The legal basis for exclusive state regulation of insurance prior to 1944 was predicated upon a series of cases holding insurance not to be interstate commerce and, therefore, outside the commerce power of the Federal government. The first case, *Paul v. Virginia*, 8 Wall. 168 (1869), upheld the state law regulating insurance agents on the grounds that Virginia could properly deny a license to Paul, who was an agent, for not having complied with the state laws regulating agents. This case laid the foundation for the cases which followed concerning the interpretation that insurance was subject to exclusive state jurisdiction.[11]

[11] See E. W. Sawyer, *Insurance as Interstate Commerce* (New York: McGraw-Hill Book Company, 1945), pp. 1—10.

Some advantages of state regulation are these:

1. The present size and scope of the private insurance business testifies to the fact that state regulation has created a regulatory environment which has assured a financially strong, solvent, and vital insurance industry.

2. Insurance contracts are purchased to meet local exposures and risks. Local administration and supervision at the state level seem implicit in resolving any difficulties the insurance consumer may have concerning the interpretation of his contract and dealing with insurers.

3. While state supervision lacks uniformity, it nevertheless encourages the innovations and new developments which private enterprise must make to meet the needs of the insurance consumer. Differences in state law, although seeming a burden to insurance supervision and administration, actually encourage insurers to follow a pattern of greater service and a variety of experimentation and development in the interests of all concerned. In several instances where uniformity is desirable, the NAIC has served as a forum for discussion and persuasion.

4. Federal supervision of insurance could be totally inadequate if poorly administered, with the result that it would be a detriment to the entire private insurance business, whereas spotty or inept insurance supervision in a limited number of states does not seriously impair the activities of the insurers and the needs of the insurance consumer in the other states where supervision is proper and fair.

It would be incorrect, however, to gather the impression that state regulation was not challenged during the years from 1869 to 1944. The inadequacy of state regulation served as the basis for legislation which was proposed in Congress in 1868, 1905, 1906, 1914, 1915, and 1933. In each of these years sponsors of legislation contended that state insurance regulation was inadequate and that the Federal government should exercise control.[12]

It was not until the Temporary National Economic Committee conducted its investigations in 1939 and 1940 that a specific critique of state insurance regulation was registered. On the basis of study and investigation, this report indicated the following abuses in the structure of state regulation:[13]

1. State insurance commissioners were not appointed on the basis of qualification, their tenure of office was too short, and their salaries were inadequate to attract competent people.

[12] See the *Congressional Record*, Vol. 40, p. 748.
[13] *Temporary National Economic Committee Reports, Final Report and Recommendations*, 77th Congress, Document 77 (Washington, D.C.: U.S. Government Printing Office, 1940).

2. Budget and staff of commissions were totally inadequate in terms of the job to be fulfilled. Insurers should not pay the salaries of examiners directly.

3. There should be closer regulation of agency practices and training and closer scrutiny of the competence and activities of agency managements.

4. The number of policy forms was much too great for intelligent consumer decision, and greater standardization of coverage was in the public interest.

5. Intercompany agreements and interlocking boards of directorates existed which tended to reduce the competitive environment for insurance.

6. Certain types of insurance, particularly certain types of industrial insurance, were viewed to be against the public interest because of high distribution costs which the consumer was asked to pay.

THE SOUTHEASTERN UNDERWRITERS ASSOCIATION DECISION

The criticisms developed by the TNEC culminated in an important decision and case involving an action against the Southeastern Underwriters Association alleging that 200 stock fire insurers had violated Sections 1 and 2 of the Sherman Act. Specifically, the indictment contained the following claims: Not only did the insurers involved sell over 90 per cent of the fire insurance in the six states in which they operated, but by continued agreement and concert of action they were able to fix premium rates and agents' commissions and often used boycotts and coercion to force the purchase of a particular insurer's insurance. The following coercive devices were scored in the indictment:

1. Failure to provide reinsurance for noncomplying insurers

2. Withdrawal of agents' licenses where there was representation of competing insurers

3. Threatening consumers doing business with non-SEUA insurers with boycotts when they attempted to satisfy their other insurance needs

4. Policing by the rating bureaus and local boards of insurance agents of the activities of their members and imposing boycotts and intimidations in attempting to carry out their program

Litigation first developed on the issue of the jurisdiction of the Federal government over insurance and was raised on demurrer by the insurers. The demurrer was sustained in the lower courts but reversed by the United States Supreme Court in a 4-to-3 decision. The opinion of the Court, written by Justice Black, distinguished the line of cases starting with *Paul v. Virginia* on the basis that the earlier cases involved the validity of state statutes, and that this was the first case squarely presenting the question of whether the commerce clause grants Congress power to regulate insurance when conducted across state lines. The court determined that the Federal government could regulate insurance either as interstate commerce or as a matter that affects interstate commerce and pointed out that the practices attacked under the indictment were violative of the Sherman Anti-trust Act. The trial on the facts never took place, since the indictment was dismissed by agreement between the parties after the decision on jurisdiction.

THE CONSEQUENCES OF THE SEUA DECISION

In retrospect, the SEUA decision clearly appears to have established Federal jurisdiction over the activities of insurance conducted across state lines. This does not mean, however, that state regulation is entirely precluded, since there may be practices and activities of insurance which are predominantly intrastate in character or subject to only state regulation. It follows then that as a consequence of this important case, the courts have essentially established a dual system of regulation, with the state commissions assuming the role of an administrative agency to enforce state law with respect to intrastate commerce and with respect to interstate commerce to the extent that it would be privileged by the Federal government.[14]

The most important Federal statutes involved in any interstate regulation of insurance are:

1. *The Sherman Act.* The Sherman Act is designed essentially to prevent restraints to free competition in business and commercial transactions. In particular this act would apply to insurance practices which involve cooperative or joint service in the auditing, production, adjustment, investigation, or inspection of particular insureds or losses. It would make illegal agreements or concerted actions with reference to the making of rates and the apportionment of risks taken under reinsurance pools. Agreements which relate to the appointment of agents, levels of commission, rating plans, and cooperative insurance activities would all be subject to question under the provisions of the Sherman Act.

2. *The Clayton Act.* Section 14 of the Clayton Act prohibits time contracts and agreements of sale or lease "where the effect of such activities substantially lessen competition or tend to create a monopoly." The Clayton Act would prohibit in the insurance field certain stock acquisitions, interlock-

---

[14] See Alice Chelberg, "Dual Regulation: It Has Happened Here," *The Annals of the Society of Chartered Property and Casualty Underwriters*, X, No. 1 (January, 1958), 2–13.

ing directorates, price discrimination, and brokerage compensations which may substantially lessen competition.[15]

3. *Robinson-Patman Act.* Section (*a*) of the Robinson-Patman Act prohibits unlawful price discrimination between different purchasers of commodities of like kind and quality which tends to create a monopoly.[16]

4. *Federal Trade Commission Act.* Under this act, the Federal Trade Commission is given power to investigate within reason and to restrain unfair trade practices.

ENACTMENT OF THE MCCARRAN-FERGUSON ACT (PUBLIC LAW 15, 15 U.S.C.A. 1012)

As a result of the Southeastern Underwriters case, Congress was petitioned by the insurance business and the state insurance departments to enact clarifying legislation which would establish the jurisdiction of the states over insurance. In attempting to draw the dividing line between the areas of jurisdiction of the Federal and state governments, Congress sought to establish by Public Law 15 the preeminence of the state insurance laws in the first instance.[17] In order to cover any gaps that may exist in inadequate state legislation, however, the act further suggested that "the Sherman Act, the Clayton Act, and the Federal Trade Commission Act would be applicable to the business of insurance to the extent that such business is not regulated by state law"[18] except that agreements to boycott, coerce, or intimidate remain subject to the Sherman Act. The purpose of this provision essentially was to place responsibility on the states to set their regulatory houses in order and to dispel the threat of Federal intervention unless state legislation proved inadequate.

ACTION BY THE STATES SINCE 1944

The NAIC, operating through its established Federal Legislation Committee and the Rate and Rating Organizations Committee, conducted many meetings and hearings to help determine the course of action to be followed by the states as a result of Public Law 15. Basically, the committees' objectives were to develop standard rating laws which could be adopted by the states as well as be in compliance with the congressional intent behind Public Law 15. Because of the Federal pressure implied by Sections 2(*b*) and

[15] See Irwin Stelzer, "The Insurance Industry and the Anti-Trust Laws," *Insurance Law Journal*, No. 386 (March, 1955), 137–52, for comments on whether insurance is a commodity and hence subject to this law.
[16] See Henry Glassie, "Insurance and the Robinson-Patman Act: Revisited," *Insurance Law Journal*, No. 409 (February, 1957), 85–100.
[17] See the enactment clause, Public Law 15, for a statement of the purpose and intent of Congress.
[18] Sections 2(*b*), 3(*a*), and 3(*b*).

3(a) of Public Law 15, most state legislatures acted rapidly by enacting in substance the model rating laws proposed by the NAIC and described briefly earlier in this chapter. These laws recognized the desirability of competition in rates as well as the necessity of cooperative rate making where such cooperative practices were controlled and supervised. At the same time, the laws sought to avoid the charge of inadequate regulation under the Sherman Act and the other antitrust laws by requiring rate approval or disapproval by the state commissioners.[19]

In accordance with and in some cases prior to the mandate given to the states under Public Law 15 to enact legislation which would adequately regulate insurance, about three-fourths of the states have passed what is referred to as the *Unfair Trade Practices Act for Insurance*. The purpose of this statute is "to prohibit and define unfair methods of competition and unfair and deceptive acts or practices in the business of insurance."[20] The other states, while not enacting the model bill, have (according to the brief filed by the American Mutual Alliance in the *National Casualty Co. v. Federal Trade Commission*, C.C.A. 6th Cir. No. 12944) laws which have the same effect in regulating insurance advertising and trade practices.

Under these laws, unfair methods of competition are defined as follows:

1. Misrepresentation and false advertising in policy contracts
2. False information in advertising generally
3. Defamation of persons engaged in insurance
4. Boycott, coercion, and intimidation
5. Filing of false financial statements
6. Paying or receiving rebates
7. Unfair rate discrimination

Because of the difficulties in enforcing insurance regulations against out-of-state unlicensed insurers, the National Conference of Commissioners on Uniform State Laws has proposed a model *Unauthorized Insurers Process Act* which attempts to give jurisdiction over foreign insurance companies operating within a given state. Section 5 provides that

> . . . issuance or delivery of a policy of insurance by an unauthorized and unlicensed insurer to a citizen or resident of the adopting state shall be deemed to constitute designation of that state's insurance official as the attorney in fact upon whom legal process may be served.

---

[19] Some states, notably California, did not require rate filings. Instead they adopted a more competitive law. See p. 617.
[20] See *Wis. Stats.*, 1957, Sec. 207–04.

The specific practice which this legislation is an attempt to control is the mail-order insurer operating in unlicensed areas.[21] Thus far the legislation or parts of it have been enacted in over forty states.

ACTION BY THE FEDERAL GOVERNMENT SINCE 1944

The enactment of Public Law 15, when attempts to establish the preeminence of state regulation, does not necessarily mean that the Federal government has been sitting on its hands. On the contrary, certain activities on the part of the Federal government have threatened the whole structure of continued state regulation.

Among these activities are the following:

1. Hearings of the Cellar subcommittee on Study of Monopoly Power (81st Congress, 1949), which investigated the possible existence of economic concentration and monopoly practices in insurance, particularly life insurance, which might indicate the need for Federal intervention. No specific legislative proposal resulted from the hearings.

2. Regulation by the Federal Trade Commission of fraud committed in mail-order insurance.

3. Hearings before a subcommittee of the Committee on Interstate and Foreign Commerce on the fraudulent misclassification of insured purchasers of financed automobiles by some insurers, the "packing" of the finance instrument with excessive insurance charges, and the failure to refund premiums on canceled or lapsed policies.

4. Various actions by the Securities and Exchange Commission with respect to the sale of variable annuities.

5. Statutory disclosure and bonding requirements designed to correct certain abuses in the administration of employee benefit plans whether insured or not.

6. Numerous prosecutions of health insurers by the Federal Trade Commission with respect to alleged deceptive advertising. This activity of the FTC was the first major test of the statement in Public Law 15 that certain Federal acts were applicable to insurance "to the extent that such business is not regulated by state law."

---

[21] Another troublesome problem confronting state insurance regulation is related to supervision and control of unauthorized and unlicensed companies doing business within the boundary of the state through the mail. An important landmark decision was recently made by the U.S. Supreme Court in *State Board of Insurance et al. v. Todd Shipyards Corporation*, 370 U.S. 451(1962). The Court held that the state of Texas could not tax the insurance premiums paid on coverage of property located in Texas when the insurance contract was entered into in another state. This decision, while vague on several points, suggests that state insurance commissioners may be powerless to impose supervision over unauthorized insurers that are not licensed within their states and over contracts of insurance entered into in another state.

7. Antitrust prosecutions in cases of boycott, coercion, and intimidation.[22]

8. Regulation of variable annuities and other equity-type contracts offered by life insurers, which were held by the Supreme Court as *not* constituting "the business of insurance" (as described by the McCarran Act) and therefore not exempt from the Securities and Exchange Act of 1933 and the Investment Company Act of 1940. This decision established jurisdiction of the Securities and Exchange Commission over these types of investments. See: *Securities and Exchange Commission v. Variable Annuity Life Insurance Company of America,* 359 U.S. 65 (1959).

9. Special studies on automobile insurance have been conducted by the Interstate Commerce Committee of the United States House of Representatives and by the Department of Transportation. The DOT studies, parts of which are reported in Chapter 33, examined in great detail (1) the economic consequences of automobile accidents and the performance of present reparation systems, (2) the causes of automobile accidents, and (3) the structural trends and operational activities of automobile insurers in serving the needs of the consumer.

10. The investigations of the insurance industry by the Subcommittee on Antitrust and Monopoly of the United States Senate have involved a variety of subjects and were performed on the basis of a continuing probe of the substance and quality of state supervision of insurance. Subjects investigated or under investigation include: Aviation and Ocean Marine Insurance, Critique of State Supervision, Rate Regulation, Alien Insurers, Insolvencies of Insurers, High Risk and Substandard Automobile Insurers, and Insurance Availability to Problem Risks. Out of these investigations Federal legislation has been proposed for a Federal Guaranty Insurance Corporation for insolvent companies and rating law revisions for the District of Columbia.

Just where these Federal investigations and probes will lead is anyone's guess. The insurance industry has generally supported the system of state supervision as providing the best protection for the consumer and preservation of a strong private insurance institution. On the other hand, if these investigations show that state supervision has failed to protect the public adequately, the McCarran Act itself gives the Federal government power to regulate "to the extent that such business is not regulated by state law." New legislation undoubtedly will be introduced from time to time to test the climate for or against further Federal regulation of this industry. The continuing threat to state jurisdiction is best summarized in the words

---

[22] The two leading cases are *United States v. The Insurance Board of Cleveland,* 144 F. Supp. 684 (Ohio, 1956), and *United States v. New Orleans Insurance Exchange,* Civil No. 42–92, Eastern District, La., 1957.

of the Subcommittee on Antitrust and Monopoly in its report on state supervision: "It remains to be seen how long such a regulatory structure (state) can stand without substantial improvement in substance and administration."[23]

Criticism of state regulation was brought sharply into focus in the 1960 *Report of the United States Senate Antitrust and Monopoly Subcommittee on the Insurance Industry.* Paraphrased, some of the conclusions reached with respect to state regulation were as follows:

1. Separation of insurance regulatory duties from other state services is highly desirable. Most states have operated their insurance departments with positive results in this fashion.

2. Insurance commissioners should be selected on the basis of their administrative and professional talents. The elective processes for selection of a commissioner appear to be somewhat suspect on this score.

3. Better supervision of insurance would be served by establishing longer terms of office (at least four years) in several states.

4. Many state insurance departments are both understaffed and poorly staffed in terms of the qualifications of their personnel. Many do not use the civil service method for hiring personnel.

5. The budgets of insurance departments are generally inadequate for the responsibilities placed on them. Budget figures reveal that only about 4 per cent of the total revenue collected by way of taxes on premiums (usually 2 per cent) is spent on insurance regulatory activities.

6. Premium taxes often discriminate in favor of domestic insurers as opposed to foreign insurers. They also favor certain types of insurers over others.

7. The admission and licensing of foreign insurers has not been conducted in as efficient, prompt, and direct a manner as public interest dictates.

8. Many states had not conducted examinations within the five years preceding the investigation.

9. The capital and surplus requirements for the organizing of new insurers in many states appear inadequate. Local differences do not justify the wide variations in minimum capital and surplus requirements for solvency or organization for new insurers. On the other hand, the capital and surplus requirements for an operating insurer should be quite different from the requirements for newly formed insurers.

10. The states have not dealt effectively with insurance mergers. In the period between 1953 and 1957, 187 mergers were reported, and in no case were any of the mergers disapproved by the respective insurance commissioners.

[23] *The Insurance Industry,* 86th Congress, 1960, p. 247.

11. A substantial number of liquidations have occurred based either upon a laxity of examination procedures, inadequate minimum capital and surplus requirements, or a failure to scrutinize underwriting and reserve activities of the insurers operating within each state's jurisdiction.

12. Over two-thirds of the states reported no formal actions with respect to restraint of trade, monopoly, and unfair trade practices. This lack of activity may indicate lax supervision.

Since 1960 the states have made substantial progress in improving salaries and budgetary support for their administration of insurance laws. The caliber of state insurance commissioners has been improving and one state, Wisconsin, has been developing what it considers to be a model insurance code on the basis of carefully structured research findings. Also, the National Association of Insurance Commissioners has established a research department, has added personnel, and has obtained new facilities and expanded budgetary support for their activities. Still, many would agree that state supervision has many inherent limitations in dealing effectively with a giant interstate industry such as insurance.

CONCLUSIONS

Regulation of the private insurance industry appears to be in a state of flux, with the areas of Federal and state activity rapidly changing. The trend of expanding Federal activities indicates a narrowing of state jurisdiction and a reformation of the present system of regulation. The carving out of specific jurisdiction for the Federal government either by legislation enacted in Congress or by a court decision will be a burdensome process. The need for clarification of the boundary lines between Federal and state jurisdiction, which are still very blurred in many areas, and the overlapping of jurisdiction and interest as regards the activities of this business point to increased conflict and litigation in the future. Continued investigations by various federal agencies appear very likely.

The role of the private insurance institution in the economy is an important one. The challenge which confronts government is the working out of a system of regulation—through effective legislation and effective enforcement—to adequately protect the public interest and to preserve the many benefits of private insurance.

REVIEW QUESTIONS

1. "Permitting insurance practices to be determined under conditions approximating perfect competition is neither desirable nor possible." Comment on the truth or falsity of this statement.

2. What are the objectives of current insurance regulation? How have these objectives been influenced by the "age of consumerism"?
3. a. What was the nature of insurance regulation prior to the appointment of state insurance commissioners?
  b. Trace the development of state insurance commissioners.
  c. Explain the increasing emphasis upon administrative law.
4. The state insurance department has extensive regulatory authority over the solvency of insurers. Indicate the scope of this authority with specific examples.
5. Another important objective of insurance regulation is the prevention of unfair trade practices. Indicate the scope of this authority with specific examples.
6. a. An insurer wishes to raise its automobile liability insurance rates 10 per cent. In most states, what procedure must it follow?
  b. Can this insurer join with other insurers to establish a common price? Explain your answer.
7. a. What competition is possible under the model rating laws?
  b. Some states have laws that restrict competition more than the model rating law, while others have less restrictive laws. What is the probable nature of these laws?
  c. Which method of rate regulation do you prefer?
8. a. How do FAIR plans improve the supply of insurance in urban core areas?
  b. How do FAIR plans and civil disorder charges socialize the risk of environmental hazards?
  c. How serious would riot losses have to be before the National Insurance Development Fund would be forced to borrow from the U.S. Treasury to pay reinsured losses?
9. What is the relative responsibility of the Federal government and private insurers in the national flood insurance program?
10. a. What are some implications of possible inadequate rates of return for property and liability insurers?
  b. Do you favor state insolvency funds? Explain your answer.
11. Prior to 1944 the states had the exclusive right to regulate insurance. What was the legal basis for this authority?
12. a. What was the nature of the Federal complaint against the Southeastern Underwriters Association which gave rise to a history-making decision by the United States Supreme Court?
  b. What ruling did the Court make, and how did it reach this decision?
13. In the absence of any qualifying Federal legislation, what would be the impact upon insurance of
  a. The Sherman Act?
  b. The Clayton Act?

c. The Robinson-Patman Act?

d. The Federal Trade Commission Act?

14. According to Public Law 15, what is the dividing line between state and Federal jurisdiction over insurance?

15. What actions have been taken by the Federal Government since 1944?

16. Would you favor state or Federal regulation of insurance? Why?

SUGGESTIONS FOR ADDITIONAL READING

Kimball, S. L.: *Insurance and Public Policy* (Madison, Wis.: University of Wisconsin Press, 1960).

————, and Denenberg, H. S.: *Insurance, Government, and Social Policy* (Homewood, Ill.: Richard D. Irwin, Inc., 1969).

Meeting the Insurance Crisis of Our Cities, a Report by the President's National Advisory Panel on Insurance in Riot-affected Areas (Washington, D.C.: U.S. Government Printing Office, 1968).

Mertz, A. C.: *The First Twenty Years* (Chicago: National Association of Independent Insurers, 1965).

New York State Insurance Department: *Examination of Insurance Companies* (New York: New York State Insurance Department, 1953–1956).

Patterson, E. W.: *The Insurance Commissioner in the United States* (Cambridge, Mass.: Harvard University Press, 1927).

Proceedings of the National Association of Insurance Commissioners (biannually).

"Regulation of Insurance," *Law and Contemporary Problems*, XV, No. 4 (Autumn, 1950).

Reports of the Subcommittee on Antitrust and Monopoly, U.S. Senate, on various aspects of the insurance industry (Washington, D.C.: U.S. Government Printing Office, periodically since the late fifties).

Sawyer, E. W.: *Insurance as Interstate Commerce* (New York: McGraw-Hill Book Company, 1945).

31

social insurance

In addition to concerning itself indirectly with risk management through the regulation of insurers, the government is more directly involved through social insurance. Because social insurance programs provide the first layer of protection in most family insurance programs, they are clearly a major tool of family risk management. A risk manager of a firm, of course, cannot turn to social insurance to handle the risks to the firm itself, but as noted in Chapter 8, he has reason to be interested in the losses facing the employees and the way they are handled. Five important reasons why he should have a specific interest in social insurance as a risk management tool are the following:

1. In counseling individual employees, he must understand the important social insurance benefits to which each employee is entitled.

2. The existence of social insurance programs reduces the gap to be filled by employee benefit plans sponsored by private industry and by public and private charities.

3. Tax savings may depend upon the proper integration of a social insurance program with an employee benefit plan.

4. The cost of social insurance programs is almost always borne completely or in part by employers.

5. All private enterprises (and all citizens) should be concerned about the proper sphere of government action and the administration of government programs.

This chapter provides some background material on the nature and objective of social insurance in general and describes the leading specific programs.

What Is Social Insurance?

For the purposes of this text, social insurance includes all insurance required by law for substantial numbers of the general population, administered or closely supervised by the government, and supported primarily by earmarked contributions, with a benefit structure that usually redistributes income to achieve some social objective, not private equity.[1] Several features of this definition are worthy of brief comment.

First, although all current social insurance programs deal with personnel risks, the concept may be extended in the future to property and liability risks. Indeed the national flood insurance program (see Chapter 30), the Massachusetts automobile compensation plan (see Chapter 33), and some other public property or liability insurance programs already have some of the characteristics of social insurance. Social insurance programs have emphasized personnel risks because all members of society may incur important economic losses occasioned by death, old age, poor health, or unemployment.

Second, the term is reserved for programs that apply to large segments of the general population and that are compulsory for most eligible persons. Plans established by the government solely for its present or former employees, such as the Civil Service Retirement System, are not considered social insurance. Federal government life insurance programs for veterans are omitted for the same reason and because they are voluntary.

Third, although some government agency is commonly the insurer, the level of direct supervision by the government may be limited to the settlement of contested cases or checking compliance with insurance requirements, most of the daily operations being conducted by private insurers.

Fourth, although the definition does not rule out some financial support from general government funds, most of the financing comes from contributions made specifically for this purpose. Although others may sometimes make these contributions, usually they are paid by employees or their employers.

Fifth, like all insurance, social insurance pools the risks associated with covered perils, such as death, poor health, and unemployment. In addition social insurance benefit structures usually stress "social adequacy" rather than "private equity." Instead of relating the benefits for any indi-

---

[1] This definition was developed by the Committee on Social Insurance Terminology of the American Risk and Insurance Association.

vidual directly to the contributions made by him or by others in his behalf, the system usually favors some groups whom it is considered socially desirable to help. For example, the program may favor persons with low former wages or a large number of dependents. As will be demonstrated later, however, in the United States there has been a reluctance to ignore completely private equity considerations.

Social insurance, therefore, need not be government or public insurance. Furthermore, not all public insurance is government insurance. With one exception (Supplementary Medical Insurance) this chapter is limited to social insurance programs.

SOCIAL SECURITY, SOCIAL INSURANCE, AND PUBLIC ASSISTANCE

Social insurance is part of a social security system. A *social security* system includes all government measures designed to protect its citizens against (1) perils such as death, poor health, unemployment, and superannuation and (2) poverty and substandard wages, hours, or conditions of employment. A social security system includes preventive measures (e.g., safety regulations, "full" employment measures, and public health activities) and alleviative approaches, of which social insurance is the principal example. The other major alleviative methods are *public assistance* and *income supplements*, both of which are described in the next chapter. The major distinction between social insurance and public assistance is that public assistance benefits are paid, in principle, only to those persons who can demonstrate their individual need, and then only to the extent of that need. Public assistance programs are usually financed out of general revenues. Social insurance benefits, on the other hand, do not require the demonstration of individual need and are usually related in some way, however crude, to contributions made by the beneficiary or on his behalf. Income supplements, represented by the recently proposed Family Assistance System, are closely related to public assistance. Payments are based on need, but need is determined not through a demonstration of individual needs but by the difference between some guaranteed minimum income and the family's actual income.

Is Social Insurance "Insurance"?

One question that has generated considerable heat for many years is whether social insurance is "insurance." Many observers believe that the answer is clearly "no" with respect to many social insurance programs. They point to the emphasis upon social adequacy, the absence of a legal contract, and the method of financing, which often defers many of the costs to future generations. They believe that the benefits are better described as transfer payments from one sector of the population to another. They believe that public acceptance of social insurance programs is often influenced by the "halo effect" of the insurance label and that unfair comparisons are often drawn between the relative performance and efficiency of social insurance and of private insurance.

The answer to the question depends upon how one defines insurance. If an insurance program must possess all of the characteristics typical of private insurance, social insurance is not insurance, as will be demonstrated below. On the other hand, social insurance is a device for pooling and sharing the risks of death, old age, unemployment, and poor health. Consequently it possesses the only necessary conditions for insurance specified in the definition on page 193.

Private insurance differs from social insurance, however, in several important respects. (1) Each individual decides how much, if any, private insurance he wants to purchase. Employees, it is true, may have no choice under employee benefit plans, but the decision is made voluntarily by someone other than the insurer, e.g., their employer or union. (2) Benefits and premium rates are prescribed by a contract which cannot be changed except by mutual consent. (3) The benefits are related on an actuarial basis to the contributions paid; i.e., private equity is an important goal of private-insurance pricing. (4) Numerous insurers compete with one another for business. Social insurance programs are compulsory for most people; benefits and contribution rates are not prescribed by law but are subject to change; social adequacy is usually stressed; and, although numerous private insurers may be involved, the program is often administered by a single government insurer.

Certain characteristics of social insurance enable it to encompass some risks, such as unemployment, that private insurers have been reluctant to write. The compulsory feature avoids adverse selection; the flexibility in benefits and contribution rates plus the compulsory feature enables the program to be adapted to changing conditions.

Reasons for Social Insurance

The first social insurance program in the United States, workmen's compensation, is almost sixty years old, but it was not until the Social Security Act of 1935 that the United States adopted an extensive social insurance system. The reasons for the various social insurance programs are not the same, but certain basic changes in our economy explain the increasing interest in the general concept of social security.

In a predominantly agricultural community, families had relatively few needs, were largely self-sufficient, and were bound together by common interests. It was not too much of a burden for the family to maintain disabled, aged, widowed, orphaned, or unemployed family members, because their needs were modest, they could perform some of the family household tasks, and there was usually ample space.

With increasing industrialization and urbanization, the picture changed. First, continued employment depended upon the ability of the employer to provide a job, and this ability, in turn, depended upon the functioning of a complex interdependent economy. Second, it created new occupational accidents and injuries, particularly around the turn of the century. Third, families became less self-sufficient. More and more household products and services were purchased from outsiders. An extra hand became less useful unless he added cash to the family budget. What is more important, the loss of the breadwinner's check became a financial catastrophe. Fourth, families became more widely separated geographically, and this separation, together with a divergence in interests among generations, tended to weaken family ties. Fifth, it became more of a burden to assist an unfortunate family member because of smaller living quarters, increased obligations to children, and a desire to maintain or improve the standard of living of the immediate family.

Since it was no longer so easy to turn to relatives in time of need, more families (in the narrow sense) had to handle their risks themselves or turn to outsiders for assistance. Few families could accumulate enough assets in advance to meet the losses caused by death, poor health, unemployment, or superannuation. Private charities, churches, labor unions, fraternal organizations, and the like provided valuable but limited assistance. Private life insurance had been developing steadily since the Civil War, but by the time of the Great Depression of the 1930s, most of the population had very limited coverage at best. The insurance protection against poor health and old age was even less effective; unemployment insurance was limited to some trade-union plans and a few employer plans. Some persons could not afford private insurance protection; others were ineligible because of poor health; and still others did not appreciate their need for insurance. Government assistance during the nineteenth century and the early twentieth century took the form of poorhouses or "outdoor" relief for needy persons. The relief was either an outright grant in cash or services or was given in exchange for some services such as work on a public project. This meager assistance was usually provided by state or local governments.

By the close of the nineteenth century, the inability of individual families to provide a minimum "floor of protection" for themselves and the dissatisfaction with the stigma associated with accepting relief caused Germany to adopt a fairly complete social insurance system. Great Britain acted during the first two decades of the present century. Other countries followed the lead of these two nations. The United States, however, did not adopt a comprehensive program until 1935.

The United States was slower to act for several reasons. First, our population enjoyed a more favorable economic status. Second, our nation stressed the freedom and responsibility of the individual for his own future. Third, the life insurance industry, although limited by today's standards, was more fully developed. Fourth, it was not clear whether the states or the national government should take the lead in developing social insurance. Fifth, states varied in their need for, and attitude toward, social insurance programs. Sixth, states feared that some businesses would leave or not enter their state if their taxes were higher than those of other states. The Great Depression, however, shook our confidence in individual responsibility, made us more aware of the risks facing our population, and caused more people to turn to the Federal government for assistance. Further industrialization and improved education also increased our social conscience. The Social Security Act of 1935 was a response to this important change in our attitudes, but, as will become apparent in the discussion of our social insurance system, the circumstances which retarded the development of any social insurance program influenced the nature of the programs adopted. Since 1935, the factors favoring an extensive social insurance program have become more important. In addition, as the economy has prospered, we have revised our standards for social insurance upward because our concept of a minimum floor of protection has changed, and our ability to bear the taxes involved has improved.

Although the preceding paragraphs offer a sufficient explanation for the passage of the Social Security Act, other reasons must be cited for the adoption of other social insurance programs. Workmen's compensation, for example, arose out of dissatisfaction with the employer's liability method of handling industrial injuries and diseases. The defects in the employer's liability system and the historical beginnings of workmen's compensation have been outlined in Chapter 7 and need not be repeated here. The Medicare program, established in 1965, reflected dissatisfaction in many quarters with the efforts of private health insurers to provide medical expense coverage for the aged.

Social Insurance System of the United States

A summary view of the social insurance system of the United States will help the reader to view each individual program in its proper perspective. The major social insurance programs providing protection for large segments of the general public against each of the four personnel perils included under these programs are as follows:[2]

A. Death
    1. Old-Age, Survivors, and Disability Insurance
    2. Federal and state workmen's compensation legislation (occupational death only)
B. Old-age
    1. Old-Age, Survivors, and Disability Insurance
C. Accidental injury and sickness
    1. Disability income benefits
        a. Old-Age, Survivors, and Disability Insurance
        b. Federal and state workmen's compensation legislation (occupational illness only)
        c. Temporary nonoccupational disability insurance legislation in Rhode Island, California, New Jersey, New York, and Hawaii
    2. Medical expense benefits
        a. Medicare—Hospital Insurance and Supplementary Medical Insurance
        b. Federal and state workmen's compensation legislation (occupational illness only)
        c. Temporary nonoccupational disability insurance legislation in California (hospital benefits)
D. Unemployment
    1. State unemployment insurance

The widespread effects of these programs, their relative importance, and their growth are indicated by the estimates in Table 31.1 of the cash benefit and medical expense payments under these programs in 1950, 1960, and 1969.

Old-Age, Survivors, and Disability Insurance

Old-Age, Survivors, and Disability Insurance is one of the three components of Old-Age, Survivors, Disability, and Health Insurance. The other two parts are Hospital Insurance and Supplementary Medical Insurance—popularly known as Medicare. OASDI was established under the Social Security Act of 1935. This act, which was a landmark in social legislation, also introduced

---

[2] The major omissions are the Railroad Retirement System, Railroad Temporary Disability Insurance, and Railroad Unemployment Insurance, which apply only to workers in one industry, and veterans' programs.

Table 31.1 Cash benefit payments and medical expense payments under selected social insurance programs (in $ million)

Type of benefit and program	1950	1960	1969
Cash benefits:			
OASDI	$ 961	$11,245	$26,751
State unemployment insurance	1,408	2,867	2,262
Federal and state workmen's compensation	415	860	1,720
State temporary disability insurance	89	311	615
Medical expense payments:			
Hospital Insurance			4,739
Supplementary Medical Insurance			1,865
Federal and state workmen's compensation	200	435	920

Source: Social Security Bulletins, monthly.

a Federal-state program of unemployment compensation; Federal-state programs of public assistance to the needy aged, needy blind, and dependent children; and Federal-state programs creating and extending public health services, health and welfare services for children, and vocational rehabilitation services. Although these other programs are extremely important, OASDI is much larger in scope and is often misleadingly termed "social security."

The OASDI sections of the Social Security Act have been amended frequently; the most recent major amendments were made in early 1971. Some important changes considered recently by Congress but not yet passed will be summarized following the discussion of the program as it now operates. Originally the system was designed primarily to provide retirement benefits, but OASDI today also provides important death (added in 1939) and disability (added in 1954) benefits. Although the many details involved make a complete explanation of the system impossible, the major characteristics of OASDI can be outlined. Because future changes in this legislation are likely, a more detailed discussion is impractical.[3]

ELIGIBILITY REQUIREMENTS

In order to receive benefits, a worker must have qualified himself by working in *covered* employment for a specified period of time. Over nine out of ten types of employment are covered on a compulsory basis. Student workers in institutions of learning, hospitals, college clubs, fraternities, or sororities are excluded. Railroad workers are protected by a separate federally operated

[3] Following each change in the legislation, the Social Security Administration publishes a booklet entitled *Your Social Security,* which describes the major features of OASDI. The changes are also summarized in an issue of the *Social Security Bulletin.*

railroad retirement system, but under some circumstances they may receive OASDI benefits in addition to or in lieu of the railroad retirement benefits. Ministers and members of religious bodies, employees of state and local governments, and employees of nonprofit organizations may be covered under the system under varying circumstances. Self-employed persons, domestic workers, and farm laborers are covered on a compulsory basis if they earn at least some small specified amount.

To receive OASDI benefits, the worker must usually be "fully insured," "currently insured," or both. Most old-age benefits are payable if the worker is fully insured. Most death benefits are payable if the insured is either fully or currently insured, but one important benefit, the widow's benefit, is not available unless the worker was fully insured. Disability benefits are payable if the worker is fully insured and if he has at least 20 "quarters of coverage" in the 40 calendar quarters prior to his disability. Blind persons and workers disabled before age 31 can qualify with less than 20 quarters of coverage.

A quarter of coverage for most workers is a calendar quarter (January through March, for example) during which the worker is paid $50 or more in wages. To be fully insured, a worker must have quarters of coverage equal to at least the number of years elapsing since 1950 or, if later, since the end of the year in which the worker was 21. However, the worker never needs more than 40 quarters of coverage and must have at least 6 quarters. For example, a worker aged 38 on January 7, 1972, will be fully insured in 1972 if he has at least 16 quarters of coverage.[4] To be currently insured, a worker must have at least 6 quarters of coverage among the last 13 quarters, including the current quarter. Thus it is possible for a worker who enters covered employment in December, 1971, to be currently insured after he earns $50 in January, 1973.

Under a transitional provision persons who became 72 before 1968 receive payments (subject to certain deductions for other government pension payments) of $48.30 a month ($72.50 for a married couple) even though they are not fully insured or in fact though they never worked in covered employment.

BENEFITS

Benefits are paid if the worker (1) retires, (2) dies, or (3) is totally and permanently disabled.

Retirement The basic benefit is a monthly retirement income for life to a worker, aged 65 or over. The worker may elect to retire as early as age

[4] These quarters may have been earned prior to 1951.

62, but the benefit is reduced. The retirement income is equal to the worker's primary insurance amount, which usually depends upon the worker's average monthly earnings during the period beginning with 1951 or the year in which he became 22, if later, and ending with the year before he becomes (or would become) age 65 (62 if a female), dies, or becomes disabled, whichever happens first. The earnings counted in computing this average include all wages subject to an OASDI tax over this period. During 1951 to 1954, the maximum annual amount taxed was only $3,600; during 1955 to 1958, the maximum amount taxed was $4,200; from 1959 to 1965, it was $4,800; from 1966 to 1967, $6,600; and since 1968 the maximum amount has been $7,800. The worker, however, may exclude the five years of lowest earnings in computing the average.[5] For example, if a person retiring in January, 1972, earned $10,000 each year from 1966 to 1971, inclusive, in covered employment but nothing prior to that date, his average monthly wage would be 2($6,600) + 4($7,800) or $44,400, divided by 12(21 − 5), or $231.

Except for low average monthly earnings, the primary insurance amount is determined by multiplying by 1.265 the amount developed by the following formula:

71.16% of the first $110 of average monthly earnings plus
25.88% of the next $290 plus
24.18% of the next $150 plus
28.43% of the next $100

For example, if the average monthly earnings were $550, the primary insurance amount would be 1.265 times the sum of 0.7116($110) + 0.2588($290) + 0.2418($150), or 240. The minimum primary insurance amount is $70. If a worker elects to retire prior to age 65, this amount is reduced by $5/9$ of 1 per cent for each month that his retirement date precedes his sixty-fifth birthday.

The primary insurance amount increases directly with the average monthly wage, but it is clear that the formula favors relatively persons with lower average monthly wages. The benefit formula represents a compromise between the desire to provide socially adequate benefits for all workers and the wish to preserve some elements of private equity.

The dependents' benefits, all of which are expressed as a percentage

[5] This option will help workers who were not in covered employment during part of this period, whose earnings during part of the period were very low, or who earned the maximum amount each year but whose average monthly wage is reduced because of the small maximum amounts prevailing in the early years. Nevertheless, a $650 average monthly wage will still be impossible for workers now in their thirties or older unless they work beyond the first day of the year in which they reach age 65 (62 for women) and are fully insured. Their earnings during these years can be substituted for lower earnings in earlier years and thus raise the average.

of the primary insurance amount, are summarized in Table 31.2. The total monthly benefits paid to one family are limited to a specified maximum that is a function of the average monthly earnings.

The family of a retired worker will lose in benefits (1) one-half of the first $1,200 that the worker earns after retirement in excess of $1,680 plus (2) all that he earns in excess of $2,880. For example, the family loses $100 if he earns $1,880, $600 if he earns $2,880, and $1,600 if he earns $3,880. However, no reduction in benefits is made if the worker is aged 72 or over. Moreover, the monthly benefit is not reduced for any month in which the retired person did not earn wages of more than $140 or perform substantial services in self-employment. A retired person may thus earn $10,000 in one month and lose only one monthly benefit. Dependent beneficiaries are subject to the same rules, except for the fact that only their own benefits are affected by their employment.

Death   The survivorship benefits that are payable in case the insured worker dies are presented in Table 31.3. The family maximums discussed in connection with the retirement benefits also apply here, and the same rules apply with respect to earnings in excess of $1,680. Two points that deserve special emphasis are (1) the magnitude of the survivorship benefits for a young man with a large family and (2) the gap that exists in the protection between the times when the youngest child attains age 18 and the widow reaches age 62.

Disability   The major disability benefits are a disability "freeze" and disability income payments. To receive these two benefits, the worker must

Table 31.2   OASDI dependents' retirement benefits

Type of benefit	Amount expressed as a per cent of the worker's primary insurance amount*
Monthly life income for wife aged 62 or over	50, reduced by 25/36 of 1% for each month benefit starts before sixty-fifth birthday
Monthly income for dependent children to age 18 or, if they go to school, to age 22	50 for each child
Monthly income for mother until youngest dependent child is aged 18	50
Monthly life income for dependent husband aged 65 or over	50

*If a worker's primary insurance amount is reduced because he retired before age 65, these percentages are applied to the unreduced amount.

Table 31.3 OASDI survivorship benefits

Type of benefit	Amount expressed as a per cent of the worker's primary insurance amount*
Monthly life income for widow aged 62 or over	82.5
Monthly income for dependent children to age 18 or, if they go to school, to age 22	75 for each child
Monthly income for mother until youngest dependent child is aged 18	75
Monthly life income for dependent widower aged 65 or over	82.5
Monthly life income for dependent parent (mother aged 62 or over or father aged 65 or over)	75 for each parent; 82.5 if one parent
Lump-sum payment to widow or widower or to person who paid burial expenses	300, or $255 if less

*Computed as if the insured were applying for retirement benefits as of the date of death.

be unable to engage in any substantially gainful activity,[6] his disability must have lasted at least 6 months, and the condition must be expected to result in death or to continue for at least twelve calendar months.

The first benefit freezes the worker's earnings record as of the date of disability. In other words, the worker's insured status for retirement and survivor's benefits and his average monthly wage are determined by ignoring the time that elapsed since the disability began.

The second benefit provides an income for the disabled worker and his dependents beginning 6 months after the start of the disability. The benefit amounts are determined in the same way as the retirement benefit amounts. At age 65 the disability payments cease and the retirement payments begin.

Disability benefits are also available for dependent children, aged 18 or over, who become totally and (presumably) permanently disabled before age 18. These children may receive retirement payments or survivor's payments as dependent children, and their mothers may receive a mother's benefit despite the fact that for other children these benefits stop at age 18.

[6] A special provision applies to the totally blind.

Disabled widows can, under certain conditions, receive survivorship benefits as early as age 50.

Some examples   Retirement, death, and disability benefits for some selected family situations are presented in Table 31.4. The examples serve as a review of the preceding discussion.

TAXES

Employees and their employers contribute equally to the cost of OASDI. A self-employed person pays about 40 per cent more than an employee. The present scheduled tax rates for 1971 and latter are shown in the table on page 653.

At present these tax rates are applied to the first $7,800 of earnings. Thus in 1971, a worker who earns at least $7,800 a year pays 4.6 per cent of $7,800, or $359, and his employer must contribute an equal amount. In 1972 the taxable wage base will rise to $9,000. According to the present schedule, which, of course, is subject to change, the ultimate tax rate is 5.15 per cent. These rates do not include the charges for Hospital Insurance presented in the next section.

FUNDING

Congress has expressed its intent to maintain OASDI on a self-supporting basis, and the tax schedule is designed to achieve this result for at least the next 75 years, if some underlying assumptions regarding mortality, interest rates, total employment, and the like are correct.

The taxes deemed necessary to meet the administrative expenses and the costs of the retirement benefits, the death benefits, and some disability benefits such as the "freeze" are placed in the Old-Age and Survivors Insurance Trust Fund. The remainder are placed in the Disability Insurance Trust Fund. Most of the assets remaining after current expenditures are invested in interest-bearing government securities.

The program is not "fully funded," a term described under "Actuarial Cost Method" in Chapter 22. If OASDI were to cease operations today, the money in the trust funds would not be enough to support continued benefits to those already receiving them and to return a "fair" amount to other contributors. In fact, if the program were to be terminated today, payments to persons already receiving benefits could not be continued. The present intent, apparently, is to maintain the program on a partial reserve basis, with the interest on the assets in the fund reducing to a limited extent the financial burden on future taxpayers. So long as the system operates

Table 31.4 Illustrative monthly cash benefits under Old-Age, Survivors, and Disability Insurance*
(Social Security Amendments of 1971)

Family situation	Average monthly earnings							
	$76 or less	$150	$250	$350	$450	$550	$650
Primary insurance amount	$ 70	$112	$146	$178	$209	$240	$276
Retirement:							
Worker, aged 65	70	112	146	178	209	240	276
Worker, aged 62	56	90	116	142	167	192	221
Wife, aged 65	35	56	73	89	104	120	138
Wife, aged 62	26	42	55	67	78	90	104
One child	35	56	73	89	104	120	138
Survivorship:							
Widow, aged 62	70	92	120	147	172	198	228
Widow, aged 60, no child	61	80	104	127	149	172	197
Widow under 62 and 1 child	106	168	218	267	313	360	414
Widow under 62 and 2 children	106	168	223	309	390	435	483
Lump-sum death benefit	182	255	255	255	255	255	255
Disability:							
Worker	70	112	146	178	209	240	276
Wife with child in her care	35	56	77	131	181	195	202
One child	35	56	73	89	104	120	138
Disabled widow at age 50	43	56	73	89	104	120	138
Maximum family benefit	106	168	223	309	390	435	483

* Rounded to nearest dollar.

indefinitely, a "full reserve" is not required for the plan to meet its obligations on a self-supporting basis. In fact, it can be argued that a full reserve
would be unwise for various reasons, one of which would be the excuse
it would offer for unwarranted liberalization of benefits.

Calendar year	Employer, %	Employee, %	Self-employed, %
1971–1972	4.6	4.6	6.9
1973–1975	5.0	5.0	7.0
1976 on	5.15	5.15	7.0

Issues   Only a sample of the many issues surrounding OASDI can be discussed here. These issues will be categorized according to whether they
affect coverage, benefits, or financing.

Because most employments are now covered under OASDI, there is
much less pressure than in the past for the inclusion of new occupations.
However, there is some support for coordinating the Civil Service Retirement
System with OASDI in the same way as the Railroad Retirement System.
The ultimate goal, in the eyes of many, is universal coverage. A related
proposal would grant some OASDI benefits immediately to all aged persons.
The transitional benefits to those aged 72 before 1968 are a step in this
direction. This extension of benefits has been justified mainly on the grounds
that it would improve the situation of aged nonbeneficiaries, reduce public
assistance costs, and correct the discrimination against aged persons who
were not covered under OASDI simply because they were born too soon.
In opposition it has been suggested that this proposal would destroy the
fundamental principle underlying OASDI that benefits be related to contributions to the program, benefit some aged persons who elected not to join
the system, and shift the tax burden from progressive income taxes that
provide the main support for public assistance to regressive payroll contributions. The relationship between the benefit amounts to be received by these
persons and those received by contributors to the system also poses some
interesting philosophical questions.

Several features of the benefit structure are highly controversial. First,
there is strong support for increasing the minimum benefit, but supporters
disagree on what the increase should be. One often-quoted suggestion is
that regular full-time workers at low earnings levels should receive enough
money to make it unnecessary for them to apply for public assistance.
A separate minimum benefit would be paid to persons with low average
monthly earnings who had not been regular full-time workers. Second, the
balance between social adequacy and private equity implicit in the present
benefit structure is not acceptable to many. One proposal, not seriously con-

sidered at this time, is that all beneficiaries receive the same benefit, regardless of their past earnings records. At the other extreme, a few critics argue that benefits should be related proportionately to average monthly earnings. Between these two extremes there are numerous possible positions. For example, each of the percentages in the present benefit formula could be raised or lowered. The highest per cent in the present formula could be applied to a higher or lower portion of average monthly earnings than $110. The desired relationship between benefits and contributions depends, among other things, on one's preferred balance between public and private responsibility for protection above the minimum benefit level, one's concept of a fair redistribution of income, and one's degree of concern about possible adverse effects upon the private insurance business. Third, there are several philosophies concerning the maximum earnings base. Because the maximum benefit depends upon the maximum average monthly earnings, one's philosophy concerning this base has benefit implications as well as financing implications. The choice, therefore, depends in part upon the three factors just mentioned. In addition, some persons suggest maintaining the relationship between the proportion of total payroll that is taxed or the proportion of workers with all their earnings covered that existed during some earlier period;[7] others would equate the base to the average wage of full-time workers. Fourth, the earnings test that causes some beneficiaries earning more than $1,680 a year to lose their benefits or to receive reduced benefits has been attacked on the grounds that it forces some able aged persons out of the labor force or prevents them from obtaining benefits to which they are allegedly entitled because they have paid for them through contributions to the program. Removing the test, however, would increase the cost of the program by about 10 per cent to meet what many consider to be a relatively unimportant need. Finally, it has been suggested that the benefits and the earnings base be subject to certain automatic adjustments instead of depending upon *ad hoc* adjustments by Congress. For example, benefits could be adjusted according to changes in the Consumers' Price Index, or the earnings base could be adjusted according to one of the principles noted above. Such automatic adjustments, it is argued, would eliminate the delays associated with the ad hoc adjustments that Congress has made in the past. Proponents also contend that automatic adjustments would make it possible for Congress to study more carefully other proposed changes. No action has been taken on this suggestion primarily because the legislators cannot agree on the principles to be built into the system, because they

---

[7] For example, under the original $3,000 base, 92 per cent of the covered payroll was taxed in the late 1930s. Ninety-eight per cent of the workers had all their earnings covered. A base of $14,500 woud have been necessary in 1965 to maintain this relationship.

believe that a frequent review of the entire program is in the public interest, and because they do not want to lose the political credits associated with increasing benefit levels.

One important financing issue is whether contributions should be increased by raising the earnings base or the contribution rate. The relative impact upon high- and low-paid workers is a major consideration, as is the effect of the maximum earnings base upon the maximum benefit. It is also argued that a high earnings base would permit the program to capture more contributions in periods of economic prosperity and to reduce contributions in periods of economic decline. A second major financing issue is the role of the trust funds. Some would favor higher contribution rates now to build up the trust funds to avoid passing to future generations the cost of benefits to this generation and to make the public more conscious of the additional costs of proposed liberalizations in the program. On the other hand, others are concerned about the "fiscal drag" imposed upon the economy by the current or higher contribution rates. Future generations, it is argued, will benefit from many expenditures financed by the current generation through other taxes. Furthermore, large trust funds may provide an excuse for undue liberalizations in the program instead of discouraging them. The most recent and most controversial issue is the use of general revenues to pay part of the cost of the system. Because of the windfall benefits provided many aged persons during the early years of the program and the emphasis upon socially adequate benefits for workers with low earnings or many dependents, the contributions paid by many younger workers and their employers have reached the level at which they could be used to obtain superior benefits from private insurers, assuming no further liberalizations in the benefits. To correct this situation and to make possible some benefit increases and other liberalizations, it has been suggested that one-third of the cost of the benefits be financed out of general revenues. Current employees and their employers would then be paying approximately the cost of the benefits for current employees. The fundamental principle of contribution-related benefits would be retained and benefit liberalizations would require increased contributions. In opposition it has been argued that employer contributions are not made in behalf of their own employees but as their share of the cost of the entire program, that it is unfair to shift the burden of OASDI benefits to general revenues, that benefits will be unduly liberalized when the new funds are made available, and that the role of general revenues will be expanded beyond the proposed one-third.

In a recent comprehensive study of OASDI Drs. Joseph Pechman, Henry Aaron, and Michael Taussig argued that the United States has been attempting to solve two problems with one instrument: (1) basic income support for the aged poor and (2) retirement benefits for others that are related to their previous standard of living.[8] Both problems, they believe, are legitimate areas for public action, but they recommend two separate systems to eliminate the system's split personality. First, the basic income for the aged poor would be provided by a negative income tax or guaranteed minimum income plan (see Chapter 32) covering all poor families. Second, a social insurance system would pay a retirement benefit equal to a stated percentage (50 per cent is the example used) of each aged family's past average earnings. The maximum earnings base would be the median earnings level. There would be no additional dependents' benefits under this second system. Both programs would be financed completely out of general revenues, not payroll taxes. In favor of their proposal the three authors cite its efficiency and flexibility.

Like the negative income tax, this separation of the two functions of OASDI has supporters in both conservative and liberal circles. Some conservatives favor the establishment of two systems, but would make the social insurance program voluntary and self-supporting. The present OASDI program could not survive on a voluntary basis, but individual options would be possible in a program that relates benefits actuarially to contributions. Those favoring a compulsory system argue that many individuals with adequate incomes lack either the willpower or the ability to prepare on their own for retirement, that private pension plans have many shortcomings, and that failure of an individual to provide for his retirement imposes substantial costs upon society.

The effect of such extensive changes in the OASDI benefit and tax structure would be enormous. Some persons, mainly the poor, would improve their economic position significantly under a two-part economic security system supported by general revenues while others, especially those in high income tax brackets, would, at least relatively, be less well off. Because of these economic impacts, the controversial value judgments that are inherent in the new benefit and tax structure, and a natural reluctance to substitute an untried plan for a successful program that is widely accepted by persons of varying political faiths, Congress has not yet given the two-system idea serious consideration. However, if the Nixon Administration family assistance proposal or some other version of a guaranteed minimum income plan is enacted, the stage may be set for a comprehensive public debate on whether OASDI should continue to have a split personality.

Proposed changes   In 1970 the House of Representatives passed a bill that would have made some significant changes in OASDI. The Senate also considered a bill cleared by the Senate Finance Committee, but the session

[8] J. A. Pechman, H. J. Aaron, and M. K. Taussig, *Social Security: Perspectives for Reform* (Washington: The Brookings Institution, 1968), pp. 215–217.

ended before any action could be taken. In early 1971 more modest changes were enacted. Benefits were increased 10 per cent and, effective January 1, 1972, the taxable wage base was increased to $9,000. Because other extensive changes proposed in 1970 are expected to receive more serious consideration later, they are summarized briefly below:

1. An increase in the minimum primary insurance amount to $100.
2. Automatic increases in benefits whenever the Consumer Price Index increases more than 3 per cent in one year.
3. Automatic adjustments in the wage base in the future in accordance with increases in the average annual earnings paid to covered workers.
4. An increase to $2,000 in the amount a beneficiary could earn and still receive benefits.
5. A revised tax schedule calling for higher ultimate rates.
6. More liberal benefits for widows and widowers.
7. Elimination of the present discrepancy in the law favoring females over males in the calculation of the average monthly earnings used to determine retirement benefits.

Hospital Insurance

All employments covered under OASDI plus railroad employment are covered under the new (1965) Hospital Insurance (HI) program, also known as Part A of Medicare. OASDI and Railroad Retirement System beneficiaries, aged 65 or over, are eligible for HI benefits. Also eligible are those aged persons who would be receiving OASDI benefits except for the fact that their current earnings cause them to lose their benefits. As a transitional feature, benefits are also paid to most persons, aged 65 or over before 1968, who are not covered under OASDI or the railroad program. Persons aged 65 after 1967 but before 1973 (1971 for women) must have some quarters of coverage but they need not be fully or currently insured.

The program provides (1) hospital benefits, (2) extended-care-facility benefits, and (3) home health-services benefits. The hospital benefits include such items as room and board in a semiprivate room, general nursing services, operating room, laboratory tests and X-rays, drugs, dressings, and the services of interns and residents in training. The maximum duration is 90 days in a single "spell of illness," which begins on the first day that the person receives hospital or extended care services and ends when a person has not been in any hospital or extended care facility for 60 consecutive days. Each person also has a "lifetime reserve" of 60 additional benefit days which can be used to supplement the 90 days provided for each spell of illness. Each time this reserve is used, the number of days remaining is reduced. There is a $52 deductible applicable to each spell of illness, and after the person has received 60 days of care in a hospital, there is a deductible of $13 a day for the next 30 days. A deductible of $26 applies to expenses incurred during each "reserve" day. The program provides for automatic adjustment of these deductibles to reflect changes in hospital costs. The first adjustment became effective in 1969. For example, until 1969 the deductible applicable to each spell of illness was $40.

Similar services are covered in an extended care facility after the person has been in the hospital for at least three days and, although he is not well, he no longer needs intensive hospital care. The maximum duration is 100 days in a spell of illness. There is a deductible of $6.50 a day (subject to future automatic adjustments) after the first 20 days.

Home health services following a hospitalization period of three days include such items as part-time visiting-nursing care and use of medical appliances but not full-time nursing care or drugs. The maximum duration is 100 visits in the year following discharge from a hospital or extended care facility.

The transitional benefits for aged persons not covered under OASDI are financed through general revenues, but most HI benefits are financed through a contribution rate levied on the OASDI maximum earnings base. The scheduled contribution rates are as follows:

Year	Employee	Employer	Self-employed
1971–1972	0.6 %	0.6 %	0.6 %
1973–1975	0.65	0.65	0.65
1976–1979	0.7	0.7	0.7
1980–1986	0.8	0.8	0.8
1987 on	0.9	0.9	0.9

These contributions are appropriated to a Hospital Insurance Trust Fund from which benefits and expenses are paid.

An unusual feature of this program is the involvement of private insurers in the administration of the program. Each hospital or other provider of services can deal directly with the Federal government, but most have elected to receive their payments through a fiscal intermediary approved by the Federal government—usually a Blue Cross association or some commercial insurer. These fiscal intermediaries are reimbursed for their reasonable costs of administration. The experience of these agencies in dealing with overutilization of services and excessive charges was partially responsible for involving them in the program. Hospitals and other agencies are themselves required to meet certain standards and to take steps to discourage overutilization of their services.

Supplementary Medical Insurance

Unlike the other OASDHI programs, Supplementary Medical Insurance (SMI), also known as Part B of Medicare, is voluntary. Subject to certain exceptions, all aged persons are eligible to participate. However, in order to avoid adverse selection against the program, persons wishing to participate must elect coverage during specified enrollment periods.

The benefits include doctors' services, certain medical services and supplies such as artificial limbs and ambulance services, and the home health services covered under HI, but the patient need not be hospitalized first to receive these services. Except for a limit of 100 visits in a calendar year applicable to home health services and a special limit on the treatment of mental disorders, there is no limit on the protection afforded. However, there is a deductible equal to the first $50 of expenses incurred in a calendar year plus 20 per cent of the excess.

Aged participants will pay a monthly premium of $5.60, effective July 1, 1971, which is matched by the Federal government out of general revenues. These moneys are appropriated to a Supplementary Medical Insurance Trust Fund. Because these premiums are based upon short range cost estimates, they are subject to frequent changes. When the program started in July, 1966, the premium was $3.

Like HI, SMI involves private agencies in its administration. However, unlike HI, SMI provides two methods for paying doctors' bills. The doctor, like the hospitals under HI, may submit the claim directly to the fiscal agency; but if the doctor refuses to submit his bill to the administering agency, the patient can submit an itemized but unpaid bill for payment.

Issues

Pressures have developed to cover persons other than the aged under these public medical-expense programs, to add new types of benefits, and to tighten controls over the rapidly rising cost of services provided under the programs. One proposal receiving serious consideration at the moment would provide HI and SMI benefits to disabled OASDI beneficiaries (and possibly survivor beneficiaries). Proposals have also been made to increase the number of days of hospital coverage, to eliminate or reduce the deductible amounts, to add prescription drug coverage, and to freeze the premium charge for SMI at present levels. Because (1) medical care costs rose about 31 per cent from 1966 to September, 1970 (hospital daily service charges rose 76 per cent) while the Consumer Price Index for all goods and services rose only 21 per cent, and because (2) it has been necessary to increase HI and SMI contributions substantially, the Federal government has been investigating ways in which it might exercise more control over the cost of medical services. One possibility is the use of group-practice plans described on pages 391–392 to provide these services.

Many observers believe that a health care crisis exists and that a national medical expense insurance program covering all citizens, coupled with more emphasis on coordinated planning of health services and cost controls, is inevitable and highly desirable. To support their case they point to (1) high and rising medical costs, (2) the two-thirds of private expenditures for medical services that are not covered by private health insurance because many persons have no coverage or limited coverage and all contracts have some limitations, and (3) inefficiencies and wastes in the health delivery system (for example, manpower shortages, too much use of hospitals, gaps and overlaps in medical care facilities, and too little incentive for cost controls). Although they admit that there may be other explanations, they also note that despite superior technical medical knowledge and equipment the United States lags behind other countries in life expectancy.

These current proposals illustrate the widely varying approaches being suggested:

1. The Committee for National Health Insurance plan would cover the cost of most medical expenses for the entire population. Their plan would replace present public plans and most private health insurance. About 60 per cent of the cost would be financed through earmarked taxes, the remainder being met out of general revenues. On the basis of fiscal 1969 costs employers would pay a tax equal to 2.8 per cent of payrolls; employees would pay 1.8 per cent of their income (not limited to wages) up to $15,000. The plan would be administered by the Department of Health, Education, and Welfare through a Federal board and regional, subregional, and local offices.

This plan would include numerous service and cost controls. For example, medical facilities would be coordinated regionally. Prepaid group-practice plans would be encouraged. Hospital rates, doctors' charges, and other prices would be set locally within guidelines established by the Department of Health, Education, and Welfare. Boards representing consumers would make annual reports on medical services and costs.

A bill that would implement this plan was introduced in the Senate in 1970 by Senator Edward Kennedy with some bipartisan support. In January, 1971, he introduced a slightly modified version.

2. The National Health Insurance and Health Services Improvement

Act of 1970, sponsored by Senator Jacob Javits, would establish a comprehensive government program but permit employees to "elect out" if they had adequate private coverage. Present Medicare benefits would be expanded in scope, and coverage gradually extended to include all citizens by 1973. The public plan would be financed by employer and employee taxes and by general revenues. The program would be administered by the Department of Health, Education, and Welfare, either directly or through contracts with state governments. Private insurers or quasi-government organizations would be involved as fiscal intermediaries.

3. The American Medical Association favors tax credits for private health insurance meeting certain standards. Families whose Federal income tax liability was $300 or less would receive a "credit" equal to 100 per cent of the premium paid for a qualified health insurance policy (estimated at $219 for an individual and $663 for a family of four). If the premium exceeded the tax liability of the family, they would be excused from paying the tax and would in addition receive from the government a payment voucher for the excess. For families with a tax liability higher than $300 the maximum tax credit would be reduced from 98 per cent of the premium for a tax liability of $301 to 10 per cent for a tax liability of $1,300 or more. These higher-income families would not receive a payment voucher if their tax credit exceeded their tax liability. This plan would be financed out of general revenues.

4. The Aetna Life and Casualty Insurance Group, one of the nation's leading private group insurers, has proposed a three-part protection plan: (1) a voluntary plan of basic medical-expense benefits for the poor, who would pay nothing; the nonpoor, who would pay part of the cost; and the uninsurables, who would pay surcharged rates; (2) a major medical expense plan covering at first the same groups as the basic plan but later extended to cover the entire population; and (3) a 50 per cent income tax deduction instead of 100 per cent for premiums paid by employers for private employee benefit plans not meeting certain standards. Private insurers would underwrite these plans individually or through pools. The Federal government would subsidize the first two plans out of general revenues. The plan also includes several measures designed to achieve quality and cost controls.

In January, 1971, the Health Insurance Association of America announced its support of a plan similar to the Aetna proposal.

5. The Nixon Administration has submitted a three-part proposal to Congress. Under a National Health Insurance Partnership employers would pay at least 65 per cent (later 75 per cent) of the cost of employee-benefit plans including both hospital and physician's services. Medical bills would be covered up to $50,000, but beneficiaries would bear 25 per cent of the first $5,000 of expenses plus certain other deductibles. Private insurers,

subject to new Federal controls, would underwrite these plans. A Family Health Insurance Program would provide a national minimum package of benefits at little or no cost to low-income families. Supplementary Medical Insurance premiums paid by aged persons would be replaced by increased OASDHI taxes.

The proposal would also encourage health maintenance organizations—group practice plans, expansion of medical school enrollments, and location of doctors, nurses, and clinics in less popular areas.

Workmen's Compensation

In this text, workmen's compensation has been discussed in connection with property and liability risk management because from the viewpoint of the firm, this legislation creates an absolute liability where formerly only negligence liability existed. Workmen's compensation is given brief mention here in order to remind the reader that it is social legislation and that, from the viewpoint of the worker, workmen's compensation insurance is social insurance. The discussion will be limited to two sets of issues surrounding this program.

ISSUES OTHER THAN METHODS OF INSURANCE

Despite the fact that workmen's compensation has existed since the early part of this century (or perhaps because of it), this program is subject to frequent and severe criticism. Management often claims that industrial commissions are too liberal in their interpretation of occupationally caused injuries and occupational diseases; labor claims the opposite. Some observers argue that the difficulties inherent in these interpretations would be eliminated by replacing workmen's compensation with a program covering both occupational and nonoccupational illnesses. Critics claim that more workers should be covered under the program, that there is still too much litigation, that benefits are not paid as promptly as they should be, that maximum weekly benefits have not increased as rapidly as average weekly wages, that the goal of rehabilitation has received too little attention, and that state programs vary greatly with respect to some major characteristics (e.g., whether a totally and permanently disabled person will receive benefits for life). Because workmen's compensation is overshadowed by OASDI, the critics believe that it receives little attention from the public and the state legislatures and that for this reason improvements will come slowly. Although agreeing with the direction of many of these criticisms, supporters believe that the deficiencies of present programs have been overemphasized. They believe that there have been substantial improvements in the programs since their introduction and that more can be expected in the future.

METHODS OF INSURANCE

One issue of particular interest in this text is the method of insuring the workmen's compensation obligation. In forty-four of the fifty states insurance of workmen's compensation is provided by private insurers. In twelve of these states insurance is also provided by state funds, i.e., insurers operated by the state, it being optional for a private employer to insure either with a private insurer or with the fund. In eight of these twelve states some or all public employers are required to insure with the fund. In six states the state fund is the exclusive means of insurance, and in only two of these may the employer "self-insure," an option which is available in all but one of the other forty-four states. In order to self-insure, however, the employer must receive specific permission from the industrial commission or other administering agency. Such permission is usually conditioned upon proof of the employer's financial ability. In many states a deposit of some sort is required. A few employers elect to retain this obligation but, because they are generally large employers, they pay about 13 per cent of the claims.

State funds are a subject of much controversy, ranging from the broad question whether such institutions should exist to the practical performance of individual funds. Proponents of the exclusive fund argue that the state should have full control of the administration of workmen's compensation in order that the interest of the workman may be fully protected; that a single fund makes for economy by eliminating expenses of competition; and that it is contrary to the spirit of workmen's compensation to permit it to be made a subject of private profit. Against the exclusive fund are brought the arguments that it is contrary to the American principle of private enterprise; that it is subject to political influence in appointments and operation; that its economy is illusory because of hidden subsidies, the general inefficiency of public administration, and failure to render as high grade service as do private insurers.

Proponents of competitive funds support them by arguing that employers who are required to insure should not be forced to patronize a private insurer; that the state should offer insurance that will serve as a yardstick to measure the performance of private insurers; and that employers who are unable to obtain insurance with private insurers should have access to a public source of coverage rather than be forced out of business. Opponents argue, but less vehemently than in the case of exclusive fund, that even the competitive fund is contrary to the American way; that it is unnecessary, since private insurance is available and since, through assigned risk plans, they provide for insurance of the unwanted risk; and that private business operation is more efficient than public business operation.

Temporary Disability Insurance Legislation

Five states have legislation that requires employers to pay cash benefits to employees who are temporarily disabled. The primary intent of this legislation is to cover nonoccupational illnesses. The five states, in the order in which they enacted this legislation, are Rhode Island (1942), California (1946), New Jersey (1948), New York (1949), and Hawaii (1969).

The details of the legislation in the five states are too complicated and too numerous to discuss at length. Some major features of this legislation, however, and some of the differences among the states are described below.

RELATIONSHIP TO UNEMPLOYMENT INSURANCE

California, New Jersey, and Rhode Island relate their temporary disability insurance programs to their unemployment insurance programs. The coverage, qualifications for benefits, and the benefits are similar to those in the unemployment insurance program, and the two programs are administered by the same public agency. This tie-in is natural because of the administrative savings made possible by such an integration and because of the desirability of continuing approximately the same payments to an unemployed person who becomes disabled and thus becomes ineligible for unemployment insurance benefits.[9] New York, on the other hand, considered nonoccupational disability to be more closely related to occupational disability. Consequently, New York's temporary disability insurance legislation is an amendment to that state's workmen's compensation law. Hawaii created a new administrative division in its Division of Labor and Industrial Relations.

COVERAGE

All five states cover employers of one or more employees. Agricultural work, domestic employment, government service, employment for nonprofit organizations, self-employment, and work for interstate railroads are common exclusions.

QUALIFICATION FOR BENEFITS

Qualifications for benefits vary, but in general the claimant must be unable to perform his regular and customary work, he must have earned at least a certain amount or have worked at least a specified period of time prior to his disability, and he must demonstrate continued attachment to the labor force. All laws exclude or limit benefits for disability due to pregnancy.

[9] Nine other states have amended their unemployment insurance laws to provide for the continuance of unemployment insurance payments to unemployed job seekers who become disabled.

BENEFITS

The weekly benefit amounts depend upon the worker's wages in some previous period, within certain maximum and minimum amounts. In all states there is a waiting period of approximately one week before benefits begin, but in California the waiting period does not apply to hospitalized patients. In New Jersey the waiting period is compensable after benefits have been paid for three consecutive weeks. The maximum potential duration of benefits is a uniform 26 weeks in Hawaii and New York. In the other states, the maximum potential period is also 26 weeks, but the individual potential period depends upon the worker's earnings in some previous period.

California has the highest maximum weekly benefit, $87. Hawaii, New Jersey, and Rhode Island express their maxima as a per cent of the state average weekly wage.

Only one state, Rhode Island, pays additional amounts for dependents ($3 per dependent child up to $12).

Other sources of income, such as workmen's compensation, wages, private pensions, and OASDI benefits usually reduce or terminate the benefits. No state permits a person to receive unemployment compensation and temporary disability insurance benefits at the same time.

INSURING AGENCY

In Rhode Island all benefits are provided through a monopolistic state fund. In California and New Jersey all employers are insured under a competitive state fund unless they apply for and secure approval of a privately insured plan or a self-insured plan. In California a private plan (insured or self-insured) must provide more liberal benefits than the state plan in at least one respect and be at least as liberal in all other respects. Private insurers are also prevented from selecting only those groups whose age, sex, and wage composition might create adverse selection against the state plan. New Jersey requires that a private plan be at least as liberal as the state plan. New York requires that the employer insure through a competitive state fund or a private insurer unless he obtains permission to self-insure this program. New York permits a private plan that provides temporary-disability-income benefits somewhat below the statutory benefits if it provides other types of benefits, such as medical-expense benefits, to make up the difference. Private plans insure less than 10 per cent of the covered employees in California, about half in New Jersey, and over 90 per cent in New York. Hawaii requires employers to purchase insurance from private insurers unless they secure permission to self-insure. A special state fund pays benefits to unemployed workers.

FINANCING

Employees pay the entire cost of the state plan in Rhode Island (1 per cent of the first $4,800 in wages) and California (1 per cent of the first $7,400). The New Jersey state plan is supported by employees (0.5 per cent of the first $3,600 of wages) and employers (0.25 per cent), but the employers' contributions are experience-rated. In New York employees may be asked to contribute up to 0.5 per cent of their first $60 weekly earnings, with employers paying the excess. Private plans in the three states permitting these plans may cost more or less than the state plan and the employer may pay for all of these benefits. Employee contributions in Hawaii are limited to half the cost but not more than 0.5 per cent of weekly earnings up to two-thirds of the state average weekly wage.

ISSUES

The spread of private employee benefit plans providing incomes for workers who are temporarily disabled has diminished the interest in these programs, but state legislatures still debate the advisability of this form of social insurance. Some persons would favor including a benefit of this sort under OASDI; some believe that OASDI should through a comprehensive temporary disability insurance program replace both compulsory temporary disability insurance and workmen's compensation. Eligibility requirements and benefits levels are frequently debated, but the most critical issue in existing programs has been the place of private insurance. The questions are similar to those considered in the preceding section with regard to workmen's compensation, but the problem of adverse selection has received much more attention.

Unemployment Insurance

As we have stated earlier, the Social Security Act of 1935 introduced a system of grants to states that had unemployment insurance programs. Wisconsin was the only state with a program at the time the act was passed, although a few other states had legislation that was not yet effective. This situation soon changed because of the nature of the Federal legislation. By 1937 all states had unemployment insurance systems.

THE ROLE OF THE FEDERAL GOVERNMENT

The Social Security Act levied a 3 per cent payroll tax on all employers of eight or more persons, but the legislation did not apply to certain types of employment such as domestic service, agricultural work, casual labor, and work for most nonprofit organizations. The employer could credit against this tax his contributions to an approved state program (including any reduction in these contributions as a result of "experience" rating), but the credit could not exceed 90 per cent of the Federal tax. For example, if the state tax was 2.7 per cent, the effective Federal tax was only 0.3 per cent. If the state had no unemployment insurance program, the Federal tax would be 3 per cent. Essentially, the same rules apply today, except that since 1939 the tax has applied only to the first $3,000 of each employee's earn· ings; since 1955 the tax has been levied on employers of four or more persons; and from 1961 through 1969 the tax rate was 3.1 per cent, 0.4 per cent being the effective Federal tax. Effective January 1, 1970, under the Employment Security Amendments of 1970, the tax rate became 3.2 per cent, 0.5 per cent being the net Federal tax. These 1970 amendments made other important changes, described near the end of this unemployment insurance discussion, most of which will become effective in 1972.

The incentive to establish a state unemployment insurance program was further strengthened by the fact that the Federal government uses its tax income to defray the administrative costs of the state systems and to establish a fund from which the state funds may, under certain conditions, obtain interest-free loans.

The Federal government does not prescribe any eligibility requirements or benefit levels for approved plans, but it does require that benefits shall not be denied to any person who refuses employment which (1) is available because of a labor dispute, (2) requires or prohibits union membership, or (3) is subject to substandard conditions. Another important requirement is that the state taxes be placed in an unemployment trust fund maintained by the Federal government but in which a separate account is established for each state. Withdrawals from the fund are to be used almost exclusively for unemployment benefits to insureds. Under some conditions, some of the state moneys may be used to pay administrative expenses, but the bulk of these expenses are met by the Federal grants. As we mentioned earlier, states that required employees to contribute at some time are authorized to make withdrawals in connection with temporary disability insurance legislation.

STATE PROGRAMS

State unemployment insurance programs vary greatly with respect to coverage, qualifying requirements, benefit levels, and financing. Only a brief summary of the major provisions is presented here.[10]

---

[10] For the more details, see U.S. Department of Labor, Bureau of Employment Security, *Comparison of State Unemployment Insurance Laws,* revised periodically.

Coverage   States have been generally more liberal than the Federal government in covering employees; many state plans, for example, cover employment for state and local government and employers of one employee. Otherwise the types of employment covered have been very close to those subject to the Federal tax.

Eligibility for benefits   To be eligible for benefits, a worker must first demonstrate his attachment to the labor force. In most states he demonstrates this attachment by having earned certain minimum wages (usually some multiple such as $1\frac{1}{2}$ or $\frac{30}{26}$ times his high-quarter earnings) during his base period, which is generally the first four of the last five completed calendar quarters prior to the date he files a claim. In addition, he must be unemployed (or working less than full time and earning less than some specified amount), he must (except in 9 states) be physically able to work, and he must be available for work; i.e., he must be willing and able to take any suitable employment. In over half the states he must in addition be actively seeking work. In all states he must register for work with the state employment service. His benefits may be postponed, reduced, or canceled if he leaves his job voluntarily without good cause, is fired because of misconduct, refuses suitable work, is idle because of a labor dispute, misrepresents the facts to receive benefits to which he is not entitled, or receives other forms of income such as wages in lieu of notice, dismissal payments, workmen's compensation benefits, OASDI benefits, or a pension. Benefits are postponed in many states for some of these causes instead of being canceled for the duration of the worker's unemployment on the theory that after the passage of the postponement period, the person's unemployment is not attributable to the reason for which he was disqualified.

Benefits   All states except four require that an unemployed person be unemployed for one week before benefits are payable. However, once a person has satisfied this waiting-period requirement, he need not satisfy it again with respect to future spells of unemployment during a "benefit year." A benefit year is usually the year beginning with the date he files an unemployment claim.

About two-thirds of the states relate the worker's benefit during a benefit year to his earnings during that calendar quarter of his base period in which he had the highest earnings. About one-third of these states multiply these high-quarter earnings by $\frac{1}{26}$, which would give a worker with 13 full weeks of employment about 50 per cent of his average weekly wage as a benefit. About half the states basing benefits on high-quarter earnings use lower fractions to allow for some periods of unemployment during the base quarter. All but one of the remaining high-quarter-earnings states use a lower fraction for persons with high earnings than for those with low earnings. That state pays half of the full-time average weekly wage in the high-earnings quarter. The remaining jurisdictions relate their benefit to the worker's earnings during the entire base period. About one-fifth of the states pay additional weekly allowances for dependents.

The benefits developed by these formulas are subject to both minimum and maximum limits. Maximum benefits without dependents' allowances range from $40 to $79, with $45 to $60 being the most common limits. If maximum dependents' allowances are included, the range is $40 to $114. Almost half the states now automatically adjust the maximum benefit according to changes in the average weekly wage in covered employment. Minimum benefits without dependents' benefits range from $3 to $25

Benefits for partial unemployment are usually the weekly benefit amount less the wages earned in the week, but some portion of the wages earned, usually $2 to $10, is disregarded in this computation.

Seven jurisdictions pay benefits for a uniform period during a benefit year to all unemployed workers. The remainder limit the maximum duration in two ways. First, they specify some maximum period, such as 26 weeks. Second, if this would produce a shorter period, they either limit (1) the maximum dollar payout to some fraction, such as $\frac{1}{3}$ or a fraction that declines as the earnings increase, of the base-period wages or (2) the maximum number of weeks to some fraction, such as $\frac{3}{4}$, of the number of weeks of employment in the base period. Forty-two jurisdictions have a maximum duration of 26 weeks; 8 have a longer potential duration, 36 weeks being the highest value. Eight jurisdictions provide for extended benefits, usually by 50 per cent up to a maximum of 13 weeks, when unemployment in the state reaches a specified level.

Some states impose special requirements on seasonal workers. For example, wage credits earned in seasonal employment may be counted only in connection with unemployment during the operating season.

Financing In all but three states employers pay the entire cost of the program. In almost one-half of the states the taxable wage base is higher than the $3,000 Federal base and in a few cases it is tied to the state average wage. Most states have a standard tax rate of 2.7 per cent, but in all states the rates paid by employers depend upon their experience and the status of the state unemployment trust fund. Maximum rates are usually 4.5 per cent or less, but one state has a 7.2 per cent maximum. Minimum tax rates are usually 0.1 to 0.5 per cent, but in 15 states they can be zero. Some states have substantial accounts in the Unemployment Trust Fund; others have less than the maximum amount they have paid in a 12-month period.

EMPLOYMENT SECURITY AMENDMENTS OF 1970

The Employment Security Amendments of 1970 will result in several significant changes in unemployment insurance by 1972. Coverage will be increased by (1) extending the Federal Unemployment Tax Act to employers
of one or more workers and (2) requiring states to extend coverage to
certain types of employees not presently covered (employees of state hospitals, state colleges and universities, and certain nonprofit institutions) or
have their employers lose their existing credit against the 3.2 per cent
Federal tax.

By January 1, 1972, to preserve the tax offset, states must also establish a program to pay extended unemployment insurance benefits to workers
who exhaust regular state unemployment benefits during periods of high
unemployment at either the state or national level. A worker's extended
benefits cannot exceed 13 times his weekly benefit; his total regular and
extended benefits are limited to 39 times his weekly benefit. The Federal
government will reimburse the state for half of the cost of these extended
benefits. States that wish to do so can establish these programs before
1972.

The increase in the tax rate under these amendments has already
been mentioned. In part this increase will finance the new extended benefit
program. In 1972, the taxable wage base will rise from $3,000 to $4,200.

SOME IMPORTANT ISSUES

Unemployment compensation plans have been subjected to much criticism
in recent years. Some of the major issues are described briefly in the
following passage.

Since unemployment is in many respects a national problem, it is
argued that one Federal system should replace the heterogeneous state plans.
Less radical suggestions are that the Federal government be responsible
for unemployment beyond a certain stated period of time or that state plans
be required to meet certain Federal standards. The Employment Security
Amendments of 1970 described above are a step in this direction. In opposition to these arguments, it is claimed that the state plans have performed
satisfactorily and that Federal intervention would ignore local conditions
and needs and violate states' rights.

Benefits are said to be inadequate because they have dropped to between 30 and 40 per cent of wages instead of reaching the original goal
of 50 to 65 per cent. The major reason for this declining percentage benefit
is that, as in workmen's compensation, maximum benefit increases have
lagged behind increases in wages. The coverage and the duration of benefits,
particularly for low-income workers in a state where the duration depends
upon the wages earned in the base period, are commonly considered inade-

quate. On the other hand, the plans may be too liberal with respect to part-time working wives and similar groups who may obtain the benefits designed for low-income breadwinners.

Because the program must be administered with discretion, the state administrations have been called too restrictive by some and too lax by others.

The financing of the plans has been a prime target for criticism. The financial status of the plans as a result of low tax rates and some recent recessions is a matter of universal concern. The merits of experience rating have been debated at length. Critics argue that (1) a single employer has little control over his unemployment rate, (2) some employers fire employees before they become eligible for benefits in order to cut their losses, and (3) experience rating feeds inflation and deepens depressions by producing low rates during boom periods and high rates during recessions. Several technical questions have also been raised concerning the application of experience rating. The principal pro argument is that experience rating provides an incentive for employers to stabilize employment.

REVIEW QUESTIONS

1. a. Is "social insurance" insurance?
   b. If so, what distinguishes social insurance programs from other insurance programs?
2. Distinguish among social security, social insurance, and public assistance.
3. a. Discuss the impact of the Industrial Revolution and other economic and social changes upon the quest for security.
   b. Was the United States a leader in the development of social insurance programs? Why or why not?
4. Social insurance programs have often been criticized on the ground that they are not "actuarially fair."
   a. Explain this criticism.
   b. In what other ways do social insurance programs differ from private individual insurance?
5. What programs were established under the Social Security Act of 1935?
6. a. How would you determine whether a person was fully insured under OASDI at the present time? currently insured?
   b. Why is the person's status important?
7. Construct examples to illustrate how OASDI benefits favor persons (a) with low incomes and (b) with many dependents.
8. One person worked continuously in OASDI-covered employment from 1951 to 1972, when he retired. Another person, who worked about half that time, also retired in 1972.

     a. Are both persons eligible for retirement benefits?

     b. How would their monthly checks compare?

9. A man, aged 35, has a wife, aged 35, and two children, aged 3 and 8. His average monthly wage for OASDI purposes is $550.

     a. If this man is currently insured, what benefits will his family receive if he dies today?

     b. If this man is fully insured, what benefits will his family receive if he dies today?

10. What types of losses caused by disability are covered under OASDI?

11. Is OASDI "actuarially sound"?

12. Identify some of the leading current issues with respect to OASDI, and discuss the arguments presented for and against each issue.

13. Compare Hospital Insurance and Supplementary Medical Insurance with respect to (a) eligibility requirements, (b) benefits, and (c) financing.

14. Which of the national health insurance proposals, if any, do you prefer?

15. Is workmen's compensation insurance social insurance? Explain.

16. a. What is the relationship between temporary disability insurance and unemployment insurance?

     b. Compare the approaches in the five states with TDI programs with respect to (1) the determination of benefits, (2) the type of insurer, and (3) the financing.

     c. Since only five states have TDI programs, some persons argue that these programs are not very important. Do you agree?

17. What is the role of the Federal government with respect to unemployment insurance?

18. Comment on each of the following criticisms of state unemployment insurance programs:

     a. The eligibility and benefit provisions favor secondary wage earners, such as working wives and part-time and seasonal workers.

     b. The maximum weekly benefits are too low.

     c. The system encourages strikes and quitting without good cause.

     d. The system does not protect the worker against long-term unemployment.

19. a. How is unemployment insurance financed?

     b. Comment upon the desirability of experience rating unemployment insurance.

SUGGESTIONS FOR ADDITIONAL READING

Brinker, P. A.: *Economic Insecurity and Social Security* (New York: Appleton-Century-Crofts, Co., Inc., 1968).

Burns, E. M.: *Social Security and Public Policy* (New York: McGraw-Hill Book Company, 1956).

Carlson, Valdemar: *Economic Security in the United States* (New York: McGraw-Hill Book Company, 1962).

Gagliardo, Domenico: *American Social Insurance* (rev. ed., New York: Harper & Row, Publishers, Incorporated, 1955).

Haber, W., and Cohen, W.: *Social Security Programs, Problems, and Policies* (Homewood, Ill.: Richard D. Irwin, Inc., 1960).

Lester, R. A.: *The Economics of Unemployment Compensation* (Princeton: Industrial Relations Section, Princeton University, 1962).

Myers, R. J.: *Social Insurance and Allied Government Programs* (Homewood, Ill.: Richard D. Irwin, Inc., 1965).

Osborn, Grant: *Compulsory Temporary Disability Insurance in the United States* (Homewood, Ill.: Richard D. Irwin, Inc., 1958).

Pechman, J. A., Aaron, H. J., and Taussig, M. K.: *Social Security: Perspectives for Reform* (Washington: The Brookings Institution, 1968).

Turnbull, J. G., Williams, C. A., Jr., and Cheit, E. F.: *Economic and Social Security* (3d ed., New York: The Ronald Press Company, 1967), chaps. 1, 4, 7, 10, 11, 13, and 18.

Wilcox, Clair: *Toward Social Welfare* (Homewood, Ill.: Richard D. Irwin, Inc., 1969).

32

poverty and ways to reduce it

The plight and treatment of the poor and the near-poor is one of the most-discussed topics of the day. As a nation we are becoming more aware that for most of the poor poverty is not a matter of their own making. Instead it is an accident of birth, technological change, hard luck, or some other chance factor. All of us face the risk of poverty before and after birth.

Both businesses and families have a major stake in the reduction of poverty. The analysis and treatment of the poverty risk is not generally considered to be risk management as defined in this text, but the degree of poverty does influence the pure risks to which businesses and families are exposed. Furthermore, social insurance, which is clearly a tool of risk management, is in part a poverty instrument. Consequently in order to understand more fully social insurance and the directions it is likely to take, one needs to know more about poverty and the other methods used to attack it.

This chapter describes briefly (1) the poor and the near-poor—their number and their characteristics, (2) the limitations of social insurance as a device for treating poverty, (3) several programs developed specifically to help the poor—public assistance, food programs, housing programs, and programs initiated under the Economic Opportunity Act of 1964, and (4) some recent proposals dealing with poverty—family allowances, guaranteed minimum income, and the family assistance system.

The Poor and the Near-poor

At the close of 1968 over 25 million persons, or 13 per cent of the total population, were poor according to standards used by the Bureau of the Census.[1] The index of poverty is a minimum income that varies depending upon the size of the family, its composition, and whether it lives on a farm. In 1968 for four-person families headed by a male not living on a farm, the index minimum annual income was $3,555. For farm families of the same size and composition the index minimum annual income was $3,031. The median income of all families in the United States in 1968 was $8,632.

Several important facts about the poor in 1968 are summarized below:

1. Over 42 per cent of the poor were children under age 18. These poor children were about 15 per cent of their age group in the total population. Poor persons 65 or over were less numerous, but over one-fourth of the aged were poor.

2. Over 11 per cent of the family households with children were poor, the proportion ranging from 8 per cent for families with one child to 34 per cent for families with six or more children.

3. Almost 69 per cent of the poor lived in white households, but these poor included only about 10 per cent of the total persons in white households. Fewer poor persons lived in non-white households, but these poor were more than 33 per cent of the total non-white population.

4. Children under age 18 were a much more important component of the non-white poor than the white poor.

5. About the same number of poor persons lived in metropolitan and nonmetropolitan areas. The proportion living in cities, however, has been increasing.

6. Families with a female head or unrelated females comprised about 41 per cent of the poor. About 39 per cent of this group in the total population were poor compared with about 8 per cent of those in families with a male head or unrelated males. About 58 per cent of the persons in non-white households with female heads were poor, compared with 32 per cent of the persons in corresponding white households.

7. Among poor families headed by men under age 65, over 80 per cent of the heads worked for at least part of 1968, and most of those

[1] For more details than can be presented here, see the following:
Mollie Orshansky, "The Shape of Poverty in 1966," *Social Security Bulletin*, XXXI, No. 3 (March, 1968), 3–32.
Carolyn Jackson and Terri Velten, "Residence, Race, and Age of Poor Families in 1966," *Social Security Bulletin*, XXXII, No. 6 (June, 1969), 3–11.
"Poverty in the United States, 1959 to 1968," *Consumer Income, Current Population Reports*, Series P-60, No. 68, December 31, 1969.

who did not work at all were disabled. About half worked all year, but their earnings were not sufficient to raise their income above the poverty level. Almost 4 per cent of all families with a male head under 65 who worked all year were poor.

About half of the female heads under age 65 of poor families worked some time during 1966; about one-sixth worked all year.

The working poor were engaged primarily in farming, unskilled labor, or domestic service.

8. The total number of poor persons has declined from 39.5 million, or 22 per cent of the population, in 1959 largely because of the favorable economic conditions that have existed since that time. The poverty index, however, has been revised only to reflect changes in the cost of living, not the standard of living. Furthermore, the groups that have benefited the least are children under age 18, the aged, the non-white population, and families with female heads.

Social Insurance as a Poverty Instrument

Social insurance contributes much to the reduction of poverty in our society, but there are limitations on its potential accomplishments. According to data collected by the Bureau of the Census in the *Current Population Survey* for 1966, 37 per cent of the households defined as poor in 1965 received OASDI benefits. If it had not been for OASDI benefits, the number of poor households would have been 14.8 million instead of 11.2 million. About 7 per cent of the poor households received some public-program cash payments other than OASDI or public assistance—primarily unemployment compensation, workmen's compensation, or veterans' pensions and compensation. If it had not been for these payments, another 1.1 million families would have been poor.

Social insurance payments benefit some segments of the poor more than others. The aged are the principal beneficiaries because of their OASDI retirement benefits. Over three-quarters of the unrelated poor aged 65 or over or poor families with an aged head received OASDI benefits. Except for these OASDI payments the number of poor households with an aged head would have been 7.1 million instead of 4.1 million. On the other hand, only 14 per cent of the younger poor households received any OASDI benefits —these benefits being limited to survivor benefits or disability benefits or to retirement benefits paid to an older family member. The younger poor would be the major recipients of unemployment compensation and workmen's compensation, but these benefits replace interrupted income and for various reasons are almost always considerably less than the earnings they replace.

The benefits provided poor families under social insurance programs are considerably below the level required to raise these recipients above the poverty level. For example, about 31.8 per cent of the families receiving OASDI benefits in 1965 were still poor. To raise substantially the benefits based on low former wages would require either (1) stressing social adequacy far more than is true at present or (2) raising the benefit level for all recipients. Unless the latter could be justified on other grounds, this would be a costly way to help the poor.

Another limitation of present social insurance programs is that bene-fits are limited to families whose incomes are interrupted by old age, death, poor health, or unemployment. The programs do not benefit the working poor or the persons who are unemployed but cannot prove a recent attach-ment to the labor force.

Family allowances described later in this chapter under "Some Recent Proposals" could be attached to the present social insurance system to overcome some of these difficulties, but such allowances would be a substan-tial departure from past practices.

Public Assistance

Public assistance programs provide cash benefits or medical services for eligible persons who can demonstrate their individual need. Benefits depend upon the amount of the demonstrated need. These programs, patterned after the English Poor Law of 1601, have existed in the United States since the seventeenth century, but only limited financial assistance was provided to the poor in this way until the Social Security Act of 1935, which created some new programs supported by Federal grants. Current public assistance programs can be divided into two groups: (1) state programs supported by Federal grants and (2) state and local general assistance programs.

STATE PROGRAMS SUPPORTED BY FEDERAL GRANTS

Under the Social Security Act the Federal government makes grants-in-aid to states having each of the five types of public assistance programs de-scribed below meeting certain minimum standards. Although more far-reach-ing standards have been proposed,[2] present standards deal primarily with administrative questions (e.g., administration by a single state agency and right to a fair hearing) and some broad eligibility requirements. For the most part, eligibility requirements and benefits are determined by the states and the program is administered by the state government or by local govern-ments under the supervision of the state government. State programs vary markedly in eligibility requirements and benefit levels.

[2] See later in this chapter, under "Some Recent Proposals."

Old-age assistance   All states have programs providing cash benefits for the needy aged. Usually the recipients must be at least 65 and have insufficient income or other resources to provide reasonable subsistence compatible with decency and health. Some earnings may be disregarded in determining whether a person is needy. Almost all states also limit the amount of property that recipients may own. The recipient's need is determined by subtracting from the claimant's personal requirements (based on state standards adapted to his individual situation) his other resources, but sometimes the assistance payment is less than this need. In July, 1970, over 2 million aged persons received average monthly payments of about $74. Average monthly benefits ranged from $49 in South Carolina to $166 in New Hampshire.

The Federal government pays (1) 50 per cent of the reasonable administrative expenses incurred by the state program, (2) 75 per cent of the cost of providing certain "social services" designed to help persons attain or retain some ability for self-care or self-support, and (3) the following portion of the average monthly pension per aged person:

$31\frac{1}{37}$ of the first $37, plus
50 to 65 per cent of the next $38

For states with per capita incomes equal to or in excess of the national average, the second fraction is 50 per cent. States with below-average per capita incomes receive a larger percentage, depending upon how much their per capita income is below the national average. The purpose of this "equalization" procedure is to help the poorer states to improve their benefits.

In many states Old-age Assistance has been combined, as permitted under the Federal law, with Aid to the Blind and Aid to the Permanently and Totally Disabled.

Aid to the blind   The Federal grants to state programs providing aid to needy blind people are calculated in the same way as Federal grants for Old-Age Assistance. All states have such programs; most impose no age requirement.

Aid to the permanently and totally disabled   All states except Nevada have federally supported programs providing aid to the needy permanently and totally disabled. These plans are, on balance, slightly less liberal than Aid to the Blind. The Federal-grant formula is the same as for Old-Age Assistance.

Aid to families with dependent children   Needy families with dependent children receive benefits under the most controversial public assistance program. Federal aid is provided for benefits in cases (1) where the father has died, become mentally or physically disabled, or is continually absent from the home because of a divorce or desertion on his part or (2) where the parents are unemployed. No payments are made to needy families if the father is present and working but at low wages. Furthermore many state programs do not cover situations in which the parents are unemployed. In most recipient families either the parents are divorced or the father is absent from the home, the recipients being a mother and her legitimate or illegitimate children. In July, 1970, over 2.2 million families, including over 2.2 million adults and 6.2 million children, received average monthly benefits per recipient of $48. Average monthly benefits ranged from $12 in Mississippi to $74 in Minnesota. The Federal government pays (1) 50 per cent of the reasonable administrative expenses, (2) 75 per cent of the cost of certain "social services," and (3) the following portion of the average monthly benefit per recipient (not family):

$5/6$ of the first $18, plus
50 to 65 per cent of the next $14

The fraction in the 50 to 65 per cent range depends upon the state per capita income relative to the national average.

AFDC, like the other public assistance programs, has been criticized because of the complex, expensive administrative machinery required to make individual determinations, the stigma associated with the receipt of "charity," and the invasion of the privacy of recipients. The heterogeneity of state programs has also been a matter of great concern. AFDC in particular has been under fire on the grounds that it encourages desertion by the father, condones illegitimacy, and provides too little incentive for employment. The program has been accused of perpetuating need instead of attacking the root causes of poverty. Amendments to the Social Security Act in 1962 and 1967 were designed to correct some of these difficulties. For example, new emphasis was placed on social services and rehabilitation, but most states have not taken advantage of Federal grants available for this purpose. In order to provide more incentives for employment, states were permitted to disregard some earnings under AFDC and still receive Federal grants. In addition states were required to deny payments to any adult or teen-ager who refused employment or training deemed suitable for him. To reduce administrative costs and the prying into personal affairs of claimants, by administrative rule the Welfare Administration of the Department of Health, Education, and Welfare now permits states to use simplified, more objective procedures for determining need. Nevertheless, there appears to be some consensus that much more can be done to improve the administration of public assistance and to reduce the heterogeneity among the states.

Some authorities would supplement or supplant public assistance with the proposals discussed later in this chapter.

Medical assistance   Under Title XIX of the Social Security Act, popularly known as Medicaid, the Federal government pays (1) half of the administration costs and (2) 50 to 83 per cent of the payments made under state programs to vendors of medical care (e.g., doctors and hospitals) for a broad range of services to needy persons or the medically indigent (persons who are needy only with respect to medical expenses). The fraction depends upon the relationship between the state and national per capita incomes, the poorer states receiving the larger percentage grants. For the present, state programs can be limited to the types of needy persons eligible under the four categorical programs described above, but the Federal government will contribute to the cost of benefits for the medically indigent in these categories, as well as the indigent, and will in addition support the cost of benefits to *all* needy children. The Federal government will not pay for benefits to anyone earning more than 133 per cent of the income limit used in the state's related cash-benefit assistance plan.

In order to qualify for Federal funds, state programs must provide at the minimum many types of medical services and may not impose any deductible on hospital services. Consequently the benefits may be much more generous than Medicare benefits. To receive Federal funds, the states must also demonstrate that they are making efforts to broaden the services and liberalize the eligibility requirements so that by 1977 all indigent or medically indigent persons, not just those under the four categorical programs, will receive comprehensive care and services.

State programs differ greatly with respect to eligibility requirements and benefit levels. Most states, however, have established an income limit of around $3,500 for a family of four and provide more than the Federal minimum on types of services.

GENERAL ASSISTANCE

Needy persons who are not eligible for aid under the Federal-state programs must turn to general assistance programs financed entirely by state and local funds. Payments are made in cash or in services. Benefits tend to be much less adequate in amount and duration than those under the Federal-state programs.

Prior to the Social Security Act of 1935, general assistance was the major program in the United States economic security system. As the social insurance and Federal-state public assistance programs have been extended and liberalized, the role of general assistance has been drastically reduced, but it still is an important program for many families.

Food Programs

Three food programs specifically designed to help the poor are (1) the food stamp program, (2) a direct food distribution program, and (3) a national school lunch program.

Under the food stamp program, poor families are given stamps at no charge or reduced charges that will enable them to buy food of their own choice at retail stores. Retailers can redeem the stamps at a bank which in turn is reimbursed by the Federal government.

Under the second program, agricultural surpluses purchased by the government under its farm price support program are distributed to states requesting such food supplies. The states in turn pass this food on to local authorities who distribute it to charitable institutions or persons on relief.

Under the school lunch program, the Federal government pays one-quarter of the cost of lunches provided children at participating schools. Poor children are supposed to receive these meals at no charge or a lower charge than other children, but many schools in poor areas do not participate because they lack cafeterias. Related programs are those providing school breakfasts and, for preschool children, lunches in settlement houses and the like.

Housing Programs

Under the Housing Act of 1937 the Federal government has been actively involved in public housing for the poor. The Federal government provides almost all of the capital for projects initiated by municipal housing authorities and approved by the Federal government. The local government authority operates the project and collects rent sufficient to cover its operating costs. To qualify for this housing the poor family must not have an annual income exceeding five times the rent but must have sufficient income to pay the subsidized rent.

Urban renewal projects instituted under the Housing Act of 1947 are designed to replace substandard buildings in blighted areas with new buildings. After the Federal Urban Renewal Administration has approved a plan prepared by a local public agency, the agency acquires the land, moves out the residents, makes public improvements, and sells or leases the land to a private developer. The developer obtains the land at a bargain price, a subsidy being provided by the city and the Federal government. In the process the residents, many of whom are poor, are supposed to be relocated in better quarters at rents within their budget, but the success of this effort has been questioned. Few can afford to pay the rents charged for the new housing.

The Housing and Urban Development Act of 1968 expanded some existing housing programs and created some new ones. The existing programs were public housing, urban renewal, demonstration cities (attempts authorized in 1966 to change all phases of life in blighted areas through better housing, employment, education, health, and social facilities and services), and rent supplements (started in 1965) paid on behalf of persons eligible for public housing who instead rent housing from nonprofit groups such as churches and social agencies. Under new programs the Federal government (1) guarantees payments on securities issued by private developers to build new towns outside present cities and (2) subsidizes the payment of interest on home mortgages or rent by families that have low incomes but who earn too much to qualify for public housing.

Programs under the Economic Opportunity Act

The Economic Opportunity Act of 1964 was a comprehensive piece of legislation billed as the major thrust in a "war on poverty." Instead of making cash payments to the poor, the act concentrates on education, training, work experience, health centers, and other social services. An Office of Economic Opportunity established in the Executive Office of the President is supposed to coordinate the entire "war on poverty." This war includes several new programs described below and established programs such as social insurance payments to the poor, public assistance, veterans' benefits, food programs, and public housing. In practice the OEO has limited its direct attention to the new programs, which constitute about one-tenth of the total poverty effort, and has delegated administrative responsibility for some of these programs to other public agencies or private groups. The Economic Opportunity Act itself assigned some programs to the Department of Labor and to the Department of Health, Education, and Welfare.

Community action programs are the most novel approach in the Economic Opportunity Act. Private citizens and public agencies are encouraged to determine the needs of the poor in their community, prepare long-range plans for dealing with this problem, and establish an organization to implement the plans. If OEO approves the application for funds submitted by this organization, it becomes a Community Action Agency. Since 1967 the CAA must be a state or local government or private agency designated by the government. Most CAAs are private groups. To be approved, one-third of the members of the governing board have to be "representatives" of the poor. In many, but by no means all, instances, these representatives have been elected by poor communities.

Community action programs fall in two categories: (1) national-emphasis programs and (2) local-initiative programs. Congress has made the national-emphasis programs mandatory, and more than half the CAP funds have been devoted to these programs. They include:

Head Start—Preparation of poor preschool children for primary school through early physical and educational development

Head Start Follow-through—An extension of Head Start services into the first year of regular school

Upward Bound—Preparation and motivation of low-income high school students for college and counseling and academic support while in college (This program was recently placed under the Department of Health, Education, and Welfare.)

Comprehensive health services—Neighborhood health centers designed to provide comprehensive one-stop medical care for the poor

Family planning—Family planning services and devices for the poor, much of which is channeled through Planned Parenthood—World Population

Legal services—Legal services for the poor in family, consumer, employment, administrative (e.g., claims under social insurance and public assistance), criminal, and tort cases

Local-initiative programs developed by CAAs themselves include a wide variety of approaches dealing with the social and economic development and well-being of the poor. One expert has noted that the "projects supported by these funds ranged from cultural uplift—taking poor children to a museum or giving them a music lesson—to providing housing for Indians living on remote reservations or remedial education to migrants."[3] Most of the funds go to neighborhood service centers which provide for the poor in their area employment counseling, job placement, health, education, and welfare services. The poor are also supposed to be involved as employees of the centers and in establishing center policies. Many national-emphasis programs such as Head Start and legal services operate out of these "one-stop" neighborhood centers.

Other major programs established under the Economic Opportunity Act are as follows:

VISTA—Volunteers in Service to America, a domestic Peace Corps, designed to recruit and train volunteers to work with community action agencies or other EOA programs.

Job Corps—Remedial education, job training, and work experience for school dropouts, aged 16 to 21, at rural and urban residential centers.

---

[3] Sar A. Levitan, *The Great Society's Poor Law: A New Approach to Poverty* (Baltimore: The Johns Hopkins Press, 1969), p. 127. This book provides an excellent analysis of the Economic Opportunity Act.

Enrollees receive an allowance, clothing, food, medical and dental care, and travel payments. (In 1969 responsibility for this program, which involved high costs, was transferred to the Department of Labor and over half the centers were closed.)

Neighborhood Youth Corps—Counseling, remedial education, and employment for disadvantaged youths on projects initiated and sponsored by local public or private nonprofit organizations. NYC is administered by the Department of Labor.

Work experience and training—Work experience, training, and education for heads of families on relief who were previously unemployable. This program is administered by the Department of Health, Education, and Welfare, which also conducts an Adult Basic Education program.

Three programs aimed at the rural poor are a rural loan program, aid to migrant and seasonal farm labor, and help for Indians living on Federal reservations. The Small Business Administration makes loans to low-income businessmen on more liberal terms than under its standard program.

The Economic Opportunity Act is a multi-faceted approach to poverty. As might be expected, some of its programs have been highly successful while others have been severely criticized.

Some Recent Proposals

Because of the increasing awareness of the poverty problem in the United States, three proposals that would change significantly the way our economic security system deals with poverty have aroused considerable public and legislative interest. These proposals include (1) family allowances, (2) a guaranteed minimum income, and (3) a family assistance system.

FAMILY ALLOWANCES

Family (or children's) allowances are payments to families that depend upon the number and perhaps the ages of the children in each family. All families with children would be eligible for these payments, regardless of their income. The "risk" handled by family allowances is the risk of a large family.

Those who favor family allowances point out that almost half of the poor are children and that a substantial proportion of the large families are poor. Consequently family allowances would contribute much to the elimination of poverty. Other supporting arguments are as follows: (1) Family allowances are superior to public assistance because there would be no means test and the benefit amounts would be certain and objectively determined. (2) Public assistance programs for needy families with children could be eliminated or reduced. (3) Discrimination of various sorts against children born into large families would be diminished. (4) Family allowances would make it possible for parents to assume more parental responsibility and to command more respect from their children because they would not have to be away from home so often to earn the same income or because the increased income would enable them better to care for their children's needs. (5) The nation's progress and strength depend largely upon the optimum use of its young manpower. Society as a whole, therefore, should be interested in the welfare of its children and be willing to contribute to the cost of family allowances. (6) Family allowances are an important part of the social security system of many nations and no nation with a family allowance system has ever abandoned it.

Arguments against family allowances, which have prevailed up to the present time, are as follows: (1) Even a modest program would be extremely costly. (2) The redistribution of income to large families is not "fair." (3) Incentives to work would be adversely affected. (4) The program would contribute to the problem of population growth, particularly among the poor. (5) Parental responsibility would decrease because the government has assumed financial responsibility. (6) Most families in the United States do not require assistance through family allowances. To counter this argument and to reduce the cost of family allowances, it has been suggested that income tax exemptions for children be eliminated and any allowances received be subject to income taxes. Such a change in the income tax would affect higher-income families much more than poor families.

GUARANTEED MINIMUM INCOME

Guaranteed-minimum-income proposals guarantee each family an income that varies according to the family size. If the family has some income, this income would be taxed at some rate less than 100 per cent. The government in effect would subsidize families out of general revenues up to the point where the tax paid on income would equal the supplement for a family with no income. For example, Professor Milton Friedman, a noted conservative economist, has proposed a minimum income equal to 50 per cent of a family's tax exemptions and minimum standard deduction and a 50 per cent tax on earnings. For a family including two adults and two children with no income, at the time Professor Friedman made his proposal, the government payment would be 50 per cent of [4($600) + $600 = $3,000] or $1,500. If the family had earnings of $2,000, the government subsidy would be $1,500 less a tax equal to 50 per cent of $2,000, or $500. The total family income would be $2,000 + $500 = $2,500. The subsidy would disappear if the family income were $3,000 or more. Other proposals, of which there are many, differ with respect to the minimum income guaranteed, the tax rate applicable to earnings, and the income level at which the subsidy disappears. These variables determine how many families would be raised above the poverty level, the effect on work incentives, and the number of families above the poverty level who would nevertheless receive subsidies.[4] The plans also differ in their treatment of existing programs. Most would abolish or greatly reduce the role of public assistance but would continue social insurance programs. Professor Friedman's proposal on the other hand, would abolish both public assistance and social insurance programs.

Guaranteed-minimum-income proposals have been supported on one or more of the following grounds: (1) Poverty would be eliminated or at least reduced. (2) Public assistance could be eliminated or at least reduced in importance. (3) The tax system already serves certain welfare objectives, as evidenced by special deductions for the aged and the exemptions for dependents, but these features benefit most those with higher incomes. (4) The proposal would eliminate discrimination against large families, at least among low-income families, and achieve the other advantages of a family allowance program.

Criticisms of these proposals usually center upon the following points: (1) The plan would reduce incentives to seek work. It is better to train the unskilled to do the many jobs that will have to be done. (2) The plan would substitute an untried experiment for an economic-security system based upon an entirely different philosophy and tested over a long period of time. (3) If the minimum income is set near the poverty level, the plan would be extremely costly, even assuming abandonment or reduction of the present system. (4) The arguments that family allowances would encourage large families, result in an "unfair" redistribution of income, and reduce parental responsibility also apply to this proposal.

The future of the guaranteed-minimum-income concept is uncertain, but these proposals are receiving far more serious consideration today than was thought possible only a decade ago.

FAMILY ASSISTANCE SYSTEM

In 1969 President Nixon proposed a family assistance system with the following features: (1) All families with children would be guaranteed a basic

---

[4] For example, Robert Theobald in 1963 proposed a minimum income of $3,200 for a family of four and a tax rate of 90 per cent on earnings. Theobald is concerned about the vast unemployment that he expects technological change to produce in the future, particularly among unskilled workers.

Professor Robert Lampman of the University of Wisconsin and Professor James Tobin of Yale have also developed widely quoted plans. For a concise statement of their proposals, see Clair Wilcox, *Toward Social Welfare* (Homewood, Ill.: Richard D. Irwin, Inc., 1969), pp. 254–257.

minimum income of $500 a year for each of the first two family members plus $300 for each additional child. Thus a family of four with no income would receive $1,600 a year. A minimum income of $65 a month[5] would be established for adults who are blind, aged, or disabled. (2) The head of a household receiving family assistance benefits would, unless she was a mother with a preschool child, have to accept a job or enter a job training program if a suitable one were available. Manpower development programs and child care centers would be expanded to remove impediments to work. (3) Earnings up to $720 a year would be disregarded. For each dollar in excess of $720, welfare benefits will be reduced by 50 cents. For a family of four the benefit would be reduced to zero when the family earnings reached $3,920. (4) The Federal government would pay the entire cost of the new family minimum and an increased share of other assistance payments.

A major effect of this plan would be to bring benefits in several states up to the Federal minima and to make many more persons in those states eligible for assistance. States with higher benefits at present would be required to continue their present payment levels, but the Federal government would under the plan pay a larger share of these payments than it does at the present time.

This plan, which would remove many of the objections to public assistance, has supporters of varying political persuasions. On the other hand, it has been attacked by others because the minimum income level is below the poverty level, because of the compulsory work requirements—especially for mothers of school children—because states with more generous public assistance benefits at present would gain little from the plan, because it would greatly increase welfare costs, and because it would substantially federalize public assistance. The House of Representatives, but not the Senate, approved the Family Assistance Act of 1970. In his State of the Union message in January, 1971, the President indicated his continuing interest in having Congress pass his family assistance plan.

REVIEW QUESTIONS

1. In 1968 about one-eighth of the population were poor.
   a. Describe and evaluate the poverty index.
   b. Describe briefly the effect of age, race, sex, and marital status upon poverty levels.
   c. Are most poor persons unemployed?
2. What are the contributions and limitations of social insurance as a tool for combating poverty?

[5] $110 a month under the legislation considered in 1970.

3. Compare and contrast Old-Age Assistance and Aid to Families with Dependent Children with respect to: (a) eligibility requirements; (b) benefits; (c) financing.
4. Compare and contrast Medicare and Medicaid.
5. Is the Federal housing program limited to public housing? Explain your answer.
6. The community action programs under the Economic Opportunity Acts include national-emphasis programs and local-initiative programs. Describe the leading programs under each group.
7. Which of the basic tools of risk management is illustrated by VISTA? by the Neighborhood Youth Corps?
8. Would you favor family allowances? Why?
9. Would you favor a guaranteed minimum income? If so, what minimum income and tax rate would you prefer? If not, why not?
10. How would the family assistance plan differ from present public assistance?

SUGGESTIONS FOR ADDITIONAL READING

Batchelder, Alan B.: *The Economics of Poverty* (New York: John Wiley & Sons, Inc., 1966).

Brinker, Paul A.: *Economic Insecurity and Social Security* (New York: Appleton-Century-Crofts Co., Inc., 1968).

Green, Christopher: *Negative Income Taxes and the Poverty Problem* (Washington, D.C.: The Brookings Institution, 1967).

Levitan, Sar A.: *The Great Society's Poor Law: A New Approach to Poverty* (Baltimore: The Johns Hopkins Press, 1969).

Poverty Amid Plenty: The American Paradox, The Report of the President's Commission on Income Maintenance Programs (Washington: U.S. Government Printing Office, 1969).

Rejda, G. E.: *Public Assistance and Other Income Maintenance Programs* (Bryn Mawr, Pa.: The American College of Life Underwriters, 1970).

Turnbull, J. G., Williams, C. A., Jr., and Cheit, E. F.: *Economic and Social Security* (3d ed., rev. printing, New York: The Ronald Press Co., 1968).

Vadakin, James C.: *Children, Poverty, and Family Allowances* (New York: Basic Books, Inc., 1968).

Wilcox, Clair: *Toward Social Welfare* (Homewood, Ill.: Richard D. Irwin, Inc., 1969).

33

automobile insurance
problems and issues

Because the automobile plays such an important role in the lives of American families and businesses, both the Federal and state governments have demonstrated an intense interest in the problems and operations of automobile insurers. Of particular interest have been (1) the plight of innocent victims of financially irresponsible drivers, (2) the availability of insurance at a reasonable price for all qualified drivers, (3) the protection of insureds and liability claimants against insurer insolvencies, and (4) proposed changes in the legal liability system based on the law of negligence.

The High Cost of Automobile Accidents

According to the American Insurance Association, in 1969 the nation's traffic accidents cost about $16.5 billion.[1] These losses include incomes not earned because of disability or death, medical expenses, property damage, legal costs, and the administrative costs of insurers. This total cost has been mounting steadily as follows:

1950	$ 3.7 billion
1955	5.5 billion
1960	7.5 billion
1965	11.0 billion

[1] *Insurance Facts, 1970* (New York: Insurance Information Institute, 1970), p. 51.

Motor vehicle accident costs are determined by the number of accidents and their average severity. As the number of vehicles registered has multiplied at an amazing rate (about 87 million passenger cars registered in 1969, compared with about 62 million in 1960), the number of automobile accidents has increased significantly, but, according to the most reliable trend data available, the number of accidents per vehicle may have plateaued or even declined. For example, during the period 1963–1969 bodily-injury-liability-insurance-claim frequencies declined from 2.61 to 2.23 claims per 100 insured car-years.[2] A car-year is one car insured for one year. One car insured for half a year is $\frac{1}{2}$ car-year. Property-damage-liability-claim frequencies have been fairly stable, fluctuating around 7.90 claims per 100 car-years. These frequencies, however, are disturbingly high, particularly since paid-claim frequencies, being limited to situations involving both legal liability and liability insurance, understate actual automobile accident rates. These frequencies also vary greatly among states, largely because of traffic density differences. For example, in 1968, the latest year for which accurate Massachusetts data are available, the bodily-injury-claim frequencies per 100 car-years were 6.74 in Massachusetts and 3.99 in New York but only 0.74 in Wyoming and 0.84 in both North Dakota and South Dakota.

Unlike accident frequency, accident severity has increased. Average automobile bodily-injury-liability-insurance-claim payments increased from $1,031 in 1959 to $1,583 in 1969, an increase of 53 per cent. Average property-damage-liability-insurance claims increased 77 per cent, from $159 in 1959 to $280 in 1969. During this same period the Consumers' Price Index increased only 26 per cent. Wages, however, have risen more than the price index. So have medical-care and automobile-repair costs, particularly the cost of repairing damaged cars. Finally, juries have also become notably more liberal in determining awards.

Clearly the social cost of automobile accidents, measured in dollar terms, let alone human suffering, is staggering. For the victims and those held legally responsible for their losses, the results can be catastrophic. Great stress must be placed upon improving driver attitudes and skills, making automobiles safer, building better highways, developing more satisfactory traffic controls, enacting more adequate traffic laws, and enforcing existing laws most effectively. The remainder of this chapter, however, will concentrate on the ways in which the financial losses associated with automobile accidents can be alleviated.

Financial-responsibility Requirements for Drivers

In too many cases automobile accident victims have not been compensated for their losses, despite the fact that, under the law of negligence, they

[2] Data supplied by Insurance Rating Board.

have a legal right to recover their losses from negligent drivers, the reason being that these drivers are financially irresponsible. The uninsured-motorists coverage described on pages 322–323 was a private response to this problem. This section deals with three types of state laws designed to protect automobile accident victims against financially irresponsible drivers: (1) financial-responsibility laws, (2) compulsory automobile liability insurance, and (3) unsatisfied-judgment funds.

FINANCIAL-RESPONSIBILITY LAWS

Forty-seven states[3] and the District of Columbia have financial-responsibility laws. In general the purpose of these laws is to require proof of financial responsibility only of those who have shown that such proof is needed in order to protect the public. An operator or registrant who has not been involved in an occurrence on account of which proof is required may register and operate his car without giving evidence of financial responsibility.

State laws vary somewhat in details, but the following description of the operation of a typical law indicates the basic approach. First, if a person is convicted of certain offenses such as drunken driving, reckless driving, or speeding, he must prove that he would be financially responsible for motor vehicle losses he may cause in the next three years up to $10,000 for bodily injuries incurred by one person and $20,000 per accident, and up to $5,000 per accident for property damage. The proof usually takes the form of an automobile liability insurance contract,[4] but cash, certain securities, and surety bonds are also acceptable. Failure to meet this requirement will cause the operator to lose his driver's license and the owner to lose his registration.

Second, on occurrence of an accident involving bodily injury or a stated minimum of property damage, the license of the operator and the registration of any car are suspended unless, or until, evidence of financial responsibility is filed with state authorities covering, up to the limits stated earlier, any damage for which a judgment might later be incurred. Mere involvement in the accident is sufficient to trigger the requirement; the driver need not be the guilty party, the one exception being that in some obvious cases, such as a legally parked car being hit by a negligent driver, the innocent driver may be excused. The proof may take the form of an insurance contract, cash, or a surety bond. If such proof is not forthcoming, the requirement is generally terminated only by exoneration of blame for the accident; release

[3] The four states with unsatisfied-judgments funds and financial-responsibility laws are included in this number.
[4] Under contracts used as proof the insurer is obligated to pay any damages, even though the insured may have violated the contract. However, the insured must reimburse the insurer for any payments it would not have made except for this special obligation under the financial responsibility law.

by or agreement with, the injured party; or lapse of a year without suit being filed.

In less than half the states, motorists involved in accidents must also furnish proof of future financial responsibility for, say, 3 years. In practically all states, if a judgment is returned against an uninsured motorist, he must satisfy that judgment up to the financial-responsibility-law limits or his license and registration will be suspended until the judgment is satisfied up to those limits and proof of financial responsibility for, say, the next 3 years is provided.

Financial-responsibility laws encourage but do not require motorists to be financially responsible.[5] The laws have been praised for their voluntary approach and the absence of extensive enforcement machinery. They have been criticized because they are only partially effective. Many motor traffic victims go uncompensated because many automobiles are not insured (about 10 per cent nationally and much larger percentages in some states) and their drivers and owners are not otherwise financially responsible. Some financially irresponsible drivers regain their licenses after 1 year because the victim, realizing that the defendant has no assets, decides not to file a suit.

The uninsured-motorists coverage, described on pages 322–323, is the insurer's answer to this objection. All but a few of the states with financial-responsibility laws now require that insurers include uninsured-motorists coverage in all automobile liability insurance contracts. Most of these states permit the insured to reject this coverage, but he must specifically do so. In addition to providing a source of payment for the innocent victim, this coverage strengthens the operation of the financial-responsibility law because 1 year is much less likely to elapse without a suit being filed. Those who object to this approach argue principally that the insured motorists pay the cost of accidents caused by uninsured motorists.

UNSATISFIED-JUDGMENT FUNDS

Four states—Maryland, Michigan, New Jersey, and North Dakota—have unsatisfied-judgment funds supplementing their financial-responsibility laws. These funds serve the same purpose and were in fact the inspiration for private uninsured-motorists coverage. North Dakota having pioneered this concept in 1947. The four funds differ somewhat in details, but basically if the innocent victim of a motor vehicle accident secures a judgment against a negligent motorist who is unable to pay the judgment, the victim may apply to the state unsatisfied-judgments fund for payment up to the limits

---

[5] Some states with financial-responsibility laws also impound the vehicle or require the owner to store it until the owner or operator meets the requirements of the financial-responsibility law.

of the state's financial-responsibility law. If part of the judgment is recoverable outside the fund, this amount is subtracted from the amount otherwise payable by the fund. The fund must receive notice of the accident and has the right to defend the uninsured motorist if this seems desirable. This state fund is supported by assessments on both insured and uninsured resident owners of vehicles, but only insured resident motorists and uninsured non-car owners are eligible for benefits. Once the fund pays the judgment, it becomes subrogated to the victim's claim against the negligent driver. These funds thus aid the innocent victim and strengthen the financial-responsibility law in the same manner as private uninsured-motorists coverage. Uninsured motorists have an additional incentive to purchase insurance, as their assessment approaches the cost of insurance, particularly since they are not protected under the fund.

The laws differ with respect to whether they have any reciprocal relations with other states, whether they include property damage liability claims, the minimum amount that must be involved before the loss will be entertained by the fund, whether a small deductible is applied to claims against the fund, whether the fund is willing to settle the claim without the benefit of a court judgment if the uninsured motorist consents and agrees to reimburse the fund, whether insured motorists pay their assessments direct or through a levy on insurers, the relative proportion of the costs paid by insured and uninsured owners, and whether the fund is administered solely by the state or by the state and private insurers.

Many persons prefer this approach to private uninsured-motorists coverage because the uninsured motorists share part of the costs. On the other hand, this approach as practiced has been criticized on the grounds that the procedures are too complicated, the coverage is sometimes not as broad as that provided under uninsured-motorists coverage, some funds are in severe financial straits, and uninsured motorists do not pay their fair share of the costs. Some observers object on philosophical grounds to the existence of a state fund where, in their opinion, it is not necessary.

COMPULSORY AUTOMOBILE INSURANCE

A much discussed question is whether all registrants of motor vehicles or operators of licensed vehicles should be required to provide evidence of minimum financial responsibility as a condition for registering their vehicles or securing their drivers' licenses. Because this evidence would usually take the form of insurance, such a requirement is usually termed "compulsory automobile liability insurance."

Many classes of registrants and licensed operators must already provide such evidence. Registrants of public vehicles, such as taxicabs, school buses, and other passenger-carrying buses, must generally demonstrate minimum financial responsibility. Interstate motor vehicle common carriers are required to have insurance or some other evidence that they will be able to pay claims occasioned by bodily injuries to passengers or others or damage to cargo or other property. Young drivers or registrants must post proof of financial responsibility in Connecticut, Maryland, and Rhode Island.

The emphasis in discussions on compulsory automobile insurance, however, is whether *all* registrants or drivers should be required to give such evidence. Three states—Massachusetts, New York, and North Carolina—have adopted this approach. In 1970 Massachusetts also enacted a partial compensation plan, described later in this chapter. Owners in these states must give evidence of financial responsibility before they can register their vehicles. Non-owners need not demonstrate similar responsibility to secure their drivers' licenses. The Massachusetts Commissioner of Insurance establishes the common initial premium rates to be charged by all insurers (subject in recent years to downward deviations), but in New York insurers establish their own rates subject to possible disapproval by the state insurance department. North Carolina requires all insurers to belong to a single rating bureau and permits no deviations from bureau rates.

The major attraction of compulsory automobile liability insurance is its straightforward approach to this problem. If completely successful, it would allocate the costs more equitably and simplify collections by injured victims. Critics, however, observe that the law is not completely effective. For example, the law does not protect the victim against financially irresponsible drivers from other states, stolen vehicles, hit-and-run drivers, insured owners whose insurers become insolvent, and owners who elect to violate the law. New York, recognizing this fact, requires that all insurance contracts issued under its law include uninsured-motorists coverage with respect to accidents occurring within that state. This special coverage is underwritten by a Motor Vehicle Accident Indemnification Corporation managed by the insurers authorized to write motor vehicle liability insurance in New York and supported by assessments levied on insurers and self-insurers. The MVAIC also protects residents who are not insured and who at the time of the accident are not operating an uninsured vehicle. Uninsured-motorists coverage for accidents outside the state is voluntary. Massachusetts and North Carolina each require that automobile insurers operating in their state include uninsured-motorists coverage in all their contracts unless the insured rejects this coverage.

Opponents, particularly insurers, also observe that people become more claims-conscious and courts more liberal when they know that every driver and owner is supposed to be insured. They point to the enforcement difficulties and expenses incurred in the three states that currently require all registered cars to be insured. Insurers object to having a state review board force them to insure people they would prefer to reject, but some review process is necessary because denial of insurance is, except for those with other financial resources, denial of the right to drive. Insurers also associate compulsory automobile insurance with inadequate rates. Insurers have suffered underwriting losses in Massachusetts during the period, taken as a whole, since 1927 when the Massachusetts law went into effect. Insurers also report that it has been more difficult to get requests for rate increases approved in New York since 1957 and in North Carolina since 1958, when the laws of these two states became effective. They blame increased political pressures upon the state insurance departments. Finally, they believe that compulsory automobile insurance is an unwarranted interference with voluntary action, and they fear that compulsory automobile insurance will lead eventually to a demand for a competitive or monopoly state fund.

Proponents of compulsory automobile insurance either deny these assertions, e.g., the denial of rate increases on political grounds or the threat of a state fund, or argue that these are minor matters relative to the benefits afforded by this approach. The debate continues, but no state has acted for over a decade.

Availability of Insurance

Many drivers who wish to protect themselves against the potential financial losses associated with automobile accidents have been unable to secure insurance through normal channels or have lost existing protection when their insurance was canceled or not renewed. In other cases insurance may be available but at rates the drivers are unwilling or unable to pay.

To provide insurance for those who cannot secure insurance through normal channels, insurers have voluntarily or in accordance with state law established Automobile Insurance Plans, formerly called "Automobile Assigned Risk Plans." Under most of these plans persons entitled to coverage are assigned to individual automobile insurers in the state in proportion to the premiums each· insurer writes in the state.[6] Under a less common approach a few insurers service insureds for an underwriting pool to which all of the automobile insurers in the state belong. Automobile Insurance Plans typically have eligibility requirements that deny insurance to some licensed drivers, that limit coverage to the minimum bodily injury liability and property damage liability protection specified in financial-responsibility laws, and that require premium payments in cash. Currently, as a result

---

[6] Incentive credits are usually granted insurers who voluntarily insure the types of persons (e.g., young male auto owners) who most often seek insurance through this voluntary market.

of voluntary action, principles adopted by the National Association of Insurance Commissioners, or changes in state laws, many Automobile Insurance Plans have been considerably liberalized. All persons with a valid driver's license are entitled to coverage; higher liability limits, medical payments coverage, and physical damage insurance are available on an optional basis; and premiums are payable in installments.

To make insurance more readily available through channels other than the Automobile Insurance Plans, insurers specializing in less desirable insureds have been organized at a rapid rate and insurers servicing the conventional market have adopted more highly refined pricing structures that produce a higher premium for the less desirable applicants. The trend toward rating laws stressing price competition has facilitated this movement. Indeed, one major argument in favor of rating laws that are less restrictive is that they will improve the supply of insurance for less desirable insureds. The price, however, may be higher than these persons are willing or able to pay. To solve this problem, however, may require the socialization of certain risks and government intervention.[7]

Over half the states restrict by statute the cancellation or nonrenewal rights of insurers. Whether justified or not, the public questioned in the late sixties whether automobile insurance cancellations and nonrenewals were arbitrary and too frequent.[8] Usually those laws apply only to the owners of private passenger automobiles. Some legislation covers only liability coverages, but other laws add physical damage insurance. Insurers retain the right to cancel new contracts within a specified period (typically 60 days) after their effective date, but after this date they can cancel new or renewal contracts only for specified reasons. A few states, such as California, Pennsylvania, and North Dakota, limit these reasons to (1) nonpayment of premiums or premium installments and (2) suspension or revocation of the driver's license of the named insured or any customary operator of the insured automobile. At the other extreme the list is much longer, including such reasons as the following: fraudulent misrepresentation in obtaining the policy; proneness to epilepsy or heart attacks; addiction to narcotics or other drugs; habitual use of alcoholic beverages to excess; operation of a vehicle during

---

[7] Some observers believe that because the loss ratios on Automobile Insurance Plans have been much above the expected ratios, other insureds and insurers are already subsidizing these plans.
More formal arrangements might include an extra charge paid by all insureds similar to the civil disorder charge described in Chapter 30 under "Urban property insurance programs." Professor John Hall has suggested a national mandatory rating bureau that would establish a uniform set of pure premiums (no expense or profit loadings), coupled with a plan for leveling out differences in actual loss experience. See John W. Hall, *The Automobile Insurance Underwriting Problem* (Atlanta: The Center for Insurance Research, Georgia State College, July, 1969).

[8] The only data available suggest a 1 per cent cancellation rate except for nonpayment of premiums and a 2 per cent nonrenewal rate.

a period of revocation or suspension of an operator's license, conviction of or forfeiture of bail for any felony, criminal negligence in the operation of an automobile, theft of an automobile, or leaving the scene of an accident without reporting; use of an unsafe automobile; or presentation of a false claim.

Most states with cancellation notices also require that insurers give written notice of their intent not to renew contracts at some specified period, such as 20 days, prior to the expiration date of contracts in force.

In many jurisdictions most insurers use cancellation provisions that are more liberal than those required by law. However, the action by the states and the threat of further action no doubt influenced the voluntary restrictions.

Protection against Insurer Insolvencies

According to testimony presented to the United States Senate Antitrust Subcommittee in 1967, about 80 insurers specializing in automobile insurance for persons considered substandard by other insurers were placed in liquidation or receivership. Although the alleged $100 million plus losses to claimants and insureds caused by these insolvencies has been disputed, the fate of these insurers attracted considerable attention in the press and renewed congressional interest in a Federal Motor Vehicle Insurance Guaranty Corporation first proposed in 1966.[9] Although only a tiny segment of the insurance business was involved, these failures tarnished the excellent solvency record of insurers. They also reminded the public how serious an insurer insolvency could be and how the possibility of an insolvency interfered with an insurer's principal function—the removal of uncertainty.

The proposed Federal corporation, which has since been extended to cover all property and liability insurance, would accumulate funds by charging insurers guarantee fees based on premiums written. The corporation would be able to examine each covered insurer and recommend changes in its operations. Supporters believe that an insolvency fund would be highly desirable and that a Federal fund would be less costly, more efficient, and more effective in dealing with interstate insurers than separate state funds would be. Furthermore, until recently only a few states had insolvency funds. Some persons oppose any insolvency fund for the reasons listed on page 627. Others oppose only a Federal fund. They argue that state funds can be at least as economical, efficient, and effective. They also believe that a Federal fund would threaten continued state regulation.

New York, New Jersey, and Maryland had automobile insurance guaran-

---

[9] Robert W. Strain, "An Analysis of the Proposed Federal Motor Vehicle Insurance Guaranty Corporation," *CPCU Annals*, XXII, No. 1 (June, 1969), 139–146.

tee funds prior to the first Federal bill. New Hampshire established a motor vehicle security fund in 1969. The same year New York extended its motor vehicle security fund to all family and small business property and liability insurance lines. Wisconsin established a solvency fund applicable to virtually all lines to be supported by assessments on insurers following an insolvency. Post-assessment funds applicable to many property and liability insurance lines including automobile insurance were created in California and Michigan. By the middle of 1970 over twenty states had insolvency funds. Some leading insurer trade associations are urging the adoption of similar legislation by all states. The post-assessment approach is supposed to involve less machinery and be more economical than accumulating funds in advance, particularly if, as expected, there are few insolvencies.

Most states require automobile insurers to include the uninsured-motorists coverage described on pages 322–323 in their contracts. In these states and for most insurers in the remaining states this coverage permits the policyholder to collect claims against insolvent insurers from his own insurer.

Proposed Changes in the Legal System

A person suffering a bodily injury in an automobile accident can shift some of his losses to others through five reparations systems:[10]

1. Legal-liability systems, including the tort system and workmen's compensation
2. Private loss (life and health) insurance systems
3. Sick-leave and employee benefit plans covering nonoccupational disability
4. Social insurance
5. Noninsurance public programs, such as public assistance and veterans' benefits

According to an investigation of the 1958 automobile accidents in Michigan that involved some personal injuries, victims recovered about $85 million from these five systems. About 55 per cent of the reparation came from the tort liability system, 38 per cent from the victims' own private loss insurance, and the remaining 7 per cent from the other three sources. About $8 million additional reparation was expected in the future, but the sources were not identified. The estimated economic loss—loss of income and expenses incurred—was $178 million. Consequently, 47 per cent of the losses

[10] See A. F. Conard, et al., *Automobile Accident Costs and Payments: Studies in the Economics of Injury Reparation* (Ann Arbor: The University of Michigan Press, 1964) for more details on these five systems and the survey described below.

were not shifted at all. Furthermore, a substantial share of the burden was shifted because of the victims' own efforts in securing private loss insurance. Tort settlements amounted to only 26 per cent of the loss. Only 37 per cent of the approximately 86 thousand persons sustaining economic loss received any tort settlement.

A more recent investigation by the Department of Transportation[11] of deaths and serious injuries in the nation's 1967 automobile accidents, as part of its comprehensive study of automobile accident compensation systems and automobile insurance, revealed similar results. Of the $5.1 billion of "compensable" losses, victims recovered about 50 per cent from all sources. Tort liability claims (including those paid by automobile liability insurers) accounted for about one-third of the amount recovered. Other sources were life insurance (14 per cent), medical expense insurance, including automobile medical payments insurance (15 per cent), collision insurance (6 per cent), and wage replacement sources such as OASDI, sick-leave, and workmen's compensation (27 per cent).

The adequacy of tort settlements has been of particular interest to state legislatures because these settlements potentially shift the losses from those who should not bear them to those who should. Because tort settlements are based upon the law of negligence, they are subject to some criticisms reminiscent of those made over 60 years ago with respect to employer's liability:

1. Correct apportionment of blame is almost impossible. The outcome is too frequently determined by chance, the skill of the victim's lawyer, the composition of the jury, and other extraneous factors. Automobile accidents pose a special problem because the speed with which they occur makes it extremely difficult for witnesses to describe what happened. Drivers and victims are tempted to be dishonest in their description of the accident because of the ease with which this can be done and their economic interests.

2. Recovery is delayed for months or even years because of lengthy investigation periods, court congestion, and appeals. In the Michigan study, 31 per cent of the serious-injury cases were settled within 6 months after the accident, but 22 per cent had to wait for more than 2 years. In one of the DOT reports, the Federal Judicial Center concluded that more than half of the motor vehicle claims filed in court required more than 2 years to be resolved. Most claims, however, never involve the courts. According to another DOT study of insurance claims, about 58 per cent of *all* liability claims were settled in 6 months.

[11] "Economic Consequences of Automobile Accident Injuries," *Department of Transportation Automobile Insurance and Compensation Study* (Washington, D.C.: U.S. Government Printing Office, 1970).

3. Tort settlements are not net benefits. Instead, the victim usually incurs some collection expenses, such as lawyers' charges, lost wages, and transportation costs. Almost 70 per cent of the serious cases in the Michigan study reported some collection expenses, the average expenses for the group incurring some expense being 32 per cent of the tort settlement. About 4 per cent of the serious-injury cases reported collection expenses of 60 per cent or more of the tort settlement. In the DOT study of death and serious injury cases legal costs in tort cases were one-fourth of the total recovery. In addition to the collection expenses borne by the victims, society must maintain an expensive court system.

4. Tort settlements are not related to the economic loss but, like the determination of blame, are affected by many other considerations. On the basis of their analysis of serious cases, the University of Michigan investigators concluded that it "looks as though the amounts of settlement were a random choice or at least completely unrelated to amount of economic loss." However, when the cases were classified by the amount of economic loss sustained, low rates of settlement were most common in the large-loss cases. Over 80 per cent of the cases with losses under $1,000 received tort settlements equal to more than three-fourths of their loss. Only 23 per cent of those with losses over $5,000 but under $25,000 were this fortunate. In the DOT study victims with losses over $25,000 recovered only one-quarter of their losses; victims with losses less than $500 recovered four and a half times their loss.

Other criticisms, not leveled against employers' liability, include the following:

5. Courts have become so prone to find negligence in automobile cases that, if current trends continue, few defendants will escape a finding of negligence on their part.

6. Because of the trend in court decisions and the existence of liability insurance, tort law is much less effective than it was formerly as a method for placing the blame on careless drivers and encouraging them to drive more carefully.

7. Pain and suffering allowances, which are highly subjective, account for too large a proportion (over half, on the average) of the total settlements.

Criticisms such as these have caused some persons to propose that the present negligence system be replaced by a motor vehicle compensation system similar to workmen's compensation. These proposals are discussed below.

THE COLUMBIA PLAN

Proposals to abandon, at least in part, the tort system for handling automobile claims are not new, but the mounting costs of automobile accidents and the changes in the social, political, and economic climate have granted them a much more receptive audience than greeted the original proposals. The newer proposals have also benefited from earlier mistakes, and their proponents have devoted countless hours toward developing and selling their ideas. Nevertheless, to date only Massachusetts and Puerto Rico have adopted automobile compensation plans.

Credit for the first carefully worked-out proposal of this sort is usually given to a Columbia University study team whose 1932 proposal became known as the Columbia plan. The concept was first proposed in 1916 by Arthur A. Ballantine, and in 1924 Judge Robert S. Marx made more specific proposals that received considerable publicity.[12] The Columbia plan, like workmen's compensation, would have imposed upon the owners of motor vehicles absolute liability for personal injuries caused by the operation of their motor vehicles. The amount of that liability was to be determined by a schedule similar to that used in workmen's compensation, and the scheduled benefit was to be the exclusive remedy of the injured party. In other words, all common-law remedies were to be abolished. In the case of a two-car accident, the injured victims in each car would collect from the owner of the car in which they were riding. Owners would be required to purchase insurance to cover their potential liability under the plan. A special board would be created to administer this system. The plan was bitterly opposed on many grounds, chief of which were the objections noted earlier with respect to compulsory automobile insurance, the reluctance to abandon the law of negligence because of its alleged ability to punish the guilty and deter negligence, the potential cost of the program, the inadequacy of the benefits proposed, the difficulties inherent in devising one schedule of benefits for victims of much more widely varying means and need (e.g., housewives and skilled surgeons) than is true under workmen's compensation, and the absence of controls over driving habits analogous to employer controls over workmen. Insurers and lawyers were the most active opponents of the proposal.

THE SASKATCHEWAN PROGRAM

Although no state in the United States ever adopted the Columbia plan, one Canadian province—Saskatchewan—enacted a modified version of this

---

[12] C. A. Kulp, *Casualty Insurance* (rev ed.; New York: The Ronald Press Co., 1942), p. 219.

law in 1946. The principal modifications are that (1) victims can obtain damages in addition to the scheduled benefits from the compensation plan by pursuing a common-law action based upon negligence and (2) compulsory insurance against the compensation benefits and liability claims in excess of those benefits must be purchased from the Saskatchewan Government Insurance Office, a monopoly government insurer. The Saskatchewan experiment has been observed with great interest, but Saskatchewan is a rural, isolated area whose experience may not be relevant to any state in the United States. Some writers have observed that although the opportunity to pursue a claim based on negligence helps to solve the problem of low compensation benefits, it might encourage negligence actions, which would include pain and suffering, because the victim has nothing to lose.

KEETON–O'CONNELL BASIC PROTECTION PLAN

The proposal that sparked the recent strong interest in automobile compensation plans was the Basic Protection Plan developed by Professor Robert Keeton, of the Harvard Law School, and Professor Jeffrey O'Connell, of the University of Illinois Law School.[13] In this plan, the product of years of research, the authors attempted to build upon earlier proposals. The basic features of the plan, as it was originally announced, can be summarized as follows:

1. Compulsory basic-protection insurance would compensate all persons injured in automobile accidents, regardless of fault. Pedestrians would collect from the insurer of the car that injures them. Occupants of a car would collect from the insurer of that car.

2. Compensation benefits would cover net economic losses only—primarily medical expenses and work loss (loss of earnings and the expenses of hiring someone else to provide services, normally household services, ordinarily provided by the injured party)—not pain and suffering. Property losses were not covered, but the plan could be and was later modified to provide this protection.

3. Net economic losses would be determined by subtracting from gross losses (1) 15 per cent of any income loss to allow for tax savings and reduction in work expenses, (2) reimbursement from other sources as private life and health insurance, and (3) a deductible equal to $100 or, if higher, 10 per cent of the work loss. To illustrate, if the victim suffers a loss of $5,000 in medical expenses and $4,000 in earnings, his recovery, assuming a $2,000 recovery under private health insurance would be $9,000 —

---

[13] R. E. Keeton and J. O'Connell, *Basic Protection for the Traffic Victim* (Boston: Little, Brown and Company, 1965).

0.15($4,000) − $2.000 − 0.10($4,000) = $6,000. The deductible under (3) was omitted in later versions of the plan.

4. The maximum benefit would be $10,000 per person and $100,000 per accident, but if the accident claims exceed $100,000, provision is made for recovery from an assigned-claims plan. Work-loss benefits would also be limited to $750 per month.

5. Benefits would not be paid in one lump sum but instead would usually be payable monthly as losses accrue.

6. If tort damages for pain and suffering would exceed $5,000 or if other tort damages would exceed $10,000, the injured victim could start a tort action. Any recovery, however, would be reduced by these amounts.

7. Private insurers would write the necessary insurance and an assigned-case plan would provide benefits when the vehicle was uninsured or a hit-and-run car.

8. Resident liability insurance could be purchased to cover accidents in states not adopting the plan.

Professors Keeton and O'Connell argue that their plan would replace the shortcomings of the present system with respect to benefit adequacy, equity, and promptness. It would reduce significantly the wastes of litigation but preserve the tort remedy for those with serious losses. They believe that it would properly treat automobile losses as a cost of motoring generally. Merit rating could be included, if this seemed desirable, to punish the guilty and to deter negligent driving. One unique feature of their study was that it included a draft of the statute necessary to introduce the plan. According to some actuarial studies prepared for Professors Keeton and O'Connell, Basic Protection Plan premiums in New York and in Michigan in recent years would have been less than premiums for typical automobile liability insurance. More persons would have collected benefits, but the average benefit would have been considerably less because it would contain no allowance for pain and suffering and would be subject to various deductions.

Many critics deny that the present system has as many shortcomings or that they are as serious as those described earlier in this chapter under "Proposed Changes in the Legal System." For example, a study of 1964 Wisconsin accidents revealed that victims had to bear only 8 per cent of their losses out of personal funds and 30 per cent out of their own private loss insurance.[14] Only 5 per cent of the claims took a year or more to settle; 63 per cent were settled in 6 months. They recognize that some shortcomings do exist, but they prefer reformation of the present system to adopting a new, untried approach. For example, claims may be settled

---

[14] William T. Hold, "Critique of Basic Protection for the Traffic Victim," *Insurance Law Journal*, No. 541 (February, 1968), p. 82.

more promptly in Wisconsin because of that state's comparative negligence statute and the assignment of additional judges to areas with a heavy case load. Opponents believe that the Basic Protection Plan would be more costly than its authors suggest and that it is almost impossible at this time to determine the relative cost of the plan by actuarial methods. They note that the plaintiff often loses in court and that many current disputes involve the amount of the damages, not whether any liability is involved. The Basic Protection Plan, they maintain, would not remove arguments on this phase of the claim. They ask whether eliminating the fault concept might affect drivers' attitudes adversely. Moreover, they argue, some allowance for pain and suffering is legitimate, even in the less serious cases. They emphasize the many differences between automobile accidents and industrial accidents, and they ask why automobile accidents, but not hunting or boating accidents or product liability claims, should be singled out for compensation treatment. The deduction of benefits from other sources in their opinion penalizes those who have the foresight to protect themselves. If, to counteract this effect, these outside sources took steps to excuse themselves from payments in basic-protection cases, this would increase the cost of the plan. Finally, they point out that if prices are to be related to expected losses and expenses, many drivers who are now considered substandard because of their high loss potential would pay lower rates because their passengers tend to suffer smaller economic losses. On the other hand, some drivers who currently pay relatively low rates would have their rates increased because their passengers tend to suffer higher economic losses.

THE AMERICAN INSURANCE ASSOCIATION NO-FAULT PLAN

In October, 1968, the American Insurance Association, a stock-insurer trade association, proposed an automobile compensation plan that, unlike the three programs described above, would completely abolish the tort system with respect to automobile bodily injury claims and property damage claims. Its major features are as follows:

1. Compulsory automobile insurance would compensate all persons injured in automobile accidents regardless of fault. This insurance would cover the car owner and his family against losses sustained in any automobile accident and other occupants of the insured car not otherwise insured. However, losses to passengers in a public vehicle would be assessed against the insurer of the vehicle. The AIA program would also cover damage to property other than automobiles and their contents. Through an exemption from any tort liability for damage to automobiles and their contents, owners

would be made responsible for damage to their own cars, but property insurance on the car would be optional.

2. Compensation benefits for bodily injury losses would be limited to (1) net economic losses, as defined under the heading "Keeton-O'Connell Basic Protection Plan" above, and (2) extra payments for permanent impairment or disfigurement. Pain and suffering losses are excluded.

3. Net economic losses would be equal to the gross loss less 15 per cent of the income loss to reflect tax savings. Collateral sources of reimbursement, such as private life and health insurance, would be ignored in determining net economic loss.

4. The maximum benefit per person would be unlimited. However, work loss benefits would be limited to $750 a month and funeral and burial expenses to $1,000. The permanent impairment or disfigurement benefits, which were later eliminated from the plan, would vary with the nature of the injury but would not exceed half of the medical expenses.

5. Benefits would be paid periodically as they accrue.

6. With a few minor exceptions, automobile tort actions would be completely eliminated.

7. Private insurers would write the necessary insurance and an assigned case plan would provide benefits for accidents involving uninsured cars, hit-and-run cars, or nonresidents.

8. Residual liability insurance *must* be purchased to cover accidents in states not adopting this plan.

These eight features can be readily compared with the eight features of the Keeton-O'Connell plan. The two most important differences are (1) the complete elimination of auto tort liability under the AIA plan and (2) the treatment of collateral sources. The arguments pro and con the AIA plan repeat most of the arguments presented in the discussion of the Keeton-O'Connell plan. A cost study that accompanied the AIA plan claimed savings at least as great as under the Keeton-O'Connell plan. Critics disputed the claimed savings.

The AIA prefers its proposal to the Keeton-O'Connell plan because it believes that fault is not a proper factor to determine reimbursement for *any* automobile accident losses and that pain and suffering awards cannot be determined objectively. Furthermore, a "split" system is inefficient and uneconomical. Proponents of the "split" system argue that many of their objections to the negligence system disappear when that system is limited to large excess losses. For example, when juries know that the plaintiff has received basic compensation, they should be more objective in their negligence determinations. Moreover, the effort and expense involved in negligence determinations would be less than the amounts at stake. "Split" system proponents also believe that when victims suffer large losses and can prove negligence, they deserve to be completely indemnified, including some allowance for pain and suffering. Furthermore, negligent drivers who cause serious losses should be held responsible for the total amount of these losses, and possible tort liability for serious losses should have some deterrent value.

SOCIAL PROTECTION PLAN

Starting in 1969 Puerto Rico has had a Social Protection Plan which provides through a tax-supported (taxes on gas, automobile licenses, and drivers' licenses), government-administered program medical expense, disability, and death benefits to all motor traffic victims. This plan was designed by Professors Juan Aponte and Herbert S. Denenberg of the University of Pennsylvania.[15] The plan provides unlimited medical services provided by hospitals and doctors under contract with the plan, $500 toward funeral expenses, 50 per cent of a disabled victim's weekly salary with a $50 maximum for 52 weeks and a $25 maximum for a second 52 weeks, scheduled benefits up to $5,000 for dismemberments, and scheduled benefits up to $5,000, depending upon who are the survivors, if the victim dies. Many benefits were scheduled to eliminate lengthy evaluations of the losses. There are no payments for pain and suffering. Tort liability is preserved for pain and suffering claims over $1,000 and for economic losses over $2,000.

Although these compensation benefits are much lower than would be necessary in the fifty states and the replacement of private insurance with government insurance in those states would be a much more radical step than in Puerto Rico, Social Protection Plan operations will be observed closely by many insurers, consumer groups, and public officials.

COTTER PLAN

In January, 1969, Connecticut Insurance Commissioner Cotter proposed a package of proposals that would make some significant changes in automobile insurance contracts and in the law of negligence but would not substitute compensation for tort liability.[16] Parts of the package have been adopted in some states.

The major proposals are as follows:

1. All automobile liability insurance policies would include at least a $2,000 medical payments coverage and a disability income coverage provid-

---

[15] J. B. Aponte and H. S. Denenberg, "The Automobile Problem in Puerto Rico: Dimensions and Proposed Solution," *Journal of Risk and Insurance*, XXXV, No. 2 (June, 1968), 227–236.
[16] "Connecticut to Take Middle of Road in Auto Hassle?," *The National Underwriter* (January 31, 1969), pp. 1, 9.

ing 52 weeks of benefits ($6,000 maximum) for the insured, his family, guest passengers, and pedestrians injured by the insured's car. The injured party would thus receive benefits immediately but he would retain the right to sue negligent parties responsible for his losses. The insurer would have subrogation rights to recover the benefits paid under the health insurance coverages.

2. Comparative negligence would be substituted for contributory negligence.

3. Pain and suffering would continue to influence tort liability awards, but in the less serious cases general damages would be limited to some fraction of the medical expenses. In cases of death, dismemberment, disfigurement, or permanent impairment higher amounts could be awarded.

4. Damages for loss of income would be reduced to reflect income tax savings. (Many persons are surprised to find out this has not always been true.)

5. Advance payments by insurers in clear-cut liability cases would be encouraged.

6. Attorneys' fees would not be permitted to exceed 25 per cent.

7. To expedite the settlement of small claims and reduce the number of cases handled by the courts, claims under $3,000 would be submitted to a new arbitration system.

Proponents favor these proposals as a balanced, evolutionary approach that would correct the leading defects in the negligence system without destroying its virtues and substituting some untested program. Automobile compensation proponents favor the proposals but believe that they represent only a partial, inadequate solution.

DEFENSE RESEARCH INSTITUTE PROPOSAL

The Defense Research Institute, an educational and research organization serving defense lawyers, also favors an evolutionary approach. Its proposal closely resembles the Cotter plan but differs in some important respects. For example, the Institute would permit local decisions to determine (1) the details and amounts of the medical payments and disability income coverages and (2) whether comparative negligence should be substituted for contributory negligence. The insured would also be permitted to reject the medical expense and disability income coverages for himself and his family. Instead of relating pain and suffering awards to medical expenses in less serious cases, the Institute would conduct research to determine guidelines for determining these awards. Finally, under the Institute's proposal attorneys' fees would not be limited to any stated percentage, but they would be subject to strict regulation by local court rule or regulation.

THE STATE OF NEW YORK INSURANCE DEPARTMENT PROPOSAL

In early 1970 the State of New York Insurance Department proposed a no-fault plan that was endorsed by Governor Rockefeller but strongly opposed by many critics. The Department proposal resembled the AIA plan in its basic approach but differed in the following major respects. First, automobile insurance benefits would be secondary to collateral sources, such as group and individual disability income and medical expense insurance. Second, there would be no monthly limit on recoveries for loss of earnings. Third, commercial vehicle owners or their insurers would be responsible for all losses in accidents involving commercial vehicles and private passenger vehicles. Fourth, because of some special constitutional questions in New York, survivors would retain the right to sue in death cases. The New York Department actuaries, like the AIA actuaries, claim that insureds would pay substantially lower premiums under their plan than under the present system. Critics dispute this claim.

MASSACHUSETTS NO-FAULT INSURANCE LAW

In August, 1970, Massachusetts became the first state to enact a no-fault insurance law. Under this partial no-fault law an insurer must pay, regardless of fault, the first $2,000 of economic bodily injury losses sustained by its insureds. Injured persons can still bring claims under the law of negligence, but any recoveries are reduced by the amount paid under the no-fault provision. Pain and suffering awards will be considered under these tort claims only if the injured party's medical expenses exceed $500 or if the injury causes death, dismemberment, permanent and serious disfigurement, loss of sight or hearing, or a fracture. It is expected that most injured persons will be fully compensated for their economic losses by the no-fault insurance and consequently will not seek a recovery through a tort action. Property damage is still covered under the present tort liability system.

The law mandated a 15 per cent rate reduction from 1970 Massachusetts automobile bodily injury liability insurance rates. The willingness of insurers to accept this reduction is noteworthy because the 1970 rates were generally considered to be inadequate for liability insurance under the old system. Insurer experience under these lower rates should shed considerable light on the cost aspects of "no-fault" plans.

Two versions of the current law were enacted. The first required insurers to renew all policies unless the insureds were guilty of fraud in their original or renewal applications for insurance, had been convicted of driving under the influence of alcohol or dangerous drugs, or had not paid their premiums. Insurers protested that they could not operate under such a liberal renewal provision. The second version, passed about 2 weeks later, added several new grounds for nonrenewal, including conviction on one moving violation and involvement in one reportable accident in a 12-month period. The second version also permits insurers to increase the premiums charged certain drivers (e.g., speeders and drunk drivers).

THE AMERICAN MUTUAL INSURANCE ALLIANCE AND THE
NATIONAL ASSOCIATION OF INDEPENDENT INSURERS PROPOSALS

In December, 1970, two insurer organizations whose members write over half of the private passenger automobile insurance in the United States announced similar proposals that in their opinion combine the best features of the present liability system and the no-fault concept. The approach suggested by the American Mutual Insurance Alliance (called the Guaranteed Protection Plan) and the National Association of Independent Insurers (called the Dual Protection Plan) is basically a revision of the Cotter plan, which previously had been supported by these two groups. Under the plans of both organizations all drivers would be required to buy immediate-pay, no-fault coverage of at least $2,000 in medical expense benefits and $6,000 in wage loss benefits to all persons injured while riding in or struck by the insured car. The NAII would in addition require insurers to offer to all policyholders and their families catastrophe coverage extending the scope of the immediate-pay protection to at least $100,000 per person for medical expenses and wage loss and $25,000 in death benefits. Both organizations would permit tort actions for economic losses beyond those afforded by the immediate-pay coverage as well as "reasonable" compensation for noneconomic losses. In other respects the two proposals resemble the Cotter plan.

Both the AMIA and the NAII also stressed the need for increased research and action to reduce the frequency and severity of accidents, to improve automobile design, and to lower automobile repair costs.

FEDERAL NO-FAULT PROPOSALS

Two extensive studies by the Federal government generated one no-fault proposal in 1970 and the possibility of a second in 1971. In September, 1970, Senator Philip Hart, chairman of the Senate judiciary antitrust committee, introduced a "Uniform Motor Vehicle Insurance Act" that would pay an accident victim, regardless of fault, all of his medical and rehabilitation expenses and reimburse him for lost wages up to $1,000 a month for 30 months. Up to $30,000 would be paid to survivors of deceased victims. Tort actions would still be possible for those whose economic losses exceeded the compensation payments. Permanently disabled or disfigured persons could also seek reimbursement for pain and suffering. Senator Hart's proposal would in addition guarantee a noncancellable policy to all licensed drivers, void all state laws prohibiting the development of group automobile insurance plans, and give group automobile insurance plans the same favorable tax advantages as group health insurance.

The Secretary of Transportation has promised that in 1971 his department will present to Congress a program to deal with the several problems that it discovered in a 2-year, $2 million study of automobile insurance and the underlying legal system. Parts of this study, based mainly on an analysis of the nation's 1967 automobile accidents, have already been discussed. The DOT study also included extensive reports on automobile accident litigation, insurance accessibility for the hard-to-place driver, assigned risk plans, variability in automobile insurance premiums, insolvencies among automobile insurers, mass marketing of property and liability insurance, public attitudes toward automobile insurance, structural trends and conditions in the automobile insurance industry, and other important topics.

In March, 1971, the Secretary of Transportation recommended that Congress urge states to move gradually toward a no-fault system. His Department would monitor state programs and in two years determine whether further Federal action is desirable.

The Future

Whether automobile compensation programs will replace the tort liability system is still a matter of conjecture, but there is no doubt that the next decade will witness many significant changes in automobile reparations systems and the operations of automobile insurers. As a result insurance should become more readily available, the insurer's promise should become more secure, and the victims of automobile accidents should receive more prompt, adequate compensation for their losses.

REVIEW QUESTIONS

1. Why have automobile insurance costs risen so rapidly in the past decade?
2. In your state must a person have insurance to operate a vehicle? If not, what action has your state legislature taken to protect the public against uninsured motorists? Is your state typical?
3. Compare unsatisfied-judgments funds with private uninsured-motorists coverage with respect to the benefits they provide and how they are financed.
4. Do you favor compulsory automobile insurance? Present arguments for and against this approach.

5. What steps have state legislatures and insurers taken to make automobile insurance more readily available?

6. What steps have state legislators and insurers taken to protect insureds and claimants against insurer insolvencies? Evaluate these steps.

7. Compare the Keeton-O'Connell Basic Protection Plan and the American Insurance Association No-Fault Plan with respect to the following:

   a. Compensation benefits for disability
   b. Compensation benefits for medical expenses
   c. Compensation benefits for disfigurement
   d. Maximum compensation benefits
   e. Compensation benefits for property damage
   f. Effect of collateral sources
   g. Excess tort liability
   h. Role of private insurers

8. Compare the American Insurance Association No-Fault Plan with the Social Protection Plan.

9. How would the Cotter proposal reduce the delays, costs, and inequities associated with the tort liability system?

10. What is the position of (a) the insurance business and (b) the Federal government on the concept of no fault insurance?

11. Has any state enacted a no-fault compensation plan? If so, explain its plan briefly.

12. What changes would you make in the present tort liability system? Why?

SUGGESTIONS FOR ADDITIONAL READING

An Analysis and Critique of an Automobile Insurance Proposal Prepared for Study and Comment by the American Insurance Association (Milwaukee: The Defense Research Institute, Inc., 1969).

Automobile Insurance . . . For Whose Benefit? (New York: State of New York Insurance Department, 1970).

Blum, W. J., and Kalven, H., Jr.: *Public Law Perspectives on a Private Law Problem: Auto Compensation Plans* (Boston: Little, Brown, and Company, 1965).

Conard, A. F., et al.: *Automobile Accident Costs and Payments* (Ann Arbor: The University of Michigan Press, 1964).

Department of Transportation Automobile Insurance and Compensation Study (Washington, D.C.: U.S. Government Printing Office, 1970).

Hallman, G. V.: *Unsatisfied Judgment Funds* (Homewood, Ill.: Richard D. Irwin, Inc., 1968).

Keeton, R. E., and O'Connell, J.: *Basic Protection for the Traffic Victim* (Boston: Little, Brown, and Company, 1965).

Kulp, C. A., and Hall, J. W.: *Casualty Insurance* (4th ed., New York: Ronald Press Co., 1968), chaps. 10 through 13.

Report of Special Committee to Study and Evaluate the Keeton-O'Connell Basic Protection Plan and Automobile Accident Reparations (New York: American Insurance Association, 1968).

Responsible Reform: A Program to Improve the Liability Reparations System (Milwaukee: The Defense Research Institute, Inc., 1969).

index of authors and sources cited

subject index

Straight life insurance, 346–349
Subrogation rights:
  in personnel insurance, 272
  in property and liability insurance,
    270–271
Suicide, 204, 362
Suits against insurer, 533, 536, 538,
  539
Superannuation (see Old Age)
Supervision (see Government regulation of insurance)
Supplemental unemployment
  benefits, 408, 419
Supplementary Medical Insurance,
  659
Supplementary workmen's
  compensation benefits, 418
Surety Association of America, 552
Surety bonds, 332–334, 577
  contract bonds, 333
  court bonds, 333–334, 577
    fiduciary bonds, 334
    litigation bonds, 333–334
  distinction between insurance and
    suretyship, 194–195
  license and permit bonds, 334
  miscellaneous bonds, 333
Surgical expense insurance (see
  Contracts, individual health
  insurance)
Surplus:
  and dividend distribution, 506–507
  policyholders', 465, 479–480
Surplus line broker, 454
Surplus-share reinsurance, 476

Taussig, Michael, 655–656
Tax-free death benefit insurance, 401
Taxes:
  and annuities, 425
  business interest purchase
    plans, 399
  group property and liability
    insurance, 432, 710

Taxes:
  health insurance benefits,
    401–402, 414
  key-men indemnification
    plans, 397
  life insurance as an invest-
    ment, 353
  life insurance benefits, 366, 367,
    401, 413
  pensions, 149, 176, 402–403,
    404, 420, 425, 427
  premium, 177, 635
  property and liability insur-
    ance, 176
  retention decisions, 176, 177
Teachers Insurance and Annuity
  Association, 358
Temporary disability insurance
  legislation, 664–666
  benefits, 665
  coverage, 664
  financing, 666
  issues, 666
  qualifications for benefits, 664
  relationship to unemployment
    insurance, 664
  types of insurer, 665
Temporary National Economic Committee, 628, 629
Term life insurance, 345–346
Theft insurance:
  for business, 292–293, 296–298,
    307–308
  for families, 568–572, 575–576
Title insurance, 335
Torrens system, 335, 449
Torts, 107–112
  concept of, 107–108
  intentional, 108–110
  unintentional tort of negligence,
    110–112
  (See also Liability)
Transfer, 189–191
  business, 189–191
  definition, 189
  family, 566, 588